FOUNDERS WITHOUT LIMITS

Big Tech has flourished on the US public markets in recent years with numerous blue-chip IPOs, from Google and Facebook to new kids on the block such as Snap, Zoom and Airbnb. A key trend is the burgeoning use of dual-class stock. Dual-class stock enables founders to divest of equity and generate finance for growth through an IPO, without losing the control they desire to pursue their long-term, market-disrupting visions. Bobby V. Reddy scrutinises the global history of dual-class stock, evaluates the conceptual and empirical evidence on dual-class stock and assesses the approaches of the London Stock Exchange and ongoing UK regulatory reforms to dual-class stock. A policy roadmap is presented that optimally supports the adoption of dual-class stock while still protecting against its potential abuses, and which will more effectively attract high-growth, innovative companies to the UK equity markets, boost the economy and unleash the true potential of 'founders without limits'.

Bobby V. Reddy teaches Company Law and Corporate Governance at the University of Cambridge, and is a Fellow of the Cambridge Endowment for Research in Finance and a Fellow of Churchill College. He is a former corporate partner at the global law firm Latham & Watkins LLP and was a director and trustee of the charitable corporate governance think tank Tomorrow's Company.

CAMBRIDGE UNIVERSITY PRESS

International Corporate Law and Financial Market Regulation

Corporate law and financial market regulation have major implications for how the modern economy is organized and regulated and for how risk is managed and distributed – domestically, regionally and internationally. This series seeks to inform and lead the vibrant scholarly and policy debate in this highly dynamic area by publishing cutting-edge, timely and critical examinations of the most pressing and important questions in the field.

Series Editors

Founders without Limits

DUAL-CLASS STOCK AND THE PREMIUM TIER OF THE LONDON STOCK EXCHANGE

BOBBY V. REDDY
University of Cambridge

CAMBRIDGE
UNIVERSITY PRESS

CAMBRIDGE
UNIVERSITY PRESS

University Printing House, Cambridge CB2 8BS, United Kingdom

One Liberty Plaza, 20th Floor, New York, NY 10006, USA

477 Williamstown Road, Port Melbourne, VIC 3207, Australia

314–321, 3rd Floor, Plot 3, Splendor Forum, Jasola District Centre,
New Delhi – 110025, India

103 Penang Road, #05–06/07, Visioncrest Commercial, Singapore 238467

Cambridge University Press is part of the University of Cambridge.

It furthers the University's mission by disseminating knowledge in the pursuit of education, learning, and research at the highest international levels of excellence.

www.cambridge.org
Information on this title: www.cambridge.org/9781108839358
DOI: 10.1017/9781108989893

First published 2021

A catalogue record for this publication is available from the British Library.

Library of Congress Cataloging-in-Publication Data
NAMES: Reddy, Bobby V., author.
TITLE: Founders without limits : dual-class stock and the premium tier of the London Stock Exchange / Bobby V. Reddy, University of Cambridge.
DESCRIPTION: Cambridge, United Kingdom ; New York, NY : Cambridge University Press, 2021. | Series: International corporate law and financial market regulation | Based on author's thesis (doctoral – University of Cambridge, 2020). | Includes bibliographical references and index.
IDENTIFIERS: LCCN 2021041801 (print) | LCCN 2021041802 (ebook) | ISBN 9781108839358 (hardback) | ISBN 9781108989893 (ebook other)
SUBJECTS: LCSH: Stockholders – Legal status, laws, etc. – Great Britain. | Dual class stocks – Law and legislation – Great Britain. | Corporate governance – Law and legislation – Great Britain.
CLASSIFICATION: LCC KD2100 .R43 2021 (print) | LCC KD2100 (ebook) | DDC346.41/0666–dc23
LC record available at https://lccn.loc.gov/2021041801
LC ebook record available at https://lccn.loc.gov/2021041802

ISBN 978-1-108-83935-8 Hardback

Contents

List of Figures — *page* xi
List of Tables — xii
Preface — xiii
Acknowledgements — xv
Table of Cases — xvi
Table of Legislation and Regulation — xviii
List of Abbreviations — xxii

Introduction 1
Overview 4
Scope 6
Publicly Listed Companies 6
Dual-Class Stock as a Means to Control 8
Terminology 11

PART I PUTTING DUAL-CLASS STOCK INTO CONTEXT 13

1 **The Cult of Dual-Class Stock in the Era of Big Tech** 15
1.1 Introduction 15
1.2 The Rise of Dual-Class Stock in the United States 16
1.3 The United Kingdom's Position on Dual-Class Stock 21
1.4 It's All about Control 24
1.5 Putting Dual-Stock into Context 32
1.5.1 The Decline of the Public Equity Markets in the United Kingdom, and the Dearth of Listed Tech Companies 33
1.5.2 How Dual-Class Stock May Encourage Further Listings 36
1.5.3 Why Not Just Stay Private? 39
1.5.4 Why Bother with the Premium Tier? 46

1.5.5 The Hut Group Case Study 54
1.5.6 Deliveroo Case Study 57
1.5.7 The UK Listing Review 61
1.6 Conclusion: The Premium Tier Prohibition of Dual-Class Stock Matters 68

2 **A Tale of Two Cities and Beyond** 70
2.1 Introduction 70
2.2 The United Kingdom and the Institutional Investor Effect 71
2.3 The US Context 81
2.4 The Asian Experience 90
2.4.1 Hong Kong 91
2.4.2 Singapore 96
2.4.3 Tokyo 99
2.4.4 China 104
2.4.5 India 107
2.5 Mainland Europe 110
2.6 Conclusion – Making Sense of Global Policies on Dual-Class Stock 113

3 **First among Equals? Other Methods of Creating a Divergence between Voting and Cash-Flow Rights** 119
3.1 Introduction 119
3.2 Board Appointment Rights 120
3.3 Shareholders' Agreements 122
3.4 Pyramid Structures 124
3.5 Cross-Ownerships 128
3.6 Derivative Instruments 132
3.7 Preference Shares 136
3.8 Loyalty Shares 137
3.9 Conclusion 140

4 **Shareholder Democracy and Corporate Purpose** 142
4.1 Introduction 142
4.2 Shareholder Democracy 143
4.3 The Purpose of the Firm and Dual-Class Stock 150
4.3.1 Corporate Purpose 150
4.3.1.1 Theory of the Firm 151
4.3.1.2 The Dominance of Shareholder Primacy and the Application to Dual-Class Stock 155
4.3.2 The Approach in Part II to the Purpose of the Firm 157
4.3.2.1 Stakeholder Considerations in Part II 157
4.3.2.2 The Public Shareholder Focus of Part II 160
4.4 Conclusion 161

PART II EVALUATING DUAL-CLASS STOCK 163

5 From Controlling Shareholders to Dual-Class Stock 165
5.1 Introduction 165
5.2 The Provenance of the United Kingdom's Regulatory Attitude to Dual-Class Stock 166
5.3 Why the Distrust? 168
5.4 Why Not Prohibit Controlling Shareholder Firms? – The Controlling Shareholder Tradeoff 172
5.5 Empirical Evidence on One Share, One Vote Controlling Shareholder Companies 176
5.5.1 Summary of Major Empirical Studies on Controlling Shareholder Structures 177
5.5.1.1 Why the Inconclusiveness? 180
5.6 The Changing Dynamic with Dual-Class Stock 184
5.7 Conclusion 186

6 Theoretical Benefits and Detriments of Dual-Class Stock 188
6.1 Introduction 188
6.2 Theoretical Detriments to Inferior-Voting Shareholders of Dual-Class Stock 189
6.2.1 Tunnelling 190
6.2.2 High Executive Remuneration 193
6.2.3 Inefficient Decision-Making 195
6.2.4 Management Entrenchment 197
6.2.5 Non-Pecuniary Controller Benefits 201
6.2.6 Takeover Probability 203
6.2.7 Control Premia 208
6.3 Theoretical Benefits to Inferior-Voting Shareholders of Dual-Class Stock 212
6.3.1 Beneficial Related-Party Transactions 213
6.3.2 Diversification 214
6.3.3 Bonding Hypothesis 216
6.3.4 Higher Takeover Prices 221
6.3.5 Project Choice 223
6.3.6 Post-IPO Equity Funding 224
6.3.7 Long-Termism 226
6.3.8 Risk-Taking 235
6.4 The Dual-Class Stock Tradeoff 238
6.4.1 The Tradeoff – Literature Review 238
6.4.2 The Dual-Class Stock Tradeoff in Terms of Types of Controller Benefits 241
6.5 Conclusion 245

7 **The Empirical Evidence on Dual-Class Stock** 249
7.1 Introduction 249
7.2 A Note about Diversity of Firms and Controllers 252
7.2.1 Diversity of Firms 252
7.2.2 Diversity of Controllers 253
7.2.3 Impact of Diversity on Empirical Studies 255
7.3 Event-Based Studies 256
7.3.1 Summary 257
7.3.2 Detailed Analysis 257
7.3.3 Words of Warning 261
7.4 Firm Valuation Studies 265
7.4.1 Summary 267
7.4.2 Detailed Analysis 269
7.4.3 Words of Warning 276
7.5 Buy-and-Hold Stock Return Studies 279
7.5.1 Summary 280
7.5.2 Detailed Analysis 282
7.5.3 Words of Warning 284
7.6 Operating Performance Studies 285
7.6.1 Summary 286
7.6.2 Detailed Analysis 286
7.6.3 Words of Warning 293
7.7 Conclusion 296
7.7.1 General Trends 296
7.7.2 Explaining the General Trends 297
7.7.3 Are There Other Justifications for the Discounts Applied to Dual-Class Firm Values? 298
7.7.4 So What Does the Empirical Evidence Tell Us? 301
7.7.5 Does the Empirical Evidence Prove that Dual-Class Stock Is Superior to One Share, One Vote? 303
7.7.6 The Way Forward 304

PART III FORMULATING A POLICY ON DUAL-CLASS STOCK 309

8 **The Existing Constraints** 311
8.1 Introduction 311
8.2 Legal/Regulatory Restrictions 312
8.2.1 Directors' Duties 312
8.2.2 Unfair Prejudice 315
8.2.3 Takeovers 316
8.2.4 Relationship with the Controller 319
8.2.5 Independent Directors 323
8.2.6 Amendments to the Articles of Association 325

8.2.7 Post-IPO Recapitalisations of One Share, One Vote into Dual-Class Stock 327
8.3 Market Constraints 332
8.3.1 Equity Markets 332
8.3.2 Debt Markets 334
8.3.3 Product Markets 335
8.3.4 Interplay between Market Forces and Voluntary Constraints 336
8.4 Psychological Constraints 336
8.5 Conclusion 337

9 A Balanced Protection Package for Inferior-Voting Shareholders 339
9.1 Introduction 339
9.2 The Rule-Making Challenge 341
9.2.1 Mandatory, Presumptive or Permissive 341
9.2.2 Legislative, Regulatory or Soft-Law 345
9.2.3 The Role of the FCA 346
9.3 What's Not Proposed 348
9.4 Restricting the Use of Dual-Class Stock to Specific Firms or Controllers (Eligibility) 353
9.4.1 Type of Firm Restrictions around the World 353
9.4.2 Type of Controller Restrictions around the World 356
9.4.3 UK-Proposed Premium Tier Listing Criteria 358
9.5 As the Sun Sets in the West, It Is Rising in the East – Listed Company Inferior-Voting Shareholder Protections 361
9.6 The Balanced Sunset Clause 362
9.6.1 Time-Dependent Sunsets 362
9.6.2 Transfer-Driven Sunsets 368
9.6.3 Director-Linked Sunsets 374
9.6.4 Ownership-Linked Sunsets 377
9.6.5 Other Event-Driven Sunsets 384
9.6.6 Consequences of Sunset Clauses 387
9.7 The Balanced Sunrise Package 389
9.7.1 Majority of the Minority Provisions 389
9.7.2 Restrictions on Further Share Issuances 394
9.7.3 Independent Directors 395
9.7.4 Related-Party Transactions 399
9.7.5 Disclosure of Inferior-Voting Shareholder Votes 401
9.7.6 Inferior-Voting Shareholder Proposed Resolutions 404
9.7.7 Greater Disclosure 405
9.8 Further Listing Rules and Takeover Code Considerations 406
9.8.1 LR 9.2.21 R 406

9.8.2 Takeover Code 407
9.8.3 Limiting Dual-Class Stock to New Issuers 412
9.9 Conclusion 414

Epilogue 417

Appendix: Comparison of Inferior-Voting Shareholder Protections on Major Dual-Class Stock Exchanges 422

Index 442

Figures

1.1	Google stock ownership as of 31 December 2019	*page* 17
1.2	'Large' US dual-class IPOs as a percentage of total IPOs	19
1.3	UK IPOs on the LSE's Main Market and AIM 1996–2020	34
3.1	Basic pyramid structure	124
3.2	Basic cross-ownership structure	129
7.1	Dual-class stock event-based studies	258
7.2	Dual-class stock firm value studies	268
7.3	Dual-class stock buy-and-hold stock return studies	281
7.4	Dual-class stock operating performance studies	287
9.1	Equity ownership required for majority control varying by voting ratio	379

Tables

1.1 Voting and equity ownership of the principal controllers of the twenty largest US dual-class corporations by market capitalisation *page* 29
1.2 Large (over £100 m) acquisitions of UK private technology companies between 2014 and mid-2019 43
1.3 Large (over £100 m) foreign buyouts of UK listed technology companies between 2014 and mid-2019 45
2.1 Approaches to dual-class stock on major global exchanges 117

Preface

When I first started researching the topic of dual-class stock, in earnest, in 2015, the world was a different place. The United Kingdom was still part of the EU, Donald Trump was a reality TV star, the term global pandemic harked back to distant memories of the Spanish flu and, after an accounting scandal at Tesco plc, the executives of British listed companies were accused of taking short-term, shareholder value-destructive approaches to business. Well, maybe not everything has changed. Nevertheless, the economic turmoil since 2015 re-emphasises the need to develop a coherent long-term strategy to invigorate and stimulate the economy of the United Kingdom and around the world. A healthy economy is fuelled by the visions and innovations of entrepreneurs. I first started getting to know founders and entrepreneurs as a corporate partner at a global law firm, and really started delving into the area of controlling shareholders and dual-class stock while working with a corporate governance think tank prior to joining academia. It struck me that the concept of dual-class stock, much derided by UK institutional investors, could conversely, in certain circumstances, promote the listing of successful companies which in turn could benefit public shareholders, and, indeed, the economy, as a whole. My focus has been on technology companies, but the concepts in this book equally apply to any founder-led company seeking options for growth.

During the course of my research, it became evident that there was no comprehensive published book collating and discussing the evidence, theory and practicalities of dual-class stock even though the subject matter had been a significant corporate governance controversy for many decades. In particular, the academic discourse on dual-class stock from a UK perspective was only sparse. This led to me pitching this book with a view to scrutinising the London Stock Exchange's premium tier approach to dual-class stock, and, also, assessing dual-class stock generally in a manner relevant to jurisdictions around the world. I was, of course, very pleased to find Cambridge University Press to be supportive and enthusiastic, and was also grateful to the Cambridge Endowment for Research in Finance for their cross-disciplinary and financial support. Since commencing the book, a number of jurisdictions have relaxed their rules on dual-class stock, and, indeed, the UK has commenced along the path toward making dual-class stock more accessible. What was once a niche area of interest outside the US has become a hot button topic internationally, forming an essential part of the dialogue in corporate governance and corporate finance courses and discussions around the globe. A thorough investigation into dual-class stock from both UK and international perspectives is long overdue. This book is the resultant labour of love, and I hope that it will inspire discussion and influence policy-makers in the United Kingdom and abroad.

Acknowledgements

During what has been a tumultuous time for many, it would be remiss of me not to acknowledge the help and succour given to me by those who have made life, and the completion of this project, so much more bearable. First and foremost, I would like to thank my parents for all their love, support and dedication over the years, and their willingness to entertain a wholly unexpected late change in vocation. Additionally, the patience of, and encouragement given by, my amazing wife over the last few years has also been invaluable to me in completing this book. After foregoing a lucrative career as a corporate lawyer to become an academic, at least I now know she did not marry me for the money! Finally, I would also like to extend special thanks to Brian Cheffins for his insightful thoughts, comments and guidance, and the informal mentoring he has given me throughout my new career … and introducing me to Thursday afternoon 5-aside football.

Table of Cases

AUSTRALIAN CASES

Brunninghausen v. *Glavanics* (1999) 32 ACSR 294 313

NEW ZEALAND CASES

Allen v. *Hyatt* (1914) 30 *TLR* 444 313

UK CASES

Allen v. *Gold Reefs of West Africa Ltd.* [1900] 1 Ch. 656 326
Astec (BSR) plc, Re [1998] 2 BCLC 556 316
Automatic Self-Cleansing Filter Syndicate v. *Cuninghame* [1906] 2 Ch. 34 65
Beattie v. *E. F. Beattie Ltd.* [1938] Ch. 708 346
Birch v. *Cropper and Others In re The Bridgewater Navigation Company Limited* (1889) 14 App. Cas. 525 . . . . 71, 72, 143
Blue Arrow plc, Re [1987] Ch.D 585 316
Bridge v. *Daley* [2015] EWHC 2121 (Ch) 314
BTI 2014 v. *Sequana* [2016] EWHC 1686 (Ch). . 155
Burland v. *Earle* [1902] AC 83 . . . . 207, 352
Bushell v. *Faith* [1970] AC 1099 . . . . 72, 120
Carruth v. *Imperial Chemical Industry* [1937] AC 707 . . . . 330, 332
Charterhouse Capital Ltd, Re [2015] EWCA Civ 536 327
Citco Banking Corp. v. *Pusser's Ltd.* [2007] 2 BCLC 483 . . . . 327, 329
Coleman v. *Myers* [1977] 2 NZLR 255 313
Continental Assurance Company of London plc, Re [2007] 2 BCLC 287 200
Cumbrian Newspapers Group Ltd v. *Cumberland & Westmorland Herald Newspaper & Printing Co Ltd* [1987] Ch. 1 . . . . 326, 329
Dimbula Valley (Ceylon) Tea Co Ltd v. *Laurie and another* [1961] Ch. 353 326
Dorman Long & Co Ltd, Re (1934) 1 Ch 635 . . . 330
Eley v. *Positive Government Security Life Assurance Co. Ltd.* (1875) 1 Ex.D 20 326
Equitable Life Assurance Society v. *Bowley* [2004] BCLC 180 200
Estmanco (Kilner House) Ltd. v. *Greater London Council* [1982] 1 W.L.R. 2 . . . . . . 326, 385
Foss v. *Harbottle* (1843) 67 ER 189. . . . . . 313, 314
Greenhalgh v. *Arderne Cinemas Ltd and another* [1946] 1 All ER 512 . . . . 326, 329
Greenhalgh v. *Arderne Cinemas Ltd.* [1951] Ch. 286 327
Greenhalgh v. Mallard [1943] 2 All ER 234 . . . 122
Greenwell v. *Porter* [1902] 1 Ch 530 122
Hawk Insurance Company Ltd, Re [2001] EWCA Civ 241 330
Hickman v. *Kent or Romney Marsh Sheepbreeders Association* [1915] 1 Ch. 881 346
Hodge v. *James Howell & Co* [1958] The Times, December 13 . . . . 326, 329
House of Fraser v. *ACGE Investments Ltd* [1987] AC 38. 392
Iesini v. *Westrip Holdings* [2011] 1 BCLC 498 313
John Shaw & Sons (Salford) Ltd. v. *Shaw* [1935] 2 KB 113 313
Kallakis v. *AIB Group plc and Others* [2020] EWHC 460 (Comm). 314
MacDougall v. *Gardiner* (1875) 1 Ch. D. 13 . . . . .313, 346
Macro (Ipswich) Ltd., Re [1994] 2 BCLC 354 316
Mission Capital plc v. Sinclair [2008] EWHC 1339 314
O'Neill and Another v. *Phillips and Others* [1999] 1 W.L.R. 1092 . . . . 315, 316

Percival v. *Wright* [1902] 2 Ch 401 313
Prudential Assurance Co. Ltd. v. *Newman Industries Ltd. (No. 2)* [1982] Ch. 204 313
Puddephatt v. *Leith* [1916] 1 Ch 200 122
Ransomes plc, Re [1999] 1 BCLC 775 393
Ratners Group plc, Re [1988] BCLC 685. . . . 393
Rights and Issues Investment Trust Ltd v. *Stylo Shoes Ltd and Others* [1964] 3 All ER 628. . . 329
Robert Glew & Denton and Co Trustees Ltd and another v. *Matossian-Rogers and others* [2019] EWHC 3183 (ch). 314
Russell v. *Northern Bank Development Corp. Ltd.* [1992] 1 W.L.R. 588 . . . . 122, 123
Saul D Harrison & Sons plc, Re [1994] B.C.C. 475 316
Scottish Insurance Corp v. *Wilson & Clyde Coal Co* [1949] AC 462. 392
Shuttleworth v. *Cox Bros. & Co.* [1927] 2 KB 9. . 327
Smith v. *Croft* [1986] 1 WLR 580. 314
Smith v. *Fawcett* [1942] Ch. 304 . . . . 207, 314, 352
Southern Foundries (1926) Ltd. v. *Shirlow* [1940] A.C. 701 123
Spokes v. *Grosvenor Hotel Co.* [1897] 2 QB 124. . 314
T&N Ltd, Re [2004] EWHC 2361 (Ch). 330
Thorn EMI plc, Re (1988) 4 BCC 698. 393
Tottenham Hotspur plc, Re [1994] 1 BCLC 655. 316
Vald Nielsen Holding A/S v. *Baldorino* [2019] EWHC 1926. 313
Wallersteiner v. *Moir (No. 2)* [1975] QB 373 . . . 314
West Mercia Safetywear v. *Dodd* [1988] 4 BCC 30. 155
White v. *Bristol Aeroplane Co* [1953] Ch.65. . . . 326

US CASES

Abraham v. *Emerson Radio Corp.*, 901 A.2d 751, 759 (Del. Ch. 2006). 326, 350
Air Products & Chemicals, Inc. v. *Airgas, Inc.*, C.A. No. 5249—CC (Del. Ch. Feb. 15, 2011) 65
Blasius Indus. v. *Atlas Corp.*, 564 A.2d 651 (Del. Ch. 1988) 146
Citizens United v. *Federal Election Commission*, 558 U.S. 310 (2010). 151
Estate of Simplot v. *Commissioner*, 249 F.3d 1191, 1195 (9th Cir. 2001) 210
In re Caremark International, Inc. Derivative Litigation, 698 A.2d 959 *(Del. Ch. 1996)*. 350
IRA Trust FBO Bobbie Ahmed v. *Crane*, C.A. No. 12742-CB (Del. Ch. Dec. 11, 2017) 264, 330, 351
Ivanhoe Partners v. *Newmont Mining Corp.*, 535 A.2d 1334, 1344 (Del. 1987). 326, 350
Kahn v. *Lynch Communication Systems, Inc.*, 638 A.2d 1110, 1115–16 (Del. 1994). 295, 351
Kahn v. *M&F Worldwide Corp.*, 88 A.3d 635, 644 (Del. 2014) 295, 351
Kahn v. *Tremont Corp.*, 694 A.2d 422, 428 (Del. 1997) 295, 351
Moran v. *Household Intl, Inc.*, 500 A.2d 1346 (Del. 1985). 65
Weinberger v. *UOP, Inc.*, 457 A.2d 701, 703 (Del. 1983). 295, 351

Table of Legislation and Regulation

CANADA

Toronto Stock Exchange Company Manual
s. 624 (l) 211

CHINA

CSRC, 'Rules Governing the Listing of Stocks on the Science and Technology Innovation Board of Shanghai Stock Exchange (Revised in 2019)' (April 2019)
Article 4.5.2 412
Article 4.5.3 . . . . 357, 375, 380
Article 4.5.4 378
Article 4.5.6 394
Article 4.5.7 . . . . 393, 404
Article 4.5.10 . . . . 369, 389, 397

EU

Application of International Accounting Standards Regulation (1606/2002)
Article 4 320
Market Abuse Regulation (596/2014)
Article 12 135
Article 19 . . . . 37, 406
Markets in Financial Instruments Directive (2014/65/EU) 22
Shareholder Rights Directive II (2017/828) 116, 320
Short-Selling Regulations (236/2012) 135
Takeover Directive (2004/25/EC)
Article 5 . . . . 319, 407
Article 11(4) 103, 378
Article 12(1) 103, 378
Transparency Directive Amending Directive (2013/50/EU) 135

HONG KONG

Companies Ordinance (Cap 622)
s. 588(4) 91
HK Listing Rules
Rule 5.05 397
Rule 5.05A 397
Rule 5.07 398
Rule 730(B) 397
Chapter 8A 93
Rule 8A.04 95
Rule 8A.05 412
Rule 8A.9 393
Rule 8A.10 378
Rule 8A.11 . . . . 357, 375
Rule 8A.12 . . . . 380, 381
Rule 8A.13 . . . . 393, 394
Rule 8A.17 357
Rule 8A.18 369
Rule 8A.18(2) 371
Rule 8A.23 404
Rule 8A.24 . . . . 389, 397

INDIA

Companies (Issue of Share Capital with Differential Voting Rights) Rules, 2001
Rule 9 107
Companies (Share Capital and Debentures) Rules, 2014
Rule 4 107
Companies (Share Capital and Debentures) Amendment Rules, 2019
Rule 2 108
SEBI (Issue of Capital and Disclosure Requirements) (Third Amendment) Regulations, 2019 . . . . 108, 109
Rule 3(II) 108, 354, 358, 375, 378, 382, 412

Rule 3(IV) 387
SEBI (Listing Obligations and Disclosure Requirements) Regulations, 2015
Regulation 17(1)(b) 398
SEBI (Listing Obligations and Disclosure Requirements) (Fourth Amendment) Regulations, 2019................ 108, 110
Rule 3(I) 398
Rule 3(VII) 108, 358, 363, 369, 375, 389, 393, 397

JAPAN

Companies Act (Act No. 86 of July 26, 2005)
Article 115........................ 103
Article 188 100
Tokyo Stock Exchange, 'New Listing Guidebook:1st and 2nd sections' (2018).............. 102
p. 140 412
p. 142 355
pp. 142–143........................ 357
p. 143 .... 355, 363
p. 144 375
p. 145 369
p. 146 355
p. 159 .... 103, 371, 377
p. 161 394

SINGAPORE

Companies Act 2006
s. 64........................ 96
s. 64(1) 96
Companies Act 2006 (Revised Edition) (November 2018)
s. 64A........................ 96
SGX Mainboard Rules
Chapter 2........................ 97
Chapter 7 97
Chapter 8 97
Rule 210(5)(c) 397
Rule 210(10)............ 357, 369, 375, 404
Rule 210(10)(b)..................... 98
Rule 210(10)(c)..................... 412
Rule 210(10)(d)..................... 378
Rule 210(10)(h) 393
Rule 730B 389, 397
Rule 803A 393
Rule 803A(3) 394
Singapore: Newspaper and Printing Presses Act (Chapter 206)
s.10........................ 96

UK

Civil Procedure Rules
Practice Direction 19B, para. 6.1A........ 350
Rule 19.10........................ 350
Rule 44.2(2)(a) 314, 349
Rule 44.2(2)(b)..................... 314
Companies Act 1948
s. 184 .... 72, 75
Companies Act 2006 .... 155, 314, 404
s. 1 129
s. 17 24
s. 21 .... 25, 64, 123, 146, 325, 328
s. 33 147
s. 77 25
s. 97 25
s. 136 .... 128, 129
s. 168 .... 24, 72, 75, 120, 155, 165, 197
s. 170(1) 313, 349, 386
s. 172 .... 155, 313, 323, 359
s. 172(1)........................ 155
s. 172(2) 155
s. 173 .... 313, 323
s. 174 .... 313, 323
s. 175 313
s. 190 25
s. 197 25
ss.232–4 315
s.239........................ 25
ss.260–4 313
s. 261(2) 313
s. 263(2) 313
s. 263(3) 314
s. 282 .... 24, 331
s. 283 .... 25, 328, 394
s. 284 .... 65, 72, 143
s. 303 .... 64, 120, 394
s. 307A........................ 25
s. 310 405
s. 311........................ 405
s. 321........................ 72
s. 338 .... 64, 120, 405
s. 366 25
s. 403 320
s. 414C(1) 155
s. 414CZA 155
s. 420 .... 37, 194
s. 421........................ 194
s. 423 405
s. 430 194
s. 439 .... 25, 64, 193, 195, 402, 403
s. 439A.............. 25, 64, 140, 193, 403

Companies Act 2006 (cont.)
s. 441 . . . 194
s. 489(4) . . . 25
s. 489A(3) . . . 391
s. 489A(6) . . . 392
s. 491 . . . 392
s. 510(2) . . . 25
s. 551 . . . 25, 331, 377
s. 571 . . . 25, 331
s. 618 . . . 331
s. 630 . . . 326, 392
s. 641 . . . 25, 392
s. 694 . . . 25
s. 701 . . . 25
s. 755 . . . 46
s. 830 . . . 137
s. 899 . . . 26, 330
s. 899(1)) . . . 330
s. 955 . . . 408
s. 979 . . . 206
s. 994 . . . 315, 323
s. 1159(1)(c) . . . 128
Company Directors Disqualification Act 1986
s.2 . . . 386
Consumer Rights Act 2015
Schedule 8, Part 1 . . . 350
Corporate Governance Code . . . 25, 49, 324, 333
Principle H . . . 200
Provision 5 . . . 155
Provision 9 . . . 324
Provision 10 . . . 323, 324, 396
Provision 11 . . . 121, 235, 324, 396
Provision 18 . . . 25
Provision 24 . . . 392
Disclosure and Transparency Rules
DTR 1B.1.10R . . . 320
DTR 4 . . . 37
DTR 5 . . . 406
DTR 5.3.1(b)R . . . 135
DTR 7 . . . 37
DTR 7.1 . . . 391
DTR 7.3.3R . . . 321
DTR 7.3.7R . . . 321
DTR 7.3.8R . . . 321, 401
DTR 7 Annex 1 . . . 321
European Union (Withdrawal) Act 2018c.16 . . 135
Finance Act 1986
s. 77(3)(f) . . . 369
Financial Services and Markets Act 2000
Part II . . . 46
Part XVIII . . . 22
s. 21 . . . 46
s. 31 . . . 320
s. 89F . . . 135
s. 91 . . . 320, 346
Income Tax (Earnings and Pensions) Act 2003
Schedule 5, Part 6, para. 40(3) . . . 369
Income Tax Act 2007
s. 247(5) . . . 369
s. 257(5) . . . 369
Insolvency Act 1986
s.84 . . . 25, 391
Listing Rules . . . 136, 321, 400
Chapter 6 . . . 346
Chapter 7 . . . 22
Chapter 9 . . . 346
Chapter 10 . . . 37, 63, 140, 196, 390, 391
Chapter 11 . . . 37, 167, 192, 319
Chapter 15 . . . 346
Chapter 16 . . . 346
Chapter 21 . . . 172, 192, 213, 255, 346
LR 2.2.7R . . . 356
LR 3.3.1 . . . 347
LR 3.3.3 . . . 347
LR 3.3.7 . . . 347
LR 5.2.5R(2) . . . 391
LR 6.5.4R . . . 167, 192, 322
LR 6.9.1 . . . 346
LR 6.14R . . . 48, 84, 167, 328, 347
LR 6.14.2R . . . 387
LR 7.1.2G . . . 22
LR 7.1.3G . . . 22
LR 7.2.1AR . . . 135
Premium Listing Principles . . . 121, 123, 132, 140, 406
Premium Listing Principle 3 . . . 22, 79
Premium Listing Principle 4 . . . 22, 23, 79
Premium Listing Principle 6 . . . 135
LR 8.2 . . . 320
LR 8.6 . . . 320
LR 9.2.2R . . . 37, 399
LR 9.2.2ADR(1) . . . 167, 192, 322
LR 9.2.2DG . . . 325
LR 9.2.2ER . . . 167, 325, 396
LR 9.2.2FR . . . 325, 396
LR 9.2.6CR . . . 321
LR 9.2.6DR . . . 321
LR 9.2.15R . . . 48, 84, 167, 328, 347
LR 9.2.21R . . . 23, 79, 406, 407
LR 9.3.11–9.3.12R . . . 391
LR 9.3.11R . . . 331
LR 9.8.4 . . . 37
LR 9.8.5 . . . 37
LR 9.8.6 . . . 37
LR 9.8.6(1)R . . . 406
LRs 9.8.6(5)R . . . 25, 37, 324
LR 9.8.6(6)R . . . 25, 37, 324
LR 10.2.2R . . . 63

LR 10.5.1R . . . 63
LR 10 Annex 1 . . . 63, 319
LR 11.1.1AR . . . 192, 322
LR 11.1.1CR . . . 322
LR 11.1.4R . . . 319
LR 11.1.5R . . . 193, 319
LR 11.1.6R . . . 193, 320
LR 11.1.7R . . . 319
LR 11.1.10R . . . 320
LR 11 Annex 1 . . . 320
LR 11 Annex 1.1R . . . 193
LR 14.2.2R . . . 84, 167, 328, 347
LR 14.3.25R . . . 321
LR 14.3.26R . . . 321
LR 21.5.2R . . . 320
LR App 1.1 . . . 166, 192, 320
Prospectus Regulation Rules . . . 406
Representation of the People Act 1983
s. 113 . . . 146
Takeover Code . . . 317, 408, 411
Definitions . . . 408
Introduction Section 3 . . . 316, 407
Rule 9 . . . 9, 125, 205, 209, 216, 316, 407, 408, 410
Rule 9.1 Note 4 . . . 408
Rule 9.1 Note 8 . . . 125
Rule 9.1 Note 12 . . . 318, 370
Rule 9 Notes on Dispensations, Note 6 . . . 410
Rule 9.5 . . . 209, 317
Rule 10 . . . 26
Rule 14 . . . 211
Rule 14.1 . . . 209, 317, 409
Rule 14.1 Notes . . . 209, 317, 409
Rule 14.1 Note 1 . . . 78
Rule 36 . . . 206
Rule 36.5 . . . 206
Rule 37.1 . . . 410
Rule 37.1 Note 1 . . . 410, 411
The Companies (Directors' Remuneration Policy and Directors' Remuneration Report) Regulations 2019 . . . 194
The Companies (Miscellaneous Reporting) Regulations 2018 . . . 194
The Companies (Model Articles) Regulations 2008 (SI 2008/3229) . . . 24
The Companies Act 2006 (Strategic Report and Directors' Report) Regulations 2013
reg.7 . . . 37
The Financial Services and Markets Act 2000 (Regulated Activities) Order 2001
Article 60(L) . . . 400
The Financial Services and Markets Act 2000 (Financial Promotion) Order 2005 (SI 2000/1529) as amended . . . 46
Article 48 . . . 46
Article 50 . . . 46
The Financial Services and Markets Act 2000 (Regulated Activities) (Amendment) (No. 2) Order 2013
Article 6 . . . 400
The Large and Medium-Sized Companies and Groups (Accounts and Reports) (Amendment) Regulations 2013 . . . 194

US

Code of Federal Regulations, Title 17, Chapter 2, Part 240 § 240.19c-4 (repealed) . . . 87, 88
Delaware General Corporation Law (Title 8, Chapter 1 of the Delaware Code)
§141(a) . . . 145
§141(d) . . . 24
§141(k)(1) . . . 25
§151(a) . . . 83
§212(a) . . . 83
The Securities Exchange Act of 1934
§13d . . . 10
US Federal Rules of Civil Procedure (2019 edition)
Rule 23(a) . . . 350

Abbreviations

1934 Securities Act	The Securities Exchange Act of 1934
Adaptimmune	Adaptimmune Therapeutics plc
Adelphia	Adelphia Communications Corporation
Agent Provocateur	Agent Provocateur Limited
AGM	annual general meeting
AIM	Alternative Investment Market
Airbnb	Airbnb, Inc.
Alibaba	Alibaba Group Holding Limited
Allianz	Allianz SE
Alphabet	Alphabet Inc.
Amazon	Amazon.com, Inc.
AMC	AMC Entertainment Holdings, Inc.
AMEX	American Stock Exchange (now known as NYSE America)
AMTD	AMTD International Inc.
Antofagasta	Antofagasta plc
Apple	Apple Inc.
Application of International Accounting Standards Regulation	Regulation (EC) No 1606/2002 of the European Parliament and of the Council of 19 July 2002 on the application of international accounting standards
ARM	Arm Holdings
articles	Articles of Association
Asia Resource Minerals	Asia Resource Minerals plc (formerly known as Bumi plc)
Autolus Therapeutics	Autolus Therapeutics plc
Aveva	Aveva plc
Aviva	Aviva plc

BEIS	Department for Business, Energy and Industrial Strategy
BIS	Department for Business, Innovation and Skills (now merged into BEIS)
BlackRock	BlackRock, Inc.
BP	BP plc
British Energy	British Energy plc
Burton Group	Burton Group plc
CA 2006	Companies Act 2006
CBS	CBS Corporation (now merged into ViacomCBS Inc.)
CCGG	Canadian Coalition for Good Governance
CEO	Chief Executive Officer
CFA	Chartered Financial Analysts Institute
Chewy	Chewy, Inc.
CII	Council of Institutional Investors
CMA	Competition and Markets Authority
Comcast	Comcast Corporation
Countrywide	Countrywide plc
CPR	Civil Procedure Rules
CSRC	China Securities Regulatory Commission
Cyberdyne	Cyberdyne Inc.
Daily Mail	Daily Mail and General Trust plc
Daimler-Benz	Daimler-Benz AG (now Daimler AG)
Debenhams	Debenhams plc
DeepMind	DeepMind Technologies
Del. C.	Delaware General Corporation Law (Title 8, Chapter 1 of the Delaware Code)
Deliveroo	Deliveroo Holdings plc
Dell	Dell Inc.
Delphi	Delphi Technologies plc
Disney	The Walt Disney Company
Dodd-Frank	The US federal Dodd-Frank Wall Street Reform and Consumer Protection Act, Pub. L. No. 111–203, § 951, 124 Stat. 1376 (2010)
Dodge Motors	Dodge Brothers Motor Car Company
DoorDash	DoorDash, Inc.
DTR	The FCA Handbook's Disclosure Guidance and Transparency sourcebook and the rules derived thereunder
EasyJet	EasyJet plc

EBITDA	earnings (sales less costs and expenses) before interest, tax, depreciation and amortisation
EC	European Commission
ECMH	Efficient Capital Markets Hypothesis
EDF	EDF S.A.
EDS	Electronic Data Systems
EEA	European Economic Area
Endava	Endava plc
ENRC	Eurasian Natural Resources Corporation plc
EU	European Union
Evans Cycles	Evans Cycles Limited
Exillon Energy	Exillon Energy plc
Facebook	Facebook, Inc.
FarFetch	FarFetch Limited
FCA	Financial Conduct Authority
Ferrexpo	Ferrexpo plc
Findel	Findel plc
First Data	First Data Corporation
FPO 2005	The Financial Services and Markets Act 2000 (Financial Promotion) Order 2005 (SI 2000/1529) as amended
Fraser Group	Fraser Group plc
FRC	Financial Reporting Council
French Connection	French Connection Group plc
Fresnillo	Fresnillo plc
FSA	Financial Services Authority (predecessor to the FCA)
FSMA 2000	Financial Services and Markets Act 2000
Game Digital	Game Digital plc
GAN	GAN Limited
GDP	gross domestic product
GLO	group litigation order
GM	General Motors Company
Google	Alphabet Inc. (and its predecessor as parent company of the group, Google Inc.)
Great Universal Stores	Great Universal Stores plc
Hansa	Hansa Investment Company Limited
Helen Curtis	Helene Curtis Industries Inc.
Hikma Pharmaceuticals	Hikma Pharmaceuticals plc
HIS Markit	HIS Markit Limited
HKEX	Hong Kong Exchanges and Clearing Limited

HM Treasury	Her Majesty's Treasury (also known as the UK Exchequer)
Hollinger International	Hollinger International Inc.
House of Fraser	House of Fraser plc, or the business known as House of Fraser, as applicable
IA 1986	Insolvency Act 1986
IAS	International Accounting Standards
Imagination Technologies	Imagination Technologies Group plc
Independent Shareholders	Shareholders only holding inferior-voting shares, and no enhanced-voting shares (see Section 9.6.2)
Industrial Rayon	Industrial Rayon Corporation
International Game Technology	International Game Technology plc
IPO	initial public offering
ITV	ITV plc
JPXR	Japan Exchange Regulation
Just Eat	Just Eat plc (now merged into Just Eat Takeaway .com N.V.)
KAZ Minerals	KAZ Minerals plc
Kensington Health Clubs	Kensington Health Clubs Limited
Levi Strauss	Levi Strauss & Co.
LinkedIn	LinkedIn Corporation
Listing Rules	the Listing Rules sourcebook, as published by the FCA exercising its primary market functions
LivaNova	LivaNova plc
LR	a listing rule under the Listing Rules
LSE	London Stock Exchange
Lyft	Lyft, Inc.
M&A	mergers and acquisitions
Main Market	Main Market of the LSE
Manchester United	Manchester United plc
MAR	Regulation (EU) No 596/2014 of the European Parliament and of the Council of 16 April 2014 on market abuse (market abuse regulation) and repealing Directive 2003/6/EC of the European Parliament and of the Council and Commission Directives 2003/124/EC, 2003/125/EC and 2004/72/EC (forming part of UK domestic law pursuant to the European Union (Withdrawal) Act 2018 c. 16)
Marks & Spencer	Marks and Spencer Group plc
Matomy Media	Matomy Media Group Limited
MaxLinear	MaxLinear, Inc.

Members States	Member States of the EU
MiFID II	Markets in Financial Instruments Directive (2014/65/EU)
Mimecast	Mimecast Limited
Model PLC Articles	Model Articles for public companies as set out in the Companies (Model Articles) Regulations 2008 (SI 2008/3229)
NASD	National Association of Securities Dealers (now merged into the Financial Industry Regulatory Authority)
NASDAQ	National Association of Securities Dealers Automated Quotations
News Corp.	News Corporation
NYSE	New York Stock Exchange
Ocado	Ocado Group plc
OECD	Organisation for Economic Co-Operation and Development
OIBD	operating income before depreciation *plus* interest income
Okta	Okta, Inc.
ONS	Office for National Statistics
Orchard Therapeutics	Orchard Therapeutics plc
Oxford Immunotec Global	Oxford Immunotec Global plc
PE	private equity
Persimmon	Persimmon plc
Pinterest	Pinterest, Inc.
Prospectus Regulation Rules	The FCA's Prospectus Regulation Rules sourcebook
Pure Storage	Pure Storage, Inc.
R&D	research and development
Rank	Rank Group plc
Regus	IWG plc (formerly Regus plc)
Rightmove	Rightmove plc
RingCentral	RingCentral, Inc.
ROA	return on assets (EBITDA divided by assets)
ROE	return on equity (net earnings divided by equity)
ROIC	return on invested capital (operating income (adjusted for tax) divided by total debt and shareholder equity less cash)
Rolls-Royce	Rolls-Royce Holdings plc
Royal Dutch Shell	Royal Dutch Shell plc
Saga	Saga plc

Schroders	Schroders plc
SEBI	Securities and Exchange Board of India
SFC	Securities and Futures Commission of Hong Kong
SG CA 2006	Singapore: Companies Act 2006
SGX	Singapore Exchange
Shake Shack	Shake Shack Inc.
Shell	see Royal Dutch Shell
Short-Selling Regulations	Regulation (EU) No. 236/2012 of the European Parliament and of the Council of 14 March 2012 on short selling and certain aspects of credit default swaps
Sky	Sky plc (now Sky Group Limited)
Slack	Slack Technologies, Inc.
Snap	Snap, Inc.
Sofa.com	Sofa.com Limited
Softbank	Softbank Group Corp.
Sports Direct	Sports Direct International plc (now Fraser Group plc)
Square	Square, Inc.
SRD II	Directive (EU) 2017/828 of the European Parliament and of the Council of 17 May 2017 amending Directive 2007/36/EC as regards the encouragement of long-term shareholder engagement
SSE	Shanghai Stock Exchange
State Street	State Street Corporation
STI	Sci-Tech Innovation Board of the SSE (also known as the STAR market)
Takeover Code	The Takeover Code as published by the UK's Panel on Takeovers and Mergers
Takeover Directive	Directive 2004/25/EC of the European Parliament and of the Council of 21 April 2004 on takeover bids
Tesla	Tesla, Inc.
Texas Roadhouse	Texas Roadhouse, Inc.
The Hut Group	The Hut Group plc
The New York Times	The New York Times Company
Tokyo Guidebook	Tokyo Stock Exchange, 'New Listing Guidebook 2018: 1st and 2nd sections' (October 2018)
Transparency Directive Amending Directive	Directive 2013/50/EU of the European Parliament and of the Council of 22 October 2013 amending Directive 2004/109/EC of the European

	Parliament and of the Council on the harmonisation of transparency requirements in relation to information about issuers whose securities are admitted to trading on a regulated market, Directive 2003/71/EC of the European Parliament and of the Council on the prospectus to be published when securities are offered to the public or admitted to trading and Commission Directive 2007/14/EC laying down detailed rules for the implementation of certain provisions of Directive 2004/109/EC
Trinity Mirror	Trinity Mirror plc (now Reach plc)
TSB	TSB Bank plc
TSE	Tokyo Stock Exchange
TSX	Toronto Stock Exchange
Twenty-First Century Fox	Twenty-First Century Fox, Inc.
Uber	Uber Technologies, Inc.
UCloud	UCloud Technology Co. Ltd
UK CGC	The UK Corporate Governance Code
UK/EU Withdrawal Agreement	Agreement on the withdrawal of the United Kingdom of Great Britain and Northern Ireland from the European Union and the European Atomic Energy Community, OJ L 29 31.1.20, p. 7–187
UK Listing Review	HM Treasury, 'UK Listing Review' (3 March 2021)
Unilever	Unilver plc / Unilever N.V.
ValueAct	ValueAct Capital
Vanguard	Vanguard Group
VC	venture capital
Veeva	Veeva Systems, Inc.
Viacom	Viacom Inc. (now merged into ViacomCBS, Inc.)
WeWork	WeWork Companies, Inc.
Whitbread	Whitbread plc
Xiaomi	Xiaomi Corporation
Yelp	Yelp, Inc.
Zillow	Zillow Group, Inc.
Zoom	Zoom Video Communications, Inc.
Zynga	Zynga, Inc.

Introduction

With great power comes great responsibility.[1]

The titular phrase 'founders without limits' describes an environment in which founders of high-growth companies, especially in the tech sphere, are given the scope, tools and incentives to grow their businesses as listed companies and to pursue their long-term visions for success without having to succumb to the short-term pressures which many have argued have haunted the capital markets for decades. Dual-class stock is a mechanism which can give founders that latitude, and, consequently, attract such founders to the listed company markets. However, the quote at the start of this Introduction, 'With great power comes great responsibility', from comic book lore, can easily pertain to the debate surrounding dual-class stock. Dual-class stock is a company share capital structure that embraces multiple classes of shares. In this book, as in the literature on 'dual-class stock', it will be assumed that at least one of those classes of shares will grant to the holder of shares of that class voting rights that are disproportionately greater than the holder's cut of the company's dividends, distributions and residual proceeds upon a winding-up – 'cash-flow' or 'equity' rights. In its simplest form, a 'dual-class company' will have issued two classes of stock. One such class will comprise shares each of which possesses a single vote that can be exercised at general meetings of shareholders – classically referred to as 'one share, one vote'. The other class will comprise shares which possess multiple voting rights: ten, twenty or more votes per share. The cash-flow rights attached to each class of shares will be identical. The controversy that has bedevilled dual-class stock ascribes to the fact that a dual-class structure can be used by a shareholder to retain or amass sufficient voting control over material decisions of the company, while only holding a small proportion of the equity. Correspondingly, the decisions made

[1] The quote has been attributed to S. Lee and S. Ditko, 'Amazing Fantasy #15, "Spider-Man!"' (August 1962).

by that shareholder do not proportionately impact its wealth. Those in control of the company fail to fully feel the consequences of their actions.[2] The shareholder has great power, but little of the responsibility.

Although the premise of dual-class stock can apply to companies with all manner of characteristics, in this book, dual-class stock will be discussed in the context of publicly listed companies.[3] The literature and research on the subject almost invariably relates to listed companies. The controversial aspects of dual-class stock are more keenly felt where those holding shares with inferior-voting rights, and, often, the majority of the equity in the company, comprise thousands of public shareholders who have little, if any, influence on the capital structure of the company and who may be prejudiced by the acts of the holders of enhanced-voting shares. In contrast to the controversial aspects, the public equity markets are where dual-class stock can shine. Many have bemoaned the short-term approach taken by corporations as a result of pressure from public shareholders with short-term profit aspirations. With dual-class stock, a shareholder holding control through the ownership of enhanced-voting shares can take decisions on behalf of the company largely insulated from the views of the public shareholders. A balance exists between the risks to public shareholders in the use of dual-class stock and the benefits that dual-class structure can bring to the health of the company and its shareholders over the longer term.

In the United Kingdom, as of the time of writing, dual-class stock is essentially prohibited on the most prestigious tier of the Main Market of the London Stock Exchange – the 'premium tier'. Although proposals have been made to expand the scope of capital structure permissible on the premium tier,[4] as will be discussed in this book, such proposals do not constitute 'genuine' dual-class stock.[5] 'Genuine' dual-class stock is, though, permitted on many of the world's most prominent stock exchanges, including the NYSE, NASDAQ, Hong Kong, Singapore, Tokyo, Shanghai, Mumbai and Toronto. If dual-class stock is nothing but trouble, it begs the question why evidently sophisticated markets are open to the implementation of dual-class structure. In this book, the probity of dual-class stock will be assessed, with a view to evaluating the sagacity of the United Kingdom's premium tier approach to dual-class stock. The underlying context to this book is the dearth of new listings on the London Stock Exchange, particularly by technology companies, which have, in other jurisdictions, been prolific adopters of dual-class stock upon their IPOs. The

2 F. Easterbrook and D. Fischel, 'Voting in Corporate Law' (1983) 26 *J. Law Econ.* 395, 409; J. Dammann, 'The Controlling Shareholder's General Duty of Care: A Dogma That Should Be Abandoned' (2015) 2 *U. Ill. L. Rev.* 479, 494; F. Easterbrook and D. Fischel, eds., *The Economic Structure of Corporate Law* (Harvard University Press, 1991) at 73; C. Li et al., 'Ownership Structure and the Cost of Corporate Borrowing' (2011) 100 *J. Financ. Econ.* 1, 2; H. Hu and B. Black, 'The New Vote Buying: Empty Voting and Hidden (Morphable) Ownership' (2006) 79 *S. Cal. L. Rev.* 811, 851; HKEX, 'Concept Paper: New Board' (June 2017) at 18.

3 The rationale for such a limitation is discussed in more detail below in the section 'Scope'.

4 HM Treasury, 'UK Listing Review' (3 March 2021).

5 See Section 1.5.7 of Chapter 1.

lack of an option to adopt dual-class stock on the premium tier could be deterring the listing of UK tech companies. Founders of tech companies may fear losing control, and therefore the potential to be removed from the business if short-term profits are not robust, through a premium tier IPO. Dual-class stock allows a founder to sell and issue substantial levels of equity on the public markets while retaining voting control. However, institutional shareholders, who dominate the UK public markets,[6] are concerned that opening the doors to dual-class stock will enable founders to amass vast fortunes upon IPO, and subsequently exploit public shareholders through abusing their powers as corporate controllers with no effective oversight. The core of this book examines whether such 'founder without limits' should be hailed or feared on the premium tier.

The subject matter of this book has broad appeal. Dual-class stock has been described as 'the most important issue in corporate governance today',[7] and the topic has, in numerous jurisdictions, vexed practitioners, academics and regulators alike for decades. Accordingly, this book will be of interest to scholars, students and purveyors of the fields of controlling shareholders, shareholder rights and corporate governance. Since the kernel of the book correlates dual-class stock with the potential to breathe life into the UK tech sector, it will additionally be of interest to legal practitioners, economists and business schools. Many elements of the book also serve as an essential roadmap for regulators, and, if the United Kingdom's rules are relaxed, as a continuing adjunct to policy-making going forward. Although the book mainly focuses on the implications of dual-class stock in the United Kingdom, it collates a body of work that has been progressed across multiple jurisdictions over many years. In particular, the book retains relevance in the United States, where, notwithstanding the recent widespread use of dual-class stock by tech companies, there has been a backlash of sorts against the structure, returning the theme to prominence, and, also, in jurisdictions such as Hong Kong and Singapore, which have more recently commenced their journeys to accepting dual-class companies on their public markets.

This book touches upon corporate law, economics and policy-making, but prior detailed knowledge of any of these disciplines is not required by a reader. It is assumed that a reader will be unfamiliar with the nuances and technical details of dual-class structure and the associated laws and regulations, and, therefore, these are spelled-out, at least in broad terms, throughout the book. I hope that this book will prove informative and illuminating, and, above all, enjoyable, to readers, whether or not you believe that the United Kingdom should welcome 'founders without limits' with open arms.

[6] After excluding individuals, charities and public sector bodies, institutional shareholders, both in the United Kingdom and globally, hold the remainder of UK equities, amounting to 77.77 per cent of UK listed shares as of 31 December 2018 (calculated using data from: ONS, 'Ownership of UK Quoted Shares: 2018' (January 2020)).

[7] J. Coffee, 'Dual Class Stock: The Shades of Sunset' *CLS Blue Sky Blog* (19 November 2018), http://clsbluesky.law.columbia.edu/2018/11/19/dual-class-stock-the-shades-of-sunset/

OVERVIEW

I wish to tell the story of dual-class stock in the United Kingdom – from the history of its prohibition through to a compelling blueprint for a renaissance on the premium tier. The laws and regulations, and the discussions appertaining thereto, referenced in this book are generally current as of 1 January 2021 (unless otherwise stated), although some references to later material have been possible, including the more recent proposals of the UK Listing Review which are discussed throughout. The book is divided into three parts. Part I sets the scene for an analysis of dual-class stock firms, by putting dual-class stock into context. Chapter 1 outlines the rise of the phenomenon in the United States, particularly in the technology sphere, and its pertinence to the United Kingdom's dwindling level of technology, and other company listings. From the perspective of a founder, the possibilities available to foster a high-growth company in the United Kingdom will be assessed, together with the scope that dual-class stock offers to enhance the options available. As will be noted further in Chapter 1, the US experience of dual-class stock will consistently be drawn upon in the book, since the largest listed dual-stock companies exist in, and the majority of existing dual-class stock research pertains to, that jurisdiction, and the breadth, investor base, maturity and ownership structure of publicly listed firms in the United States make them the most appropriate comparators to issuers on the LSE. Chapter 1 will also outline the proposals of the UK Listing Review in the context of dual-class stock, and it will be discussed that those proposals fall far short of 'true' dual-class stock and may not attract to the premium tier the types of firms envisaged. Chapter 2 chronicles the history of the LSE's path toward proscribing dual-class stock from a position where such structures were largely accepted. This history will be juxtaposed with a history of the NYSE's attitude to dual-class stock, which has moved from a strict prohibition to a generally permissive environment. The histories of those stock exchanges that have recently relaxed their rules on dual-class stock, including the Tokyo, India, Hong Kong, Singapore and Shanghai exchanges, will also be delineated, together with an account of the approaches taken by the other major global exchanges. Chapter 3 describes some of the other mechanisms that can be used to create a divergence between voting and cash-flow rights within companies and determines that an equivalence cannot be presumed between those mechanisms and dual-class stock. Chapter 4 discusses some of the more esoteric arguments against dual-class stock, so that they can promptly be dismissed as pertinent factors.

Part II investigates the benefits and detriments of dual-class stock from the perspective of founders and public shareholders. Chapter 5 discusses the controlling shareholder phenomenon. It is not intended that this book should provide a detailed exposition of the considerations appertaining to one share, one vote firms in the presence of controlling shareholders, with the subject well-served by other controlling shareholder focused literature,[8] but given the link between control and dual-class stock, a brief elucidation of the presence of controlling shareholders in the United Kingdom provides a launching point for the dual-class discussion to follow. The differing dynamics between one share, one vote, and dual-class stock, controlling shareholder firms will be outlined. Chapter 6 provides a normative assessment of dual-class firms, comparing and contrasting the potential benefits and detriments to public shareholders of founder behaviour incentivised by dual-class structure. The gamut of international literature on the topic is corralled and digested into a UK-centric framework, with a view to distinguishing the United Kingdom from a number of other jurisdictions on the basis of its legal, regulatory and market environment. The chapter concludes with the formulation of a 'tradeoff' methodology which emphasises the nature of the actions incentivised by dual-class structure, and which can be utilised to develop policy. Chapter 7 evaluates the existing empirical evidence on dual-class firms from around the world. Unlike traditional empirical reviews, the chapter collates studies that analyse dual-class firms using different performance measures to attain a holistic view of dual-class stock. It will be shown that, in fact, dual-class firms suffer from a discount in share price that is not warranted by any deficiencies in the subsequent performance of such firms. The chapter suggests that by giving public shareholders more comfort that they will not be expropriated by the holders of enhanced-voting stock, the cost of capital for such companies can be reduced. A route forward for the United Kingdom is proposed that combines an acceptance of dual-class stock (above and beyond the limited proposals of the UK Listing Review) with judicious protective measures for public shareholders.

Part III continues the roadmap for regulators and policy-makers. Chapter 8 identifies and critically examines the potential for existing legal, regulatory, psychological and market factors in the United Kingdom to constrain the ability of controlling shareholders holding enhanced-voting stock to abuse public shareholders, if dual-class firms were to emerge on the LSE's premium tier. Chapter 9 points the way forward and discusses the efficacy of various types of further protective measures for public shareholders that could form part of a proposed balanced package of provisions accompanying a relaxation of the LSE's premium tier prohibition on dual-class stock. It is discussed that the key consideration in a balanced

[8] For example, see C. Holderness and D. Sheehan, 'The Role of Controlling Shareholders in Publicly Held Corporations: An Exploratory Analysis' (1988) 20 *J. Financ. Econ.* 317; R. Gilson and J. Gordon, 'Controlling Controlling Shareholders' (2003) 152 *U. Pa. L. Rev.* 785; B. Reddy, 'The Fat Controller: Slimming Down the Excesses of Controlling Shareholders in UK Listed Companies' (2018) 38 *OJLS* 733; B. Cheffins, 'Corporate Law and Ownership Structure: A Darwinian Link?' (2002) 25 *UNSW Law Journal* 346; R. Gilson, 'Controlling Shareholders and Corporate Governance: Complicating the Comparative Taxonomy' (2006) 119 *Harv. L. Rev.* 1641; J. Hill et al., eds., *The Research Handbook on Shareholder Power* (Edward Elgar, 2015); L. Enriques and T. Tröger, eds., *The Law and Finance of Related Party Transactions* (Cambridge University Press, 2019); A. Boyle, *Minority Shareholders' Remedies* (Cambridge University Press, 2002).

protection package is that the relevant protective measures should be sufficiently robust to prevent the most egregious forms of abuse by enhanced-voting shareholders and to assuage the anxieties of public investors in dual-class firms, without falling into the potential trap of the UK Listing Review and being so severe that they blunt the qualities of dual-class structure that create value for all shareholders or substantively discourage the listing of firms that the approval of dual-class structure is intended to attract.

The book finishes with concluding remarks, summarising the proposals made in the book and the connotations going forward.

SCOPE

The parameters surrounding the discussion to follow are summarised in this section. An unconstrained examination of dual-class stock could easily subsume several volumes, and, therefore, as a matter of pragmatism, the scope of this book will be limited in some respects. The limits are based upon the context within which dual-class stock is considered controversial and the likelihood of the manner in which dual-class stock would be utilised in a jurisdiction where it is permitted.

Publicly Listed Companies

Dual-class stock can be implemented by private companies or publicly listed companies. However, the topic is mainly discussed, both academically and in policy circles, in the context of publicly listed companies, and this book will follow a similar approach. As discussed in Chapter 2, private companies are permitted to use dual-class structures with a great deal of freedom, and such capital structures are widespread in the private company world. However, with a private company, those contemplating investment in such a company, generally, will be able to negotiate the terms directly with the other investors or owners, particularly at the time the business is founded, and, to a lesser degree, at later stages. For example, at the set-up stage, investors will have a level of input into the capital structure of the company. Additionally, to the extent that a dual-class structure is, or has been, implemented, investors can, and often do, demand minority investor protection rights, not necessarily attached to the shares that they hold, whether that be at the set-up or later stages of the company's development. There is complete freedom of choice as to whether a person makes an investment in a private company, and, in most instances, private companies will, in the United Kingdom, be prohibited from soliciting investments from unsophisticated retail investors.[9]

Unlike private companies, public companies can offer their securities to the public and solicit investments, albeit in accordance with strictly defined and

[9] See Section 1.5.3 of Chapter 1 for more details.

prescribed requirements and offering documentation.[10] Also, at the time of an IPO, although the views of prospective investors are often pre-emptively solicited to ensure the success of the listing, the issuer, in coordination with the relevant listing authority, has full control over the choice of capital structure. Any rights protecting the public shareholders will generally be secured indirectly as a result of market forces to ensure the success of the listing, rather than through direct negotiation. Furthermore, subsequent to the IPO of a public company, any acquirors of shares in the secondary market or any further investors upon future issuances of shares (unless the capital structure is changed mid-stream) are subject to the capital structure already adopted at the time of the IPO. The investors in publicly listed companies comprise a broad church, including not only sophisticated hedge funds, banks, private equity funds, mutual funds and other institutional investors but also individuals who form part of the general public. Markedly, even if individuals are not investing directly, they may be exposed to the whims of publicly listed companies through interests in pension funds, insurance products and investment funds. A greater level of scrutiny is therefore essential where 'unsophisticated' retail investors directly or indirectly invest in public companies, and where dual-class stock represents a take-it-or-leave-it structure.[11] The need for greater protection for public shareholders generally is reflected by the enhanced regulatory rules that apply to listed companies.[12]

Additionally, companies listed on the premium tier of the LSE's Main Market can comprise part of the FTSE-indices, at which point freedom of choice can become a luxury. The significance of the indices is further outlined in Chapter 1, but, in summary, certain funds track specific indices, essentially requiring them to invest in constituent companies to adhere to the relevant investment strategy. Many pension, insurance and investment funds, to which retail investors may be exposed, pursue such 'passive' strategies in whole or in part. Accordingly, freedom of choice is very much curtailed in the event that a listed company that has undergone an IPO with dual-class stock subsequently becomes a constituent of an index. Investors with no discretion as to whether to invest in a dual-class firm are deserving of greater protection.[13]

[10] *ibid.*

[11] See D. Ratner, 'The Government of Business Corporations: Critical Reflections on the Rule of One Share, One Vote' (1970–1971) 56 *Cornell L. Rev.* 1, 17, where it is discussed that the equity in privately owned companies is owned by people who are, or have been, actively involved in the business, or are related by personal or business ties to people who are, whereas the equity in a publicly listed company is owned by a substantial number of people who acquired it in the open market and have no other connection with the corporation and its business.

[12] For example, UK publicly listed companies are subject to the Listing Rules, if listed on the Main Market, the AIM Rules for Companies, if listed on AIM, and the Takeover Code.

[13] This may be the very reason why certain US indices have excluded dual-class stock (for further details, see Section 2.3 of Chapter 2), and it is also an indirect justification for excluding premium listings of dual-class structures, since non-premium listed firms are excluded from the FTSE indices.

Finally, although it is accepted that large private companies exist, in comparison, the scale of publicly listed companies is, on average, greater. Listed companies can be immense, with individual businesses employing tens of thousands of workers, and their actions can have significant impacts on a network of stakeholders, including customers, suppliers, consumers, the environment and society generally. Publicly listed companies, and the equity capital markets generally, serve an important purpose in a capitalist market-based system.[14] From the perspective of the issuers, public investors represent a substantial and valuable source of financing for companies, and the equity capital markets provide an avenue for owners of companies to exit their investments in whole or in part. From the perspective of investors, the listing of securities by public companies allows hands-off 'outsiders' the opportunity to share in the potential success of large organisations in which they would only otherwise have had the opportunity to invest if they were intrinsically involved in the business, had close relationships with the 'insiders', or if they were sophisticated investors with a professional specialisation in private company investment. Given the lack of effective negotiating ability of public investors, the absence of freedom of choice for certain investors and the sprawling influence of publicly listed companies, an examination of dual-class stock is most critical in the publicly listed company arena.

Dual-Class Stock as a Means to Control

Lessons from the United States suggest that the implementation of dual-class structure is primarily accompanied by a single shareholder (or connected shareholders) retaining effective control of a publicly listed company while holding a disproportionately smaller portion of the equity, and dual-class firms without controlling shareholders are rare.[15]

Conversely, if both inferior-voting and enhanced-voting shares were listed and made freely available to public shareholders, a dispersed ownership system for both classes of shares could develop where voting control is diffuse. The creation of divergences between voting and cash-flow rights on an investor-by-investor basis in a diffused ownership dual-class firm can confuse the dynamics of a simple one share, one vote diffused-ownership system and create a variety of consequences that diverge from those relevant to a dual-class firm where the enhanced-voting shares are not offered to the public and, instead, are owned by insiders. Those shareholders wishing to hold shares with voting rights would be able to acquire those shares in the market, whereas those with no volition to exercise voting rights would still be

[14] By way of analogy, see the comments in D. Walker, 'A Review of Corporate Governance in UK Banks and Other Financial Industry Entities: Final Recommendations' (26 November 2009) at 70.

[15] L. Bebchuk and K. Kastiel, 'The Perils of Small-Minority Controllers' (2019) 107 *Geo. L.J.* 1453, 1496 found that 83.6 per cent of Russell-3000 dual-class companies have a controlling minority shareholder (an earlier draft noted the figure as 96.7 per cent of S&P-1500 dual-class firms).

able to share in the economic prospects of the company, presumably at a discounted price.[16] Such a development does not, initially, raise, to the same level of materiality, considerations of the mischief that could be entertained by controllers being able to detach their voting and cash-flow rights. Even if, subsequent to IPO as a dispersed ownership firm, a shareholder were to acquire control through the purchase of enhanced-voting shares, as discussed in more detail in Chapters 6 and 8, for many UK listed companies, the acquiring shareholder would be required to make an offer to all the shareholders in the company, preventing minority shareholders from being subjugated to a controller without a fair exit mechanism.[17] Indeed, there is an argument that a truly dispersed ownership dual-class structure could generate significantly positive outcomes for firms from stewardship and governance perspectives. Enhanced-voting shares could be issued to shareholders interested in active stewardship based upon detailed research, and inferior-voting shares could be issued to passive shareholders with little interest in stewardship or voting, ensuring that voting stock is in the hands of public institutional shareholders who ascribe value to the vote and can exercise influence undiluted by votes in the hands of uninformed shareholders or shareholders apathetic toward voting.[18] As the markets organically align themselves amongst the two classes of shares, the company will reduce agency and transaction costs,[19] and thereby lower its costs of capital.

However, this ideal model faces a number of challenges. Firstly, it is not clear that even those shareholders who actively buy and sell shares with a view to making market-beating profits, and are assumed to benefit from informed stewardship, are, in fact, truly incentivised to incur significant expenditure on detailed research.[20] It cannot be guaranteed that placing voting stock in the hands of such shareholders will be any more effective in that regard than a one share, one vote system that does not discriminately allocate voting rights between different types of public shareholders.

[16] In relation to the discount applied to inferior-voting shares, see Section 7.4 of Chapter 7. However, the level of discount may in fact be small if enhanced-voting shares are dispersed and not held by a controller or associated group of controllers (see Section 6.2.7 of Chapter 6), and if inferior-voting shareholders perceive that management is being kept in check by a group of shareholders willing to, and adept at, monitoring the executive.

[17] Takeover Code, Rule 9.

[18] D. Lund, 'Nonvoting Shares and Efficient Corporate Governance' (2019) 71 *Stanf. L. Rev.* 687; also see A. Alchian and H. Demsetz, 'Production, Information Costs, and Economic Organization' (1972) 62 *Am. Econ. Rev.* 777, 789.

[19] Lund (2019) (n 18 above 724).

[20] B. Reddy, 'The Emperor's New Code? Time to Re-Evaluate the Nature of Stewardship Engagement Under the UK's Stewardship Code' (2021) 84 *MLR* 842, 857-861; R. Gilson and J. Gordon, 'The Agency Costs of Agency Capitalism: Activist Investors and the Revaluation of Governance Rights' (2013) 113 *Columb. L. Rev.* 863, 891–893; L. Bebchuk et al., 'The Agency Problems of Institutional Investors' (2017) 31 *J. Econ. Perspect.* 89, 99; A. Reisberg, 'The UK Stewardship Code: On the Road to Nowhere' (2015) 15 *JCLS* 217, 233; D. Arsalidou, 'Shareholders and Corporate Scrutiny: The Role of the UK Stewardship Code' (2012) 3 *ECFR* 342, 364; I. Chiu, 'Turning Institutional Investors into "Stewards": Exploring the Meaning and Objectives of "Stewardship"' (2013) 66 *Curr. Leg. Probl.* 443, 461.

Secondly, the model does not countenance the possibility that the publicly available enhanced-voting shares could fall into the hands of shareholders with different investment objectives to the majority of the inferior-voting shareholders. For example, enhanced-voting shares could be acquired by short-term orientated hedge funds, or, even worse, nefarious conduct could develop in a takeover scenario where a shareholder has a significant economic interest in a one share, one vote target, and a significant voting, but small economic, interest in a dual-class bidder through holding enhanced-voting shares.[21] The scenario could create incentives for the shareholder to exercise its votes in the dual-class firm for the benefit of the target by using its voting power to support the bidder overpaying for the target. These considerations, and the fact that a dispersed ownership of enhanced-voting shares will make it difficult for any potential investor to ascertain where the balance of power will land at any given moment, have led to certain jurisdictions, such as Hong Kong and Singapore, requiring enhanced-voting shares to remain unlisted.[22]

Given the uncertainties surrounding the use of enhanced-voting stock in a dispersed ownership structure, and the fact that dual-class stock is utilised in the United States almost ubiquitously to ingrain control, this book will assess dual-class stock on the assumption that a shareholder or a group of related shareholders controls the company, in what would effectively represent a 'controlling shareholder' structure. The term 'controller' can also have different connotations. A plethora of literature exists in relation to the impact and consequences of large 'blockholders' in companies. The definition of 'blockholder', though, is often nebulous,[23] and much of the US academia labels any shareholder owning more than 5 per cent of the voting rights in a corporation as a 'blockholder' on the somewhat arbitrary basis that such shareholdings in public corporations are required to be disclosed pursuant to Section 13d of the 1934 Securities Act. However, a true 'controlling shareholder' is one that has the ability to replace the directors of the company, and therefore is able to have a fundamental influence on the appointment and removal of managers. Therefore, in this book, the term 'controller' will be used to refer to a shareholder or an associated group of shareholders that controls a majority of the votes (or at least a sufficiently large proportion of the votes to give them effective control where the remainder of the voting rights are substantially dispersed between small shareholders).[24] The singular, 'controller', will mainly be

21 With respect to this concept of 'empty voting', see, for example, Hu and Black (2006) (n 2 above 811 and 816).

22 For more detail, see Chapters 2 and 9.

23 For a discourse in the inconsistencies in defining 'blockholder', see A. Edmans, 'Blockholders and Corporate Governance' (2014) 6 *Annu. Rev. Financ. Econ.* 23, 35; A. Edmans and C. Holderness, 'Blockholders: A Survey of Theory and Evidence' in *The Handbook of the Economics of Corporate Governance*, eds. B. Hermalin and M. Wesibach (Elsevier, 2017) at 548.

24 As discussed further in Section 1.4 of Chapter 1, in the United Kingdom, for most listed companies, holding a majority of the votes will give a controller the ability to appoint and remove directors unilaterally.

used herein, but the term should also be taken to comprise a group of connected controllers. Whether such a controller participates as part of the management team becomes a moot point, since even where third-party managers have been appointed, they will have been appointed at the behest of, and will owe their continued employment to, the controller. Controllers come in a variety of forms, including individuals, companies, public bodies, management and non-management investors, and founders (included within the term 'family controllers' in this book) and their heirs.

TERMINOLOGY

Throughout this book, the terms 'dual-class stock' and 'dual-class structure' will be used to describe capital structures encompassing share classes with differing voting rights, which are not necessarily restricted to two classes of shares. The term 'dual-class firm' will be used to describe firms that utilise dual-class stock, with 'dual-class board', 'dual-class founder' and 'dual-class controller' referring to boards, founders and controllers, respectively, of dual-class firms. Dual-class structures are also variously described in the literature as multiple voting rights and weighted voting rights structures. The nature of multiple voting rights is relative, and, in the appropriate circumstances, such as where non-voting shares are in issue, one share, one vote shares could be considered to be multiple voting right shares in that they possess more votes than another class of shares in existence. Throughout this book, the terms 'enhanced-voting shares' and 'inferior-voting shares' will be used to describe shares with greater and lesser voting rights, respectively, within a specific company's capital structure. Within a company, or in the context of a specific shareholder's ownership of shares, the divergence between voting and cash-flow rights will be termed the 'voting/cash-flow divergence', with a disproportionately greater level of voting rights attached to shares, as compared to cash-flow rights, being a larger voting/cash-flow divergence. The expression 'expropriate' will be used to describe the behaviour of a controller of a company in operating the company in a manner that is detrimental to shareholder value – where the controller possesses a large voting/cash-flow divergence, it is able to exercise voting control for its own personal benefit, while the holders of a majority of the cash-flow rights suffer financial downside. The cash-flow that would otherwise flow to the non-controlling shareholders is thereby 'expropriated'.

Although this book squarely deals with companies, and therefore corporate forms, the terms 'firm' and 'issuer' will also be used, reflecting the common terms utilised to describe companies that issue shares on the capital markets. The term 'premium tier' will be used for the Premium Tier of the Main Market of the LSE, and 'premium listed' will refer to an issuer listed on the premium tier. Additionally, even though subtle differences exist between the terms 'shares' and 'stock', the two will be used interchangeably throughout this book, with an acknowledgement that the former term is more prevalently used in the United Kingdom and the latter in the United

States. In some cases, the common terms 'insiders' and 'outside investors' or 'outside shareholders' will also be used. 'Insiders' are those significant shareholders, employees or directors with informational or control benefits over 'outside investors'. In the context of dual-class stock, the insiders will generally be the controllers, and the outside investors, the public shareholders.

The concept 'theory of the firm' has been widely discussed in the literature, in relation to the purpose and theoretical underpinnings of the corporate form. The approach that this book takes to evaluating dual-class stock is delineated in Chapter 4, and it is, therein, discussed that this book steers clear of developing a new theory of the firm in the context of dual-class stock. Since this book will not be engaging with the 'theory of the firm' or a normative assessment of the 'purpose of the firm' in relation to its evaluation of dual-class stock, the references throughout this book to 'theory' do not implicate an examination based upon the theory of the firm, or corporate purpose. 'Theory' will be used in the colloquial sense, and, throughout this book, unless otherwise expressed, 'theory' will denote a conceptual evaluation of the hypothetical pros and cons of dual-class stock as a contrast to the real-world empirical evidence.

PART I

Putting Dual-Class Stock into Context

1

The Cult of Dual-Class Stock in the Era of Big Tech

... the whole point of technology ... creates an appetite for immortality on the one hand ... threatens universal extinction on the other[1]

1.1 INTRODUCTION

Dual-class stock refers to a capital structure where a listed company issues two (or more) classes of stock to which are attached differing rights to vote at a meeting of shareholders but identical cash-flow or equity rights to distributions by the company through dividends, through share buybacks or upon a winding up. For example, in simple terms, a company could issue two classes of stock. One class will be 'inferior-voting stock', with each share in the class receiving one vote. The second class will be 'enhanced-voting stock', with each share in the class receiving, for instance, ten votes. Since the cash-flow rights for each class are identical, a holder of enhanced-voting stock can amass greater voting control in the company than the holders of inferior-voting stock for the same equity interest. In bygone times the United Kingdom's London Stock Exchange (LSE) was very much open to listings by companies with dual-class stock, with mainstays of the City such as Marks & Spencer, Shell, Whitbread, ITV, Burton Group, Rank and House of Fraser all implementing dual-class stock structure. However, now the Main Market of the LSE is divided into tiers, with the premium tier being the most prestigious, and, as of the time of writing, genuine dual-class stock is not admissible to a premium listing.[2]

The attitude to dual-class stock fluctuates wildly in other jurisdictions. The US stock exchanges and Toronto's TSX, for example, are broadly permissive of dual-class stock. This contrasts with jurisdictions, such as Australia, that maintain a prohibition on the listing of dual-class shares. In between, jurisdictions such as Hong Kong, Singapore, India and Tokyo permit dual-class stock, but subject to prescriptive requirements. In Shanghai, the SSE, like the LSE, permits dual-class

[1] D. DeLillo, *White Noise* (Viking Press, 1985) at 285.

[2] Notes 32–41 below and accompanying text.

stock, but not on all tiers of the exchange. In the decade after the financial crash of 2008, a number of exchanges relaxed their previous prohibitions of dual-class stock, manifestly to attract the listings of innovative, high-growth companies, especially from the technology sector. As will be noted in this book, the founders of tech companies have in the decades following the dotcom crash of the early 2000s discerned significant benefits in listing their companies with dual-class stock. Although numerous industries have availed themselves of dual-class stock over the years, recently, Big Tech, which refers to the current trend of major tech companies with inordinate market, public and societal influence,[3] has driven a resurgence in the structure, and it is with Big Tech that we commence the discussion.

1.2 THE RISE OF DUAL-CLASS STOCK IN THE UNITED STATES

In the context of dual-class stock, 19 August 2004 was a seminal day, marking the IPO of Google.[4] Google's founders redesignated a proportion of their stock as Class B stock, which remained unlisted, and listed new Class A stock. The Class A stock issued to the public embraced the concept of 'one share, one vote', the euphemistic term describing voting allocation where each share enjoys a single vote. In contrast, the Class B stock retained by the founders enjoyed ten votes per share.[5] The cash-flow rights attached to both classes of stock were identical. Google had adopted the classic dual-class stock structure.

The dual-class structure enabled Google's 'insiders' to retain control of the firm that they had founded by holding a majority of the voting rights, whilst, by relinquishing the majority of cash-flow rights in the company, crystallising significant wealth and tapping the public markets for finance. The situation was further exacerbated in April 2014, when, as depicted in Figure 1.1, Google split its Class A stock into Class A and non-voting Class C stock, allowing it to issue stock without further diluting the insiders' control of the corporation.[6] As of 31 December 2019, the founders of Google, Larry Page and Sergey Brin, owned 51.2 per cent of the voting rights of the company, but only 11.4 per cent of the cash-flow rights.[7]

[3] R. Foroohar, 'We Need to Talk about Big Tech' *Financial Times* (3 October 2017), www.ft.com/content/64a20c34-a769-11e7-93c5-648314d2c72c. All URLs were last accessed on 1 May 2021 unless otherwise stated.

[4] Alphabet, Inc. became the new listed holding company of Google on 2 October 2015. However, throughout this book, the more common brand name, 'Google', will be used.

[5] Form S-1 Registration Statement of Google Inc. (29 April 2004) at iii.

[6] In fact, Google announced the stock split in 2012 (Form 8-K of Google Inc. (12 April 2012) at Item 8.01), but did not issue any such stock until 2014 due to shareholder litigation, subsequently settled, against the proposed stock split.

[7] Total number of issued shares discerned from Form 10-K of Alphabet, Inc. for fiscal year ended 31 December 2019; Class A, Class B and Class C stock ownership information gathered from Form 4 Statement of Changes in Beneficial Ownership filing by Sergey Brin (filed 8 November 2019), and Form 5 Annual Statement of Changes in Beneficial Ownership filing by Larry Page (filed 8 February 2018).

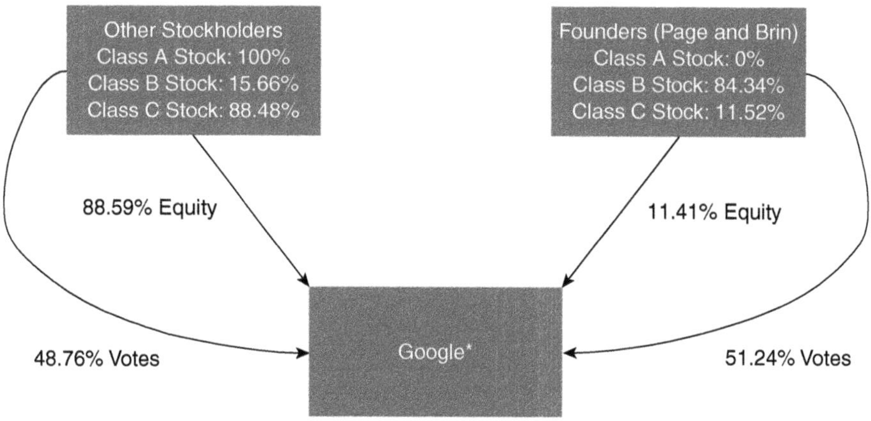

FIGURE 1.1 Google stock ownership as of 31 December 2019
* The holding company is now named Alphabet Inc.

Google's capital structure was unusual, but not rare. Several US blue-chip companies had listed with dual-class stock in the past, including Ford Motor Company, Nike, CBS, Viacom, Twenty-First Century Fox, The New York Times and Berkshire Hathaway. More noteworthy, though, was that Google had unintentionally established itself as a trailblazer of the tech company IPO scene. Numerous tech companies followed Google's lead in adopting dual-class stock at IPO. For example, upon listing in 2012, Mark Zuckerberg and other initial investors of Facebook retained a class of stock to which was attached ten votes per share, while public investors were only offered one share, one vote stock.[8] A few months before, LinkedIn had listed with a similar structure,[9] and Groupon soon followed with an even more extreme voting variance, with the founders and other insiders retaining shares to which were attached 150 votes each.[10] Most controversially, Snap, in 2017, completely abandoned the veneer of token voting rights by only offering non-voting stock to public shareholders. Like Google, Snap's voting structure consists of three classes of stock, but, unlike Google, both classes of voting stock are not listed – certain initial investors and insiders retained one share, one vote stock, and the co-founders, Bobby Murphy and Evan Spiegel, retained stock with ten votes per share.[11] Household names such as Zillow, Yelp, First Data, Square and Zynga also implemented dual-class stock on the public markets after

8 Form S-1 Registration Statement of Facebook, Inc. (1 February 2012) at 8.

9 Amendment No. 5 to Form S-1 Registration Statement (Form S-1/A) of LinkedIn Corporation (17 May 2011) at 26. The company was subsequently taken private by Microsoft Corporation in 2016.

10 Amendment No. 7 to Form S-1 Registration Statement (Form S-1/A) of Groupon, Inc. (1 November 2012) at 134. In 2016, the capital structure of Groupon was unified into a single class of one share, one vote stock (Form 8-A/A Amendment No. 1 of Groupon, Inc. (31 October 2016); see Chapter 9 for further details).

11 Form S-1/A Amended Registration Statement of Snap Inc. (8 February 2017) at 8.

Google's IPO, and the vogue in dual-class structure has continued, almost becoming a cult in the technology sphere, with the highly publicised listings of Lyft, Slack, Zoom and Pinterest in 2019, and Airbnb in 2020.[12] Indeed, since Google's IPO, the proportion of IPOs implementing dual-class stock generally has increased, and it has positively surged in the tech industry. Only 1 per cent of US IPOs in 2005 adopted dual-class structure, as compared to 15 per cent in 2014 and 24 per cent in 2015[13] (even taking listings generally, rather than IPOs, 13.5 per cent of companies listing shares on US exchanges in 2015 involved dual-class structure, compared to 1 per cent in 2001[14]). More recently, 19 per cent of US IPOs adopted dual-class structure in 2019.[15] Notably, the market capitalisation of US listed dual-class firms rose from $700 billion in 2009 to $3.8 trillion in 2019.[16] The trend is more glaring when considering 'large'[17] technology listings. Figure 1.2 shows the trend in dual-class firm IPOs for larger US companies, splitting out data for technology companies.

The US experience of dual-class stock will be drawn upon consistently in this book. The vast majority of research and literature on the topic has originated from the United States, and the largest and most high-profile listed companies with dual-class stock are based on the US exchanges. The United States has a rich, modern history of dual-class stock, and the manner in which Big Tech has embraced dual-class stock on the US exchanges makes an understanding of the US experience pertinent in many regards. The NYSE and NASDAQ are also the two largest stock markets on the basis of total market capitalisation and, therefore, deserve close attention.[18] Additionally, although it is dangerous to draw absolute equivalence between the United Kingdom and the United States (since there are critical

[12] Lyft, Pinterest and Airbnb implement a 20:1 voting ratio (although Airbnb's capital structure also includes non-voting stock, only one share, one vote stock was issued to the public at IPO, with insiders retaining shares with twenty votes per share), and both Slack Technologies and Zoom implement a 10:1 voting ratio, between enhanced-voting shares and inferior-voting shares (Form S-1 Registration Statement of Lyft, Inc. (filed 1 March 2019) at 194; Form S-1 Registration Statement of Pinterest, Inc. filed (22 March 2019) at 163; Form S-1/A Amendment No. 2 to Form S-1 Registration Statement of Airbnb, Inc. (filed 7 December 2020) at 321; Form S-1 Registration Statement of Slack Technologies, Inc. (filed 26 April 2019) at 154; Form S-1/A Amendment No. 2 to Form S-1 Registration Statement of Zoom Video Communications, Inc. (filed 16 April 2019) at 125).

[13] S. Feldman, 'Companies Opting to Go Public Offer Investors Class A One-Vote-Per-Share Stock, While Founders and Other Insiders Retain the Class B Super-Voting Shares for Themselves' (2016) 47 *SRLR* 1342.

[14] S. Solomon, 'Shareholders Vote With Their Dollars to Have Less of a Say' *The New York Times* (4 November 2015), www.nytimes.com/2015/11/05/business/dealbook/shareholders-vote-with-their-dollars-to-have-less-of-a-say.html.

[15] Council of Institutional Investors (CII), 'Dual-Class IPO Snapshot: 2017–2019 Statistics' (January 2020), www.cii.org/files/Jan%202020%20Dual%20Class%20Update%20for%20Website.pdf.

[16] B. Anh et al., 'Synthetic Governance' (2020) 101, 130, https://ssrn.com/abstract=3645312.

[17] AMEX, NYSE and NASDAQ IPOs with an offer price of at least $5.00.

[18] As of the end of February 2019, the total market capitalisation of the NYSE was US$20.679 trillion, comfortably exceeding the market capitalisation of NASDAQ, the second largest exchange (source: World Federation of Exchanges, 'Annual Statistics Guide 2018' (May 2019).

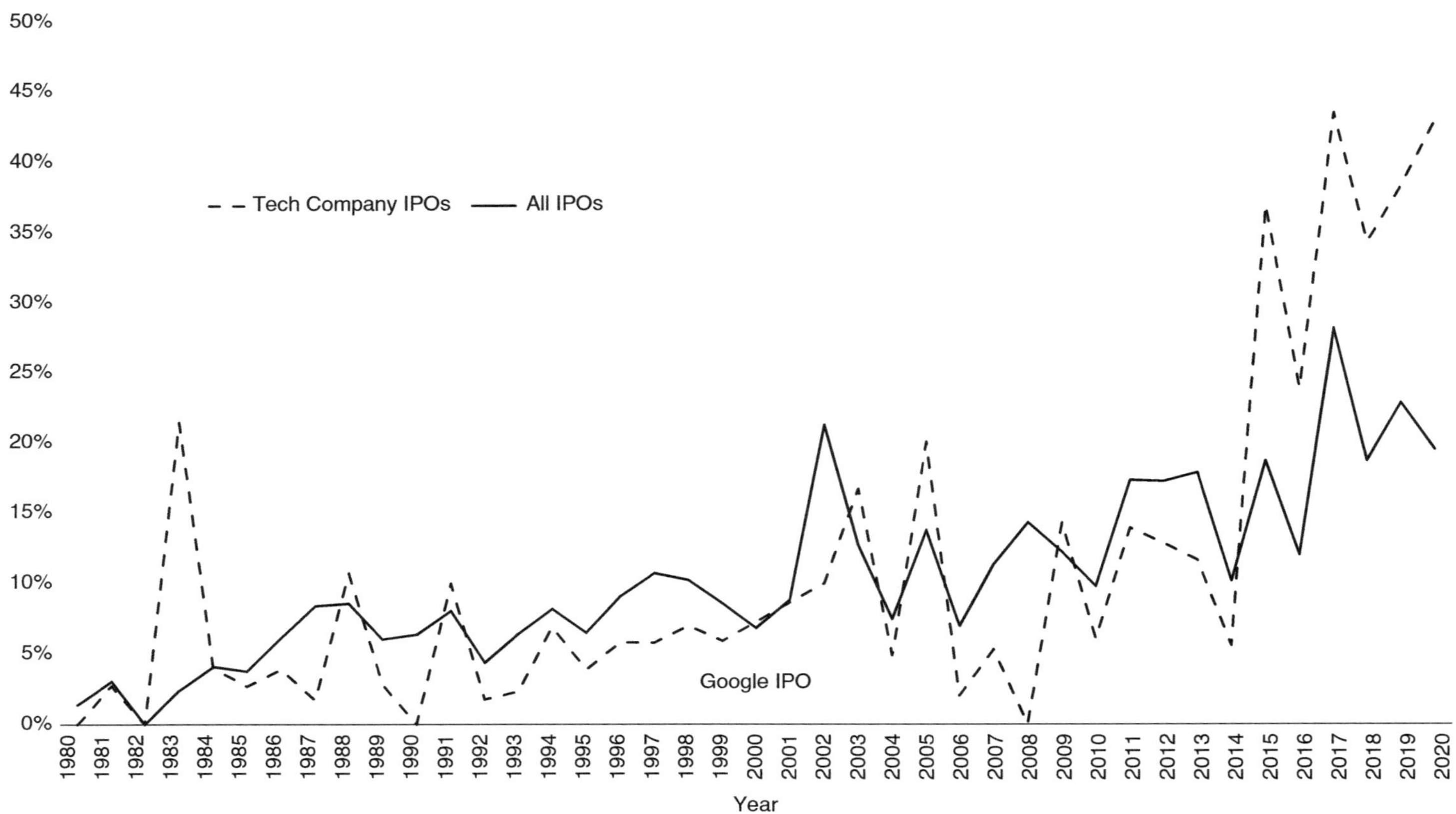

FIGURE 1.2 'Large' US dual-class IPOs as a percentage of total IPOs
Data derived from: J. Ritter, 'Initial Public Offerings: Dual Class Structure of IPOs Through 2020' (29 December 2020) https://site.warrington.ufl.edu/ritter/files/IPOs-Dual-Class.pdf

differences between the two markets[19]), in many respects, the United States represents the jurisdiction that is the closest test laboratory for dual-class stock in the United Kingdom. Although there are differences, the US public markets more closely mirror those of the United Kingdom, in terms of breadth, investor base and maturity, than any other jurisdiction. Particularly, it is often remarked that the character of the US stock exchanges parallels that of the LSE, in terms of a dispersed ownership structure,[20] whereunder the majority of companies lack a dominant blockholder or controlling shareholder, resulting in equity ownership being dispersed among numerous small shareholders. Even for those listed companies with a controlling shareholder, the remaining stock will usually be distributed amongst numerous dispersed public shareholders. Also, the majority of publicly listed stock in both the United Kingdom and the United States is held by institutional investors,[21] although it appears that such investors dominate the UK markets to an even greater extent.[22] A consideration of the US experience is therefore felicitous.

[19] For instance, there are substantial divergences in the litigation culture and environment in the United Kingdom and the United States (for further details, see Section 9.3 of Chapter 9).

[20] In relation to the United Kingdom specifically: J. Franks and C. Mayer, 'Evolution of Ownership and Control Around the World: The Changing Face of Capitalism' (2017) *ECGI Finance Working Paper No. 503/2017* 1, 36 and 43; C. Holderness, 'Blockholders Are More Common in the United States Than You Might Think' (2010) 22 *J. Appl. Corp. Finance* 75, 79; G. Aminadav and E. Papaioannou, 'Corporate Control Around the World' (2016) *NBER Working Paper 23010* 1, 19 and Appendix Table 1; B. Cheffins, 'The Undermining of UK Corporate Governance (?)' (2013) 33 *OJLS* 505 and 509. In relation to the similarities between the United Kingdom and United States: OECD Corporate Governance Factbook 2017 at 11; R. La Porta et al., 'Corporate Ownership Around the World' (1999) 54 *J. Financ.* 471, 492; J. Franks et al., 'Ownership: Evolution and Regulation' (2009) 22 *Rev. Financial Stud.* 4009, 4009; R. Gilson, 'Controlling Shareholders and Corporate Governance: Complicating the Comparative Taxonomy' (2006) 119 *Harv. Law Rev.* 1642, 1645; W.-G. Ringe, 'Deviations from Ownership-Control Proportionality – Economic Protectionism Revisited' in *Company Law and Economic Protectionism: New Challenges to European Integration*, eds. U. Bernitz and W.-G. Ringe (Oxford University Press, 2010) at 221. In relation to the US specifically: R. Daniels and P. Halpern, 'Too Close for Comfort: The Role of the Closely Held Public Corporation in the Canadian Economy and the Implications for Public Policy' (1996) 26 *Can. Bus. L.J.* 11, 12. Although some commentators have speculated that the characterisation of the ownership of equity on US markets as being predominantly dispersed is somewhat of a myth, the contention is generally based upon a prevalence of blockholders at the 5 per cent level, rather than true controlling shareholders: C. Holderness, 'The Myth of Diffuse Ownership in the United States' (2009) 22 *Rev. Financial Stud.* 1377, 1378 and 1394; A. Shleifer and R. Vishny, 'Large Shareholders and Corporate Control' (1986) 94 *J. Political Econ.* 461, 462; A. Edmans and C. Holderness, 'Blockholders: A Survey of Theory and Evidence' in *The Handbook of the Economics of Corporate Governance*, eds. B. Hermalin and M. Wesibach (Elsevier, 2017) at 51.

[21] R. Chan and J. Ho, 'Should Listed Companies Be Allowed to Adopt Dual-Class Share Structure in Hong Kong?' (2014) 43 *Comm. L. World Rev.* 155, 176; D. Langevoort, 'The SEC, Retail Investors, and the Institutionalization of the Securities Markets' (2008) *Georgetown Law, Faculty Working Papers* 1; ONS, 'Ownership of UK Quoted Shares: 2018' (January 2020) at 4.

[22] The ONS assessed that as of 31 December 2018, the proportion of UK quoted shares beneficially owned by individuals was only 13.5 per cent (ONS (2008) (n 21 at 8)). In contrast, the Securities Industry and Financial Markets Association (Securities Industry and Financial Markets Association, 'Capital Markets Fact Book 2019'(2019) at 60) showed that, in 2018, 'households' owned 37.6 per cent

However, it is not only US tech companies that have determined dual-class stock to be the capital structure of choice. Of the 'big-4' Chinese tech companies – Baidu, Alibaba, Tencent and Xiaomi[23] – three have implemented dual-class structure, with the fourth, Alibaba, implementing an alternative mechanism that grants enhanced board appointment rights to insiders.[24] Baidu, Tencent and Alibaba listed in the United States at a time when Hong Kong and mainland China did not permit the listing of dual-class companies (or the board mechanic adopted by Alibaba). Xiaomi's IPO in Hong Kong occurred after Hong Kong relaxed its restrictions on dual-class stock and was followed by secondary listings in Hong Kong by Alibaba and Baidu. Even in the United Kingdom, the tech companies Farfetch and Endava rebuffed premium tier listings in favour of opportunities to list with dual-class stock on the NYSE.[25] For the tech industry, dual-class stock matters.

1.3 THE UNITED KINGDOM'S POSITION ON DUAL-CLASS STOCK

A company desiring to list in the United Kingdom and offer shares to the public has, at least at face value, a plethora of options. The LSE's Main Market is divided into three principal categories – the premium tier, the standard tier and the high-growth segment. A fourth category, the specialist-fund segment, is designated for investment funds which may only market to institutional or professionally advised investors. Outside of the Main Market, companies may choose AIM or an independent exchange such as the Acquis Stock Exchange.[26] As a matter of company law, both private and public companies incorporated in England and Wales may issue dual-class stock.[27] Therefore, in relation to ascertaining whether dual-class stock is permitted to be listed on an exchange, the rules of that exchange will be pertinent. It is only on the premium tier, which is the most prestigious tier of the LSE, that dual-class stock issuances by companies, wherever they are incorporated, are, as of the time of writing, effectively prohibited.

of US equities. However, the figure for the United States may be overstated, by including holdings by non-profit organisations, and presumably certain indirect retail ownership through institutional funds, and the percentage of US equities held directly by individuals (pure retail investors) may be closer to that of the United Kingdom (Chan and Ho (2014) (n 21 above 175)).

23 The acronym 'BATX' is sometimes used to describe this group of Chinese tech companies (B. Reddy, 'Finding the British Google: Relaxing the Prohibition of Dual-Class Stock from the Premium-Tier of the London Stock Exchange' (2020) 79 *CLJ* 315, 315).

24 Form F-1 Registration Statement of Alibaba Holding Limited (6 May 2014) at 209. See Section 3.2 of Chapter 3 for more details.

25 Form F-1/A Amendment No.1 to Form F-1 Registration Statement of Farfetch Limited (5 September 2018); Form F-1/A Amendment No. 2 to Form F-1 Registration Statement of Endava plc (filed 23 July 2018).

26 Acquis Exchange plc acquired the NEX Exchange, which was subsequently renamed the Acquis Stock Exchange, in 2020 (Aquis Exchange plc Announcement (RNS No. 0363F), 'FCA Approval of NEX Exchange Acquisition' (4 March 2020)).

27 For further details, see Chapter 2.

The LSE operates its primary markets by virtue of being authorised as a recognised investment exchange by the FCA,[28] an independent public body with a statutory foundation under FSMA 2000. The FCA, in exercising its primary market functions,[29] is therefore the regulator for Main Market companies. The dichotomy between the FCA and the LSE is reflected by a premium tier 'listing' being a two-stage process. In fact, the term 'listing' only applies to the first stage, but the expression is commonly used euphemistically to denote the entire process. For a premium tier (or standard tier) company seeking an IPO, the first stage involves admission to the FCA's Official List, with the second stage being the admission of the applicant's securities to trading by the LSE. Therefore, not only must an applicant comply with the rules of the exchange itself,[30] but it must also apply the rules of a regulatory body sometimes described as 'quasi-governmental'.[31] The FCA's key admission and continuing requirements for companies seeking a premium listing are laid out in the Listing Rules.

The Listing Rules include a set of principles, six of which are only applicable to premium listed companies.[32] The purpose of the principles is to ensure that listed companies pay due regard to the fundamental role they play in maintaining market confidence and ensuring fair and orderly markets,[33] and are designed to assist listed companies in identifying their obligations and responsibilities under the Listing Rules and other disclosure, transparency and corporate governance rules.[34] As such, the principles are drafted broadly and should be considered when determining compliance with other more specific provisions – effectively, the premium listing principles should govern the overarching conduct of premium listed companies when interpreting the application of various listing requirements. Two premium listing principles are particularly relevant when considering dual-class stock:

- 'All equity shares in a class that has been admitted to premium listing must carry an equal number of votes on any shareholder vote.'[35]
- 'Where a listed company has more than one class of equity shares admitted to premium listing, the aggregate voting rights of the shares in each class should be broadly proportionate to the relative interests of those classes in the equity of the listed company.'[36]

[28] See FSMA 2000, Part XVIII and the Markets in Financial Instruments Directive (2014/65/EU).
[29] The FCA has retired the traditional moniker, the 'UK Listing Authority', and, instead, now refers to its 'primary market' functions (FCA, 'Primary Market Bulletin' (February 2019/No. 20) at 1).
[30] See LSE, 'Admission and Disclosure Standards' (1 October 2018).
[31] For example, see B. Tricker, *Corporate Governance: Principles, Policies, Practices*, 3rd ed. (Oxford University Press, 2015) at 378. Although the FCA is an independent body, it is accountable to the Treasury and Parliament (FCA, 'About the FCA' (2016), www.fca.org.uk/about/the-fca).
[32] Listing Rules, Chapter 7.
[33] LR 7.1.2G.
[34] LR 7.1.3G.
[35] Listing Rules, Premium Listing Principle 3.
[36] Listing Rules, Premium Listing Principle 4.

Therefore, for a premium listed company, all premium listed shares must carry votes proportional to their equity rights in the company, in effect prohibiting the premium listing of more than one class of shares with diverging voting rights, assuming that such shares only differ by way of voting rights. Theoretically, it would be possible to remain in compliance with the strict wording of the premium listing principles by listing inferior-voting shares, with enhanced-voting shares remaining unlisted in the hands of, for example, the founders. Such a structure would mimic Google's original IPO capital structure, and, indeed, the current capital structures of US tech behemoths such as Facebook, Square and Zoom. However, it is unlikely that the FCA would admit such a structure to a premium listing.[37] The listing principles were introduced to ensure adherence to the spirit as well as the letter of the Listing Rules,[38] and the FCA has noted that 'the purpose of Premium Listing Principle 4 is to prevent artificial structures involving multiple classes with different voting powers, which are designed to allow control to rest with a small group of shareholders'.[39] The capital structures of Facebook, Square and Zoom have been designed exactly for such a purpose, notwithstanding the enhanced-voting shares remaining unlisted. In any event, even if inferior-voting shares of a dual-class structure, where the enhanced-voting shares remained unlisted, were, as unlikely as it may be, to be admitted by the FCA to the premium tier, further provisions of the Listing Rules make this an unpalatable avenue for founders. For premium listed companies, certain matters that are required to be approved by a shareholder vote under the Listing Rules must be decided by a resolution of the holders of the premium listed shares;[40] the significance of this is that in many instances where the Listing Rules require a shareholder vote,[41] the votes of the unlisted shares will not be counted, negating the very advantage sought by the founders. For all intents and purposes, dual-class stock is proscribed from the premium tier.

However, perhaps change is in the air. On 3 March 2021, the UK Listing Review was published, making reform proposals for the LSE with a view to encouraging 'more high-quality UK equity listings and public offers'.[42] The headline proposal was to relax

37 The adherence of the FCA to the spirit of the Listing Principles is evidenced by the recent listing of The Hut Group being restricted to the standard tier as a result of a capital structure that replicates certain of the qualities of dual-class structure (see Section 1.5.5 later in this chapter).

38 FCA Technical Note FCA/TN/203.4, 'Compliance with the Listing Principles and Premium Listing Principles' (October 2019).

39 FCA Policy Statement PS14/8, 'Response to CP13/15 – Enhancing the Effectiveness of the Listing Regime' (May 2014) at 31.

40 LR 9.2.21R.

41 For example, cancellation of listings, certain transfers between listing categories, establishment of employee share schemes, long-term incentive plans and discounted share options, implementation of deep discount open offers, vendor consideration placings, share issues out of treasury and equity share subscription offers, undertaking of significant transactions or related-party transactions, certain repurchases of securities and material changes to investment policy or conversion of listed equity shares of closed-end investment funds.

42 HM Treasury, 'Policy Paper: Terms of Reference: Lord Hill's Review on Listings' (19 November 2020).

the premium tier prohibition of dual-class stock.[43] Notwithstanding the UK Listing Review merely constituting recommendations and subject to FCA consultation, the proposals regarding dual-class stock appear to be regarded as a 'done-deal', with potential new issuers on the LSE being informally advised that the Listing Rules will be revised for premium listed companies along the lines of the relevant proposals.[44] Although one may therefore conjecture that the United Kingdom is already on the path toward relaxing the premium tier prohibition of dual-class stock, in fact, as discussed later in this chapter,[45] the conditions that would be attached to the issuance of dual-class stock under the relevant proposals result in a capital structure that cannot be described as 'true' dual-class stock. The UK Listing Review has purportedly opened the door to dual-class stock, but what is actually described is nothing of the sort, and therefore, even if the recommendations of the UK Listing Review become effective, the premium tier prohibition of 'genuine' dual-class stock will continue.

1.4 IT'S ALL ABOUT CONTROL

Having established the United Kingdom's premium tier prohibition of dual-class stock in juxtaposition to the rise of dual-class stock listings in the United States, natural questions are why would a company list with dual-class structure, and why would a regulator prohibit its use? It's all about control. For a company incorporated in England and Wales, voting rights bring with them a variety of benefits, the most critical of which is participation in electing the board of directors. For most such companies, the company's constitution, mainly the articles of association (articles),[46] will specify that directors may be appointed by ordinary resolution, or by resolution of the board (provided that, in the latter case, for public companies, such directors retire at the subsequent annual general meeting and be reappointed by ordinary resolution).[47] An ordinary resolution will be passed if approved by a simple majority of the votes exercised at the relevant general meeting of shareholders.[48] Directors may also be removed at any time by an ordinary resolution of the shareholders, a critical right of shareholders from which the company cannot derogate,[49] that contrasts with more director-friendly regimens in other jurisdictions, such as the United States.[50]

43 UK Listing Review at 19–24.

44 T. Bradshaw, 'Deliveroo Targets £10 bn Valuation in London IPO' *Financial Times* (4 March 2021), www.ft.com/content/f8108b89-419f-40e8-97c9-ce2c15b905e9.

45 See Section 1.5.7 later in this chapter.

46 CA 2006, s. 17.

47 The Companies (Model Articles) Regulations 2008 (SI 2008/3229) (the Model PLC Articles), articles 20 and 21. In the absence of bespoke articles, the Model PLC Articles will apply (CA 2006, s. 20), and, commonly, public companies adopt an amended version of the Model PLC Articles.

48 CA 2006, s. 282.

49 CA 2006, s. 168.

50 In Delaware, for example, although, prima facie, shareholders (by way of majority vote) possess the power to remove directors, a company can instil a 'staggered' or 'classified' board, pursuant to which only one-third of the directors submit themselves for re-election each year (8 Del. C., §141(d)), in

Furthermore, premium listed companies are required to apply the UK CGC.[51] The UK CGC recommends principles and provisions on a 'soft law' basis,[52] with premium listed companies being required to disclose how they have applied the principles, and whether they have complied with the provisions, and, if not, the reasons for non-compliance ('comply-or-explain').[53] The UK CGC recommends that all directors be subject to annual re-election,[54] which would give shareholders, by way of ordinary resolution, the capacity to opine upon the continued tenure of every director on an annual basis. Although the provision is not mandatory, nearly all FTSE-350[55] companies comply with this provision.[56] Voting rights also give shareholders of publicly listed companies a variety of other powers, with certain actions of the company, many of which are described throughout this book, requiring an ordinary resolution[57] or a special resolution,[58] which is passed upon the approval of at least 75 per cent of the votes cast at a general meeting of shareholders.[59] However, the right to remove directors is arguably the most effective and influential right that shareholders possess. With most companies, the board will have the power to hire and fire management.[60] Since it is the board that determines company strategy and management that puts the strategy into practice on a day-to-day basis, shareholders will have direct and indirect influence upon how the company is operated. Although shareholders cannot directly remove managers from their employment roles, the mere shadow of shareholder power to remove directors can result in those directors ensuring that management positions are occupied by persons amenable to the shareholders with voting control. Accordingly, directors, and, by extension, management will operate the company in a manner aligned with the demands of those shareholders with voting control. The power balance within a company will lie with whoever has control over the board of

which case, the shareholders may only remove those directors at the expiry of the relevant director's term, unless removal is 'for cause' (8 Del. C., §141(k)(1)).

51 FRC, 'The UK Corporate Governance Code' (July 2018).

52 In relation to application of the UK CGC, see, for example, B. Reddy, 'Thinking Outside the Box – Eliminating the Perniciousness of Box-Ticking in the New Corporate Governance Code' (2019) 82 *MLR* 692.

53 LR 9.8.6(5)–9.8.6(6).

54 UK CGC, Provision 18.

55 In relation to the FTSE-indices, see n 173 below and accompanying text.

56 In 2020, 'annual re-election of directors' was not one of the most commonly breached provisions of the UK CGC by FTSE-350 companies, meaning that less than 1.4 per cent of such companies did not comply with the provision (Grant Thornton, 'Corporate Governance Review 2020' at 10–11).

57 For example, under CA 2006, an ordinary resolution is required to allot shares (s. 551), approve executive remuneration (ss. 439 and 439A), approve loans to directors (s. 197), approve substantial property transactions (s. 190), ratify the acts of directors (s. 239), authorise political donations (s. 366), appoint and dismiss the auditor (ss. 489(4) and 510(2)) and approve share buybacks (ss. 694 and 701).

58 For example, under CA 2006, a special resolution is required to amend the articles (s. 21), change the name of the company (s. 77), re-register the company as a private company (s. 97), reduce general meeting notice periods (s. 307A), disapply pre-emption rights (s. 571) and reduce share capital (s. 641). A special resolution is also required to voluntarily wind up the company (IA 1986, s. 84).

59 CA 2006, s. 283.

60 The board has the power to employ and dismiss managers under the Model PLC Articles, article 3.

directors. Furthermore, voting rights give the holders control over takeovers, with at least a majority of the voting rights being required to approve a takeover of the company.[61] Boards can become concerned that a decline in share price will open up the company to a predatory takeover bid, subsequent to which the board and management team are replaced. Therefore, voting power can be everything. In Chapter 6, the potential benefits and detriments to public shareholders of dual-class stock will be discussed in detail, but in this section, we will briefly take a view of the consequences of ingraining such voting power in founders through the use of dual-class stock, firstly from the perspective of a founder seeking to take his or her company public, and secondly from the perspective of a regulator seeking to protect the public markets.

Upon IPO, the existing owners of a company's stock will offer part of their stock to the public, cause the company to issue new shares to the public or both. The IPO allows the existing owners to immediately, and in the future, cash-out part of their investment in the company, and also, if the company is issuing new shares, raise further finance for the company's business. Since a premium listing in the United Kingdom entails one share, one vote, a premium tier IPO would require the existing owners to relinquish a proportion of their voting rights in the company through selling shares they own and/or dilution of their ownership from the issuance of further shares. Unless the existing owners retain a significant portion of their interest in the company, which limits the extent to which they can diversify wealth and the company can generate equity funding, they will lose control, since decision-making over the composition of the board will shift to the public shareholders. In a dispersed ownership system like the United Kingdom,[62] control would therefore be distributed among a disparate group of investors with varying investment horizons and agenda. For a founder considering an IPO of his or her company, losing control is a critical juncture. It exposes management to the public markets. The public shareholders will be able to replace directors (who in turn can replace management), and the founder cannot block a takeover of the company, which could, itself, lead to a change of management. This is of particular concern to a founder who also leads, or is part of, the management team. The founder could himself or herself be indirectly removed from his or her management role by the public shareholders through their control of the board. The founder who inaugurated the company, and tenderly nurtured it into a mature business, could be unceremoniously dumped at

[61] Generally, a hostile takeover offer must proceed by way of takeover offer, the minimum acceptance condition for which must result in the bidder acquiring at least a majority of the target's voting rights (Takeover Code, Rule 10). Although a takeover may also proceed by way of a court-approved scheme of arrangement, which requires approval by a majority in number holding 75 per cent of the votes of members exercising votes at a Court Meeting (Companies Act 2006, s. 899), since control over the scheme documentation for the takeover will, in the normal course, be in the hands of the target's board, it becomes impractical for a hostile takeover to be launched by way of scheme of arrangement. Either way, the holder of a majority of the voting rights in the company can block a takeover.

[62] See n 20 above and accompanying text.

the exact moment when his or her aspirations for the business can finally come to fruition. As a result, the founder will feel pressure to operate the company in accordance with the preferences of the public shareholders. For such a founder, dual-class stock could be an elixir. If dual-class stock were permitted, the founder could create and retain enhanced-voting shares, and issue only inferior-voting shares to the public. By carefully engineering the voting divergence between the two classes of shares, the founder could retain a majority of the voting rights in the company while still crystallising a significant portion of its investment in the company and generating new equity finance. Going forward, further equity funding can be procured while retaining control by only distributing newly issued inferior-voting shares to the public. Since the public shareholders will not attain sufficient voting control to remove directors from the board[63] or to approve takeovers, the founder's position at the company is protected, and the founder can continue to manage the company or ensure that its vision for the business is maintained by electing managers who share the same objectives.

In the United States, dual-class firms are indeed primarily associated with a single shareholder (or connected shareholders) retaining effective control while holding a disproportionately lower level of cash-flow rights,[64] and tend to develop from founder or family ownership.[65] This is further evidenced by the wedge that develops between the voting and cash-flow rights held by the controllers of the company. US studies from 1985[66] and 2010[67] found that the average of such divergences for US

[63] See n 49 above and accompanying text.

[64] L. Bebchuk and K. Kastiel, 'The Perils of Small-Minority Controllers' (2019) 107 *Geo. L. J.* 1453, 1496 found that 83.6 per cent of Russell-3000 dual-class companies have a controlling minority shareholder (an earlier draft noted the figure as 96.7 per cent of S&P-1500 dual-class firms).

[65] In examining Russell-3000 dual-class firms listed as of 2001, it was found that nearly all arose from entrepreneur and family ownership, and from 2001 through 2015, 89 per cent of them still had the founding family as owners (R. Anderson et al., 'The Dual Class Premium: A Family Affair' (2017) 1, 6, https://ssrn.com/abstract=3006669). Amoako-Adu et al.'s (2013) sample of dual-class firms (2001–2007) consisted of 83.2 per cent family-controlled firms (B. Amoako-Adu et al., 'Dual Class Discount, and the Channels of Extraction of Private Benefits' in *Advances in Financial Economics* Vol. 16, eds. S. Ferris et al. (Emerald Publishing, 2013) at 185). A more recent study assessing dual-class firms between 1994 and 2019 found that the most common controllers of dual-class firms are founders (D. Aggarwal et al., 'The Rise of Dual-Class Stock IPOs' (2020) 1, 3 https://ssrn.com/abstract=3690670) – although the study found that a slim majority of dual-class firms were not founder-controlled, a large proportion of the remainder were VC- or PE-controlled, and, as discussed further in Chapter 9, often these firms adopt transfer-driven sunset clauses, meaning that when the VC or PE firms exit (usually not long after IPO), the selling parties' shares are converted into inferior-voting shares, often leaving the founders solely with enhanced-voting shares, and therefore in control; the authors also note that recent years have seen an increasing proportion of dual-class firms being either founder-controlled or joint founder/VC-controlled. Also, see Table 1.1.

[66] H. DeAngelo and L. DeAngelo, 'Managerial Ownership of Voting Rights: A Study of Public Corporations with Dual Classes of Common Stock' (1985) 14 *J. Financ. Econ.* 33, 46 – finding insiders on average holding 56.9 per cent and 24.0 per cent of the voting and cash-flow rights, respectively.

[67] P. Gompers et al., 'Extreme Governance: An Analysis of Dual-Class Firms in the United States' (2010) 23 *Rev. Financial Stud.* 1051, 1053 – finding insiders on average holding 60 per cent and 40 per cent of the voting and cash-flow rights, respectively.

dual-class stock listed companies was between 20 and 35 per cent. A further US study, examining the ten largest dual-class stock listed companies in the United States in 2015, found that divergences were significant and tended to increase post-IPO.[68] Even in the United Kingdom, before dual-class firms were discouraged by the LSE, a study of firms adopting dual-class structure between 1955 and 1982 found that insiders held only 17.5 per cent of the cash-flow rights on average.[69] In Table 1.1, the twenty largest US dual-class stock companies by market capitalisation have been enumerated,[70] along with hand-collected data for the voting rights and cash-flow rights held by the controllers of each company as of IPO and as of the most recently available public filings. In most cases, the controllers at IPO retained majority voting control, or effective voting control (a sufficiently large proportion of the voting rights that, although below a majority, will give the controller effective control due to the dispersed ownership of the other shares in the company), while holding a minority of the cash-flow rights. Even for those who did not hold effective control at IPO, post-IPO, many have, through the operation of dual-class structure, entrenched control, while reducing their cash-flow rights further, allowing them to manage their companies broadly free from the pressures of public shareholders – founders without limits.

In contrast, from the perspective of a regulator, a view could be taken that a founder, with dual-class stock, wants to have his or her cake and eat it too. The founder seeks to liquidate his or her investment off the back of public investor funds, but he or she does not want to award those public investors with a proportionate level of voting rights. The founder wishes to sell out, yet retain control. For purveyors of private ordering theory,[71] it may be suggested that the scenario simply represents a business transaction between parties. However, for a regulator, such as the FCA, which has at its heart a mission to protect consumers, protect and enhance the integrity of the UK financial system and promote competition,[72] the ongoing

68 L. Bebchuk and K. Kastiel, 'The Untenable Case for Perpetual Dual-Class Stock' (2017) 4 *Va. Law Rev.* 585, 608.

69 J. Ang and W. Megginson, 'Restricted Voting Shares, Ownership Structure, and the Market Value of Dual-Class Firms' (1989) 12 *J. Financ. Res.* 301, 317.

70 Market capitalisation rankings determined as of 17 September 2020 from the constituents of the MSCI USA Index, www.msci.com/constituents.

71 It is not intended that corporate law theory be scrutinised in detail in this book. In brief, though, private ordering theory predicts that firms will choose the governance structures that are most beneficial to their, and other transaction parties', success, pursuant to value maximising notional 'contracts' between shareholders and management (in relation to the economic contractarian model of corporations, see Section 4.3.1.1 of Chapter 4). Therefore, the theory assumes that imposing uniform regulatory requirements on companies will not be socially optimal (for example, see D. Fischel, 'Organized Exchanges and the Regulation of Dual Class Common Stock' (1987) 54 *U. Chi. L. Rev.* 119, 140; M. Barzuza, 'Inefficient Tailoring: The Private Ordering Paradox in Corporate Law' (2018) 8 *HBLR* 131, 139; D. Larcker et al., 'The Market Reaction to Corporate Governance Regulation' (2011) 101 *J. Financ. Econ.* 431; B. Sharfman, 'A Private Ordering Defense of a Company's Right to Use Dual Class Share Structures in IPOs' (2018) 63 *Villanova L. Rev.* 1).

72 FCA, 'Our Mission 2017: How We Regulate Financial Services' (2017) at 5.

TABLE 1.1 *Voting and equity ownership of the principal controllers of the twenty largest US dual-class corporations by market capitalisation (as per the MSCI USA Index as of 17 September 2020)*

No.[a]	Company	IPO Year	Principal Controller	Founder/ Family Control Y/N	Controller Estimated Voting Ownership at IPO[b]	Controller Estimated Equity Ownership at IPO[c]	Controller Estimated Voting Ownership 2020[d]	Controller Estimated Equity Ownership 2020[e]
1	Facebook	2012	Zuckerberg	Y	54.21%	23.55%	57.88%	12.90%
2	Alphabet	2004	Page Brin	Y	31.59%	28.07%	51.20%	11.40%
3	Berkshire Hathaway	NA[f]	Buffet	N	Not available	Not available	31.00%	16.00%
4	Comcast	1972	Roberts family	Y	Not available	Not available	33.81%	0.92%
5	Nike	1980	Knight family	Y	Not available	Not available	Control over 75% of board[g]	22.96%
6	Regeneron	1991	Schleifer	Y	Not available	Not available	15.23%	3.60%
7	Estee Lauder	1995	Lauder family	Y	Not available	Not available	75.32%	34.07%
8	Workday	2012	Duffield Bhusri	Y	72.50%	63.25%	76.37%	25.91%
9	Square	2015	Dorsey McKelvey	Y	32.73%	30.29%	64.72%	17.09%
10	Constellation	1973	Sands family	Y	Not available	Not available	59.00%	16.00%

TABLE 1.1 *(continued)*

No.	Company	IPO Year	Principal Controller	Founder/ Family Control Y/N	Controller Estimated Voting Ownership at IPO	Controller Estimated Equity Ownership at IPO	Controller Estimated Voting Ownership 2020	Controller Estimated Equity Ownership 2020
11	Veeva	2013	Gassner Wallach	Y	16.50%	14.89%	53.50%	11.47%
12	Twilio	2016	Lawson	Y	11.70%	10.40%	28.80%	5.20%
13	Okta	2017	McKinnon Kerrest	Y	16.60%	14.60%	49.90%	8.90%
14	Ford Motor Company	1956	Ford family	Y	Not available	Not available	40.00%[h]	1.78%
15	Zoom	2019	Yuan family	Y	20.90%	19.08%	34.40%	16.18%
16	IAC	NA[i]	Diller family	Y	Not available	Not available	47.49%	15.32%
17	Brown-Forman	1933	Brown family	Y	Not available	Not available	66.90%	Not available (stated to be 'over 50%')
18	RingCentral	2013	Shmunis Vendrow	Y	28.94%	25.74%	48.20%	10.83%
19	Tyson Foods	1963	Tyson family	Y	Not available	Not available	70.97%	20.93%
20	Snap	2017	Murphy Spiegel	Y	88.84%	36.10%	99.46%[j]	28.62%[k]

Notes

[a] Certain companies have been excluded, which would otherwise have been constituents of the twenty largest dual-class companies by way of market capitalisation, since although their structures technically comprise dual-class stock, the applicable terms exclude them from consideration as dual-class stock controlling structures, which

are the focus of this book: (1) Visa – the company's dual-class structure was constructed principally to implement redeemable shares and a mechanism to provide for potential pre-envisaged litigation settlement costs; (2) Charter Communications – the company's dual-class controlling structure as of IPO has been largely unified into one share, one vote; (3) United Parcel Service – the terms of the capital structure impose a cap such that where a shareholder controls 25 per cent of the total voting rights, further shares held by that shareholder only enjoy 1/1000th of a vote per share; (4) Aflac – the capital structure reflects time-phased (loyalty share) voting rights, which are not considered in detail in this book (see Chapter 3); and (5) McCormick – the terms of the capital structure impose a cap such that votes in excess of 10 per cent held by the same owner may not be voted.

[b and c] Information was hand-collected from the SEC's 'Edgar website'. Data derived from disclosed information in Form S-1 (or S-1/A) registration statements of companies at time of IPO – actual figures will vary depending upon further share sales immediately after IPO, underwriter purchases at IPO, treatment of restricted stock units and final public take-up of the offering. 'Not available' indicates that IPO was pre-1994, in which case, the relevant information is not publicly accessible on the SEC's Edgar website. Percentage figures are estimates, due to lack of transparency in disclosed material as regards family and trust interests.

[d and e] Information was hand-collected from the SEC's 'Edgar website'. Unless otherwise referenced, data derived from disclosed information in the latest (as of 17 September 2020) Form DEF 14A annual proxy statements of companies. Percentage figures are estimates, due to lack of transparency in disclosed material as regards family and trust interests.

[f] Berkshire Hathaway stock was traded prior to the effectiveness of the Securities Act of 1933.

[g] Nike Class A stock as a class gives the holders the right to appoint 75 per cent of the board.

[h] Ford Motor Company Class B stock as a class gives the holders the entrenched right to exercise 40 per cent of the votes in the company, irrespective of the proportion that the Class B stock forms of the total outstanding share capital of the company.

[i] The provenance of IAC/InterActiveCorp can be traced back to a 1992 spin-off of the Silver King Broadcasting Company to Home Shopping Network shareholders, and the current company was further spun-off a larger group in 2020.

[j and k] Snap has not filed DEF 14A annual proxy statements since all of its publicly issued stock (Class A) is non-voting – therefore voting and equity percentages are as disclosed in Snap's latest (as of 17 September 2020) filed Form 10-K.

consequences of dual-class stock post-IPO will be of concern. A potential mischief, as discussed further in Chapter 6, is that the controller could install a management team (of which the controller may be a part) that prioritises the private interests of the controller over shareholder wealth maximisation. However, control is not, in and of itself, the determinative factor. After all, controlling shareholder one share, one vote firms, where the controller owns a sufficient proportion of the shares in the company to be able to appoint the board, are permitted on the premium tier. Indeed, the companies Fraser Group,[73] Ferrexpo, Fresnillo and Antofagasta are well-known examples of premium listed companies where a single shareholder or group of affiliated shareholders hold more than 50 per cent of the shares (and therefore voting rights) in the company. However, the mischief identified is mitigated in a one share, one vote system, where the controller will necessarily need to own a large level of cash-flow rights in order to maintain control. With dual-class structure, where the potential for a voting/cash-flow divergence exists, the fear emerges that those in control of the company fail to fully feel the consequences of their actions.[74] To the extent that actions of the company are detrimental to shareholder value, the controller will only suffer pain commensurate with its cash-flow interest in the company, which could be small if its voting/cash-flow divergence is large. The public shareholders, holding inferior-voting shares, will not have any ability to replace the management team, since control will reside with the holders of the enhanced-voting shares, and the incentive on the controller to replace a management team that does not maximise shareholder value reduces as its cash-flow rights fall; a state of affairs that is exacerbated where the controller himself or herself serves as part of management. In essence, the regulators have determined that dual-class structure incentivises the potential mischiefs of controllers, and, at least in the United Kingdom, the FCA has determined that founders require limits on the premium tier.

1.5 PUTTING DUAL-STOCK INTO CONTEXT

Rather than debating dual-class stock within a theoretical vacuum, the discussion to follow will be well-served by putting dual-class stock into a UK context, and grounding dual-class stock within the real-world machinations that may induce the regulators to retreat from their prevailing trepidation of dual-class firms. Although the discourse is UK-centric, the reasoning will also apply to a number of

[73] Previously known as Sports Direct.

[74] F. Easterbrook and D. Fischel, 'Voting in Corporate Law' (1983) 26 *J. Law Econ.* 395, 409; J. Dammann, 'The Controlling Shareholder's General Duty of Care: A Dogma That Should Be Abandoned' (2015) 2 *U. Ill. L. Rev.* 479, 494; F. Easterbrook and D. Fischel, eds., *The Economic Structure of Corporate Law* (Harvard University Press, 1991) at 73; C. Li et al., 'Ownership Structure and the Cost of Corporate Borrowing' (2011) 100 *J. Financ. Econ.* 1, 2; H. Hu and B. Black, 'The New Vote Buying: Empty Voting and Hidden (Morphable) Ownership' (2006) 79 *S. Cal. L. Rev.* 811, 851; HKEX, 'Concept Paper: New Board' (June 2017) at 18.

jurisdictions, and similar considerations have influenced the approaches of the United States, Hong Kong and Singapore amongst others.

1.5.1 *The Decline of the Public Equity Markets in the United Kingdom, and the Dearth of Listed Tech Companies*

In 2020, Tim Ward, Chief Executive of the Quoted Companies Alliance, stated: 'The sun set on the UK's public equity markets in 2019.'[75] The sentiment related to the dwindling number of IPOs in the United Kingdom. As shown in Figure 1.3, the number of completed IPOs on the Main Market or AIM in 2019 and 2020 were at their lowest levels since 2009, which was in the aftermath of the 2008 financial crisis. Even prior to 2019, IPO levels were not recovering to anywhere near the levels evident immediately prior to the 2008 financial crisis. The absolute number of Main Market companies in the United Kingdom has also fallen, decreasing by 57 per cent between 1999 and 2016.[76] The statistics on UK listed companies are particularly apposite in light of the growth of private sector businesses. Between 2000 and 2019, the number of private sector businesses in the United Kingdom increased by 69 per cent.[77] While the number of UK companies has continued to swell, an increasingly smaller proportion of them have determined that a UK listing would be the most conducive option for growth.

In the tech sector, the picture is even more jarring. The Main Market, especially the FTSE-100, an index comprising the largest 100 LSE listed firms by market capitalisation, is dominated by banks, mining companies and the oil and gas industry.[78] Companies from 'new economy' industries[79] that have listed between 2007 and 2017 on the LSE make up only 14 per cent of total market capitalisation, compared with 60 per cent and 47 per cent on NASDAQ and the NYSE, respectively.[80] Only two tech companies have been consistent members of the FTSE-100 since the dotcom bubble burst of the early 2000s.[81] Those two companies,

75 Institutional Asset Manager, 'New Research Shows UK Public Markets in Decline' (27 January 2020), www.institutionalassetmanager.co.uk/2020/01/27/282336/new-research-shows-uk-public-markets-decline.

76 FCA Discussion Paper DP17/2, 'Review of the Effectiveness of Primary Markets: The UK Primary Markets Landscape' (February 2017) at 42. Even taking into account all Main Market, AIM and Acquis Stock Exchange listed companies, the number of quoted companies has declined from 2,178 to 1,831 between 1999 and 2016 (FCA (2017) (*ibid* 43)).

77 House of Commons Library Briefing Paper No. 06152, 'Business Statistics' (16 December 2019) at 3.

78 M. Tubbs, 'The British Software Sector Stars Investors Should Buy Now' *MoneyWeek* (11 October 2018), https://moneyweek.com/496376/the-british-software-sector-stars-tech-stocks-to-buy-now/.

79 The 'new economy' has been variously defined, but generally references the economic structure resulting from the intersection of globalisation and information technology (M. Pohjola, 'The New Economy: Facts, Impacts and Policies' (2002) 14 *Information Econ. & Policy* 133, 134).

80 HKEX Concept Paper (2017) (n 74 above 11).

81 N. Fildes, 'Busy Buyers Leave Only Two UK Tech Giants Standing' *Financial Times* (14 January 2018), www.ft.com/content/39bc9b86-f464-11e7-88f7-5465a6ce1a00. More recently, the companies Aveva and Rightmove, which could both be described as tech companies, have moved into the FTSE-100. Ocado has also, in some quarters, been described as a technology company, but its technology offerings are dwarfed by its online grocery operations.

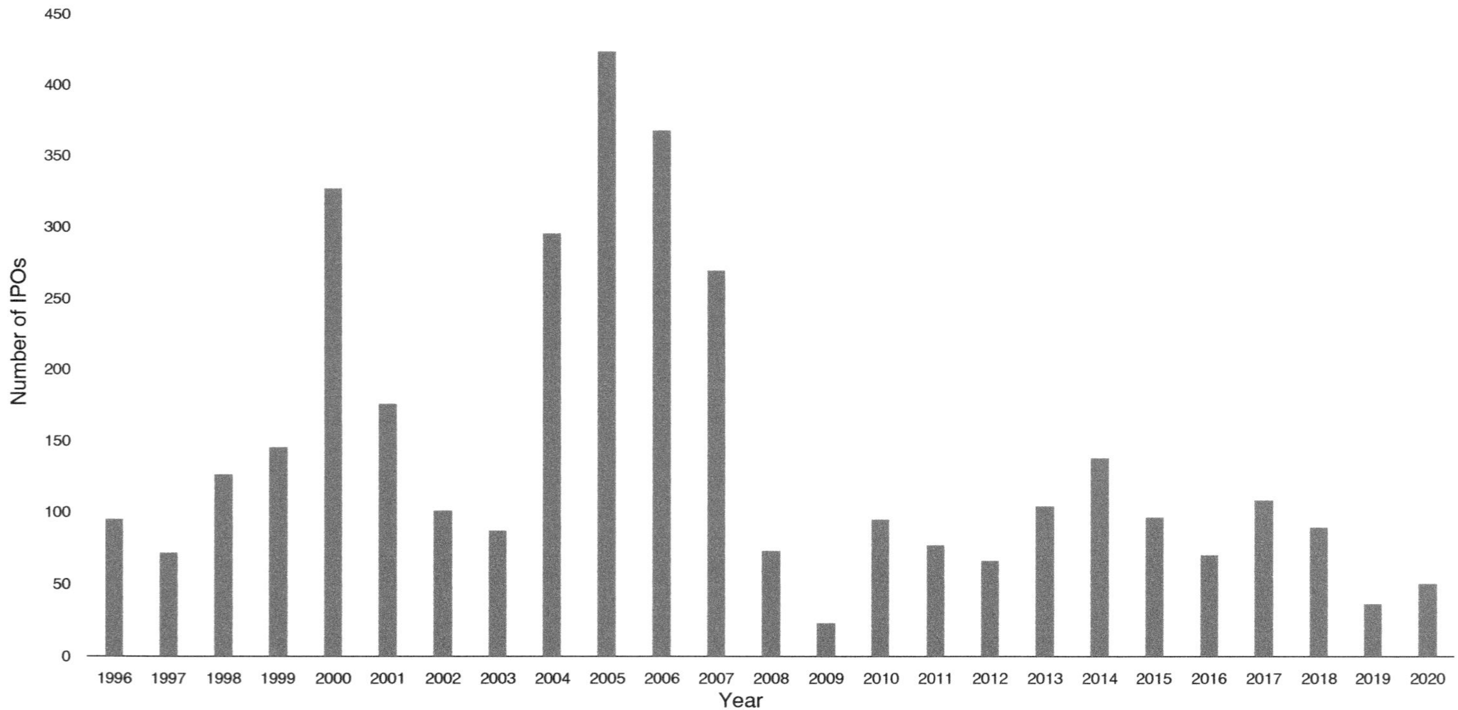

FIGURE 1.3 UK IPOs on the LSE's Main Market and AIM 1996–2020
Data derived from: London Stock Exchange, 'Reports: Primary markets, New issues and IPOs' www.londonstockexchange.com/reports?tab=new-issues-and-ipos&accordionId=0-838a7e19-eb32-49ba-a1b5-3e4eaea7021b

Micro Focus plc and Sage Group plc, are established companies which listed in the 1980s. There is no British Google or Facebook on the LSE. The dearth of UK tech firms on the market does not appear to lie in factors such as skills gaps, infrastructure obstacles or local culture – as of mid-2020, the United Kingdom was home to 24 'unicorns' (private company start-ups with individual valuations of over $1 billion), nearly half of the European total.[82] Sixteen of those UK unicorns have been described as tech companies.[83] The United Kingdom has the third highest number of unicorns globally, although it is some way behind the United States and China.[84] Therefore, the United Kingdom does not lack the capacity to develop large, successful tech companies, but such companies appear to be growing to a substantial size without pursuing the traditional scale-up route via an IPO. Outside of the unicorns, the UK pipeline is substantial, with the technology research company Megabuyte, in 2018, identifying 134 private UK tech companies that could be prime candidates for large flotations.[85] However, if the trend in UK listings continues, it is unlikely that many of those prospects will debut on the Main Market. In contrast, the period from 2012 to 2019 did not see a decline in global unicorn IPO numbers, and total global unicorn IPO value has grown substantially since 2012.[86]

The UK Government has pinpointed attracting tech firms to the LSE as a policy priority.[87] The Government's concern does not simply stem from a desire to find a British Google as a matter of self-esteem. The underlying rationale concords with the identification of innovation and investment in R&D as critical to the future competitiveness and growth of the UK economy,[88] and the potential for the public equity markets to support such innovation and investment. For a growing tech firm, equity funding could be crucial. Absent the close bank-ownership relationships found in jurisdictions such as Germany and Japan,[89] significant levels of debt financing may not be available to innovative tech firms with little or no profits history.[90] Pertinently, many recent US listings have involved pre-profit companies,

82 Data derived from CB Insights, 'The Global Unicorn Club: Private Companies Valued At $1B+ (as of June 2020)'.

83 *ibid.*

84 *ibid.* However, on a unicorns per capita basis, the United Kingdom is substantially ahead of China, and only marginally behind China when comparing the number of unicorns to GDP.

85 N. Fildes, 'Why the UK Tech Scene is Disappearing into Private Hands' *Financial Times* (22 October 2019), www.ft.com/content/27f48fac-f0f8-11e9-ad1e-4367d8281195.

86 KPMG Private Enterprise, 'Venture Pulse Q4 2019' (15 January 2020) at 19.

87 BEIS Green Paper, 'Building Our Industrial Strategy' (January 2017) at 67; FCA (2017) (n 76 above ch. 4); HM Treasury, 'Financing Growth in Innovative Firms: Consultation' (August 2017) at 33; UK Listing Review at 7.

88 BEIS (2017) (n 87 above 25).

89 J. Franks and C. Mayer, 'Ownership and Control of German Corporations' (2001) 14 *Rev. Financial Stud.* 943, 948; J. Franks et al., 'The Ownership of Japanese Corporations in the 20th Century' (2014) 27 *Rev. Financial Stud.* 2580; E. Von Thadden, 'Long-Term Contracts, Short-Term Investment and Monitoring' (1995) 62 *Rev. Econ. Stud.* 557.

90 Reddy (2020) (n 23 above 318).

particularly in the high-growth technology sphere – for example, in 2016, 68 per cent of US IPOs involved pre-profit companies, rising to 75 per cent and 92 per cent of technology and biotechnology listings, respectively.[91] A lack of available debt financing is especially acute in high asset specificity industries, like high technology, which require investment in risky, long-term projects.[92] R&D spending can therefore be hampered where access to equity markets is more limited and firms are reliant on debt financing.[93] Accordingly, external equity investment becomes essential for those pre-profit firms seeking to commercialise R&D.[94] Additionally, the incurrence of large amounts of debt, which is also a consequence of private equity buyouts, can lead to a firm shrinking to an inefficiently small size, with significant, regular interest payments throttling the ability of the company to invest and grow,[95] and could discourage the pursuit of risky, potentially lucrative projects since the company will need to retain cash to pay-off debt without becoming insolvent. Furthermore, large levels of debt may be unserviceable by a growth-phase company making little in the way of profits. The public equity markets, on the other hand, represent an immense source of funds for tech companies, and, therefore, encouraging tech listings on the LSE can foster the growth of those companies, thereby driving innovation and R&D. Supporting the growth of companies through the provision of public equity financing should benefit the economy as a whole, increasing economic growth and creating jobs.[96] With the tech sector predicted to become one of the largest providers of employment in the United Kingdom,[97] the UK economy will significantly benefit from encouraging its growth.

1.5.2 *How Dual-Class Stock May Encourage Further Listings*

Given the dwindling numbers of UK tech company IPOs, the increasing usage of dual-class structure by large US listed technology firms, and the UK Government's stated ambition to attract more science and technology companies to the Main Market, dual-class stock is a corporate governance issue that merits serious

[91] HKEX Concept Paper (2017) (n 74 above 15).

[92] M. Maher and T. Andersson, 'Corporate Governance: Effects on Firm Performance and Economic Growth' (1999) *OECD Publication* 1, 36.

[93] K. Gugler, *Corporate Governance and Economic Performance* (Oxford University Press, 2001) at 29; M. Bradley et al., 'On the Existence of an Optimal Capital Structure: Theory and Evidence' (1984) 39 *J. Financ.* 857, 874.

[94] HM Treasury (2017) (n 87 above 9).

[95] L. Bebchuk et al., 'Stock Pyramids, Cross-Ownership, and Dual Class Equity: The Mechanisms and Agency Costs of Separating Control from Cash-Flow Rights' in *Concentrated Corporate Ownership*, ed. R. Morck (University of Chicago Press, 2000) at 309.

[96] K.-H. Bae and J. Kang, 'Does the Stock Market Benefit the Economy?' (2017) *EFMA Symposium: Finance and Real Economy Accepted Papers* March 2017.

[97] Tech Nation, 'UK Tech on the Global Stage: Tech Nation Report 2019' (2019).

discussion. Of course, permitting dual-class firms to list on the premium tier will not guarantee that a plethora of large technology firms will seek listings on the Main Market, since a variety of factors will impact a founder's decision to commence an IPO on the premium tier, including the more extreme regulatory environment applicable to listed companies, and the increased public exposure of all aspects of the company's business, operations, corporate governance arrangements and remuneration practices.[98] Also, particularly in the tech sphere, at IPO, as a result of commercial and competitive sensitivities, a tech company may not be able to disclose detailed long-term plans, nor elaborate on product direction and revenue generation, and the consequent mismatch in information between the founder and potential investors can lead to the shares of the company being undervalued, further deterring the founder from listing.[99] Additionally, the burgeoning availability of private financing in the United Kingdom will also impact on the willingness of founders to list. Disregarding uncertainty surrounding the United Kingdom's withdrawal from the EU, from 2012 through 2019, private venture capital investment in UK companies grew continually, both in terms of numbers of investments and deal size.[100] The trend also shows a greater willingness of the venture capital market in the United Kingdom to invest in late-stage companies,[101] when, traditionally, such companies would otherwise be considering an IPO. Policy-makers will need to holistically evaluate the UK public equity market ecosystem to optimise it as a welcoming environment for listings. However, the one share, one vote prescription on the premium tier will be one factor that deters founders from listing.

As discussed earlier in this chapter, dual-class stock is all about control. It is worth reiterating that if a founder were to list his or her company with a one share, one vote structure and the majority of shares were to become dispersed among public

98 Premium listed companies are subject to detailed disclosure requirements over and above private companies. For example, they must make disclosures regarding capital structure, distributions and directors' interests (LRs 9.8.4–9.8.6; MAR, article 19), produce corporate governance statements (LRs 9.8.6(5) and 9.8.6(6)), publish directors' remuneration reports (CA 2006, s. 420), make periodic financial reports (DTR 4), and disclose carbon emissions (The Companies Act 2006 (Strategic Report and Directors' Report) Regulations 2013, reg. 7). Additionally, premium listed companies are subject to restrictions or requirements in relation to related-party transactions (LR Ch. 11), large transactions (LR Ch. 10), the appointment of independent directors in the presence of a controlling shareholder (LR 9.2.2) and audit committees (DTR 7). For a detailed summary of obligations, see PWC, 'Continuing Obligations for Companies Listed in the UK' (January 2018).

99 M. Cremers et al., 'The Life-Cycle of Dual Class Firms: From IPO to Sunset' (2018) *ECGI Working Paper No. 550/2018* 1, 8; L. Bebchuk, 'Asymmetric Information and the Choice of Corporate Governance Arrangements' (2002) *Harvard Law School Discussion Paper No.* 398 1; Z. Goshen and A. Hamdani, 'Corporate Control and Idiosyncratic Vision' (2016) 125 *Yale L. J.* 560, 579. It has been suggested that dual-class stock could persuade a founder to accept such undervaluation, since the retention of control will allow it to compensate itself through the extraction of other benefits ascribed by such control (J. Gordon, 'Ties that Bond: Dual Class Common Stock and the Problem of Shareholder Choice' (1988) 76 *Cal. L. Rev.* 1).

100 KPMG (2020) (n 86 above 55).

101 *ibid* 4 and 55.

shareholders, the founder will lose control of the board.[102] The fear of such loss of control will be one deterring factor in a founder taking his or her company public. The founder will not be able to preserve management's long-term vision, since it will lose the indirect ability to protect the managers from removal by public shareholders or opportunistic takeover approaches, as a result of short-term moribund share performance.[103] If the founder is involved in management, the founder will be anxious that the public shareholders could remove him or her from leading the company, and, correspondingly, as discussed in more detail in Chapter 6, the founder's scope to pursue his or her vision for the business may be curtailed by a need to placate the public shareholders. Of course, a founder could, even with one share, one vote, list on the premium tier but retain sufficient shares to ensure that it can similarly insulate the management team. However, in order to retain more than 50 per cent, or at least effective control, of the voting rights, the founder will have to limit both the proportion of its shares that it sells and the level of new equity issued. The founder will crystallise less of its wealth locked-up in the company, and the company will generate less equity funding for growth than would otherwise be the case if the founder were content for the company to become a dispersed ownership listed firm. Without sufficient equity funding (which dilutes the founder's control), the founder may not be able to fund its vision, and, in any case, the founder may be averse to the risks implicit in a large proportion of its net worth being bound to a single investment. One share, one vote entails the founder either listing and losing control or listing and retaining control but relinquishing some of the benefits from listing in the first place.[104] Dual-class stock could enter the fray as a solution to founders' concerns, allowing them to crystallise wealth and procure funding for growth while also retaining control. Additionally, with control in the hands of a founder implementing dual-class stock, post-IPO, the founder will be able to block a takeover of the company by a third party. If control were in the hands of public shareholders in a one share, one vote system, the public shareholders could sell-out control to a third party, irrespective of the views of the founder. As part of a package designed to attract flotations, dual-class stock could negate one of the primary benefits of remaining private.

The spectre of dual-class stock has preoccupied UK policy-makers in recent years. A UK Government Green Paper, in the context of supporting high-growth and innovative companies, raised the prospect of revisiting whether it should be easier for dual-class firms to list so that those companies can continue to take long-term business views without being beholden to short-term market tensions.[105] Subsequently, the FCA published a discussion paper exploring the effectiveness of

[102] See nn 47–56 above and accompanying text.
[103] See n 60 above and accompanying text.
[104] This has been described as a 'catch-22' scenario for founders, deterring them from taking their companies public (Reddy (2020) (n 23 above 324)).
[105] BEIS (2017) (n 87 above 67).

the UK primary markets,[106] including the support of science and technology company growth, specifically examining potential market enhancements to encourage the provision of scale-up and patient capital to such companies.[107] It recognised that dual-class structure may be a method enabling founders to focus on long-term company performance, and that a new listing segment may be appropriate for large international companies with premium tier incompatible control rights structures in place.[108] Speculation intensified that UK policy-makers were preparing to relax the premium tier prohibition of dual-class stock after dual-class stock recommendations in a UK Government-endorsed review of the fintech sector,[109] and a HM Treasury 'call for evidence' on, amongst other things, dual-class stock.[110] Although, ultimately, the final recommendations of the UK Listing Review fell short of propositioning what this book would describe as 'genuine' dual-class stock,[111] the subject continues to dominate corporate governance discourse in the United Kingdom as much as in other jurisdictions.

1.5.3 *Why Not Just Stay Private?*

Judging by the UK's dominance of the European unicorn scene,[112] clearly an aversion to listing in the United Kingdom is not a complete pre-requisite to growth and success. A number of UK companies, including tech companies, have grown to significant scale without tapping the public markets for equity finance. However, unicorns may be the exception rather than the rule, and a lack of attractiveness of public funding may be suffocating the capacity of many UK companies to grow. Although late-stage private VC funding has grown in the United Kingdom in recent years,[113] late-stage VC-funding deals are much larger in the United States than in the United Kingdom,[114] and a gap has been identified in available financing in the 'scale-up' phase when start-ups seek to emerge as large, established businesses.[115] Such companies are often

106 FCA (2017) (n 76 above).
107 *ibid* chapter 4.
108 *ibid* 8 and 22. Also, see HM Treasury (2017) (n 87 above 33).
109 R. Kalifa, 'Kalifa Review of UK Fintech' (26 February 2021) at 1, 65.
110 HM Treasury, 'Policy Paper: Call for Evidence – UK Listings Review' (19 November 2020).
111 See Section 1.5.7 later in this chapter.
112 See n 82 above and accompanying text.
113 See n 101 above and accompanying text.
114 FCA (2017) (n 76 above 26). More recently, European (dominated by the United Kingdom) VC late-stage-funding deal sizes have increased, but the levels generally still lag behind the levels observed in the United States, KPMG (2020) (n 86 above 27 and 58).
115 FCA (2017) (n 76 above 26) – 'scale-up companies' are those with average growth in employees or turnover of more than 20 per cent per annum over three years, with a minimum of twenty employees at the start. Also, see HM Treasury (2017) (n 87 above 11); A. Bravo-Biosca, 'Firm Growth Dynamics Across Countries' (2016) *NESTA Working Paper No.16/03*, https://media.nesta.org.uk/documents/wp16-03_firm_growth_dynamics-17.pdf; S. Rigos, 'The UK Equity Gap, "Why is There No Facebook or Google in the UK?"' *Greater London Authority* (2011) at 25.

found within the science and technology industries and attain a size that is beyond further VC funding.[116] One study examined UK start-ups forming in 1998, and found that only 11 per cent of such firms survived more than fifteen years,[117] and only 0.05 per cent evolved into 'large' firms employing more than 250 employees.[118]

In the absence of late-stage VC finance, the 'private equity' industry could ride to the rescue. Private equity firms are sitting upon vast sums of 'dry powder' (raised funds not yet invested) and regularly make investments or acquisitions that dwarf the average sums invested by the VC industry.[119] A typical private equity transaction, though, is conditional upon the ceding of extensive control to the private equity sponsor, particularly over important strategic decisions, where the sponsor acquires a majority, and usually a significant majority, of the business, and procures enhanced board-voting rights. It also usually involves the incurrence of significant debt, and the sponsor will be able to compel the founders into a sale or listing of the company through, for example, the use of drag-along rights and demand registration rights. Therefore, in its traditional form, private equity may not be the natural path for a tech founder. However, in recent years, the delineation between VC and private equity has begun to blur, with large funds, such as Softbank, making huge VC investments in tech companies,[120] and traditional private equity firms abandoning full-scale buyouts in favour of large minority investments.[121] Such minority investments could allow a founder to procure significant financing (or liquidate wealth), at a later stage than conventional VC financing, without having to cede overall control of the company. Minority investment pursuits by private equity are not, however, a panacea. Although perhaps preferable to debt financing or a majority private equity buyout, such transactions will still involve substantial minority shareholder protections in favour of the private equity firm, including possibly veto rights over major transactions and decisions of the company, board seats, and exit rights.[122] The private equity investor may also be issued with instruments such as preference shares or convertible debt securities which will require the company to generate regular distributable

116 FCA (2017) (n 76 above).

117 M. Hart and M. Anyadike-Danes, 'ERC Insights: UK's Hidden Growth Champions' *Enterprise Research Centre* (June 2014) at 2, www.enterpriseresearch.ac.uk/wp-content/uploads/2014/06/ERC-Insight-Conf-2014-Demography.pdf.

118 *ibid* 3; HM Treasury (2017) (n 87 above 12).

119 For example, see McKinsey, 'Global Private Markets Review 2019: Private Markets Come of Age' (February 2019) at 17 and 24.

120 S. Ghosh and P. Leskin, 'SoftBank is Reportedly Taking Control of WeWork. Here's a Running List of All the Japanese Giant's Major Investments in Tech' *Business Insider* (22 October 2019), www.businessinsider.com/running-list-softbank-investments-2017-7?r=US&IR=T.

121 Globally, minority buyouts by private equity firms rose from an average of 13 per cent of all private equity deals between 2004 and 2007 to an average of 27 per cent between 2008 and 2014 (A. Schneider and C. Henrik, Boston Consulting Group, 'Private Equity Minority Investments: Can Less Be More?' (2 April 2015), www.bcg.com/en-gb/publications/2015/private-equity-minority-investments-can-less-be-more.aspx); also see Herbert Smith Freehills, 'European Private Equity Review' (Autumn 2017).

122 Baker McKenzie, 'Beyond COVID-19 PE Playbook' (2020) at 11.

profits.[123] In any event, such transactions still only form a minority pursuit of private equity firms, particularly in Europe,[124] and the incompatibility with traditional private equity control models and restrictions in fund documentation will likely prevent large-scale private equity minority investments.[125]

Therefore, late-stage VC funding or minority private equity investment may not always be an option for UK tech companies in the scale-up phase. For those that are fortunate enough to procure such funding, another life-cycle phase must be further considered – the 'exit phase'. The primary driver of the private equity investor will be to exit at a significant profit within a reasonable period of time,[126] and the focus of the company can shift from long-term success to ensuring a timely exit for the private equity firm. Private equity funds have finite lives, and the model is built upon acquiring portfolio companies, making them more attractive and selling at a profit. Although the success of any secondary buyout or IPO will be dependent upon the new investors determining that the business has encouraging growth prospects, *ceteris paribus*, the existing owners will likely have to show at least a degree of visible short-term progress in order to garner a profit on investment, which could chafe against the achievement of the founder's long-term vision. Additionally, VC investors, albeit with lengthier time horizons than private equity outfits, will be seeking an exit eventually, whether as part of a buyout or IPO, in order to crystallise their investments and distribute the funds to beneficiaries. If successful private companies are not listing, it begs the question as to what eventually happens to such companies, and how the scale-up investors exit their investments?

All of which brings us to M&A. A founder may see growth potential by putting the company up for sale, and allowing a larger company with greater resources to acquire the firm, prior to later-stage VC or private equity funding, or, subsequent to late-stage funding, the founder along with the investors may determine that a buy-out is the most optimal exit option. From the founder's perspective, putting the company up for sale and allowing a larger company with greater resources to acquire the firm can be a catalyst to further growth. Although a takeover of the company implicitly involves the founder ceding authority to the acquiror, a founder will have a much stronger preference for a takeover than a one share, one vote listing, if that acquiror shares the vision of the founder and has a reputation for long-term decision-making. The founder may be content to sell-out with confidence that he or she will be given a degree of free reign in continuing to manage the company without fear of dismissal on the basis of short-term considerations. The consideration for the

123 *ibid* 10. It is likely that, in the private equity context, a sponsor will require the terms of preference shares to provide that distributions must be made in accordance with those terms whenever profits are available for the purpose.

124 Herbert Smith Freehills (2017) (n 121 above).

125 Baker McKenzie (2020) (n 122 above 10).

126 *ibid* 10. Softbank's period of ownership of ARM is a pertinent example (n 141 below and accompanying text).

acquisition may also include the grant of a not insubstantial equity award in the acquiring entity. Although there may be case-specific reasons why a tech company may prefer a takeover to a premium listing, including more extensive data sharing or economies of scale, apprehension of numerous public shareholders entering the picture will be one reason. With an acquisition, the acquiror will be known to the founder, whereas, with a listing where the founder does not retain control, the initial IPO investors will not be certain, and, subsequently, such investors may regularly change over time and are likely, in the United Kingdom, to be dispersed, each only holding a small interest.[127] The attraction of dealing with one known quantity as opposed to numerous unknown shareholders is obvious. With the latter, share price becomes a proxy for success.

UK technology companies are disproportionately the subject of M&A activity compared with their international peers.[128] In the United States, rumours abound that the founders of Snap listed the company in 2017 after turning down a takeover offer from Google that exceeded the IPO valuation of the company, and a previous smaller offer from Facebook in 2013.[129] Similarly, Groupon rejected a takeover offer from Google soon before its IPO.[130] However, in the United Kingdom, as shown in Table 1.2, between 2014 and 2019, numerous examples exist of large,[131] private UK technology companies being acquired rather than listing on the UK markets. The acquirors were mainly 'strategic' acquirors (corporations in a similar industry to the target), with the remainder being private equity purchasers (which will then be seeking a subsequent secondary exit). Pertinently, the acquirors in Table 1.2 are exclusively foreign. Also notable is that two of the target tech companies were unicorns, with the others well on their way to becoming unicorns. The prevalence of foreign M&A activity in the tech company world will be particularly concerning to policy-makers. Although such companies may not be moving abroad wholesale in every case, there is often a drip-feed of operations, management, jobs and talent to other jurisdictions. As an example, although Google is a large employer in the United Kingdom, after acquiring the British-based DeepMind, segments of its business, including units dedicated to the commercialisation of DeepMind's technology, have been moved to the United States.[132] The takeover of businesses of national strategic importance by foreign acquirors has been on the UK Government's radar for quite some time. In 2019, the UK Government proposed extended powers to block takeovers on the grounds of

[127] Note 20 above.

[128] FCA (2017) (n 76 above 26).

[129] J. Constine, 'Google Reportedly Offered $30 Billion to Acquire Snapchat' *TechCrunch* (3 August 2017), https://techcrunch.com/2017/08/03/google-buy-snap/.

[130] O. Thomas, 'Why Groupon Really Turned Down Google's $6 Billion Offer' *Business Insider* (2 June 2012), www.businessinsider.com/groupon-google-deal-turn-down-2012-6?r=US&IR=T.

[131] Acquisition values greater than £100 m.

[132] M. Murgia, 'DeepMind Co-Founder's Leave of Absence Signals Transition' *Financial Times* (23 August 2019), www.ft.com/content/45bb157a-c4f6-11e9-a8e9-296ca66511c9.

TABLE 1.2 *Large (over £100 m) acquisitions of UK private technology companies between 2014 and mid-2019*

UK Private Company Target	Year of Acquisition	Acquiror	Jurisdiction of Acquiror	Acquisition Price
DeepMind	2014	Google	USA	$650 m
Vero Software	2014	Hexagon AB	Sweden	Unannounced
Swiftkey	2015	Microsoft Corporation	USA	$250 m
Onefinestay	2016	Accor	France	£177 m
Skyscanner	2016	Ctrip.com International, Ltd	China	$1.4 b
Magic Pony Technology	2016	Twitter, Inc.	USA	$150 m
Shazam	2017	Apple Inc.	USA	$400 m
Momondo	2017	Booking Holdings	USA	$550 m
Silverrail	2017	Expedia	USA	$148 m
Vocalink	2017	Mastercard	USA	$700 m
Nyx Games	2018	Scientific Games	USA	$626.5 m
Callcredit	2018	TransUnion	USA	$1.4 b
Ziylo	2018	Novo Nordisk	Denmark	$800 m
Foundry	2019	Roper Technologies	USA	$544 m

Sources: ONS, 'Mergers and Acquisitions Involving UK Companies' (publications from Q3 2014 to Q2 2019); A. Sword, '6 of the Biggest UK Tech Acquisitions by Overseas Giants' *C. B. R.* (18 July 2016), https://techmonitor.ai/techonology/data/6-of-the-biggest-uk-tech-acquisitions-by-overseas-giants-4952343; A. Hern, 'Is the Global Desire to Buy British a Bad Thing for UK Tech Firms?' *The Guardian* (16 December 2017), www.theguardian.com/business/2017/dec/16/uk-tech-companies-bought-by-overseas-giants-apple-shazam.

national security,[133] including in relation to intervention in potentially any sector designated by the Secretary of State for BEIS[134] and to transactions of any deal size, and a further inquiry was commenced on the UK's Foreign and Commonwealth Office's role in blocking foreign asset stripping in the United Kingdom.[135] Global

133 Prime Minister's Office, 'The Queen's Speech 2019' (19 December 2019), at 104. As of the time of writing, a National Security and Investment Bill (2020) had commenced its passage toward law through the House of Commons.

134 It is currently envisaged that the sectoral scope will be broad and include tech industries such as 'artificial intelligence', 'communications', 'computing hardware', 'data infrastructure' and 'quantum technologies', with a further power for the Secretary of State to intervene even in other industries if the relevant acquisition poses a national security risk (BEIS, 'National Security and Investment: Sectors in Scope of the Mandatory Regime – Consultation' (November 2020)).

135 UK Parliament, 'FCO's Role in Blocking Foreign Asset Stripping in the UK: Report and Government Responses' (2020), https://committees.parliament.uk/work/252/the-fcos-role-in-blocking-foreign-asset-stripping-in-the-uk/publications/.

governments have also become concerned that companies, vulnerable after the 2020 pandemic-related financial crisis, could be targeted by sovereign-backed foreign acquirors.[136] Clearly, the loss of British tech businesses to foreign acquirors is not palatable for policy-makers. An example of the tensions created in the United Kingdom was apparent in the takeover of Imagination Technologies in 2017. The company was considered strategically important to UK national security owing to the capacity of its technology to identify network vulnerabilities. Although the acquiror was notionally a US-based private equity firm, the majority investor in that firm was a state-owned Chinese company.[137] When reports emerged that the Chinese investor was intending to take control of the board of Imagination Technologies, and that the company's technologies may be transferred outside the United Kingdom, an investigation was triggered by the UK's Foreign Affairs Committee.[138] Remaining private, without a credible IPO exit option, brings perils from a public policy perspective.

Another related aspect to companies remaining private is the fate of the handful of tech companies that do list on the LSE. As shown in Table 1.3, the period between 2014 and 2019 saw a number of tech companies listed in the United Kingdom taken private. Again, all the acquirors were foreign-based enterprises, which will be of further concern to UK policy-makers. The business community has also identified a lack of replacement tech flotations for listed technology companies that have been taken private as a big problem for the UK economy and UK tech sector.[139] As discussed earlier, once a company has listed with one share, one vote, it becomes open to a takeover, broadly based upon the views of the public shareholders. Even if the board opposes the takeover, a hostile takeover can be completed if shareholders holding over 50 per cent of the shares approve the bid.[140] Even if, from the perspective of jobs and operations remaining locally viable, the relevant takeover is benign, future secondary acquisitions of the company, now private, can eventually jeopardise those jobs and operations. An example is the take-private acquisition of ARM, formerly a British listed company, by Softbank in 2016. Softbank mainly maintained the operations of the company in the United Kingdom even after the takeover, but as a VC/private equity firm it was always contemplating a future sale of the company. The announcement of a secondary buyout of ARM by a US tech company in 2020 was described as an

[136] The EU is seeking such powers; for example, S. Fleming et al., 'EU Seeks to Curb State-Backed Foreign Rivals' *Financial Times* (2 June 2020), www.ft.com/content/8f8fc72d-1c05-488e-93f0-f60a4dce18b6; see EC, 'White Paper on Levelling the Playing Field as Regards Foreign Subsidies' COM(2020) 253 final (17 June 2020); also see Baker McKenzie (2020) (n 122 above 13).

[137] J. Adebiyi et al., 'Skadden Discusses How Covid-19 Prompts EU Nations to Protect against Foreign M&A' *The CLS Blue Sky Blog* (28 April 2020).

[138] *ibid.* The events at Imagination Technologies prompted a wider inquiry by the Foreign and Commonwealth Office (UK Parliament) (n 135 above).

[139] Fildes (2019) (n 85 above).

[140] Often, though, a bidder will make its offer conditional upon a greater proportion of the shares accepting the offer.

TABLE 1.3 *Large (over £100 m) foreign buyouts of UK listed technology companies between 2014 and mid-2019*

UK Listed Company	Year of Acquisition	Acquiror	Jurisdiction of Acquiror	Acquisition Price
Invensys	2014	Schneider	France	£3.4 b
CSR	2015	Qualcomm	USA	$2.4 b
Advanced Computer Software	2015	Vista	USA	£725 m
ARM	2016	SoftBank	Japan	£24 b
KBC	2016	Yokogawa	Japan	$180.3 m
XChanging	2016	CSC	USA	$720 m
PACE	2016	Arris	USA	$2.1 b
Telecity	2016	Equinix	USA	$3.8 b
E2V Technologies	2017	Teledyne Technologies	USA	£620 m
Imagination	2017	Canyon Bridge	USA	£550 m
Worldpay	2018	Vantiv Inc	USA	$10.63 b
Sophos	2019	Thoma Bravo	USA	$3.9 b

Sources: ONS, 'Mergers and Acquisitions Involving UK Companies' (publications from Q3 2014 to Q2 2019); J. Kollewe, 'UK Cybersecurity Firm Sophos Agrees £3.1bn Takeover' *The Guardian* (14 October 2019), www.theguardian.com/business/2019/oct/14/uk-cybersecurity-sophos-takeover-thoma-bravo

'absolute disaster' by one of ARM's co-founders, who was unable to block the transaction.[141] Whether tech companies remain private or float, it does not appear that the UK public equity markets are providing a stable, long-term home for UK tech companies. Dual-class stock could protect UK companies from such takeovers, since if control is retained by a founder, the acquiescence of the founder will be required for the takeover to be successful.

A final factor that will influence regulators to promote public listings is that flotations give UK individuals, or retail investors, the opportunity to participate and share in the success of issuers.[142] Such participation may be through direct investments, or indirectly through investments in pensions, insurance products and investment funds that are open to retail investors. Detailed rules govern the promotion of investment products, meaning that private companies, unlike public

[141] M. Farrer et al., 'UK Tech Giant ARM Holdings to be Sold to US Company Nvidia in $40bn Deal' *The Guardian* (14 September 2020), www.theguardian.com/business/2020/sep/14/uk-tech-giant-arm-holdings-to-be-sold-to-us-company-nvidia-in-40bn-deal.

[142] D. Cipollone, 'Risky Business: A Review of Dual Class Share Structures in Canada and a Proposal for Reform' (2012) 21 *Dalhousie J. Legal Stud.* 62, 69; S. Feldman, 'BNA Insights: IPOs in 2016 Increasingly Include Dual-Class Shareholder Voting Rights' (2016) *Bloomberg BNA* 1, 3, reproduced with permission from 47 SRLR 1342; A. Friedman, 'The Promise of Market Reform: Reigniting America's Economic Engine' *Harvard Law School Forum on Corporate Governance and Financial Regulation* (18 May 2017).

companies, are not, subject to restricted exemptions, able to offer securities to the general public or proactively solicit such investments,[143] unless the promotor of the investment has been authorised by the FCA (or the contents of the relevant financial promotion has been approved by such an authorised person),[144] or if the potential investor is a 'high net worth individual'[145] or a 'sophisticated investor'.[146] If nearly all successful high-growth UK tech companies are remaining private, only sophisticated investors will be able to participate in their growth. It is notable that of the lead investors listed for the United Kingdom's twenty-four unicorns in mid-2020, none are UK pension schemes.[147] Most of the lead investors are VC funds, private equity investors or sovereign wealth funds, which are not open to investment by retail investors themselves. A smattering of unicorn lead investors are strategic investors, which could possibly portend future takeovers of those companies. US research has shown that the net gain of the US stock markets over time has been driven by only a handful of firms.[148] Missing out on the British Google or British Facebook could be a significant loss to a UK investor's portfolio.[149]

1.5.4 *Why Bother with the Premium Tier?*

The premise of the discussion above is that the inaccessibility of dual-class stock in the United Kingdom could be deterring the listing of companies, particularly tech companies, which has a variety of negative consequences for the UK economy, retail investors and policy-makers. However, dual-class stock is only prohibited on the premium tier. If prohibition of dual-class stock is a gating issue toward IPO for founders, why not list on the standard tier, the high-growth segment, AIM or on an independent exchange, where dual-class stock is permitted?

Firstly, let's look outside the Main Market. In comparison to the Main Market, AIM was established for smaller and growing companies,[150] with less onerous listing requirements,[151] and therefore embraces an investor base reflective of the types of companies that list on the exchange. The average market capitalisation of primary

143 CA 2006, s. 755; FSMA 2000, Part II; also see FPO 2005.
144 FSMA 2000, s. 21.
145 FPO 2005, article 48.
146 FPO 2005, article 50.
147 CB Insights (2020) (n 82 above).
148 The net gain for the US stock markets between 1926 and 2016 can be attributed to only 4 per cent of listed companies (H. Bessembinder, 'Do Stocks Outperform Treasury Bills?' (2018) 129 *J. Fin. Econ.* 440, 456).
149 As noted by Sharfman, in the context of US sunset clauses (see Chapter 9 for further details on sunset clauses), '... inhibiting one company from becoming the next Alphabet or Facebook, it is one company too many' (B. Sharfman, 'The Undesirability of Mandatory Time-Based Sunsets in Dual Class Share Structures: A Reply to Bebchuk and Kastiel' (2019) 93 *S. C. L. J.* 1, 10). Also see the example of The Hut Group (n 219 below and accompanying text).
150 White Page Ltd in association with the London Stock Exchange, 'A Guide to AIM' (2010) at 4.
151 AIM companies are not subject to the Main Market's minimum capitalisation (£700,000), three-year trading record, nor free-float requirements (*ibid* 6).

issuers on AIM, as of May 2020, was just short of £120 million as compared to around £2.75 billion on the Main Market.[152] In 2019, the average money raised from new and further issues of shares was approximately £2.5 million per issuance on AIM, compared to around £23.5 million per issuance on the Main Market.[153] For a growing mid-stage tech company with high funding requirements, or a unicorn, it is unlikely that AIM would represent a suitable market to promote the levels of liquidity or raise the levels of finance required. Furthermore, informally, the LSE, as the controller of AIM,[154] has suggested that it is unlikely that it would admit dual-class stock to an AIM listing.[155] Similar considerations of scale apply to the Acquis Stock Exchange. The exchange is divided into a main market and growth market, with the main market focused on small mid-cap IPOs (generally small- and medium-sized enterprises) and the growth segment focused on even smaller companies at an earlier stage in their growth.[156] Acquis sits below AIM with respect to the size of companies it is attempting to attract, and neither of the Acquis segments would be suitable for a unicorn, or even a successful young, high-growth company with ambitions to grow to a large size reasonably quickly. Most companies that are listed on Acquis or AIM will aspire to graduate to the Main Market to access the levels of equity finance and liquidity available to larger companies. Therefore, even if a company were to list on AIM or Acquis with a dual-class structure,[157] the rules of the Main Market pertaining to such structures will still be pertinent.

Moving now into the Main Market, which is divided into the premium tier, the standard tier and the high-growth segment. Although the high-growth segment was established to attract companies too large for AIM,[158] and, in particular, high-growth tech companies, it is still considered as only a market for mid-sized companies.[159]

152 As of May 2020, the market capitalisation of a total of 832 primary issuers on AIM was £98,611.7 million (LSE, 'AIM Primary and Secondary Markets Factsheet' (May 2020)), and the market capitalisation of a total of 1,130 primary issuers on the Main Market was £3,104,247.3 million (LSE, 'Main Market Equity Factsheet' (May 2020)).

153 Data derived from LSE, 'AIM Primary and Secondary Markets Factsheet' (December 2019), and LSE, 'Main Market Equity Factsheet' (December 2019).

154 AIM embraces a 'self-regulatory' approach, whereby authorised nominated advisors are responsible to advise and regulate compliance by issuers with the rules of AIM.

155 T. Egan et al., 'The Revival of Dual Class Shares' *IFLR* (Spring 2020), www.iflr.com/article/b1lmx6clj4l38j/the-revival-of-dual-class-shares.

156 AQSX, 'Market Consultation Paper' (1 May 2020) at 1 and 4.

157 Arbuthnot Banking Group is a recent example of a company implementing dual-class structure in the United Kingdom – the company listed non-voting stock on the NEX Exchange (now Acquis Stock Exchange), to accompany its listing of one share, one vote shares on AIM (Announcement of Arbuthnot Banking Group (RNS No: 2487U), 'Diversification as New Businesses Commence' (28 March 2019)).

158 LSE, 'High Growth Segment', https://docs.londonstockexchange.com/sites/default/files/documents/hgsflyer.pdf. Note that although the high-growth segment forms part of the Main Market, firms listed on the segment do not join the FCA's Official List.

159 Practical Law Company, 'Introduction to the High Growth Segment' (2017), https://uk.practicallaw.thomsonreuters.com/7-525-8411?transitionType=Default&contextData=(sc.Default)&firstPage=true.

Furthermore, the envisaged benefit of the high-growth segment over the premium and standard tiers is that the free-float requirement – the proportion of shares that must be available to the public for the issuer to be admitted to trading – is lower on the high-growth segment.[160] Essentially, the high-growth segment is a launching pad for the premium or standard tiers, with issuers being able to move to those higher tiers once they meet the relevant eligibility requirements.[161] It gives founders the opportunity to test the waters of the public markets. However, for a founder looking to crystallise a significant portion of its wealth and/or raise substantial new capital through a fresh issue of shares, it is unlikely that the high-growth segment would be considered the appropriate forum. It is possible that the high-growth segment was attempting to bridge a gap between AIM and the Main Market that does not really exist. Since the establishment of the high-growth segment in 2013, as of 2020, only two IPOs have taken place on the segment.[162] Of those two companies, Just Eat very quickly upgraded to the premium tier within a month of its IPO after it had ascertained the level of interest in the flotation,[163] and the remaining high-growth segment company, Matomy Media, only floated on the high-growth segment after it had to abandon its initial plans for an IPO on the premium tier after failing to secure sufficient investor interest to satisfy the premium tier's free-float requirements.[164] Even if a founder were to list with dual-class stock on the high-growth segment, the fact that it is expected that the company will shift to the premium or standard tiers as it grows and intends to issue further stock to the public, means that, as with AIM and Acquis listings, the rules of the premium and standard tiers will nevertheless be germane.

A distinction between the premium tier and the standard tier has existed since 2010.[165] Although dual-class shares have always been permitted on the standard tier, there are several reasons why leaving only the standard tier as open for dual-class stock is not ideal. The LSE has marketed the premium tier as its most prestigious

160 The minimum free float on the high-growth segment is 10 per cent with a value of at least £30 million (the majority of which must be raised at admission). The free float requirement for the premium and standard tiers is 25 per cent, although the FCA has discretion to lower the threshold in individual cases (LRs 6.14R, 9.2.15R).

161 LSE (n 158 above).

162 See Practical Law Company, 'What's Market, IPOs: Main Market', https://uk.practicallaw.thomsonreuters.com/9-386-8913?transitionType=Default&contextData=(sc.Default).

163 Announcement of Just Eat (RNS No. 1985G), 'Application for Admission to a Premium Listing' (2 May 2014). Just Eat was subsequently acquired by Takeaway.com (Announcement of Just Eat (RNS No. 7089B) 'Statement re Suspension of Listing and Trading' (3 February 2020)).

164 A. Armstrong, 'Matomy Uses High Growth Segment for Second Listing Attempt' *The Telegraph* (8 July 2014), www.telegraph.co.uk/finance/newsbysector/mediatechnologyandtelecoms/media/10953669/Matomy-uses-High-Growth-Segment-for-second-listing-attempt.html.

165 Prior to the divergence into the premium and standard tiers, the Main Market was divided into the primary- and secondary-tiers. UK issuers were not permitted to list on the secondary-tier, which encompassed the minimum EU listing requirements, and could only list on the primary-tier with its super-equivalent requirements. This led to a secondary-tier solely existing as a market for foreign issuers.

tier, to which the highest standards of corporate governance are applicable.[166] More stringent admission requirements apply, including the need to appoint a sponsor, evidence a three-year revenue earnings track-record, have had control over the majority of its assets for a three-year period and evidence three years of unqualified audited accounts. After listing, premium listed companies are subject to more stringent requirements related to, for example, the implementation of large and related-party transactions, pre-emption rights and minority investor protections in the presence of controlling shareholders, and are required to apply the UK CGC. The greater corporate governance standards associated with the premium tier lends it prestige, attracting greater levels of investment by a larger number of sophisticated investors, and, consequently, attracts issuers, since such companies will be able to draw a greater level of investment at a potentially better price. As such, advisors often recommend to issuers not to list on the standard tier,[167] and separating the Main Market into two tiers has created a lack of clarity and uncertainty as to the purpose of the standard tier.[168] The FCA itself has admitted that a standard listing is often considered unattractive for many potential issuers, with the very name connoting 'second-best' status.[169] A dual-class firm that would otherwise satisfy the premium tier requirements would not be able to take advantage of the prestige attached to a premium listing, and even a high-quality dual-class share issuer may struggle to attract premium tier levels of investment when listing on the standard tier. Although a sophisticated institutional investor would be unlikely to shoot itself in the foot and pass-up a 'hot' IPO merely due to the second-rate perception attached to the 'standard tier' moniker, substantively, many of the key continuing corporate governance requirements attached to a premium tier, but not standard tier, listing are exactly the types of protections that an institutional investor would regard as essential prior to investing in dual-class shares in the United Kingdom. Premium tier companies are subject to, for example, related-party transaction regulations,[170] and controlling shareholders of premium tier companies must contractually restrict certain of their actions.[171] The lower corporate governance standards of a standard listed company would most likely be even more of a deterrent to investors where the company is issuing dual-class shares. Although the relevant issuer could voluntarily adopt equivalent protections in order to assuage investor concerns, such protections

166 The premium tier requires standards that are super-equivalent to the EU's minimum mandatory requirements, and therefore 'provides protection for investors, promotes shareholder confidence and acts as a badge of quality for companies' (FSA Consultation Paper 098/28, 'Listing Regime Review: Consultation on Changes to the Listing Categories Consequent to CP09/24' (November 2009) at 4).

167 *ibid* 19.

168 *ibid* 22.

169 FCA (2017) (n 76 above 19). The UK Listing Review also noted that the standard tier suffers from an 'identity and branding crisis' (UK Listing Review at 22).

170 See Section 8.2.4 of Chapter 8 for further details. In the United States, investors can also take some comfort from constraints on related-party transactions (see Section 7.6.3 of Chapter 7).

171 Controlling shareholders must enter into 'relationship agreements' with their companies (for further details, see Section 8.2.4 of Chapter 8).

would not be subject to regulatory oversight, and therefore would likely be contractual or implemented through the constitutional documents of the issuer. The appetite of investors to examine and analyse the relevant contractual and constitutional provisions on a case-by-case basis will not be great, and it has been suggested that the ability of investors to assess more granular elements of a company's bespoke corporate governance qualities accurately is limited.[172]

Additionally, non-premium listed firms are excluded from the FTSE UK Index Series (including indices such as the FTSE-100 and the FTSE-350), which comprise sub-categories of firms ranked on the basis of market capitalisation.[173] Even if the FCA could refine the framework around standard listings to attenuate the 'second best' moniker attached thereto, as considered in its 2017 discussion paper,[174] a large dual-class firm would be considerably disadvantaged by a lack of access to the indices. Inclusion on the indices can improve liquidity and create a 'bump' in share price.[175] One reason for this is that certain investors, known as passive index trackers, slavishly track the performance of benchmark indices such as the FTSE-100 in the United Kingdom, and are therefore compelled to invest in their constituents.[176] Such passive investment funds represent significant assets under management,[177] from which standard listed shares are completely excluded. Certain active funds will also be mandated to only invest in the shares of companies included in specific indices. Additionally, the performance of fund managers of non-index trackers may be assessed against the performance of indices, in which case, the fund managers are likely to invest a portion of assets under management in the indices to hedge risk.[178] Active investors that nonetheless track indices are sometimes referred to as 'closet indexers'[179] and indirectly represent another source of demand (increasing price and liquidity) for the shares of index constituents. If a standard tier firm were to grow to a size that would otherwise be worthy of index inclusion, it would not be able to take advantage of the associated benefits, including

172 Bebchuk (2002) (n 99 above); Bebchuk and Kastiel (2017) (n 68 above 623).

173 The FTSE-indices are maintained by a subsidiary of the LSE.

174 FCA (2017) (n 76 above 14).

175 Sharfman (2018) (n 71 above 4); Anderson et al. (2017) (n 65 above 7); D. Lund, 'Nonvoting Shares and Efficient Corporate Governance' (2019) 71 *Stanf. L. Rev.* 687, 711; S. Hirst and K. Kastiel, 'Corporate Governance by Index Exclusion' (2019) 99 *B.U. L. Rev.* 1229, 1253–1254; A. Shleifer, 'Do Demand Curves for Stocks Slope Down?' (1986) 41 *J. Fin.* 579.

176 For a more detailed description of index funds and the way in which they operate, see L. Bebchuk and S. Hirst, 'Index Funds and the Future of Corporate Governance: Theory, Evidence, and Policy' (November 2018) 1, 15, https://papers.ssrn.com/sol3/papers.cfm?abstract_id=3282794; Cheffins (2013) (n 20 above 508); D. Solomon, 'The Importance of Inferior Voting Rights in Dual-Class Firms' (2019) 2 *BYU Law Rev.* 533, 562; Lund (2019) (n 175 above 732).

177 In 2018, passive funds accounted for approximately 26 per cent of all UK assets under management (rising from only 16 per cent in 2008), and 42 per cent of UK-managed equity assets were managed passively (The Investment Association, 'Asset Management in the UK 2018–2019: The Investment Association Annual Survey' (September 2019) at 45).

178 Cheffins (2013) (n 20 above 513); Hirst and Kastiel (2019) (n 175 above 1256).

179 Hirst and Kastiel (2019) (n 175 above 1250).

greater share value and lower costs of capital. An example of the importance of the indices transpired when Unilever, a company which, for historic reasons, maintained a dual listed structure with entities listed on both the Main Market's premium tier and the Amsterdam Stock Exchange, suggested, in 2018, that it would propose a resolution to abandon its Main Market listing in favour of a single Dutch listing. The suggestion created a furore among investors, both passive and active, who would be forced to sell all or some of the shares held in the company upon it leaving the FTSE-100.[180] The issue was of concern to sufficient a number of shareholders that Unilever abandoned its proposals, suspecting that the required resolution would not be passed.[181] HM Treasury's UK Listing Review noted that index exclusion was a key reason for issuers finding the standard tier unattractive.[182] A further corollary of excluding dual-class firms from the FTSE indices is that it will limit the exposure of retail investors to those firms, restricting the ability of such investors to share in their success.[183] Pension funds and insurance companies, for example, will invest much of their funds through index funds which track the indices, and if dual-class stock were to be included on the indices, it would enable such funds to participate in the growth of successful dual-class firms, while mitigating the risk from less successful dual-class firms by being diversified across the market.[184] Whereas index exclusion may be justified on grounds related to protecting retail investors, a contrary argument can be made that exclusion forces retail investors, desiring to participate in dual-class firm listings, into investing directly or using active funds which will be less diversified, and, therefore, present greater risks than index tracker funds.

The inferiority complex associated with the standard tier, and the exclusion from the indices, does indeed appear to have deterred dual-class firms from listing on that tier. Even though companies have been liberally availing themselves of dual-class structure in the United States, as of the time of writing, excluding preference shares, the only companies to list on the standard tier with disproportionate voting rights since it was established in 2010 are, in 2020, The Hut Group (which, as discussed in Section 1.5.5 later in this chapter, involved the grant of bespoke enhanced-voting rights, that were not 'full' dual-class stock rights, to the founder in specific circumstances[185]) and, in 2021, Deliveroo (which, as discussed in Section 1.5.6 later in this chapter, reports suggested had been undertaken with a view to shifting from the standard tier to the premium tier upon the UK Listing Review proposals

180 Z. Wood, 'Unilever Scraps Plan to Move HQ from London to Rotterdam' *The Guardian* (5 October 2018), www.theguardian.com/business/2018/oct/05/unilever-scraps-plan-move-london-rotterdam-uk-netherlands.

181 *ibid.* Although Unilever's stated reason to contemplate the switch to a single listing in the Netherlands was to simplify its structure, after fighting-off a bid for the company by Kraft in 2017, it may also have been influenced by the United Kingdom's listing regime being *too* 'takeover friendly'.

182 UK Listing Review at 23.

183 MSCI, 'Should Equity Indexes Include Stocks of Companies with Share Classes Having Unequal Voting Rights?' (January 2018) at 14.

184 A. Grinapell, 'Dual-Class Stock Structure and Firm Innovation' (2020) 25 *SJLBF* 40, 74.

185 See Section 1.5.5 later in this chapter.

becoming effective[186]). Although three further companies – Schroders, Hansa, and Daily Mail – do currently have non-preferential inferior-voting shares listed on the standard tier,[187] they were all long-time members of the Main Market's former 'primary-tier' and found their inferior-voting shares downgraded to the standard tier upon the prohibition of non-voting stock from the premium tier becoming effective.[188] The enhanced-voting shares of Schroders and Hansa are premium listed, and those of Daily Mail are unlisted. Schroders, Hansa and Daily Mail have not listed inferior-voting shares on the standard tier through choice, but, instead, find their shares on the standard tier as a result of regulatory exigencies.

A final possibility for a founder with his or her heart set on dual-class stock is to pursue a foreign dual-class stock listing. Manchester United, a mainstay of the English football leagues, is an example of a UK-based business that listed on the NYSE with dual-class structure,[189] foregoing other exchanges that did not permit the structure.[190] In the tech sphere, Farfetch, the online fashion retailer, and Endava, a technology services and consultancy company, listed inferior-voting stock on the NYSE in 2018.[191] With foreign exchange options available to UK companies as an avenue of growth, one may challenge the assertion that a more open premium tier is even required to support the growth of UK companies. However, UK companies have not sprinted toward the warm embrace of foreign markets. For example, there are very few UK tech companies listed on the NYSE or NASDAQ.[192] Several factors will deter UK companies from listing abroad, which limits the efficacy of such markets as a source of finance. For example, if there is an unfamiliarity in the foreign market with the brand and products of the UK company, it will not be able to improve the success of the listing by capitalising on its reputation in its home product market, and, from the opposite perspective, it may not be able to leverage the publicity of the listing into better sales in its main product market.[193] Listing costs

186 See Section 1.5.6 later in this chapter.

187 FCA's 'The Official List' as of 25 November 2019.

188 New issuances of non-voting shares were prohibited from the premium tier in 2010, and existing non-voting stock was required to be moved to the standard tier after a two-year transition period (Financial Services Authority, 'Listing Regime Review: Feedback on CP09/24 and CP09/28 with Final Rules' (February 2010) at 13; also see Section 2.2 of Chapter 2 for more details).

189 Form F-1 Registration Statement of Manchester United Ltd. (3 July 2012) at 112.

190 Chan and Ho (2014) (n 21 above 168).

191 Form F-1 Registration Statement of Farfetch Limited (20 August 2018) at 142; Amendment No. 2 to Form F-1 Registration Statement of Endava plc (filed 23 July 2018) at 126.

192 As of 3 April 2020, only five UK tech companies had stock listed exclusively on the NYSE – Farfetch, International Game Technology, Endava, IHS Markit and Delphi Technologies (NYSE, 'Current List of All Non-U.S. Issuers' (2020), www.nyse.com/publicdocs/nyse/data/CurListofallStocks.pdf). From a search of NASDAQ's 'company list' as of 1 July 2020 (https://old.nasdaq.com/screening/company-list.aspx), only two UK tech companies had stock listed exclusively on NASDAQ – Mimecast and GAN. Five UK biotechnology firms were also listed on NASDAQ (Oxford Immunotec Global, Orchard Therapeutics, LivaNova, Autolus Therapeutics and Adaptimmune).

193 M. Pagano et al., 'The Geography of Equity Listing: Why Do Companies List Abroad?' (2002) 57 *J. Financ.* 2651, 2658–2659.

will also be more extensive for a UK company listing abroad with requirements to instruct foreign as well as UK advisors, and to ensure that accounts are compatible with the foreign jurisdiction's requirements.[194] The company will also need to accommodate the litigious culture of the foreign jurisdiction, which may differ from the United Kingdom,[195] and it may be subject to greater ongoing regulatory compliance costs.[196] The provenance of the pre-IPO investors can also influence the listing jurisdiction, with a bias toward UK listings by UK-based investors.[197]

In any event, driving UK issuers to foreign markets will undermine some of the objectives of policy-makers and UK exchanges. For instance, foreign exchanges and foreign-based advisors will extract the majority of the financial benefits accruing to the listing. Commercially, the UK exchanges will face significant competition for foreign listings as foreign exchanges make it simpler for potential issuers to list. Several jurisdictions have either opened the door to dual-class firms or are contemplating the possibility, many in response to losing listings to foreign jurisdictions which permit dual-class stock. The primary exchanges of Japan,[198] Hong Kong,[199] Singapore[200] and India[201] have all recently relaxed their rules to permit the admission of dual-class firms, and Shanghai has created a new board to accommodate technology firms with dual-class structure.[202] Along with the fact that all the major US exchanges and Canada's TSX have permitted the listing of dual-class firms for thirty years or longer, the LSE will face significant competition for listings in light of the increasing trend in the use of dual-class structure in the public sphere. Additionally, foreign listings will make it more difficult for UK retail investors to participate, since direct investments will involve foreign-based investment accounts and unfamiliar regulations. Even indirect exposure to foreign listed companies through investments in UK-based pension plans, insurance products and investment

194 J. Fanto and R. Karmel, 'A Report on the Attitudes of Foreign Companies Regarding a U.S. Listing' (1997) 3 *SJLBF* 51, 66.

195 *ibid* 67.

196 For example, not only will a UK company listed on the NYSE be required to comply with certain UK requirements, such as the Takeover Code (if the company's registered office and central place of management is in the UK) and disclosure and voting rules regarding executive remuneration (CA 2006, ss. 420, 439 and 439A), but also with US exchange requirements such as the NYSE Rules and federal regulations such as the Sarbanes-Oxley Act.

197 C. Silva, 'Why the LSE Can Serve Tech Startups Better than Nasdaq or the NYSE' *The Guardian* (10 November 2016), www.theguardian.com/business/blog/2016/nov/10/lse-tech-startups-nasdaq-nyse-investors.

198 K. Yoshii, 'A New Share-listing System in Japan' *Asia Law Corp. Fin. Rev.* (July 2008) at 16.

199 HKEX, 'Research Report: Listing Regime Reforms for Dual-Class Share Structure and Biotech Industry' (November 2018).

200 SGX News Release, 'SGX Launches Rules for Listing of Dual Class Shares Companies' (26 June 2018), www.sgx.com/media-centre/20180626-sgx-launches-rules-listing-dual-class-shares-companies.

201 SEBI, 'Framework for Issuance of Differential Voting Rights (DVR) Shares' (June 2019).

202 K. Ho, 'Examining the Viability to Allow Dual-Class Share Structure Companies to List in the Financial Market of the People's Republic of China: Lessons and Experiences from Hong Kong' (2019) 1, 26, https://ssrn.com/abstract=3408873.

funds which seek to be diversified across several jurisdictions may be limited, since such UK-based institutional investors will retain a significant proportion of their investments in the United Kingdom.[203] Overall, access to foreign stock exchanges cannot be considered to be an adequate solution to the premium tier prohibition of dual-class stock on either practical or public policy grounds.

1.5.5 *The Hut Group Case Study*

The purported inadequacies of the standard tier and the importance of the premium tier as outlined earlier cannot be fully conceived without a discussion of the 2020 IPO of The Hut Group. The Hut Group IPO serves as an interesting UK case study, highlighting both the flexibility and the limitations of the UK equity market policy on dual-class stock. The Hut Group marketed itself as a tech company,[204] and the IPO, on 16 September 2020, was portrayed as one of the largest UK tech listings in history.[205] However, unusually, and, at the time, almost unique for a large UK company IPO since the split into the standard and premium tiers in 2010, the company debuted on the standard tier rather than the premium tier of the LSE.[206] The standard tier was not a voluntary choice, since the premium tier was ruled out by the FCA due to the capital structure of the company upon admission infringing the spirit of Premium Listing Principle 4.[207] Although the company was not employing a classic dual-class stock structure per se, at IPO, the founder, Matthew Moulding, was issued with a 'special share' pursuant to which voting rights will be triggered upon a 'change of control',[208] giving the founder sufficient votes to pass or veto any proposed shareholders' resolution

[203] ONS, 'MQ5: Investment by Insurance Companies, Pension Funds and Trusts: October to December 2018' (March 2019) at 26.

[204] The Hut Group in fact encompasses a variety of businesses with the tech offering only forming a minority portion of the company's business as of IPO, leading some to comment that the company is more of a retail enterprise than a genuine tech company (S. Fieldhouse, 'The Hut Group IPO: A Retailer Posing as a Tech Company?' *The Armchair Trader* (28 August 2020), www.thearmchairtrader.com/the-hut-group-ipo-a-retailer-posing-as-a-tech-company/).

[205] A. Ramnarayan and S. Cruise, 'The Hut Group Shares Soar 30% after Bumper $7 Billion IPO' *Reuters* (16 September 2020), https://uk.reuters.com/article/uk-the-hut-group-trading/the-hut-group-shares-soar-30-after-bumper-7-billion-london-ipo-idUKKBN2670QJ.

[206] Since the IPO of The Hut Group, Deliveroo also joined it on the standard tier in one of the biggest UK IPOs in a decade (T. Bradshaw et al., 'Deliveroo Tumbles 26% in London Debut' *Financial Times* (31 March 2021), www.ft.com/content/5028437e-accf-4624-8ecd-2b502d04743d); however, reports suggested that Deliveroo listed on the standard tier with the intention to graduate to the premium tier once the recommendations of the UK Listing Review become effective (see Section 1.5.6 later in this chapter).

[207] See nn 38 and 39 and accompanying text; J. Eley and S. Provan, 'Hut Group Targets £4.5bn Valuation in London Listing' *Financial Times* (27 August 2020), www.ft.com/content/481b0b9f-504b-482b-9c77-a63b20757d40.

[208] Change of control is broadly defined to be an acquisition resulting in the acquiror, together with connected persons, holding more than 50 per cent of the voting rights in the company (excluding the votes attributable to the special share) (THG Holdings plc, 'Prospectus for the Offer of up to 376,273,998 Ordinary Shares at an Offer Price of 500p per Ordinary Share and Admission to the Standard Listing Segment of the Official List and to Trading on the Main Market for Listed

of the company.[209] Therefore, the founder's enhanced-voting rights would only become effective after a post-IPO takeover of a majority of the ordinary shares in the company (and outside of a change of control the founder does not have control over the composition of the board) – the effect, and purpose, of the rights attached to the special share is to deter any change of control of the company without founder support.[210] It is unlikely that any potential bidder will desire to acquire a majority of the shares in the company if the founder will be able to control the company, and its board, after the takeover. In effect, the special share is a 'poison pill'.[211] The rights attached to the special share endure for a period of three years post-IPO.[212]

One may therefore challenge that, in fact, the status quo in the United Kingdom regarding dual-class stock works and effectively enables companies to list with dual-class stock on the standard tier. On first sight, the IPO was a roaring success, with all allocations of offered shares taken-up, institutional shareholders not shunning the offering[213] and the share price climbing steeply in the twenty-four hours after admission.[214] However, when scrutinised in detail, the case study also highlights the limitations of the current policy. Firstly, The Hut Group is not a young, high-growth company in the vibrant stages of growth as, for example, Google and Facebook were when they publicly listed in the United States. The Hut Group commenced operations sixteen years prior to IPO,[215] and several of its early investors made returns of around fifty times their investment.[216] The founder himself stated that concerns about ceding control had deterred an earlier listing, and he was also antagonistic toward a foreign listing, such as in the United States, where dual-class stock would have been permitted.[217] If the standard tier could have provided an avenue for a listing with a special share structure, why delay the listing to 2020? The answer most probably lies in the diminished status of the standard tier. As a young, growing company, the ability to attract investors on the standard tier, with its reduced liquidity as a result of the exclusion of index trackers which follow the FTSE-indices,[218] and lower corporate governance standards, will have been

Securities of the London Stock Exchange' (10 September 2020) at 186; THG Holdings plc, 'Articles of Association Adopted by Special Resolution Passed on 9 September 2020' at article 69.1).

209 THG Prospectus (2020) (n 208 above 186); THG Articles (n 208 above article 69.5).

210 THG Prospectus (2020) (n 208 above 187).

211 'Poison pill' is a US-centric term for a constitutional provision that enables management to block or deter a takeover of the company.

212 THG Prospectus (2020) (n 208 above 186); THG Articles (n 208 above article 69.6).

213 C. Williams, 'Plain Sailing for Moulding with Flotation of Hut Group' *The Sunday Telegraph* (13 September 2020), www.telegraph.co.uk/business/2020/09/12/plain-sailing-moulding-flotation-hut-group/.

214 Ramnarayan and Cruise (2020) (n 205 above).

215 THG Prospectus (2020) (n 208 above 2).

216 P. Evans and S. Chambers, 'Matt Moulding, the Shy Tycoon Who Built a €5bn Hut' *The Sunday Times* (30 August 2020), www.thetimes.co.uk/article/matt-moulding-the-shy-tycoon-who-built-a-5bn-hut-0z23nl92t.

217 Eley and Provan (2020) (n 207 above).

218 See nn 173–184 and accompanying text.

prejudiced. Only once it had become a mature company with a proven track record was it successfully able to list on the standard tier, although the result is that retail investors and other UK public investors have missed out on participating in the company during its more accelerated growth-phase. A fifty times multiple return on investment could have been shared among thousands of public shareholders, rather than being the privileged preserve of a handful of private institutional investors.[219] Additionally, the opportunity to participate in the IPO was not as widely available as one may have first thought. Newly issued shares amounted to 19.56 per cent of the issued share capital of the company as of admission, and existing shares amounting to 19.81 per cent of the issued share capital as of admission were also sold in the IPO.[220] Of the newly issued shares, nearly 67 per cent were pre-allocated to existing institutional shareholders of The Hut Group, such as BlackRock and Merian, and further institutional investor powerhouses investing in The Hut Group for the first time, such as Henderson, Drogoneer and the Qatar Investment Authority.[221] Additionally taking into account further private placements of a small proportion of the newly issued shares,[222] only around 25.2 per cent of the issued shares in the company became widely available to public shareholders for subscription upon IPO. Even casting the pre-allocations and private placements as part of the free float, the existing shareholders in the company retained a majority of the shares in the company as of IPO, and a significant majority when considering the fully diluted share capital of the company.[223] One could conjecture that the standard tier designation has impeded the ability of the company to successfully issue further shares to the public as part of a much wider-ranging offering.

Although The Hut Group has proved that it is not impossible to pursue a large dual-class-esque listing in the United Kingdom, being restricted to the standard tier has likely considerably delayed the listing of the company. Eventually, pressure from VC and private equity investors for a partial or full exit will have driven the submission to a standard tier IPO.[224] The consequences of the IPO taking place on the standard tier has circumscribed the breadth of the public offering, and has led to the perverse consequence that The Hut Group is not permitted to become a constituent of the FTSE-100, even though its market capitalisation is much larger

219 The lead time in UK companies migrating to the public markets, and the participation in the lucrative growth-phase of such companies being restricted to private investors, has been bemoaned by certain commentators (M. Webb, 'Private Equity is a Club and the Ordinary Investor is Not Invited' *Financial Times* (28 August 2020), www.ft.com/content/80ff5ee1-cc36-4140-9f25-f60b14b3720c).

220 THG Prospectus (2020) (n 208 above 170).

221 *ibid* 172.

222 *ibid* i.

223 Further ordinary shares could be issued to insiders pursuant to the operation of performance share plans, and the company also has the power to buy back up to 10 per cent of its ordinary shares which could be exercised over shares not held by insiders (*ibid* 19).

224 The founder stated that a 'request for liquidity' by private equity backers influenced the decision to go public (Eley and Provan (2020) (n 207 above)).

than many existing constituents.[225] Index trackers, and, by extension, pension funds, insurance companies and retail investors who seek diversification through passive investment, are excluded from participating in the company. Therefore, even though the FCA has shown a degree of pragmatism in permitting the bespoke capital structure of The Hut Group to the standard tier, exclusion from the premium tier has resulted in numerous compromises for the company. The lessons of The Hut Group IPO will have significantly influenced the UK Listing Review, which, as outlined later in this chapter, has proposed that, going forward, a company could design a capital structure that gives a founder the right to block takeovers and still be admitted to the premium tier. If the recommendations of the UK Listing Review had been effective at the time of The Hut Group's IPO, the company could have engineered a capital structure giving the founder equivalent takeover-blocking rights that would have been permitted on the premium tier. However, focusing on the right to block takeovers is only half the story, and it will be discussed later in this chapter[226] that the proposals of the UK Listing Review do not advocate 'genuine' dual-class stock, and, for a founder seeking true control, a flotation of its company will continue to be restricted to the standard tier in the United Kingdom and subject to the same shortcomings as The Hut Group's standard tier listing.

1.5.6 *Deliveroo Case Study*

Hot on the heels of The Hut Group's apparently successful IPO in 2020, Deliveroo, the online food delivery service, floated on the standard tier with a dual-class share structure on 31 March 2021. Unlike The Hut Group, the Deliveroo capital structure is more akin to a genuine dual-class structure, with the founder, Will Shu, holding Class B shares, to which are attached twenty votes per share, and public shareholders holding Class A shares to which are attached one vote per share.[227] At IPO, Will Shu held 57.5 per cent of the voting rights in the company, but only 6.3 per cent of the equity.[228] Enhanced-voting rights are exerciseable on all resolutions of the company, but only subsist for three years post-IPO, and will automatically expire upon the founder ceasing to be a director, the founder ceasing to provide services as an officer, employee or consultant and upon a transfer of the enhanced-voting shares to a person who is not a 'permitted transferee'.[229] Permitted transferee is defined widely

[225] From a review of the FTSE-100 on 29 April 2021, with a market capitalisation of £6.06 billion, The Hut Group would have been the eighty-sixth largest company within the FTSE-100 (data derived from LSE, 'FTSE 100').

[226] See Section 1.5.7 later in this chapter.

[227] Deliveroo Holdings plc, 'Prospectus for the Offer of up to 384,615,384 Class A Shares at an Offer Price Expected to be Between 390 and 460 Pence Per Class A Share and Admission to the Standard Listing Segment of the Official List and to Trading on the Main Market of the London Stock Exchange' (March 2021) at 27.

[228] *ibid* 3.

[229] *ibid* 170.

to include, for example, any entities or organisations exclusively owned and controlled by the founder, any trust established for the benefit of the founder or his family, any charitable organisation established by the founder, and any family member of the founder.[230] Deliveroo was held out as the poster child for a new era of tech listings in the United Kingdom,[231] and also as a vindication of the proposals of the UK Listing Review, with reports that Deliveroo's decision to list on the standard tier was in part based upon the carrot of a graduation to the premium tier once the recommendations of the UK Listing Review become effective.[232]

However, like The Hut Group, a standard tier listing entailed compromises. Only a minority of shares were offered to the public, with existing pre-IPO shareholders retaining around 70 per cent of the equity post-IPO.[233] Of those shares offered to the public, the company indicated that around 30 per cent would be allocated to three 'anchor investors'.[234] It is likely that a restriction of the listing to the standard tier, and the narrower breadth of investors willing or able to invest on that market, will have tempered the level of equity sold and issued in the offering. Compromising on the extent of the listing was not, though, sufficient to assure the success of the standard tier listing. Deliveroo's IPO was labelled an unmitigated disaster, with one of its bankers calling it 'the worst IPO in London's history'.[235] Share price plummeted by as much as 31 per cent on the day of IPO, with trading volumes only a third of what advisors had envisaged.[236] A number of reasons were given for the market's antipathy to what had been a highly anticipated flotation, including large fund managers shunning the listing due to concerns over future potential legal and regulatory risks as to the legal status of Deliveroo's delivery workers,[237] and the company simply

[230] *ibid* 211.

[231] See n 44 above.

[232] *ibid*; M. Taylor, 'Deliveroo's Shares are a Mess' *Wired* (31 March 2021). However, to graduate to the premium tier, even after the UK Listing Review recommendations become effective, Deliveroo will have to revise its capital structure to include, in particular, stricter restrictions around the exercise of voting rights and the scope of 'permitted transferees' to comply with the conditions attached to dual-class issuances under the proposals of the UK Listing Review (see Section 1.5.7 later in this chapter).

[233] Derived from data set out in Deliveroo Prospectus (2021) (n 227 above 181–182).

[234] Taylor (2021) (n 232 above).

[235] T. Bradshaw and A. Mooney, 'Disaster Strikes as Deliveroo Becomes "Worst IPO in London's History"' *Financial Times* (31 March 2021), www.ft.com/content/bdf6ac6b-46b5-4f7a-90db-291d7fd2898d.

[236] A. Massoudi et al., 'Goldman Sachs Bought £75 Million of Deliveroo Shares to Prop up IPO Price' *Financial Times* (6 April 2021), www.ft.com/content/bf75f260-33d8-42ea-85c3-6482aa1fb2ff.

[237] A number of legal cases had commenced challenging the categorisation of Deliveroo's delivery riders as independent self-employed contractors, which could result in huge payouts by the company if such workers were to be considered employees of the company (S. Butler and K. Makortoff, 'Deliveroo Sets Aside £112 Million to Cover Legal Costs of Delivery Rider Cases' *The Guardian* (8 March 2021), www.theguardian.com/business/2021/mar/08/deliveroo-losses-flotation-covid-ipo-london-stock-exchange). A number of large fund managers publicly announced that they would not be purchasing shares in the Deliveroo IPO off the back of such risks (J. Jolly and S. Butler, 'UK's Biggest Fund Manager Expected to Shun Deliveroo Float' *The Guardian* (25 March 2021), www.theguardian.com/business/2021/mar/25/another-major-asset-manager-says-it-will-not-invest-in-deliveroo).

being too late to hang on to the coattails of the global surge in tech stock that it was so desperately trying to grab.[238] More importantly, being constrained to the standard tier will also have severely hampered the success of the IPO.[239] Although, Deliveroo, as with The Hut Group, limited the size of the offering, unlike The Hut Group, Deliveroo was not a mature company upon IPO. Whereas The Hut Group waited until it had an established, profitable business prior to engaging with the standard tier, Deliveroo was founded in 2013, eight years prior to IPO (although the founder recognised that the 2020 global pandemic had accelerated the business model of the company by around three years[240]), and, critically, Deliveroo was a pre-profit company at IPO.[241] Attracting sufficient investors to a standard tier listing as a company with little or no profit track-record was an insurmountable task,[242] and, in such circumstances, the absence of the premium tier's protective measures, including, in particular, regulations pertaining to related-party transactions,[243] will have deterred investors, especially where the founder has majority control over the voting rights of the company.

Predictably, given UK institutional investor hostility to dual-class stock, after the relative fiasco of Deliveroo's IPO, institutional investors, in an attempt to quash the proposals of the UK Listing Review, stated that the company's dual-class structure also dissuaded them from investing.[244] However, notably, there was very little noise regarding Deliveroo's dual-class structure prior to IPO, with most of the publicised concerns relating to regulatory risks.[245] The same institutional investors also did not shy away from The Hut Group IPO, even though it also implemented a structure giving the founder disproportionate rights. Both The Hut Group and Deliveroo included the same three-year limitation on enhanced-voting rights. To the extent that dual-class structure had an impact on institutional investor appetite, it will have related to the nature of the company rather than dual-class stock per se. It is difficult to describe Deliveroo as an innovative company with a visionary founder who is essential to its business. The founder is a businessman rather than a tech visionary like Mark Zuckerberg at Facebook or Larry Page at Google. The company operates

[238] Massoudi et al. (2021) (n 236 above). DoorDash, a US company operating in a similar industry to Deliveroo, successfully floated on the NYSE with dual-class stock in 2020, with its shares bouncing 86 per cent on the first day of trading (T. Bradshaw, 'Deliveroo's Challenge to Serve Up Growth after IPO' *Financial Times* (11 March 2021), www.ft.com/content/5ce64d6e-8ee5-46f6-9580-f59d0708b547).

[239] *ibid.* The consequences of a standard listing were enumerated as risk factors by Deliveroo in its prospectus (Deliveroo Prospectus (2021) (n 227 above 39)).

[240] Butler and Makortoff (2021) (n 237 above).

[241] *ibid.*

[242] Taylor (2021) (n 232 above).

[243] See Chapter 8.

[244] A. Mooney, 'Investors Hit Back at Dual-class Reforms after Deliveroo IPO Flop' *Financial Times* (2 April 2021), www.ft.com/content/72de7a53-e7af-4c6b-af0f-cfd1f8fcbdf5.

[245] See n 237 above and accompanying text.

in a saturated market[246] where most industry innovation takes place outside of the delivery service sector.[247] With the nature of the business being easily observable to public shareholders, and with it being difficult to discern the quintessence of the founder to the continued success of the business, institutional investors may have doubted the benefits of dual-class stock.[248]

Although clearly a combination of factors appear to have sabotaged the success of Deliveroo's IPO, including regulatory and legal risks, poor timing, initial over-pricing and firm-specific inappropriateness of dual-class structure, foremost among them is the restriction to the standard tier. Deliveroo made certain compromises to accommodate a standard listing, but the need for finance forestalled the company's ability to delay its listing until more mature like The Hut Group. It is not certain that Deliveroo's IPO would have been a rousing success if it had taken place on the premium tier, and there is a strong case to be made that Deliveroo was the wrong company at the wrong time to attempt a dual-class structure, but listing on the standard tier, with its narrower investor base, index-exclusion and lower corporate governance standards, will have certainly had a material impact on its prospects. Deliveroo's failure may be a somewhat deflationary tale for young, high-growth tech companies seeking to list in the United Kingdom. The standard tier is not a welcoming environment for successful early-stage, pre-profit companies to list, and as the UK equity markets stand, private company investors will continue to reap the rewards of early-stage company growth – a point evidently noted by the UK Listing Review which justified its proposals regarding permitting disproportionate voting shares on the premium tier by a need to attract companies to the public equity markets at an earlier stage.[249] Moreover, the fact that Deliveroo may have been lured to the standard tier by the possibility of eventually upgrading to the premium tier[250] means that even if its IPO had been successful it would not have undermined debate regarding the importance of the premium tier and its approach to dual-class stock. In fact, if Deliveroo can graduate to the premium tier, then perhaps all is not lost for the company. Even after the plunge in share price during the first day of the float, the

246 S. Singh, 'The Soon to Be £200B Online Food Delivery Is Rapidly Changing The Global Food Industry' *Forbes* (9 September 2019), www.forbes.com/sites/sarwantsingh/2019/09/09/the-soon-to-be-200b-online-food-delivery-is-rapidly-changing-the-global-food-industry/; Bradshaw (2021) (n 238 above).

247 Singh (2019) (n 246 above).

248 In relation to the possible benefits of dual-class stock to public shareholders, and the relevance of the nature of the firm and controller to the potential for those benefits to eclipse the possible detriments of the structure, see Chapter 6. However, whether dual-class stock itself was the main issue can be questioned; since UK-based pension and insurance funds that were publicly dismissive of the capital structure post-IPO only comprise a minority of the UK equity markets (only 6.1 per cent of UK listed equities (ONS, 'Ownership of UK Quoted Shares: 2018' (January 2020) at 5)), their views on the adoption of dual-class stock could not have had such a decisive effect on the success of the IPO. Foreign investors who comprise the majority of the market do not routinely shun dual-class IPOs (see Section 7.5.2 of Chapter 7), as evidenced by the myriad of successful US dual-class IPOs.

249 UK Listing Review at 19.

250 See n 232 above and accompanying text.

market capitalisation of Deliveroo was larger than that of The Hut Group, and, upon entering the premium tier, Deliveroo could become a constituent of the FTSE-indices, attracting investment by passive index trackers.[251] However, Deliveroo's current dual-class structure is incompatible with the conditions outlined in the UK Listing Review, and, as discussed next, it is questionable that a founder seeking the control that dual-class stock achieves would be willing to genuflect to those constraints.

1.5.7 *The UK Listing Review*

The discourse in this chapter so far in relation to the potential for dual-class stock to encourage listings, and the importance of the premium tier, naturally leads us to the UK Listing Review. In November 2020, HM Treasury, in light of the United Kingdom leaving the EU and reclaiming full control over its financial regulations, commenced an investigation into the competitiveness of the United Kingdom's equity markets, and the fitness-for-purpose of the existing body of regulations relating to listed companies.[252] The results of the review were published on 3 March 2021, and, amongst other things, purportedly proposed that the premium tier prohibition of dual-class stock be relaxed. However, any such relaxation would be subject to specific conditions:[253]

(i) Dual-class structure to revert to one share, one vote within five years after IPO.
(ii) Enhanced-voting shares would only be permitted to be held by individuals who are directors.
(iii) Enhanced-voting shares to convert into inferior-voting shares upon a transfer of such shares by the holder (except transfers for estate planning or charitable purposes).
(iv) A maximum ratio between voting rights attached to enhanced-voting shares and voting rights attached to inferior-voting shares of 20:1.
(v) Enhanced-voting rights only exercisable on decisions to remove the holder from the board as a director, or in relation to approving takeovers of the company.

The premium tier dual-class stock conditions of the UK Listing Review therefore include what are known as 'sunset clauses', pursuant to which dual-class structure converts into one share, one vote upon the occurrence of certain events.[254] Specifically, the conditions require that dual-class structure must be collapsed

[251] At IPO, Deliveroo opened with a market capitalisation of £7.6 billion (n 235 above); even after first day losses, its market capitalisation was £5.6 billion, still more than the £5.4 billion market capitalisation of The Hut Group on IPO (n 213).

[252] See n 110 above.

[253] UK Listing Review at 21.

[254] For further detail on 'sunset clauses', see Section 9.5 of Chapter 9.

within five years of IPO, and that any enhanced-voting shares held by a shareholder will convert into inferior-voting shares upon a transfer of those shares or upon the shareholder ceasing to be a director of the company. Additionally, the corollary of the maximum voting ratio requirement is that an enhanced-voting shareholder wishing to retain majority control over the voting rights in the company must hold a minimum level of equity.[255] Sunset clauses and maximum voting ratios constitute protections for the public, inferior-voting, shareholders, the sagacity of which, including in the context of the UK Listing Review, is discussed in detail in Chapter 9.[256] However, for the purposes of this chapter, focus should shift to the restriction on the exercise of enhanced-voting rights – a controller will only be able to exercise those enhanced-voting rights in relation to the approval of takeovers and the controller's position on the board, and, on all other resolutions, all shares would be treated as one share, one vote.

Although the ability to block takeovers is a crucial consideration for founders, as has been discussed in this chapter, retaining control over the composition of the board is also vital for many founders.[257] A founder employing dual-class stock in conformity with the UK Listing Review's proposals would be assured of a place on the board (for up to five years post-IPO), but would not be able to guarantee his or her continued incumbency as a CEO leading the company on a daily basis. The board has decision-making capacity over management roles,[258] and without control over the composition of the board, the founder could easily be removed from his or her position as CEO, and, even though the founder would remain on the board, the ability of that founder to influence board decisions will be severely curtailed if the majority of the board is antagonistic to the founder's vision – which is likely the case if the board has removed the founder as CEO. Even the UK Listing Review acknowledges, 'When founders bring their companies to market, they often seem to be concerned mostly about their vision not being derailed by being removed as a director/CEO.'[259] For a founder of a company adopting the proposals of the UK Listing Review, in order to protect his or her position as CEO, the founder would, unless he or she has retained a majority of the equity (which would limit the extent to which the founder can crystallise its investment in the company and raise equity finance), be beholden to the desires of the public shareholders, and the board would,

[255] With a 20:1 maximum voting ratio, a controller must retain at least 4.8 per cent of the equity to maintain majority voting control (see Figure 9.1 in Chapter 9).

[256] For a detailed scrutiny of the premium tier dual-class stock proposals of the UK Listing Review, see B. Reddy, 'Up the Hill and Down Again: Dual-Class Stock and the UK Listing Review' (2021), https://ssrn.com/abstract=3812744.

[257] See Section 1.4 above.

[258] See n 60 and accompanying text.

[259] UK Listing Review at 20. Nevertheless, the UK Listing Review has instead focused solely on a founder's concern that their newly listed company could become the subject of a takeover, subsequent to which the management team is replaced, arresting the founder's pursuit of his or her vision for the business of the company – the UK Listing Review sees takeovers as the 'bigger risk' to a founder's vision (UK Listing Review at 20).

equally, need to prioritise the views of those public shareholders (with share price being a relevant proxy) above the founder's vision. The dynamic becomes especially pertinent if the company is an innovative, early-stage, high-growth tech company where the founder's vision, and the long-term investments made pursuant thereto, are not easily observable to the public shareholders. It is exactly the exposure to the caprice of public shareholders that founders are seeking to avoid through the implementation of dual-class stock.[260]

Another consequence of the UK Listing Review moving away from a 'pure' form of dual-class stock, with its limitations on the exercise of enhanced-voting rights, is that the public shareholders, if they hold a significant proportion of the equity, will continue to possess veto rights over decisions of the company which require shareholder approval. Such decisions not only comprise actions requiring approval by ordinary resolution[261] and special resolution[262] under legislation but also actions of premium listed companies subject to shareholder approval under the Listing Rules.[263] In particular, under Chapter 10 of the Listing Rules, shareholder pre-approval is required for certain large 'Class 1' transactions.[264] An early-stage company, which has yet to generate substantive profits, may find that many potential transactions will result in it crossing the thresholds for shareholder pre-approval under Chapter 10.[265] For a company seeking to grow by way of acquisitions, it will be time-consuming to obtain shareholder pre-approval, and the company will be impeded from making strategic acquisitions confidentially without alerting competitors. It will also not be beyond doubt that the public shareholders will approve the relevant transactions no matter how much the founder believes that they will create long-term benefits for the company – the public shareholders may well lack the insight that has served the founder so well in making a success of the business.[266]

260 For example, the founders of Google stated, upon IPO: 'we have set up a corporate structure that will make it harder for outside parties to take over or influence Google.' (Form S-1/A Amendment No. 8 to Registration Statement of Google Inc. (filed on 16 August 2004) at 29). Also see DeAngelo and DeAngelo (1985) (n 66 above 35); Goshen and Hamdani (2016) (n 99 above); Reddy (2020) (n 23 above 328). The UK Listing Review itself states, 'Arguably, that [IPO] is the point at which the company is most at risk of falling sway to the dangers of short-termism by both investors and directors as the public share price provides a daily report card on their decisions' (UK Listing Review at 20).

261 See n 57 above.

262 See n 58 above.

263 See n 41 above.

264 LR 10.5.1R. A Class 1 transaction is a large transaction where the 'percentage ratio' for any class test is 25 per cent or more (LR 10.2.2R). Class tests compare the size of a transaction to the size of the company factored on gross assets, profits, consideration and gross capital (LR 10 Annex 1).

265 If the profits of the target are more than 25 per cent of the profits of the acquiring company, it could constitute a Class 1 transaction (*ibid*). In relation to the preponderance of pre-profit IPOs in the United States, see n 91 above and accompanying text.

266 As an example, Facebook continued with the acquisition of Instagram for £1 billion in the face of opposition from the board and other shareholders, since the founder had majority control of the company. The acquisition proved to be extremely successful for Facebook, with Instagram becoming valued at many times its acquisition price (CFA Institute, 'Dual-Class Shares: The Good, The Bad and The Ugly' (August 2018) 1, 8).

For a company such as Deliveroo, for example, which operates in a saturated market,[267] divided between continental lines,[268] acquisitions will form an important aspect of its business strategy[269] – however, if it were to revise its capital structure to conform with the UK Listing Review and shift to the premium tier as speculated,[270] as a pre-profit company,[271] it may be hindered in achieving its goals where the founder is not able to unilaterally pass resolutions under Chapter 10 of the Listing Rules. Under the Companies Act 2006, public shareholders could also create aggravations for a founder by registering their discontent with the manner in which the company is being managed by not approving director remuneration policies pursuant to their binding vote on such policies,[272] or by not approving remuneration actually paid to the management team under the relevant pay policy, pursuant to their advisory vote on such matters (which can create significant bad publicity for the company).[273] Activist investors have started using such tactics to pressure management teams to take certain actions,[274] and it is exactly these types of extraneous influences that founders are trying to avoid through the adoption of dual-class structure.

Furthermore, beyond veto rights, it will be concerning for founders that without the ability to block ordinary, and, possibly, if the founder does not retain more than 25 per cent of the equity, special, resolutions, public shareholders with sufficient votes could proactively cause the company to take certain actions, by requiring the company to call a general meeting of the shareholders to hear shareholder-proposed resolutions,[275] or proposing resolutions for the agenda of the company's AGM.[276] The use of such mechanisms could enable those shareholders to instigate corporate actions, such as an amendment to the articles of the company.[277] If the articles so

267 See n 246 above.

268 Singh (2019) (n 246 above).

269 The industry already appears to be moving toward consolidation (T. Bradshaw and R. Milne, 'Amazon's Deliveroo Investment Approved by UK Regulator' *Financial Times* (4 August 2020), www.ft.com/content/edf8a144-a101-4ef8-80e3-7d2f1565d35c).

270 See n 232 above and accompanying text.

271 See n 241 above and accompanying text.

272 Companies Act 2006, s. 439A.

273 Companies Act 2006, s. 439.

274 A. Mooney, 'Activists Become Wolves in Sheep's Clothing' *Financial Times* (21 July 2019), www.ft.com/content/bf1e6037-bbdd-3465-a0oc-d111e301624e; specifically in relation to 'say-on-pay': J. Goldstein, 'Shareholder Activism and Executive Compensation' *Harvard Law School Forum on Corporate Governance and Financial Regulation* (18 June 2015); A. Ralph, 'Investors Revolt Over Executive Pay at De La Rue' *The Times* (26 July 2019) www.thetimes.co.uk/article/investors-revolt-over-pay-at-banknote-printer-de-la-rue-6x3r87tws.

275 For a company incorporated in England and Wales, members holding at least 5 per cent of the paid-up capital of the company (that carries the right to vote), or 5 per cent of the total voting rights in the company, can require the board to call a general meeting of the shareholders (CA 2006, s. 303).

276 For a company incorporated in England and Wales, members holding at least 5 per cent of the voting rights, or at least 100 members with a right to vote and average sum paid-up per member of at least £100, can propose resolutions at the AGM (CA 2006, s. 338).

277 A special resolution would be required under CA 2006, s. 21.

allow, shareholders could even require the board to take specific commercial actions.[278] In practice, it may be unlikely that public shareholders will be able to coral sufficient supportive votes to take those actions,[279] but one could see potential for activist shareholders to use the procedure to disrupt the business of the company by constantly requiring the calling of general meetings, and, again, exert pressure on, and agitate, the founder. As an extreme example, in the midst of a takeover offer that could otherwise be blocked by the founder under the proposals of the UK Listing Review, activists could use shareholder-proposed resolutions to coerce the founder into accepting the offer. Even outside of a firm takeover offer, activists could also use such tactics to compel the founder to voluntarily dismantle the UK Listing Review-compliant disproportionate voting structure in the hopes of subsequently opportunistically soliciting a takeover.

The adoption of a capital structure that enables a founder to block takeovers for a period of five years post-IPO in accordance with the UK Listing Review will not assuage the fears of that founder that, after undertaking a premium tier IPO, his or her long-term vision for the company will be impeded by the influence of public shareholders. The company's management team will continue to be exposed to the consequences of share price fluctuations – the founder will need to placate public shareholders in order to continue as CEO of the company. The United States serves as evidence that the ability to block takeovers is not the sole concern of founders. In the United States, even though other options subsist for listed companies to give management control over the success of takeover bids,[280] founders still consistently adopt wider dual-class stock structures,[281] even though the cost of capital for companies adopting such structures is greater than those that adopt one share, one vote.[282] Founders are prepared to accept lower share prices upon IPO in return for the ability to insulate the management team from public shareholder pressure and to control the shareholder voting process, and it is clear that dual-class stock is more valuable to

[278] With management control in the hands of the board (Model PLC Articles, article 3), shareholders can only cause the company to take, or omit to take, actions if the articles so permit (*Automatic Self-Cleansing Filter Syndicate* v. *Cuninghame* [1906] 2 Ch. 34). Under Model PLC Articles, article 4, a special resolution is required.

[279] A 75 per cent vote is required to pass a special resolution (CA 2006, s. 284).

[280] For example, 'blank-check preferred stock plans', 'poison pills' and charter supermajority requirements to approve mergers can all be used as takeover-blocking mechanisms (for a description of antitakeover devices, see T. Chemmanur et al., 'Management Quality and Antitakeover Provisions' (2011) 54 *J. Law Econ.* 651, 686–689). The Delaware Courts have approved antitakeover devices as a legitimate exercise of the board's business judgement (*Moran* v. *Household Intl, Inc.*, 500 A.2d 1346 (Del. 1985); *Air Products & Chemicals, Inc.* v. *Airgas, Inc.*, C.A. No. 5249—CC (Del. Ch. Feb. 15, 2011)).

[281] See Figure 1.2.

[282] See Chapter 7 for further details. In relation to the United States specifically, see B. Reddy, 'More than Meets the Eye: Reassessing the Empirical Evidence on US Dual-Class Stock' (2021) 23 *U. Pa. J. Bus. L.* In contrast, the empirical evidence on the effect on share price of antitakeover devices, generally, is more mixed (see the literature review in I. Wanasika and Y. Limbu, 'Effects of Antitakeover Defenses on Value in the Pharmaceutical Industry' (2015) 15 *AJM* 59, 63).

founders than simple antitakeover devices.[283] In the United Kingdom, even though it is speculated that Deliveroo will move to the premium tier,[284] it is instructive that, in the interim, the company has adopted a 'true' dual-class structure on the standard tier (rather than a UK Listing Review-compliant structure) which gives the founder the right to exercise enhanced-voting rights on all resolutions of the company.

The five-year limit on UK Listing Review-compliant premium tier 'dual-class stock' issuances also deserves scrutiny, and such 'time-dependent sunset clauses' are discussed in further detail in Chapter 9.[285] However, briefly, one can question whether the five-year limitation will be conducive to attracting high-growth innovative companies to the premium tier. Founders may well be hesitant to consider the premium tier if they will only be given a maximum of five years within which to pursue their visions before the company becomes exposed to takeovers and the 'market for corporate control';[286] at such a stage, a declining share price can expose the company to a predatory takeover bid, and, therefore, after five years, or even approaching the end of the five-year period, a founder will be struck by a need to manage the company in a manner that appeases public shareholder aspirations.[287] It can take far longer than five years for a young, innovative tech company's business to mature to the extent that the rationale for specific investments in long-term ventures and product cycles becomes easily observable to the public shareholders. Indeed, it took more than five years post-IPO for Google's operating strategy to become comprehensible and for many of its products to reach critical mass.[288] Even then, mature US dual-class firms such as Google and Facebook continue to innovate and create significant positive returns for public shareholders many years after IPO.[289] Substantive risk exists that a five-year limitation will deter many founders from utilising the relaxed premium listing requirements proposed by the UK Listing Review, and, even for those founders who do entertain the possibility of a premium tier listing under such conditions, it is likely that IPO will be delayed until later in the firm's life-cycle, after which the founder will feel sufficiently comfortable that five years is an appropriate period during which the legitimacy of its long-term vision will become evident to the public shareholders. The UK Listing Review aspires to attract companies to the LSE at an earlier stage of their life-cycles,[290] but with a five-year limitation, it is unlikely that this will be achieved.

283 D. Ashton, 'Revisiting Dual-Class Stock' (1994) 68 *St. John's L. Rev.* 863, 927.
284 See n 232 above and accompanying text.
285 Also see Reddy (2021) (n 256 above 24–29).
286 In relation to the 'market for corporate control', see Section 6.2.6 of Chapter 6.
287 The disciplining effect of the 'market for corporate control' was elucidated in H. Manne, 'Mergers and the Market for Corporate Control' (1965) 73 *J. Political Econ.* 110; also see *ibid.*
288 '. . . it took over three years just to ship our first Android handset, and then another three years on top of that before the operating system truly reached critical mass. . . . We have protected Google from outside pressures and the temptation to sacrifice future opportunities to meet short-term demands' (Alphabet's 2011 Founders' Letter (31 December 2011), https://abc.xyz/investor/founders-letters/2011/).
289 Google's IPO was in 2004, and Facebook's in 2012.
290 UK Listing Review at 19.

The proposals of the UK Listing Review undermine the control that a founder seeks when adopting dual-class stock to dictate the composition of the board, preserve his or her managerial role in the company and pass shareholders' resolutions. It is therefore unlikely that the UK Listing Review revisions to the rules of the premium tier will have other than a marginal effect on enticing founders of high-growth, innovative tech firms to the LSE. Even to the extent that the ability to block takeovers moves the needle on a founder's decision as to whether to consider the premium tier, the five-year limitation will lead to firms delaying IPO until they are more mature, continuing to restrict the gains in a firm's high growth-phase to primarily venture capital, private equity and large strategic investors. Although the UK Listing Review has labelled its proposals as 'dual-class stock', they are essentially little more than a five-year, takeover-blocking golden share and a five-year guaranteed founder board seat. The UK Listing Review proposals do not constitute 'genuine' dual-class stock, and, therefore, the remainder of this book will scrutinise the possibility of relaxing the premium tier prohibition of 'true' dual-class stock, where the exercise of enhanced-voting rights are not restricted to blocking takeovers and founder board incumbency, and, instead, enable the founder to determine the composition of the board as a whole. The UK Listing Review has taken a different approach to all the other jurisdictions that have opened their doors to dual-class stock. As such, the proposals will not significantly alleviate the competitive threat from other jurisdictions nor provide substantial benefits beyond other existing options for large, successful private companies, including lucrative buyouts by larger firms or the exploitation of private capital. In a worst-case scenario, the UK Listing Review's proposals will not attract the high-growth firms intended, but may, instead, lead to the widespread adoption of time-limited takeover blockers by founder- or management-led firms that would have listed as simple one share, one vote firms in any case. In a bare IPO market, public shareholders are unlikely to significantly discount stock where a takeover is blocked for a short period, since few will even contemplate that a takeover would be launched so soon after flotation. Although the UK Listing Review moves the United Kingdom closer toward premium tier dual-class stock, the review has seemingly discerned that giving founders complete control over the voting process of companies through the adoption of dual-class stock will create more mischiefs than benefits for public shareholders. Whether those concerns are legitimate will be dissected in this book,[291] and it will be discussed in Chapter 9 whether 'genuine' dual-class stock could be introduced to the premium tier alongside constraints that protect public shareholders in a manner less severe than the UK Listing Review, and which do not deter the very firms the relaxation is intended to attract.

[291] In particular, see Chapters 6 and 7.

1.6 CONCLUSION: THE PREMIUM TIER PROHIBITION OF DUAL-CLASS STOCK MATTERS

To summarise, UK IPOs on the Main Market have been in free-fall, especially in the tech industry, despite a flourishing tech sector and private business enterprise scene generally. Although VC and minority private equity funding has surged in the United Kingdom in recent years, the regulators have still identified a funding gap for many companies when they attain a level of later-stage maturity and emerge as established companies but are still realising substantial growth. Furthermore, for those companies that are fortunate enough to access late-stage VC or minority private equity funding, they will be haunted by the desire of such investors to exit. With the Main Market seemingly shunned, M&A has thrived, with UK companies, particularly in the tech sector, being disproportionately the subject of acquisitions as compared to other developed nations. The handful of those tech companies that do list on the Main Market are also often targeted by take-private transactions. With foreign acquirors dominating, the UK authorities are understandably concerned, and there is a clear intention on the part of the UK Government and regulators to make the public markets more accessible and stable.

Relaxing the premium tier prohibition of dual-class stock could encourage further listings on the Main Market. A founder, otherwise fearful of ceding control to a dispersed group of unknown public shareholders, could, with dual-class stock, retain control while still crystallising significant wealth and generating finance for growth. Although a founder could list with dual-class stock on AIM, the Acquis Stock Exchange, the Main Market's high-growth segment or the Main Market's standard tier, with the exception of the standard tier listings of The Hut Group and Deliveroo (the IPOs of which, as outlined in this chapter, involved various compromises and nuances), it is unlikely that any of those exchanges or listing tiers will regularly be a preferred option for high-growth tech companies. The premium tier is the most prestigious tier of the United Kingdom's public markets, and companies pondering a UK IPO with aspirations to join the ranks of Big Tech will either seek a premium listing or will anticipate a graduation to the premium tier from a lesser tier or exchange in the future. Opting for a foreign IPO on an exchange that permits dual-class stock is always an option, but significant hurdles are required to be overcome by the potential issuer, which has resulted in the process remaining relatively uncommon. UK regulators also have an interest in promoting local IPOs by UK companies over foreign listings.

A greater prevalence of UK dual-class IPOs could encourage the growth of UK companies, aid in keeping British business British and allow retail investors, either directly or indirectly through pension funds, insurance companies or investment funds, to more easily participate in the growth and success of such companies. As an added bonus, if a dual-class stock IPO were to become a viable option for founders, it could encourage even greater earlier VC and minority private equity investment, since such listings would represent another avenue of exit for those investors. All these considerations have led to the UK authorities actively investigating the use of dual-class stock as a means of encouraging listings, especially in the tech sector. However, the recommendations of the UK Listing Review fall short of 'genuine' dual-class stock, and it is unlikely that those proposals will significantly attract the tech firm IPOs envisaged. The UK Government and regulators have determined that the benefits of genuine dual-class stock do not outweigh the potential costs to public shareholders. In this book, that determination will be scrutinised, and a different approach will be proposed that will enable the listing of genuine dual-class structures on the premium tier, but with more judicious public shareholder protective measures that will be more conducive to attracting the founders of innovative, high-growth firms. Dual-class stock is a topic that bears serious consideration from a variety of angles, and in Chapter 2, we will take a look at the history of how the United Kingdom and the United States have seemingly arrived at opposite ends of the spectrum.

2

A Tale of Two Cities and Beyond

Two nations divided by a common language.[1]

2.1 INTRODUCTION

The history of one share, one vote in the United Kingdom, and the path taken toward the premium tier's prohibition of dual-class firms, is chronicled in this chapter. It will be explained that one share, one vote was not always the norm in the listed-company sphere, but it came to the fore as a result of the influence of institutional investors that began to dominate the UK markets. The LSE's history will be juxtaposed with that of the NYSE. Given the similarities in market profile, breadth and dispersal of equity ownership between the two exchanges, it would have been reasonable for one to have presumed that the LSE and NYSE would have arrived at the same conclusions regarding dual-class stock. However, it will be shown that in the United States, when the NYSE was debating whether to relax its own prohibition on dual-class firms, issuers and their managers had a greater degree of influence than in the United Kingdom, and were therefore able to impel the NYSE's direction of travel, particularly at a time when various US exchanges were competing for issuers, and the NYSE was facing significant pressure from a large existing issuer openly flouting the exchange's rules. It would appear that the regulators of both the LSE and the NYSE have been reactionary over time and have been largely compelled by the viewpoints of the dominant factions in each market, rather than being proactive in rigorously scrutinising the merits of dual-class structure with a view to justifying their approaches on normative grounds. Although the focus of this chapter is the United Kingdom and the United States, the major Asian exchanges will also be discussed, in the context of their more recent journeys into the world of dual-class stock. A summary of the approaches to dual-class stock taken by other large global exchanges will also be included, and it

[1] The derivation of the quote has been attributed to Bernard Shaw's comment, 'England and America are two countries separated by the same language' (M. Browne, 'How Now, Mr. Shaw?' *The Christian Science Monitor* (5 September 1942) WM1, WM7.

will be shown that the dual-class stances taken by the major exchanges are diverse and inconsistent. It is time for the LSE to take the lead and formulate a coherent and justifiable policy on dual-class firms.

2.2 THE UNITED KINGDOM AND THE INSTITUTIONAL INVESTOR EFFECT

A detailed exposition of the history of dual-class stock in the United Kingdom and elsewhere could easily subsume the entirety of a legal historian's magnum opus, and this book does not allude to such delusions of grandeur. However, a brief elucidation of the progression toward a formal one share, one vote criterion for premium listed companies would be conducive to fully understanding the impetus and motivation leading to the FCA's position.

It would be remiss not to commence with the late-nineteenth century case of *Birch* v. *Cropper*.[2] The Court assessed whether the assets of an unlisted private company, The Bridgewater Navigation Company Limited, upon winding up, should be distributed equally to all ordinary and preference shareholders based upon capital subscribed rather than capital paid-up. The Court determined that since any shareholder who has subscribed to the same amount of capital must meet losses equal to such subscribed capital, in relation to the distribution of assets, after the return of all capital to all classes of shareholder, the surplus assets should be distributed equally between all shareholders holding equal shares in the company's equity.[3] Lord Fitzgerald and Lord Macnaghten recognised, on the basis of equality and justice, that unless otherwise provided in the articles of association of the company (articles) or renounced by a shareholder, every holder of shares of equal amount is entitled to an equal proportion in the capital and property of the company per share.[4] Although this case concerned the application of surplus assets upon a winding up rather than voting rights per se, it is acknowledged as the launching point for the assertion that absent any specific regulation (of the company or the law), each shareholder is entitled to equal rights in the company proportional to its subscribed capital, including the right to vote.[5]

Prior to the case *Birch* v. *Cropper*, one share, one vote was not the most common policy for UK companies. In particular, joint stock banks, railway companies and canal companies often implemented voting schemes that prevented investors acquiring voting control simply by making large capital investments.[6] Voting rights were

2 *Birch* v. *Cropper and Others In re The Bridgewater Navigation Company Limited* (1889) 14 App. Cas. 525.

3 *ibid* 538.

4 *ibid* 541–543 and 546.

5 It should also be noted that, in the normal course, it is likely that potential investors in companies would expect voting and cash-flow rights to be allocated on a one share, one vote basis, and so, as a matter of practicality, the decision in *Birch* v. *Cropper* represents a 'presumptive' approach to company law which reduces the transaction costs of companies in having to specifically implement rules that would be expected by the vast majority of investors (see Chapter 9 on the 'presumptive' approach).

6 B. Cheffins, *Corporate Ownership and Control: British Business Transformed* (Oxford University Press, 2008) at 32.

either capped or were determined pursuant to schemes where those voting rights would increase at a slowing rate with greater investment.[7] The intention was to prevent company policy being dominated by a small cabal of wealthy investors, and the voting system was included as a provision in the default articles for companies.[8] Such structures, sometimes labelled 'prudent-mean voting', began to become less popular in the early twentieth century, as one share, one vote began to dominate,[9] and the default articles for companies were amended in 1905 to reflect one share, one vote.[10]

Notwithstanding the aspirations toward equality, the decision in the case of *Birch* v. *Cropper* is clear that one share, one vote is not a mandatory prerequisite. Although one share, one vote constitutes the default position, and this has been ingrained statutorily,[11] a company is free to deviate from such a construction through provisions set out in its articles.[12] Even the entitlement of shareholders holding a majority of the votes in a company to remove the directors under s. 168 of CA 2006, which is expressed to be non-waivable, does not preclude the use of a dual-class structure. The case *Bushell* v. *Faith* involved a provision in the articles of the private company Bush Court (Southgate) Ltd. that gave directors three votes per share in relation to any resolution to remove that director from the board.[13] The Court held that the provision was not a circumvention of the predecessor of CA 2006, s. 168, that gave shareholders the right to remove directors by ordinary resolution.[14] Therefore, from a purely legislative and common law basis, companies are ascribed a degree of flexibility in the rights attached to their capital structures; but taking the trajectory of the history of one share, one vote into the listed-company realm, other factors will also influence the ability of companies to implement dual-class structure. For example, as discussed in Chapter 1, a 'listing' on the Main Market requires an issuer to be admitted to the FCA's Official List and for the issuer's securities to be admitted to trading. Accordingly, an issuer must obtain permission from both the FCA, which will, amongst other things, insist on compliance with the Listing Rules, and the LSE. Additionally, the exigencies of investors will also pressure companies to structure capital rights in a manner that attracts maximum investment. As such, the rules and customs of the stock exchange itself, and market forces, are wholly relevant to a discourse on the path of the United Kingdom's premium tier toward one share, one vote.

7 *ibid* 33.

8 C. Dunlavy, 'Social Conceptions of the Corporation: Insights from the History of Shareholder Voting Rights' (2006) 63 *Wash. & Lee L. Rev.* 1347, 1360.

9 Cheffins (2008) (n 6 above 33).

10 Dunlavy (2006) (n 8 above 1360).

11 CA 2006, s. 284. Although when voting is conducted by way of a 'show-of-hands', each member is entitled to one vote notwithstanding the extent of its shareholding, the chair of a shareholders' meeting can call a 'poll' (counting votes-per-share) and is required to do so where demanded by at least five shareholders, or by shareholders representing at least 10 per cent of the voting rights or paid-up share capital with voting rights attached (CA 2006, s. 321).

12 *Bushell* v. *Faith* [1970] AC 1099.

13 *ibid.*

14 Companies Act 1948, s. 184.

At the listed-company level, deviations from one share, one vote were not always restricted in the United Kingdom. Indeed, deviations from one share, one vote were not uncommon during the nineteenth and twentieth centuries.[15] It has been supposed that one reason for such deviations was due to the imposition by the LSE, from the mid-nineteenth century to the late 1940s,[16] of a rule requiring that at least two-thirds of securities the subject of a public offering be allotted to the public.[17] Although there were a number of potential loopholes to the rule, including through arranging for shares to be traded on the LSE by way of 'special settlement',[18] for a company owner seeking an orthodox LSE quotation of one share, one vote stock, majority control could not be retained at the time of IPO. Although the relevant owner could subsequently re-acquire further shares on the public markets after the IPO in order to, once again, build up a controlling position, an obvious approach to avoid the transaction costs inherent therein would be to only float non-voting shares and retain voting stock, since the rule applied only to the class of shares being listed.[19] Although the application of the two-thirds rule would have influenced some issuers to adopt dual-class structure, in fact, dual-class structure began to grow more rapidly only after the rule was repealed.

The emergence of hostile takeover activity was the true precursor to a rapid growth of dual-class structure in the UK public markets. Previously, takeovers had been mainly consensual with boards approving the relevant takeovers, but a new game was in town, where bidders would bypass the board and put offers directly to the shareholders.[20] The first UK hostile takeover was launched in 1953 for the shoe chain J. Sears Holdings.[21] There were two dual-class stock related consequences of the ascension of the hostile takeover in the 1950s and a burgeoning takeover market generally. On the first consequence, in response to the escalation of hostile takeovers, companies and their boards began issuing dual-class stock, whereby a discrete set of shareholders, friendly to the board, would acquire the vast majority of

[15] By 1958, the proportion of listed industrial and commercial one share, one vote companies in the United Kingdom was only 41 per cent, having reduced steadily from 55 per cent in 1896 (F. Braggion and M. Giannetti, 'At the Origins of the Non-Voting Shares' Discount: Investor Preferences vs. Fundamentals' (2012) *Unpublished* 1, 32, https://pdfs.semanticscholar.org/a48e/53a18141d21de29615ed9cdc4e472c6e2c5a.pdf).

[16] Cheffins (2008) (n 6 above 76).

[17] L. Hannah, 'The "Divorce" of Ownership from Control from 1900 Onwards: Re-calibrating Imagined Global Trends' (2007) 49 *Bus. Hist.* 404, 416; B. Cheffins et al., 'Ownership Dispersion and the London Stock Exchange's "Two-Thirds Rule": An Empirical Test' (2013) 55 *Bus. Hist.* 670, 686.

[18] Cheffins et al. (2013) (n 17 above 673).

[19] Cheffins (2008) (n 6 above 226–227).

[20] *ibid* 123.

[21] J. Franks et al., 'Spending Less Time with the Family: The Decline of Family Ownership in the United Kingdom' in *A History of Corporate Governance Around the World: Family Business Groups to Professional Managers*, ed. R. Morck (NBER and University of Chicago Press, 2005) at 584; A. Johnston, 'Takeover Regulation: Historical and Theoretical Perspectives on the City Code' (2007) 66 *CLJ* 422, 427.

enhanced-voting shares.[22] In this way, boards were able to insulate themselves from hostile predators who would otherwise be able to secure control by acquiring shares from public shareholders. For example, Whitbread foresaw the emerging market for corporate control as early as 1948, when it joined the public markets with a dual-class structure that preserved control in the hands of the Whitbread family.[23] In 1956, as hostile takeovers became more prevalent, Whitbread established the Whitbread Investment Company to invest in brewing industry participants.[24] Through a combination of dual-class stock and cross-ownership structure,[25] Whitbread and the Whitbread Investment Company became 'takeover-proof'.[26] The structure allowed the company and the brewers and retailers within its 'Whitbread umbrella' to remain largely protected from the height of takeover activity in the brewing industry in the 1960s.[27] On the second consequence, listed companies began to use inferior-voting stock as consideration for acquisitions themselves. After the Second World War, many listed companies were thought to be undervalued, making them prime targets for takeovers.[28] Where the acquiror was a listed company, rather than using cash as consideration for the takeover, publicly listed stock could, instead, be issued to sellers. However, with one share, one vote, the use of stock as consideration would significantly dilute the ownership of existing shareholders. Where a controlling shareholder existed, that shareholder could lose control if significant further stock were to be issued as consideration, and, therefore, controlling shareholders could derive significant benefit through the utilisation of dual-class stock. In fact, J. Sears Holdings, subsequent to its partial takeover in 1953, conducted a number of acquisitions itself using non-voting stock as consideration.[29] Similarly, General Universal Stores and the House of Fraser, listed firms with controlling shareholders in the 1950s, carried out several acquisitions using non-voting or inferior-voting stock as consideration, so that the controlling shareholders could retain control, notwithstanding a dilution of their cash-flow rights.[30] Unlike the use of dual-class stock to circumvent the LSE's erstwhile two-third free-float rules, where the enhanced-voting shares would remain unlisted, the 1950s saw dual-class stock in the form of listed inferior- and enhanced-voting shares. Franks et al.

22 Franks et al. (2005) (n 21 above 584 and 604).

23 J. Bower, 'The Whitbread Umbrella: A Structural Response to Shareholder Activism' (2016) 17 *Enterp. Soc.* 874, 883.

24 *ibid* 885.

25 In relation to 'cross-ownership' structures, see Chapter 3.

26 Bower (2016) (n 23 above 885).

27 *ibid* 875; Franks et al. (2005) (n 21 above 584).

28 J. Armour et al., 'The Evolution of Hostile Takeover Regimes in Developed and Emerging Markets: An Analytical Framework' (2011) 52 *Harv. Int. L. J.* 219, 233 – it was suggested that real estate had been undervalued in the accounts of listed companies, and the discrepancies between book and market value were not reflected in share price, since the primary determinant of share price at the time was dividend yield.

29 Cheffins (2008) (n 6 above 316).

30 *ibid* 316.

(2005)[31] estimated that in a fifteen year period from 1953, 7.5 per cent of listed companies issued dual-class shares of this nature.[32] However, an advance toward an equity capital market composed of numerous companies controlled by small groups of voting-privileged shareholders came to a screeching halt. Three crucial qualities of the corporate governance environment in the 1960s instigated the handbrake.

Firstly, the rise of the institutional shareholder in the United Kingdom in effect cut dual-class stock off at the knees. In the 1950s and 1960s, after the Second World War, the proportion of listed company shares owned by institutional shareholders rose significantly, as the proportion held by individual investors fell.[33] Institutional investors were averse to dual-class structure generally.[34] Dual-class structure gave insiders the ability to block takeovers, which institutional investors cherished for their potential to generate windfall returns,[35] and, to the extent that takeovers did proceed, insiders could garner, to the exclusion of institutional investors, a control premium from a potential offeror on the basis that such offeror would be able to acquire voting control merely by acquiring the insiders' enhanced-voting shares. Institutional investors were also concerned, to a lesser extent given the passivity of institutional investors during this period,[36] that their powers to influence the composition of the board,[37] and therefore discipline managers, would be curtailed. For example, in the late 1950s, the British Insurance Association, a representative body for insurance companies, advised its members not to purchase inferior-voting shares, and, in 1962, reiterated its view that the right to vote was a fundamental shareholder right and that control should not be divorced from financial interest.[38] The clear distaste by institutional investors for dual-class structure, and the ensuing increases in cost of capital, led to a number of existing dual-class firms reunifying into one share, one vote in order to raise equity finance at a commercially practical price.[39] High-profile companies such as Burton Group, Marks & Spencer, Rank and House

[31] Franks et al. (2005) (n 21 above 584).

[32] Also see Cheffins (2008) (n 6 above 31) – 'During the mid-1950s some 7 per cent of the market value of the industrial and commercial sector of the UK equity market took the form of "non-voting" ordinary shares . . . '.

[33] Cheffins (2008) (n 6 above 88 and 244–245); Franks et al. (2005) (n 21 above 585); J. Moyle, *The Pattern of Ordinary Share Ownership: 1957–1970* (Cambridge University Press, 1971); J. Armour and D. Skeel, 'Who Writes the Rules for Hostile Takeovers, and Why? – The Peculiar Divergence of U.S. and U.K. Takeover Regulation' (2007) 95 *Geo. L. J.* 1727, 1768–1770.

[34] Franks et al. (2005) (n 21 above 584 and 604); Armour and Skeel (2007) (n 33 above 1736); F. Braggion and M. Giannetti, 'Changing Corporate Governance Norms: Evidence from the Dismissal of Dual Class Shares in the U.K.' (2016) 1, 9, https://ecgi.global/sites/default/files/working_papers/documents/SSRN-id2138949.pdf.

[35] Cheffins (2008) (n 6 above 360).

[36] B. Cheffins and S. Bank, 'Corporate Ownership and Control in the UK: The Tax Dimension' (2007) 70 *MLR* 778, 808.

[37] The Companies Act 1948 (s. 184) introduced the non-waivable right of shareholders to remove directors from the board by ordinary resolution (now reflected in CA 2006, s. 168).

[38] Cheffins (2008) (n 6 above 317).

[39] J. Franks and C. Mayer, 'Evolution of Ownership and Control Around the World: The Changing Face of Capitalism' (2017) *ECGI Finance Working Paper No. 503/2017* 1, 13 noted that, in 1965,

of Fraser all experienced enfranchisement of existing non-voting shares between 1959 and 1979.[40]

Secondly, with institutional investor domination of the London capital markets came increased influence. In relation to an individual investment, the axiomatic remedy for an institutional investor displeased with the governance of an investee company was to exit, but in relation to market-wide rules, customs and regulations, exiting the entire market as a whole was not really an option for domestic institutional investors; this led to collaborative lobbying of the regulators by institutional investors for shareholder-friendly regulations beneficial to them.[41] Although institutional investors could simply factor the risks inherent in investing in dual-class firms into the price they were willing to pay for inferior-voting shares, the clear preference was to avoid the transaction costs intrinsic to making such assessments. This could be ensured by pressing for uniform levels of corporate governance across all companies, including harmonised voting structures geared toward one share, one vote.[42] It is not surprising, therefore, that institutional investors heavily petitioned the regulators against the issue of restricted voting rights shares by listed companies.[43] The views of the Jenkins Committee[44] of 1960, which was charged with reviewing the adequacy of corporate legislation, were also germane. Although it concluded that an outright prohibition of non-voting stock would be 'too drastic a step' and would 'encourage alternative methods of vesting control in the holders of particular shares or classes of shares',[45] the report was marked by substantially divergent opinions amongst the witnesses to the committee, and a robust dissenting opinion by a minority of the committee.[46] The dissenting element noted in particular that objection to the use of non-voting shares was strongest in the ambit of publicly quoted companies,[47] but, importantly, further noted that it was open to the British stock exchanges to refuse new issues of non-voting shares on their markets, which

approximately 15 per cent of LSE-listed companies had dual-class stock, but nearly all of these companies had enfranchised their non-voting shares by the 1990s.

40 Cheffins (2008) (n 6 above 309 and 317).

41 Armour and Skeel (2007) (n 33 above 1771); L. Enriques et al., 'The Basic Governance Structure: Minority Shareholders and Non-Shareholder Constituencies' in *The Anatomy of Corporate Law*, eds. R. Kraakman et al. (Oxford University Press, 2017) at 104.

42 W.-G. Ringe, 'Deviations from Ownership-Control Proportionality – Economic Protectionism Revisited' in *Company Law and Economic Protectionism: New Challenges to European Integration*, eds. U. Bernitz and W.-G. Ringe (Oxford University Press, 2010) at 229.

43 Armour and Skeel (2007) (n 33 above 1771) noted that institutional investors had significant influence over an assortment of other corporate governance measures, such as pre-emption rights, shareholder consent for major corporate transactions under the Listing Rules and the Combined Code on Corporate Governance, as well as being 'involved at every stage of the drafting of the [Takeover] Code'; S. Wei and A. Young, 'Dual Share Plan in Context: Making Sense of Hong Kong's Decision Not to Embrace Alibaba's Listing' (2015) 26 *I.C.C.R.R.* 4, 7.

44 The Report of the Company Law Committee presented to Parliament in June 1962, chaired by Lord Jenkins (the Jenkins Report).

45 *ibid* 48.

46 *ibid* 207.

47 *ibid* 208.

would negate the requirement to legislate in this area.[48] In fact, this is exactly the process that entailed. In response to pressure from powerful institutional investors, the LSE made it clear that it discouraged the quotation of inferior-voting shares;[49] although there was no outright prohibition on their issuances, the LSE would use its discretionary powers to refuse applications to list inferior-voting shares on its market in the majority of cases.[50] This curbed the listing of new dual-class firms.

The third change in the corporate governance environment deterring the use of dual-class structure was the emergence of rules governing the conduct of public company takeovers. In 1959, guidance on takeovers was published through a collaborative effort between the Bank of England and the LSE known as the Notes on the Amalgamation of British Business.[51] Unsurprisingly, given the rising influence of institutional investors, they were heavily involved in the drafting of the guidance,[52] and ensconced within the principles was the genesis of a concept of equality of treatment during takeover offers as between all shareholders.[53] This concept was elaborated and reinforced when it was more formally ingrained into the 'City Code on Take-overs and Mergers' (the Takeover Code) in 1968.[54] The new Takeover Code was administered by a Takeover Panel promoted by institutional investors and issuing houses as well as by the original backers of the principles.[55] It has occasionally been stated that the United Kingdom formally prohibited the listing of dual-class structure in 1968,[56] but, in fact, the relevant change in that year was the introduction of certain Takeover Code rules that diluted their utility rather than a formal prohibition. The new Takeover Code specified that partial bids for shares were unwelcome, and to the extent a partial offer was made, a pro rata offer would have to be made to all shareholders unless otherwise agreed by the Takeover Panel,[57] and the same price offered to all shareholders of the same class of shares in the company.[58] These equality provisions were further supplemented by a 1971 revision

48 *ibid* 209.

49 Cheffins (2008) (n 6 above 317).

50 Franks et al. (2005) (n 21 above 604); Cheffins (2008) (n 6 above 317 and 32); Ringe (2010) (n 42 above 223); B. Cheffins, *Company Law: Theory, Structure and Operation* (Oxford University Press, 1997) at 472 and 475; M. Brennan and J. Franks, 'Underpricing, Ownership and Control in Initial Public Offerings of Equity Securities in the UK' (1997) 45 *J. Financ. Econ.* 391, 395.

51 Armour and Skeel (2007) (n 33 above 1759); Cheffins (2008) (n 6 above 334); Franks et al. (2005) (n 21 above 604).

52 Armour and Skeel (2007) (n 33 above 1771); Armour et al. (2011) (n 28 above 237).

53 Armour and Skeel (2007) (n 33 above 1760); Cheffins (2008) (n 6 above 334).

54 Armour and Skeel (2007) (n 33 above 1759); Cheffins (2008) (n 6 above 335); Franks et al. (2005) (n 21 above 604); J. Franks et al., 'Ownership: Evolution and Regulation' (2009) 22 *Rev. Financial Stud.* 4009, 4045.

55 Armour and Skeel (2007) (n 33 above 1760); Cheffins (2008) (n 6 above 335).

56 For example, see K. Rydqvist, 'Dual-Class Shares: A Review' (1992) 8 *Oxf. Rev. Econ. Policy* 45; M. Faccio and L. Lang, 'The Ultimate Ownership of Western European Corporations' (2002) 65 *J. Financ. Econ.* 365, 386.

57 R. Pennington, 'Takeover Bids in the United Kingdom' (1969) 17 *Am. J. Comp. Law* 159, 174.

58 *ibid* 175.

to the Takeover Code that first implemented a mandatory bid provision whereunder any person acquiring 40 per cent (subsequently reduced to 30 per cent in 1974) or more of the company's shares would be required to make a bid for the remaining shares in the company.[59] Two consequences of the new Takeover Code were that it prohibited discriminatory price offers, and deterred post-IPO stake-building of large blockholdings, since acquirors would be wary of being required to make a full takeover offer for all the shares in the company upon surpassing the mandatory bid threshold.[60] The requirements outlined therein gradually morphed into the detailed takeover conduct provisions contained in the modern day Takeover Code, as outlined in Chapter 8. Turning back to the effect on dual-class structure, it is clear that the Takeover Code can have indirect deterrence effects on their employment. Upon a takeover offer, within classes of shares, the same price must be offered to all shareholders, and between classes, comparable offers must be made, and, therefore, the ability of a holder of enhanced-voting shares to garner a significant premium on the sale of those shares is necessarily limited. Although 'comparable' is not precisely defined, in effect, the offeror cannot offer a disproportionate premium over market price to enhanced-voting shareholders as opposed to inferior-voting shareholders.[61] Of course, the enhanced-voting shares and inferior-voting shares may be trading at different prices on the market, meaning that the offer price for each will not be identical, but the percentage premium over market price for each would likely have to be identical,[62] reducing the ability of the enhanced-voting shareholders to generate a substantial control premium. Thus, one of the incentives for insiders to adopt or retain dual-class structure was eliminated.

Through a combination of institutional shareholder apathy, LSE discouragement and rules governing takeovers, listed companies with dual-class structure became rare in the United Kingdom,[63] with new listings of dual-class firms almost completely extinguished by the 1980s.[64] By the early 1990s, only three FTSE-100 companies retained dual-class voting structures, and two of those, Great Universal Stores and Whitbread, unified their share voting rights in 1993.[65]

59 Armour and Skeel (2007) (n 33 above 1764).
60 Franks et al. (2005) (n 21 above 585).
61 Takeover Code, Note 1 to Rule 14.1.
62 Although the position is not free from doubt, where the enhanced-voting shares are not listed, the ability to offer divergent prices for inferior-voting shares and enhanced-voting shares will likely be limited even further (see Chapters 6 and 8).
63 Cheffins (2008) (n 6 above 32); Ringe (2010) (n 42 above 223); Franks et al. (2005) (n 21 above 604).
64 Franks et al. (2005) (n 21 above 585).
65 Practical Law Company, 'Whitbread Equalises Shares' (1993) *Practical Law UK Articles* 2–100–444; J. Shepherd, 'Whitbread Puts End to Two-Tier Voting Structure: Brewing Giant Decides to Purchase Remainder of Investment Company' *Independent* (7 October 1993), www.independent.co.uk/news/business/whitbread-puts-end-to-two-tier-voting-structure-brewing-giant-decides-to-purchase-remainder-of-1509176.html. In fact, the 'Whitbread Umbrella' (n 27 above and accompanying text) was unwound together with the dual-class structure partly in response to new competition rules designed to limit the dominance of the large brewers (Bower (2016) (n 23 above 894)). The third company was

The status quo which effectively deterred dual-class structure without imposing a formal prohibition remained in place until the situation was finally set-in-stone for premium listed companies. In 2010, the two tiers of the Main Market were re-labelled the premium tier and the standard tier, and non-voting shares were prohibited from the premium tier.[66] In 2014, the Listing Rules were further amended to introduce two new high-level principles with which premium listed companies must comply (Premium Listing Principles): (i) 'All equity shares in a class that has been admitted to premium listing must carry an equal number of votes on any shareholder vote';[67] and (ii) 'Where a listed company has more than one class of equity shares admitted to premium listing, the aggregate voting rights of the shares in each class should be broadly proportionate to the relative interests of those classes in the equity of the listed company.'[68] Therefore, for a premium listed company, all premium listed shares must carry votes proportional to their cash-flow rights in the company, in effect prohibiting the premium listing of more than one class of shares with diverging voting rights, assuming that such shares only differ by way of voting rights. Theoretically, on a strict reading of the Premium Listing Principles, it would be possible to premium list inferior-voting shares with enhanced-voting shares remaining unlisted in the hands of, for example, the founders. However, it is unlikely to be palatable to founders to pursue this avenue due to the introduction of a rule providing that, for premium listed companies, certain matters that are required to be approved by a shareholder vote under the Listing Rules must be decided by a resolution of the holders of the premium listed shares;[69] the significance of this is that in many instances where the Listing Rules require a shareholder vote,[70] the votes of the unlisted shares will not be counted, negating the very advantage sought by the founders. It is also unlikely that the FCA would admit such a structure to a premium listing, considering it to be contrary to the spirit of the Premium Listing Principles. The FCA noted that 'the purpose of Premium Listing Principle 4 is to prevent artificial structures involving multiple classes with different voting powers, which are designed to allow control to rest with a small group of shareholders'.[71] Schroders, Hansa and Daily Mail, dual-class firms

Schroders, which still maintains a dual-class structure, although the non-voting shares are only standard listed.

66 FSA, 'Listing Regime Review: Feedback on CP09/24 and CP09/28 with Final Rules' (February 2010).

67 Listing Rules, Premium Listing Principle 3.

68 Listing Rules, Premium Listing Principle 4.

69 LR 9.2.21R.

70 For example, cancellation of listings, certain transfers between listing categories, establishment of employee share schemes, long-term incentive plans and discounted share options, implementation of deep discount open offers, vendor consideration placings, share issues out of treasury and equity share subscription offers, significant transactions or related-party transactions, certain repurchases of securities, and material changes to investment policy or conversion of listed equity shares of closed-end investment funds.

71 FCA Policy Statement PS14/8, 'Response to CP13/15 – Enhancing the Effectiveness of the Listing Regime' (May 2014) at 31. The refusal of the FCA to permit a premium listing of The Hut Group is a case in point (see Section 1.5.5 of Chapter 1).

with non-voting stock that were admitted prior to the 2010 prohibition, had to move their inferior-voting shares to the standard tier, resulting in them not enjoying the greater liquidity and price premium ascribed by a premium listing. Schroders and Hansa maintained their enhanced-voting shares on the premium tier, while Daily Mail, whose enhanced-voting shares are unlisted, now only maintains a standard listing (of its non-voting stock).

Unsurprisingly, as discussed earlier, the United Kingdom's approach to dual-class structure was strongly influenced by the dominant stakeholders in the market – the institutional investors. That approach emerged without any public consultations on dual-class structure, and without any formal research into the benefits and detriments of dual-class structure and whether they are, in fact, harmful to public shareholders. However, the United Kingdom's story with respect to dual-class firms does not halt here. The debate is ongoing, and contemporary dialogue has raised the topic once again. Both the UK Government and the FCA have noted the potential value of dual-class stock, and have acknowledged it as an area for discussion,[72] and a recent UK Listing Review call for evidence on the subject galvanised the debate in the United Kingdom, and finally instigated serious debate as to whether dual-class stock should be permitted on the premium tier.[73] Consequently, the proposals of the UK Listing Review were published, and once implemented, they may further move the United Kingdom toward a potential relaxation of the premium tier prohibition of dual-class stock. Under the UK Listing Review proposals, a director of a company (who is an individual) will be permitted to hold shares that allow him or her to block takeovers and ensure his or her continued incumbency on the board for a period of five years post-IPO.[74] Although, as discussed in Chapter 1, the recommendations of the UK Listing Review, clearly influenced by the views of UK institutional investors, do not constitute 'genuine' dual-class stock, the fact that a form of disproportionate shareholder control is apparently being endorsed so soon after the FCA's 2014 amendments to the Listing Rules, even in the face of continued institutional investor hostility,[75] is

[72] BEIS Green Paper, 'Building Our Industrial Strategy' (January 2017) at 67; FCA Discussion Paper DP17/2, 'Review of the Effectiveness of Primary Markets: The UK Primary Markets Landscape' (February 2017); HM Treasury, 'Policy Paper: Call for Evidence – UK Listings Review' (19 November 2020). Also see R. Kalifa, 'Kalifa Review of UK Fintech' (26 February 2021) at 65.

[73] HM Treasury (2020) (n 72 above).

[74] UK Listing Review at 21. For further details, see Section 1.5.7 of Chapter 1.

[75] Both the UK Government and the FCA have noted that institutional shareholders are still generally averse to dual-class structure (BEIS (2007) (n 72 above 67); FCA (2017) (n 72 above 8)). As an example, in relation to the US listing of Lyft, institutional investors, including a number of UK-led organisations, flexed their muscles by publicly decrying the proposed dual-class structure (S. Bond, 'Investors Call for Lyft to Scrap Dual-Class Share Structure Plans' *Financial Times* (17 March 2019), www.ft.com/content/7d26dca6-4747-11e9-b168-96a37d002cd3); the signatories were institutional investors with over $3.2 trillion assets under management, including the UK-led institutions Legal and General Investment Management, Hermes Equity Ownership Services, and the Local Authority Pension Fund Forum.

indicative of the subject's divisiveness and that, perhaps, the United Kingdom's adherence to one share, one vote is not as inexorable as recent history seemingly suggests.

2.3 THE US CONTEXT

As of the end of 2016, the largest stock market on the basis of total market capitalisation was the NYSE.[76] Given its significance, an examination of one share, one vote and dual-class stock as they pertain to the LSE would be facilitated by traversing the historical course of one share, one vote and dual-class stock on the NYSE. Additionally, it is often remarked that the character of the US stock exchanges parallels that of the LSE, in terms of a dispersed ownership structure,[77] where the majority of companies lack a dominant blockholder or controlling shareholder, resulting in equity ownership being dispersed amongst numerous small shareholders. Also, the majority of publicly listed stock in both the United Kingdom and the United States is held by institutional investors,[78] although it appears that such investors dominate the UK markets to an even greater extent.[79] Furthermore, the vast majority of the existing literature and academic discourse on the merits of

[76] As of the end of 2018, the total market capitalisation of the NYSE was US$20.679 trillion, comfortably exceeding the market capitalisation of NASDAQ, the second largest exchange (source: World Federation of Exchanges, 'Annual Statistics Guide 2018' (May 2019)).

[77] In relation to the United Kingdom specifically, Franks and Mayer (2017) (n 39 above 36 and 43); C. Holderness, 'Blockholders Are More Common in the United States Than You Might Think' (2010) 22 *J. Appl. Corp. Finance* 75, 79; G. Aminadav and E. Papaioannou, 'Corporate Control Around the World' (2016) *NBER Working Paper* 23010 1, 19 and Appendix Table 1; B. Cheffins, 'The Undermining of UK Corporate Governance (?)' (2013) 33 *OJLS* 505 and 509. In relation to the similarities between the United Kingdom and the United States: OECD Corporate Governance Factbook 2017 at 11; R. La Porta et al., 'Corporate Ownership Around the World' (1999) 54 *J. Finance* 471, 492; Franks et al. (2009) (n 54 above 4009); R. Gilson, 'Controlling Shareholders and Corporate Governance: Complicating the Comparative Taxonomy' (2006) 119 *Harv. L. Rev.* 1642, 1645; Ringe (2010) (n 42 above 221). In relation to the United States specifically, R. Daniels and P. Halpern, 'Too Close for Comfort: The Role of the Closely Held Public Corporation in the Canadian Economy and the Implications for Public Policy' (1996) 26 *Can. Bus. L. J.* 11, 12. Although some commentators have speculated that the characterisation of the ownership of equity on US markets as being predominantly dispersed is somewhat of a myth, the contention is generally based upon a prevalence of blockholders at the 5 per cent level, rather than true controlling shareholders (C. Holderness, 'The Myth of Diffuse Ownership in the United States' (2009) 22 *Rev. Financial Stud.* 1377, 1378 and 1394; A. Shleifer and R. Vishny, 'Large Shareholders and Corporate Control' (1986) 94 *J. Political Econ.* 461, 462; A. Edmans and C. Holderness, 'Blockholders: A Survey of Theory and Evidence' in *The Handbook of the Economics of Corporate Governance*, eds. B. Hermalin and M. Wesibach (Elsevier, 2017) at 51).

[78] R. Chan and J. Ho, 'Should Listed Companies Be Allowed to Adopt Dual-Class Share Structure in Hong Kong?' (2014) 43 *Comm. L. World Rev.* 155, 176; D. Langevoort, 'The SEC, Retail Investors, and the Institutionalization of the Securities Markets' (2008) *Georgetown Law, Faculty Working Papers* 1, 1; ONS, 'Ownership of UK Quoted Shares: 2018' (January 2020) at 4.

[79] The ONS assessed that as of 31 December 2018, the proportion of UK-quoted shares beneficially owned by individuals was only 13.5 per cent (ONS (2020) (n 78 above 8)). However, the Securities Industry and Financial Markets Association (Securities Industry and Financial Markets Association 'Capital Markets Fact Book 2019' (2019) at 60) showed that, in 2018, 'households' owned 37.6 per cent

dual-class structure was published in the mid-1980s in relation to a proposed controversial relaxation by the NYSE of its one share, one vote tenet,[80] and a subsequent attempt by the Securities and Exchange Commission (SEC) to harmonise voting rights across all US exchanges.[81] A consideration of the United States' experience is therefore felicitous.

The course of voting standards of corporations in the United States initially followed a similar track to the United Kingdom (although with a larger degree of volatility), interestingly, also driven by those stakeholders holding the greatest influence at the time. Historically, one share per stockholder was the prevalent voting norm in the United States, developing into a one share, one vote standard toward the end of the eighteenth century and the beginning of the nineteenth century, following pressure from large existing and potential stockholders.[82] However, Alexander Hamilton, who, prior to his stint on Broadway, was better known as the father of the first National Bank of the United States, in conceiving of the bank's voting structure was hesitant to settle on one share, one vote on the basis that it would allow just a few shareholders to 'monopolize the power and benefits of the bank'.[83] He also acknowledged that one vote per person would not give sufficient deference to the investments made by large stockholders and the protection that they required, so he advocated for 'prudent-mean voting rights' which, as discussed in relation to the United Kingdom earlier, essentially, placed a cap on the votes exercisable by individual stockholders.[84] Accordingly, as with the United Kingdom, the prudent mean system became somewhat of the norm in the United States in the early nineteenth century,[85] driven by public concerns as to the concentration of control of large corporations by a small number of financial institutions.[86] Prudent mean voting, though, soon came under pressure from large stockholders, and, by the end of the nineteenth century, corporations were struggling to raise capital without appeasing shareholders with full compensation in terms of voting power for their investments.[87] The situation therefore evolved, and it became rare for statutory rules to mandate such restraints. As such, one share, one vote without restrictions became

of US equities. However, the figure for the United States may be overstated, by including holdings by non-profit organisations, and presumably certain indirect retail ownership through institutional funds, and the percentage of US equities held directly by individuals (pure retail investors) may be closer to that of the United Kingdom (Chan and Ho (2014) (n 78 above 175); C. McGrath, '80% of Equity Market Cap Held by Institutions' *Pensions & Investments* (25 April 2017), www.pionline.com/article/20170425/INTERACTIVE/170429926/80-of-equity-market-cap-held-by-institutions).

80 See n 122 below and accompanying text.

81 See n 130 below and accompanying text.

82 D. Ratner, 'The Government of Business Corporations: Critical Reflections on the Rule of "One Share, One Vote"' (1970) 56 *Cornell L. Rev.* 1, 6.

83 *ibid* 6; Dunlavy (2006) (n 8 above 1356).

84 *ibid.*

85 Dunlavy (2006) (n 8 above 1358).

86 Ratner (1970) (n 82 above 6); T. O'Neil, 'Rule 19c-4: The SEC Goes Too Far in Adopting a One Share, One Vote Rule' (1989) 83 *Nw. U. L. Rev.* 1057, 1062.

87 O'Neil (1989) (n 86 above 1063).

the default rule in most States, and once again became the voting standard followed by the majority of US corporations.[88] Currently, in Delaware, the most popular US State for business organisation incorporations, one share, one vote is the default standard,[89] although corporations may deviate from that standard through the use of different classes of stock in their certificates of incorporation.[90]

Since one share, one vote was only a default maxim, and not mandatory, in the absence of federal encroachment, the ability for listed companies to issue shares that deviated from that standard was a function of the rules of the relevant stock exchange. In the early twentieth century, the NYSE permitted dual-class stock. The first known instance of a US listed company issuing true dual-class stock was when International Silver Company issued non-voting stock in 1898.[91] As listed corporations thrived, it became more common for them to begin issuing dual-class shares, since, amongst other things, additional finance could be raised without diluting existing large stockholders.[92] The attitude of investors had shifted as such corporations became more profitable, with them seeing the benefits of investing in successful companies notwithstanding that shares carried restricted voting rights.[93] The situation, though, came to a head in the mid-1920s, after two high-profile listings on the NYSE adopting extreme dual-class structures. In 1925, the controllers of Dodge Brothers listed non-voting common stock, while retaining control through holding voting stock, and, strikingly, the investment bank (and controller of Dodge Brothers), Dillon, Read and Company, was able to retain 100 per cent control while holding less than 2 per cent of the equity.[94] In the same year, the controllers of Industrial Rayon procured the NYSE listing of 598,000 shares of non-voting Class A stock, while retaining control through holding only 2,000 shares of voting Class B stock.[95] These listings resulted in a great deal of adverse publicity and academic criticism. Professor William Ripley, at the time a professor of political economy at Harvard University, in particular, railed against the notion that banks were acquiring private businesses, and recouping the purchase price, and more, through subsequent issues of stock to the public without relinquishing any semblance of control.[96]

88 Ratner (1970) (n 82 above 8); *ibid* 1063; J. Seligman, 'Equal Protection in Shareholder Voting Rights: The One Common Share, One Vote Controversy' (1985–1986) 54 *Geo. Wash. L. R.* 687, 693; Ringe (2010) (n 42 above 224); Dunlavy (2006) (n 8 above 1359).

89 8 Del. C., §212(a).

90 8 Del. C., §151(a).

91 J. Howell, 'The Survival of the U.S. Dual-Class Share Structure' (2017) 44 *J. Corp. Finance* 440, 444.

92 D. Ashton, 'Revisiting Dual-Class Stock' (1994) 68 *St. John's L. Rev.* 863, 892.

93 O'Neil (1989) (n 86 above 1063).

94 Seligman (1985–1986) (n 88 above 694 and 700); P. Loomis and B. Rubman, 'Corporate Governance in Historical Perspective' (1979) 8 *Hofstra Law Rev.* 141, 152; M. Warren III, 'One Share, One Vote: A Perception of Legitimacy' (1988) 14 *J. Corp. L.* 89, 92.

95 Seligman (1985–1986) (n 88 above 694).

96 W. Ripley, 'Two Changes in the Nature and Conduct of Corporations' (1926) 11 *Proc. Acad. Pol. Sci.* 695, 696. As to concerns relating to the powers of, and potential abuses by, the banking houses through the use of dual-class stock, also see A. Berle, 'Non-Voting Stock and "Bankers' Control"' (1926) 39 *Harv. L. Rev.* 673, 676; W. Ripley, *Main Street and Wall Street* (Little, Brown, 1927) at 77.

Through a series of public addresses, articles and texts, Ripley's influence grew, with his diatribes against the use of dual-class stock entering the public conscience, leading to a discussion with President Calvin Coolidge on the subject.[97] Adolf Berle, a noted lawyer who later published a groundbreaking text on company governance and the separation of ownership from control,[98] also joined the pantheon of preeminent academics criticising non-voting stock, stressing that 'power without responsibility is, philosophically, a perilous matter'.[99]

The escalating public anxiety led to the NYSE, in 1926, adopting an informal policy which, even though cast in opaque terms, in effect established an assertion not to permit the listing of non-voting stock. The NYSE publicly stated, 'Without at this time attempting to formulate a definite policy, attention should be drawn to the fact that in the future the committee, in considering applications for the listing of securities, will give careful thought to the matter of voting control.'[100] Although many reasons, treading the topography of the academic arguments, were tendered as to the reasons for the policy, it is clear that the primary impetus was the emergent public hysteria, and the NYSE's fear that it would lead to unwelcome top-down regulation.[101] It was even pointed out that the informal policy was 'devoid of content', and '[not] based . . . on a principle or theory that could clarify the ambiguities in the policy'.[102] The policy was formalised in 1940 with the publication of the NYSE's 'Statement of Listing Requirements as to Preferred Stock Voting Rights', which stated: 'Since 1926, The New York Stock Exchange has refused to list non-voting common stock.'[103] Beyond simple non-voting shares, other forms of dual-class structure were also subject to scrutiny by way of a requirement that 'any allocation of voting power under normal conditions to classes of stock other than common stock should be in reasonable relationship to the equity interests of such classes'.[104] It should be noted, though, that in enforcing this policy, the NYSE still showed a degree of pragmatism, much in the same way as the LSE displays in exercising its discretion as to whether to waive its free-float requirement that at least 25 per cent of listed shares be in public hands.[105] In particular, in 1956, the Ford Motor

97 Seligman (1985–1986) (n 88 above 695).

98 A. Berle and G. Means, *The Modern Corporation and Private Property* (Macmillan, 1932).

99 Berle (1926) (n 96 above 674).

100 Seligman (1985–1986) (n 88 above 697); Loomis and Rubman (1979) (n 94 above 152); O'Neil (1989) (n 86 above 1064); Ashton (1994) (n 92 above 893).

101 Loomis and Rubman (1979) (n 94 above 153). Also see Seligman (1985–1986) (n 88 above 698) quoting a 1953 memorandum from the vice president to the president of the NYSE referencing the reason for the prohibition as being the political reaction to the notion of 'banker control' and specifically referring to Ripley's criticism.

102 Seligman (1985–1986) (n 88 above 700).

103 *ibid* 699.

104 *ibid* 690; Warren III (1988) (n 94 above 92); R. Gilson, 'Evaluating Dual Class Common Stock: The Relevance of Substitutes' (1987) 73 *Va. L. Rev*. 807, 808.

105 LRs 6.14R, 9.2.15R and 14.2.2R. The FCA has used its discretion to lower the threshold for a number of controlling shareholder companies, such as ENRC, Ferrexpo and Fresnillo, in the past.

Company was permitted to issue stock with disproportionate voting rights – evidently the prestige of the company and the benefit to the NYSE of admitting the company's listing outweighed a strict adherence of the exchange to one share, one vote.[106]

The NYSE's policy on dual-class structure continued, albeit with the occasional exception as referenced earlier, until the mid-1980s, when, as with the United Kingdom in the 1950s,[107] there was a rash of hostile takeover activity.[108] Corporations saw the issue of dual-class stock as an effective takeover defence. A review of policy was again elicited by a burst of pragmatism when confronted with divergence by another large corporation, more significantly in this case by a corporation already listed on the NYSE. In 1984, General Motors issued restricted voting stock[109] in conjunction with its acquisition of EDS.[110] The significance of General Motors already being NYSE listed is that the NYSE's only means of recourse would have been to delist General Motors, a perceptibly more severe corollary than merely rejecting a corporation's IPO. The NYSE did not delist General Motors, and, as a result, many other NYSE listed corporations subsequently issued stock with disproportionate voting rights.[111] Consequentially, the NYSE declared a moratorium in 1984 on enforcement against divergences from one share, one vote.[112] Some have speculated that it was happenstance that prompted the NYSE to modify its position on dual-class structure,[113] in that it was such a high-profile corporation challenging the status quo through the issue of restricted-voting stock for what was, at the time, an unorthodox purpose rather than for a more commonly castigated purpose such as entrenchment of control. Indeed, the NYSE had in the past delisted smaller firms for breaches of its listing standards.[114] However, another element was also at play – competition from other domestic stock exchanges. Historically, the NYSE could rely upon its position of prestige and

106 Seligman (1985–1986) (n 88 above 700).

107 Franks et al. (2005) (n 21 above).

108 J. Gordon, 'Ties that Bond: Dual Class Common Stock and the Problem of Shareholder Choice' (1988) 76 *Cal. L. Rev.* 1, 4; Ringe (2010) (n 42 above 225); S. Bainbridge, 'The Short Life and Resurrection of SEC Rule 19C-4' (1991) 69 *Wash. U. L. Q.* 565, 571.

109 The restricted voting stock carried only half the votes of the common stock, justified on the basis that the new class of stock would be tied to the performance of the acquired company, and, therefore, had lesser entitlement to voting rights over the whole, larger, enterprise.

110 O'Neil (1989) (n 86 above 1064); Ashton (1994) (n 92 above 894); Warren III (1988) (n 94 above 93).

111 In a three-year period ending June 1987, more than forty-six corporations listed on the NYSE had either issued inferior-voting shares or had restricted the voting power of large shareholders (Warren III (1988) (n 94 above 93)). General Motors itself also issued further inferior-voting shares in conjunction with a second acquisition.

112 Warren III (1988) (n 94 above 93).

113 Ashton (1994) (n 92 above 895).

114 The NYSE delisted Cannon Mills in 1962 superficially as a result of a breach of its proxy solicitation rules, but the underlying polemic was the distribution of non-voting stock by the corporation; in many other cases, the NYSE used the threat of delisting to dissuade corporations from issuing non-voting stock (Seligman (1985–1986) (n 88 above 699–700)).

enhanced liquidity to attract listings, but this competitive advantage was gradually eroded through uniformly applicable federal regulations and better use of technology throughout the capital markets, and sponsors began to recognise the American Stock Exchange (AMEX)[115] and the National Association of Securities Dealers (NASD), including its computerised trading system, NASDAQ, as viable alternatives.[116] At the time, the NASD had not instigated any constraints on the listing of dual-class structure.[117] Although AMEX had prohibited the listing of pure non-voting stock in 1972, it permitted the listing of stock with disproportionate voting rights, subject to prescribed requirements.[118] These competitive pressures, further underscored by the General Motors' issuances, resulted in the NYSE, in 1984, forming a subcommittee[119] to review its policy on dual-class structure.[120] It seems that, fundamentally, the NYSE took these actions under protest, heavily influenced by competitive pressures.[121] The subcommittee recommended an amendment to the NYSE's listing standards, subject to certain safeguards, following which the NYSE, in 1986, proposed a relaxation to its rules on one share, one vote.[122]

Digressing briefly, given the history of the United Kingdom's journey to one share, one vote, and the significance of institutional investor predilection, one may ask where were the institutional investors in the United States during this period? However, during the period when the NYSE was considering a relaxation of its

115 AMEX became the NYSE MKT, and is now known as NYSE American.

116 Gordon (1988) (n 108 above 6); Warren III (1988) (n 94 above 92); Seligman (1985–1986) (n 88 above 701); Bainbridge (1991) (n 108 above 576–577).

117 Warren III (1988) (n 94 above 92); Gilson (1987) (n 104 above 807).

118 AMEX implemented, inter alia, a voting ratio maximum of 10:1 between enhanced-voting and inferior-voting shares, and a rule requiring that inferior-voting shareholders be able to elect not less than 25 per cent of the board (Seligman (1985–1986) (n 88 above 704–705); Warren III (1988) (n 94 above 92); Ashton (1994) (n 92 above 896); Gilson (1987) (n 104 above 807)).

119 The NYSE's Subcommittee on Shareholder Participation and Qualitative Listing Standards.

120 Seligman (1985–1986) (n 88 above 700); Warren III (1988) (n 94 above 93); Bainbridge (1991) (n 108 above 577).

121 In 1985, the chair of the NYSE extolled the virtues of one share, one vote and that, from a 'philosophical perspective', the NYSE did not desire to relax its policy on one share, one vote, and the preference would be for all exchanges to implement the same policy; however, competitive pressures forced the NYSE to pursue the relaxation (Warren III (1988) (n 94 above 93)). This is in contrast to the reasons officially propounded by the NYSE Subcommittee, being that shareholders should be given greater flexibility to determine capital structure, and that other NYSE listing requirements already provided sufficient protections for public shareholders (Ashton (1994) (n 92 above 897)).

122 The NYSE proposed that any dual-class stock outstanding at the time of a corporation's IPO would be permitted to listing. However, any such stock either issued at a later date or created by way of the modification of existing stockholder rights would be required to be approved by a majority of independent directors and public stockholders. The prohibition of purely non-voting stock would remain in place (Gilson (1987) (n 104 above 807); Warren III (1988) (n 94 above 93); Ashton (1994) (n 92 above 898). The subcommittee had in fact proposed even greater protections than finally published by the NYSE, including approval by two-thirds of all stockholders, a maximum voting ratio of 10:1, and a requirement that, other than voting rights, all classes of common stock should have equivalent rights attached (Warren III (1988) (n 94 above 94)).

one share, one vote rules, institutional investor influence was not at the levels seen in the United Kingdom.[123] Although the holdings of institutional investors were rising dramatically, they did not account for a majority of equity holdings on the NYSE,[124] and institutional investors were only just beginning to become a significant voice in the 1990s.[125] With issuers holding sway, the period was labelled 'managerialism'.[126]

Since the change to NYSE's listing standards required SEC approval,[127] it triggered federal reaction. The SEC endeavoured to broker an agreement between the main national exchanges – the NYSE, the NASD and AMEX – in an attempt to seek voluntary adoption of a uniform voting standard on dual-class stock.[128] However, the efforts were unsuccessful, leading to the SEC, in 1988, influenced again by public and academic opprobrium toward the proposed NYSE reforms,[129] enacting a federally mandated listing requirement – the infamous Rule 19c-4.[130] Rule 19c-4 provided that US exchanges would be required to delist any corporation that 'issues any class of security, or takes other corporate action, with the effect of nullifying, restricting or disparately reducing the per share voting rights of holders of an outstanding class or classes of common stock of such issuer'.[131] Although Rule 19c-4 restricted deviations from one share, one vote in certain circumstances, it is often overlooked that the rule did not go as far as to mandate a one share, one vote requirement for issuers. Rule 19c-4 essentially only prohibited post-IPO recapitalisations that had the effect of disenfranchising existing public stockholders by converting their stock into stock with lesser voting rights, or converting insiders' stock into stock with superior voting rights. The significance that Rule 19c-4 would still permit the exchanges to determine the validity of dual-class firm IPOs should not be neglected; notwithstanding all the previous public excoriation regarding dual-class stock, the SEC was willing to tacitly approve their existence. In 1989, as

123 A. Gurrea, 'Theory, Evidence, and Policy on Dual-Class Shares: A Country-Specific Response to a Global Debate' (2019) *Ibero-American Institute for Law and Finance Working Paper Series 3/2019* para. 6.1; J. Coffee, 'Liquidity Versus Control: The Institutional Investor as a Corporate Monitor' (1991) 91 *CLR* 1277, 1310.

124 Institutional investors held 28.2 per cent of the equity of NYSE-listed corporations in 1970, rising to 41.4 per cent in 1990 (NYSE Factbook data as published by NYX data). Another study determined that institutional stockholders held, on average, 24 per cent of a NYSE firm's equity in 1980, rising to 44 per cent in 2000 (R. Sias et al., 'Changes in Institutional Ownership and Stock Returns: Assessment and Methodology' (2006) 79 *J. Bus.* 2869, 2877).

125 Armour and Skeel (2007) (n 33 above 1767).

126 A. Sorkin, 'How Shareholder Democracy Failed the People' *New York Times* (20 August 2019), www.nytimes.com/2019/08/20/business/dealbook/business-roundtable-corporate-responsibility.html?smid=nytcore-ios-share>.

127 Gordon (1988) (n 108 above 7); Bainbridge (1991) (n 108 above 577).

128 Gilson (1987) (n 104 above 808); Gordon (1988) (n 108 above 7); Bainbridge (1991) (n 108 above 577).

129 For example, Gordon (1988) (n 108 above 4).

130 Code of Federal Regulations, Title 17, Chapter 2, Part 240 § 240.19c-4 'Governing certain listing or authorization determinations by national securities exchanges and associations'. The short-lived Rule 19c-4 was promulgated by the SEC and adopted in 1988 under Section 19(c) of the 1934 Securities Act.

131 *ibid* subsection (a).

a consequence of Rule 19c-4, the NYSE abandoned the proposed amendment to its listing requirements, and, instead, adopted requirements that mirrored the SEC's new rule. However, the SEC's efforts spawned controversy, and a representative organisation for large publicly listed corporations, the 'Business Roundtable', no doubt motivated by the interests of its members who would have been predisposed toward flexibility to issue dual-class stock as a takeover defence, filed a lawsuit against the SEC. In 1990, the Court of Appeals for the District of Columbia struck down Rule 19c-4, rendering it invalid, on the basis that the SEC had exceeded the powers that had been imbued by Congress.[132] The resultant scenario was that voting right requirements would remain purely in the hands of the individual exchanges. In 1993, the SEC suggested that the main exchanges should follow a voluntary uniform policy, which reflected the spirit of Rule 19c-4 while incorporating a greater deal of flexibility.[133] AMEX and NASD quickly adopted this policy, followed by the NYSE in 1994. The rule still exists today and, in tribute to Rule 19c-4, gives greater attention to post-IPO disenfranchisements of existing stockholders, while broadly permitting other issuances of dual-class stock, including at IPO.[134]

Without outlining the background of one share, one vote amongst the US public markets, history may, on first sight, suggest that, eventually, through a careful progress of normative and empirical analysis over the course of decades, the NYSE determined that capital flexibility rather than one share, one vote was the most beneficial system for modern-day equity markets. However, as the background shows, the reasons and reactions to one share, one vote over the years were not so much governed by judicious scrutiny of the pros and cons of dual-class structure, but more through a combination of public reaction, competitive pressure, the influence of the primary stakeholders of the relevant times and the serendipity of a mammoth corporation flouting the listing requirements. The controversy relating to dual-class structure does not seem to have been tempered over time. Prior to settling on the suggestion of a voluntary uniform policy amongst the exchanges in 1993, the SEC had sought, again, to negotiate a mandatory one share, one vote standard.[135] Even

132 *Business Roundtable* v. *SEC*, 905 F.2d 406 (D.C. Cir. 1990).

133 Howell (2017) (n 91 above 447).

134 The current version of the NYSE Listed Company Manual states in §313.00 (A): 'Voting rights of existing shareholders of publicly traded common stock . . . cannot be disparately reduced or restricted through any corporate action or issuance. Examples of such corporate action or issuance include, but are not limited to, the adoption of time phased voting plans, the adoption of capped voting rights plans, the issuance of super voting stock, or the issuance of stock with voting rights less than the per share voting rights of the existing common stock through an exchange offer.' Of further note, §313.40 gives a greater degree of flexibility to foreign issuers where the issuer's capital structure is in compliance with its local laws stating that, 'The Exchange will accept any action or issuance relating to the voting rights structure of a non-U.S. company that is in compliance with the Exchange's requirements for domestic companies or that is not prohibited by the company's home country law.'

135 V. Goldwasser, 'Differential Voting Rights and the Super Share – In Search of an Accommodation on the Merits' (1994) 7 *Corp. & Bus. L. J.* 215.

politicians have criticised the concept of dual-class stock,[136] with, in 2013, Senator Elizabeth Warren (D-MA) sending a letter to the vice presidents of the NYSE and NASDAQ, urging them to consider rules mandating one share, one vote. Furthermore, institutional shareholders, through the representative body, the Council of Institutional Investors (CII), have intensified their lobbying efforts with the regulators and private-sector indices,[137] and individual and groups of institutional investors have consistently disparaged dual-class structure, influencing proxy advisors and the development of voluntary corporate governance principles.[138] The efforts have not been in vain. S&P Dow Jones, in 2017, declared that it would not include any potential new entrants to its S&P Composite 1500 indices with dual-class structure.[139] Existing constituents of the indices would remain as members however. FTSE Russell, also, since 2017, omits any new entrants of dual-class stock from its indices unless at least 5 per cent of the voting rights are freely available to the public.[140] Existing constituents of the indices are grandfathered until September 2022. For new entrants, although FTSE Russell's transmutation was not as severe as S&P Dow Jones, the decision rules out index inclusion for firms only issuing non-voting stock to the public (as Snap has done) or from implementing an extreme voting ratio. After a long consultation, MSCI narrowly declined to omit dual-class firms from its regular indices; instead, it resolved to launch new benchmark indices that would either only comprise one share, one vote firms or weight firms for voting rights.[141] MSCI was no doubt influenced by the machinations of

[136] On 5 June 2013, Senator Elizabeth Warren (D-MA) sent a letter to the vice presidents of the NYSE and NASDAQ urging them to consider rules mandating one share, one vote, www.warren.senate.gov/newsroom/press-releases/senator-elizabeth-warren-urges-nyse-nasdaq-to-propose-rules-requiring-and-quotone-share-one-vote-and-quot-structures.

[137] B. Sharfman, 'A Private Ordering Defense of a Company's Right to Use Dual Class Share Structures in IPOs' (2018) 63 *Villanova Law Rev*. 1, 3; D. Lund, 'Nonvoting Shares and Efficient Corporate Governance' (2019) 71 *Stanf. Law Rev*. 687, 709.

[138] L. Bebchuk and K. Kastiel, 'The Untenable Case for Perpetual Dual-Class Stock' (2017) 4 *Va. Law Rev*. 585, 597–599; A. Winden, 'Sunrise, Sunset: An Empirical and Theoretical Assessment of Dual-Class Stock Structures' (2018) 3 *CBLR* 852, 856; B. Nicholas and B. Marsh, 'Dual-Class: The Consequences of Depriving Institutional Investors of Corporate Voting Rights' *Harvard Law School Forum of Corporate Governance and Financial Regulation* (17 May 2017); CII, 'Dual-Class Stock', www.cii.org/dualclass_stock; ProxyInsight, 'An Interview with W. Robert Main III, Head of Portfolio Company Engagement, Analysis and Voting at Vanguard' *Proxy Monthly* (July 2017) at 4; Calpers Investment Committee, 'Dual Class/Non-Voting Shares Update' (April 2018) at 9.

[139] S&P Dow Jones Indices, 'S&P Dow Jones Indices Announces Decision on Multi-Class Shares and Voting Rights' (31 July 2017), www.spice-indices.com/idpfiles/spice-assets/resources/public/documents/561162_spdjimulti-classsharesandvotingrulesannouncement7.31.17.pdf?force_download=true.

[140] FTSE Russell, 'Voting Rights Consultation – Next Steps' (July 2017), www.ftse.com/products/downloads/FTSE_Russell_Voting_Rights_Consultation_Next_Steps.pdf.

[141] MSCI Press Release, 'MSCI Will Retain the MSCI Global Investable Market Indexes Unchanged and Launch a New Index Series Reflecting the Preferences of Investors on Unequal Voting Structures' (30 October 2018), www.msci.com/documents/10199/0b548379-fbe7-71c7-b392-7140b2215cc9>; MSCI, 'MSCI Voting Rights-Adjusted Indexes Methodology' (March 2019), www.msci.com/eqb/methodology/meth_docs/MSCI_Voting_Rights_Adjusted_Indexes_Methodology_Mar2019.pdf.

BlackRock, the leading asset manager of US equities (by assets under management).[142] In an open letter by the vice chair of BlackRock, the firm underlined its preference for one share, one vote, but conveyed its opinion that corporate governance standards should be set by regulators and exchanges.[143] BlackRock acknowledged that in certain instances, at least for limited periods of time, dual-class structure could be beneficial, and, therefore, its preference, as eventually followed by MSCI, was for the maintenance of broad indices covering the entire investable universe, with separate bespoke indices that screen-out specific corporate governance traits. Vanguard and State Street, the second and third largest asset managers of US equities, subsequently expressed similar sentiments.[144] Clearly, even in the United States, which is often held-out as the paragon of successful companies utilising dual-class structure, the debate on one share, one vote has not yet been decisively won.

2.4 THE ASIAN EXPERIENCE

Unlike the United States, the Asian equity markets do not closely resemble that of the United Kingdom. They are dominated by companies with concentrated, often family or government, ownership, or, in the case of Japan, by companies with complicated cross-ownership structures often involving banks. However, Asian exchanges, especially Tokyo and Hong Kong, represent significant markets[145] which have recently made journeys toward dual-class friendly systems. It is also worth considering these jurisdictions, since they have taken a different approach to admitting dual-class firms, foregoing the permissive environment of the United States, in favour of a regime that incorporates mandatory safeguards. Although Hong Kong and Singapore, and, to a lesser extent, Tokyo, have dominated the conversation on dual-class shares in the Far East in recent years due to the pivotal and momentous change in direction that their respective exchanges have made in relation to dual-class stock, it would be remiss to not at least also note the approaches of China and India, both of which have made partial manoeuvres toward the relaxation of one share, one vote standards. All five jurisdictions are therefore discussed in the following sections, and, judging by the

142 J. Fichtner, 'Hidden Power of the Big Three? Passive Index Funds, Re-Concentration of Corporate Ownership, and New Financial Risk' (2017) 19 *Bus. Polit.* 298, 304.

143 BlackRock, 'Open Letter Regarding Consultation on the Treatment of Unequal Voting Structures in the MSCI Equity Indexes' (19 April 2018), www.blackrock.com/corporate/literature/publication/open-letter-treatment-of-unequal-voting-structures-msci-equity-indexes-041918.pdf.

144 S. Hirst and K. Kastiel, 'Corporate Governance by Index Exclusion' (2019) 99 *B.U. L. Rev.* 1229, 1234; J. Koren and P. Dave, 'Snap Won't Give Shareholders Voting Rights. For That, It's Being Shunned by a Major Stock Index' *Los Angeles Times* (28 July 2017), www.latimes.com/business/la-fi-snap-russell-indices-20170727-story.html.

145 As of the end of February 2019, the Tokyo Stock Exchange was the third largest market by way of total market capitalisation, and the Hong Kong Stock Exchange was the sixth (slightly ahead of the LSE) (source: World Federation of Exchanges, 'Annual Statistics Guide 2018' (May 2019)).

conditions attached to dual-class listings, each jurisdiction has been circumspect in the relaxation of their respective listing regimes.

2.4.1 *Hong Kong*

The Hong Kong listed-company market is dominated by controlling shareholder companies.[146] As a matter of legislation, in Hong Kong, although one share, one vote remains the default rule, a company is permitted to deviate from the standard by provision in its articles.[147] In relation to listed companies, though, in response to proposals by three large listed companies to engage in first time issuances of shares with disproportionate voting rights, in 1987, the controller of the Hong Kong Stock Exchange, HKEX, informally prohibited the listing of new disproportionate voting shares.[148] Prior to 1987, listed companies were permitted to, and did, issue shares with disproportionate voting rights. The step change occurred in the context of the looming handover of Hong Kong to China in 1997. A prime concern was that dual-class structures could be used to channel capital to China while maintaining control in Hong Kong[149] – a concern that caused a large decline in the Hang Seng Index upon the announcement of the plans by the three companies to issue such shares.[150] The prohibition was formalised in 1989 with a change to the HKEX Main Board Listing Rules (HK Listing Rules),[151] which provided that the listing of new disproportionate voting shares, and further issuances of disproportionate voting shares by existing issuers, would not be permitted, other than in exceptional circumstances or where the shares were being issued by way of scrip dividend of capitalisation by an issuer with existing dual-class structure where the proportion of enhanced- to inferior-voting shares did not change.[152]

The status quo remained for nearly three decades. However, attitudes began to shift after the loss of a number of Chinese listings to foreign exchanges that accepted dual-class structures. In particular, there was a great deal of disquiet over the 2014 blue-chip listing of Alibaba, which was, at the time, the largest IPO in

[146] J. Ho, 'Revisiting the Viability to Allow Dual-Class Share Structure Companies to List in the Financial Market of Hong Kong' (2018) 47 *Common Law World Rev*. 167, 179; D. Donald, *A Financial Centre for Two Empires* (Cambridge University Press, 2014) at 55; J. Ho, 'Examining the Viability to Allow Dual-Class Share Structure Companies to List in the Financial Market of the People's Republic of China: Lessons and Experiences from Hong Kong' (2019) 1, 13, https://ssrn.com/abstract=3408873.

[147] Companies Ordinance (Cap 622), s. 588(4).

[148] HKEX, 'Concept Paper: Weighted Voting Rights' (August 2014) at 26; H. Huang et al., 'The (re) introduction of dual-class share structures in Hong Kong: a historical and comparative analysis' (2019) JCLS 1, 3.

[149] *ibid* 27; Ho (2019) (n 146 above 18).

[150] HKEX (2014) (n 148 above 26).

[151] *ibid* 25.

[152] HK Listing Rules, Rule 8.11.

history,[153] taking place on the NYSE rather than Hong Kong Stock Exchange.[154] In fact, the listing of Alibaba on the NYSE also caused some naval gazing by the FCA in the United Kingdom, since the LSE had also been attempting to attract Alibaba.[155] As Alibaba's IPO proceeded, HKEX commenced a consultation on whether to, once again, permit dual-class stock.[156] In 2015, HKEX published conclusions to its consultation, pursuant to which it proposed a framework for the admission of dual-class structures to Hong Kong's Main Board, and recommended a second consultation.[157] The framework broadly endorsed the admission of dual-class stock, subject to minimum market capitalisation requirements, restriction to firms with particular characteristics making them well-suited to, and which presented low risks as, dual-class structures, restriction to new issuers, and constraints around the identities of holders of enhanced-voting shares and the proportion of equity held by them.[158] However, before the second consultation could proceed, the SFC, the principal regulator of Hong Kong's securities and futures markets, expressed its opposition to the admission of dual-class stock.[159] The SFC extolled the importance of preserving the high reputation of the exchange, and, although recognising the competitive pressure from other exchanges, noted that such pressure fluctuates over time and that the SFC has a duty to balance short-term and long-term objectives. In particular, the SFC was not convinced by the safeguards proposed by HKEX, namely that the size of the issuer does not guarantee fairness in treatment of shareholders, enhanced suitability criteria would create undesired subjectivity on the part of HKEX resulting in regulatory uncertainty and existing issuers would be able to circumvent the provisions restricting dual-class structures to new issuers.[160] HKEX suspended its process on examining dual-class structures in the face of the opposition by the SFC.[161]

HKEX did not, though, abandon its drive to admit dual-class stock for long. In 2017, HKEX published a modified proposal for consultation pursuant to which a new board or listing sector would be established, alongside the Main Board, which would permit dual-class stock,[162] even though in a previous paper, HKEX noted that limiting dual-class structures to a separate board could stigmatise companies implementing dual-class stock.[163] Only so-called new economy companies

153 F. Huang, 'Dual Class Shares around the Top Global Financial Centres' (2017) 2 *J. Bus. L.* 137, 137.
154 HKEX Concept (2014) (n 148 above 31).
155 Huang (2017) (n 153 above 145).
156 HKEX Concept (2014) (n 148 above).
157 HKEX, 'Consultation Conclusions to Concept Paper on Weighted Voting Rights' (June 2015) at 44.
158 *ibid* 44.
159 SFC statement on the SEHK's draft proposal on weighted voting rights (25 June 2015), www.sfc.hk/edistributionWeb/gateway/EN/news-and-announcements/news/doc?refNo=15PR69.
160 *ibid.*
161 HKEX, 'Listing Committee Announces Way Forward on Weighted Voting Rights' (5 October 2015), www.hkex.com.hk/News/Regulatory-Announcements/2015/151005news?sc_lang=en.
162 HKEX, 'Concept Paper: New Board' (June 2017).
163 HKEX Conclusions (2015) (n 157 above 37).

would be permitted to list on the new board.[164] Highlighting the mercurial attitude of global regulators to dual-class stock, the SFC, barely two years after dismissing dual-class stock, indicated a new found belief in the possible benefits such structures could bring to the Hong Kong economy in attracting the listings of innovative, high-growth companies.[165] Interestingly, noting the premium tier/standard tier dichotomy in the United Kingdom, the SFC was sceptical that restricting dual-class stock to a new board was the most conducive method of introducing them to the market.[166] The SFC's scepticism, and the responses to its consultation, led HKEX to conclude that the new board concept should be discarded and that dual-class stock should be permitted to its Main Board.[167] HKEX noted concerns that restricting dual-class stock to a new board would introduce another layer of complexity to the market and would discourage the highest-quality issuers from listing with HKEX.[168] A new board would create a second-class citizen regime, akin to the distinction between standard listings and premium listings in the United Kingdom.[169] With the new board abandoned, the SFC endorsed recommendations to permit dual-class stock on the Main Board,[170] and HKEX amended the HK Listing Rules to permit such structures in April 2018.[171] HKEX's relaxation and the SFC's endorsement were not without caveats. Both institutions acknowledged the preference for one share, one vote and the risks inherent in dual-class structures and, therefore, required that dual-class firms only be admitted if certain conditions were satisfied.[172] The current position is that dual-class firms are now permitted to list on Hong Kong's Main Board, subject to the following principal conditions:[173]

- Minimum capitalisation of HK$40 billion (or HK$10 billion with revenue of at least HK$1 billion in the last audited financial year).
- New listings only.
- Enhanced-voting shares may not be listed.
- Holders of enhanced-voting shares must be directors.

164 See Chapter 9 for more details.

165 E. Yiu, 'Regulator's U-Turn Paves Way for Dual-Class Companies to Raise Funds in Hong Kong in Pilot Plan' *South China Morning Post* (27 October 2017), www.scmp.com/business/companies/article/2117159/regulators-u-turn-paves-way-dual-class-companies-raise-funds-hong.

166 Speech by the CEO of the SFC, A. Alder, at the HKSI Institute Roundtable Luncheon Series, 'Front-Loaded, Transparent and Direct: A New Approach to Regulation for Changing Markets' (13 July 2017), www.sfc.hk/-/media/EN/files/ER/PDF/Speeches/CEO-speech-at-HKSI-final_13-Jul.pdf.

167 HKEX, 'Consultation Conclusions: New Board Concept Paper' (December 2017).

168 *ibid* 10.

169 In relation to the United Kingdom, see Chapter 1, and earlier in this chapter.

170 E. Yiu, 'Securities Commission Backs Introduction of Dual-Class Shares on Hong Kong Stock Exchange' *South China Morning Post* (20 December 2017), www.scmp.com/business/companies/article/2124972/securities-commission-backs-introduction-dual-class-shares-hong.

171 HK Listing Rules, Chapter 8A.

172 HKEX, 'Research Report: Listing Regime Reforms for Dual-Class Share Structure and Biotech Industry' (November 2018).

173 HK Listing Rules, Chapter 8A.

- Conversion of a holder's enhanced-voting shares into one share, one vote upon death, incapacity or cessation of directorship of such holder, or upon a transfer of such shares to another person.
- Enhanced-voting shares to only confer enhanced-voting rights at general meetings, with all other rights equal to those of inferior-voting shares.
- Ratio of enhanced-voting share voting rights to inferior-voting share voting rights not to exceed 10:1, and the holders of enhanced-voting shares must hold at least 10 per cent of the cash-flow rights (although HKEX may approve a lower percentage for high-market capitalisation companies (for example, over HK$80 billion)).
- Inferior-voting shareholders who do not also hold enhanced-voting shares must be entitled to exercise at least 10 per cent of the voting rights.
- Shareholders holding 10 per cent of the voting rights, calculated on a one share, one vote basis, must be able to convene a shareholders' general meeting.
- Voting rights will revert to one share, one vote on any decisions to amend the constitutional documents, vary the rights attached to a class of shares, appoint and remove independent directors, appoint and remove auditors and voluntarily wind-up the company.
- The proportion that enhanced-voting shares form of the total issued share capital cannot be increased post-IPO, and, conditional upon such a proviso, post-IPO, further enhanced-voting shares may only be issued, with prior HKEX approval, if offered to all shareholders pro rata to their existing holdings, pursuant to scrip dividend, or pursuant to a stock split or other capital reorganisation.
- Rights attached to enhanced-voting shares cannot be modified post-IPO to grant them even greater voting rights.
- Requirements on the roles of independent directors, and to implement a nomination committee composed of a majority of independent directors, that are otherwise imposed on a 'comply-or-explain' basis under a corporate governance code are mandatory for dual-class firms, and the chair of the nomination committee must be an independent director.
- Independent directors to be subject to retirement by rotation every three years.
- Requirement for a corporate governance committee, comprised of solely independent directors, to monitor compliance with the dual-class conditions, provide recommendations on potential conflicts with enhanced-voting shareholders and publish semi-annual reports on its activities.
- Required appointment of a permanent compliance advisor and imposition of director, senior management and company secretary training on the risks of dual-class structures.
- Disclosure of the dual-class structure on the front page of any documents issued by the firm, with explanations within those documents for the rationale for the structure and the risks inherent therein.

- Interim and annual reports must disclose the holders of enhanced-voting shares and set out the circumstances in which enhanced-voting shares may convert into one share, one vote shares, together with the impact of any such conversions.
- All dual-class firms to be designated with a dual-class stock marker.

Overarching all the aforementioned conditions, HKEX retains discretion as to whether a dual-class firm is eligible and suitable for listing.[174] HKEX has provided guidance as to when it will grant admission for a dual-class firm.[175] The relevant applicant must demonstrate that it is an innovative company with a track record for high business growth.[176] Any holder of enhanced-voting shares must have been materially responsible for the growth of the business, through skills, knowledge or strategic direction, where the value of the company is largely attributable to intangible human capital. The relevant holders must also be actively involved in an executive capacity at the time of IPO and serve, and post-IPO continue to serve, as a director on the board. The applicant must have previously received meaningful investment from at least one-third party sophisticated investor, who must retain at least 50 per cent of its investment for at least six months post-IPO. HKEX has further noted that it may reject a dual-class share applicant if it represents 'an extreme case of non-conformance with governance norms', such as in the case of non-voting shares.[177] Importantly, unlike the conditions for listing which have been included in the HK Listing Rules (as set out in the bullet points above), these eligibility and suitability requirements, which on their face appear restrictive, have been included as guidance rather than as part of the HK Listing Rules. This resonates with HKEX's desire for flexibility and discretion. The requirements have, in fact, intentionally been drafted in a broad manner to allow that level of flexibility and discretion – for example, HKEX notes that, in considering 'innovation', the term will necessarily be defined by the industry and market in which the business operates, and could change over time.[178] A determination by HKEX that a particular company is innovative may not apply to an identical applicant requesting admission many years later.

HKEX's relaxation of the one share, one vote rule has borne almost immediate dividends. The high profile listings of Xiaomi and Meituan-Dianping took place on the Hong Kong Stock Exchange with dual-class structures not long after the relaxation became effective.[179] Just as notable are 'homecomings' of sorts for Alibaba and Baidu, which have chosen the Hong Kong Stock Exchange for secondary listings. Such early successes are even more considerable in light of competing political

174 HK Listing Rules, Rule 8A.04.

175 HKEX Guidance Letter HKEX-GL93-18, 'Suitability for Listing with a WVR Structure' (April 2018).

176 See Chapter 9 for further details on what could construe an 'innovative company', and the criteria for 'high growth'.

177 HKEX Guidance (2018) (n 175 above para. 4.7).

178 *ibid* para. 4.2.

179 Xiaomi and Meituan-Dianping were within the top ten global IPOs (by way of proceeds) in 2019 (KPMG, 'Mainland China and Hong Kong – 2019 Review: IPOs and Other Market Trends' (2020) at 4).

considerations that may influence Chinese companies to list on foreign exchanges,[180] and, no doubt, the LSE's premium tier, will be monitoring the Hong Kong Stock Exchange's progress carefully.

2.4.2 *Singapore*

As with Hong Kong, Singapore's public markets display a prevalence of concentrated ownership, mostly family-controlled, companies. Singapore's journey toward dual-class structure has only been marginally less torturous than Hong Kong's. Prior to a company law review which commenced in 2007, under Singaporean companies legislation, one share, one vote was the default standard and, generally, only private companies were permitted to deviate.[181] Except for an exemption for listed newspaper companies, which were required to issue shares to approved persons with enhanced-voting rights with respect to the appointment and removal of directors and staff,[182] public companies could not issue dual-class shares.[183] Rather than simply leaving decisions as to whether to permit dual-class stock to the exchanges, Singapore imposed a direct company law prohibition on public companies adopting dual-class stock.

However, in 2011, the Ministry of Finance's Steering Committee recommended that public companies be given similar flexibility to private companies to issue dual-class shares provided that any such issuances are approved by a special resolution, and one share, one vote will apply on any resolution to wind-up the company or vary rights attached to shares.[184] The rationale was that public companies should be granted flexibility in their capital management, and matters pertaining to the listing of dual-class firms was a matter for the SGX. Notwithstanding the rationale given, mirroring Hong Kong's reaction to losing out on the Alibaba IPO, Singapore was in the midst of introspection with respect to potentially missing out on the listing of the British company and sporting goliath, Manchester United.[185] After courting SGX, Manchester United eventually listed on the NYSE mainly due to SGX's inability to offer a dual-class listing. Therefore, it is likely that the Steering Committee will also have been influenced by a desire to give SGX greater flexibility to permit dual-class stock in order to compete with other exchanges.[186] The revised law became effective in 2016.[187]

Technically, SGX's Mainboard Rules (SGX Listing Rules) did not prohibit the listing of dual-class firms, but the entirety of the rules were predicated on one share, one vote, and therefore, in practice, dual-class firms were excluded from SGX

180 See nn 240–241 below and accompanying text.
181 Formerly Singapore: Companies Act 2006 (SG CA 2006), s. 64.
182 Singapore: Newspaper and Printing Presses Act (Chapter 206), s. 10.
183 Formerly SG CA 2006, s. 64(1).
184 Ministry of Finance, 'Consultation Paper: Report of the Steering Committee for Review of the Companies Act' (June 2011) at 3-3.
185 Chan and Ho (2014) (n 78 above 168).
186 *ibid* 168.
187 See, for example, SG CA 2006 (Revised Edition) (November 2018), s. 64A.

admission.[188] Notwithstanding the revisions to companies' legislation recommended in 2011, SGX, for its part, procrastinated in making any amendments to its listing rules. However, a review of Singaporean economic strategy, which commenced in 2016, resulted in a recommendation, in 2017, that dual-class firms be permitted for admission to SGX, with appropriate safeguards.[189] Concurrently, SGX made a reference to the Listing Advisory Committee (LAC). The LAC, in turn, also recommended that dual-class firms be permitted on SGX subject to a variety of safeguards, including a holistic assessment of the suitability of any applicant to list with dual-class stock.[190] Both recommendations led to SGX commencing a consultation on a 'possible' framework for dual-class stock in 2017,[191] followed by a 'proposed' framework in 2018.[192] Finally, on 26 June 2018, SGX introduced amendments to the SGX Listing Rules to formally permit the listing of dual-class stock.[193]

The SGX Listing Rules did not give potential dual-class firm applicants carte blanche. Similar to Hong Kong, and in line with the recommendations of the LAC and SGX consultations, various conditions are attached to dual-class listings:[194]

- New listings only.
- Enhanced-voting shares may not be listed.
- Holders of enhanced-voting shares must be directors, or a director must be appointed on behalf of a permitted holder group.
- Unless approved by shareholders on a one share, one vote basis, conversion of a holder's enhanced-voting shares into one share, one vote upon cessation of directorship of such holder (or permitted holder group's appointed director), or upon a transfer of such shares to another person (unless within a permitted holder group).
- Other than enhanced-voting rights at general meetings, rights of enhanced-voting shares to be equal to those of inferior-voting shares.
- Ratio of enhanced-voting share voting rights to inferior-voting share voting rights not to exceed 10:1.
- Inferior-voting shareholders who do not also hold enhanced-voting shares must be entitled to exercise at least 10 per cent of the voting rights.

188 SGX, 'Consultation Paper: Possible Listing Framework for Dual Class Share Structures' (16 February 2017) at 2.

189 Committee on the Future Economy, 'Report: Pioneers of the Next Generation' (7 February 2017) at 31 and 86.

190 SGX Consultation (2017) (n 188 above 23).

191 *ibid*.

192 SGX, 'Consultation Paper: Proposed Listing Framework for Dual Class Share Structures' (28 March 2018).

193 SGX News Release, 'SGX Launches Rules for Listing of Dual Class Shares Companies' (26 June 2018), www.sgx.com/media-centre/20180626-sgx-launches-rules-listing-dual-class-shares-companies.

194 SGX Mainboard Rules, Chapters 2, 7 and 8.

- Shareholders holding 10 per cent of the voting rights, calculated on a one share, one vote basis, must be able to convene a shareholders' general meeting.
- Voting rights will revert to one share, one vote on any decisions to amend the constitutional documents, vary the rights attached to a class of shares, appoint and remove independent directors, appoint and remove auditors, effect reverse takeovers, de list and voluntarily wind-up the company.
- Further enhanced-voting shares may not be issued post-IPO, except through rights issue, bonus issue, scrip dividend scheme or consolidation or subdivision of shares, in each case in conjunction with the issuance of inferior-voting shares and as approved by special resolution.
- The total voting rights of the enhanced-voting share class compared to those of the inferior-voting share class may not increase post-IPO.
- Majority of the members of the audit, remuneration and nomination committees (as well as their respective chairs) to be independent directors.
- Disclosure of the dual-class structure on the front page of any documents issued by the firm, with explanations within those documents of the rationale for the structure and the risks inherent therein, and of decisions which will implement a one share, one vote process.
- Documents issued to shareholders or potential investors must disclose the holders of enhanced-voting shares, together with their holdings of, and voting rights attached to, enhanced-voting and inferior-voting shares, and their total voting rights.
- Holders of enhanced-voting shares may not transfer or dispose of any shares for at least twelve months post-IPO.
- All dual-class firms to be designated with a dual-class share stock marker.

As in Hong Kong, SGX reserves the right to adjudicate on the suitability of a dual-class firm for listing.[195] SGX will assess the business model of the company (including evaluating whether the company has a long-term plan that predicts high-growth); the operating track record of the business; the role, contribution to the success of the business and level of active involvement in the business of the proposed enhanced-voting shareholders; the level of participation of sophisticated investors; and any other features of the business that may be benefitted by dual-class structure.[196] SGX has followed HKEX's approach in creating as much flexibility as possible while making it clear that it will evaluate whether the benefits of dual-class stock will outweigh the potential risks on an applicant-by-applicant basis. SGX has further stated that its guidance in relation to suitability will evolve as more dual-class applicants approach the exchange over time.

Even though the conditions imposed by the SGX regarding dual-class firms are broadly equivalent to those introduced by Hong Kong, the Singapore Stock

195 SGX Mainboard Rules, Rule 210(10)(b).
196 SGX Consultation (2018) (n 192 above 2).

Exchange has not seen similar levels of success in attracting dual-class IPOs. As of the date of writing, only one firm, AMTD, which was a secondary listing of a US firm, has listed on the Singapore Stock Exchange with dual-class stock. However, that lack of dual-class listings should be viewed in conjunction with the comparatively low numbers of listings in Singapore generally,[197] and, therefore, the success or otherwise of Singapore's relaxation of a one share, one vote standard can only be properly assessed over a longer period of time.

2.4.3 *Tokyo*

Tokyo is the largest non-US exchange by market capitalisation of listed equities.[198] However, it bears greater similarity to the markets of Hong Kong and Singapore than the NYSE or LSE. As of the end of 2018, 17.5 per cent of all listed companies on the TSE had controlling shareholders holding (along with associates) a majority of the voting rights in the relevant company.[199] TSE listed companies are also associated with uncommonly high levels of cross-ownerships,[200] with banks, especially, holding significant stakes in multiple listed companies through the keiretsu model.[201]

Historically, Japan's corporate laws had been largely hostile to the implementation by companies of classes of shares with differing voting rights, particularly in the public company arena. Although Japanese companies could issue different classes of stock, with respect to voting rights, prior to 2002, it was only possible to issue voting stock and non-voting stock, and further provided that the non-voting stock had preferential dividend rights attached.[202] Amendments to Japan's Commercial Code in 2002, though, introduced greater flexibility such that voting rights could be restricted in any class of share, provided that, for public companies, the total number of shares with limited voting rights did not exceed half the total issued shares.[203] In theory, that flexibility was partially dented by corporate laws not permitting public companies to issue shares with more than one vote per

197 In 2019, there were only eleven IPOs in Singapore, and there have not been more than twenty IPOs in any calendar year since 2015, www.statista.com/statistics/1022801/number-of-ipos-in-singapore/. Hong Kong, in contrast, saw 160 IPOs in 2019 (KPMG (2020) (n 179 above 17)).

198 Source: World Federation of Exchanges, 'Annual Statistics Guide 2018' (May 2019).

199 Tokyo Stock Exchange, Inc., 'TSE-Listing Companies White Paper on Corporate Governance 2019' (2019) at 10.

200 *ibid* 24. C. Goodman, *The Rule of Law in Japan: A comparative analysis* (Wolters Kluwer, 2017) §13.03A. For more detail on cross-ownerships, see Chapter 3.

201 Franks and Mayer (2017) (n 39 above 8); J. Franks et al., 'The Ownership of Japanese Corporations in the 20th Century' (2014) 27 *Rev. of Financ. Stud.* 2580. However, recent trends have suggested a decline in such bank-orientated ownership relationships (Tokyo Stock Exchange (2019) (n 199 above 24); Franks and Mayer (2017) (n 39 above 29)).

202 International Financial Law Review, 'Local Insights: Japan' (1 March 2002), www.iflr.com/article/b1ltxqrr5h4pz1/japan.

203 *ibid.*

share.[204] However, in practice, Japanese public companies could implement a structure that resembled a dual-class stock model through the use of a 'unit share system'.[205] The unit share system allows a company to split each class of stock into units. One vote would be attached to each unit, and each unit divided into shares. A company could, for example, issue one class of stock with units divided into 100 shares each, and one class of stock with units divided into 10 shares each.[206] A shareholder of the second class holding the same number of shares as a shareholder of the first class will enjoy ten times the votes. In effect, a dual-class system of inferior-voting and enhanced-voting stock can be constructed, although the number of shares per unit cannot exceed 1,000.[207]

As with Japan's corporate law, stock exchange rules have become progressively more welcoming to dual-class stock. Notwithstanding the capacity of companies to engineer dual-class stock style structures under corporate law, before amendments implemented in 2008, the TSE would not permit the rights of an issuer's shareholders to be 'unreasonably restricted', which was interpreted as an effective prohibition of dual-class stock.[208] The listing of non-voting preference stock, to the extent that an issuer had already listed common stock, was permitted.[209] Although the TSE's proclamations were construed restrictively, it is interesting to speculate how the TSE would have reacted if it had been tested by a proposed high-profile IPO, as the NYSE was with Ford Motor Company in 1956,[210] or by a high-profile existing issuer, in the manner that General Motors tested the NYSE's appetite to delist an existing large issuer in 1984.[211] By analogy, the TSE's position was also seen as prohibiting the use of 'golden shares' to which were attached veto rights over certain decisions of companies, but, as an exception, it did not delist the company Inpex Corporation when it issued golden shares to the Japanese Government in 2004. The TSE subsequently confirmed that an issuer of veto shares would not be delisted if there is 'minimal risk to the interests of investors given the scope of activities of the issuer, the purpose of issuing the veto shares, the nature of the subscriber, the details of the granted power, and other terms and conditions of the veto shares'.[212] Therefore, the TSE may well have been afflicted with a dose of pragmatism if it had been tested on dual-class stock in the same way as the NYSE.

204 K. Lebrun, 'Making a Private Equity/Venture Capital Investment in Japan: Implementing Techniques Commonly Used in U.S. Transactions' (2002) 23 *U. Pa. J. Int'l. L.* 213, 226 (fn 27).

205 For example, see Japan's Companies Act (Act No. 86 of July 26, 2005), article 188.

206 See, for example, Shearman & Sterling LLP, 'Proportionality between Ownership and Control in EU Listed Companies: Comparative Legal Study Exhibit C (Part II)' (2007) at 332; T. Watanabe, 'Shareholder Rights and Powers in Japan' *Lexology* (10 July 2018), www.lexology.com/library/detail.aspx?g=13339d10-32be-446f-91b6-04f74e9efe64.

207 Shearman Part II (2007) (n 206 above 333).

208 *ibid* 333.

209 K. Yoshii, 'A New Share-listing System in Japan' (2008) 4 *Asia Law Corp. Financ. Rev.* 16.

210 See n 106 above and accompanying text.

211 See n 110 above and accompanying text.

212 Shearman Part II (2007) (n 206 above 363).

In 2008, however, after a two-year discussion period, the TSE formally relaxed its rules on dual-class stock. The rationale was to provide investors with more choice, with a perception that there was a demand by issuers to raise capital utilising dual-class stock, and that it was beneficial to provide options to investors.[213] In fact, resonating with critical junctures in the United Kingdom and United States, the TSE may have been influenced by the views of potential issuers after a spate of attempted hostile takeovers in the mid-2000s.[214] Pursuant to the 2008 amendments, new public company issuers finally became permitted to issue inferior-voting common shares (whether or not preferred stock) and maintain unlisted enhanced-voting shares.[215] Cyberdyne was the first company to avail itself of dual-class shares on the TSE, issuing inferior-voting shares on the exchange in 2014.[216] The founder, Yoshihuki Sankai, and two associated foundations retained enhanced-voting shares, giving them 87.7 per cent of the total voting rights, but only 41.7 per cent of the cash-flow rights.[217] The reason given by the company for the use of dual-class stock was that it would ensure that control would remain with the founder, therefore ensuring that the company's technology, centred around an autonomously controlled robotic hybrid assistive limb, would be used only for peaceful purposes.[218] When the TSE considered the structure for admission to listing, the importance of Sankai to the continued success of the business weighed heavily, and it was determined that dual-class stock would safeguard Sankai's commitment to the business, and the fact that enhanced-voting shares were only held by Sankai and related parties would make the structure acceptable to investors.[219]

The TSE is a good example of the way in which exchanges can nimbly evolve based upon experience. After the Cyberdyne IPO, the TSE took stock of its rules on dual-class stock, and introduced, in 2014, further restrictions on potential dual-class issuers. The new rules were developed to better protect public shareholders and provide more clarity than otherwise palpable from the Cyberdyne listing.[220] In contrast to the relatively prescriptive requirements subsequently adopted by Hong Kong and Singapore, the TSE's restrictions are more conceptual in nature and give the TSE broad scope as to how and when to apply its judgment. Most of the conditions describe general types of protections for public shareholders without specifying the details that must be included, with the presumption that those details must be negotiated with the TSE prior to a decision on admission. The principal

[213] See quotes by the executive managing director of the TSE in CFA Institute, 'Dual-Class Shares: The Good, The Bad, And The Ugly' (2018) at 46.

[214] K. Toshima, 'Cyberdyne's Dual-Class IPO' *IFLR* (2014), www.iflr1000.com/NewsAndAnalysis/Cyberdynes-dual-class-IPO/Index/1662.

[215] Yoshii (2008) (n 209 above 17).

[216] CFA Institute (2018) (n 213 above 39); Toshima (2014) (n 214 above).

[217] Toshima (2014) (n 214 above).

[218] *ibid*; CFA Institute (2018) (n 213 above 39).

[219] Toshima (2014) (n 214 above).

[220] Huang (2017) (n 153 above 153); CFA Institute (2018) (n 213 above 47).

conditions applied to dual-class structures by the TSE's regulator, the JPXR, are as follows:[221]

- The dual-class structure must be in the common interest of the shareholders (such as to ensure that a specific person with appropriate knowledge and skill continues in management), and should not provide undue benefits to holders of enhanced-voting stock.
- Only new issuers.
- Only one class of voting shares may be listed, and enhanced-voting shares may not be listed.
- When the need for the dual-class structure no longer exists, it is expected that the structure will dissolve.
- If the controller holds only a small proportion of the cash-flow rights, it is expected that the dual-class structure will dissolve – breakthrough or sunset provisions will be expected.[222]
- Enhanced-voting shares to be converted into inferior-voting shares upon transfer (although the JPXR may, on a case-by-case basis, permit an exception for transfers between existing holders of enhanced-voting shares).
- Dual-class stock should not be used primarily as a takeover defence mechanism.
- Purpose and need for dual-class stock to be appropriately disclosed in the initial listing application.
- Normally, it will be expected that the holders of enhanced-voting stock will be individuals and directors, although JPXR will consider exceptions on a case-by-case basis.
- Dual-class issuers must implement mechanisms that protect the rights of inferior-voting shareholders from being disproportionately modified.
- Controlling shareholder related-party transaction protections must be implemented by the issuer.
- In the case of non-voting preferred stock (in relation to which less restrictive conditions apply), the extent to which it is likely that the issuer will generate profits to pay preferential dividends will be examined by the JPXR to prevent a circumvention of the rules relating to non-voting stock with no preferential dividends attached.
- Corporate governance practices must respect the rights of inferior-voting shareholders.
- It is unlikely that the issue of further enhanced-voting stock will be approved post-IPO, but JPXR to assess on a case-by-case basis.

[221] TSE, 'New Listing Guidebook 2018: 1st and 2nd Sections' (October 2018).

[222] For an explanation of breakthrough provisions, see n 226 below and accompanying text. In relation to sunset provisions in this context, see Section 9.6.4 of Chapter 9.

One aspect of Tokyo's conditions on dual-class issuers bears further scrutiny. The corporate law relevant to public companies still applies, such that a company that issues shares with restricted voting rights (so less than one vote per share, or one vote per unit), such as non-voting stock, must still ensure that such shares do not represent more than a half of the issued share capital.[223] A Snap-style capital structure,[224] with substantial levels of non-voting stock issued to the public, would therefore violate Japan's corporate laws. With a simple non-voting stock/one share, one vote system, a founder wishing to retain control would, if the maximum number of non-voting shares were issued, need to hold at least a majority of the remaining one share, one vote shares issued, meaning that it would have to hold over 25 per cent of the equity. Furthermore, even if dual-class stock were to be implemented through the founder holding enhanced-voting stock, and issuing one share, one vote stock to the public, the TSE requires that either sunset provisions be implemented such that enhanced-voting shares convert into inferior-voting shares upon the holders of enhanced-voting shares owning below a threshold level of equity[225] or breakthrough provisions should be included. Breakthrough provisions allow a bidder for the company to 'breakthrough' the dual-class structure such that upon acquiring a threshold proportion of equity, all shares will be treated on a one share, one vote basis in relation to the approval of the bid and appointments to the board.[226] Although the TSE does not mandate a percentage threshold, it has indicated that the appropriate percentage would be 75 per cent.[227] Therefore, a founder would need to retain more than 25 per cent of the equity to ensure that it can block takeovers. If the sunset provision option were taken, it is likely that the threshold would similarly be set so that the enhanced-voting shareholders would have to retain more than 25 per cent of the equity to avoid the enhanced-voting shares converting into inferior-voting shares. Therefore, in Japan, absent an exemption from the JPXR, a controller seeking to retain control through the implementation of dual-class stock will have to retain more equity than would be the case in Hong Kong, Singapore or the United States.

As of the time of writing, Cyberdyne remains the only dual-class stock issuer on the TSE. The plethora of issuers seeking to utilise dual-class stock envisaged by the

223 Japan Companies Act (2005) (n 205 above article 115); also, see note 203 above and accompanying text.

224 See Section 1.2 of Chapter 1.

225 See Section 9.6.4 of Chapter 9.

226 Toshima (2014) (n 214 above). The EU has also introduced a breakthrough rule, with a 75 per cent threshold (Takeover Directive, article 11(4)). Member States were, however, given the right to derogate from the breakthrough rules (Takeover Directive, article 12(1)), and only three Member States – Estonia, Lithuania and Latvia – applied the rules (Report from the Commission to the European Parliament, the Council, the European Economic and Social Committee and the Committee of the Regions, 'Application of Directive 2004/25/EC on takeover bids' at 3), reflecting a concern that the rule essentially undermines any structures that deviate from one share, one vote (G. Ferrarini, 'One Share – One Vote: A European Rule?' (2006) 3 *ECFR* 147).

227 TSE Guidebook 2018 (2018) (n 221 above 159).

TSE when it amended its rules have not emerged. Although market specificities, including the preponderance of cross-ownership banking relationships and investor preferences, will have played a role in the lack of issuers taking advantage of dual-class stock, the TSE experience may be a salutary lesson in ensuring that conditions applied to dual-class issuers are not too restrictive. In particular, the application of the breakthrough rule may exclude potential founders of dual-class companies seeking to crystallise significant wealth and/or raise substantial equity capital.

2.4.4 *China*

As discussed earlier, part of the drive by Hong Kong to permit dual-class stock was to attract mainland Chinese technology companies that were otherwise listing on foreign exchanges, and, therefore, it is pertinent to assess whether mainland China has also sought to entertain the listing of dual-class issuers. In China, joint stock companies may only issue one share, one vote common shares unless the State Council of China determines that other classes of shares may be issued.[228] However, in the 1990s, the laws and guidance for joint stock limited companies flip-flopped somewhat in relation to the acceptance of shares with differing voting rights, with some confusion as to whether non-voting preferred stock was permitted.[229] In 2014, though, it was confirmed that at least preferred stock was permitted as a separate class of stock, which reignited the debate on dual-class stock.[230] Finally, in 2018, the State Council of China published a guideline advocating for the support of technology start-ups, including the amendment of legislation and regulations to permit the use of differential voting rights.[231] Such guidelines are imperative in China given that the two main markets, the Shanghai and Shenzhen exchanges, are owned by the government.[232] A softening in the approach to dual-class stock will have been influenced by the flood of Chinese companies to the US stock exchanges partly to protect themselves from an emerging hostile takeover market by the adoption of dual-class stock.[233] Accordingly, the CSRC, in 2019, published final proposals for a separate board of the SSE specifically for science and technology companies (the STI Board).[234] Dual-class issuers would be permitted to list on the STI Board, and,

[228] Ho (2019) (n 146 above 23); G. Fei, 'Rethinking Dual-Class Share Structure in the Context of China' (2019) 1, 6, https://ssrn.com/abstract=3480313.

[229] Ho (2019) (n 146 above 23–24).

[230] *ibid* 25.

[231] H. Yongqi, 'Promising Start-ups to Get Backing for Listing' *China Daily* (27 September 2018), http://english.www.gov.cn/policies/latest_releases/2018/09/27/content_281476320340892.htm.

[232] G. Brouwer and W. Pupphavesa, eds., *Asia Pacific Financial Deregulation* (Taylor & Francis, 1999) at 150.

[233] F. Chen and L. Zhao, 'To Be or Not to Be? An Empirical Study on Dual-Class Share Structure of US Listed Chinese Companies' (2017) 16 *J. Int'l Bus. & L.* 215, 219.

[234] CSRC, 'Administrative Measures on the Registration of Initial Public Offering of Shares on the Science and Technology Innovation Board (for Trial Implementation)' (1 March 2019).

therefore, the capacity for joint stock companies to issue dual-class stock had now been adopted as public policy.[235] Crucially, only issuers on the STI Board may issue dual-class stock, and not issuers on the Main Board of the SSE – in some ways, the approach mirrors the traditional premium tier/standard tier approach of the LSE, with dual-class stock not permitted on the most prestigious tier of the exchange. Following the adoption of the STI Rules on dual-class stock, in October 2019, mainland Chinese investors were permitted to invest in dual-class issuers listed on the Hong Kong Stock Exchange pursuant to the Shanghai-Hong Kong Stock Connect and Shenzhen-Hong Kong Stock Connect programmes.[236]

Echoing Hong Kong and Singapore, the STI imposes stringent conditions on issuers wishing to avail themselves of dual-class structure, including the following:[237]

- New issuers only.
- Enhanced-voting shares may not be listed.
- Expected market capitalisation of at least RMB 10 billion, or an expected market capitalisation of at least RMB 5 billion with an operating revenue of at least RMB 500 million during the previous financial year.
- Enhanced-voting shareholders must be persons who have made material contributions to the development of the business.
- Enhanced-voting shareholders must have been directors pre-IPO and continue to be directors post-IPO (and in the case of a corporate enhanced-voting shareholder, the individual controlling such shareholder must be a director).
- Conversion of a holder's enhanced-voting shares into inferior-voting shares upon death, cessation of directorship, change of control of a corporate enhanced-voting shareholder or transfer of enhanced-voting shares (or delegation of voting rights attached thereto).
- Conversion of all enhanced-voting shares into inferior-voting shares upon a change of control of the company.
- Enhanced-voting shares to only confer enhanced-voting rights at general meetings, with all other rights equal to those of inferior-voting shares.
- Ratio of enhanced-voting share voting rights to inferior-voting share voting rights not to exceed 10:1.
- Enhanced-voting stock must comprise at least 10 per cent of the total issued share capital, with a conversion of all enhanced-voting shares into inferior-voting shares if enhanced-voting shares no longer represent at least 10 per cent of the issued share capital.

235 I. Wong, 'The Revival of Dual Class Shares' *IFLR* (2020), www.iflr.com/article/b1lmx6clj4l38j/the-revival-of-dual-class-shares.

236 S. Shen and A. John, 'China Revises Stock Connect Rules to Include HK-Listed Dual-Class Shares' *Reuters* (19 October 2019), https://uk.reuters.com/article/us-china-connect-inclusion/china-revises-stock-connect-rules-to-include-hk-listed-dual-class-shares-idUKKBN1WY07E.

237 See CSRC, 'Rules Governing the Listing of Stocks on the Science and Technology Innovation Board of Shanghai Stock Exchange (Revised in 2019)' (April 2019).

- Inferior-voting shares must comprise at least 10 per cent of the voting rights in the company.
- Shareholders holding 10 per cent of the voting rights must be able to convene a shareholders' general meeting, and shareholders holding 3 per cent of the voting rights may propose resolutions at the shareholders' general meeting.
- Enhanced-voting share voting rights to be identical to inferior-voting share voting rights on any decisions to amend the constitutional documents, to vary the voting rights attached to the enhanced-voting shares (requiring a super-majority vote), to appoint and remove independent directors, to appoint and remove auditors, and on the combination, division, dissolution and change of legal form of the company.
- No further enhanced-voting shares may be issued, and the proportion of enhanced voting-shares may not be increased, post-IPO, except pursuant to a proportional rights issue.
- Full disclosure at IPO and in periodic reports of the dual-class structure, its risks, corporate governance implications and implemented investor protection measures.
- Board of supervisors to report annually on adherence to dual-class conditions and whether the enhanced-voting shareholders have abused their voting rights or damaged the legitimate interests of investors.

As of the time of writing, only one large issuer, UCloud, has listed on the STI with dual-class stock. It is early days, but the stringent conditions, and the fact that dual-class issuers are still prohibited from the Main Board of the SSE, may see some firms deterred from taking advantage of the greater capital structure flexibility granted by the STI Board. Additionally, the fact that the CSRC insisted on further restrictions on the founders of UCloud when applying for admission,[238] and the exclusion of retail investors from the STI,[239] may further discourage issuers. Other considerations may also be salient, though. For example, most Chinese listed companies are state-owned or controlled, either directly or indirectly, and political considerations weigh heavily on listing jurisdiction decisions.[240] It has been speculated that government-backed entities may have a preference to list on foreign exchanges to politically leverage the resulting publicity and influence.[241] Therefore, it is not clear whether the opening-up of the STI Board to dual-class stock will have a significant effect in curtailing the listing of Chinese companies in other jurisdictions.[242]

[238] M. Yan, 'Differentiated Voting Rights Arrangement under Dual-Class Structures in China: Expectation, Reality and Future' (2020) *Queen Mary Legal Studies Research Paper* No. 344/2020 1, 17.

[239] *ibid* 15.

[240] Ho (2019) (n 146 above 27).

[241] *ibid* 27.

[242] However, clearly China still sees dual-class stock as a viable route to IPO, given the recent announcement that the smaller Shenzhen Stock Exchange will admit dual-class stock on its 'tech startups' board, ChiNext (W. Sheng, 'Shenzhen Looks to Draw Tech Firms with New Dual-Class

2.4.5 *India*

India has also had a storied history when it comes to dual-class stock. The underlying corporate law position in India was silent as to whether shares with differential voting rights could be issued by companies,[243] although some commentators presumed that the laws were permissive.[244] In 2001, regulations were introduced that referenced shares with differential voting rights (DVRs) for the first time.[245] However, for companies seeking a listing, the rules prohibited the issuance of stock deviating from one share, one vote, until after one share, one vote shares had been first listed, and to the extent that DVRs were listed subsequent to the IPO of one share, one vote shares, they could only form up to 25 per cent of the total share capital.[246] A handful of firms, such as Tata Motors, Gujarat NRE Coke, Future Enterprises, Jain Irrigation Systems and Stampede Capital issued dual-class stock in this manner, with all such firms issuing one share, one vote shares, and inferior-voting shares with restricted voting rights.[247] Commonly, the inferior-voting shares also included preferential dividend rights.[248] The scope for listed companies was further limited though in 2009, when the Indian securities regulator, SEBI, pronounced that listed companies would not be permitted to issue shares with superior rights. The proclamation brought with it significant ambiguity,[249] but it was eventually established that it did not prohibit stock with enhanced dividend rights, nor the issuance of shares with voting rights inferior to one share, one vote.[250] Essentially, the prohibition only applied to shares with voting rights greater than one share, one vote. However, with the requirement that one share, one vote shares be listed prior to the listing of inferior-voting shares, and for those inferior-voting shares to form no more than 25 per cent of the issued share capital (in 2014, the 25 per cent limitation was marginally amended to 26 per cent of the total issued share capital[251]), the scope for founders to use dual-class stock in the manner of tech founders in the United States was severely limited.

Share Rule' (27 August 2020), https://technode.com/2020/08/27/shenzhen-looks-to-draw-tech-firms-with-new-dual-class-share-rule/.

243 P. Sanjanwala, 'India – DVR Shares – A Timeline' *Conventus Law* (27 September 2019), www.conventuslaw.com/report/india-dvr-shares-a-timeline/–ftn2.

244 A. Jadhav, 'Dual Class Shares – Is India Ready For It?' (2012) 5 *Macroec. Financ. Emerg. Mkt. Econ.* 124, 127.

245 Sanjanwala (2019) (n 243 above).

246 Jadhav (2012) (n 244 above 127); Companies (Issue of Share Capital with Differential Voting Rights) Rules, 2001, Rule 9.

247 SEBI, 'Consultation Paper: Issuance of Shares with Differential Voting Rights [DVRs]' (20 March 2019) at 10.

248 *ibid* 13.

249 Jadhav (2012) (n 244 above 123).

250 For example, see Letter from SEBI to S. Sethna, Company Secretary Tata Motors, 'Request from Tata Motors Limited for Interpretative Letter under SEBI (Informal Guidance) Scheme, 2003 – Guidance in Relation to Clause 28A of Equity Listing Agreement' (23 April 2010), www.sebi.gov.in/sebi_data/commondocs/sebiletter_p.pdf.

251 Companies (Share Capital and Debentures) Rules, 2014, Rule 4.

In 2019, however, India shifted its stance, and like Hong Kong and Singapore, moved toward a more permissive environment for dual-class stock, after SEBI consulted on a framework proposal on dual-class stock.[252] The framework was adopted into law, and now permitted the listing of companies with DVRs with voting rights greater than one share, one vote. Completing the volte-face, existing listed companies would be prohibited from issuing shares with lesser voting rights than one share, one vote, such as non-voting stock.[253] Two significant limitations applied for listed companies, however, with only 'technology' firms being able to issue such shares,[254] and the shares would have to be in existence at the time of IPO, with only one share, one vote shares permitted to be freshly issued at IPO.[255] Additionally, in 2019, the rule requiring that DVRs do not form more than 26 per cent of the issued share capital was substantively amended, and now it provides that the voting rights attached to DVR shares must not exceed 74 per cent of the total voting rights of the company (in India, certain resolutions require a super-majority vote of at least 75 per cent of the votes).[256] The shift in focus from limitations around equity to limitations around voting rights portend a future trend toward a greater use of DVRs with superior-voting rights, rather than DVRs that were restricted-voting preference shares. SEBI also enacted further legislation which mirrored the requirement that the holders of enhanced-voting shares may not hold more than 74 per cent of the voting rights in the company,[257] and also, evidencing its cautious approach to dual-class stock in listed companies imposed numerous conditions, including the following:[258]

- Only 'technology companies'[259] permitted to list with enhanced-voting shares.
- Enhanced-voting shares must be in existence (and held for at least six months prior to publication of the red herring prospectus) pre-IPO, and only one share, one vote shares may be issued at IPO.
- Enhanced-voting shares technically listed, but locked-up until at least the conversion of such shares into inferior-voting shares.
- Only one class of enhanced-voting shares permitted.

252 Parivathan, 'Explained: Dual-Class Shares in India' (21 March 2019), http://iksa.in/gs3/explained-dual-class-shares-in-india/6975/.

253 A. H and H. Srivastava, 'Another Step Forward by India Inc: DVR Shares' *Nishith Desai* (13 September 2019), www.nishithdesai.com/information/news-storage/news-details/article/another-step-forward-by-india-inc-dvr-shares.html.

254 The issuer must 'be intensive in the use of technology, information technology, intellectual property, data analytics, bio-technology or nano-technology to provide products, services or business platforms with substantial value addition' (SEBI (Issue of Capital and Disclosure Requirements) (Third Amendment) Regulations, 2019, Rule 3(II)).

255 *ibid* Rule 3(II).

256 Companies (Share Capital and Debentures) Amendment Rules, 2019, Rule 2.

257 SEBI (Listing Obligations and Disclosure Requirements) (Fourth Amendment) Regulations, 2019, Rule 3(VII).

258 See SEBI (Third Amendment) Regulations, 2019 (n 254 above); SEBI (Fourth Amendment) Regulations, 2019 (n 257 above).

259 See n 254 above.

- Pre-IPO, enhanced-voting shares must have been held by promotors or founders in executive positions, with total net worth (not including the shares) of no more than Rs 500 crores.
- Enhanced-voting shareholders may not hold more than 74 per cent of the voting rights in the company.
- Enhanced-voting shares to automatically convert into one share, one vote shares five years post-IPO, unless extended for one further five-year period by a vote of the shareholders, excluding the votes of enhanced-voting shareholders.
- Conversion of a holder's enhanced-voting shares into one share, one vote upon death, resignation of executive position, merger or acquisition resulting in loss of control by the enhanced-voting shareholders, change of control of a corporate enhanced-voting shareholder, or transfer of enhanced-voting shares.
- Enhanced-voting shares to only confer enhanced rights of voting at general meetings, with all other rights equal to one share, one vote shares.
- Ratio of enhanced-voting share voting rights to inferior-voting share voting rights not to exceed 10:1, and to be a minimum of 2:1.
- Enhanced-voting share voting rights to be treated as one share, one vote on any decisions to amend the constitutional documents, to appoint and remove independent directors, to appoint and remove auditors, on voluntary winding ups or insolvency processes, on related-party transaction approvals involving an enhanced-voting shareholder, to approve changes of control instigated by a voluntary transfer of enhanced-voting shares, to approve substantial value transactions, on de listings, on share buybacks, and to utilise funds for purposes other than the company's business.
- Further enhanced-voting shares may only be issued to existing holders pursuant to a bonus, split or rights issue.
- At least half the board to be independent directors.
- Remuneration, nomination, risk management and stakeholder relationship committees to comprise at least two-thirds independent directors, and audit committee to be comprised exclusively of independent directors.

As of the time of writing, it is too early to assess the impact of India's regulatory relaxation regarding dual-class stock, since changes were only implemented in 2019, and enhanced-voting shares must have been held for at least six months prior to the date of publication of a company's 'red herring prospectus'[260] – a pre-IPO unapproved prospectus issued to evaluate market interest in the IPO. However, India has introduced fairly onerous conditions to dual-class issuances, which go beyond the restrictions applied by Hong Kong, Singapore and mainland China. Notably, India is the first jurisdiction to impose a mandatory time-dependent sunset clause, requiring that enhanced-voting shares convert into inferior-voting shares

260 SEBI (Third Amendment) Regulations, 2019 (n 254 above), Rule 3(II).

after five years, unless extended for one further period of five years by a vote of the shareholders, excluding the enhanced-voting shareholders,[261] and enhanced-voting shareholders are prevented from passing super-majority votes.[262] As discussed further in Chapter 9, in relation to investor protections, time-dependent sunset clauses, in particular, can be blunt instruments, and it will be intriguing to observe, going forward, whether such a mandatory requirement has a chilling effect on dual-class listings in India, particularly since similar proposals have been made by the UK Listing Review.

2.5 MAINLAND EUROPE

Europe comprises a vast and diverse set of policies on dual-class stock, and it is not intended to delineate in detail the policies applied across the continent. However, briefly, the permissiveness of the primary jurisdictions in mainland Europe will be described.

In Germany, dual-class structures equivalent to those implemented by Google and Facebook in the United States are not possible. In 1998, Germany prohibited new issuances of multiple-voting stock (shares with more than one vote per share), with existing multiple voting rights shares mainly phased out in 2003.[263] The 2003 legislation confirmed that only two classes of shares could be issued by German companies – ordinary one share, one vote shares, and non-voting preference shares.[264] Therefore, pure non-voting shares without preferential dividend rights are not permitted. As discussed further in Chapter 3, the use of preference shares cannot adequately replicate the dynamics created through pure dual-class structures. Additionally, in Germany, non-voting preference shares may not form more than 50 per cent of the total share capital,[265] further limiting their expediency to a founder seeking to divest of significant investment and generate equity funding, whilst retaining control.

Non-voting preference shares are permitted in France.[266] It is debateable whether non-voting shares without preferential dividend rights attached are permitted, but, in any case, non-voting shares may only form a maximum of 25 per cent of the issued

261 SEBI (Fourth Amendment) Regulations, 2019 (n 257 above), Rule 3(VII).

262 See n 257 above and accompanying text. Additionally, in India, it is common for lenders to require founders to offer their shares as security – therefore, the automatic conversion of enhanced-voting shares into one share, one vote upon transfer could encumber the ability of dual-class firms to raise debt finance (H and Srivastava (2019) (n 253 above).

263 M. Goergen et al., 'Is the German System of Corporate Governance Converging Towards the Anglo-American Model?' (2008) 12 *J Manage Governance* 37, 47; A. Betzer et al., 'Index Membership vs. Loss of Voting Power: The Unification of Dual-Class Shares' (2017) 49 *J. Int. Financ. Markets Inst. Money* 140, 142.

264 K. Bentel and G. Walter, 'Dual Class Shares' *Penn Law: Legal Scholarship Repository* (2016) 1, 10, https://scholarship.law.upenn.edu/fisch_2016/2.

265 Betzer et al. (2017) (n 263 above 142).

266 Shearman & Sterling LLP, 'Proportionality between Ownership and Control in EU Listed Companies: Comparative Legal Study Exhibit C (Part I)' (2007) at 248.

share capital, reducing their effectiveness in creating a divergence between voting and cash-flow rights.[267] Outside of non-voting preference shares, in the listed company arena, genuine dual-class stock is not permitted in France.[268] A divergence between voting and cash-flow rights may be created, though, through the use of loyalty shares which are discussed in further detail in Chapter 3. Prior to 2016, French companies could 'opt-in' (via a two-thirds super-majority shareholders' vote) to loyalty share structures pursuant to which the votes attached to ordinary one share, one vote shares would double after a specified period of ownership by the same shareholder of not less than two years.[269] On 29 March 2014, France passed laws, known as the Loi Florange rules, requiring, inter alia, loyalty share structures, encompassing two-year holding periods, to become the default mechanism for all companies with registered stock from 3 April 2016.[270] Therefore, currently, any French company undergoing an IPO will be subject to a loyalty share structure unless the shareholders (by way of two-thirds super-majority vote) 'opt-out'. Those firms that had already listed in April 2016 automatically converted to loyalty share structures unless disapplied by a super-majority (two-thirds) vote of the shareholders.[271] Prior to the effectiveness of the Loi Florange rules, if any such firm had desired to implement a loyalty share structure, it would have required a similar super-majority vote to create the structure.[272] Loyalty shares do not form a separate class of shares to the ordinary shares,[273] and, as discussed in Chapter 3, present a different set of considerations than pure dual-class structure.

Non-voting shares can be issued by non-listed Italian companies. For listed companies, although it is debatable as to whether non-voting shares can be issued without preferential dividend rights, many commentators believe that such shares can be issued by listed companies.[274] However, as with Germany and France, their effective use by founders is limited, since non-voting stock may not exceed 50 per cent of the company's shares capital. Until 2014, generally, it was not permissible for Italian companies to issue multiple voting rights shares.[275] However, following the relocation

267 *ibid* 244. Investment certificates that are non-voting have, though, been issued in conjunction with capital raisings (C. Muus, 'Non-Voting Shares in France: An Empirical Analysis of the Voting Premium' (1998) *Goethe University Working Paper Series: Finance & Accounting, No. 22* 1, 6, www.econstor.eu/bitstream/10419/76962/1/wp022.pdf).

268 Shearman Part I (2007) (n 266 above 240); A. Santoro et al., 'Deviations from the "One Share – One Vote" Principle in Italy: Recent Developments – Multiple Voting Rights Shares and Loyalty Shares' (2015) 5 *Bocconi Legal Papers* 141, 147.

269 M. Becht et al., 'Loyalty Shares with Tenure Voting – A Coasian Bargain? Evidence from the Loi Florange Experiment' (2018) *European Corporate Governance Institute Law Working Paper No. 398/2018* 1, 3.

270 *ibid* 6.

271 *ibid* 4.

272 *ibid* 3.

273 Shearman Part I (2007) (n 266 above 240).

274 *ibid* 322.

275 *ibid* 321.

of the Fiat Group from Italy to the Netherlands, partly in response to the restrictive approach of the Italian stock exchange to multiple voting rights shares,[276] new laws were introduced in 2014 that permitted Italian private companies to issue multiple voting rights stock with a maximum of three votes per share.[277] A public company is entitled to list with such multiple voting rights shares provided that they were issued pre-IPO.[278] Although the jurisdiction imposes a three votes per share maximum, by combining such shares with non-voting shares, which cannot exceed 50 per cent of the total issued capital, a founder could list one share, one vote and non-voting shares, while retaining shares with three votes per share, and therefore retain control while only holding just over 12.5 per cent of the equity.[279] Listed companies can, since 2014, additionally adopt loyalty share structures with any ordinary one share, one vote shares receiving two votes per share if ownership is maintained by a shareholder for at least two years.[280] Unlike France, the structure must be 'opted-in' by way of appropriate shareholder vote.[281]

Traditionally, in Spain, other than non-voting stock, which could not form more than 50 per cent of the total issued share capital, multiple voting rights shares were not permitted.[282] As a further restriction for listed companies, public companies could only issue non-voting shares if preferential economic rights were attached.[283] However, in 2020, Spain validated a draft bill on loyalty shares, which commences the path toward allowing listed companies to 'opt-in' to loyalty share schemes that grant shareholders who hold their shares for at least two years, double voting rights.[284]

Beyond Germany, France, Italy and Spain, the markets of Euronext should also be considered, as well as Sweden where listed dual-class firms are almost as prevalent as listed one share, one vote firms. Euronext is a pan-European exchange that comprises markets in Amsterdam, Brussels, Dublin, Lisbon, Oslo and Paris. For Euronext, the applicable rules on dual-class stock will be those of the jurisdictions of incorporation of the issuers and the regulations imposed by the regulator in which the market is located. France has been described earlier, but the other Euronext markets and Sweden employ disparate rules on dual-class shares. The Netherlands,[285] Sweden,[286] Norway[287] and

[276] Santoro et al. (2015) (n 268 above 142).
[277] *ibid* 153.
[278] *ibid* 154.
[279] *ibid* 155.
[280] *ibid* 143.
[281] T. Vos, 'Conference Report: The ECGI Roundtable on Loyalty Shares' *Oxford Business Law Blog* (8 September 2018).
[282] Shearman Part I (2007) (n 266 above 198).
[283] *ibid* 199.
[284] N. Martín, 'Loyalty Shares in Listed Companies' *Osborne Clarke Insights* (25 March 2020), www.osborneclarke.com/insights/loyalty-shares-listed-companies/.
[285] Shearman Part I (2007) (n 266 above 113); Vos (2018) (n 281 above).
[286] Shearman Part II (2007) (n 206 above 233).
[287] P. Lekvall, ed., *The Nordic Corporate Governance Model* (SNS Förlag, 2014) at 53.

Ireland[288] are more welcoming than the United Kingdom to both loyalty shares and genuine dual-class stock for listed companies (at least at IPO), although in the Netherlands, since all shares must have voting rights proportional to their nominal value, a dual-class system involves the application of differing contributions on inferior- and enhanced-voting stock.[289] In Sweden, dual-class firms form a majority by market capitalisation (and nearly a majority by number) of listed firms,[290] but no share may carry more than ten times the voting rights of any other shares issued.[291] In contrast, in Norway, notwithstanding the legally permissible environment, dual-class listed firms are rare as a result of the Norwegian Code of Practice for Corporate Governance recommending that listed companies should only have one class of shares, and the listing rules of the Oslo Stock Exchange specifying that votes attached to shares may only be limited on reasonable grounds.[292] In Belgium, although non-voting shares are permitted, listed companies may not issue multiple-voting rights shares of the type used in classic dual-class structures.[293] However, recent legislation has opened the door to the utilisation of 'opt-in' loyalty shares by Belgium-listed companies.[294] Finally, Portugal does not permit the use of multiple-voting shares by listed companies, although there has been some debate as to whether loyalty shares are similarly prohibited.[295]

2.6 CONCLUSION – MAKING SENSE OF GLOBAL POLICIES ON DUAL-CLASS STOCK

Attitudes in the United Kingdom and the United States have seemingly flip-flopped between favouritism toward one share, one vote and dual-class structure, although the course of history of the two jurisdictions eventually settled on opposite sides of the argument. The exchanges in both jurisdictions were influenced by the dominant stakeholders at the relevant times. The United Kingdom's passage

[288] P. White, 'Ireland' in *The Law Reviews: The Corporate Governance Review*, ed. W. Calkoen (The Law Reviews, 2020).

[289] Vos (2018) (n 281 above). Since share premium is not considered to represent the nominal value of the shares, inferior-voting shares with nominal value of EUR 10 and enhanced-voting shares with nominal value EUR 100, for example, could be issued, with EUR 100 being required to be paid for both classes of share – in such a way, the enhanced-voting shares can validly possess ten times more votes per share than the inferior-voting shares (since their nominal value is ten times that of the inferior-voting shares), even though the consideration for each is the same.

[290] Committee on Capital Markets Regulation, 'The Rise of Dual Class Shares: Regulations and Implications' (April 2020), www.capmktsreg.org/wp-content/uploads/2020/04/The-Rise-of-Dual-Class-Shares-04.08.20-1.pdf.

[291] Shearman Part II (2007) (n 206 above 233). However, certain companies in Sweden have grandfathered larger voting ratios pursuant to capital structures implemented prior to regulatory changes (T. Baums et al., eds., *Institutional Investors and Corporate Governance* (De Gruyter, 1993) at 293).

[292] Lekvall (2014) (n 287 above 214–215).

[293] Shearman Part I (2007) (n 266 above 4); Vos (2018) (n 281 above).

[294] Vos (2018) (n 281 above).

[295] P. Cunha and C. Miranda, 'Portugal' in Calkoen (2020) (n 288 above).

toward a one share, one vote standard on its highest listing level was steered by the aspirations of institutional investors, the foremost players in the UK capital markets at the time.[296] In the United States, the critical juncture of General Motors disregarding the one share, one vote paradigm in 1984[297] occurred at a time when institutional investors did not quite have the sway that they had in the United Kingdom at the time the United Kingdom adhered to one share, one vote, and, as such, in the United States, managers of corporations were able to be more assertive.[298] It is unlikely that, present day in the United Kingdom, a current premium listed company would test the determination of the LSE and FCA to enforce its rules on one share, one vote, or that a group of large listed companies would challenge any such regulatory requirements in the manner that the Business Roundtable proceeded in the United States in the late 1980s. The influence of institutional shareholders is too strong in the United Kingdom, and given the need to raise capital, UK companies would not wish to 'bite the hands that feed them'. Also significant, in the United States, was the competition that the NYSE faced from other US exchanges which were more amenable toward dual-class firms. The LSE did not face the same levels of domestic competition, with regional exchanges effectively merging into the LSE in 1965,[299] and, even pre-1965, those regional exchanges determined not to deviate from the LSE's position on one share, one vote.[300] Furthermore, with responsibility for the Listing Rules being in the hands of a public body regulator since 2000, the FCA will be less concerned with competition for listings than a self-regulatory exchange.[301] All these considerations will have led to the recent proposals of the UK Listing Review, which purportedly opened the door to premium tier dual-class stock, falling short of 'true' dual-class stock.[302]

Although the UK and US exchanges have arrived at different places, it could be argued that, with rising institutional investor influence in the United States, the two are now not quite so divided by that common language as it first appears. The US institutional investors have successfully lobbied the S&P, and to a lesser extent FTSE Russell, to exclude dual-class firms, at least partially, from some of their indices. The FCA's premium tier prohibition of dual-class stock effectively arrives at a similar position, since only premium listed companies can be

[296] It has been said that the influence of institutional shareholders stretches to such an extent that their 'interests dominate the institutions of lawmaking and enforcement' (Enriques et al. (2017) (n 41 above 104).

[297] See n 110 above and accompanying text.

[298] The ability of managers to be more assertive may also have been a factor of the more 'manager-friendly' corporate legislative environment in the United States (Ringe (2010) (n 42 above 230); M. Roe, *Strong Managers, Weak Shareholders: The Political Roots of American Corporate Finance* (Princeton University Press, 2004)).

[299] Cheffins (2008) (n 6 above 75).

[300] *ibid* 317.

[301] Cheffins (1997) (n 50 above 378).

[302] See Section 1.5.7 of Chapter 1.

constituents of the FTSE UK Index Series, which includes prominent indices such as the FTSE-100, FTSE-350 and FTSE SmallCap.[303] Not only has the FCA sought to restrict the premium tier to those companies with the highest standards of corporate governance, but, in conjunction with the rules of FTSE Russell, by restricting dual-class stock from the premium tier, the FCA is protecting passive index-tracking investors from being obliged to invest in dual-class firms, emblematic, in the view of the FCA, of lower corporate governance standards. It would not be a huge leap for the FCA to permit dual-class firms on the premium tier, but with those companies continuing to be omitted from the indices. Excluding companies with structures that could be detrimental to unsophisticated retail investors (investing through passive funds, insurance products and pension plans) and other passive investors with little proactive choice in the companies in which they invest could be considered a laudable goal. However, critically, the approach presumes that dual-class firms are riskier investments and that passive investors will inevitably be worse off having to invest in dual-class firms. If, as discussed in Chapter 7, there is little evidence that dual-class firms underperform one share, one vote firms, exclusion from the indices could harm the very stakeholders the FCA is seeking to protect. Additionally, excluding dual-class firms from the indices may prejudice their underlying concept. For example, it would be perverse that a passive fund desiring to track, say, the largest 100 firms by market capitalisation would not be capturing the performance of dual-class firms otherwise large enough to be constituents, but excluded from the index.[304] For example, reverting back to the current regulatory environment, if a tech company were to list with dual-class stock on the standard tier and attain the levels of success of a behemoth such as Google in the United States, such a passive tracker would not be able to participate in the success of that company. The Hut Group and Deliveroo, for example, which as discussed in Chapter 1 have pursued standard listings, are not constituents of the UK FTSE indices, even though, as of the time of writing, their market capitalisations are large enough to otherwise be constituents of the FTSE-100.[305] As has been remarked, the index would no longer represent the underlying economy, and the investable universe of companies that an investor may wish to track within a specific index will be curtailed.[306] Furthermore, index omission diminishes the ability of retail investors to invest in dual-class firms – retail investors would

303 FTSE Russell, 'FTSE UK Index Series: An Accurate and Consistent Measurement of the UK Equity Market' (October 2017) at 6.

304 Sharfman (2018) (n 137 above 32).

305 As of 29 April 2021, the market capitalisations of The Hut Group and Deliveroo were £6.06 billion and £4.73 billion, respectively, and the companies would have been the 86th and 100th largest companies, respectively, within the FTSE-100 (data derived from LSE, 'FTSE 100').

306 Sharfman (2018) (n 137 above 32); D. Solomon, 'The Importance of Inferior Voting Rights in Dual-Class Firms' (2019) 2 *BYU Law Rev.* 533, 564; Hirst and Kastiel (2019) (n 144 above 1247). Furthermore, research suggests that had the S&P 500 included new dual-class stock issuers since 2017, when, as discussed earlier, such firms were excluded from the index, returns would have been significantly higher for a notional investor tracking the index (B. Sharfman and V. Deluard, 'How

have to make investments in individual firms directly, or pay expensive management fees to invest in actively managed funds,[307] which, counter-intuitively, increases the risks to retail investors, since they will be less diversified than otherwise would be the case if invested across a broad index.[308] Although institutional investors in the United States continue to be publicly hostile to dual-class stock, these index-related considerations will have led to the backlash of sorts by large institutional investors against the exclusion of dual-class firms from indices.[309] It is also concerning that the US treatment of dual-class firms is being impacted by the decisions of, broadly unregulated, for-profit index providers rather than by regulators or exchanges. Therefore, simply excluding dual-class firms from the indices, while remaining largely permissive to the structure, is not an ideal approach, and it would be ill-conceived if the FCA were to follow this path.[310]

The positions in both jurisdictions may not yet be settled, as evidenced recently by the United Kingdom's re-examination of whether dual-class structure may be appropriate in certain circumstances, and the United States' relaxed policy being subject to criticism from politicians and institutional investors, and re-assessment by certain indices. However, it is worrying that the policy decisions in both the United Kingdom and United States have been directed quixotically rather than based upon a clear assessment of the benefits and burdens of dual-class structure, and how they relate to existing ownership, regulatory and shareholder-protection factors.

The debate on dual-class firms is not confined to the United Kingdom and the United States. Numerous jurisdictions have, in recent times, deliberated on the admission of dual-class firms to their exchanges. Tokyo, Hong Kong, Singapore and India have recently relaxed their rules to permit dual-class firms, and the Shanghai Stock Exchange has introduced a new listing segment for science and technology companies that permits dual-class firms. In the EU, given the more general trend toward harmonisation of corporate laws, it is intriguing that the regulations on dual-class stock are somewhat disparate in European nations, although an encouragement by the EU to permit loyalty shares is seemingly gathering momentum, with several European jurisdictions modifying their regulations on loyalty share systems.[311]

Discretionary Decision-Making Has Created Performance and Legal Disclosure Issues for the S&P 500 Index' (2021) 1, 33, https://papers.ssrn.com/sol3/papers.cfm?abstract_id=3794306).

307 Solomon (2019) (n 306 above 564); Speech by Robert J. Jackson Jr., Commissioner of the SEC, 'Perpetual Dual-Class Stock: The Case against Corporate Royalty' (15 February 2018, San Francisco, California); HKEX Concept (2017) (n 162 above 24).

308 A. Grinapell, 'Dual-Class Stock Structure and Firm Innovation' (2020) 25 *SJLBF* 40, 74.

309 See nn 143–144 and accompanying text.

310 In fact, the direction of travel appears to be in the opposite direction with the UK Listing Review urging index providers to reconsider the exclusion of at least certain standard listed firms from the indices (UK Listing Review at 23–24).

311 Although the EU does not mandate the use of loyalty shares, SRD II encourages long-term shareholder engagement. Early drafts of the SRD II went further by including provisions that would have required Member States to implement mechanisms to promote long-term shareholdings, with loyalty shares specifically referenced as a possible mechanism.

Table 2.1 summarises the approaches to genuine dual-class structure of the twelve largest stock exchanges by way of market capitalisation.[312] It is immediately apparent that no coherent approach to dual-class firms has been adopted amongst the major

TABLE 2.1 *Approaches to dual-class stock on major global exchanges*

No.	Stock Exchange	Dual-Class Stock Approach
1	NYSE	Dual-class firms broadly permitted. Mid-Stream recapitalisations that disenfranchise existing shareholders prohibited.
2	NASDAQ	Dual-class firms broadly permitted. Mid-Stream recapitalisations that disenfranchise existing shareholders prohibited.
3	Tokyo	Dual-class structures permitted, but subject to extensive conditions. Only new issuers.
4	Hong Kong	Dual-class structures permitted, but subject to extensive conditions. Only new issuers.
5	Shanghai	Dual-class structures, but subject to extensive conditions, and only permitted (i) on a separate science and technology listing segment; or (ii) through the Stock Connect Programme that links the exchange with companies listed on the Hong Kong Stock Exchange that can adopt dual-class structure. Only new issuers.
6	Euronext (Eurozone)	Laws of local stock exchange jurisdictions applied.
7	LSE	Dual-class structures prohibited from the premium tier. Dual-class structures permitted on the standard tier, and on the high-growth segment.
8	Shenzhen	Firms listed through the Stock Connect Programme can adopt dual-class structure (see Shanghai earlier). From late 2020, firms listed on the 'tech startup' segment, ChiNext, can adopt dual-class stock.
9	Bombay	Dual-class structures permitted, but subject to extensive conditions. Only new issuers.
10	National Stock Exchange of India	See Bombay earlier.
11	Deutsche Börse	Genuine dual-class structures prohibited. Non-voting stock only permitted through the use of 'preference-style' shares. Any non-voting shares must be entitled to a guaranteed dividend amount in priority to payments on other shares (preference shares are additionally entitled to share in any further distributions to shareholders once the guaranteed sum has been paid to the preference and other shareholders).
12	Toronto	Dual-class structures broadly permitted. All dual-class firm admissions since 1987 must implement coattail provisions (see Chapters 6 and 9).

312 Source: World Federation of Exchanges, 'Annual Statistics Guide 2018' (May 2019).

exchanges, with some prohibiting dual-class firms in totality, others providing a permissive environment and some permitting dual-class firms, but with stringent conditions applied. The rules in each jurisdiction are determined by an assortment of laws pertaining to companies generally and the rules of individual exchanges that apply to companies listed thereon. Many jurisdictions have not commissioned detailed consultations on dual-class firms, with their approaches to dual-class firms being largely determined by competitive pressures and/or the influence of the dominant market players on the relevant exchange. Even though Hong Kong and Singapore did undertake comprehensive consultations on dual-class firms prior to adopting their current policies,[313] they were heavily influenced by a desire to retain international competitiveness, especially in relation to technology company floats, not least between themselves.[314] In relation to the United Kingdom, specifically, a detailed assessment of the merits of dual-class structure is long overdue, and Part II of this book endeavours to commence that process. However, before doing so, in the next chapter, other mechanisms that can create divergences between voting and cash-flow rights will be described. In order to dispel accusations that a dialogue on relaxing the rules on dual-class stock is entirely moot, it will be shown that, from a UK perspective, such mechanisms do not enable founders to reap benefits equivalent to those that could otherwise be garnered through the use of dual-class stock.

[313] In relation to Hong Kong, see HKEX Concept (2014) (n 148 above); HKEX Conclusions (2015) (n 157 above); HKEX Concept (2017) (n 162 above); HKEX Conclusions (2017) (n 167 above). In relation to Singapore, see Ministry of Finance Consultation (2011) (n 184 above); SGX Consultation (2017) (n 188 above); Committee on the Future Economy (2017) (n 189 above); SGX Consultation (2018) (n 192 above).

[314] Chan and Ho (2014) (n 78 above 168). Singapore has been described as Hong Kong's 'arch-rival' and, therefore, Singapore's moves toward relaxing its approach to dual-class stock will have driven Hong Kong's reforms (Ho (2018) (n 146 above 186)).

3

First among Equals?

Other Methods of Creating a Divergence between Voting and Cash-Flow Rights

That's not a choice, it's a lack of options.[1]

3.1 INTRODUCTION

As discussed in Chapter 1, dual-class stock can be used by founders to create a divergence between voting and cash-flow rights. That divergence can enable founders to list their firms, crystallise value and generate significant equity finance for the company while retaining control. However, the same divergence can incentivise a variety of behaviours, some of which may be beneficial, and some of which detrimental, to public shareholders. These benefits and detriments are discussed further in Chapter 6. Before delving into the merits of dual-class stock, and whether a United Kingdom premium tier prohibition of the structure is justified, the very premise that founders require dual-class stock to create the desired divergence should first be challenged. Assuming that retention of control, while divesting of equity, is the key driver for the use of dual-class stock, there are other methods to achieve the same goal that could potentially create a divergence between voting and cash-flow rights – so-called 'control-enhancing mechanisms'. Accordingly, two competing contentions deserve consideration: if other methods are available to attain the de facto position, is there any need to debate the availability of dual-class stock and, if such other methods are permitted, surely a prohibition on dual-class stock is not warranted? However, it will be shown in this chapter that such control-enhancing mechanisms may create environments similar to those created by dual-class stock, but cannot be considered to be equivalent. Dual-class stock fills a gap in the panoply of capital structures available to founders.

[1] Harry Stamper, 'Armageddon' (Touchstone Pictures, 1998).

3.2 BOARD APPOINTMENT RIGHTS

Rather than a founder retaining stock with enhanced-voting rights, a founder could, instead, construct the articles of a UK company to provide that the founder has the exclusive right to nominate a majority of the board. Since, for UK-listed companies, by default, the board is responsible for appointing the management team of the company,[2] the founder could retain effective indirect control over the day-to-day operations of the company with a right to appoint a majority of the board. Alibaba is an example of a Big Tech company that incorporated a similar mechanism when listing on the NYSE – the constitutional documents of the company provide that a group of founders and management has the right to nominate and appoint a majority of the board.[3] A structure such as Alibaba's may, though, pose some challenges for an English-incorporated company. The right of shareholders of English-incorporated companies to remove directors by ordinary resolution, requiring a majority of votes cast, cannot be excluded.[4] As discussed in Chapter 2, unlike Alibaba's structure, the use of class rights attached to different classes of shares can be used to circumvent the rule. In the case of *Bushell* v. *Faith*,[5] the articles specified that the shares held by a director would enjoy three votes per share on any resolution to remove that director from office. The other shareholders proposed a resolution to remove that director from the company, and the Court confirmed the validity of the provision in the articles, such that the other shareholders' votes were not sufficient to pass an ordinary resolution to remove that director when he exercised his enhanced votes at the shareholders' meeting. In many respects, the voting system in *Bushell* v. *Faith* represented a scaled-down dual-class stock structure; rather than a shareholder possessing enhanced-voting rights on all resolutions, the enhanced-voting rights only 'activated' upon a resolution to remove a director. However, Alibaba's nomination rights are not tied to classes of shares and simply give a group of persons the right to nominate a majority of the directors. Director nomination and appointment rights in articles are not uncommon for English-incorporated companies, especially in the private company sphere, but the operation of such a right must be reconciled with rights to remove directors from the board, and, therefore, is not as neat a solution as dual-class stock. For example, shareholders holding a majority of voting rights in the company can always remove any directors nominated by the entitled shareholder by calling a general meeting[6] and passing an ordinary resolution. The

2 See Model PLC Articles, articles 3 and 5. Companies can adopt articles that deviate from the Model PLC Articles, but it would be extraordinary for a listed company to remove the power of the board to select, and delegate management to, the managers of the company.

3 Amendment No. 7 to Form F-1 Registration Statement of Alibaba Holding Limited (15 September 2014) at 238.

4 CA 2006, s. 168.

5 *Bushell* v. *Faith* [1970] AC 1099.

6 Under CA 2006, s. 303, shareholders holding 5 per cent of the paid-up capital as carries the right to vote can require the calling of a general meeting of the shareholders. Members holding 5 per cent of the voting rights (or 100 members with the right to vote who each hold on average £100 of the paid-up capital) can also require a resolution to be moved at the annual general meeting (CA 2006, s. 338).

shareholder with the relevant right could nominate and appoint a new director, or even the same director, immediately after removal pursuant to its rights under the articles, but that director could then be removed in the same way by the other shareholders. The situation would clearly be absurd, and, in practice, it is unlikely that, for a listed company, public shareholders holding a majority of the voting rights would waste time and effort collaborating in such a manner to remove a director who can simply be reappointed immediately after removal. Therefore, director appointment and nomination rights over a majority of the board could, in theory, be used by a founder to attain a position broadly similar to dual-class stock. Additionally, if the company is incorporated outside of England and Wales, the laws of the foreign jurisdiction will apply to director removal rights, in which case, the technical machinations for an English-incorporated company would not apply. Although the right of a shareholder to appoint a majority of the board would be contrary to the UK CGC provision for premium listed companies to constitute a board at least half of which (excluding the chair) comprises independent non-executive directors, a premium listed company can simply explain non-compliance without any regulatory consequences.[7]

However, notwithstanding the theoretical legitimacy, it is unlikely that a company implementing a structure in its constitutional documents giving certain persons the right to appoint a majority of the board would be admitted to a premium tier listing. As discussed in Chapter 2, the underlying purpose of Premium Listing Principle 4 of the Listing Rules that effectively prohibits dual-class stock from the premium tier is 'to prevent artificial structures involving multiple classes with different voting powers, which are designed to allow control to rest with a small group of shareholders'.[8] Clearly, the right to appoint a majority of the board would ingrain control of the company in the holder of that right. By analogy, the Hong Kong Stock Exchange, prior to it modifying its rules to permit dual-class stock, rejected Alibaba's director nomination structure on the basis that it undermined its one share, one vote standard.[9] At one stage, the LSE was attempting to attract Alibaba to the exchange,[10] but the FCA, which was, at the time, formalising its premium tier prohibition of dual-class stock by implementing the Premium Listing Principles,[11] supported the Hong Kong Stock Exchange's stance,[12] and Alibaba listed on the NYSE. Therefore,

7 UK CGC, Provision 11. In relation to the 'comply-or-explain' application of the UK CGC, see Chapter 8.

8 FCA Policy Statement PS14/8, 'Response to CP13/15 – Enhancing the effectiveness of the Listing Regime' (May 2014) at 31.

9 P. Davies, 'LSE Joins Race for $60bn Alibaba Listing' *Financial Times* (22 October 2013) www.ft.com/content/7ef904f6-3b03-11e3-87fa-00144feab7de.

10 *ibid.*

11 See Chapters 1 and 2 for further detail as to how the substance of the Listing Rules' Premium Listing Principles effectively prohibit dual-class listings on the premium tier.

12 E. Yiu, 'British Regulator Backs Hong Kong Stance on Alibaba IPO' *South China Morning Post* (20 March 2014) www.scmp.com/business/money/markets-investing/article/1452681/british-regulator-backs-hong-kong-stance-alibaba.

on the premium tier, it is unlikely that board appointment rights could be used as a substitute for dual-class stock. However, if dual-class stock were to be permitted on the premium tier, clearly any rejection of majority board appointment rights on the basis that they deviate from the principle of one share, one vote would become less justifiable, assuming that any conditions that the FCA were to apply to the use of dual-class stock could be equivalently applied to board appointment rights.

3.3 SHAREHOLDERS' AGREEMENTS

In the private company sphere, shareholders' agreements are common, particularly in private equity, joint venture and venture capital contexts. A shareholders' agreement is a contractual arrangement between shareholders, and often also the company, pursuant to which the parties agree to the grant of specific rights and the incurrence of obligations, bolstered by covenants to exercise votes attached to shares to effectuate those rights and obligations. Minority shareholders can secure rights and protections in shareholders' agreements. A founder, for instance, could preserve the right to appoint directors to the board in a shareholders' agreement, rather than in the constitution of the company, and all the shareholders who are parties to the agreement would be required to vote their shares in the appropriate manner to respect those rights. Even though the right of shareholders under statute to remove directors by ordinary resolution will still apply, if shareholders were to vote to remove the founder's nominee director in a manner contrary to the shareholders' agreement, the founder would have a valid claim against those non-complying shareholders for breach of contract.[13] However, shareholders' agreements between shareholders of a publicly listed company will be unworkable. In the United Kingdom, where most Main Market listed companies display dispersed ownership with potentially tens of thousands of shareholders, self-evidently it would be impractical to ensure that a sufficient number of shareholders enter into the shareholders' agreement to make it effective. Furthermore, unlike the constitutional documents of a company, a shareholders' agreement only binds those shareholders who have executed the agreement. If a shareholder transfers its shares, the transferee will not be automatically bound by the terms of the shareholders' agreement.[14] Although private companies solve this issue by the parties to the shareholders' agreement agreeing that they will not transfer shares unless the proposed transferee has entered into a deed of adherence to the shareholders' agreement, for a listed company, such

[13] By way of analogy, see *Russell* v. *Northern Bank Development Corp. Ltd.* [1992] 1 W. L. R. 588 at 593, where it was discussed that contractual requirements to vote shares in a particular manner could be valid even in the face of a non-waivable right of shareholders to amend the articles of association by way of special resolution. Also see *Greenwell* v. *Porter* [1902] 1 Ch 530; *Puddephatt* v. *Leith* [1916] 1 Ch 200.

[14] For example, see *Greenhalgh* v. *Mallard* [1943] 2 All ER 234.

a requirement would encumber the freely transferable nature of the shares and would not be acceptable to institutional shareholders.

Another, more attainable, option for a listed company would be for an agreement to be entered into between only the shareholder to whom rights are being granted, such as the founder, and the company itself. Although an English-incorporated company cannot bind itself to not amend its articles,[15] it can be contractually bound by an agreement that requires it to act in a particular manner.[16] For example, if the shareholder's agreement between the founder and the company states that the founder may appoint a director to the board, the other shareholders cannot be prevented from amending the articles of the company by way of special resolution[17] to provide that, instead, all directors must be appointed by majority vote, but if the company were to then act upon that amended article and appoint all of its directors by majority shareholder vote, rather than respecting the shareholder's agreement, the founder could potentially make a contractual claim against the company. Companies listed on the LSE have made use of such agreements in the past. For example, in 2016, the activist investor ValueAct secured a board seat at Rolls-Royce constituted by a 'relationship agreement'[18] between the shareholder and the company.[19] Similarly, the founders of ENRC each had the right to appoint one director to the board (for so long as the founder group held 10 per cent of the voting rights in the company), pursuant to a relationship agreement entered into between each of the founders and the company.[20]

However, similar to director appointment rights in the constitution of a company, shareholders' agreements can be employed on a theoretical foundation, but, in practice, they will not be of much utility to a founder seeking to retain control while substantially divesting of its investment. Notably, the founders' rights to appoint directors to the board of ENRC were subject to the board maintaining a majority of independent non-executive directors.[21] In order to retain control, the founder would need to safeguard in the relevant shareholders' agreement the right to appoint a majority of the board. Such a right would clash against the spirit of the Premium Listing Principles of the Listing Rules in the same way as constitutionally implemented board appointment rights. Therefore, a shareholders' agreement between a founder and the company that has the effect of embedding control in the hands of that founder is unlikely to be acceptable to the FCA if such a company were to apply to be admitted to listing on the premium tier.

15 *Russell* v. *Northern Bank Development Corp. Ltd.* (n 13 above at 593).

16 *Southern Foundries (1926) Ltd.* v. *Shirlow* [1940] A.C. 701 at 740–741.

17 CA 2006, s. 21.

18 For more detail on the nature of 'relationship agreements', see Chapter 8.

19 For example, see Rolls-Royce Holdings plc, '2018 Annual Report' (2019) at 74 and 201. ValueAct's board representative relinquished his seat in 2019 (P. Hollinger, 'Rolls-Royce's biggest shareholder ValueAct quits board' *Financial Times* (10 December 2019) www.ft.com/content/d4e45da8-1b25-11ea-9186-7348c2f183af.

20 For example, see Eurasian Natural Resources Corporation plc, '2012 Annual Report and Accounts' (2013) at 63. ENRC subsequently delisted from the LSE in 2013.

21 *ibid* 63.

3.4 PYRAMID STRUCTURES

Another method of embedding control would be to use what is known as a 'pyramid structure'. In its simplest form, the intended controller would hold its interest in the listed company through an interest in a controlled intermediate company. As with dual-class stock, a pyramid structure allows the controller to implement a divergence between voting and cash-flow rights. For example, as shown in Figure 3.1, if the controller owns 51 per cent of a parent company that itself owns 51 per cent of a listed company, in effect, the controller has majority control over the listed company by possessing a majority of the voting rights throughout the chain. However, the controller will have only 26 per cent of the cash-flow rights in the listed company, since it loses 49 per cent of the cash-flow rights at each tier. In mainland Europe[22] and Asia,[23] more complicated pyramid structures are often used encompassing multiple tiers of less than wholly owned controlled entities. By increasing the number of tiers, so long as a majority interest is held at each tier, the proportion of cash-flow rights can be progressively reduced while still maintaining operational control.[24]

Pyramid structures are permissible in the United Kingdom. A founder could hold a controlling interest in a body corporate, which itself could hold a majority

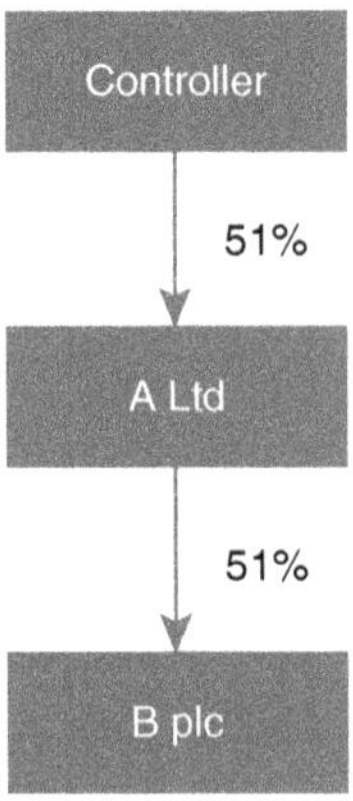

FIGURE 3.1 Basic pyramid structure

[22] J. Franks and C. Mayer, 'Ownership and Control of German Corporations' (2001) 14 *Rev. Financ. Stud.* 943, 948; R. La Porta, F. Lopez-de-Silanes and A. Shleifer, 'Ownership Around the World' (1999) 54 *J. Financ.* 471, 499; M. Faccio and L. Lang, 'The Ultimate Ownership of Western European Corporations' (2002) 65 *J. Financ. Econ.* 365.

[23] S. Claessens et al., 'The Separation of Ownership and Control in East Asian Corporations' (2000) 58 *J. Financ. Econ.* 81, 92; L. Bebchuk et al., 'Stock Pyramids, Cross-Ownership, and Dual Class Equity: The Mechanisms and Agency Costs of Separating Control from Cash-Flow Rights' in *Concentrated Corporate Ownership*, ed. Randall K. Morck (University of Chicago Press, 2000) at 299; La Porta et al. (1999) (n 22 above 499).

[24] For example, see H. Almeida and D. Wolfenzon, 'A Theory of Pyramidal Ownership and Family Business Groups' (2005) *NBER Working Paper Series* No. 11368 1.

interest in a listed company. If such structures are already permitted, is dual-class stock even needed? The prevalence of dual-class structures and pyramids in various jurisdictions has been extensively studied,[25] but the distinction between the two, and how their utilisation by a controller could differ, has not been widely discussed.[26] Evidently, a key condition of an effective pyramid structure is that a majority interest, but less than wholly owned interest, is held in the listed operating company. Therefore, the pyramid could be formed by a founder before or after the listing of the operating entity. However, if formed after the IPO of the listed entity, as the founder transfers interests in the listed operating company, and subsequently new tiers above it, to newly formed tier entities, it will need to be cautious about triggering mandatory offer requirements. The United Kingdom and a number of European jurisdictions require an acquiror of a material interest (30 per cent or more of the total voting rights in the company in the case of the UK Takeover Code[27]) in a listed company to make an offer for the remaining shares in the company.[28] Such requirements could, if applicable, apply to the listed operating entity itself, or any listed entities in the pyramidal chain above it. Even if entities in the chain above the listed operating company are not themselves listed companies, under the United Kingdom's Takeover Code, which applies to most Main Market listed companies, transfers of interest above the listed operating entity could trigger mandatory offer requirements pertaining to the listed operating company through application of the 'chain principle'.[29] The founder would therefore have to tread carefully to ensure that the implementation of the pyramid structure does not trigger requirements to make an offer for the shares of any pyramidal tier entity, or the listed operating company itself. The founder could, instead, hive-down the business of the listed entity to a new corporate body, and then list that new corporate body, but it is likely that the minority shareholders of a listed entity will have to acquiesce to the hive-down, creating further administrative burden and uncertainty.[30] Listing first, and subsequently creating a pyramid, is not a path in relation to which a founder can possess any degree of certainty.

25 For example: La Porta et al. (1999) (n 22 above).

26 The most enlightening study in this regard is Almeida and Wolfenzon (2005) (n 24 above), although even that study was focused on the usage of pyramid structures rather than contrasting them with dual-class stock per se.

27 Takeover Code, Rule 9.

28 See Chapter 8 for more details.

29 Takeover Code, Rule 9.1 Note 8. In a separate context, the chain principle was applied when Disney acquired NASDAQ-listed Twenty-First Century Fox. Twenty-First Century Fox owned more than 30 per cent of the UK-listed Sky, and, therefore, the Takeover Panel ruled that Disney would have to make an offer for the entire issued share capital of Sky (The Takeover Panel, 'Panel Statement 2018/4' (12 April 2018)). Events were superseded, however, by a successful bid for Sky by Comcast.

30 If the upper tier entity is, itself, listed, such a hive-down to an entity initially controlled by the founder would likely be a substantial related-party transaction, which, in many jurisdictions, would require minority shareholder approval (in relation to the United Kingdom, see Chapter 8).

To create a pyramid prior to listing the operating entity, a founder would have to incorporate tiers between itself and the operating business, and attract unaffiliated investors at each tier. This can occur in one or a combination of three ways: intentionally building tiers upwards, intentionally building tiers downwards or the structure organically emerging. Starting with intentionally building tiers upwards, the founder would need to impose a holding company above the operating entity, and sell a minority interest (the closer to just under 50 per cent, the more enhanced the control/cash-flow divergence effect) in that holding vehicle. If the founder desires to reduce his or her cash-flow rights to a nominal level, several tiers with unaffiliated investors would be necessary, requiring the founder to attract unaffiliated minority investors at each level. The ability to attract unaffiliated investors at each tier could also become progressively more difficult, since with each added tier, there will be an increase in the founder's divergence between control and cash-flow rights at the operating company level, with a correspondingly greater incentive on the founder to manage the operating company for his or her own private benefit. With an additional tier being proposed, any potential minority investors will be concerned that the structure is being put in place to assist the founder in extracting ever more private benefits from the listed operating company, leaving even less profits available for distribution up the corporate pyramid. For any tiers above the listed operating company that are private companies (which is likely to be the case in most instances since they will not be operating companies), it is likely that the minority investors will require significant constitutional or contractual protections, which will further make the structure less efficient and more unwieldy for a founder as compared to a simple dual-class stock issuance. Alternatively, tiers could be built downwards. This would involve the founder first selling a minority interest (again, preferably just below 50 per cent to enhance the control/cash-flow divergence effect) in the operating entity. The founder would then hive-down the business of the operating entity (or perhaps even just a partial hive-down if the entity encompasses numerous standalone businesses) to a new corporate body. Critically, though, the initial investors may have negotiated veto rights over such a hive-down, since hiving-down the business and listing it, rather than just listing the business outright, prejudices the ability of those initial investors to exit the business completely – only a minority proportion of the shares of the hive-down entity owned by the parent would be sold at IPO, and those initial investors would not have liquidity of their shares in the parent entity (which remains unlisted) after the IPO of the hive-down entity. In the United Kingdom, IPOs represent an avenue for exit by non-management shareholders, and, in most cases (excepting controllers who desire to remain in control post-IPO), non-management shareholders dispose of substantially all of their shareholdings in the company relatively soon after IPO.[31] Furthermore, to

[31] M. Brennan and J. Franks, 'Underpricing, Ownership and Control in Initial Public Offerings of Equity Securities in the UK' (1997) 45 *J. Financ. Econ.* 391, 408.

create a substantial divergence between control and cash-flow rights, further hive-downs of the business would be required with unaffiliated investors having to be attracted at each tier (with, as the number of tiers increases, the same potential struggles to attract such investors as when building upwards). Whether building upwards or downwards, clearly the process is extremely cumbersome and expensive, and it does not entail the same levels of certainty that can be accrued through the use of dual-class stock.

Given the inefficiencies in using a pyramid structure to intentionally create a control/cash-flow divergence, other reasons usually exist for the emergence of a pyramid structure over and beyond engineering such a divergence.[32] More likely, a pyramid structure will have developed organically. Almeida and Wolfenzon (2005) show that pyramid structures are not necessarily implemented in order to construct a control/cash-flow divergence,[33] and, in fact, in jurisdictions where dual-class stock is permitted, pyramid structures are more common. Furthermore, even where there were restrictions on the degree of control/cash-flow divergence that can be incorporated through dual-class structure, the pyramid structures in general did not create divergences beyond those possible with dual-class stock. Therefore, the authors contend that pyramids are used for reasons beyond creating control/cash-flow divergences, since the relevant divergence could more easily be created using dual-class stock.[34] It appears that pyramids often appear in jurisdictions with poor investor protection regulations.[35] In such jurisdictions, the cost of capital in the public markets is high (due to the fear of public investors of being expropriated),[36] so it is more financially advantageous to finance new businesses using internal resources from an existing business. At a later time, the controller may sell-off part of an upper tier's interest in a lower tier entity, either to a single outside investor or discrete group of private investors, or through publicly listing the entity (by that stage, the business may be sufficiently established that public investors see the risk of expropriation being less, or the listing may occur in a different jurisdiction where minority investor rights are stronger, in each case reducing the cost of outside equity financing). Additionally, any such subsequent sell-off may be to other entities in which the original controller itself has an interest. In this way, a mature, sprawling group of entities can form. Pyramid structures can commonly occur where certain investors have diverse interests in numerous businesses, leading to ultimate control through pyramid structures being held by those investors rather than

32 Almeida and Wolfenzon (2005) (n 24 above).

33 *ibid* 13.

34 Also see M. Bennedsen and K. Nielsen, 'The Principle of Proportional Ownership, Investor Protection and Firm Value in Western Europe' (2006) *ECGI Working Paper No. 134/2006* 1, 23: '… dual class shares are frequently implemented in firms through IPOs or during successions in family firms, whereas a pyramidal structure often is the result of firm acquisitions'.

35 *ibid* 18.

36 See Section 8.3 of Chapter 8.

a founder per se – a clear example noted in the late 1990s is Daimler-Benz in Germany.[37] In the United Kingdom, it is likely that a structure that entails the listing of a lower tier entity with a pyramidally implemented control/cash-flow divergence will have formed naturally over time, rather than with a specific view to creating that divergence in the UK listed company.

Although academic studies have often grouped pyramid structures with dual-class stock as mechanisms to create a control/cash-flow divergence, as discussed, from a practical perspective, it is difficult to foresee scenarios where a pyramid structure would be implemented to specifically create such a divergence in a listed company. The divergence is a consequence of the implementation of a pyramid structure, but, practically, the pyramid structure would more likely have developed for other reasons. Pyramids are not currently an adequate substitute for dual-class stock in the United Kingdom.

3.5 CROSS-OWNERSHIPS

Cross-ownership is a type of corporate structure where companies own circular interests in each other, which could enable the disposal of a disproportionate level of cash-flow rights by a founder while maintaining control.[38] The concept of cross-ownership does, though, present some obstacles from an English law perspective. In the United Kingdom, under s. 136 of CA 2006, a 'body corporate' cannot be a member of a company that is its 'holding company'. Taking the simple example of two companies with ownership interests in each other, if they are both English-incorporated companies, the validity of the structure lies in whether one company is considered to be a 'subsidiary' of its 'holding company'. Under CA 2006, a company will be a 'subsidiary' of a 'holding company' if that second company holds (or controls pursuant to an agreement with other members) a majority of the voting rights in the first company, or has the right to appoint or remove a majority of the board of the first company.[39] Therefore, although the question is not free of doubt, absent other agreements or rights, it is likely that a company will not be a holding company of the other if it holds less than a majority of the votes in the other company. Accordingly, as long as a founder together with external shareholders, for example, holds a majority of the votes in the two companies, in the model described, neither company will be a holding company of the other, and the cross-ownership should be permitted in the United Kingdom. More complicated cross-ownership groups could be structured in this way to avoid a breach of s. 136, and, potentially, s. 136 could also be avoided by using overseas holding entities, since the use of the word 'company' under this section presumably indicates the intention of

37 Franks and Mayer (2001) (n 22 above 949); La Porta et al. (1999) (n 22 above 487).

38 M. Levy and A. Szafarz, 'Cross Ownership: A Device for Management Entrenchment' (2017) 21 *Rev. Financ.* 1675.

39 CA 2006, s. 1159(1)(c).

the framers that the holding entity must be a company formed and registered under CA 2006.[40] Therefore, although the position is not free of doubt, technically, a cross-ownership structure could also be created where an English-incorporated company is a subsidiary of a holding entity incorporated in a foreign jurisdiction, and itself holds an interest in that foreign entity (even if that foreign entity holds a majority of the votes in the subsidiary), assuming that it is permitted under the laws of the foreign jurisdiction.[41]

Bebchuk et al. (2000) presented a simple cross-ownership structure that can be used to ingrain control while divesting of a disproportionate level of equity.[42] Adapting to the listed company controller models discussed in this book, the structure would involve a controller initially majority-owning two companies – company A and company B. Company A would, in turn, own a minority interest in company B, and company B would own a similar cross-ownership minority interest in company A. At this stage, the controller has direct majority interests in companies A and B, and can, therefore, appoint friendly boards to both companies. Having appointed those boards, the controller can then cede direct majority control in both companies A and B and still retain control of those companies. One or both of companies A and B may be listed. If the controller's direct interest in company A, when aggregated with the cross-holding that company B owns in company A is greater than 50 per cent, the board of company A will be entrenched.[43] The same logic applies for company B. Figure 3.2 shows a hypothetical structure with the controller holding direct interests in companies A and B of 35 per cent, and

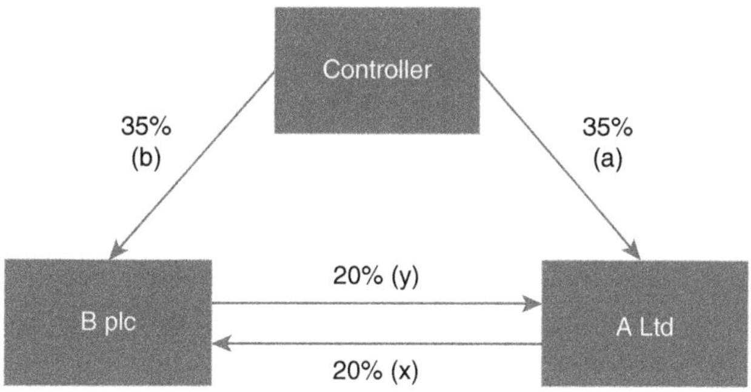

FIGURE 3.2 Basic cross-ownership structure

40 CA 2006, s. 1.

41 KPMG Insights, 'Can UK companies hold shares in their overseas parent companies?' (14 September 2016) at 3. The article points out, though, that if the UK subsidiary owns enough shares in its overseas holding entity to itself become the holding company of that entity, then CA 2006, s. 136 could be breached.

42 Bebchuk et al. (2000) (n 23 above 300).

43 Bebchuk et al. (2000) (n 23 above 300).

companies A and B holding cross-ownership interests of 20 per cent in each other. Let's assume company B in Figure 3.2 is listed and company A unlisted. If the public shareholders in company B wish to change the board, they will require the support of company A's votes in company B, which are controlled by the board of company A, which is friendly to the controller. Equally, a proposal by the external shareholders in company A to change the board of that company will require the support of company B's votes in company A, which are also controlled by a controller-friendly board. That circularity entrenches the boards of both companies A and B.

In terms of cash-flow rights, the overall picture is complicated. Take the example in Figure 3.2, and consider the controller's cash-flow interest in the listed company B plc. Clearly, the controller holds a 35 per cent direct cash-flow interest in company B. Through the controller's 35 per cent ownership of company A, the controller also owns an indirect cash-flow interest of 7 per cent (35% × 20%) in company B. Company B, though, also essentially holds an interest in its own cash-flow of 20 per cent of the 20 per cent interest in company B's cash-flow owned by company A; the controller also owns 35 per cent of that interest. The calculation soon becomes circular, since company A also owns an interest in the interest that company B owns in the interest that company A has in company B. For the 'simple' type of cross-ownership structure in Figure 3.2, Almeida et al. (2008)[44] adapted formulae developed by Brioschi et al. (1989)[45] and Flath (1992)[46] to determine the cash rights ('c') of the controller in B plc as (with letters in the formula corresponding to the same letters used in Figure 3.2):

$$c = \frac{b}{1 - xy} + \frac{ax}{1 - xy}$$

Therefore, under the arrangement set out in Figure 3.2 and applying the formula, the controller has 43.75 per cent of the cash-flow rights in the listed company B plc, but the board is effectively entrenched. The cross-ownership creates a divergence between control and cash-flow rights.[47] However, as an author, one feels the need to apologise for the tortuous narrative of cross-ownership. Likewise, the practicalities for a founder in implementing such a structure are similarly tortuous, with potentially the costs outweighing the benefits, since, as calculated for the Figure 3.2 example, the founder would still own a significant proportion of the cash-flow rights (albeit a minority). The extent to which a divergence can be created is somewhat

44 H. Almeida et al., 'Beyond Cash Flow and Voting Rights: Valuation and Performance of Firms in Complex Ownership Structures' (2008) 1, 9 https://ssrn.com/abstract=1101865.

45 R. Brioschi, L. Buzzacchi and M. Colombo, 'Risk Financing and the Separation of Ownership and Control in Business Groups' (1989) 13 *J. Bank Financ.* 747.

46 D. Flath, 'Indirect Shareholding within Japan's Business Groups' (1992) 38 *Econ. Lett.* 223.

47 G. Ferrarini, 'Corporate Ownership and Control Law Reform and the Contestability of Corporate Control' presented at: Company Law Reform in OECD Countries: A Comparative Outlook of Current Trends (Stockholm, 2000) www.oecd.org/corporate/ca/corporategovernanceprinciples/1931676.pdf.

limited by the fact that the aggregate of the ownership interest in company B of company A and of the controller must be more than 50 per cent to entrench the board of company B, which, in the case of the simple cross-ownership structure as represented in Figure 3.2, limits the extent to which cash-flow rights can be reduced. As described by studies,[48] and further elucidated by a number of mathematical models,[49] the cash-flow rights could be further reduced, without the founder ceding control of listed company B plc, by introducing further entities into the group structure, and by combining a pyramid structure with numerous cross-holdings. However, given the complexities of the simple structure outlined earlier (together with the complexities in developing pyramid structures as already described), and the need to attract external shareholders to invest in multiple companies, it would take a specific type of masochism for a founder to choose cross-ownership structures specifically to create a sufficiently large control/cash-flow divergence. As with pyramids, cross-ownerships that are effective are likely to develop organically across much larger, complicated group structures, usually also involving pyramids. Cross-ownerships are especially common in Asia,[50] and, to an extent, also in mainland Europe.[51] Allianz has been cited as an example of a complex cross-ownership structure in Germany, where the company has become insulated from outside control.[52] Often the cross-ownership is implemented for reasons other than developing a control/cash-flow divergence, or the cross-ownership is interposed into an already complex ownership pattern. In the case of Allianz, it appears that the structure developed over time through numerous acquisitions, expansions and restructurings, leading to the effective entrenchment of the management team,[53] long after the founder had departed, rather than as an attempt by a founder to divest of investment while retaining control. Cross-ownership is a particularly treacherous form of splitting cash-flow and control rights, since the complexity of the structure can obscure any assessment by the public shareholders of the extent of that divergence, and, in the worst cases, makes the identification of the ultimate controller or

[48] Bebchuk et al. (2000) (n 23 above 300); OECD Steering Group on Corporate Governance, 'Lack of Proportionality between Ownership and Control: Overview and Issues for Discussion' (December 2007) at 13.

[49] For example, Almeida et al. (2008) (n 44 above 9); Brioschi et al. (1989) (n 45 above); Flath (1992) (n 46 above); Levy and Szafarz (2017) (n 38 above 1675); K. Ritzberger and J. Shorish, 'Cross-Ownership among Firms: Some Determinants of the Separation of Ownership from Control' (2001) *IHS Economics Series Working Paper* 113 1.

[50] Claessens et al. (2000) (n 23 above 92); Bebchuk et al. (2000) (n 23 above 300); La Porta et al. (1999) (n 22 above 499); Levy and Szafarz (2017) (n 38 above 1676).

[51] Franks and Mayer (2001) (n 22 above 952); La Porta et al. (1999) (n 22 above 499); Levy and Szafarz (2017) (n 38 above 1676).

[52] La Porta et al. (1999) (n 22 above 486); Levy and Szafarz (2017) (n 38 above 1687); Institutional Shareholder Services, Shearman and Sterling LLP and European Corporate Governance Institute, 'Report on the Proportionality Principle in the European Union, as commissioned by the European Commission' (2016) 1, 101.

[53] Levy and Szafarz (2017) (n 38 above 1689).

controllers rather opaque,[54] which, in some cases, may well be the reason for implementing the structure in the first place.

Another wrinkle is that it is unlikely that a simple cross-ownership structure such as that set out in Figure 3.2 would be admitted to a premium listing by the FCA. Although it would not entail any express breach of the Premium Listing Principles, clearly the structure does not adhere to the spirit of the principles in that it effectively creates a control/cash-flow divergence; a simple structure as per the example would have obviously been developed to create such a divergence. In any case, as discussed, a founder is unlikely to derive significant benefit from a simple cross-ownership structure since the divergence between control and cash-flow rights is minimal. If a more complicated cross-ownership/pyramid structure has developed organically, the FCA may be more accommodating to the listing of a group entity, notwithstanding the possibility of a control/cash-flow divergence, but such a structure is, as discussed, likely to have developed over time for numerous reasons, not specifically related to the manufacture of such a divergence in favour of a founder. Rather than complicated cross-ownership patterns being associated with the presence of a controlling shareholder with a disproportionate level of control as compared to cash-flow rights, they are more commonly associated with management teams being insulated from *all* their shareholders. Complicated cross-ownership patterns will likely only develop at a mature stage of a company's life-cycle subsequent to numerous acquisitions and expansions, by which stage the principal reason for an IPO of a group entity will not be to crystallise a founder's investment while it retains control. Therefore, in the United Kingdom, it is unlikely that cross-ownership would be used by a founder of a growing tech company to create a control/cash-flow divergence, and it is certainly not a substitute for dual-class stock.[55]

3.6 DERIVATIVE INSTRUMENTS

Another relevant theme that is not well-studied pertains to the nubilous world of derivatives. A plethora of derivative instruments exist in the equity markets that may have the effect of separating voting and cash-flow rights. The sheer variety of instruments can be mind-boggling, but some categorised general forms can be described. Stock lending or borrowing, for instance, in simplified form, usually entails a stock lender transferring stock to a borrower for a fee, with the borrower

[54] See the description of Korean *chaebols* in Alemida et al. (2008) (n 44 above 3), where the cross-ownership structures are difficult to analyse in spite of mandatory ownership information disclosure requirements. Also see Bebchuk et al. (2000) (n 23 above 300). In relation to Germany, often cross-ownership structures are disguised since proponents can take advantage of flying under the radar of relevant disclosure thresholds (Franks and Mayer (2001) (n 22 above 952)).

[55] Although UK sample sizes were small, a number of studies have suggested that cross-ownership structures are not prevalent in the United Kingdom – La Porta et al. (1999) (n 22 above 499); OECD (2007) (n 48 above 21); Institutional Shareholder Services et al. (2016) (n 52 above 34).

then selling the shares in the market with a view to acquiring the same number of shares in the market at the term of the arrangement when the shares must be returned to the lender. In effect, the borrower is banking on share price declining during the term of the arrangement – a comportment known as 'shorting'. Stock borrowing is a beloved strategy of the hedge fund industry; where a hedge fund already holds shares in a company, it can hedge some of its economic risk on those shares by concurrently shorting the company through stock borrowing.[56] Essentially, the hedge fund's economic interest in the company is no longer proportionate to its voting interest.

Similarly, with an equity swap, parties to the instrument 'swap' different cash-flows. One of the parties (the 'long' party) may become entitled to the returns attached to specific shares over the term of the instrument (or, more likely, payments tied to the extent to which those shares outperform an index) with the other party entitled to a different cash-flow, pegged to, for example, a floating interest rate (the 'short' party).[57] The short party may hedge some of its exposure to the shares by itself acquiring shares in the relevant company, in which case, a dissociation develops between that party's voting interest in, and financial exposure to, the company. Hu and Black (2006) called the dissociations created through stock borrowing and equity swaps 'empty voting', and noted, in a takeover context, how a voting shareholder with zero economic interest (100 per cent hedged) in an acquiror could use voting rights to encourage that acquiror to overpay for shares of a target in which the shareholder has an economic interest.[58]

A further strategy is that of the 'collar', which comprises put and call options.[59] Under the put option, a shareholder would have the right, in return for a fee, to sell its shares to a counterparty at a specific price within the term of the option. The shareholder is therefore able to put a limit on any loss resulting from a decline of share price during the term. Under the call option, a counterparty will have the right to acquire shares from the shareholder, in return for paying a fee to the shareholder, at a specific price after the same term as the put option. The shareholder therefore earns a regular income from the call option, but its potential profit from the shares increasing in value during the term is limited. Combining the put and call options, the shareholder is able to put a collar around its potential economic loss and gain from the shares, thereby effectively creating a divergence between the voting rights held by the shareholder and its economic exposure. It is acknowledged that derivative instruments, including stock borrowing instruments, equity swaps and collars, can serve a useful purpose in the market – they allow investors to hedge risk, increase

56 H. Hu and B. Black, 'The New Vote Buying: Empty Voting and Hidden (Morphable) Ownership' (2006) 79 *S. Cal. L. Rev.* 811, 815.

57 Hu and Black (2006) (n 56 above 816). Also see A. Khachaturyan, 'Trapped in Delusions: Democracy, Fairness and the One-Share-One-Vote Rule in the European Union' (2007) 8 *EBOR* 335, 353.

58 Hu and Black (2006) (n 56 above 816).

59 Khachaturyan (2007) (n 57 above 354); H. Hu and B. Black, 'Empty Voting and Hidden (Morphable) Ownership: Taxonomy, Implications, and Reforms' (2006) 61 *Bus. Law* 1011, 1026.

liquidity and allow arbitrage activity which smooths out mispricing in the market[60] – and it seems that such instruments are consistently utilised by management insiders, and, to a greater extent, institutional shareholders.[61] It seems perverse that institutional investors regularly deride the use of dual-class structures by controllers, yet are content to create divergences between their own voting and cash-flow rights.[62]

Reverting to founders, can such derivative instruments be used by founders to create an effective divergence between voting and cash-flow rights? The ability of founders to amass control while shorting their own companies through stock borrowing, although theoretically possible, would be infeasible in practice. From a commercial perspective, it would stretch credulity to surmise that a sophisticated investor would entertain acting as a willing counterparty to such a rigged transaction; the counterparty would know that the founder has control over the prospects of the company and is putting himself or herself in a position where he or she could proactively destroy share value. Unlike dual-class stock, where the founder's wealth is largely insulated from share price declines, with stock borrowing, the founder can positively profit from declines in share price during the term of the instrument. Questions of market abuse, breach of directors' duties and fraud would also be applicable. In any case, the founder will struggle to borrow sufficient shares to meaningfully hedge against its controlling interest in the company, and the founder would only be hedging against share price declines during a finite term, and not crystallising its investment in the company (which, as discussed in Chapter 1, is one of the presumed aims of founders in utilising dual-class structure). With an equity swap, again, it would be challenging for a controlling founder to enter into sufficient instruments to meaningfully impact its financial exposure to the company, and, in any case, any such instruments would only be effective for their terms. Equity swaps also do not permit a founder to crystallise wealth in the company; other than giving the founder a revenue stream in the event that share price declines, an equity swap is of little value to a founder in the context of the founder-driven reasons for utilising dual-class stock (namely divesting of investment in, and growing, the company while retaining control). Critically, with both stock borrowing and equity swaps, if the price of the relevant shares were to increase, the founder's share of that price increment (through its controlling interest in the company) will be moderated by having to satisfy its obligations under the relevant instruments, which, if it does not have sufficient resources, may require a transfer, in the case of stock borrowing, or

60 K. Sill, 'The Economic Benefits and Risks of Derivative Securities' (1997) *Bus. Rev.* (January/February 1997) 15, 18.

61 Institutional Shareholder Services et al. (2016) (n 52 above 13). It should also be noted that when hedge funds utilise derivative instruments, institutions will be the natural counterparties.

62 R. Adams and D. Ferreira, 'One Share-One Vote: The Empirical Evidence' (2008) 12 *Rev. Finance* 51, 72. The authors also attest that even the simple situation where an institutional investor (such as a pension or investment fund) invests funds on behalf of clients is an example of a divergence between voting and cash-flow rights, since the trustee of the fund exercises the voting rights, while the cash-flow rights accrue to the underlying beneficiaries.

a sale, in the case of an equity swap, of its shares in the company, reducing its voting interest. Additionally, once information is publicly disclosed that the founder, who controls the company and whose optimism as to the future success of the company will be carefully tracked by the market, is proactively hedging its economic interest in the company, through stock borrowing or equity swaps, it would surely cause a commensurate change to the market price of the shares. Such transactions would have to be disclosed since a loophole in the FCA's DTRs that previously only required changes in voting interests, or rights to acquire or requirements to dispose of votes, to be disclosed was closed in 2009; now the disclosure of derivative instruments with similar economic effects is also required.[63] Even before entering into the transaction, the controller would also have to consider whether it would be falling foul of prohibitions on creating a false market in shares or other market abuse.[64] In relation to collars, the practice is widespread amongst US management teams.[65] Collars can serve a useful purpose in allowing management to diversify their wealth without eliminating all economic exposure to the prospects of their firm.[66] One could speculate that it could also give controllers the ability to diversify in the same manner, akin to what they would be able to effect through dual-class structure. However, put and call options operate by necessarily requiring, unless the price of the shares remain within the collared price created by the interaction of the two options, the controller to sell its shares to the counterparty. The controller would, therefore, lose votes if share price strayed outside of the collar and, potentially, control of the firm. As such, collars do not serve the same purpose as dual-class stock.

Therefore, it is wholly unlikely that a founder would be able to create benefits equivalent to those generated by dual-class stock through the use of traditional derivative instruments. In any event, to the extent that derivatives are used to create a voting/cash-flow divergence, although the market, to a degree, will be able to assess movements in interests through the use of such derivatives, like post-IPO recapitalisations from one share, one vote to dual-class structure, these would be mid-stream changes, and, therefore, do not give the investors the opportunity to evaluate risk and the holistic consequences of the disconnect within the framework of the type of firm and controller at the time of investment.[67] Therefore, a good argument could also be

[63] DTR 5.3.1(b)R (also see FSMA 2000, s. 89F, and FCA, 'Indicative list of financial instruments that are subject to notification requirements by virtue of section 89F(1)(b)(iii) of Financial Services and Markets Act 2000 (FSMA) and according to DTR 5.3.1R' (1 January 2021)). The DTRs were tightened even further with respect to disclosures by borrowers and lenders of stock lending transactions in 2015 to incorporate aspects of the EU's Transparency Directive Amending Directive. Extensive disclosures are also required in relation to short-selling pursuant to the EU's Short-Selling Regulations (which, after the United Kingdom left the EU, became part of UK domestic law pursuant to the European Union (Withdrawal) Act 2018 c. 16).

[64] For example, under MAR, article 12; Premium Listing Principle 6, LR 7.2.1AR.

[65] J. Bettis et al., 'Managerial Ownership, Incentive Contracting, and the Use of Zero-Cost Collars and Equity Swaps by Corporate Insiders' (2001) 36 *J. Financ. Quant. Anal* 347, 354.

[66] Hu and Black (2006) (n 59 above 1026).

[67] The analogy to dual-class recapitalisations was noted by Hu and Black (2006) (n 59 above 1027).

made that dual-class stock is, in fact, less egregious than the use of derivative instruments, given that dual-class structures are more transparent and allow investors to 'know what they are getting into'.[68]

3.7 PREFERENCE SHARES

Preference shares award the holders of such shares preferential dividend rights and/or preferences in distributions upon returns of capital or a winding up of the company. Usually, there will be no further right of preference shareholders to share in distributions beyond their fixed preferences. Most commonly, the preference shareholders will receive a fixed dividend, to the extent that profits are available for distribution and a dividend is declared by the company, in priority to distributions made to the holders of ordinary shares, and the preference shares will not carry any voting rights (until, in some cases, preferential dividends have remained unpaid for a certain period of time). As with dual-class stock, since only 'equity shares' are permitted on the premium tier, preference shares with only fixed returns on dividend or capital (with no further right to share in surplus) are prohibited from the premium tier.[69] Theoretically, non-voting preference shares could, though, allow a controller to raise finance while maintaining control. Indeed, in the late-nineteenth and early-twentieth centuries, William Lever built Lever Brothers into one of the largest companies in the world by generating finance through the issuance of non-voting preference shares while retaining control.[70]

However, the dynamics of preference share structure are different from pure dual-class stock. It is not credible that a founder would be able to divest of significant wealth in the company by converting a proportion of its shares into preference shares, and selling them on the market – investors will be paying for an income stream rather than equity capital in the company, and the price that investors would be willing to pay for such shares will additionally be determined by the number of preference shares being issued; if too many preferences shares are issued, investors will begin to doubt the ability of the company to pay the relevant fixed distributions on a regular basis. Significantly, if the company is a pre-profit company at IPO, as is the case with many high-growth tech companies that have recently listed in the United States,[71] investors will be even more sceptical that the preference shares will

[68] Hu and Black (2006) (n 56 above 858).

[69] Under the Listing Rules, 'equity share capital' is defined to be 'issued share capital excluding any part of that capital which, neither as respects dividends nor as respects capital, carries any right to participate beyond a specified amount in a distribution'.

[70] B. Cheffins, *Corporate Ownership and Control: British Business Transformed* (Oxford University Press, 2008) at 71 and 178. In 1929, the listed behemoth, Unilever, was formed through a merger between Lever Brothers and the Dutch company, Margarine Unie.

[71] In 2016, 68 per cent of US IPOs involved pre-profit companies, rising to 75 per cent and 92 per cent of technology and biotechnology listings, respectively (HKEX, 'Concept Paper: New Board' (June 2017) at 15).

have any value until many years have passed. Additionally, if the preference share terms provide that preferential distributions must be made whenever profits are available for the purpose[72] (and, to the extent that profits are not available, are cumulative, meaning that the sum outstanding is carried over to future years), which may give investors greater confidence to invest in preference shares, a sizeable issuance of preference shares could place a significant burden on the business by requiring it to service the preferential distributions from profits, potentially constraining the actions of the controller in a similar manner to debt financing. Therefore, from a practical perspective, it becomes unfeasible for a founder to divest of significant wealth through the use of preference shares. Preference shares are a different beast to regular dual-class stock, and although they could be utilised by a firm to generate finance for the company without the controller of that firm losing control, they do not represent a suitable method of creating the voting/cash-flow divergence desired through the use of dual-class stock.

3.8 LOYALTY SHARES

'Loyalty shares', or 'tenured voting shares', award greater voting rights to those shareholders who have held shares for a specified period of time. Any voting rights so awarded would only attach to the shares to the extent that they are still held by the shareholder who initially received those shares at the commencement of the relevant period of time, and such voting rights would revert to one share, one vote upon a transfer of those shares by such shareholder. While those enhanced-voting rights are activated, certain long-term shareholders will hold shares with equity rights equivalent to all other ordinary one share, one vote shares that have been issued, but will hold greater voting rights than those ordinary shareholders; as such, it is obvious that loyalty shares are a sub-category of dual-class stock. Therefore, even if loyalty shares could be used to create a voting/cash-flow divergence, it would not be an option open to a founder seeking a premium tier listing for its company, since such shares would be subject to the same prohibition on dual-class stock.

Listed companies with loyalty shares are common in France, and, as outlined in Chapter 2, recently a number of European jurisdictions, including Italy, Spain and Belgium, have either relaxed or are in the process of relaxing their rules to permit the listing of loyalty share structures. In the United States, companies have been known to voluntarily adopt similar 'tenured voting' or 'time-phased voting' mechanisms, although the practice is not widespread.[73] Currently, issuers on the NYSE are

[72] CA 2006, s. 830 – distributable profits must be available to make a distribution.

[73] D. Berger et al., 'Tenure Voting and the U.S. Public Company' (2016) *Berkeley Center for Law, Business and the Economy and Wilson Sonsini Goodrich & Rosati* 1, 16 www.wsgr.com/publications/PDFSearch/tenure-voting.pdf. It has been suggested that a number of US companies that adopted tenure voting systems in the United States did so to protect management against hostile takeovers during a period of uncertainty as to the validity of mid-stream recapitalisations into straight dual-class

permitted to undergo IPOs with time-phased voting right systems but cannot adopt such plans mid-stream where the effect would be to disparately reduce or restrict the voting rights of any existing public shareholders.[74] The principal intention behind the concept of loyalty shares is to ensure that voting control is in the hands of long-term shareholders with, presumably, the long-term interests of the company at heart.[75] Transitory shareholders, and those with more short-term inclinations, such as activist hedge funds, would be less able to exert influence. Over time, enhanced-voting shares could become concentrated in the original controller or founder of the firm, giving those shareholders holding shares over a long-term horizon the opportunity to create a voting/cash-flow divergence, since, after their shares receive the enhanced-voting rights, they will be able to maintain control with a lower proportion of the equity than previously. Accordingly, some commentators have described loyalty shares as another form of entrenchment mechanism.[76] However, even if loyalty shares were permitted on the premium tier as a softer exception[77] to the general rule against dual-class stock, it is unlikely that they would be considered by founders to be an adequate substitution for regular dual-class stock. A founder wishing to preserve control would need to retain over 50 per cent of the shares at IPO, since enhanced-voting rights will not attach to that founder's shares until the specified loyalty period has expired post-IPO, and the loyalty share structure would be an extremely slow method for a founder to divest of equity while preserving control. In Europe, the loyalty period is commonly required to be at least two years. Upon receiving enhanced-voting rights, the founder would be able to divest of further equity (or generate further equity financing) without losing control, even if the founder's total equity falls below 50 per cent, but the extent to which divestment and/or equity financing can ensue without losing control will be limited by the fact that other shareholders who have retained their shares post-IPO will also receive enhanced-voting rights. Furthermore, the increase in voting rights after the loyalty period will also be restricted, with European regulations usually limiting loyalty shares to a maximum of two or three times the votes of other shares. Therefore, not only will the maximum extent of voting/cash-flow divergence be restricted but also that maximum will only be achieved after all other non-founder shareholders have transferred their shares, and therefore lost loyalty privileges, post-IPO. In the context of attracting tech listings to the premium tier, it is unlikely that the availability of loyalty share structures would move the needle significantly.

stock (L. Dallas and J. Barry, 'Long-Term Shareholders and Time-Phased Voting' (2016) 40 *DJCL* 541, 595; A. Pacces, 'Exit, Voice and Loyalty from the Perspective of Hedge Funds Activism in Corporate Governance' (2016) 4 *ELR* 199, 214). Chapter 2 discusses the development of the United States' approach to dual-class stock.

74 NYSE Listed Company Manual, §313.00.

75 Berger et al. (2016) (n 73 above 20); Dallas and Barry (2016) (n 73 above 570).

76 Pacces (2016) (n 73 above 214).

77 Although, the description of loyalty shares as a softer form of dual-class structure can be challenged (see the text accompanying n 78 below).

If the premium tier lifted its prohibition on dual-class stock in an unrestricted manner, loyalty share structures, as a sub-category of dual-class stock, would be permitted. However, scrutinising the merits of loyalty shares evinces a variety of considerations that are not applicable to classic dual-class structures which are implemented at the time of IPO. Although loyalty shares are sometimes discussed as a softer form of dual-class stock[78] (since in relation to the right to receive enhanced-voting rights, all shareholders are treated equally and loyalty shares do not specifically grant enhanced-voting rights to the controller of a firm), in fact, loyalty shares can be more testing to assess for public shareholders. With loyalty share structures, unlike with classic dual-class stock implemented at IPO, it would not be unequivocally clear, upon IPO, as to where voting control will lie down the line after shareholders receive enhanced-voting rights, since it cannot be determined with certainty as to who will hold shares sufficiently long enough to receive those rights. With the identity of the future controller not perfectly known, it makes it difficult for the market to 'price-in' the risks and rewards of the structure. Complications for public shareholders in assessing firms on a case-by-case basis will be exacerbated if loyalty share mechanisms can be implemented post-IPO (especially if the controller possesses sufficient voting power to do so unilaterally) – at IPO, a potential investor will not be able to ascertain whether the relevant company will be subject to a loyalty share mechanism in the future that could shift the control and power dynamics within the company (a criticism that was made against proposed loyalty share regulations in Spain[79]). As will be discussed in Chapter 6, many of the arguments in favour of dual-class stock revolve around control being in the hands of specific individuals; if investors are not able to ascertain who those individuals are at the time of investment, the ability of an investor to determine whether the structure is net-beneficial is curtailed. Loyalty share mechanisms can also be practically challenging to implement, since it can be difficult to track the beneficial ownership of shares – if the beneficial ownership of shares is being regularly transferred in the background, awarding loyalty voting rights to a long-term legal owner of the shares could undermine the intended benefits of the loyalty share programme, especially if the legal owner is required to vote in accordance with the instructions of the beneficial owner from time to time.[80] Therefore, loyalty shares that create enhanced-voting stock post-IPO are not the principal focus of this book.[81] Loyalty share structures will not promote further premium tier listings to any substantive degree, and their adoption can, in some ways, be more perilous for public shareholders. In a departure

[78] Dallas and Barry (2016) (n 73 above 577).

[79] A. Martínez, 'Un análisis crítico sobre la posibilidad de permitir las acciones de lealtad en las sociedades cotizadas españolas' (2019) *Instituto Iberoamericano de Derecho y Finanzas Working Paper Series 4/2019* 1, 12.

[80] Berger et al. (2016) (n 73 above 24).

[81] Similarly, mid-stream post-IPO recapitalisations of one share, one vote shares into dual-class stock (as opposed to implementation of dual-class stock as of IPO) are also not advocated in this book (see Section 9.8.3 of Chapter 9).

from the approach of many other European jurisdictions, if the FCA were to open up the premium tier to dual-class stock, as revisited in Chapter 9, a strong argument exists to continue to restrict the use of loyalty shares and other structures where existing shares are directly or indirectly disenfranchised post-IPO.

3.9 CONCLUSION

The discussion on alternative control-enhancing mechanisms suggests two points. Firstly, with a view to creating a control/cash-flow divergence, dual-class stock presents various advantages over other control-enhancing mechanisms, and, at least for premium listed companies, certain of those other mechanisms arguably would not be permitted. For example, preference shares (which are, in any case, currently excluded from the premium tier) and derivative instruments would not, from both structural and practical perspectives, fulfil the needs of controllers in creating control/cash-flow divergences, and board appointment rights, shareholder's agreements between founders and companies and cross-ownership structures created specifically to create a control/cash-flow divergence are likely to fall foul of the FCA's Premium Listing Principles and not be permitted on the premium tier. Even if a cross-ownership structure were permitted, as with a pyramid structure, it would be much more complicated, as compared to dual-class stock, to use to produce a control/cash-flow divergence that is sufficiently adequate to allow a founder to economically diversify meaningfully while retaining control. Similarly, even if board appointment rights over a majority of the board were to be permitted by the FCA on the premium tier, they are not as attractive to founders as dual-class stock, since they do not allow the founder to control other aspects of the company's business that depend upon controlling voting rights generally (for example, the founder would not be able to unilaterally pass a resolution to approve the remuneration policy of the directors[82] or approve large transactions[83]). Finally, loyalty shares, if permitted on the premium tier, would be a convoluted method for a founder to divest of substantial equity while retaining control, with the structure mainly intended to reward and incentivise long-term shareholdings. If it is contended that dual-class stock can create an environment that, overall, benefits the public markets of the United Kingdom, then the discussion should evolve on to how it can be prescribed while mitigating the risks to inferior-voting shareholders, rather than on to whether greater ambit should be given to other types of control-enhancing structures that can create the same environment but not as smoothly or effectively.

Secondly, permitting dual-class stock on the premium tier would not be opening the door to a greater use of other control-enhancing mechanisms that may currently be prohibited or discouraged by the FCA. If dual-class stock were permitted, it may

82 CA 2006, s. 439A.
83 For example, Class 1 transactions under Chapter 10 of the Listing Rules.

well be more difficult to justify a discouragement of other control-enhancing mechanisms based upon an ideological distaste for control/cash-flow divergences, but clearly, if creating such a divergence is the intention, founders are unlikely to choose other control-enhancing mechanisms over dual-class stock given the practical difficulties with those other structures outlined earlier. In any case, there would still be an argument for the FCA to take a stricter view of pyramid, cross-ownership, derivative instrument and loyalty share structures since they can be opaque to public shareholders compared to dual-class stock. For public investors, an analysis of the consequences of a dual-class structure would be simpler than that of a complicated pyramid, cross-ownership, derivative instrument or loyalty share structure. In relation to board appointment rights, one could argue that it is notionally a softer arrangement than dual-class stock, and should therefore be permitted on the premium tier if dual-class stock were permitted, but it is submitted that board appointment rights would also be less transparent to the public, especially retail, shareholders. Instead clearly designating shares as inferior- or enhanced-voting makes it obvious where the balance of power lies in a listed company, and would be the preferred option of controllers.

In the world of control-enhancing mechanisms, dual-class stock is top of the tree, and given the practical and regulatory challenges in utilising other control-enhancing mechanisms, for a founder seeking to list its company and divest of a substantial portion of its investment and/or generate significant equity financing while preserving control, there are currently no other viable options on the premium tier. However, being on a pedestal means that there are plenty looking to knock dual-class stock off its perch. In the next chapter, some of the conceptual arguments against dual-class stock will be critically analysed. Additionally, prior to investigating the benefits and detriments of dual-class stock from the perspective of founders and public shareholders in Part II of this book, the next chapter will also set out where the discussion in Part II sits within the concept of ‘firm purpose’.

4

Shareholder Democracy and Corporate Purpose

In theory there is no difference between theory and practice, while in practice there is.[1]

4.1 INTRODUCTION

Before evaluating the merits of dual-class stock in Part II, we will complete putting dual-class stock into context in this Part I by discussing two conceptual aspects that deserve consideration. The assertion of shareholder democracy was once often levied against the use of dual-class stock. One share, one vote was regarded as the 'fairer' option. However, it will be discussed later in this chapter that a comfortable analogy cannot be made between notions of shareholder democracy and corporate capital structure. The second aspect considered is the concept of 'firm purpose'. Determining the purpose of the firm, especially in relation to whether companies should be managed for the benefit of shareholders or other stakeholder groups, is a dialogue closely linked to the theory of the firm, the theoretical foundation of the corporate form. Although it is not intended to develop a new theory of the firm in this book, it is germane to discuss on what basis the merits of dual-class stock will be evaluated in Part II. It will be discussed later in this chapter that dual-class stock could indeed support exponents of a model where boards are enabled to take decisions in the interests of stakeholders rather than just in the interests of shareholder wealth maximisation. However, for the purposes of this book, dual-class stock will mainly be assessed from the perspective of public shareholders, rather than other stakeholders. UK law and regulation is generally geared toward shareholder interests, and any proposed approach to dual-class stock on the premium tier will need to consider the impact on public shareholders, particularly the institutional investors who dominate the UK equity markets.

[1] B. Brewster, 'Free Government' in *The Yale Literary Magazine Volume 47*, eds. the Students of Yale College (Published by the Editors, 1882) at 202.

4.2 SHAREHOLDER DEMOCRACY

The judgment in the case *Birch* v. *Cropper*,[2] outlined in Chapter 2, settled the default position that absent provision in a company's articles, every holder of shares of equal amount is entitled to an equal proportion in the capital and property of the company per share. The position has been extrapolated to embrace the concept of one share, one vote, which is now statutorily embedded as a default.[3] The judgment appears to have been influenced by the principles of equality and justice.[4] Some commentators have extended that line of thought to argue that companies should always employ one share, one vote, and that dual-class stock offends the principles of democracy and fairness and taints the bargain that has been implicitly struck between investors and management – investors expect influence commensurate to their investment in the company. The natural conclusion to those arguments is that a company should not be permitted to deviate from the default one share, one vote model in its articles even though the Court in *Birch* v. *Cropper* acknowledged it was technically possible. Moving into the public equity market arena, the arguments become more apposite, since investors have less input, as compared to investors in private companies, into the capital structures adopted by issuers, and such investors can encompass unsophisticated retail shareholders.

Easterbrook and Fischel (1983) classically espoused that the very basis of attaching voting rights to shares is the fact that the shareholders are the residual claimants in the company.[5] Upon a winding up of the company, the shareholders' equity rights are the last to be paid out, long after the claims of lenders, employees and other creditors. The shareholders bear the ultimate risk that upon a failure of the company, their investments will be lost, and, as such, they should enjoy voting rights during the lifetime of the company, giving them a modicum of control over the manner in which the business of the company is conducted. Using the residual claimant's argument as a foundation, an analogy can be drawn to the political arena, thereby linking one share, one vote to democratic principles. The key similarity between the political and corporate spheres is that both states and companies are governed by constitutional principles, and, therefore, those who submit to those principles should possess votes to, amongst other things, influence the behaviour and election of those to whom power to manage has been delegated.[6] Commentators have even linked the premise of 'corporate governance' to the

2 *Birch* v. *Cropper and Others In re The Bridgewater Navigation Company Limited* (1889) 14 App. Cas. 525.

3 CA, s. 284.

4 For example, see Lord Fitzgerald in *Birch* v. *Cropper* (note 2 above 541 and 542).

5 F. Easterbrook and D. Fischel, 'Voting in Corporate Law' (1983) 26 *J. Law Econ.* 395, 409.

6 Ripley drew an analogy between the design of corporate voting rights to the US constitution's design of political government (W. Ripley *Main Street and Wall Street* (Little, Brown, 1927) at 130). Also see P. Flocos, 'Toward a Liability Rule Approach to the "One Share, One Vote" Controversy: An Epitaph for the SEC's Rule 19c-4' (1990) 138 *U. Pa. L. Rev.* 1761, 1785; B. Cheffins *Company Law: Theory, Structure and Operation* (Oxford University Press, 1997) at 474.

operation of governmental institutions: 'corporate governance is associated with representative government and is aimed at mirroring social, economic and political institutions of a wider society into the level of corporations'.[7] In advocating one share, one vote on the basis of political analogy, equivalence is drawn between the equality of citizens and the equality being ascribed to each unit of investment in a company; a person investing £1 should not be treated differently to another person investing the same sum. This has led to commentators labelling one share, one vote as representative of 'fair corporate suffrage'[8] and the 'democracy of the dollar',[9] and opining that attaching a single vote to each and every share is an immutable or inherent right.[10] In particular, stock exchanges have used the concept of 'democracy' in justifying one share, one vote as a preferred voting structure.[11]

However, even if one were to accept the political analogy, it can be doubted that one share, one vote truly represents a democratic ideology. Dunlavy (2006) concluded that one share, one vote is, in fact, plutocratic in nature – it concentrates voting power in the hands of those with the most financial wealth rather than distributing that power equally amongst shareholders.[12] Even in a dispersed voting system where one share, one vote is less prone to monopolisation of power in the hands of the few, it is still difficult to conceive of the system as being democratic. If democratic arguments are germane, then the prevailing system would be one vote per shareholder rather than one share, one vote.[13] One share, one vote is more akin to a political system where a person's voting power is commensurate to the level of taxes

[7] *Corporation Finance*, E. Mead (D. Appleton and Company, 1922) cited in A. Khachaturyan, 'Trapped in Delusions: Democracy, Fairness and the One-Share-One-Vote Rule in the European Union' (2007) 8 *EBOLR* 335, 341.

[8] M. Warren III, 'One Share, One Vote: A Perception of Legitimacy' (1988) 14 *J. Corp. L.* 89, 95.

[9] C. Rohrlich, 'Corporate Voting: Majority Control' (2014) 7 *St. John's L. Rev.* 218, 218.

[10] L. Lowenstein, 'Shareholder Voting Rights: A Response to SEC Rule 19c-4 and to Professor Gilson' (1989) 89 *Colum. L. Rev.* 979, 1006; *ibid* 219.

[11] For example, prior to the NYSE permitting dual-class stock in the late 1980s, the NYSE declined to admit such stock to the exchange based upon the statement in the NYSE Listed Company Manual: 'Consistent with the Exchange's long-standing commitment to encourage high standards of *corporate democracy* [emphasis added], every listed company is expected to follow certain practices aimed at maintaining appropriate standards of corporate responsibility, integrity and accountability to shareholders.' (J. Seligman, 'Equal Protection in Shareholder Voting Rights: The One Common Share, One Vote Controversy' (1985) 54 *Geo. Wash. L. Rev.* 687, 699). In relation to the United Kingdom, Hong Kong and Singapore, see S. Wei and A. Young, 'Dual Share Plan in Context: Making Sense of Hong Kong's Decision Not to Embrace Alibaba's Listing' (2015) 26 *I.C.C.L.R.* 4, 8. The Australian Stock Exchange's devotion to one share, one vote is said to 'enshrine the shareholder democracy rule' (V. Goldwasser, 'Differential Voting Rights and the Super Share – In Search of an Accommodation on the Merits' (1994) 7 *Corp. & Bus. L.J.* 205, 219). In discussing the arguments against dual-class stock, the Singapore Stock Exchange noted that 'Shareholder democracy demands that voting powers should match economic incentives' (SGX Consultation Paper, 'Possible Listing Framework for Dual Class Share Structures' (16 February 2017) at 7).

[12] C. Dunlavy, 'Social Conceptions of the Corporation: Insights from the History of Shareholder Voting Rights' (2006) 63 *Wash. & Lee L. Rev.* 1347, 1355; Y. Allaire, 'The Case for Dual-Class of Shares' (2019) *IGOPP Policy Paper No. 11* 1, 16.

[13] Dunlavy (2006) (n 12 above 1354).

paid by that person.[14] Similarly, Ratner (1970) discussed the premise of the 'equal protection clause' of the Fourteenth Amendment to the US Constitution applying to corporations broadly in the context of the imposition of one person, one vote rather than one share, one vote.[15] As such, one share, one vote has sometimes been viewed with caution. For example, when the father of the first National Bank of the United States, Alexander Hamilton, conceived of its voting structure, he was hesitant to settle on one share, one vote on the basis that it would allow just a few shareholders to 'monopolise the power and benefits of the bank'.[16] He also acknowledged that one vote per person would not give sufficient deference to the investments made by large shareholders and the protection that they required, so advocated for what became known as 'prudent-mean voting rights', which, essentially, placed a cap on the votes exercisable by individual shareholders that would otherwise be governed by one share, one vote.[17] The prudent-means system found favour on both sides of the Atlantic, becoming somewhat of the norm in the United States in the early nineteenth century,[18] and being introduced, in a format similar to default model articles of association, in the United Kingdom until one share, one vote was implemented in 1905.[19] If the political analogy is taken further, dual-class structure could be deemed to epitomise oligarchies, a governmental structure that is closer to the plutocracy of one share, one vote than the democracy of one person, one vote. From a political standpoint, dual-class structure is not quite as divergent from one share, one vote as the democratic argument first postulates, and one share, one vote does not conform to the democratic principles presumed by some commentators.

Therefore, it is not obvious that one share, one vote truly represents a democratic course of action, but, in any case, the very basis of the political analogy has been widely discredited.[20] In particular, in the United States, the analogy has been doubted on fundamental grounds. In Delaware, the default power to manage the corporation is vested in the board by statute,[21] and, therefore, since the power of the board does not flow from the voters – the shareholders – corporations cannot be considered to be democratic institutions.[22] Accordingly, with dispersed ownership, a separation of ownership by the shareholders from control by the managers[23] has been described in the

[14] D. Ratner, 'The Government of Business Corporations: Critical Reflections on the Rule of "One Share, One Vote"' (1970) 56 *Cornell L. Rev.* 1, 19 made a similar comment in the context of school district elections.

[15] *ibid* 44.

[16] *ibid* 6; Dunlavy (2006) (n 12 above 1356).

[17] *ibid*; also see Section 2.3 of Chapter 2.

[18] Dunlavy (2006) (n 12 above 1358).

[19] *ibid* 1360.

[20] Goldwasser (1994) (n 11 above 212).

[21] 8 Del. C., §141(a).

[22] J. Cox et al., 'Understanding the (Ir)relevance of Shareholder Votes on M&A Deals' (2019) 69 *Duke L. J.* 503, 515.

[23] A. Berle and G. Means, *The Modern Corporation and Private Property* (Macmillan, 1932) at 355.

United States as being a structure closer to a technocracy,[24] where the control is ascribed to those with technical expertise rather than ownership. Further, although shareholder voting has been endorsed in the Delaware Courts on the basis that it justifies the exercise of power by managers over the property of others,[25] at a societal level, the need for democracy is far more legitimate since the state can enforce its powers over the liberty and freedom of its citizens through police and enforcement powers; in a publicly listed company, shareholders, with limited liability, can simply sell their shares if they do not agree with the manner in which the company is being managed – an endeavour much simpler than attempting to change citizenship.[26] Even in the United Kingdom, where the management power of the board is derived from the articles,[27] which can be adopted and amended at the will of the shareholders,[28] a number of significant divergences exist between the political and corporate spheres. For instance, one of the principal qualities of the public markets is the ability of shareholders to freely buy and sell shares in the market. It is, though, illegal for a citizen to sell his or her votes in a political election.[29] The share represents a commercial interest in an entity that can be traded, whereas a citizen's rights and interests are personal. As Ratner (1970) stated: 'The shareholder under the present system is not voting as a person at all, but as the temporary trustee of a piece of paper embodying values to which shareholders and management alike have agreed to adhere in making their 'corporate' decisions, whether or not they accept them in their personal lives.'[30] There is no equivalence in the electoral sphere, for example, of high-frequency traders, who continuously buy and sell shares based upon momentary incongruities in share pricing. The transitory nature of share ownership also does not sit well with polity when considering the right to vote – a visitor to a country cannot vote in that jurisdiction, whereas, generally (with one share, one vote), any shareholders of voting stock as of the relevant record date can vote at a shareholders' meeting.[31] In fact, rather than one share, one vote, loyalty shares would be more akin to democratic elections, where the right to vote is only granted after citizenship is gained.[32]

24 Dunlavy (2006) (n 12 above 1365).

25 *Blasius Indus.* v. *Atlas Corp.*, 564 A.2d 651 (Del. Ch. 1988); H. Hu and B. Black, 'The New Vote Buying: Empty Voting and Hidden (Morphable) Ownership' (2006) 79 *S. Cal. L. Rev.* 811, 815.

26 Flocos (1990) (n 6 above 1788); H. Manne, 'Some Theoretical Aspects of Share Voting: An Essay in Honor of Adolf A. Berle' (1964) 64 *Colum. L. Rev.* 1427, 1445.

27 For example, see Model PLC Articles, article 3.

28 The incorporators of the company can adopt different or modified articles to the Model PLC Articles. After incorporation, shareholders can subsequently amend the articles by special resolution (CA 2006, s. 21).

29 For example, in the United Kingdom, see Representation of the People Act 1983, s. 113. Also see Manne (1964) (n 26 above 1445). Although, Khachaturyan (2007) also notes the practice of 'vote trading' by legislators in the political sphere (n 7 above 353).

30 Ratner (1970) (n 14 above 38).

31 Allaire (2019) (n 12 above 16).

32 In relation to loyalty shares, tenured voting and time-phased voting, see Section 3.8 of Chapter 3. Theoretically, a voting system could be designed such that certain stock is non-voting until a specific period of ownership has expired.

The political analogy also falls down when considering that the underlying drive of shareholders is, generally, homogenously financial wealth maximisation, whereas, in society, broader issues are also pertinent,[33] and, significantly, one share, one vote only confers voting rights on those with property rights – the shareholders. Other stakeholders such as employees, consumers, suppliers and any community affected by the actions of the corporation are not automatically endowed with voting rights unless they also own shares. In contrast, governments, in a manner more direct than corporate management, must take these interests into consideration since all such stakeholders hold voting rights.[34] The nature of rational apathy also has a greater bearing on the corporation than government. It is accepted that voters can be apathetic to political elections, but interest can be piqued through the collective bargaining of political parties and factions. With corporations, a voter's interest is, generally, driven by his or her financial interest in the company. In a dispersed ownership system, if each shareholder only holds a very small interest in the company, a separation between ownership and control is created, and a shareholder may not be particularly committed to the voting process, where the effort and costs incurred in determining how to vote outweigh the possible benefits accruing to the shareholder's small holding. As a corollary, with one share, one vote, in a dispersed ownership system, if one shareholder holds even a marginally large interest (even as small as 10 per cent), that shareholder can exert significant and disproportionate influence.[35] The identity of that dominant shareholder can also change over time. Although gerrymandering can cause shifts in the distribution of voting rights on a constituency basis, the frequency of such shifts cannot be compared to the potential for the dynamic shifting of power that can occur within a public company. Finally, it has also been underscored that the voting rights within business organisations are generally determined on a contractual basis, meaning that, in theory, the participants can either negotiate their rights or, to the extent that the participant does not possess the requisite bargaining power, decide whether to invest in the relevant business organisation.[36] The contractual nature of the relationship lends itself to a consideration that different organisations may benefit from

[33] D. Fischel, 'Organized Exchanges and the Regulation of Dual Class Common Stock' (1987) 54 *U. Chi. L. Rev.* 119, 141; Manne (1964) (n 26 above 1442). Although, it is also acknowledged that the wealth-maximising strategies of shareholders may not be quite so homogenous, with, for example, shareholders operating on the basis of differing time horizons and possessing differing views on takeovers and other restructurings (R. Chan and J. Ho, 'Should Listed Companies Be Allowed to Adopt Dual-Class Share Structure in Hong Kong?' (2014) 43 *Comm. L. World Rev.* 155, 158; J. Ho, 'Examining the viability to allow dual-class share structure companies to list in the financial market of the People's Republic of China: Lessons and experiences from Hong Kong' (2019) https://ssrn.com/abstract=3408873).

[34] Fischel (1987) (n 33 above 141); Ratner (1970) (n 14 above 38).

[35] Fischel (1987) (n 33 above 141); Ratner (1970) (n 14 above 19).

[36] Fischel (1987) (n 33 above 141). The articles of association of a company have contractual effect (CA 2006, s. 33). It should be noted, though, that passive investors may not have the discretion as to whether to invest in a corporation (see Section 1.5.4 of Chapter 1).

different voting structures.[37] A one-size-fits-all mentality is less credible in the face of the diversity of business relationships as compared to a constant and stable society.

Even if the political analogy does not hold, the argument that one share, one vote is 'fair' can still be persuasive. The rationale here is that certain investors need to be protected, and, by ensuring equality of treatment, such shareholders are less likely to be taken advantage of by those with informational and resource privileges.[38] A further argument has been put forth that equality of treatment leads to a desirable redistribution of wealth, and therefore equality of treatment prevents those with greater wealth and power from appropriating opportunity from those who are not as well-positioned.[39] Salient arguments, though, can be made against 'fairness' and 'equality' notions. In relation to both 'protection of investors' and 'redistribution of wealth', it is difficult to see how this would be appropriate in the context of one share, one vote. In a well-developed public market, like the LSE, institutional shareholders dominate.[40] Such shareholders are sophisticated and make decisions with their eyes open. As referenced in Chapter 8, through the operation of market forces, institutional shareholders can also exert significant influence on management teams even in the absence of voting power. In a stock market dominated by retail investors with lower levels of financial acumen and sophistication, 'fairness' is a more convincing proposition. In the United Kingdom, though, unsophisticated shareholders are mainly exposed to the market indirectly through pension and insurance funds, the fund managers of which are experienced individuals and institutions.[41] Retail investors investing directly in the market are likely to possess at least non-insubstantial levels of financial experience and resources, and be well-diversified. Furthermore, one share, one vote prioritises those shareholders with the greatest resources. The shareholder investing the most possesses the greatest voting power. One person, one vote would represent a better form of redistributive justice. Even dual-class structure, where the founder possesses the enhanced-voting shares, could be argued to be a fairer system of redistribution than one share, one vote by giving the founder, often with lesser resources than institutional investors, greater parity with the wealthy investors.

Cheffins (1997), in discussing equality of shareholders generally, outlined three concepts that could undermine the rationale for equality – the 'pass-along', 'puniness' and 'crudeness' problems.[42] These three problems can be specifically applied to equality and fairness arguments in favour of one share, one vote. The 'pass-along' problem relates to the tendency of market participants to adjust their behaviours in response to regulations demanding equality to an extent that permitted deviations

37 Fischel (1987) (n 33 above 141).
38 Cheffins (1997) (n 6 above 472).
39 *ibid* 473.
40 As of the end of 2018, if individuals, charities and public sector bodies are excluded, UK and global institutions hold the remainder of UK equities, amounting to 77.77 per cent of UK-listed shares (calculated using data from ONS, 'Ownership of UK quoted shares: 2018' (January 2020)).
41 Individuals directly own only 13.5 per cent of UK-listed shares (*ibid* 4).
42 Cheffins (1997) (n 6 above 476–479).

from equality are created that are as pernicious or worse than would be the case if the relevant regulations were not in place. In the context of one share, one vote, in some jurisdictions, founders may find other means of creating control/cash-flow divergences, such as pyramid, cross-ownership or derivative instrument structures that are more opaque and detrimental to outside investors than dual-class stock. Although, in the United Kingdom, as discussed in Chapter 3, those alternative control-enhancing mechanisms may not be possible or practical for a founder, the pass-along problem can also manifest itself in a founder simply deciding not to list. In a way, the costs of implementing the prohibition on dual-class stock are 'passed-on' to investors and potential investors, since, in the case of a visionary founder, they may not be able to participate in the success generated by the talent of that founder if the firm remains unlisted.[43] Even if the founder does list, as discussed further in Chapter 6, without dual-class stock, an important mechanism that bonds the founder to the firm is lacking – with one share, one vote, the founder may cede control, disincentivising the founder to remain with the company for the long term or preventing the founder from implementing a vision that is profitable for all investors. Where the founder is talented, again, public investors lose out. 'Puniness' refers to a case where the relevant regulatory solution may have a minor effect compared to other mechanisms that could be used. The premium tier prohibition of dual-class stock only has a marginal impact on most investors – using the United States as an example, although the use of dual-class stock has been progressively increasing, in 2019, less than one-fifth of IPOs adopted dual-class stock.[44] Additionally, as will be discussed in Chapter 7, of those companies that do adopt dual-class structure, it is likely that public shareholders are rarely excessively expropriated. Rather than prohibiting dual-class stock outright, other regulatory tools could be used to ensure that the most egregious abuses of public shareholders are prevented. Those regulatory rules may apply solely to dual-class stock, to all control-enhancing mechanisms, or to all types of listed companies; such regulatory rules may protect public shareholders far more effectively than simply prohibiting dual-class stock. 'Crudeness' describes laws that act as blunt instruments. In relation to the redistribution of wealth, as before, with a market dominated by institutional investors, it is difficult to ascertain how a system that favours those investors with the greatest resources will create the desired redistribution. In fact, dual-class stock could potentially represent a better redistributive strategy in taking the power away from those with the greatest resources, and putting the power in the hands of founders who would be able to take decisions with a longer-term focus free from the influences of wealthy institutional investors. If fairness and equality are the priorities, more incisive methods to ensure that the controllers of companies do not act in a manner that prejudices non-controlling

43 See Section 1.5.5 of Chapter 1 for an example of a company that remained unlisted for a prolonged period of time, thereby limiting substantial returns during its main growth-phase to a handful of sophisticated investor.

44 Council of Institutional Investors (CII), 'Dual-Class IPO Snapshot: 2017–2019 Statistics' www.cii.org/files/Jan%202020%20Dual%20Class%20Update%20for%20Website.pdf.

shareholders may better achieve those goals. Jurisdictions such as Hong Kong, Tokyo, India and Singapore, for example, have taken more pragmatic approaches, with the implementation of tailored public shareholder protections, in place of a wholesale prohibition of dual-class structure. We will revert to this topic in Chapter 9.

Although fairness and democratic arguments seem in the first instance to be cogent reasons to prescribe one share, one vote, both concepts suffer from significant flaws. Having determined that it is tenuous to impugn deviations from one share, one vote on the basis of fairness to, and equality of, shareholders, another fundamental question, discussed in the following section, is whether the merits of dual-class stock should be discussed in terms of shareholder interests at all.

4.3 THE PURPOSE OF THE FIRM AND DUAL-CLASS STOCK

We will complete Part I of this book, which puts dual-class stock into context, by identifying against what measures dual-class stock will be evaluated in Part II. 'One man's meat is another man's poison',[45] or, more appropriately, one person's private benefit is another person's loss. Clearly, dual-class stock creates potential benefits for founders. However, judging by the attitudes of the FCA and institutional investors to dual-class stock, there are also clearly concerns that dual-class stock could be detrimental to public shareholders. The key task in evaluating dual-class stock is to ascertain from which perspective its merits should be extolled and its costs apprehended. Beyond public shareholders and founders, dual-class stock could be assessed from the perspective of other stakeholders, such as employees, customers, suppliers, and even the economy or society generally. From a conceptual standpoint, determining the 'purpose' of a company – essentially for whose benefit should a company be managed – could be deemed persuasive in identifying the parameters around the assessment of dual-class stock. However, from a practical standpoint, determining 'corporate purpose' may have less relevance. In this section, the theory of corporate purpose will be discussed briefly, before pulling the discussion back from a conceptual orientation to the realms of pragmatism, and it will be explained that a consideration of the real world reasons for the premium tier's approach to dual-class stock will dominate the context of the discussion in Part II.

4.3.1 *Corporate Purpose*

The 'purpose' of the firm has been debated for over 200 years,[46] and it is not intended that a thorough synopsis of the history of that debate be included here. However, a brief overview of the continuing dialectic, and the approach taken by this book, will benefit the discussion to follow in Part II. Although somewhat of a simplification,

45 T. Middleton, *Plato's Cap: Cast at this yeare 1604, being leape-yeere* (Bushell and Chorlton, 1604).

46 A. Page, 'Has Corporate Law Failed? Addressing Proposals for Reform' (2009) 107 *Mich. L. Rev.* 979, 979 (f/n 1).

broadly, the contemporary debate has fluttered between two concepts: 'shareholder primacy' and 'stakeholder pluralism'. Shareholder primacy asserts that managers should manage corporations primarily in the interests of its shareholders.[47] In contrast, stakeholder pluralism can be associated with 'managerialism', where managers have the discretion to manage companies in the interests of their stakeholders as they see fit rather than merely prioritising shareholder value.[48] The 'purpose' of the firm, or, more appropriately, in 'whose interests should firms be managed?' is a live debate, with academic and cultural discourse on the topic enlivened in recent years.[49] Managerialism, and its connection with stakeholder pluralism, has spilled into the real world with the pronouncements by the Business Roundtable, an association of US company CEOs, that companies should not be required to prioritise short-term shareholder profits over all other stakeholder interests,[50] swiftly followed by a denouncement of that view by institutional investors through the CII.[51]

4.3.1.1 Theory of the Firm

Various theories of the firm have been used to justify both shareholder primacy and stakeholder pluralism. Early theoretical arguments regarding the theory of the firm mainly revolved around the essence of the company itself, and considerations as to its 'corporate personality'.[52] That debate, however, had dissipated by the 1930s with recognition that the company had a legal form beyond a mere amalgamation of compacts between shareholders. Reflections on the functional basis of the company began to dominate over determinations of its abstract conception.[53]

[47] C. Smith and D. Rönnegard, 'Shareholder Primacy, Corporate Social Responsibility and the Role of Business Schools' (2016) 134 *J. Bus. Ethics* 463, 465.

[48] For a description of managerialism, see A. Dignam and M. Galanis, *The Globalization of Corporate Governance* (Ashgate Publishing Limited, 2010) at 25 *et seq*. Managerialism does not sit completely comfortably with stakeholder pluralism, however, since managers could act in their own self-serving interests in a manner that does not benefit any other stakeholders (see n 76 below and accompanying text, and n 78 below).

[49] For example, see C. Mayer, *Better Business Makes the Greater Good* (Oxford University Press, 2018) at 37–40; L. Stout, 'New Thinking on Shareholder Primacy' (2012) 2 *Account. Econ. Law* 1; B. Choudhury and M. Petrin, *Corporate Duties to the Public* (Cambridge University Press, 2018) at 41–46; J. Fisch and S. Solomon, 'Should Corporations Have a Purpose?' (2020) https://ssrn.com/abstract=3561164.

[50] Business Roundtable, 'Statement on the Purpose of a Corporation' (August 2019) https://opportunity.businessroundtable.org/ourcommitment/. From a UK perspective, also see The British Academy, 'Principles for Purposeful Business' (2019) www.thebritishacademy.ac.uk/publications/future-of-the-corporation-principles-for-purposeful-business.

[51] CII, 'Council of Institutional Investors Responds to Business Roundtable Statement on Corporate Purpose' (19 August 2019) www.cii.org/aug19_brt_response.

[52] For a more detailed overview of the early theoretical underpinnings of corporate form, including the contractual, concession, legal fiction, aggregate and corporate realism theories, see Dignam and Galanis (2010) (n 48 above 9–14).

[53] B. Cheffins, 'The Trajectory of (Corporate Law) Scholarship' (2004) 63 *CLJ* 456, 479. However, the debate on 'corporate personality' was resurrected in a different context in the US Supreme Court's judgment in *Citizens United* v. *Federal Election Commission*, 558 U.S. 310 (2010), where a majority

A corollary to accepting that the company has legal form with its own interests is that the 'interests of the company' must be defined. The early 1930s saw a popular academic discourse between two prominent lawyers. In one corner, Dodd (1932) tackled the challenge of defining the interests of the company by espousing that the managers of a company are fiduciaries for the company rather than for its individual members.[54] Dodd argued that, as a legal person, a company should be equated to any professional person, and, therefore, 'employ its funds in a manner appropriate to a person practising a profession and imbued with a sense of social responsibility'.[55] In the other corner, Berle (1932),[56] although he had sympathy for Dodd's views, rejected what was essentially a stakeholder pluralism paradigm on pragmatic grounds. Berle believed that the shareholder wealth maximisation purpose of the corporation cannot be abandoned without first determining the accountability of managers.[57] Building upon his earlier seminal work on the separation of ownership from control, where in a dispersed ownership system outside managers control firms,[58] Berle determined that the pluralist approach extolled by Dodd would give managers free reign to make self-serving decisions.[59] Although Berle was attracted to the social responsibility aspects of Dodd's articulation, he felt, at least in his early work,[60] that non-shareholder stakeholder interests were better served by legal developments rather than assuming that managers will act in the most socially optimal manner.[61] Shareholder primacy was the most prudent course.[62]

The legal debate between Dodd and Berle gave way to an economic formulation of the theory of the firm. An early protagonist was Coase (1937), who based his theory upon a transaction costs rationale.[63] He built upon the economic theory that the market operates through a pricing mechanism which automatically allocates resources efficiently, by continually matching supply to demand,[64] but deduced that transaction costs are inherent in the contracts entered into by market participants.[65] Those transaction costs could be mitigated through 'a system of relationships which comes into existence when the direction of resources is

court decision judged that corporations, as 'associations of citizens', have a First Amendment right to free speech much in the same way as private individuals.

54 E. Dodd, 'For Whom Are Corporate Managers Trustees?' (1932) 45 *Harv. L. Rev.* 1145, 1160.

55 *ibid* 1161.

56 A. Berle, 'For Whom Corporate Managers Are Trustees: A Note' (1932) 45 *Harv. L. Rev.* 1365.

57 *ibid* 1367.

58 A. Berle and G. Means, *The Modern Corporation and Private Property* (Macmillan, 1932).

59 Berle (1932) (n 56 above 1368).

60 Berle, in his later work, embraced more of a pluralist approach (for example, see *Power without Property*, A. Berle (Harcourt, Brace, 1959)).

61 Berle (1932) (n 56 above 1372).

62 *ibid* 1368.

63 R. Coase, 'The Nature of the Firm' (1937) 4 *Economica* 386.

64 F. Hayek, 'The Trend of Economic Thinking' (1933) 40 *Economica* 121, 129.

65 Coase (1937) (n 63 above 390–391).

dependent on an entrepreneur'.[66] The firm was the mechanism by which the entrepreneur could direct those resources. Although such an approach could invoke stakeholder pluralism, since the entrepreneur is responsible for directing all stakeholder relationships in an efficient manner,[67] economists in the 1970s began to use Coase's theorem as a foundation to take corporate purpose roundly in a shareholder primacy direction. The firm began to be described as a market in and of itself within which contracts are continually renegotiated by management.[68] The firm was designated as a 'nexus of contracts',[69] and 'contractarians'[70] prioritised the primacy of shareholders underpinned by their position as the residual claimants in the company.[71] The shareholders, as residual claimants, would be incentivised to monitor the other contracting parties, whose performance may otherwise be difficult to discern, in the interests of the company's success, and should, therefore, be granted voting rights and the ability to change management to undertake such monitoring efficiently.[72] Furthermore, stakeholders, such as creditors, suppliers and employees, are able to contract for a fixed sum, whereas shareholders as residual claimants cannot contractually protect themselves, particularly in the context of a dispersed ownership system, and, therefore, their interests should be prioritised in the manner in which companies are managed.[73] The discourse naturally led to the pathbreaking work of Jensen and Meckling (1976).[74] The authors focused on the 'contract' between the owners of the firm (or, from a legal perspective, the owners of the residual cash-flow rights of the firm) and management, and framed it in the context of an (economic, rather than legal) 'agency relationship' – 'a contract under which one or more persons (the principal(s)) engage another person (the agent) to

66 *ibid* 392–393.

67 Cheffins (2004) (n 53 above 484).

68 A. Alchian and H. Demsetz, 'Production, Information Costs, and Economic Organization' (1972) 62 *Am Econ. Rev.* 777. The authors, however, rejected Coase's description of the existence of an authority relationship between the entrepreneur and stakeholders.

69 For example, the term 'nexus of contracts' was used by M. Jensen and W. Meckling, 'Theory of the Firm: Managerial Behavior, Agency Costs and Ownership Structure' (1976) 3 *J. Financ. Econ.* 305, 310.

70 Under the economic nexus of contracts model, the company can be considered to be an 'association of people formed to carry on business' (Cheffins (1997) (n 6 above 32)).

71 Cheffins (2004) (n 53 above 484).

72 Alchian and Demsetz (1972) (n 68 above 788). In the US context, the authors noted that the right to change management in a dispersed ownership firm is more correctly a manifestation of a shareholder's right to sell its shares – management can be replaced through the operation of the market for corporate control (in relation to the market for corporate control, see Section 6.2.6 of Chapter 6), and that threat influences management to act in accordance with shareholder objectives. Also see Easterbrook and Fischel (1983) (n 5 above 403).

73 F. Easterbrook and D. Fischel, 'The Corporate Contract' (1989) 89 *Colum. L. Rev.* 1416, 1447.

74 Jensen and Meckling (1976) (n 69 above). Jensen and Meckling, and Alchian and Demsetz, were likely inspired by an influential article by Milton Friedman: M. Friedman, 'The Social Responsibility of Business Is to Maximise Its Profits', *New York Times Magazine* (13 September 1970) (although it has also been commented that Friedman's influence on the shareholder primacy debate has been overblown – B. Cheffins, 'Stop Blaming Milton Friedman!' (2020) https://ssrn.com/abstract=3552950).

perform some service on their behalf which involves delegating some decision making authority to the agent'.[75] In this case, the agents are the managers, and the principals are the shareholders. It was noted that the agents will not always act in the best interests of the principals and may, instead, pursue their own wealth maximisation, leading to 'agency costs', which increase as the residual ownership rights of management decline.[76] An implication is that efficiency is fostered by implementing mechanisms that ensure that management operates the company to pursue the best interests of the shareholders.[77]

Although shareholder primacy, accordingly, dominated much of the literature in the 1980s and 1990s, the concept did not have it all its own way. Theorists were also able to justify stakeholder pluralism on contractarian grounds, rationalising that, due to divergences in market power, non-shareholder stakeholders are not able to negotiate their contracts in an optimal manner and are, therefore, as deserving of protection as shareholders.[78] Similarly, emphasising the vicissitudes of the debate, arguments for shareholder exceptionalism on the basis that, unlike non-shareholder stakeholders who can constantly renegotiate their contracts, shareholders invest for the life of the firm,[79] have been disputed through the identification of stakeholder interdependencies that can render the renegotiation power of non-shareholder stakeholders ineffective in certain scenarios.[80] Contemporary theoretical studies have developed variations of existing themes,[81] with one 2017 study looking at the debate from the opposite angle, recognising that giving shareholders too much power can itself create costs for companies.[82] The theory of the firm has not solved the conundrum of shareholder primacy versus stakeholder pluralism and, largely,

75 Jensen and Meckling (1976) (n 69 above 308).

76 *ibid* 312–330. The authors defined agency costs to be the aggregate of monitoring costs, costs expended in aligning the respective interests of the agents and the principals, and any losses incurred through the agents nevertheless pursuing their own interests over those of the principals (*ibid* 308).

77 Easterbrook and Fischel (1989) (n 73 above 1421).

78 C. Hill and T. Jones, 'Stakeholder-Agency Theory' (1992) 29 *J. Manag. Stud.* 131, 136–139. The authors noted that non-shareholder stakeholders suffer 'utility losses' in the same way that shareholders suffer agency costs, and, therefore, mechanisms should be implemented to align the interests of the company with all stakeholders, not just shareholders. Also see A. Licht, 'The Maximands of Corporate Governance: A Theory of Values and Cognitive Style' (2004) 29 *Del. J. Corp. Law* 649, 652 – the claims of non-shareholder stakeholders are not necessarily fixed, and, therefore, it could be argued that those stakeholders also have residual claims.

79 O. Williamson, 'Corporate Governance' (1984) 93 *Yale L.J.* 1197, 1202 and 1204.

80 R. Freeman and W. Evan, 'Corporate Governance: A Stakeholder Interpretation' (1990) 19 *J. Behav. Econ.* 337, 353. Also see the 'team production' formulation used to justify a pluralist approach by M. Blair and L. Stout, 'A Team Production Theory of Corporate Law' (1999) 85 *Va. L. Rev.* 247, 292.

81 Contemporary theories of the firm have generally used Coase's theorem as an initial foundation, although some have delved into new territory, such as the 'adaptation costs' theorem proposed by Wernerfelt, 'The Comparative Advantages of Firms, Markets and Contracts: a Unified Theory' (2015) 82 *Economica* 350, and the 'director primacy' concept of S. Bainbridge, *The New Corporate Governance in Theory and Practice* (Oxford University Press, 2008) at 66.

82 See the discussion in Sections 6.3.5 and 6.4.1 of Chapter 6 on the notion of 'principal costs', as expounded in Z. Goshen and R. Squire, 'Principal Costs: A Theory for Corporate Law and Governance' (2017) 117 *Colum. L. Rev.* 767.

similar theories of the firm can be adopted to justify both ideologies. Therefore, since the aim of this book is not to develop a new theory of the firm, placing dual-class stock squarely within a particular 'theory of the firm' is not practically necessary to progress the assessment of dual-class firms. However, as discussed next, it is useful to briefly outline where dual-class stock sits within the shareholder primacy/stakeholder pluralism debate, from a practical, rather than 'theory of the firm', perspective, as a first step to establishing the footing on which dual-class stock will be assessed.

4.3.1.2 The Dominance of Shareholder Primacy and the Application to Dual-Class Stock

Although academics and economists have long debated the shareholder primacy/stakeholder pluralism juxtaposition, it would appear that, legally, in the United Kingdom, shareholder primacy has won the day. Under CA 2006, s. 172, in satisfying their duty to act in the interests of the company, directors must, as a default,[83] 'promote the success of the company for the benefit of its members as a whole'. Although directors must also have regard to various non-stakeholder interests, those considerations are tied to acting to benefit the shareholders.[84] This 'enlightened shareholder value' concept recognises that by taking into account the interests of non-shareholder stakeholders, long-term profits for shareholders can also be enhanced.[85] Furthermore, shareholders possess the underlying right to change the board of the company (and, therefore, indirectly, the management team).[86] The intervention rights of shareholders in this regard underpin a shareholder primacy approach.

However, with dual-class stock, the dynamics shift to such an extent that one could challenge whether in such circumstances shareholder primacy remains extant. Assuming that a founder has listed his or her company, divested of a majority of the equity and retained control through the adoption of dual-class stock, the majority equity holders of the dual-class firm cannot remove the directors.

83 A company is free to express in its articles a purpose other than the benefit of its members (CA 2006, s. 172(2)). Additionally, creditor interests may intrude as the company approaches insolvency (CA 2006, s. 172(3); *West Mercia Safetywear* v. *Dodd* [1988] 4 BCC 30; *BTI 2014* v. *Sequana* [2016] EWHC 1686 (Ch)).

84 CA 2006, s. 172(1)(a)–(f). However, note recent efforts to require certain companies to disclose how directors have considered the interests of non-shareholder stakeholders in their decision-making (CA 2006, ss. 414CZA and 414C(1); and UK CGC, Provision 5).

85 The wide-ranging review of UK companies legislation by the UK Company Law Review Steering Group, which resulted in the formulation of CA 2006, considered the concept of stakeholder pluralism when determining that directors' duties should be codified into statute, but eventually settled on the 'enlightened shareholder value' approach (see UK Company Law Review Steering Group, 'Modern Company Law for a Competitive Economy: Completing the Structure' (2000) at 34).

86 CA 2006, s. 168. The board generally has the power to appoint and remove managers under Model PLC Articles, article 3.

In turn, the managers therefore remain insulated from those equity holders, and the accountability of those managers to the public shareholders will be significantly undermined. Economically, decision-making authority has been delegated to the managers (which will generally include the founder) by the equity holders, and those managers may pursue self-serving (or, more appropriately, founder-serving) actions to the detriment of the equity holders. The founder, with voting control in the company, has little in the way of personal economic incentive to desist from such behaviour if its equity holding is small, and the economic incentives to pursue shareholder wealth maximisation progressively diminish as the founder's equity-holding declines.[87] From a less dystopian standpoint, a socially conscious or altruistic founder could ensure that the company is managed for the benefit of its stakeholders, notwithstanding any detrimental effect on shareholder wealth, or a founder that prioritises the long-term health of his or her company can take appropriate actions even if detrimental to shareholder wealth in the short term. Is dual-class structure therefore managerialism in disguise, and potentially a route toward stakeholder pluralism?

From an economic and control perspective, where the founder leads the management team of a dual-class firm, clearly managers have discretion to take decisions for the benefit of non-shareholder stakeholders. The law does, though, effectuate a realignment of dual-class structure with shareholder primacy. In Chapter 8, the various legal and regulatory measures that could protect the interests of inferior-voting shareholders in dual-class firms are outlined. In particular, CA 2006, s. 172, would still apply to directors of dual-class firms in the same way as it does to directors of one share, one vote firms, requiring them to promote the success of the company for the benefit of its members as a whole (not just the enhanced-voting shareholders). Other regulatory measures, such as related-party transaction regulations, also prevent certain actions being taken by management without the consent of the inferior-voting shareholders. Although the efficacy of those protections can, to a degree, be doubted,[88] dual-class firm managers do not have complete free reign to make decisions as they see fit. Therefore, dual-class firms sit somewhere between shareholder primacy and stakeholder pluralism in their form. Managers of dual-class firms have practical discretion to make decisions that do not prioritise shareholder wealth maximisation, but cannot completely ignore the interests of the public shareholders due to constraints that exist under law and regulation (and, to a lesser degree, through the application of other psychological and market forces[89]). With those considerations in mind, we can now establish the basis on which dual-class firms will be assessed in Part II.

87 For further discussion in relation to the shifting conflict dynamics as capital structure changes, see Section 5.6 of Chapter 5.

88 See Chapter 8.

89 *ibid.*

4.3.2 *The Approach in Part II to the Purpose of the Firm*

The debate on the purpose of the firm has long fluttered between shareholder primacy and stakeholder pluralism,[90] and it is outside the scope of this book to present a normative appraisal of the purpose of the firm. Moreover, the purpose of this book is to explicate the merits of dual-class stock with a view to developing a framework within which the LSE could welcome dual-class stock to the premium tier most effectively. However, it is expedient to outline whether, in Part II, the merits of dual-class firms are to be assessed on the basis of shareholder primacy or stakeholder pluralism, particularly since, as above, dual-class firms sit somewhere close to the dividing line between the two concepts. The recent discord between the Business Roundtable and CII indicates that this is a topical issue.[91] Although that debate was not specifically related to dual-class structure, it involved contentions as to the degree to which shareholder power can influence management to prioritise short-term shareholder interests; clearly dual-class structure is relevant in this regard, since it gives management a level of insulation from the influence of public shareholders. An argument in favour of, or in opposition to, dual-class stock can be made on both shareholder primacy and stakeholder pluralism grounds. The approach of Part II will straddle some elements of stakeholder pluralism, but will principally consider public shareholders.

4.3.2.1 Stakeholder Considerations in Part II

From a stakeholder perspective, it was outlined in Chapter 1 that there is a scarcity of high-growth, especially tech sector, firms listing on the UK equity markets. Dual-class structure can encourage founders to list their firms in the United Kingdom, and some of the broader economic benefits of fostering flotations and keeping British companies British were broached.[92] A fundamental argument in favour of relaxing the premium tier rules on dual-class stock, as also discussed in Chapter 1, is that a greater proportion of British society will be able to, either directly or indirectly, participate in the success of more high-growth firms. Additionally, giving founders more options with which to list their firms in the United Kingdom could slow the exodus of British tech firms to foreign acquirors, which could be critical in sustaining robust employment in the United Kingdom as the tech sector becomes a major employer. Therefore, elements that are not related to pure shareholder wealth maximisation are taken into account when considering the grounds for permitting dual-class stock on the premium tier. One could take the theme further in Part II and discuss dual-class stock in terms of stakeholder concerns and the propensity for dual-class stock to incentivise a board to

90 The debate has also been labelled 'cyclical' (Cheffins (2004) (n 53 above 498)). Even the Business Roundtable has flip-flopped between shareholder primacy and stakeholder pluralism, often influenced by the prevailing economic winds (Cheffins (2020) (n 74 above 25)).

91 See nn 50 and 51 above and accompanying text.

92 Also see B. Reddy, 'Finding the British Google: Relaxing the Premium-Tier Prohibition of Dual-Class Stock' (2020) 79 *CLJ* 315.

take stakeholder-friendly actions. This author accepts that dual-class structure could enable managerial decision-making on a broader stakeholder-friendly basis; as discussed in more detail in Chapter 6, the ability to take a long-term approach to the company's business and the incentive to take risks that could result in innovative products are facilitated by dual-class structure. Consequentially, such approaches could be beneficial for many non-shareholder stakeholders, such as employees, suppliers, customers and society generally. For example, in the face of transitory economic downturns, a dual-class firm founder with a long-term perspective may not be so inclined to commence redundancy programmes or delay supplier payment terms if such actions could prejudice the founder's long-term vision, as compared to a one share, one vote firm founder who could be removed from management by public shareholders with either less long-term aspirations or who are not as visionary as the founder, as a result of a short-term decline in profits. Additionally, advancing high-growth firms (by, for example, a dual-class stock path to flotation) could prospectively, due to growth-phase economics, benefit customers and employees through the desire of such firms to pursue market share and increase workforce. Accordingly, a justification for dual-class structure could be made on stakeholder pluralism grounds. However, such considerations should be weighed against the proposition asserted by Berle that giving management discretion to take actions that benefit all stakeholders does not necessarily result in those managers taking those actions,[93] and a detailed elaboration of the benefits (or otherwise) of long-termism and risk-taking for all stakeholders, and an evaluation of the evidence pertaining thereto, which could easily subsume the entire subject matter of a book, is not the intended focus of this book.[94] Therefore, the possible benefits to non-shareholder stakeholders of dual-class structure are not the focus of Part II, although it will be noted how a number of aspects that enable boards to take stakeholder-friendly actions can, in fact, be beneficial to public shareholders in the long term.

Similarly, Part II will not consider in detail the potential for dual-class stock to incentivise boards to take actions that could be considered to be detrimental to non-shareholder stakeholders, particularly the topical concern that there is a possible predilection for large, financially dominant tech companies to act contrary to the public interest. It is, though, worth recounting the concern herewith, and justifying its omission from Part II. Some of the most successful tech firms have adopted dual-class stock, and the pseudo-monopolies within which such firms operate can give the founders of those firms far-reaching powers. Some may argue that giving founders of dual-class companies access to vast economic resources, and granting them wide

93 See n 61 above and accompanying text.

94 Several books have been published specifically on the subject of long-termism, including, for example, C. Mayer, *Prosperity: Better Business Makes the Greater Good* (Oxford University Press, 2018); A. Rappaport, *Saving Capitalism from Short-Termism: How to Build Long-Term Value and Take Back Our Financial Future* (McGraw-Hill Education, 2011); K. Willey, *Stock Market Short-Termism: Law, Regulation and Reform* (Palgrave, 2019).

and unaccountable power, may have exacerbated some of the recent controversies in Big Tech. For example, Google was fined by the EU for anti-trust violations after leveraging its market dominance to force customers of its search products into agreeing to contractual restrictions on the publication of advertisements linked to rival search engines.[95] Facebook's alleged misuse of customer data has also attracted high-profile privacy concerns.[96] Such abuses, however, are a product of the dominance that such firms enjoy in their respective markets, which allows them to take actions that are detrimental to customers or society generally with very little commercial consequence, rather than being redolent of dual-class stock itself. For both Google and Facebook, the use of dual-class stock will have given their respective founders the scope to build their firms into tech behemoths, but, having attained such prominence, it is not dual-class stock that has caused or enabled those companies to abuse their positions. Corporate controversies of a similar nature are prevalent in one share, one vote as well as dual-class firms. For example, the one share, one vote firm Amazon, another tech behemoth, has attracted significant public opprobrium for alleged tax avoidance practices,[97] and legal claims have been made against Apple, another one share, one vote tech giant, for allegedly intentionally minimising useable product life,[98] and for abusing a dominant position vis-à-vis customers.[99] Rather than focusing on the use of dual-class stock, disquiet regarding the disproportionate market power of large tech firms are aspects that should be reflected and balanced through targeted legal and regulatory methods.[100] It is not within the purview of this book to determine whether further regulations are required to temper the success of Big Tech. The relevant concerns exist outside the dominion of dual-class stock, and, conversely, it could be argued that permitting the use of dual-class stock gives tech firms further options for growth beyond being acquired by larger tech companies, and therefore promotes greater competition, rather than ingrains dominant positions. Although there are fundamentally sound arguments that regulation to counter the power of large, dominant

[95] A. Hern and J. Jolly, 'Google fined €1.49bn by EU for advertising violations' *The Guardian* (20 March 2019) www.theguardian.com/technology/2019/mar/20/google-fined-149bn-by-eu-for-advertising-violations.

[96] J. Wong, 'Facebook expects FTC fine of up to $5bn in privacy investigation' *The Guardian* (24 April 2019) www.theguardian.com/technology/2019/apr/24/facebook-ftc-fine-first-quarter-financial.

[97] S. Butler, 'Amazon accused of handing over "diddly-squat" in corporation tax' *The Guardian* (3 September 2019) www.theguardian.com/technology/2019/sep/03/amazon-accused-of-handing-over-diddly-squat-in-corporation-tax-despite-tripling-payment.

[98] M. Murphy, 'Apple agrees to pay $500m over "iPhone slowdown" lawsuit' *The Telegraph* (2 March 2020) www.telegraph.co.uk/technology/2020/03/02/apple-agrees-pay-500m-iphone-slowdown-law suit/.

[99] P. McGee, '"Fortnite" maker goes to war over "Apple tax"' *Financial Times* 14 August 2020) www.ft.com/content/29378of7-d2f8-4f3f-aa52-752c74e2d34d.

[100] Nascent steps have already been made in the United Kingdom toward greater regulation of Big Tech, with the creation of a Digital Markets Unit to administer a new regulatory code (BEIS Press Release, 'New competition regime for tech giants to give consumers more choice and control over their data, and ensure businesses are fairly treated' (27 November 2020)).

tech firms should be effectuated, there are currently no UK-based tech firms operating on the scale of a Google or Facebook (or, indeed, on the scale of one share, one vote firms such as Amazon and Apple), and, therefore, any desire for such regulatory steps should not, at this stage, delay encouraging UK tech firms to grow.

4.3.2.2 The Public Shareholder Focus of Part II

Although the argument in favour of permitting dual-class firms on the premium tier in Chapter 1 is founded on public benefit grounds – the potential for dual-class stock to encourage more flotations – after establishing that footing, the primary focus in Part II shifts to the effect of dual-class structure on the interests of public shareholders. This author is not advocating that shareholder primacy should be the centre of attention for companies and regulators, but there are three main reasons for taking a public shareholder-focused approach in Part II. Firstly, as discussed earlier, the laws of England and Wales pertaining to directors' duties endorses shareholder primacy, with directors of dual-class firms required to promote the success of the company for the benefit of its members as a whole, and, therefore, the proclivity of the directors of dual-class firms to comply with that duty in practice should be gauged. CA 2006, s. 172 does encompass an enlightened shareholder value prospect, though, and it will be argued that dual-class structure, in fact, promotes compliance with that concept, since it is easier for dual-class firm managers to have regard to the interests of non-shareholder stakeholders, with a view to creating long-term success for shareholders, if those managers are not slavish adherents to short-term share price. Secondly, as discussed in Chapter 2, the United Kingdom's premium tier prohibition of dual-class structure stems from an institutional shareholder and regulatory bias against dual-class stock, and an assumption that the structure harms public shareholders. Accordingly, whether dual-class stock does in fact harm public shareholders should be scrutinised. Conceptually, it will be discussed in Chapter 6 that actions taken by dual-class firm founders ostensibly in the interests of the founder are not necessarily harmful to public shareholders – the outcomes may be shared with, or generate separate consequential benefits for, public shareholders. Empirically, in Chapter 7, it will be shown that there is no evidence of a correlation between dual-class structure and financial harm to public shareholders. Thirdly, the ideological distaste of institutional investors, particularly UK institutional investors, against dual-class stock cannot be completely ignored. That distaste is not reflected by those institutional investors shunning dual-class firms on exchanges where they are permitted,[101] but, as will be outlined in Chapter 7, the

[101] Finding that institutional investor ownership in dual-class firms was the same or greater than such ownership in one share, one vote firms: R. Anderson et al., 'The Dual Class Premium: A Family Affair' (2017) 1, 28 https://ssrn.com/abstract=3006669; S. Smart et al., 'What's in a Vote? The Short- and Long-Run Impact of Dual-Class Equity on IPO Firm Values' (2008) 45 *J. Account. Econ.* 94, 99; S. Smart and C. Zutter, 'Control as a Motivation for Underpricing: A Comparison of Dual- and

cost of capital for dual-class stock issuers is increased due to institutional investor discounting of dual-class firms. To win the argument that dual-class firms should be welcomed on the premium tier, a consideration of public shareholder interests is critical; therefore, it is necessary to show that dual-class stock will not harm public shareholders, and to reduce the cost of capital for such firms (and to smooth the path toward premium tier dual-class stock), mechanisms will need to be developed to give institutional investors greater comfort that the managers of dual-class firms will not egregiously act against their interests. After a body of evidence has been amassed as to the conduct of UK dual-class stock firms, if or when they are accepted on the premium tier, future research can shift to determining whether one share, one vote or dual-class stock is more conducive to other stakeholder interests, and, correspondingly, whether issuers should choose one share, one vote or dual-class stock in specific contexts. However, in the first instance, any evaluation of the premium tier's approach to dual-class stock must assess dual-class firms from the perspective of shareholder primacy, and that baton is picked up in Part II.

4.4 CONCLUSION

The concepts of shareholder democracy and corporate purpose have vexed many an academic over the decades, and both concepts have been periodically cited in the context of dual-class stock. In more recent years, however, shareholder democracy has fallen somewhat out of fashion, while corporate purpose and, in particular, an exhortation that companies should be managed for the benefit of all stakeholders, has seen a resurgence. For the purposes of this book, though, neither concept is deemed critical to the real-world assessment of dual-class firms or a discussion of the premium tier approach to dual-class stock.

Shareholder democracy, although an elegant soundbite, falters when subject to more intense scrutiny. The contention that one share, one vote represents shareholder democracy has been disputed, with many commentators opining that one share per shareholder is a better representation of democracy. Furthermore, analogies between corporate governance and political theory are tenuous, with material differences existing between the two; allusions toward shareholder democracy are built on fragile grounds.

Stakeholder pluralism, on the other hand, is a conversation that is alive and kicking, and some commentators have highlighted that dual-class stock enables founders (and therefore management) to manage companies in the interests of

Single-Class IPOs' (2003) 69 *J. Financ. Econ.* 85, 98; I. Dittmann and N. Ulbricht, 'Timing and Wealth Effects of German Dual Class Stock Unifications' (2007) 14 *Eur. Financ. Manag.* 163, 191. Finding slightly less institutional ownership of dual-class firms: K. Li et al., 'Do Voting Rights Affect Institutional Investment Decisions? Evidence from Dual-Class Firms' (2008) 37 *Financial Management* 713, 720; J. Kim et al., 'Multi-Class Shares Around the World: The Role of Institutional Investors' (November 2018) *Unpublished* 1, 19.

numerous stakeholders rather than focusing primarily on short-term shareholder wealth maximisation. This author acknowledges that those arguments do bear substantive merit, but in the context of the premium tier approach to dual-class stock, the benefit of dual-class structure to non-shareholder stakeholders is only tangentially discussed in this book. Dual-class stock can benefit society generally by encouraging founders to list their companies, allowing those companies to grow rapidly, and allowing a greater proportion of society to participate in their success. However, from a legal and regulatory perspective, the United Kingdom has, over the years, embraced the concept of shareholder primacy, and institutional shareholders dominate the equity markets. Importantly, as will be discussed in the next chapter, the provenance of the premium tier's approach to dual-class stock stems from a distrust of controlling shareholders and the possible ills that they can cause to the interests of public shareholders. Therefore, any discussion around United Kingdom policy will need to focus on the effect of dual-class stock on public shareholders, and Part II of this book will primarily take such an approach.

PART II

Evaluating Dual-Class Stock

5

From Controlling Shareholders to Dual-Class Stock

Here's the deal. What I win, I keep. What you win, I keep.[1]

5.1 INTRODUCTION

As briefly remarked in Chapter 1, part of the distrust that the regulators exhibit toward dual-class stock stems from a fear that the controller will utilise its power to extract personal benefits that are detrimental to shareholder wealth maximisation. The concept of such 'personal' or 'private benefits of control', or 'controller benefits' as they shall be described in this book, is not unique to dual-class structures. The notion that a controller can use its voting power to extract controller benefits derives from the fact that the controller has voting control, which allows the controller to influence the composition of the management team of the company, and thereby directly or indirectly dictate the company's actions.[2] Dual-class stock is not required for voting control, and a holder of more than 50 per cent of the shares in a one share, one vote listed company will possess similar powers. Although the UK listed markets are more commonly associated with dispersed ownership firms,[3] controlling shareholder one share, one vote firms exist, even on the premium tier, and such firms represent a healthy minority of listed companies in the United Kingdom. However, this chapter will commence by discussing that the distrust of controlling shareholder one share, one vote firms is the genesis of the FCA's prohibition of dual-class firms

[1] Billy the Kid, 'Bill & Ted's Excellent Adventure' (Interscope Communications, 1989).

[2] The holder of a majority of the votes in a company will have control over the removal of directors (CA 2006, s. 168) and, if the Model PLC Articles apply, over the appointment of directors (Model PLC Articles, articles 20 and 21). The board, in turn, almost ubiquitously with listed companies, has the power to appoint and remove managers (Model PLC Articles, article 3).

[3] J. Franks and C. Mayer, 'Evolution of Ownership and Control around the World: The Changing Face of Capitalism' (2017) *ECGI Finance Working Paper No. 503/2017* 1, 36 and 43; C. Holderness, 'Blockholders Are More Common in the United States Than You Might Think' (2010) 22 *J. Appl. Corp. Finance* 75, 79; G. Aminadav and E. Papaioannou, 'Corporate Control around the World' (2016) *NBER Working Paper* 23010 1, 19 and Appendix Table 1; B. Cheffins, 'The Undermining of UK Corporate Governance (?)' (2013) 33 *OJLS* 505 and 509).

on the premium tier. It will continue by outlining the wariness held by regulators as to the behaviour of controlling shareholders, but also the pragmatism displayed in admitting them to the listed markets. The empirical evidence on one share, one vote controlling shareholder firms will be described briefly, with its inconclusiveness rationalised by the existence of a controlling shareholder tradeoff that could swing in different directions on a firm-by-firm basis. The difference between dual-class stock and one share, one vote controlling shareholder firms will also be demarcated, and it will be explained why those shifting dynamics have led to the former being prohibited on the premium tier, with the latter very much tolerated.

5.2 THE PROVENANCE OF THE UNITED KINGDOM'S REGULATORY ATTITUDE TO DUAL-CLASS STOCK

Although dual-class stock is permitted as a matter of company law in the United Kingdom, the FCA created an exception to this prima facie position by proscribing such structures from the premium tier, which embraces the highest standards of corporate governance.[4] The dichotomy between company law and premium tier regulations suggests that the structure is not completely without merit, but, with certain companies, shareholders should be shielded from some menace against which they are unequipped to protect themselves. Why is dual-class structure not perceived to be correlated with the highest standards of corporate governance?

The underpinning of the premium tier prohibition of dual-class stock can be traced back to a distrust of controlling shareholders and concerns as to how they will exercise their considerable power. A controlling shareholder possesses sufficient voting control to decisively influence the composition of the board. A shareholder with a majority of the votes in the company will clearly be able to exercise such a privilege,[5] but even shareholders owning a large block of votes, somewhat less than a majority of the votes in the company, will enjoy similar faculties where the rest of the shares are significantly dispersed among tens or hundreds of thousands of other small shareholders, who will be disincentivised from acting, and will find it difficult to act in a collective manner, to oppose the large blockholder[6] (for example, under the Listing Rules, a 'controlling shareholder' is defined at the 30 per cent level[7]). The board will generally be responsible for the management of the company and will

4 For further details, see Chapter 2.

5 See n 2 above.

6 In relation to the difficulties inherent in institutional investors actively engaging in UK listed companies, see B. Black and J. Coffee, 'Hail Britannia?: Institutional Investor Behavior under Limited Regulation' (1994) 92 *Mich. L. Rev.* 1997, 2055–2073; B. Reddy, 'The Emperor's New Code? Time to Re-Evaluate the Nature of Stewardship Engagement Under the UK's Stewardship Code' (2021) 84 *MLR* 842, 854–861. Also see nn 52–54 below and accompanying text.

7 Under the Listing Rules, a 'controlling shareholder' is any person who exercises or controls on its own, or together with any person with whom it is acting in concert, 30 per cent or more of the votes that can be cast on all or substantially all matters at general meetings of the company (LR App 1.1).

retain the capacity to delegate to managers,[8] and, accordingly, the board will have the power to employ and dismiss managers. Therefore, a controlling shareholder with control over the composition of the board can indirectly also control the management of the company. Resonating with the quote, 'power tends to corrupt and absolute power corrupts absolutely',[9] the FCA's concerns are triggered by the considerable power that a controlling shareholder can wield over the management of the company.

Controlling shareholder one share, one vote structures are not prohibited on the premium tier. Indeed, the premium tier has a rich history of controlling shareholder companies. Companies such as Fraser Group (formerly Sports Direct), Antofagasta, Fresnillo, Easyjet and Regus are stalwarts of the FTSE-350, all of which feature individuals as controlling shareholders owning more than 30 per cent of the shares. Countrywide, Saga and TSB are further examples of premium listed controlling shareholder companies with corporate shareholders holding effective control. However, it cannot be said that the United Kingdom provides an open, unconstrained environment for such firms. Premium tier companies are subject to numerous restrictions where a controlling shareholder is in situ. As discussed further in Chapter 8, premium tier controlling shareholder companies must, for example, obtain, in certain cases, public shareholder approval when entering into transactions with controlling shareholders,[10] enter into contractual arrangements with controlling shareholders to limit the scope of actions of controlling shareholders[11] and give public shareholders the right to vote separately on the appointment of independent directors.[12] On the premium tier, the FCA also espouses a default minimum free-float, requiring that at least 25 per cent of listed shares be held by public shareholders (who are not insiders or shareholders related to insiders), unless the requirement is waived by the FCA.[13] The free-float prerequisites have primarily been implemented to ensure sufficient liquidity of listed shares and to reduce volatility, but also have the consequence of restricting the voting power of the controlling shareholder (however, with exactly 25 per cent of the votes in public hands, the controlling shareholder could still unilaterally pass a special resolution with 75 per cent of the votes,[14] and, therefore, institutional shareholders have lobbied the FTSE indices in the past to implement more stringent free-float requirements to curtail the voting power of controlling shareholders of firms included on the FTSE indices[15]). The regulatory

8 For example, see Model PLC Articles, articles 3 and 5.

9 The quote has been attributed to Lord Acton in a letter to the Archbishop Mandell Creighton (5 April 1887).

10 Listing Rules, Chapter 11.

11 LR 6.5.4R and LR 9.2.2ADR(1).

12 LR 9.2.2ER.

13 LRs 6.14R, 9.2.15R and 14.2.2R.

14 Special resolutions are passed by the approval of *not less than* 75 per cent of the votes exercised (CA 2006, s. 283).

15 K. Burgess, 'FTSE pushed on 50% free float' *Financial Times* (14 December 2011) www.ft.com/content/1ab7c1b4-267c-11e1-91cd-00144feabdc0.

restrictions placed on controlling shareholders, alongside the hostile environment to controlling shareholder firms presented by regulators and institutional shareholders, are indicative of the distrust held of controlling shareholders. Underscored by the FCA's suspicion of controlling shareholders, it is not surprising that a 'controlling shareholder plus' structure like dual-class stock, which is not only associated with controlling shareholders[16] but also enables controlling shareholders to more easily list their firms, is prohibited on the premium tier.

5.3 WHY THE DISTRUST?

Clearly, an apprehension exists of the power in the hands of controlling shareholders. As Holderness and Sheehan (1988) stated: '... although the reasons for the public's hostility are seldom specified, there is a vague notion that the voting power of large-block shareholders somehow harms small shareholders'.[17] The fear is that a controlling shareholder of a listed company will exercise its influence over the management of the company to cause the company to take actions that benefit the controlling shareholder personally to the exclusion of the public shareholders. Commonly, the controller, or a representative of the controller, will serve on the board of the company, and the management of the company, cognisant that their continued employment is in the gift of the controller, will likely show a level of obsequiousness to the controller in the manner in which they manage the company. Even where the controller is not itself represented on the board, it may collude with management for its benefit to the detriment of the company as a whole.[18] In some cases, the controller may even act in a management capacity itself, giving it a more direct influence on the management of the company,[19] enhancing its ability to cause the company to be managed in a manner that is personally beneficial to the controller, but that may be detrimental to shareholder wealth maximisation. Such

[16] L. Bebchuk and K. Kastiel, 'The Perils of Small-Minority Controllers' (2019) 107 *Geo. L.J.* 1453, 1496 found that 83.6 per cent of Russell-3000 dual-class companies have a controlling minority shareholder (an earlier draft noted the figure as 96.7 per cent of S&P-1500 dual-class firms).

[17] C. Holderness and D. Sheehan, 'The Role of Majority Shareholders in Publicly Held Corporations: An Exploratory Analysis' (1988) 20 *J. Financ. Econ.* 317, 318.

[18] In continental Europe, it is not unusual for blockholders to either force management to pursue actions that augment blockholder value rather than shareholder value generally, or to support management-sponsored proposals in return for compensatory side payments (M. Maher and T. Andersson, 'Corporate Governance: Effects on Firm Performance and Economic Growth' (1999) *OECD Publication* 1, 25).

[19] R. La Porta et al., 'Corporate Ownership Around the World' (1999) 54 *J. Financ.* 471, 500 showed that 69 per cent of large companies in wealth economies that are controlled by individuals or families also have board representation by such controllers at CEO or chair level. More recently, in a random sample of 375 US listed firms, in cases where the largest blockholder was an individual, a named representative served on the board in 91 per cent of the cases, and 62 per cent of individual blockholders were both directors and officers (A. Edmans and C. Holderness, 'Blockholders: A Survey of Theory and Evidence' in *The Handbook of the Economics of Corporate Governance*, eds. B. Hermalin and M. Wesibach (Elsevier, 2017) at 553).

personal benefits are often referred to as 'private benefits of control'. For reasons that will become clear in the discussion on the 'Dual-Class Stock Tradeoff' at the end of Chapter 6, private benefits of control are generally labelled 'controller benefits' in this book.

Where a controlling shareholder owns a significant proportion of the shares in the company, it is incentivised, to a degree, to exercise its power to ensure that the company maximises shareholder wealth, since actions that are detrimental to shareholder wealth maximisation will also have a considerable impact upon the controller's wealth – sometimes referred to the controller having 'highest use value'.[20] However, as the shareholding of the controller declines, the proclivity for that controller to extract controller benefits increases. Accordingly, the assumption that a controlling shareholder will act in a manner beneficial to public shareholders was once described by Ratner (1970) as akin to 'putting the lions in the same cage with the rabbits at the zoo, on the assumption that the lions will represent the rabbits' interests in negotiating with the keepers for food'.[21] With just over 50 per cent of the shares, a controlling shareholder can guarantee that it will be able to unilaterally control the composition of the board of directors, and therefore influence management to extract controller benefits on its behalf that may be detrimental to shareholder value. In such a case, the controller will receive 100 per cent of the controller benefits resulting from such actions, but only suffer just over 50 per cent of the detrimental impact on the value of the company caused by the extraction of those controller benefits. The situation would be further exacerbated where the controller holds effective control with less than 50 per cent of the shares. A controlling shareholder will be incentivised to extract controller benefits if the value of the controller benefits outweighs the harm to the price of the controlling shareholder's shares. As controller benefits are extracted, value is expropriated from the company, and, therefore, the public shareholders; the propensity for controlling shareholders to threaten the financial well-being of public shareholders in such a manner provokes the institutional and regulatory antipathy toward controlling shareholders.

A variety of means to extract controller benefits exist. Most of these overlap with the extraction of controller benefits by the controllers of dual-class firms, and will, therefore, be detailed in Chapter 6. However, examples can be noted in the one share, one vote ecosystem of the premium tier.[22] A notorious

[20] P. Flocos, 'Toward a Liability Rule Approach to the "One Share, One Vote" Controversy: An Epitaph for the SEC's Rule 19c-4?' (1989–1990) 138 *U. Pa. L. Rev.* 1761, 1797; R Gilson, 'Controlling Shareholders and Corporate Governance: Complicating the Comparative Taxonomy' (2006) 119 *Harv. L. Rev.* 1641, 1651; J. Dammann, 'The Controlling Shareholder's General Duty of Care: A Dogma That Should Be Abandoned' (2015) 2 *U. Ill. L. Rev.* 479, 481.

[21] D. Ratner, 'The Government of Business Corporations: Critical Reflections on the Rule of "One Share, One Vote"' (1970) 56 *Cornell L. Rev.* 1, 20.

[22] For further details regarding certain of the controlling shareholder controversies referenced in this chapter, see B. Reddy, 'The Fat Controller: Slimming Down the Excesses of Controlling Shareholders in UK Listed Companies' (2018) 38 *OJLS* 733.

example is that of ENRC, a Kazakhstan company that was listed on the premium tier. In 2011, two independent directors were ousted from ENRC's board by controlling blockholders acting in concert, after the directors in question criticised the corporate governance of the company and questioned the independence of the chair, leading to one ousted director describing the company as 'more Soviet than City'.[23] The controlling shareholders, with their voting power, instigated the removals, in spite of the precipitous decline in share price that the actions could, and did, cause.[24] Clearly, the scrutiny with which the ousted independent directors were casting on the governance of the company was not conducive to the manner in which the controlling shareholders desired the company to be managed. Subsequently, ENRC's conduct and dubious governance practices inspired widespread public shareholder outrage, including the sale of a subsidiary to the nephew of one of the controlling shareholders,[25] allegations of non-disclosure of other transactions with associates of the controlling shareholders[26] and allegations of bribery payments made to governmental officials in Africa.[27] By the time ENRC was delisted from the Main Market in 2013, after the founders reacquired the company, its share price had fallen to 217.25p from its listing price of 540p in 2007.[28] Over the course of its life as a publicly listed company, public shareholders had seen value expropriated from their holdings, and the travails of ENRC, in fact, prompted the FSA to propose many of the restrictions on controlling shareholder firms now evident in the Listing Rules.[29] ENRC may be the poster child for controlling shareholder abuses on the Main Market, but other firms have also shared the limelight. To illustrate, Asia Resource Minerals (formerly known as Bumi plc) suffered a dramatic decline in share price in 2012[30] after allegations of financial irregularities, and related-party transactions (including with persons

[23] G. White et al., 'ENRC "more Soviet than City", Says Ousted Board Member Ken Olisa' *The Telegraph* (9 June 2011) www.telegraph.co.uk/finance/newsbysector/epic/enrc/8564697/ENRC-more-Soviet-than-City-says-ousted-board-member-Ken-Olisa.html.

[24] H. Thomas, 'ENRC Bolsters Board to Improve Corporate Governance' *Financial Times* (25 May 2012) www.ft.com/content/393db758-a67c-11e1-968b-00144feabdc0.

[25] S. Goodley, 'ENRC Subsidiary Sold Secretly to Nephew of Co-founder' *The Guardian* (14 February 2013) www.theguardian.com/business/2013/feb/14/enrc-mining-company-subsidiary-sold-secretly.

[26] E. Rowley, 'ENRC in New Controversy as CFO Named in "Leak"' *The Telegraph* (14 March 2013) www.telegraph.co.uk/finance/newsbysector/industry/9931137/ENRC-in-new-controversy-as-CFO-named-in-leak.html.

[27] B. Thompson and C. Binham, 'Law Firm Accuses ENRC of Bribes, Sanctions-Busting and Overpayment' *Financial Times* (5 July 2018) www.ft.com/content/9b5ebe14-8069-11e8-bc55-50daf11b720d.

[28] J. Wilson et al., 'ENRC "Should Have Set Off Alarm Bells"' *Financial Times* (22 November 2013) www.ft.com/content/1995e548-5368-11e3-b425-00144feabdc0?mhq5j1.

[29] FSA Consultation Paper CP12/25, 'Enhancing the effectiveness of the Listing Regime and feedback on CP12/2' (October 2012); FCA Consultation Paper CP13/15, 'Feedback on CP12/25: Enhancing the effectiveness of the Listing Regime and further consultation' (November 2013).

[30] H. Thomas, 'Bumi Looks into Alleged Irregularities' *Financial Times* (28 September 2012) www.ft.com/content/74b8874c-08ae-11e2-b57f-00144feabdc0?mhq5j1.

connected to the controlling shareholders) without complying with the appropriate related-party transaction regulations.[31] Another foreign business with a premium listing, Exillon Energy, has been haunted by allegations of related-party transactions, including with its controlling shareholder, resulting in sanctions by the FSA in 2012,[32] and, years later, a suspension of its listing[33] after the publication of its annual results were delayed in order to investigate further transactions with uncertain counterparties.[34] The company later announced its intention to delist from the Main Market[35] as its share price tumbled.[36] Ferrexpo also suffered share price declines when a Ukrainian bank, which was controlled by Ferrexpo's controlling shareholder and which held a majority of the company's cash balance, was declared insolvent.[37] The controlling shareholder (and former CEO) of Ferrexpo was subsequently mired by reports, which the company denied, that he was being investigated in relation to the failure of the bank.[38] It is not only foreign controlling shareholder businesses that have been prone to controversies. Fraser Group, a premium listed British business with a founder holding more than 50 per cent of the shares, has been accused of a litany of poor practices, including allegedly deficient employee working conditions and minimum wage breaches,[39] transactions, or attempts to transact, with the founder's family members or close contacts,[40] expenditure on perks such as a private jet for the controlling shareholder in his role as CEO,[41] and lobbying attempts to keep retail premises open during the United Kingdom's COVID-19 lockdown of 2020.[42] In

31 See the FCA's Final Notice to Asia Resource Minerals plc, 12 June 2015.

32 FSA Final Notice to Exillon Energy plc, 26 April 2012.

33 Exillon Energy (RNS Number: 6240X), 'Suspension of share listing' (1 May 2019).

34 Exillon Energy (RNS Number: 2751X), 'Announcement of Exillon Energy plc' (26 April 2019).

35 Exillon Energy (RNS Number: 8280R), 'Notice of Intention to Delist from the LSE' (31 October 2019).

36 See share price charts as recorded and published by the *Financial Times* https://markets.ft.com/data/equities/tearsheet/charts?s=EXI:LSE.

37 J. Wilson and R. Olearchyk, 'Shares in Ferrexpo hit by bank closure' *Financial Times* www.ft.com/content/9431c744-5dd5-11e5-9846-de406ccb37f2.

38 N. Hume, 'Ferrexpo chief executive temporarily steps down' *Financial Times* (28 October 2019) www.ft.com/content/e3b6a728-f951-11e9-98fd-4d6c20050229.

39 S. Goodley and J. Ashby, 'Revealed: how Sports Direct effectively pays below minimum wage' *The Guardian* (9 December 2015) www.theguardian.com/business/2015/dec/09/how-sports-direct-effectively-pays-below-minimum-wage-pay.

40 Sean Farrell, 'Sports Direct Uses Mike Ashley's Brother's Firm for Overseas Distribution' *The Guardian* (London, 22 August 2016) www.theguardian.com/business/2016/aug/22/sports-direct-pays-mike-ashleys-older-brother-international-delivery; Sports Direct (RNS Number: 6376K), 'Statement clarifying the role of Michael Murray' (4 January 2016).

41 Fraser Group purchased a corporate plane for £51.1 million while the group's underlying EBITDA had decreased by 33.5 per cent and profits (before tax) had fallen by 57.0 per cent (see Sports Direct's interim results for the 26 weeks to 23 October 2016, dated 8 December 2016).

42 M. Sweney and S. Goodley, 'Sports Direct's Mike Ashley Apologises for Poor Covid-19 Actions' *The Guardian* (27 March 2020) www.theguardian.com/business/2020/mar/27/sports-direct-mike-ashley-apologises-for-poor-covid-19-actions.

particular, the allegations of poor working conditions and the resulting negative publicity precipitated a drastic share price drop for the company.[43]

5.4 WHY NOT PROHIBIT CONTROLLING SHAREHOLDER FIRMS? – THE CONTROLLING SHAREHOLDER TRADEOFF

If controlling shareholders' structures are nothing but a source of unhappiness for public shareholders, why does the FCA tolerate their existence on the premium tier? The FCA could simply eradicate such firms by increasing the free-float requirement to 50 per cent, or more. However, to the contrary, the FCA has shown a readiness to waive even the current free-float default requirement of 25 per cent to permit extreme controlling shareholder structures to list. The FCA has used its discretion to lower the threshold for a number of controlling shareholder companies, including ENRC, Ferrexpo and Fresnillo. Additionally, the FCA has introduced exemptions in the Listing Rules for 'sovereign-controlled commercial companies' (where the controlling shareholder is a State body), for certain provisions that restrict the acts of controlling shareholders.[44] Although the FCA will have been influenced by a healthy dose of pragmatism in attempting to attract listings on to the Main Market,[45] it is apparent that the FCA recognises that it is not a fait accompli that controlling shareholder firms will be managed in a manner solely prejudicial to the interests of public shareholders. For all the predilections for controlling shareholders to expropriate public shareholders, the controlling shareholder structure can also create shareholder value. For example, synergies between a controlling shareholder's separate businesses, particularly in the case of sovereign-controlled companies, could be beneficial commercially to the relevant listed company.[46] Also pertinent is that the management team of a controlling shareholder company, although beholden to the controlling shareholder, is insulated from the public shareholders and the market for corporate control.[47] The benefits of such insulation are discussed in more detail in Chapter 6 in the context of dual-class firms, but

43 Sports Direct shares were trading above 800p in August 2015, prior to news of the various scandals breaking, but had fallen to below 300p by the start of 2016 (see share price charts as recorded and published by the *Financial Times* https://markets.ft.com/data/equities/tearsheet/summary?s=FRAS:LSE).

44 For example, as discussed further in Chapter 8, a sovereign-controlled commercial company is not required to enter into a relationship agreement with its controlling shareholder, and related-party transaction requirements are largely dis-applied (Listing Rules, Chapter 21).

45 The exemptions provided to sovereign-controlled commercial companies (*ibid*) were purportedly introduced in an unsuccessful attempt to attract the blue chip listing of Saudi Aramco to the LSE (C. Binham and A. Raval, 'UK presses ahead on listing reforms in effort to woo Saudi Aramco' *Financial Times* ((8 June 2018)) www.ft.com/content/3a5a1b70-6aea-11e8-b6eb-4acfcfb08c11.

46 M. Gutiérrez and M. Sáez, 'A Contractual Approach to Disciplining Self-Dealing by Controlling Shareholders' (2017) 2 *JLFA* 173, 197; J Dammann, 'Corporate Ostracism: Freezing Out Controlling Shareholders' (2008) 33 *J. Corp. L.* 681, 707.

47 In relation to the market for corporate control, for further details, see Section 6.2.6 of Chapter 6.

importantly, to the extent that a controlling shareholder has a long-term outlook and is able to financially sustain short-term fluctuations in share price, it will be able to direct the company to take long-term decisions that benefit all shareholders in the long term,[48] while disregarding any short-term whims of public shareholders. Accordingly, rather than expropriating public shareholders, the actions of controlling shareholders can be shareholder wealth maximising.

Controlling shareholder structures can also present certain conceptual benefits over one share, one vote dispersed ownership structures. As elucidated by Berle and Means (1932),[49] widely held companies, as is often the case for UK listed companies,[50] may be associated with a separation between ownership and control, where the owners – notionally the shareholders in this paradigm – have delegated control to a board which has broad scope to manage the company. As discussed in Chapter 4, Jensen and Meckling (1976) framed the relationship between shareholders and managers in terms of an economic agency relationship[51] and noted that managers of companies may pursue their own wealth maximisation, rather than acting in the best interests of the shareholders. For example, managers may (i) 'shirk' by focusing excessively on leisure time; (ii) overly commit time to other diversified business interests ahead of the business of the company; (iii) engage in personal indulgences (such as 'pet projects' or 'empire building'); or, most egregiously (iv) divert the cash-flow or assets of the company for personal gain (often described as 'rent-seeking'). Such behaviours can be mitigated by shareholder monitoring of managers. However, with a dispersed ownership system, no individual shareholder will hold a sufficiently large stake in the company to motivate it to expend significant cost and effort in monitoring management;[52] such a shareholder will only garner a small proportion of the benefits (benefits which could equally be enjoyed simply by 'free-riding' on the back of another shareholder's monitoring efforts).[53] When combined with the collective action issues inherent in the shareholder having to corral a significant cabal of dispersed shareholders in order to ensure that they possess sufficient aggregate voting power to pressure management in the event that

48 Reddy (2018) (n 22 above 739).

49 A. Berle and G. Means, *The Modern Corporation and Private Property* (Macmillan, 1932).

50 See n 3 above.

51 M. Jensen and W. Meckling, 'Theory of the Firm: Managerial Behavior, Agency Costs and Ownership Structure' (1976) 3 *J. Financ. Econ.* 305, 308.

52 Note, though, the rise of hedge fund activists who may intervene while owning equity well below controlling interest levels – however, traditionally, this is not managerial monitoring as such, and more 'offensive activism' where a hedge fund acquires shares in a company with a view to instigating changes which they have already identified may create shareholder value (Reddy (2021) (n 6 above 861); B. Cheffins and J. Armour, 'The Past, Present, and Future of Shareholder Activism by Hedge Funds' (2011) 37 *J. Corp. L.* 51, 56; L. Bebchuk et al., 'The Agency Problems of Institutional Investors' (2017) 31 *J. Econ. Perspect.* 89, 105; E. Rock, 'Institutional Investors in Corporate Governance' in *The Oxford Handbook of Corporate Law and Governance*, eds. J. Gordon and W. Ringe (Oxford University Press, 2018) at 382.

53 For a succinct description of the free-riding issue, see J. Gordon, 'Ties that Bond: Dual Class Common Stock and the Problem of Shareholder Choice' (1988) 76 *Cal. L. Rev.* 1, 44.

monitoring unearths poor performance, dispersed shareholders can become 'rationally apathetic'.[54] Although mechanisms can be implemented to incentivise management to operate the company in the best interests of the shareholders,[55] such as through the formulation of performance-related executive pay packages, or the creation of proxies for shareholder monitoring (including the appointment of independent directors), those mechanisms can be costly for the company, and therefore shareholder wealth. Monitoring costs, costs expended in aligning the interests of the agents to the principals, and any losses incurred through the agents nevertheless pursuing their own interests over those of the principals are known as 'agency costs'.[56] In contrast to dispersed shareholders, controlling shareholders have sufficient motivation to monitor management – by owning a large proportion of the equity in the company, the consequences of management pursuing personal interests or not managing the company optimally will have a significant impact on the value of the controlling shareholder's stake in the company (consequently, the controlling shareholder also enjoys a large share of the benefits gained by better monitoring). Additionally, it is difficult to dispose of a large stake in a listed company without depressing the share price. This means that exit is not an easy option for controlling shareholders, and provides further motivation to monitor management. Controlling shareholders, particularly those that are individuals, are also not usually well-diversified. An inability to risk-spread in this way further accentuates the importance of managerial monitoring for controlling shareholders. Furthermore, with sufficient voting power, the controlling shareholder is able to substantially influence management by possessing the capacity to replace directors (who can, in turn, replace management). With the controlling shareholder taking on the costs of monitoring, negating the need for costly mechanisms to align the interests of management with shareholders, agency costs for public shareholders are reduced. Of course, the controlling shareholder may be part of the management team, or will significantly influence the decisions of management, in which case public shareholders will be concerned about controller benefits being extracted by the controlling shareholder, but with regard to the other managers extracting their own personal benefits, public shareholders will benefit from reduced agency costs.

Another crucial aspect that will have factored into the FCA's logic in permitting one share, one vote controlling shareholders structures is that the controlling shareholder must retain a significant proportion of equity to maintain control. A majority controlling shareholder will own over 50 per cent of the cash-flow rights as well as the votes, and even an effective, although not majority, controller will most probably need to own near to at least 30 per cent of the cash-flow rights to hold

[54] *ibid* 43; S. Marks, 'The Separation of Ownership and Control' in *Encyclopedia of Law and Economics*, eds. B. Bouckaert and G. Geest (Edward Elgar, 1999) at 694.

[55] D. Fischel, 'The Corporate Governance Movement' (1982) 35 *Vand. L. Rev.* 1259, 1263; F. Easterbrook and D. Fischel, 'The Corporate Contract' (1989) *Colum. L. Rev.* 1416, 1421.

[56] Jensen and Meckling (1976) (n 51 above 308).

sufficient voting power to decisively control the composition of the board. Although, as discussed earlier, such a controlling shareholder only suffers detriment from its own controller benefit extraction proportionate to its percentage interest in the company, that pain may still be considerable. If public shareholder protections are in place to curtail the most egregious types of controller benefit extractions, such as through related-party transaction regulations and anti-fraud laws, excessive expropriation of public shareholders should be substantively mitigated by the potential for large share price declines which will substantially affect the controlling shareholder's wealth. The equity owned by the controlling shareholder acts as an organic 'equity constraint' that theoretically limits the extent to which expropriation will take place.

In contrast to the examples of controlling shareholder controversies described earlier, numerous examples also exist of successful premium listed controlling shareholder companies, such as Hikma Pharmaceuticals, KAZ Minerals and Regus, where the public shareholders have profited from the controlling shareholder's assiduous monitoring of the management team and/or diligent management as a manager itself. Even Fraser Group, prior to revelations relating to its employee conditions in 2015,[57] had worked its way into the FTSE-100 in 2013, just six years after its IPO when known as Sports Direct. The balance between positive and negative anecdotal tales of controlling shareholder companies can be attributed to the existence of a 'controlling shareholder tradeoff', a term first coined by Gilson and Gordon (2003).[58] Essentially, this describes how, with a publicly listed company, potential equity investors will have a preference for the presence of a controlling shareholder if the benefits from decreased managerial agency costs are greater than the detriments (if any)[59] from the extraction of controller benefits by such controlling shareholder.[60] If controlling shareholders always acted in a manner such that they extracted maximum controller benefits, to the detriment of minority shareholders, it would be unlikely that the accompanying reduction in agency costs would compensate minority shareholders for such high levels of expropriation, and therefore the tradeoff would be skewed to such an extent that there would be a dearth of investors willing to invest; and so as a matter of 'Darwinian logic',[61] controlling shareholder firms would not be apparent in the publicly listed company realm.[62] The fact that controlling shareholder firms

57 See n 39 above and accompanying text.

58 R. Gilson and J. Gordon, 'Controlling Controlling Shareholders' (2003) 152 *U. Pa. L. Rev*. 785.

59 Controller benefits could also be neutral or even positive for minority shareholders (for further details, see Chapter 6).

60 It should be noted, though, that the concept of a controlling shareholder tradeoff may be tainted in an imperfectly efficient market, since there may be visibility issues with regard to potential investors discerning the levels of agency costs and controller benefit extraction.

61 For a discussion of the application of 'Darwinian logic' to the ownership structure of listed companies, see B. Cheffins, 'Corporate Law and Ownership Structure: A Link? (2002) 25 *UNSW L. J*. 346.

62 C. Holderness and D. Sheehan, 'Constraints on Large-Block Shareholders' in *Concentrated Corporate Ownership*, ed. R. Morck (University of Chicago Press, 2000) at 141.

continue to exist suggests that certain constraints on the actions of controlling shareholders tilt the tradeoff into positive territory by limiting their ability to extract controller benefits. As before, the most obvious constraint is the large equity ownership of the controller. As described further in Chapter 8 in the context of dual-class stock, legal and regulatory constraints can further tip the balance. However, promoting the benefits of the ownership structure is not as simple as completely eliminating the extraction of controller benefits, since some controller benefits may be beneficial to both the minority and controlling shareholders, and allowing at least a certain level of controller benefit extraction may be necessary to compensate the controller for increased monitoring costs, lower liquidity and a lack of diversification represented by holding a controlling block,[63] and, therefore, to persuade the controller to float the company. Thus, for all the potential for controlling shareholders to expropriate public shareholders, their presence is very much tolerated by the regulators.

5.5 EMPIRICAL EVIDENCE ON ONE SHARE, ONE VOTE CONTROLLING SHAREHOLDER COMPANIES

Over the years, a plethora of, albeit mostly dated, studies have been conducted investigating the correlation between ownership concentration and firm performance. It is not, though, intended that a comprehensive exposition of the empirical evidence on controlling shareholder companies be outlined in this book, since the primary subject matter of this book is dual-class stock. In Chapter 7, the empirical evidence on dual-class stock is evaluated in detail. As a precursor to that analysis, though, it is helpful to summarise some of the most cited studies on ownership concentration, since a broad assessment of the empirical evidence on controlling shareholder structures may reveal trends that indicate in which direction the controlling shareholder tradeoff is tilted, which can serve as a launching point as to whether that tradeoff may be distorted by the introduction of dual-class stock. However, when collating the empirical studies on controlling shareholder firms, it is difficult to establish an obvious correlation between ownership concentration and firm performance. That very inconclusiveness validates the FCA's accepting approach to one share, one vote controlling shareholder structures, and we will revert to a similar line of thinking when assessing the empirical evidence on dual-class stock in Chapter 7, in relation to which the FCA has taken a much harsher stance.

[63] Gilson and Gordon (2003) (n 58 above 785); Gutiérrez and Sáez (2017) (n 46 above 179); R. Gilson and A. Schwartz, 'Constraints on Private Benefits of Control: Ex Ante Control Mechanisms versus Ex Post Transaction Review' (2013) 169 *J. Institutional & Theoretical Econ.* 160, 169; Gilson (2006) (n 20 above 1665) – the author also supposes that in jurisdictions where the extraction of pecuniary controller benefits is constrained, the prevalence of, sometimes benign, non-pecuniary controller benefits explains the existence of controlling shareholder firms in such jurisdictions.

Most of the empirical evidence on ownership concentration has been conducted on US listed companies, with many of the studies focusing on the effect of stock ownership by managers rather than specifically controlling shareholder structures. Although several performance metrics have been used, including accounting rates of return and abnormal returns upon sale announcements featuring potential changes in ownership concentration, the most common is 'Tobin's Q' (effectively, the ratio of the market value of a firm to the replacement cost of its assets). A more precise definition of Tobin's Q, and a critical scrutiny of its use, is included in Chapter 7, which assesses the empirical evidence on dual-class stock specifically.[64] It should be noted that although a parallel is often drawn between a firm having a higher Tobin's Q than its peers and that firm being managed better than those peers (since its assets are being valued more than similar assets of its peers due to superior management of those assets), the possibility also exists that Tobin's Q merely represents the market's perception of a firm's capital structure. This potential challenge in drawing conclusions from Tobin's Q studies becomes even more consequential when the results of those studies overwhelmingly trend in a specific direction, and will, therefore, be discussed more robustly in Chapter 7.[65]

5.5.1 *Summary of Major Empirical Studies on Controlling Shareholder Structures*

A significant number of US studies, including those by Demsetz and Lehn (1985),[66] Holderness and Sheehan (1988),[67] Agrawal and Knoeber (1996)[68] (after controlling for 'interdependence'[69]), Loderer and Martin (1997),[70] and Himmelberg et al. (1999)[71] and, in relation to Japan, Prowse (1992)[72] found that firm performance, measured by accounting profit rate, was not correlated with ownership concentration.

Certain other studies seem to suggest that controlling shareholders could lead to a decrease in firm performance – a much-cited paper by Morck et al.

64 See Section 7.4 of Chapter 7.

65 *ibid.*

66 H. Demsetz and K. Lehn, 'The Structure of Corporate Ownership: Causes and Consequences' (1985) 93 *J. of Polit. Econ.* 1155, 1155.

67 Holderness and Sheehan (1988) (n 17 above 317).

68 A. Agrawal and C. Knoeber, 'Firm Performance and Mechanisms to Control Agency Problems between Managers and Shareholders' (1996) 31 *J. Financial Quant. Anal.* 377.

69 The authors hypothesised that where there is a scarcity of a particular constraint with respect to agency costs or controller benefits, another substitutes for it. Although it is unlikely that there could be perfect counterbalancing, the theory has merit in as much as it highlights that caution should be applied in isolating the impact that ownership concentration has on firm performance.

70 C. Loderer and K. Martin, 'Executive stock ownership and performance: Tracking faint traces' (1997) 45 *J. Financ. Econ.* 223.

71 C. Himmelberg et al., 'Understanding the Determinants of Managerial Ownership and the Link between Ownership and Performance' (1999) 53 *J. Financ. Econ* 353.

72 S. Prowse, 'The Structure of Corporate Ownership in Japan' (1992) 47 *J. Financ.* 1121.

(1988)[73] established what has been termed as a 'saw-toothed'[74] pattern. It was found that as management stock ownership increased from 0 per cent to 5 per cent, Tobin's Q also increased. Chiming with Jensen and Meckling's (1976) theory that agency costs decrease as management's ownership of equity rises, Morck et al. hypothesised the results to be due to increased convergence between management and shareholder interests.[75] However, between 5 per cent and 25 per cent stock ownership, a decrease in Tobin's Q was observed, attributed to management entrenchment effects dominating convergence,[76] and, therefore, a greater likelihood that management will either extract personal benefits or manage the company less assiduously when they are more insulated from removal by shareholders. Although above 25 per cent, a slight increase in Tobin's Q was demonstrated (attributed to the fact that above 25 per cent only an increase in convergence is observed, since such managers would not be significantly more entrenched than managers holding 25 per cent), overall, the data showed that firm performance did not recover to levels seen at the 5 per cent threshold until very high ownership concentrations (well beyond 50 per cent). Wruck (1989), in investigating abnormal returns on private equity sales that resulted in changing ownership concentrations, also identified greater abnormal returns at low and high changes of ownership concentration, but a negative correlation in a 'middle range'.[77] Although the precise range in which the negative effect became dominant was firm-specific, on average, it correlated well with the range delineated by Morck et al. Hermalin and Weisbach (1991) similarly showed increasing firm performance, measured by Tobin's Q, at low ownership levels (up to 1 per cent), with downward correlation at ownership levels above 20 per cent.[78] Holderness et al. (1999) found a very similar pattern to Morck et al. in relation to a 1935 sample of US firms, but the correlation was much weaker for a 1995 sample, which showed statistical significance only at ownership levels below 5 per cent.[79] However, the study by Morck et al. has been criticised in some respects,[80] with a number of authors noting that the results of the Morck et al. study are likely erroneous or accidental.[81]

73 R. Morck et al., 'Management Ownership and Market Valuation' (1988) 20 *J. Financ. Econ* 293.

74 C. Holderness, 'A Survey of Blockholders and Corporate Control' (2003) *FRBNY Economic Policy Review* (April 2003) 51, 58.

75 Although, see n 110 below.

76 Morck (1988) (n 73 above).

77 K. Wruck, 'Equity Ownership Concentration and Firm Value: Evidence from Private Equity Financings' (1989) 23 *J. Financ. Econ.* 3, 22–23.

78 B. Hermalin and M. Weisbach, 'The Effects of Board Composition and Direct Incentives on Firm Performance' (1991) 20 *Financ. Manag.* 101, 106.

79 C. Holderness et al., 'Were the Good Old Days That Good? Changes in Managerial Stock Ownership since the Great Depression' (1999) 54 *J. Financ.* 435, 460.

80 Even the authors acknowledged that the study only focused on large (usually old) firms, and that in young, faster growing firms, founders may have an important leadership role with management equity playing important signalling and compensation functions.

81 Cheffins (2002) (n 61 above 367); H. Demsetz and B. Villalonga, 'Ownership Structure and Corporate Performance' (2001) 7 *J. Corp.* 209, 230; M. Cho, 'Ownership Structure, Investment, and the

In contrast, McConnell and Servaes (1990) found a positive (although slowing) correlation between firm value (based on Tobin's Q) and inside ownership until ownership reached 40–50 per cent.[82] Beyond 40–50 per cent, a downward correlation was found, but even at ownership concentrations of 75 per cent, firm value was shown to be greater than inside ownership concentrations of 0 per cent.[83] The authors therefore rejected the findings of Morck et al.,[84] and the results are indicative of controlling shareholder firms overall performing better than dispersed ownership firms (notwithstanding the slight downward correlation beyond 40–50 per cent). A further study that presented a meta-analysis of seventy-four US studies on family-owned firms found that, overall, family-owned firms showed better 'financial firm performance' than non-family-owned firms, although the authors noted considerable variance suggesting that several of the studies found negative correlations.[85] Outside of the United States, some positive correlations were also found. In Western Europe (excluding the United Kingdom and Ireland), it was found that 'family-control' was associated with higher Tobin's Q and operating performance (measured by ROA), although 'control' in this context was delineated at the 10 per cent and greater voting level.[86] Leech and Leahy (1991) found that ownership control in UK listed companies was positively correlated with valuation ratios, greater returns of shareholder's capital, greater profit margins, and higher-growth-rates of sales and net assets.[87] In Canada, two more recent

Corporate Value: An Empirical Analysis' (1998) 47 *J. Financ. Econ.* 103, 120; Agrawal and Knoeber (1996) (n 68 above 378).

82 J. McConnell and H. Servaes, 'Additional Evidence on Equity Ownership and Corporate Value' (1990) 27 *J. Financ. Econ.* 595, 604.

83 No statistically significant correlation was found at all, though, when countenancing solely non-management shareholders (however, as noted by Holderness (2003) (n 74 above 59), the authors were unsure as to what constituted an 'outside [non-management] owner').

84 The authors opined that the difference in results from Morck et al. (1988) could be ascribed to a difference in the size of the firms sampled (n 82 above 608); also see S. Kole, 'Measuring Managerial Equity Ownership: A Comparison of Sources of Ownership Data' (1995) 1 *J. Corp.* 413, 428. However, when McConnell and Servaes attempted to replicate the Morck et al. (1988) study using a more comparable sample of firms, they only found a similar positive correlation for ownership up to 5 per cent, then no significant correlation at all after 5 per cent (note 82 above 609).

85 M. van Essen et al., 'How Does Family Control Influence Firm Strategy and Performance? A Meta-Analysis of US Publicly Listed Firms' (2015) 23 *Corp. Gov.* 3, 11. A comment on this study is that the authors do not confirm the measures of firm performance used by each of the studies, although they do confirm that their results were robust across all measures of firm performance (*ibid* 17). In testing a small sub-sample of six studies which had evaluated the impacts of ownership concentration, the authors did, however, note an 'inverted U-shaped' pattern, with positive correlations concentrated in the 'lower-ranges' of family-ownership concentration, and outperformance gradually degrading at higher ownership concentrations (*ibid* 17). The authors did not, though, specify where the turning point between beneficial concentration and negative concentration likely lies.

86 R. Barontini and L. Caprio, 'The Effect of Family Control on Firm Value and Performance: Evidence from Continental Europe' (2006) 12 *Euro. Financial Manag.* 689, 703.

87 D. Leech and J. Leahy, 'Ownership Structure, Control Type Classifications and the Performance of Large British Companies' (1991) 101 *Econ. J.* 1418, 1435.

studies by the National Bank of Canada found that 'family-controlled' Canadian firms earned better returns than non-family-controlled company portfolios.[88] However, the definition of 'family-controlled' encompassed a much wider set of companies than firms majority-owned by a controlling shareholder, and included both one share, one vote and dual-class firms.[89] The studies also did not involve any matching criteria to ensure that family-controlled firms were being compared with equivalent non-family-controlled firms, and were not peer-reviewed.

In summary, the empirical evidence is mixed as to which of controlling shareholder firms and dispersed ownership firms perform better, and a number of studies, in fact, suggest that there is no correlation at all between ownership concentration and firm performance. No matter the measure of firm performance used, there do not seem to be settled patterns. Holderness (2003), on a review of the relevant literature, remarked that it is not clear that the effect of ownership concentration on firm value was definitely positive or negative, and whatever the effect, there is little evidence that it is pronounced.[90] Pertinently, in 2001, Demsetz and Villalonga constructed a graph comparing the results of twelve major studies examining the effect of ownership concentration on Tobin's Q, and it was clear from the disarray of the illustration that there was no strong evidence that ownership concentration affected firm performance.[91] With the empirical evidence being inconclusive as to whether one share, one vote controlling shareholder structures overall harm public shareholders when compared with dispersed ownership firms, it is of no surprise that the FCA permits controlling shareholder firms on the premium tier, notwithstanding the regulator's apparent circumspection.

5.5.1.1 Why the Inconclusiveness?

In Chapter 7, the various extraneous aspects that can influence or bias the results of empirical studies on ownership structure will be discussed in more detail in the context of dual-class stock. Many of the same extraneous aspects, though, are

88 P. Fournier and A. Kastoras, 'The Family Advantage: The Sustainable Outperformance of Canadian Family-Controlled Public Companies' *National Bank of Canada* (October 2015) at 7 www.bnc.ca/content/dam/bnc/a-propos-de-nous/salle-de-presse/2015/study-the-family-advantage-national-bank-2015.pdf; A. Kastoras et al., 'The Family Advantage: The Sustainable Outperformance of Canadian Family-Controlled Public Companies' (2018) *National Bank of Canada* at 17 www.bnc.ca/content/dam/bnc/a-propos-de-nous/salle-de-presse/2018/study-the-family-advantage-national-bank-2018.pdf.

89 In Fournier and Kastoras (2015) (n 88 above 8), 'family-controlled' was defined to include firms where a family owns 25 per cent or more of the votes, and/or has significant influence over management or the board, and/or has succession power or power to name the CEO; and in Kastoras et al. (2018) (n 88 above 11), 'family-controlled' was defined to be where a founding family or founder controls 10 per cent or more of the votes, or an individual or related entities control 33.3 per cent or more of the votes.

90 Holderness (2003) (n 74 above 60).

91 Demsetz and Villalonga (2001) (n 81 above 211–212).

relevant to studies on one share, one vote controlling shareholder firms, and the inconclusiveness of the empirical studies may be attributed to those aspects. Some of those aspects are identified in this section, although a more detailed description of their likely impact is entrusted to Chapter 7.

In particular, the identity of the controlling shareholder will be an important factor in whether a controlling shareholder structure is positive or negative for public shareholders,[92] and the variety of controlling shareholder types, what was labelled by Holderness as the 'richness of blockholders',[93] will always make sweeping conclusions as to the impact of controlling shareholders imprecise. It has been speculated, for instance, that controlling shareholders who are individuals or families will act in a different manner to corporate controlling shareholders.[94] Additionally, even within the ambit of non-corporate controlling shareholders, an heir of a founder may have different incentives or lesser talents as a controlling shareholder as compared to the founder itself, and, as discussed further in Chapter 6, empirical evidence has suggested that firms controlled by heirs perform worse than those controlled by original founders. On a more granular level, there will be further distinctions relating to the personal intents, ambitions, incentives, skills and altruism of the individual controller. The age of the firm, an element that may be related to the identity of the controlling shareholder (with heirs more likely to be in control of older firms), can also have a bearing on whether the presence of a controlling shareholder is a positive or negative trait for public shareholders.[95]

The environment in which a company operates can also impact results. Although many studies that empirically evaluate controlling shareholder firms compare such firms to 'matched' dispersed ownership firms that are similar in nature, if matching criteria is not perfect, results may be biased by firm-specific qualities. For example, it has been inferred that the effect of controlling shareholder structure on firm performance will be influenced by the type of industry in which the firm operates,[96] the specificity of the assets of the company[97] and the

92 M. Barclay and C. Holderness, 'Negotiated Block Trades and Corporate Control' (1991) 46 *J. Finance* 861, 877.

93 Holderness (2003) (n 74 above 60); also see Edmans and Holderness (2017) (n 19 above 553).

94 For example, see the contrasting studies by Holderness and Sheehan (1988) (n 17 above 344), and R. Daniels and P. Halpern, 'Too Close for Comfort: The Role of the Closely Held Public Corporation in the Canadian Economy and the Implications for Public Policy' (1996) 26 *Can. Bus. L.J.* 11, 23.

95 Morck et al. (1988) (n 73 above 311).

96 Demsetz and Lehn (1985) (n 66 above 1161); Holderness et al. (1999) (n 79 above 461). For example, for regulated firms, regulation may effectively subsidise the costs of monitoring management, blunting one of the advantages of concentrated ownership (on the flipside, the shadow of regulation could constrain a controlling shareholder from extracting egregious controller benefits).

97 R. Zeckhauser and J. Pound, 'Are Large Shareholders Effective Monitors? An Investigation of Share Ownership and Corporate Performance' in *Asymmetric Information in Corporate Finance and Investment*, ed. R. Hubbard (University of Chicago Press, 1990) at 152. For example, it has been suggested that a non-management controlling shareholder has more of a positive effect on firm performance in industries with low asset specificity, such as machinery and paper product manufacturing, since it is

degree to which the company benefits from a monopoly.[98] The regulations of the relevant jurisdiction in which the company is listed can also affect the ability of controlling shareholders to extract controller benefits,[99] and the degree to which dispersed ownership firms are impinged by agency costs[100] – those regulations will in turn have a bearing on the effect of a controlling shareholder on firm performance, creating difficulties when results are collated in cross-jurisdictional studies.[101] Jurisdiction can also be linked to controlling shareholder identity. For example, in Singapore, family-controllers dominate the controlling shareholder scene,[102] whereas in China,[103] the State is the most prevalent controlling shareholder.

Another crucial aspect in evaluating empirical studies is the potential for the results to suffer from endogeneity issues. For example, certain firm-specific characteristics,[104] such as those related to the industry, life-cycle stage or amenity

easier for controlling shareholders to monitor management due to open information structures (conversely, controlling shareholders have less of an impact in industries with high asset specificities, since the benefits of controlling shareholders are less likely to accrue where a closed information structure makes monitoring difficult). However, this contention can also be challenged – with low asset specificity, the market is better able to monitor management and, in fact, the presence of a controlling shareholder in an industry with high asset specificity, particularly when involved in management itself, constrains a management team that would otherwise be difficult to monitor by the market, and, additionally, industries with high asset specificity, such as high technology, may benefit from large levels of management and employee human capital investment, which can be encouraged by a controlling shareholder ownership structure (see Section 6.3.3 of Chapter 6).

98 Maher and Andersson (1999) (n 18 above 33). For example, in a monopolistic or oligopolistic market, there may be greater opportunities for expropriation than in a competitive market.

99 B. Hall and R. Oriani, 'Does the Market Value R&D Investment by European Firms? Evidence from a Panel of Manufacturing Firms in France, Germany, and Italy' (2006) 24 *Int. J. Ind. Organ.* 971, 991; Gilson (2006) (n 20 above 1654).

100 K. Lins, 'Equity Ownership and Firm Value in Emerging Markets' (2003) 38 *J. Financ. Quant. Anal.* 159, 177.

101 It should also be noted that the 'law matters' theory predicts that controlling shareholder firms are less likely to list in jurisdictions with strong minority protection rights, since controllers will be constrained from extracting substantial controller benefits, and controllers are less likely to list with a concession of control in weak minority protection jurisdictions for fear of a new controller interjecting and excessively expropriating the original controller (R. La Porta et al., 'Law and Finance' (1998) 106 *J. Polit. Econ.* 1113, 1145). The theory has been discredited in some circles, since controlling shareholder structures continue to exist in non-trivial numbers in jurisdictions with supposedly strong minority protections (Gilson, (2006) (note 20 above 1641)), and a dispersed ownership system can develop within an environment of relatively low investor protection (B. Cheffins, *Corporate Ownership and Control: British Business Transformed* (Oxford University Press, 2009) at 35; also see J. Armour et al., 'Shareholder Protection and Stock Market Development: An Empirical Test of the Legal Origins Hypothesis' (2009) 6 *J. Empirical Legal Stud.* 343, 364).

102 L. Lan and U. Varottil, 'Shareholder Empowerment in Controlled Companies: The Case of Singapore' in *The Research Handbook of Shareholder Power*, eds. R. Thomas and J. Hill (Edward Elgar, 2015) at 579.

103 G. Liu and P. Sun, 'Identifying Ultimate Controlling Shareholders in Chinese Public Corporations: An Empirical Survey' (2003) *The Royal Institute of International Affairs Asia Programme Working Paper* No. 2 1, 8.

104 Demsetz and Lehn (1985) (n 66 above 1161–1162); Holderness (2003) (n 74 above 105).

potential[105] of the firm, or controller-specific characteristics,[106] such as those related to the identity of the controller, may lend themselves more to listing as controlling shareholder firms. It could be those characteristics that drive effects on firm performance rather than ownership structure. Although some studies control for some forms of endogeneity, it may be impossible to cover all bases without significantly prejudicing sample sizes. Relatedly, it has been suggested that the ownership structure of a firm is the endogenous outcome of a value-maximising process, and that the market essentially chooses the ownership structure appropriate to the environment in which that firm operates (for example, regulatory and economic scale considerations).[107] On that basis, ownership concentration will not be a determinant of firm performance, and ownership structure will vary systemically in a manner consistent with value maximisation; the industry in which the firm operates determines qualities such as firm size, cost of monitoring, regulations and amenity potential, which, in turn, determine the most value-maximising ownership structure.[108] Finally, reverse causation has also been raised as an issue,[109] conjecturing that individuals seek to retain or accumulate substantial shareholdings upon listing if they foresee substantial improvements in firm performance post-IPO. The possibility that management may be more likely to invest in, and be rewarded by the issue of equity in, high-performing firms could also taint those studies that focus on the impact of management equity on firm performance.[110] So much time has been spent trying to find the effect of 'A' on 'B' that not enough pause for thought has been given to the consideration that it may be 'B' causing 'A'.

105 'Amenity potential' relates to the potential for the business of the firm to allow for the creation of non-profit related utility for owners of the firm (Demsetz and Lehn (1985) (n 66 above 1161)). For example, controllers can garner non-profit related kudos, reputation and influence through the control of media and sports firms, which, accordingly, are often controlling shareholder firms (Demsetz and Lehn (1985) (n 66 above 1162)); S. Smart and C. Zutter, 'Control as a Motivation for Underpricing: A Comparison of Dual and Single-Class IPOs' (2003) 69 *J. Financ. Econ.* 85, 105).

106 D. Denis and D. Denis, 'Majority Owner-Managers and Organizational Efficiency' (1994) 1 *J. Corp.* 91, 110.

107 H. Demsetz, 'The Structure of Ownership and the Theory of the Firm' (1983) 26 *J. Law Econ.* 375, 384; also see Cheffins (2002) (n 61 above 369).

108 Value maximisation was propounded by Demsetz and Lehn (1985) (n 66 above). However, also see n 111 below.

109 Holderness (2003) (n 74 above 58).

110 McConnell and Servaes (1990) (n 82 above 611). Morck et al. (1988) also acknowledged that their positive correlation between ownership concentration and firm performance at low ownership levels could be due to endogenic factors such as: (i) managers of high Tobin's Q firms being awarded more stock; (ii) where management's value-enhancing ideas are rewarded with stock awards, high intangible asset firms will simultaneously have higher Tobin's Q and higher management equity; or (iii) high intangible asset firms will require management to hold more equity to ensure proper management of their assets (n 73 above 312), and their negative correlation between ownership concentration and firm performance at high ownership levels could be due to a positive correlation between ownership concentration, and managerial and firm attributes that themselves cause a decrease in Tobin's Q (*ibid* 312).

In summary, two concepts, which are not necessarily mutually exclusive, may explain the inconclusiveness of the empirical evidence. Firstly, it is possible that controlling shareholder structures are 'good' for some firms, and 'bad' for others, with the two types of firms cancelling themselves out when evaluated on a grouped basis, with specific firm and controller qualities influencing the direction of the controlling shareholder tradeoff on a firm-by-firm basis. Secondly, ownership structure may be an endogenous quality, and commentators have suggested that ownership structure may, in the most part, be 'chosen' to maximise firm value;[111] therefore, with an adequate sample size, no difference would be observed in firm value between dispersed ownership and controlling shareholder firms. It has been stated that 'Even a question as fundamental as the impact of blockholders on firm value remains unanswered.'[112] What is clear is that there is no strong evidence that controlling shareholders, in one share, one vote systems, are consistently prejudicial to public shareholders, and, accordingly, the FCA, albeit grudgingly, has tolerated their existence on the premium tier.

5.6 THE CHANGING DYNAMIC WITH DUAL-CLASS STOCK

Although the FCA clearly has reservations over controlling shareholder firms, it has determined that such firms are welcome, if not with open arms, on the premium tier. One may ask, therefore, what changes when a controlling shareholder lists its firm with dual-class stock? The answer lies in the shifting sands of the theoretical conflicts within the firm.

In any publicly listed firm, conflicts of interest can arise between various parties. The nature of these conflicts can vary between one share, one vote dispersed ownership, one share, one vote controlling shareholder, and dual-class stock controlling shareholder firms. Where ownership and control is separated in a one share, one vote dispersed ownership firm, as described earlier, a potential conflict exists between management and shareholders, and, in the absence of adequate monitoring by shareholders, managerial agency costs may be incurred as a result of self-serving, underperforming or indolent managers not acting in the best interests of the company, or its shareholders.[113] In contrast, in a one share, one vote controlling shareholder firm, due to the substantial equity ownership of the controller, it is sufficiently incentivised to rigorously monitor management, and management misbehaviour can be moderated. Ownership and control, which is seemingly ruptured in dispersed ownership firms, is concomitant in controlling shareholder firms. On the one hand, better monitoring by a controlling shareholder, free from the rational

111 However, scepticism could be directed at the emergence of 'efficient' value-maximising structures, and the ability for investors in public companies to 'choose' the relevant ownership structure (see Section 7.4.3 of Chapter 7).

112 A. Edmans, 'Blockholders and Corporate Governance' (2014) 6 *Annu. Rev. Financ. Econ.* 23, 44.

113 See nn 51–56 above and accompanying text.

apathy tainting disparate shareholders, solves the managerial agency costs dilemma. On the other hand, due to the incentive on the controlling shareholder to extract controller benefits, the primary conflict shifts from that between the management team and the shareholders to that between the majority shareholder and the minority shareholders; however, the incentive to extract controller benefits that reduce shareholder value is tempered by the controlling shareholder's large equity stake in the company. With dual-class stock, though, the dynamic may be distorted further. If a large voting/cash-flow divergence is created and the controller only holds a small level of equity, the incentive to monitor the management team in the interests of shareholder wealth is diminished, yet the incentive to extract controller benefits is enhanced. As the equity held by the controller decreases, the extraction of controller benefits that are detrimental to shareholder value will have less of a wealth-reducing effect on the controller, increasing the likelihood that the value of controller benefits to the controller will substantially outweigh the shareholder value cost to the controller of extracting those benefits. The conflict, now between the enhanced-voting shareholders and the inferior-voting shareholders, sees a re-emergence of managerial agency costs with little incentive on management to pursue shareholder wealth maximisation. Some have therefore opined that dual-class firms embrace the risks of one share, one vote controlling shareholder firms without the benefits, thereby combining the worst qualities of controlling shareholder and dispersed ownership constructs.[114]

It has been mathematically modelled that the incentive on a dual-class controller to extract controller benefits escalates at a sharply increasing rate as the controller's cash-flow rights decrease.[115] By way of example, as per a model outlined by Bebchuk and Kastiel (2019),[116] if controller benefit extraction is $100 million, a 30 per cent equity owner would accept a decrease in firm value of up to $333.3 million (the controller's proportion of that decrease is $100 million, so the controller will not be compensated for the decrease in firm value by the extraction of controller benefits for any decrease in firm value above that sum). For the same value of controller benefits, a 25 per cent owner would accept a decrease in firm value of $400 million, a 10 per cent owner of $1 billion and a 5 per cent owner of $2 billion. Therefore, the decrease in firm value that the controller would accept increases between a 30 per cent and 25 per cent equity owner by $66.6 million, but by $1 billion as the controller moves from 10 per cent to 5 per cent. The shifting sands of incentives to extract controller benefits as a controller's equity constraint vacillates in a dual-class stock firm seemingly underlies the FCA's approach to dual-class stock on the premium tier.

114 L. Bebchuk et al., 'Stock Pyramids, Cross-Ownership, and Dual Class Equity: The Mechanisms and Agency Costs of Separating Control from Cash-Flow Rights' in *Concentrated Corporate Ownership*, ed. R. Morck (University of Chicago Press, 2000) at 295.

115 *ibid* 301; Bebchuk and Kastiel (2019) (n 16 above 1473).

116 Bebchuk and Kastiel (2019) (n 16 above 1473).

5.7 CONCLUSION

Evidently, based upon the regulatory restrictions placed on premium tier one share, one vote controlling shareholder firms, the FCA has misgivings over controlling shareholders, but in recognition of the fact that controlling shareholder firms are not necessarily detrimental to public shareholder wealth, and could, in fact, present advantages over dispersed ownership firms, they are not prohibited from the premium tier. The presence of a controlling shareholder can be beneficial to the performance of certain firms, in the same way that dispersed ownership structure can also be detrimental to certain firms. The freedom of choice to list with a one share, one vote controlling shareholder structure enables those firms that will derive value from the structure to lock-in the benefits, and enables public shareholders to share in the success of such firms, when otherwise those firms may not list in the United Kingdom at all. The empirical evidence also suggests that one share, one vote controlling shareholders should not be feared.

However, the FCA has distinguished dual-class firms from one share, one vote controlling shareholder firms. Some of the benefits that are presented by one share, one vote controlling shareholder firms evaporate as a dual-class controller's voting/cash-flow divergence increases, and the incentive on the controller to extract controller benefits also increases. As such, the FCA, in instigating the premium tier prohibition of dual-class stock, determined that dual-class stock posed too great a risk to public shareholders on the premium tier, where the regulator is upholding the highest standards of corporate governance. Even the UK Listing Review proposals, which portend the acceptance of a form of disproportionate voting rights structure on the premium tier, restrict the exercise of enhanced-voting rights to blocking takeovers and enhanced-voting shareholder board incumbency in an attempt to limit the potential for controller benefit extraction, resulting in a proposal that does not resemble 'genuine' dual-class stock at all. However, the discussion does not end here. As discussed further in Chapter 6, the very fact that a controller of a dual-class firm has less of an equity-tie to the firm can also incentivise such a controller to take certain actions that are beneficial to all the shareholders in the company. For example, the perceived propensity for a controlling shareholder of a one share, one vote firm to take long-term decisions on behalf of the company may be tempered if the relevant decisions could cause that controlling shareholder to suffer substantial wealth deterioration as a result of short-term share price declines. Holding a smaller proportion of the equity in a dual-class stock system, with less financial exposure to short-term share price fluctuations, can liberate the controller into making such long-term decisions. Therefore, the absence of an equity constraint does not just present disadvantages as compared to a one share, one vote firm; it can also, theoretically, create advantages for shareholder wealth. If those advantages are credible, and it can be shown, as for one share, one vote controlling shareholder firms, that dual-class firms are not necessarily costly to public shareholders, surely the same approach to dual-class firms should be taken as has been applied to one share, one vote controlling shareholder firms. As with one share, one vote controlling shareholder structures, dual-class stock could be permitted, but with restrictions in place to prevent the most egregious types of expropriation of public shareholders, and to reduce the probability that the detriments of the structure will outweigh the benefits. Hence, in Chapter 6, the theoretical costs and benefits of dual-class firms will be discussed, and, in Chapter 7, the empirical evidence on dual-class stock will be evaluated, with a view to determining whether the FCA's concern that dual-class stock harms public shareholders is justified.

6

Theoretical Benefits and Detriments of Dual-Class Stock

The best men are not consistent in good; why should the worst men be consistent in evil?[1]

6.1 INTRODUCTION

As remarked in Chapter 5, part of the distrust that the regulators exhibit toward dual-class stock stems from a fear that the controller will utilise its power to extract personal benefits that are detrimental to shareholder wealth maximisation. However, as with one share, one vote controlling shareholder structures, it is not inevitable that a controller will use its power to take actions that are detrimental to other shareholders. This chapter commences with a discussion of the benefits and detriments of dual-class stock from the perspective of the public shareholders. Certain of the pros and cons will be common to both one share, one vote controlling shareholder and dual-class firms, but, as discussed in the previous chapter, dual-class stock modulates the dynamics of the relevant factor. Also discussed in the previous chapter was the nature of the (one share, one vote) controlling shareholder tradeoff. Similarly, the balance between the benefits and detriments to public shareholders of dual-class stock results in a tradeoff. Although such a tradeoff has been previously noted in the literature, it is discussed in new terms in this chapter: it will be argued that, in reality, the tradeoff represents a balance between different types of controller benefits. It is not inevitable that the extraction of controller benefits will be costly to inferior-voting shareholders. As will be discussed, the description of controller benefits in the common literature as private benefits of control may be a misnomer – the exercise of control in a manner that benefits a controller personally can, in certain cases, have consequential effects that are also beneficial for all shareholders. Where those controller benefits that are benign outweigh those controller benefits that are pernicious to public shareholders, the tradeoff can be tilted into a net-beneficial position. The likelihood that the tradeoff will be tilted into a positive direction is firm-specific and may shift over time. Dual-class structure, like

[1] W. Collins, *The Woman in White* (All the Year Round, 1860).

one share, one vote, will be optimal for some firms (at least for part of their life-cycles), but not for others. Taking dual-class stock off the table prevents those firms for which the structure is beneficial from realising the locus that is optimal for public shareholders. The discussion in this chapter sets the tone for the next chapter, in which the empirical evidence on dual-class firms will be assessed to determine how, in fact, the dual-class tradeoff is generally tilted.

6.2 THEORETICAL DETRIMENTS TO INFERIOR-VOTING SHAREHOLDERS OF DUAL-CLASS STOCK

Prior to outlining the potential merits of dual-class stock, in this section, the potential costs to public shareholders that are created by the actions of controllers theoretically incentivised by dual-class stock are discussed. As with controlling shareholder firms, many of the possible downsides of dual-class stock relate to the possibility that the controller will use its privileged position in being able to dictate the composition of the board and influence the management team (which may include or be led by the controller itself) to cause the company to take actions that are personally beneficial to the controller but costly to the interests of the company and the public shareholders. Consequently, as will be indicated, many of those potential actions will also be incentivised in a one share, one vote controlling shareholder structure. However, the situation is further exacerbated with dual-class stock. The controller is able to progressively abrogate responsibility, since its financial exposure to the well-being of the company declines as its cash-flow rights fall. The controller's voting/cash-flow divergence may in practice be sizeable,[2] tainting the motives and incentives of the controlling shareholder. Those in control of the company fail to fully feel the consequences of their actions,[3] and, therefore, even though similar controller benefits may be extracted in one share, one vote controlling shareholder firms, dual-class structure further incentivises the extraction of those controller benefits. The nature of those controller benefits that may be detrimental to public shareholder value are discussed in the following sections. However, it will also be noted that, particularly in the context of the United Kingdom's regulatory environment, in the real world, the risk that such controller benefits will be extracted to any great extent can be challenged.

[2] See Table 1.1 in Chapter 1.

[3] F. Easterbrook and D. Fischel, 'Voting in Corporate Law' (1983) 26 *J. Law Econ.* 395, 409; J. Dammann, 'The Controlling Shareholder's General Duty of Care: A Dogma That Should Be Abandoned' (2015) 2 *U. Ill. L. Rev.* 479, 494; F. Easterbrook and D. Fischel, *The Economic Structure of Corporate Law* (Harvard University Press, 1991) at 73; C. Li et al., 'Ownership Structure and the Cost of Corporate Borrowing' (2011) 100 *J. Financ. Econ.* 1, 2; H. Hu and B. Black, 'The New Vote Buying: Empty Voting and Hidden (Morphable) Ownership' (2006) 79 *S. Cal. L. Rev.* 811, 851; HKEX, 'Concept Paper: New Board' (June 2017) at 18.

6.2.1 *Tunnelling*

Perhaps the most egregious form of controller benefit extraction is through what is euphemistically labelled 'tunnelling'.[4] This is 'the transfer of assets and profits out of firms for the benefit of those who control them'.[5] The most common form of tunnelling is where the relevant company enters into transactions with other entities, in which the controller usually owns a greater proportion of the cash-flow rights than in the relevant company, on non-arm's length terms unfavourable to the relevant company. In effect, the controller is diverting cash-flow from one controlled entity to another, thereby expropriating the inferior-voting shareholders in the first entity.[6] Sweetheart deals or the simple withdrawing of corporate funds,[7] as well as the appropriation of corporate opportunities[8] have been noted as forms of tunnelling in dual-class firms. Additionally, a controller may divert resources from a company by entering into a merger with, or acquiring, a weaker firm in which the controller has a greater ownership stake, then 'bailing-out' the weaker firm using the assets of the first company.[9] Tunnelling can, of course, also occur in one share, one vote controlling shareholder firms, but, with dual-class stock, the conflict of interest between the controlling and public shareholders is more acute due to the disproportionately low equity interest held by the controller. From a theoretical perspective, the incentives to engage in tunnelling and the temptation to use voting power to heighten personal interests increase with the voting/cash-flow divergence of the controller[10] – the 'self-perpetuation of corporate princes'.[11]

In Chapter 5, a litany of one share, one vote controlling shareholder abuses that have taken place on the United Kingdom's premium tier, and which could be described as forms of tunnelling, were recounted.[12] With respect to dual-class stock, examples of tunnelling through egregious self-dealing are prevalent in weak investor protection jurisdictions,[13] but in contrast, in commonly perceived

[4] For example, R. Gilson and J. Gordon, 'Controlling Controlling Shareholders' (2003) 152 *U. Pa. L. Rev.* 785 favours laws that place limits on tunnelling by way of deviation of a corporation's ongoing earnings to controlling shareholders, but is more sanguine as to the extraction of other controller benefits such as the extraction of control premia.

[5] S. Johnson et al., 'Tunneling' (2000) 90 AEA *Papers and Proceedings* 22, 22. The authors attribute the genesis of the term to the expropriation of minority shareholders in the Czech Republic ('as in removing assets through an underground tunnel').

[6] *ibid* 7; M. Bertrand et al., 'Ferreting Out Tunneling: An Application to Indian Business Groups' (2002) 117 *Q. J. Econ.* 121, 139.

[7] D. Ashton, 'Revisiting Dual-Class Stock' (1994) 68 *St. John's L. Rev.* 863, 916.

[8] D. Solomon, 'The Importance of Inferior Voting Rights in Dual-Class Firms' (2019) 2 *BYU Law Rev.* 533, 548.

[9] Dammann (2015) (n 3 above 494).

[10] Hu and Black (2006) (n 3 above 851); M. Jensen and W. Meckling, 'Theory of the Firm: Managerial Behavior, Agency Costs and Ownership Structure' (1976) 3 *J. Financ. Econ.* 305, 313; Solomon (2019) (n 8 above 546).

[11] M. Warren III, 'One Share, One Vote: A Perception of Legitimacy' (1988) 14 *J. Corp. L.* 89, 104.

[12] See Section 5.3 of Chapter 5.

[13] See the examples in Johnson et al. (2000) (n 5 above 7); S. Johnson, 'Corporate Governance in the Asian Financial Crisis' (2000) 58 *J. Financ. Econ.* 141, 144. In Korea, it was found that an increasing

strong investor protection jurisdictions, such as the United Kingdom and the United States,[14] it has been stated that: 'At major companies with two classes of stock, horror stories are rare; champions of uniform voting rights can't cite a single example.'[15] Although that quote was made in 1985, at a time when the NYSE was just opening up to dual-class firms once again, even since 1985, at least in relation to extreme tunnelling, only two obvious US examples have emerged. Adelphia was a US cable television dual-class firm listed on NASDAQ, where the family of the founder, the Rigas family, held at the time of the relevant controversies around 63 per cent of the voting rights but only 26 per cent of the cash-flow rights.[16] In 2001, the founder and his son were convicted of obscuring liabilities, inflating earnings to meet market expectations, and more clear examples of tunnelling, such as using Adelphia's funds for personal purchases by the Rigas family, causing Adelphia to enter into purchase contracts with Rigas family-controlled entities at exorbitant rates and causing Adelphia to guarantee the debts of Rigas family-controlled entities.[17] Even though the fundamentals of Adelphia's base business were apparently strong, the company entered into bankruptcy proceedings in 2002. Similarly, in 2007, Conrad Black was convicted of expropriating more than $400 million from the media conglomerate Hollinger International.[18] Black held, directly or indirectly (through the Canadian company Hollinger Inc., which Black controlled), 73 per cent of the voting rights in Hollinger International, but only 30 per cent of the cash-flow rights. Black also served as CEO and chair of

voting/cash-flow divergence is associated with greater levels of related-party transactions, which were likely to have been implemented for the benefit of the controller (in effect, tunnelling), although the correlations were less significant for high-growth firms and those firms with strong governance where related-party transactions would be closely monitored (M. Kang et al., 'The Association between Related-Party Transactions and Control-Ownership Wedge: Evidence from Korea' (2014) 29 *Pac-Basin. Financ. J.* 272, 285).

14 The strength of investor protection in the United Kingdom and United States was deduced by an influential series of studies by La Porta et al. (R. La Porta et al., 'Legal Determinants of External Finance' (1997) 52 *J. Financ.* 1131; R. La Porta et al., 'Law and Finance' (1998) 106 *J. Political Econ.* 1113; R. La Porta et al., 'Investor Protection and Corporate Valuation' (2002) 57 *J. Financ.* 1147). However, in relation to the United States, some doubt was subsequently raised as to the strength of investor protections (for example S. Djankov et al., 'The Law and Economics of Self-Dealing' (2008) 88 *J. Fin. Econ.* 430; H. Spamann, 'The "Antidirector Rights Index" Revisited' (2010) 23 *Rev. Fin. Studies* 467). Further studies have, though, explained those doubts by suggesting that the strength of US protections lies in the accessibility and prevalence of private enforcement rather than the strength of the legal protections themselves (D. Katelouzou, and M. Siems, 'Disappearing Paradigms in Shareholder Protection: Leximetric Evidence for 30 Countries, 1990–2013' (2015) 15 *J. Corp. Law Stud.* 127).

15 Hector, 'The Flap Over Super-Shares' *Fortune* (16 September 1985) 114, 116, as cited in P. Flocos, 'Toward a Liability Rule Approach to the "One Share, One Vote" Controversy: An Epitaph for the SEC's Rule 19c-4?' (1989–1990) 138 *U. Pa. L. Rev.* 1761, 1778.

16 S. Gilson and B. Villalonga, 'Adelphia Communications Corp.'s Bankruptcy' (2010) *Harvard Business School Case* 208–071 1, 17.

17 For example, see *ibid* 6.

18 D. Cipollone, 'Risky Business: A Review of Dual Class Share Structures in Canada and a Proposal for Reform' (2012) 21 *Dalhousie J. Legal Stud.* 62, 75.

Hollinger International.[19] Black had used Hollinger International's funds to underwrite his lavish lifestyle, and had expropriated cash directly under the guise of non-compete agreements.[20] The examples of Adelphia and Hollinger International, though, appear to be exceptions, and the dearth of anecdotal evidence may be due to the fact that regulations in strong investor-protection jurisdictions, such as related-party transaction regulations, apply to curtail the most extreme forms of self-dealing. Such regulations prevent the relevant company from entering into transactions with, inter alia, the controller, or 'associates' of the controlling shareholder, unless specific conditions are fulfilled. For example, in Delaware, upon a challenge, the Courts may require a company to prove that a conflicted transaction was made on the basis of fair price and process, and was fair to the public shareholders.[21] Such requirements can deter tunnelling in dual-class firms.

Reverting to the United Kingdom, as described further in Chapter 8, related-party transactions (including those between the company and its controlling shareholder), if they exceed certain thresholds and are outside the normal course of business, are only permissible if confirmed by the company's sponsor that the terms are fair and reasonable to the shareholders, or, if the transaction is large, after the approval of the independent shareholders.[22] Additionally, in the presence of a 'controlling shareholder',[23] which would include a dual-class controller with at least 30 per cent of the votes in the company, a premium listed company must enter into a 'relationship agreement' with the controlling shareholder,[24] pursuant to which the controller must agree, inter alia, to conduct all transactions with the company on arm's length and normal commercial terms.[25] If that relationship agreement is breached by, for example, the controller entering into a transaction with the company on non-arm's length terms, the thresholds for related-party transactions are disapplied,[26] and the relevant transaction would require independent shareholder pre-approval no matter its size. The scope for tunnelling is therefore limited in the United Kingdom. However, given that tunnelling abuses have occurred in the United Kingdom in relation to one share, one vote controlling shareholder firms, as

19 B. Nicholas and B. Marsh, 'Dual-Class: The Consequences of Depriving Institutional Investors of Corporate Voting Rights' *Harvard Law School Forum of Corporate Governance and Financial Regulation* (May 17, 2017).

20 R. Siklos, 'Conrad Black Found Guilty in Fraud Trial' *The New York Times* (14 July 2007) www.nytimes.com/2007/07/14/business/13cnd-black.html.

21 *Weinberger* v. *UOP, Inc.*, 457 A.2d 701, 703 (Del. 1983).

22 Listing Rules, Chapter 11. However, note the exemption for sovereign-controlled companies (Listing Rules, Chapter 21; for further details, see Chapter 8).

23 For the purposes of the Listing Rules, a controlling shareholder is any person who exercises or controls on its own, or together with any person with whom it is acting in concert, 30 per cent or more of the votes able to be cast on all or substantially all matters at general meetings of the company (LR App 1.1).

24 LRs 6.5.4R and 9.2.2ADR(1).

25 LR 6.5.4R.

26 LR 11.1.1AR.

further discussed in Chapter 9, there may be a case to strengthen the related-party transaction regulations in the United Kingdom for dual-class firms if the premium tier were to welcome dual-class firms. Even with strong related-party transaction regulations, given the power and information advantages instilled in a controller, clandestine or subtle, even fraudulent, tunnelling could still occur in contravention of the regulations which may only be discovered after the event;[27] however, obvious and egregious examples of tunnelling in the United Kingdom, if dual-class stock were prevalent on the premium tier, would likely be rare.

6.2.2 *High Executive Remuneration*

The extraction of excessive managerial remuneration could be considered to be a form of tunnelling, and generally would not be covered by related-party transaction regulations.[28] The board, in the United Kingdom, has prima facie responsibility for the remuneration of management. Therefore, if the controller itself serves as part of the management team, that controller could use its influence over the composition of the board to substantially enhance its remuneration as a manager. Even though the same abuse could be associated with one share, one vote controlling shareholder firms, theoretically the incentive on the dual-class controller to extract significant sums through this method is greater, through a combination of suffering a smaller downside as a result of its smaller equity holding, and receiving lower regular equity income. Although, in the United Kingdom, say-on-pay voting mechanics give shareholders the right to opine on directors' executive remuneration,[29] the director concerned is not prevented from exercising his or her votes on the relevant resolutions. Therefore, a controller holding a majority of the votes in the company could unilaterally pass a say-on-pay shareholders' resolution on his or her pay as an executive director. In the United States, there is even easier scope for abuse since say-on-pay votes are advisory and do not void payments made, or proposed by the board to be made, to executives.[30] Indeed, some commentators have noted that where a dual-class controller is involved in management, this can be associated with higher levels of executive compensation,[31]

27 Hollinger International is a felicitous example from an international perspective (see nn 18–20 above and accompanying text).

28 In the United Kingdom, it is likely that the payment of directors' remuneration would be considered to be a transaction in the ordinary course of business, which is excluded from the related-party transaction regulations (LR 11.1.5R). Payments under long-term incentive schemes are also excluded from the regulations (LR 11.1.6R and LR 11 Annex 1.1R).

29 Shareholders have a binding vote on a quoted company's directors' remuneration policy (CA 2006, s. 439A), and an advisory vote on the implementation of that policy, being the sums paid to directors in the previous financial year (CA 2006, s. 439).

30 Dodd-Frank Act, § 951.

31 R. Masulis et al., 'Agency Problems at Dual-Class Companies' (2009) 64 *J. Financ.* 1697, 1708; S. Tinaikar, 'Executive Compensation Disclosure and Private Control Benefits: A Comparison of U.S. and Canadian Dual Class Firms' (2017) 29 *J. Int. Account. Aud. Tax.* 32, 41; S. Tinaikar, 'Voluntary Disclosure and Ownership Structure: An Analysis of Dual Class Firms' (2014) 18

and some have opined that this is one of the primary channels of controller benefit extraction.[32] However, although in individual cases there may be instances of astonishingly high levels of executive pay, across the board, in the United States, the higher levels of pay in dual-class firms are insignificant compared to market capitalisation.[33] As such, notwithstanding the theoretical concerns, evidence does not suggest that executive remuneration is a substantial form of expropriation.

In high investor-protection jurisdictions, requirements for public companies to disclose substantial details of executive pay mean that outrageously high levels of pay would likely attract significant shareholder, public and media opprobrium. In the United States, for example, extensive disclosure is required pursuant to the Dodd-Frank Act.[34] In the United Kingdom, quoted companies must prepare a directors' remuneration report[35] which must disclose detailed information relating to directors' remuneration (and the CEO's and deputy CEO's remuneration, even if they are not board members).[36] The contents must be filed with the Registrar of Companies,[37] and publicly disclosed on the company's website.[38] Disproportionately high levels of executive pay for dual-class controllers involved in management (assuming that they also serve on the board, or serve as CEO or deputy CEO) would therefore be publicly disclosed, and the adverse publicity that extortionate pay would attract should moderate expropriation through executive remuneration.[39] By way of analogy, in a UK one

J. Manag. Gov. 373, 394; B. Amoako-Adu et al., 'Dual Class Discount, and the Channels of Extraction of Private Benefits' in *Advances in Financial Economics Vol.* 16, eds. S. Ferris et al. (Emerald Publishing, 2013) at 195; S. Smart and C. Zutter, 'Control as a Motivation for Underpricing: A Comparison of Dual and Single-class IPOs' (2003) 69 *J. Financ. Econ.* 85, 104.

32 Amoako-Adu et al. (2013) (n 31 above 195).

33 For example, for the fiscal years ending 2000 and 2001, the average total annual compensation for managers of US dual-class corporations was only $154,000 more than those of one share, one vote corporations (Tinaikar (2014) (n 31 above 394)), and between 2001 and 2007, the average CEO compensation for dual-class firms was $5.2 million compared to $4.7 million for matched one share, one vote firms (Amoako-Adu et al. (2013) (*ibid* 183). Although Masulis et al. (2009) found more striking results showing that average US CEO total compensation between 1995 and 2003 increased by $1.054 million as the ratio of insiders' voting rights to cash-flow rights rose by one standard deviation (n 31 above 1707), and Smart and Zutter (2003) (n 31 above 104) found average US CEO pay of dual-class firms between 1990 and 1998 to be $905,649 (about twice as much as the figure for one share, one vote firms), this should be considered in the context of average market capitalisation – in 2017, the average market capitalisation of a US listed company was $7.3 billion, and even in 2001, the average was above $3 billion (Ernst & Young, 'Looking Behind the Declining Number of Public Companies' (May 2017) at 3 and 2).

34 Dodd-Frank Act, § 953.

35 CA 2006, s. 420.

36 CA 2006, s. 421, and The Large and Medium-sized Companies and Groups (Accounts and Reports) (Amendment) Regulations 2013, as amended by The Companies (Miscellaneous Reporting) Regulations 2018, and The Companies (Directors' Remuneration Policy and Directors' Remuneration Report) Regulations 2019.

37 CA 2006, s. 441.

38 CA 2006, s. 430.

39 The term 'outrage costs and constraints' was coined in this context in L. Bebchuk and J. Fried, *Pay without Performance* (Harvard University Press, 2004) at 5.

share, one vote firm, the loss of a say-on-pay vote on payments made to directors in the previous financial year, which is only advisory,[40] can still lead to substantive changes being made to executive remuneration.[41] Even with United Kingdom controlling shareholder one share, one vote companies, the managers may voluntarily not exercise the votes attached to their shares on matters of executive remuneration.[42] Accordingly, reverting to the realm of dual-class companies, it is not inevitable that a controller will extract high levels of remuneration, and a prominent US example is that of Google, where the founders famously annually only pay themselves $1 in salary.[43] Although a controlling shareholder has the legal power to pay itself any sum by way of executive compensation, other constraints seem to curtail this power.

6.2.3 *Inefficient Decision-Making*

The pursuit of controller benefits, which is incentivised in dual-class firms, can also lead to management making inefficient decisions.[44] The seminal study by Bebchuk et al. (2000) showed that controllers can 'externalise progressively more of the costs of their moral hazards' as the controller's voting/cash-flow divergence expands.[45] For example, when presented with two competing projects, one of which is better for the company, a controller may still procure that the company choose the more inefficient option if the controller benefits accruing to that project outweigh the downside risk associated with the controller's equity holding; with dual-class structure, if the controller has significantly reduced its equity holding, the likelihood of choosing inefficient projects of this nature increases.[46] The authors also show that 'decisions of scope' are influenced by dual-class structure – decisions as to whether to distribute cash-flow or expand the firm. If the firm owns an asset that generates controller benefits, a controller may cause the firm to hold on to the asset rather than sell it and

40 CA 2006, s. 439.

41 For example, the chair of the remuneration committee in 2009, and the CEO in 2012, resigned from Royal Dutch Shell and Aviva, respectively, after the loss of directors' remuneration report advisory votes, and, in 2012, the CEO of Trinity Mirror resigned ahead of a planned shareholder revolt on pay. In 2016, the remuneration committee of BP used its discretion to reduce performance-related pay to which the CEO was otherwise entitled to avoid 'formulaic outcomes', after the company had lost the advisory vote on the implementation of the remuneration policy in the previous financial year. In 2017, the chair of Persimmon resigned after shareholder and public outrage toward the CEO's £110 million pay package, followed by the resignation of the CEO in 2018.

42 For example, the executive directors of Fraser Group voluntarily agreed not to exercise the votes attached to their shares in relation to the approval of a controversial bonus scheme in 2015 (see Sports Direct (RNS Number: 1069J), '2015 Bonus Share Scheme' (9 June 2014)).

43 Proxy Statement Schedule 14(A) of Alphabet Inc. (30 April 2019) at 43.

44 Also see, from a normative perspective, the classic robust defence of one share, one vote in Easterbrook and Fischel (1983) (n 3 above 409).

45 L. Bebchuk et al., 'Stock Pyramids, Cross-Ownership, and Dual Class Equity: The Mechanisms and Agency Costs of Separating Control from Cash-Flow Rights' in *Concentrated Corporate Ownership*, ed. R. Morck (University of Chicago Press, 2000) at 301.

46 *ibid* 302.

distribute the profits, even though the sale price for the asset exceeds the benefits derived by the company from retaining it. Additionally, if the firm can acquire an asset that creates controller benefits for the controller, the firm may acquire that asset with free cash rather than distribute that cash to the shareholders. The controller benefits that lead to the making of inefficient decisions can be related to tunnelling, as described previously, but could also be more subtle and be, for example, correlated with the extraction of non-pecuniary controller benefits (see Section 6.2.5 later in this chapter). Bebchuk et al. opine that inefficient decisions can unintentionally result in dual-class firms becoming inefficiently large and evolving into unwieldy conglomerates[47] (although, as discussed later in this chapter, other factors that drive diversification, and therefore the creation of conglomerates, by one share, one vote controlling shareholder firms may be dampened by dual-class stock[48]). The determination by the UK Listing Review that rather than 'true' dual-class stock, a share structure that enables an individual to disproportionately exercise votes to block takeovers and preserve his or her board seat, but does not enable that individual to exercise votes on other shareholders' resolutions, should be permitted on the premium tier, will in part have been driven by a desire to mitigate against controllers making inefficient decisions.[49] For example, without the individual holding omnipotent voting power, larger transactions of a premium listed company will need to be pre-approved by a shareholders' vote which such a person cannot unilaterally carry unless he or she has retained a majority of the equity.[50]

The equity markets appear to acknowledge that inefficient decision-making could be taking place in the dual-class stock world, notwithstanding the existence of regulations aimed at curtailing related-party transactions. Taking the United States, Masulis et al. (2009) found that the value given by outside investors to cash holdings of dual-class firms is decreasing with the size of the controller's voting/cash-flow divergence.[51] The reasoning is that such excess cash holdings give the controller the opportunity to use firm cash in a way that extracts controller benefits. Additionally, chiming with the theoretical analysis of Bebchuk et al. (2000), as the controller's voting/cash-flow divergence increases, the authors found that acquisition decisions were greeted with greater negative market reactions, firms were less likely to withdraw from acquisitions that the market deemed as negative, and capital expenditure contributed less to shareholder value.[52] This suggests that, with dual-class stock, the market perceives that acquisition decisions are being driven by the level of controller benefits that may be generated, and that capital expenditure is being used to 'empire-build' or for other reasons personally beneficial to the

47 *ibid* 303.
48 See Section 6.3.2 later in this chapter.
49 See Section 1.5.7 of Chapter 1.
50 Listing Rules, Chapter 10; also see *ibid*.
51 Masulis et al. (2009) (n 31 above 1703).
52 *ibid* 1713–1715.

controller rather than for the benefit of the company.[53] Amoako-Adu et al. (2013) also found that the higher the cash holdings of a dual-class firm, the greater the valuation discount attributed to such firm by outside investors compared to one share, one vote firms,[54] but, unlike Masulis et al. and Bebchuk et al., did not find that capital expenditure by dual-class firms was discounted more than in one share, one vote firms, suggesting that investors did not view capital expenditure as a means of controller benefit extraction.[55] In the next chapter, though, the empirical evidence on dual-class stock will be discussed in more detail, and, in particular, it will be noted that market reaction or 'event-based' studies, and firm valuation studies, can be heavily impacted by the market's perception of events or dual-class stock generally. Beyond market perception, a more thorough picture of whether dual-class managers are making more inefficient decisions can be painted by evaluating whether there are any correlations between dual-class stock and operating performance. Noting the spoiler alert, in Chapter 7, it will be shown that there is no evidence that the operating performance of dual-class firms is worse than similar one share, one vote firms, suggesting that controller benefit extraction does not prejudice the performance of those firms to the extent that they perform worse than one share, one vote firms. Therefore, even though theory suggests that tunnelling and inefficient decision-making will be excessive in dual-class firms, this is not conclusively backed-up by the empirical evidence, and the UK Listing Review's concerns that giving wider voting powers to founders will necessarily prejudice the interests of public shareholders[56] may be misguided. Indeed, the propensity for inefficient decision-making should be balanced against the enhanced ability for dual-class firm managers to make efficient project choices as described under the benefits of dual-class structure later in this chapter.

6.2.4 *Management Entrenchment*

In the United Kingdom, the shareholders of a company can remove the directors by way of majority vote.[57] This is an important and non-waivable requirement of company law, since, in the normal course, the board has the right to remove and replace management,[58] giving the shareholders an indirect method of expressing their views on management and effectively instigating change in the management team. With the controller of a dual-class firm holding a majority of the votes, inferior-voting shareholders are unable to exercise this right without the support of the controller, who may well also be a manager. Management is completely

53 Solomon (2019) (n 8 above 550); H. Kim and R. Michaely, 'Sticking Around Too Long? Dynamics of the Benefits of Dual-Class Structures' (2018) 1, 5 https://ssrn.com/abstract=3145209.
54 Amoako-Adu et al. (2013) (n 31 above 196).
55 *ibid* 197.
56 See text accompanying nn 49–50 above.
57 CA 2006, s. 168.
58 Model PLC Articles, article 3.

insulated from removal by the public shareholders.[59] So long as the managers are acting in a manner that is satisfactory to the controller, possibly even in priority to the interests of the shareholders as a whole, they will not have any fear of losing their employment.[60] The inability to cause the removal of managers is a key detriment of, and significant risk to minority shareholders in, even one share, one vote controlling shareholder firms, since without the deterrent of removal, the risk persists that the managers may not perform efficiently or diligently, or, worse, act in a self-serving manner. With dual-class structure, though, the risks are amplified, since, as the controller's voting/cash-flow divergence expands, the less the incentive on the controller (as a, potentially, well-diversified, minority investor) to ensure that management maximises shareholder wealth and the greater the incentive on the controller to, instead, procure that management serves the interests of the controller. Therefore, in theory, there is a greater likelihood that an underperforming (from the perspective of shareholder wealth) management team will remain in situ in a dual-class firm. Such a prospect has not escaped the UK Listing Review proposals for the premium tier, which would entitle an individual to guarantee his or her board seat for a finite period but would not assure such an individual that he or she could entrench incumbent management through control over the composition of the board as a whole.[61]

The impact of management entrenchment on shareholder value could transmute over time. For example, a founder may hang on as a manager even though his or her skills and abilities have significantly waned over time and the company would be better served with fresh leadership. Even though the founder would benefit from handing over day-to-day management to a new CEO through an increase in share price (although of course, as the controller's voting/cash-flow divergence increases, the share value benefits to the founder decrease), a combination of a desire to avoid the loss of controller benefits, endowment effects[62] and a reticence to accept that the interests of the company would be further promoted by new management can lead to the founder continuing as a manager.[63] A much cited example is that of Sumner Redstone, who remained as executive chair of the US dual-class company Viacom into his nineties despite allegations that he was no longer competent to lead the company.[64]

59 J. Gordon, 'Ties that Bond: Dual Class Common Stock and the Problem of Shareholder Choice' (1988) 76 *Cal. L. Rev.* 1, 61; Cipollone (2012) (n 18 above 65); M. Moore and E. Walker-Arnott, 'A Fresh Look at Stock Market Short-termism' (2014) 41 *J. Law Soc.* 416, 440; A. Anand, 'Offloading the Burden of Being Public: An Analysis of Multiple Voting Share Structures' (2016) 10 *Va. Law Bus. Rev.* 395, 400.

60 Although such behaviour could constitute a breach of directors' duties, as discussed in Chapter 8, difficulties persist in the enforcement of such duties which blunt the deterrent effect.

61 See Section 1.5.7 of Chapter 1.

62 See n 91 below and accompanying text.

63 H. Cronqvist and M. Nilsson, 'Agency Costs of Controlling Minority Shareholders' (2003) 38 *J. Financ. Quant. Anal.* 695, 715; see n 79 below and accompanying text.

64 L. Bebchuk and K. Kastiel, 'The Untenable Case for Perpetual Dual-Class Stock' (2017) 4 *Va. Law Rev.* 585, 588.

It is not, however, inevitable that a founder will remain in charge of a company on a day-to-day basis. At Google, for example, the founders, Larry Page and Sergey Brin, voluntarily relinquished their roles as CEO and president, respectively, in 2019.[65]

A further aspect connected with management entrenchment rears its (potentially ugly) head when the original founder does resolve that there should be a change in day-to-day management. Rather than instigating an open recruitment process, the founder may determine that managerial control should be transferred to an heir or another family member. Although the original manager is no longer entrenched, family entrenchment continues, even though the new manager may not be well-suited or the best candidate for the role.[66] The change in management may also be concomitant with a transfer of the controller's enhanced-voting shares to the family member. Studies have shown that, on average, transfers of control to heirs or other family members are associated with worsening performance.[67] This has been termed the 'gravity of generations'.[68] As discussed in Chapters 7 and 9, dwindling management team efficacy upon a transfer of control to heirs could explain one of the reasons why certain studies have shown that the performance of dual-class firms declines over time. An analogy can be drawn to the fictional, dysfunctional Roy family in the television show 'Succession'.[69] Public shareholders were concerned that the patriarch had outstayed his welcome as CEO of the family-controlled company, and were ill-disposed to succession by family members. The producers of the drama conceded that they used the US dual-class firms CBS and News Corp., with their controlling families, the Redstones and Murdochs, respectively, as inspiration.[70]

65 Alphabet, 'A letter from Larry and Sergey' (December 3, 2019) https://blog.google/inside-google/alphabet/letter-from-larry-and-sergey.

66 Bebchuk and Kastiel (2017) (n 64 above 606); C. Holderness and D. Sheehan, 'The Role of Majority Shareholders in Publicly Held Corporations: An Exploratory Analysis' (1988) 20 *J. Financ. Econ.* 317, 318.

67 R. Anderson et al., 'Founding-Family Ownership and Firm Performance; Evidence from the S&P 500' (2003) 58 *J. Financ.* 1301, 1321; R. Morck et al., 'Inherited Wealth, Corporate Control, and Economic Growth: The Canadian Disease' in *Concentrated Corporate Ownership*, ed. R. Morck (University of Chicago Press, 2000) at 338; N. Bloom and J. Van Reenen, 'Why Do Management Practices Differ Across Firms and Countries?' (2010) 24 *J. Econ. Persp.* 203, 218; M. Bennedsen et al., 'Inside the Family Firm: The Role of Families in Succession Decisions and Performance' (2007) 122 *Q.J. Econ.* 647, 669; F. Pérez-González, 'Inherited Control and Firm Performance' (2006) 96 *Am. Econ. Rev.* 1559, 1574; B. Villalonga and R. Amit, 'How Do Family Ownership, Control and Management Affect Firm Value?' (2006) 80 *J. Fin. Econ.* 385, 403; N. Bloom and J. Van Reenen, 'Measuring and Explaining Management Practices Across Firms and Countries' (2007) 122 *Q.J. Econ.* 1351, 1383; R. Barontini and L. Caprio, 'The Effect of Family Control on Firm Value and Performance: Evidence from Continental Europe' (2006) 12 *Euro. Financ. Manag.* 689; M. van Essen et al., 'How does Family Control Influence Firm Strategy and Performance? A Meta-Analysis of US Publicly Listed Firms' (2015) 23 *Corp. Gov.* 3, 18; R. Adams et al., 'Understanding the Relationship between Founder-CEOs and Firm Performance' (2009) 16 *J. Empir. Financ.* 136, 149.

68 R. Gilson, 'Controlling Shareholders and Corporate Governance: Complicating the Comparative Taxonomy' (2006) 119 *Harv. Law Rev.* 1642, 1668.

69 J. Armstrong, 'Succession' *HBO* (2018-2019).

70 A. Hill, 'The Plague of Long-Running Feuds in Family Businesses' *Financial Times* (19 August 2019) www.ft.com/content/f5d1b782-bf3f-11e9-89e2-41e555e96722.

The entrenchment of management is further exacerbated by the fact that the internal monitoring mechanism provided by independent directors in dispersed ownership firms is substantially lacking in the presence of a controlling shareholder,[71] such as found in most dual-class firms. Non-executive directors in UK listed companies have traditionally had two roles: an advisory role in developing strategy, and a supervisory role in monitoring and scrutinising the performance of management.[72] Although dual-class firms can, and do, appoint independent directors, from a UK perspective, if dual-class firms were permitted on the premium tier, the controller would dictate the relevant appointments, and it can be doubted as to whether those directors are truly independent and whether they will be particularly adroit in monitoring the management team.[73] If the relevant 'independent' director attaches prestige, pride or financial benefits to the role, there is a possibility that such director's independence could display a level of obsequiousness to a controller who has appointed the director and controls his or her removal,[74] and who could also appoint compliant 'independent' directors to further positions at other companies under its control.[75] Although, as discussed in Chapter 8, the Listing Rules grant minority shareholders in controlling shareholder firms a separate right to vote, in the first instance, in relation to the appointment or re-election of independent directors, ultimately, the controlling shareholder possesses the power to finally compel any such appointment or re-election.[76] Concerns with regard to the independence of independent directors (and their ability to act, in the interests of the public shareholders, as a check-and-balance on the managers) would not be any different in a dual-class firm as compared to a one share, one vote controlling shareholder firm,

[71] Cipollone (2012) (n 18 above 75).

[72] UK CGC, Principle H. Also, see *Re Continental Assurance Company of London plc* [2007] 2 BCLC 287, 443; and *Equitable Life Assurance Society* v. *Bowley* [2004] BCLC 180, 189.

[73] J. Seligman, 'Equal Protection in Shareholder Voting Rights: The One Common Share, One Vote Controversy' (1985–1986) 54 *Geo. Wash. L.R.* 687, 722; R. Daniels and P. Halpern, 'Too Close for Comfort: The Role of the Closely Held Public Corporation in the Canadian Economy and the Implications for Public Policy' (1996) 26 *Can. Bus. L.J.* 11, 16; P. Halpern, 'Systemic Perspectives on Corporate Governance Systems' in *Corporate Governance and Globalization: Long-Range Planning Issues*, eds. S. Cohen and G. Boyd (Edward Elgar, 2000) at 29; N. Kumar and J. Singh, 'Outside Directors, Corporate Governance and Firm Performance: Empirical Evidence from India' (2012) 4 *AJFA* 39, 44; L. Bebchuk and A Hamdani, 'Independent Directors and Controlling Shareholders' (2017) 165 *U. Pa. L. R.* 1271, 1287; L. Lan and U. Varottil, 'Shareholder Empowerment in Controlled Companies: The Case of Singapore' in *The Research Handbook of Shareholder Power*, eds. Randall Thomas and Jennifer Hill (Edward Elgar, 2015) at 577; J. Erickson et al., 'Board Composition and Firm Value under Concentrated Ownership: The Canadian Evidence' (2005) 13 *Pac-Basin. Financ. J.* 387, 400; C. Chen et al., 'Board Independence as a Panacea to Tunneling? An Empirical Study of Related-Party Transactions in Hong Kong and Singapore' (2018) 15 *J. Empir. Leg. Stud.* 987, 1017; A. Gurrea, 'Towards a Credible System of Independent Directors in Controlled Firms' *Ibero-American Institute for Law and Finance Working Paper* 1/2019 1, 15.

[74] B. Reddy, 'The Fat Controller: Slimming Down the Excesses of Controlling Shareholders in UK Listed Companies' (2018) 38 *OJLS* 733, 754.

[75] D. Lin, 'Beyond Beholden' (2019) 1 https://papers.ssrn.com/sol3/papers.cfm?abstract_id=3335195.

[76] For further details, see Section 8.2.5 of Chapter 8.

but the consequences of the independent directors being ineffective or impotent will be more keenly felt where the management team is even less incentivised to act in the interests of the outside shareholders.

Therefore, in summary, if the inferior-voting shareholders of a dual-class firm are displeased with the performance of management, they will have no power to change the management team and will not be able to rely upon the controller to make the relevant change if such performance results in a decrease in share price. With controller benefits dictating over share value, the consequences of the inferior-voting shareholders not being able to remove underperforming management become more acute. High-profile managerial failures have occurred in US dual-class firms, and inferior-voting shareholders were not able to replace management. For example, the executives of Groupon survived after its auditor discovered material weaknesses in its internal controls, which precipitated a decline in share price, and, at News Corp. in the wake of the phone-hacking scandal, even after non-controlling shareholders voted against Rupert and James Murdoch remaining on the board, they were protected by their own majority control through the ownership of enhanced-voting stock.[77] The inclination of a controller to hang on in a management role (or to appoint an heir as a replacement) can be related to the capacity to extract pecuniary controller benefits such as through tunnelling, or high executive remuneration. However, as with inefficient decision-making, the driver of entrenchment could also be non-pecuniary in nature, which is discussed next.

6.2.5 *Non-Pecuniary Controller Benefits*

Most studies into controller benefits focus on the extraction of financial benefits by the controller, ignoring the numerous non-pecuniary benefits.[78] Reputation and prestige, as well as the simple psychological worth of being in control,[79] are obvious non-pecuniary benefits. Certain industries also lend themselves to specific non-pecuniary benefits, such as the influence accrued through control of the media or newspapers, and the sense of achievement through success of sports teams,[80] which may explain why such firms, even when they float, often retain concentrated ownership or, in jurisdictions where permitted, adopt dual-class structure.[81] Being the controller of a large or influential company can breed further commercial, political or reputational opportunities, unrelated to the business of the company.

77 T. Wen, 'You Can't Sell Your Firm and Own It Too: Disallowing Dual-Class Stock Companies from Listing on the Securities Exchanges' (2014) 162 *U. Pa. L. R.* 1495, 1502.

78 Gilson (2006) (n 68 above 1665) made a similar critique.

79 P. Aghion and P. Bolton, 'An Incomplete Contracts Approach to Financial Contracting' (1992) 59 *Rev. Econ. Stud.* 473, 476; A. Dyck and L. Zingales, 'Private Benefits of Control: An International Comparison' (2004) 59 *J. Financ.* 537, 540; Gilson (2006) (n 68 above 1664).

80 H. Demsetz and K. Lehn, 'The Structure of Corporate Ownership: Causes and Consequences' (1985) 93 *J. Political Econ.* 1155, 1162; Smart and Zutter (2003) (n 31 above 105).

81 Demsetz and Lehn (1985) (n 80 above 1167 and 1171).

Although often academically neglected, from the perspective of outside shareholders, non-pecuniary controller benefits can be particularly insidious, since there may be large incentives for controllers to sacrifice firm value in their pursuit,[82] especially where a dual-class controller only owns a small level of equity, and therefore only has minimal economic concern as to the effect that the pursuit of non-pecuniary controller benefits will have on the value of the company.

Further examples of the extraction of non-pecuniary controller benefits include empire-building and instigating pet projects for personal satisfaction.[83] A controller could cause the company to pursue a project purely due to it being personally interesting to the controller. In contrast, a controller may decline an otherwise profitable project or changes to the strategy of the business due to apathy, simply an inclination to work less assiduously or preference for an 'easy-life' that avoids difficult decisions that cause strife but are in the interests of the company.[84] A theoretical propensity for dual-class firms to make inefficient decisions (as discussed in Sections 6.2.1 and 6.2.3 earlier in this chapter) could well be driven by the controller prioritising the extraction of non-pecuniary controller benefits, rather than driven by an engagement in related-party transactions or the extraction of other pecuniary controller benefits. Of course, a management team in a one share, one vote controlling shareholder firm, or even a one share, one vote dispersed ownership firm, could take similar approaches. However, in a one share, one vote controlling shareholder firm, the incentive to do so is reduced due to the controller's large equity interest in the company, and, in a one share, one vote dispersed ownership firm, the outside shareholders can, at least in the United Kingdom, change the board with a view to constituting a more diligent management team. In a dual-class firm, though, outside investors will be concerned that a management team led by the controller will underperform yet remain in place since the controller derives personal satisfaction from managing the company.

As discussed further in Chapter 8, in a one share, one vote controlling shareholder company, management entrenchment even in the face of weak performance, and the extraction of non-pecuniary controller benefits to the detriment of shareholder value, may be mitigated by market forces. As the company's performance declines, its share price also declines, leading to a decrease in the wealth of the controlling shareholder. With dual-class stock, of course, as the level of equity held by the controller decreases, the efficacy of the market constraint diminishes. However, in the context of high-growth tech firms, which have, in the United States, been adopting dual-class structure in droves, other market considerations may moderate the incentives to continue

82 P. Gompers et al., 'Extreme Governance: An Analysis of Dual-Class Firms in the United States' (2010) 23 *Rev. Financial Stud.* 1051, 1085 – 'A Majority owner . . . can rationally . . . sacrifice firm value . . . to maintain [non-pecuniary] private benefits of control'.

83 Also see Section 6.2.3 earlier in this chapter.

84 M. Bertrand and S. Mullainathan, 'Enjoying the Quiet Life? Corporate Governance and Managerial Preferences' (2003) 111 *J. Political Econ.* 1043, 1047; Kim and Michaely (2018) (n 53 above 5).

with a poorly performing management team or extract non-pecuniary controller benefits that harm the company. It is likely that such companies, being within a growth-phase, will need to invest heavily in R&D, and, with debt funding scarce,[85] may, post-IPO, have to make regular excursions to the equity markets for further financing. The cost of capital for a poorly performing firm will be higher, making such equity financing much more expensive,[86] and, with the firm unable to grow, also making the extraction of non-pecuniary benefits such as reputation and prestige more difficult to extract. Therefore, even when regulatory rules do not restrain the actions of controllers, other constraints must also be considered when discerning the incentives that influence controller actions.[87] Another consideration, though, as will be detailed next, is that the incentive to extract non-pecuniary controller benefits can also have a bearing on takeover activity.

6.2.6 *Takeover Probability*

With dual-class structure, there is the potential that controlling shareholder structures could lead to certain takeovers being blocked by the controller. The determination as to whether a potential takeover can be considered 'optimal' or 'efficient' varies between studies, including considerations as to whether the relevant takeover will result in a better managed company, be optimal for society generally or enhance the financial welfare of investors. For the purposes of this section, though, as aligned with the manner in which dual-class firms are being evaluated,[88] takeovers are considered with regard to their optimality for the current public shareholders of the company: will the potential takeover be value-enhancing for the incumbent public shareholders? Clearly, an offeror cannot take control of a controlling shareholder company without itself acquiring, in a consensual manner, the controlling stake of the controller, which will not occur unless the controller is compensated for the loss of its controller benefits.[89] Moreover, mathematical models predict that the level of such compensation increases sharply with the ability of the controller to externalise the costs of controller benefits (as is possible with dual-class structure), which varies inversely with the level of equity owned by the controlling shareholder.[90]

85 See Section 1.5.1 of Chapter 1.

86 In relation to controlling shareholders generally: A. Shleifer and R. Vishny, 'A Survey of Corporate Governance' (1997) 52 *J. Financ.* 737, 749; R. La Porta et al. (1997) (n 14 above 1149). Also see Section 8.3.1 of Chapter 8.

87 B. Reddy, 'Finding the British Google: Relaxing the Prohibition of Dual-Class Stock from the Premium-Tier of the London Stock Exchange' (2020) 79 *CLJ* 315, 339.

88 See Section 4.3.2.2 of Chapter 4.

89 M. Barclay and C. Holderness, 'Private Benefits from Control of Public Corporations' (1989) 25 *J. Financ. Econ.* 371, 380; E. Schuster, 'The Mandatory Bid Rule: Efficient, After All?' (2013) 76 *MLR* 529, 547; Gilson (2006) (n 68 above 1672).

90 Bebchuk et al. (2000) (n 45 above 304); Also see Easterbrook and Fischel (1983) (n 3 above 409); R. Ruback, 'Coercive Dual-Class Exchange Offers' (1988) 20 *J. Financ. Econ.* 153, 153; Warren III (1988) (n 11 above 99).

Equally, a bidder will not compensate an incumbent controller for controller benefits unless such a bidder can accrue equivalent (or, in the case of jurisdictions with mandatory bid rules that require equality of treatment of all shareholders, enhanced) controller benefits after completion, or such a bidder believes that it can drastically improve firm performance to a level that outweighs the compensation paid. The relevant controller benefits may encompass pecuniary or non-pecuniary benefits. An example of non-pecuniary benefits deterring a takeover is the endowment effect that is particularly applicable to individual or family controlling shareholders where sentiment, loyalty or paternalistic considerations dominate pure economic considerations;[91] a takeover otherwise profitable and advantageous to public shareholders (either in terms of sale price or in terms of appreciation of share price post-completion under new control) is blocked by the controlling shareholder. It should be noted that such considerations apply only where a controller (or persons acting in concert to exercise control) exists; in rare situations where a dispersed ownership dual-class firm prevails, since the enhanced-voting shares are owned by multiple unrelated parties, each individual holder of enhanced-voting shares will not possess control and will not therefore be able to extract controller benefits. In such a case, in relation to the potential for takeovers that would otherwise be beneficial to the financial wealth of the public shareholders to be blocked, dual-class firms will be no different from one share, one vote firms.[92]

A number of theoretical US studies have also suggested that dual-class structure is not as optimal as one share, one vote from a takeover perspective, since not only will 'efficient' takeovers (where existing public shareholders will earn greater returns by the takeover proceeding rather than remaining invested in the company with the incumbent controller remaining in situ) be blocked, but 'inefficient' takeovers may also be promoted, which leave the inferior-voting shareholders subject to the control of a new, worse controller (and management team) that portends poorer firm performance.[93] These studies are not discussed in depth here, since the studies do not fully contemplate mandatory bid rules. The United Kingdom's Takeover Code is described in more detail in Chapter 8, but with respect to takeover probabilities, importantly, under the Takeover Code, a public company with a registered office in the United Kingdom, the Isle of Man or the Channel Islands and listed on the premium tier is subject to mandatory bid rules. Therefore, if dual-class stock were permitted on the premium tier, and a British tech company were to list with such

91 Daniels and Halpern (1996) (n 73 above 20). For an economic description of the term 'endowment effect', see D. Kahneman, *Thinking, Fast and Slow* (Farrar, Straus and Giroux, 2011) at 289–299.

92 Noted briefly in: M. Burkart and S. Lee, 'One Share – One Vote: The Theory' (2008) 12 *Rev. Financ.* 1, 11.

93 For example, *ibid*; M. Harris and A. Raviv, 'Corporate Governance: Voting Rights and Majority Rules' (1988) 20 *J. Financ. Econ.* 203; S. Grossman and O. Hart, 'One Share-One Vote and the Market for Corporate Control' (1988) 20 *J. Financ. Econ.* 175; Bebchuk et al. (2000) (n 45 above 295); R. Stulz, 'Managerial Control of Voting Rights: Financing Policies and the Market for Corporate Control' (1988) 20 *J. Financ. Econ.* 25, 32.

a structure, and a person (or persons acting in concert), after IPO, were to acquire 30 per cent or more of the voting rights in the company, then that person (or persons) would be required to make an offer for all the shares in the company.[94] Even outside the realm of British tech companies, as outlined in Chapter 8, mandatory bid rules inherent in other European jurisdictions also apply to many other companies currently listed on the premium tier. Accordingly, under mandatory bid rules, a bidder cannot secure control by simply acquiring only the enhanced-voting shares, and, instead, a control-seeking bidder would have to make an offer for all the shares in the company. All shareholders have the opportunity to sell their stock, and notions of inferior-voting shareholders being lumbered with a worse management team due to the nature of the capital structure are therefore less relevant. From the bidder's perspective, since the bidder will have to make an offer for all the shares which could, potentially, lead to it owning 100 per cent of the company, it will not be able to guarantee that it will own a majority of the votes and only a sliver of the equity post takeover – this will deter the bidder from making an offer for greater than the post-acquisition security benefits (the bidder will not be able to recompense itself for overpaying for the shares by expropriating inferior-voting shareholders post-acquisition if there are no or very few inferior-voting shareholders post-acquisition). This makes it less likely that the inferior-voting shareholders could become beholden to a new controller that extracts greater levels of controller benefits than the previous controller.

The US models also assume that dispersed inferior-voting shareholders will make an assessment as to whether to sell to a large extent based upon the potential for share-appreciation post-acquisition. In practice, with mandatory bid rules and the nuances of the United Kingdom's takeover environment, if the offer price is substantially above the market price of the shares, there is a good chance that individual shareholders will decide to sell. The post-acquisition share value would only be relevant to a target shareholder to the extent that such shareholder remains as a shareholder post-takeover. This is a challenging and risky assessment for a shareholder to make, since it is likely that the bidder will be at least outwardly indicating that it will only proceed with the takeover if it acquires full ownership. For companies incorporated in England and Wales, most recommended offers are structured as 'schemes of arrangement'.[95] A scheme of arrangement is a Court-approved procedure which results in all of the

94 Takeover Code, Rule 9.

95 A recommended offer is an offer that has been recommended by the board of the target company to its shareholders (as opposed to a hostile offer). Although, technically, a scheme of arrangement could be utilised in a hostile offer, as a practical matter, schemes of arrangement are only used for recommended bids, since the board of the target legally controls the scheme documentation and process. In 2019, of thirty-five takeover bids on the Main Market, twenty-three were structured as schemes of arrangements and only twelve were takeover offers. In 2018, the numbers were eighteen and five, respectively, and, in 2017, the numbers were nineteen and six, respectively (Practical Law What's Market, 'Public M&A: Trends and Highlights 2019: What's Market Data – Structure of Deal' (2020); Practical Law What's Market, 'Public M&A: Trends and Highlights 2018: What's Market Data – Structure of Deal' (2019)).

shares of the target being transferred to the bidder, and, therefore, represents an 'all-or-nothing' offer; either the bidder acquires 100 per cent of the shares or, unless the bid is converted into a takeover offer, the bid is unsuccessful. If the offer is not structured as a scheme, a straight takeover offer will be employed. For a target subject to the Takeover Code and to which CA 2006 applies, the bidder will, usually, be making an offer for all the shares in the company, since partial offers are discouraged and require the consent of the Takeover Panel.[96] The bidder will, therefore, generally include as a condition to the offer that acceptances from shareholders holding at least 90 per cent of the votes must be received, since this is the threshold at which the bidder can subsequently 'sweep-up' the remaining minority shareholders.[97] Although the bidder will inevitably reserve the right to waive the condition, this will be entirely at the discretion of the bidder. As such, the consideration of a target shareholder would be whether the offer price is more than the benefits the shareholder will receive going forward if the takeover does not succeed, rather than a consideration of the benefits received if the takeover does succeed and the shareholder remains as a shareholder post-acquisition. Therefore, in the United Kingdom, if dual-class firms were permitted on the premium tier, in theory, takeovers that could be beneficial to inferior-voting shareholders (in that they will receive a windfall on their original investments) may well be blocked; but the likelihood of 'inefficient' takeovers occurring which result in public shareholders being trapped in a dual-class firm with a worse controller in place should be no greater than would be the case with a one share, one vote firm.[98]

A consequence of takeover probability being reduced is that the market for corporate control, a valuable constraining mechanism on management, is attenuated. 'A well-functioning takeover market subjects firms to a continuous auction process. In principle, firms should therefore be ultimately owned and managed by those who maximize their value.'[99] The notion propounded by the quote correlates with the seminal work of Henry Manne. Manne noted that the market for corporate control provides a valuable check-and-balance on managerial conduct, assuring competitive efficiency among managers and protecting small shareholders.[100] If managers are not performing adequately, share price will fall, leading to it becoming easier and cheaper for a third party to acquire control of the company and install a new, more efficient, management team, thereby incentivising managers to perform to the best of their abilities.[101] Since courts usually apply the 'business

96 Takeover Code, Rule 36. Usually the Takeover Panel's consent to a partial offer will be conditional upon the approval of shareholders, independent of the offeror, holding at least 50 per cent of the votes in the target (Takeover Code, Rule 36.5).

97 CA 2006, s. 979.

98 In fact, it has been noted that mandatory bid and coat-tail requirements should block all inefficient transfers (Burkart and Lee (2008) (n 92 above 18)).

99 *ibid* 5.

100 H. Manne, 'Mergers and the Market for Corporate Control' (1965) 73 *J. Political Econ.* 110, 113; Cipollone (2012) (n 18 above 77).

101 M. Maher and T. Andersson, 'Corporate Governance: Effects on Firm Performance and Economic Growth' (1999) *OECD Publications* 1, 39.

judgment rule' in the United States, and therefore rarely second guess the business decisions of managers, Manne remarked that the market for corporate control also had a role in encouraging directors to comply with their fiduciary duties which would otherwise be difficult to enforce by the shareholders.[102] Additionally, the market for corporate control can be viewed as a mechanism that enables alternative management teams to compete for the right to manage corporate resources, thereby incentivising shareholder wealth maximisation.[103] With the market for corporate control significantly curbed in dual-class firms, the management team, which may overlap or be associated with the controller, will only be concerned with the aspirations of the controller, rather than the threat of a takeover caused by deteriorating share price.

The deduction of takeover probabilities is not a simple task though. For instance, notwithstanding that theory and models suggest takeover probability will be reduced in dual-class firms, takeovers of dual-class firms, with controller consent, do occur,[104] and empirical evidence is mixed as to whether dual-class firms are subject to fewer takeovers in the United States than one share, one vote firms.[105] A plethora of external economic and non-economic considerations, unrelated to the pure economics of the offer price, could affect a controller's decision to exit; the mathematical models rarely acknowledge the possible existence of such considerations. For example, a determination to seek new challenges, a desire to retire from the business or a simple desperation to liquidate assets may weigh heavily on the decision-making of an incumbent controller. In the United States, LinkedIn and Twenty-First Century Fox are high-profile examples of dual-class firms that have been the subject

102 Although the business judgment rule does not formally apply in the United Kingdom, the Courts have generally shown a deference to managerial decisions and will not look upon them with the benefit of hindsight (*Smith* v. *Fawcett* [1942] Ch. 304, 306; *Burland* v. *Earle* [1902] AC 83, 93). Additionally, the ability of shareholders to assert breaches of fiduciary duties through derivative claims may be practically limited (see Section 8.2.1 of Chapter 8).

103 M. Jensen and R. Ruback, 'The Market for Corporate Control: The Scientific Evidence' (1983) 11 *J. Financ. Econ.* 5, 6.

104 D. Fischel, 'Organized Exchanges and the Regulation of Dual Class Common Stock' (1987) 54 *U. Chi. L. Rev.* 119, 150; A. Khachaturyan, 'Trapped in Delusions: Democracy, Fairness and the One-Share-One-Vote Rule in the European Union' (2007) 8 *EBOR* 335, 351.

105 Finding dual-class firm takeovers to be as, or more, prevalent than one share one vote firm takeovers: S. Bauguess et al., 'Shareholder Diversification, Corporate Risk Taking, and the Benefits of Changing to Differential Voting Rights' (2012) 36 *J. Bank Financ.* 1244, 1249; S. Bauguess et al., 'Recontracting shareholder rights at closely held firms' (2007) (unpublished working paper, Arizona State University) cited in R. Adams and D. Ferreira, 'One Share-One Vote: The Empirical Evidence' (2008) 12 *Rev. Finance* 51, 64; O. Arugaslan et al., 'On the Decision to Go Public with Dual Class Stock' (2010) 16 *J. Corp. Financ.* 170, 175. Finding that the probability of an acquisition was less for dual-class firms, Smart and Zutter (2003) (n 31 above 102); M. Cremers et al., 'The Life-Cycle of Dual Class Firms: From IPO to Sunset' (2018) *ECGI Working Paper* No. 550/2018 1, 21; W. Mikkelson and M. Partch, 'The Consequences of Unbundling Managers' Voting Rights and Equity Claims' (1994) 1 *J. Corp. Financ.* 175, 197; Cronqvist and Nilsson (2003) (n 63 above 712); B. Jordan et al., 'Growth Opportunities, Short-Term Market Pressure, and Dual-Class Share Structure' (2016) 41 *J. Corp. Financ.* 304, 310.

of successful takeover bids.[106] Also, the theoretical studies do not fully contemplate the existence of non-pecuniary controller benefits, and the fact that these may well vary significantly between different controllers – in jurisdictions where mandatory bid requirements do not apply, a bidder for a company may rationally overpay for shares from a financial perspective if it values non-pecuniary controller benefits higher than the existing controller.

Importantly, from the perspective of the premium tier's approach to dual-class stock, the UK Listing Review's proposals to permit individual shareholders of premium listed companies to hold disproportionate voting rights that enable them to block takeovers for a finite period of time[107] indicates that the UK Government does not view the possibility that efficient takeovers may be blocked, or the attenuation of the market for corporate control, as show-stoppers in the consideration of disproportionate voting rights on the premium tier.

6.2.7 *Control Premia*

Outside the United Kingdom, a dual-class controller can benefit from control premia in two ways: (i) an acquiror solely acquires the enhanced-voting shares, thereby acquiring control without the inferior-voting shareholders receiving any consideration; or (ii) the acquiror acquires all the shares in the company but pays a higher price for the enhanced-voting shares as compared to the inferior-voting shares. The first scenario is potentially more egregious, and some have criticised such control premia of being, in effect, a transfer of the value of the firm from the inferior-voting shareholders to the exiting controller.[108] Even in the second scenario, although it is widely recognised that a controller may retain a premium for the sale of its controlling block (and is therefore expected by investors),[109] the inferior-voting shareholders could be regarded as having been prejudiced if the difference in offer prices for inferior- and enhanced-voting shares is greater than merely the value of the controller benefits held by the controller.[110]

106 LinkedIn was acquired by Microsoft in 2016, and Twenty-First Century Fox was acquired by Disney in 2019.

107 See Section 1.5.7 of Chapter 1.

108 Control has been described as a 'corporate asset', and accordingly should benefit all shareholders in proportion to their ownership (M. Barclay and C. Holderness, 'The Law and Large-Block Trades' (1992) 35 *J. Law Econ.* 265, 268).

109 *ibid* 267.

110 Some have postulated that where both inferior-voting and enhanced-voting shares of controlling shareholder dual-class firms are listed, the premium attached to enhanced-voting shares represents the level of controller benefits of the controller (or alternatively, the discount attached to inferior-voting shares represents the potential for controller benefit extraction that expropriates inferior-voting shareholders) (R. Lease et al., 'The Market Value of Control in Publicly-Traded Corporations (1983) 11 *J. Financ. Econ.* 439, 467; Masulis et al. (2009) (n 31 above 1721); L. Zingales, 'What Determines the Value of Corporate Votes?' (1995) 110 *Q. J. Econ.* 1047, 1071). However, also see the reasoning in the text accompanying n 123 below, which suggests otherwise.

In the United Kingdom, the ability to extract control premia is significantly mitigated by the mandatory bid regime and comparable treatment requirements.[111] With regard to the first scenario, if mandatory offer rules apply (such as under the Takeover Code),[112] a potential acquiror will not be able to acquire control of the company merely by making an offer for the enhanced-voting shares; an offer for all the shares in the company, no matter the class or voting rights attached, must be made.[113] With regard to the second scenario, if the Takeover Code applies, with multiple classes of shares, a bidder must pay to each class of shareholder at least the highest price paid by the bidder for shares of that *class* during the twelve months prior to the announcement of the offer,[114] and offers made for each class of shares must be 'comparable'.[115] 'Comparable' does not necessarily mean 'identical', and the Takeover Panel must be consulted,[116] but, prima facie, the Takeover Panel will insist that the ratio of the offer values be equal to 'the average of the ratios of the middle-market quotations taken from the Daily Official List over the course of the six months preceding the commencement of the offer period'.[117] For a British company to which the Takeover Code applies and where enhanced- and inferior-voting shares are listed in the United Kingdom,[118] it is unlikely that control premia would be large (and even if it were, investors would not be caught off-guard, since it would be based upon prevailing market prices). Although the Main Market listed company Schroders, which has implemented dual-class stock,[119] often shows a non-trivial price differential between enhanced- and inferior-voting shares,[120] a large slice of such differential is driven by the fact that the enhanced-voting shares are premium listed and the inferior-voting shares only standard listed.[121] As discussed in Chapter 1, certain index-tracker passive investors will be required to, and certain active investors will customarily, invest in the premium listed enhanced-voting shares, which are part of an index, driving the price differential (that differential

111 For further details, see Section 8.2.3 of Chapter 8.

112 With regard to the application of the Takeover Code and the mandatory offer rules of other jurisdictions applying to companies listed in the United Kingdom, see Section 8.2.3 of Chapter 8.

113 If the bidder acquires 30 per cent or more of the voting rights, a mandatory offer will be required (Takeover Code, Rule 9).

114 *ibid*, Rule 9.5.

115 *ibid*, Rule 14.1.

116 *ibid*, Rule 9.5.

117 *ibid*, Notes to Rule 14.1.

118 Note, though, in Chapter 9, it is proposed that upon any relaxation of the United Kingdom's premium tier rules, enhanced-voting shares should remain unlisted.

119 As discussed in Chapter 2, Schroders had legacy non-voting stock listed on the Main Market prior to the formal prohibition of non-voting stock from the premium tier. Subsequent to the imposition of the prohibition (and expiry of the grandfathering period), Schroders was required to move its non-voting stock to the standard tier.

120 For example, on 15 July 2020, the closing share price (as published by the LSE) for Schroders was £29.81 for voting shares and £22.85 for non-voting shares.

121 See D. Lobo, 'Crux: Schroders is a "No Brainer" Investment Opportunity' *Citywire Wealth Manager* (12 July 2017) https://citywire.co.uk/wealth-manager/news/crux-schroders-is-a-no-brainer-investment-opportunity/a1032675; I. Dittmann and N. Ulbricht, 'Timing and Wealth Effects of German Dual Class Stock Unifications' (2007) 14 *Eur. Financ. Manag.* 163, 185.

will be exacerbated by Schroders' voting shares, as of the time of writing, being part of the most prestigious UK index, the FTSE-100). If both classes of shares were premium listed, the price differential would likely be much smaller, since where a controller holds a majority of the voting rights through holding a significant majority of the enhanced-voting shares (which is usually the case based upon the US experience[122]), a minority holding of enhanced-voting shares is unlikely to be of substantially greater value to a third party as compared to a minority interest in the inferior-voting shares,[123] and a potential offeror would not be able to acquire substantive voting rights in the company merely by acquiring the enhanced-voting shares – an offer for the inferior-voting shares would also be required pursuant to the mandatory offer requirements of the Takeover Code. By way of example, Hansa also showed a not insignificant premium between voting and non-voting shares when its voting shares were premium listed and included on the FTSE-250 while its non-voting shares were standard listed and, therefore, not included on any FTSE index.[124] However, after a restructuring in 2019 which resulted in the company's voting shares being removed from the FTSE indices,[125] the share price divergence between voting and non-voting stock narrowed significantly, with the price of non-voting stock at times even marginally exceeding that of voting stock.[126] From a US perspective, it should also be noted that with Google, where the non-voting and one share, one vote shares are both listed, and the company has voluntarily adopted an equal treatment clause such that both classes of shares will receive the same sum on any takeover,[127] the voting premium between the two classes is only around 2 per cent.[128]

122 L. Bebchuk and K. Kastiel, 'The Perils of Small-Minority Controllers' (2019) 107 *Geo. L.J.* 1453, 1496 found that 83.6 per cent of Russell-3000 dual-class companies have a controlling minority shareholder (an earlier draft noted the figure as 96.7 per cent of S&P-1500 dual-class firms). H. DeAngelo and L. DeAngelo, 'Managerial Ownership of Voting Rights, A Study of Public Corporations with Dual Classes of Common Stock' (1985) 14 *J. Financ. Econ.* 33, 46 found that insiders on average hold 56.9 per cent of the voting rights in dual-class companies. Gompers et al. (2010) (n 82 above 1053) found that insiders on average hold 60 per cent of the voting rights in dual-class companies.

123 A. Stumpf and A. Cline, 'Price Differentials between Voting and Nonvoting Stock' *Stout Advisory Services* www.stout.com/en/insights/article/price-differentials-between-voting-and-nonvoting-stock/; the same point was raised in a US tax case where it was found that the value attached to a minority interest in enhanced-voting shares should be comparable to the value of a minority interest in inferior-voting shares, and should not be conflated with the value of holding a controlling interest in the company (*Estate of Simplot* v. *Commissioner*, 249 F.3d 1191, 1195 (9th Cir. 2001)).

124 For example, on 2 January 2019, the closing share price (as published by Financial Times Market Data) for Hansa was £10.40 for voting shares and £9.70 for non-voting shares.

125 Pursuant to the restructuring, a new Bermudan holding company, which did not meet the FTSE UK Index Series minimum requirements for non-UK incorporated companies, became the listed entity of Hansa (Hansa Trust (RNS Number: 1356I), 'Hansa Trust (UK): Scheme of Arrangement Informative Notice' (6 August 2019)).

126 On 15 July 2020, the closing share price (as published by the LSE) for Hansa was £1.59 for voting shares and £1.63 for non-voting shares.

127 Amended and Restated Certificate of Incorporation of Alphabet Inc. filed on 2 October 2015, Article IV, Sections 2(e) and 5(e).

128 D. Lund, 'Nonvoting Shares and Efficient Corporate Governance' (2019) 71 *Stanf. Law Rev.* 687, 731.

Of course, in most cases, the enhanced-voting shares will not be listed[129] (and in some jurisdictions, such as Hong Kong and Singapore, the enhanced-voting shares are not permitted to be listed), and the Takeover Panel will not be able to apply the aforementioned voting premium formula in assessing 'comparable' price. In such circumstances, in the event of a voluntary offer for the shares in the company, or a bidder triggering the Takeover Code's mandatory offer requirements by acquiring unlisted enhanced-voting shares, it is difficult to envisage that the Takeover Panel will not insist that the same price be paid for equal equity interests, requiring that the price paid per listed inferior-voting share be the same as the highest price paid per unlisted enhanced-voting share. After all, the underlying purpose of the comparable pricing regime is to ensure that the price payable for the listed ordinary shares reflects the value that those shares represent of the value of the whole business, and that any control premium is distributed amongst all shareholders, not just the enhanced-voting shareholders. Accordingly, it seems unlikely that control premia will be a substantive detriment of dual-class stock within the United Kingdom's regulatory environment,[130] although, as discussed in Chapter 9, it would be helpful for the Takeover Panel to clarify the meaning of 'comparable' in a dual-class stock context.[131] An important factor to note, though, is that with control premia bearing little relevance in the United Kingdom, takeovers will be even less likely to occur, since controllers can consume controller benefits but not sell them separately.[132]

An analogy can be drawn to Canada where, since 1987, new dual-class firms floating on the TSX must implement 'coat-tail' provisions which require, subject to certain exemptions, inferior-voting shares to receive the same price per enhanced-voting share upon a takeover bid.[133] This can eliminate control premia, and allow all shareholders to participate in the potentially higher takeover premia (as discussed in relation to benefits of dual-class firms in Section 6.3.4 later in this chapter) generated by dual-class firms when takeovers do occur. It has also had the effect of voting premia (the difference between the price of enhanced-voting and inferior-voting shares) in Canada being 'some of the smallest premiums in the world'.[134] Even in the United States, notwithstanding some instances of control

[129] Gompers et al. (2010) (n 82 above 1056).

[130] Similarly, it is unlikely that the extraction of control premia will be a substantive detriment of the proposals of the UK Listing Review (see Section 1.5.7 of Chapter 1) if implemented on the premium tier.

[131] In practice, however, it is likely that the Takeover Panel will require a dual-class applicant to the premium tier to specify in its issuer prospectus exactly how Rule 14 of the Takeover Code will apply to the inferior-voting shares (for more details, see Section 8.2.3 of Chapter 8).

[132] Barclay and Holderness (1992) (n 108 above 276). An assessment of the merits of mandatory offer requirements is beyond the scope of this book (in relation to which, see for example Schuster (2013) (n 89 above)).

[133] Cipollone (2012) (n 18 above 79); TSX Company Manual, s. 624(l).

[134] Cipollone (2012) (n 18 above 80).

premia,[135] on acquisitions, studies have found that often the price paid for inferior-voting shares is identical or similar to the price paid for enhanced-voting shares.[136] One explanation is the risk of litigation,[137] with it being contended that all shareholders are paid similar sums as paid to the blockholder in order to avoid accusations of unfairness. In the United States, upon a two-step reorganisation (which can be used to circumvent the equal treatment rules of tender offers), the board must be satisfied that the transaction is fair to all shareholders; by ensuring that the purchase price is not discounted, the board can evidence a degree of fairness that can pre-empt the risk of litigation holding up the transaction.[138] Another explanation is that control premia represent the valuation of controller benefits – in strong investor protection jurisdictions, the ability to extract significant controller benefits is constrained, and, therefore, the premium attached to a controller's block of shares should be correspondingly reduced.[139] In fact, this is the explanation given by a cross-country study of controlling shareholder firms which found that control premia were significantly larger in weak, as compared to strong, investor protection jurisdictions.[140] A third explanation is that US dual-class firms often voluntarily adopt coat-tail or similar provisions at IPO.[141] It would seem that market forces influence issuers to negate future control premia, ab initio, in order to ensure the success of the listing. Apparently, the potential extraction of control premia is a controller benefit too far for outside investors, and, in strong investor protection jurisdictions, even in the absence of mandatory equal treatment rules, it appears that the extraction of a control premium is not a significant concern.

6.3 THEORETICAL BENEFITS TO INFERIOR-VOTING SHAREHOLDERS OF DUAL-CLASS STOCK

As articulated earlier, many of the theoretical detriments of one share, one vote controlling shareholder structures also apply to dual-class stock, with the significant downside that those detriments are exacerbated as the controller's voting/cash-flow divergence becomes larger. However, the enigma of dual-class stock is that it can also present consequential benefits to all shareholders, some of which derive from the very controller benefits that are often derided as being insidious. Controller

135 DeAngelo and DeAngelo (1985) (n 122 above 60) – in this older study, it was found that the price paid for enhanced-voting shares in a takeover can, in some cases, exceed the price paid for inferior-voting shares by a level much larger than the variation in market price of the shares pre-takeover.

136 Bauguess et al. (2012) (n 105 above 1249); Arugaslan et al. (2010) (n 105 above 175).

137 Barclay and Holderness (1992) (n 108 above 286); C. Holderness and D. Sheehan, 'Constraints on Large-Block Shareholders' in *Concentrated Corporate Ownership*, ed. R. Morck (University of Chicago Press, 2000) 139, 162.

138 Holderness and Sheehan (2000) (n 137 above 166).

139 Dyck and Zingales (2004) (n 79 above 542); Barclay and Holderness (1989) (n 89 above 380).

140 Dyck and Zingales (2004) (n 79 above 550).

141 See n 136 above. For example, in relation to Google, see note 127 above and accompanying text.

benefits that accrue to a controller may not necessarily be detrimental to the health of the company or the interests of the other shareholders. For example, controller benefits could also be neutral to public shareholders, such as the reputational and self-worth benefits that the controller derives from being in control and management of a valuable, well-known business. Controller benefits may even be positive for public shareholders[142] – even though the controller may not be taking certain actions primarily to benefit the public shareholders, such actions could have consequential benefits for the public shareholders. As with the detriments, in some cases, the benefits to public shareholders apply equally to one share, one vote controlling shareholder companies, whereas in other cases, the benefits are amplified by the fact that a dual-class controller may not hold significant equity in the company. One may argue that where the benefits apply equally, a discussion of dual-class firms is unnecessary since the relevant benefits could simply accrue to one share, one vote controlling shareholder firms which are permitted on the premium tier, and which may, as discussed earlier in the theoretical detriments to inferior-voting shareholders of dual-class structure, present less costs to public shareholders. However, there is still much to be gained in discussing dual-class firms. As discussed in Chapter 1, dual-class structure can persuade founders to list their firms. The structure enables the founder to diversify wealth while retaining control. Without dual-class structure, such founders may decide either to not list their firms or list and cede control, becoming a one share, one vote dispersed ownership firm, and the benefits to public shareholders that would have been derived from a listed one share, one vote controlling shareholder firm are not realised. Dual-class structure therefore fosters the listing of firms with controlling shareholders (which may otherwise not list in such form), and deserves discussion even where the relevant benefits are equally applicable in a one share, one vote controlling shareholder system. A discussion of the primary benefits to inferior-voting shareholders follows next.

6.3.1 *Beneficial Related-Party Transactions*

Related-party transactions do not always necessarily entail tunnelling, and synergies between a controller's separate businesses could create efficiencies that are commercially beneficial to the relevant companies.[143] With respect to one share, one vote controlling shareholder companies, the FCA's decision to relax certain related-party transaction restrictions for sovereign-controlled companies[144] will have been

[142] R. Gilson and A. Schwartz, 'Constraints on Private Benefits of Control: Ex Ante Control Mechanisms versus Ex Post Transaction Review' (2013) 169 *J. Institutional & Theoretical Econ* 160, 171; Gilson (2006) (n 68 above 1664).

[143] M. Gutiérrez and M. Sáez, 'A Contractual Approach to Disciplining Self-Dealing by Controlling Shareholders' (2017) 2 *J. Law Financ. Account.* 173, 197; J. Dammann, 'Corporate Ostracism: Freezing Out Controlling Shareholders' (2008) 33 *J. Corp. L.* 681, 707; Chen et al. (2018) (n 73 above 1010).

[144] Listing Rules, Chapter 21.

partly driven by an acknowledgment that business relationships between various sovereign-controlled entities can be beneficial to, and necessary for, the success of the listed company.[145] The presence of a controller could also enable a company to expand successfully, particularly in environments where business information is difficult to reliably verify or where a substantial trust deficit in business exists – the attachment of a respected controller and brand to various conglomerate businesses could assuage the concerns of counterparties.[146] For example, in India, the trust attached to the name of Ratan Tata, former chair of Tata Sons, enabled the Tata business empire to successfully compete across an array of industries.[147] Dual-class structure does not substantively differ from a one share, one vote controlling shareholder structure in this regard.

6.3.2 *Diversification*

A significant benefit for a founder in adopting dual-class structure is that a significant portion of that founder's wealth which is tied-up as an investment in the company can be crystallised upon IPO without the founder ceding control of the business.[148] With one share, one vote, the founder is resigned to either crystallising wealth and losing control as ownership becomes dispersed or remaining as a controlling shareholder and retaining a significant financial investment in the company.

By the founder diversifying its own wealth, consequential benefits can accrue to the inferior-voting shareholders from the manner in which the business of the company will subsequently be conducted. For example, controlling shareholders of one share, one vote firms, with a significant proportion of their wealth tied-up in the company, may attempt to mitigate the risks of being significantly financially exposed to the industry in which the company operates by ensuring that the investee company diversifies its business operations into other, often unrelated, industries, either organically or through acquisitions. As a result of the drive to diversify, one share, one vote controlling shareholder firms are particularly associated with the development of huge, unwieldy conglomerates as they mature.[149] Such diversification may not be in the best interests of the company nor be favourable to the minority

145 The FCA will also have been heavily influenced by a desire to attract the blue-chip listing of Saudi Aramco to the LSE (C. Binham and A. Raval, 'UK Presses Ahead on Listing Reforms in Effort to Woo Saudi Aramco' *Financial Times* (8 June 2018)) www.ft.com/content/3a5a1b70-6aea-11e8-b6eb-4acfcfb08c11.

146 The attachment of named figures to businesses is particularly felicitous in certain jurisdictions, such as Italy (A. Santoro et al., 'Deviations from the "One Share – One Vote" Principle in Italy: Recent Developments – Multiple Voting Rights Shares and Loyalty Shares' (2015) 5 *Bocconi Legal Papers* 141, 164.

147 'Ratan Tata's Legacy' *The Economist* (1 December 2012) www.economist.com/leaders/2012/12/01/ratan-tatas-legacy.

148 Arugaslan et al. (2010) (n 105 above 181). For further details, also see Chapter 1.

149 B. Cheffins, 'Corporate Law and Ownership Structure: A Darwinian Link?' (2002) 25 *UNSW L.J.* 346, 364; Bebchuk et al. (2000) (n 45 above 303). Also see D. Ratner, 'The Government of Business

shareholders who can themselves self-diversify by maintaining a varied portfolio. The one share, one vote controlling shareholder company Fraser Group is an eminent example – it has evolved from its previous incarnation as Sports Direct, which focused on sportswear retail, into a holding company for various non-sports-related retail businesses.[150] Dual-class structure, and a large voting/cash-flow divergence, can alleviate the incentives on the controller to act in this way. When Hong Kong Exchanges and Clearing (HKEX) was considering lifting its prohibition of dual-class stock, two of the noted benefits were that entrepreneurs would be able to diversify their personal wealth into other entrepreneurial projects which benefits the market as a whole, and that the ability to diversify personal wealth would reduce the preponderance of intra-firm empire-building.[151] Empirically, the implementation of dual-class structure that coincides with the divestment of significant equity by the controller is associated with, going forward, greater corporate focus through the disposal of non-core operations[152] (however, it should also be noted that a will to diversify is not the only driver of empire-building or the creation of conglomerates, and other factors may persist, including, as described in Section 6.2.3 earlier, the entering into of inefficient projects driven by a desire to extract pecuniary or non-pecuniary controller benefits). Although the contention that dual-class firms are less likely to form large, sprawling conglomerates could be challenged when considering the diverse range of businesses in which large US tech firms operate, it can be explained by the nature of their businesses and the desire to collate and share data between those businesses through the integration of differing applications, with such data and its uses being the foundation upon which the firms are built. For example, the acquisitions by Google, which originated as a simple search engine, of Nest Labs, DeepMind, Android, YouTube and, as of the time of writing, the proposed acquisition of Fitbit, will have all been pursued with data-sharing in mind.[153] Equally, the acquisitions by Facebook, as, originally, a social media platform, of Instagram, WhatsApp and Oculus VR will have been influenced by data-driven models.[154] Beyond those data-driven acquisitions, a need for a controller to financially diversify

Corporations: Critical Reflections on the Rule of "One Share, One Vote"' (1970) 56 *Cornell L. Rev.* 1, 21 – '. . . the "entrepreneurial" image cultivated by the Mature Corporation merely serves as window dressing for sophisticated financial manipulations, such as those that characterized the "conglomerate" developments of the past decade'.

150 Fraser Group has been highly acquisitive since becoming a listed company, acquiring full or partial interests in companies across a broad range of different retail industries, not necessarily involved in sportswear. Notable investments include House of Fraser, Findel, Debenhams, French Connection, Agent Provocateur, Sofa.com, Evans Cycles, Kensington Health Clubs and Game Digital.

151 HKEX, 'Concept Paper: Weighted Voting Rights' (August 2014) at IV-8. However, as discussed in Chapter 9, there are sound grounds for ensuring that founders have at least some 'skin-in-the-game'.

152 Bauguess et al. (2012) (n 105 above 1252).

153 For example, in relation to the proposed acquisition of Fitbit by Google, see J. Espinoza, 'EU Signals Deeper Investigation of Google Fitbit Deal' *Financial Times* (2 July 2020) www.ft.com/content/aba45bc9-ffc8-411e-ac29-dbb3171f4886.

154 In relation to Facebook's acquisition of WhatsApp, see 'Facebook to Buy Messaging App WhatsApp for $19bn' *BBC Business* (20 February 2014) www.bbc.co.uk/news/business-26266689.

will not be a primary concern of dual-class controllers of Big Tech firms where the controller has significantly divested of its equity investment. The ability of the founder to diversify its wealth is also closely connected with a number of other potential benefits for inferior-voting shareholders, as discussed further in the following sections.[155]

6.3.3 *Bonding Hypothesis*

If outside shareholders view the controller as fundamental to the success of the business, the holding of enhanced-voting shares by that controller can benefit outside shareholders by bonding the controller to the firm.[156] If the controller has already divested the majority of its equity, it has more to lose than gain by selling its shares, since the controller will lose the pecuniary and non-pecuniary controller benefits in return for only the price of a sliver of equity.[157] The strength of the bond would be additionally reinforced in the United Kingdom, where takeover regulations, as discussed previously, would prevent the controller from receiving a premium for the voting rights. In addition, mandatory offer requirements under the Takeover Code could make the securities somewhat illiquid – a possible purchaser of shares may be deterred from acquiring the enhanced-voting shares, since an acquisition of 30 per cent or more of the voting rights would require the bidder to make an offer for all the shares in the company.[158] Accordingly, a purchaser not wishing to obtain control of the company (but wishing to acquire a significant equity stake) would be more likely to acquire inferior-voting shares and avoid triggering the mandatory bid requirement. Even if regulatory mandatory offer requirements are not in operation (such as in the United States), the controller may be unable to secure a premium due to the existence of voluntarily adopted coat-tail provisions or transfer-driven sunset clauses, further tying in the controller.[159] Additionally, where the enhanced-voting shares are unlisted, the lack of capacity to sell those shares on the market will also exacerbate the illiquidity of the securities.[160] Correspondingly, it has been noted that where enhanced-voting shares are not listed, it is indicative of a controller that has sacrificed liquidity in order to take a long-term approach – the

155 See, for example Sections 6.3.5, 6.3.7 and 6.3.8 later in this chapter.

156 Fischel (1987) (n 104 above 137); SGX, 'Consultation Paper on Possible Listing Framework for Dual Class Share Structures' (16 February 2017) at 9. Also see Santoro (2015) (n 146 above).

157 A. Choi, 'Concentrated Ownership and Long-Term Shareholder Value' (2018) 8 *HBLR* 53, 68.

158 Takeover Code, Rule 9.

159 For further details on sunset clauses and coat-tail provisions see Chapter 9; also see n 141 above and accompanying text.

160 E. Böhmer et al., 'The Effect of Consolidated Control on Firm Performance: The Case of Dual-class IPOs' in *Empirical Issues in Raising Equity* Capital, ed. M. Levis (Elsevier, 1996) at 109; J. Ang and W. Megginson, 'Restricted Voting Shares, Ownership Structure, and the Market Value of Dual-Class Firms' (1989) 12 *J. Financ. Res.* 301, 317; E. Böhmer et al., 'Managerial Bonding and Stock Liquidity: An Analysis of Dual-Class Firms' (2004) 28 *J. Econ. Financ.* 117, 117; Gompers (2010) (n 82 above 1053).

controller likely possesses private information as to the potential cash-flow success of the company over the long term, which the market should recognise when making investment decisions.[161]

The existence of controller benefits could also enhance the bonding effect in that they incentivise the controller to remain in control and not sell out.[162] If controller benefits were reduced to a minimum level (for example, if, as with the proposals of the UK Listing Review, inferior-voting shareholders were given the ability to appoint a majority of the board), the controller may garner few pecuniary and non-pecuniary benefits from retaining a controlling stake in the company, and, unless adequately compensated, may seek pastures new. If a founder has already sold much of its equity, and has therefore generated significant wealth, it is unlikely that the usual management bonding mechanism of high compensation with significant deferred consideration will be effective to retain the founder as a manager, unless the remuneration package is exorbitant. In such circumstances, only a gargantuan pay package will bond the founder. By way of analogy, the CEO of Tesla, albeit a one share, one vote dispersed ownership firm, is the company's founder, Elon Musk, whose vision is highly valued by the market. Since Musk has already generated significant wealth from the sell-down of equity in the company, the shareholders' attempts to bind Musk to the firm and incentivise him have required a breathtaking financial package that could amount to $50 billion if all performance targets are met.[163] As a one share, one vote dispersed ownership firm, Tesla's shareholders cannot rely upon the existence of controller benefits to bind Musk to the firm. Therefore, if the skills of the controller are highly valued by the other shareholders, optimally, a balance can be struck between the controller having sufficient 'skin-in-the-game' so that controller benefit extraction that is detrimental to shareholder value will not be excessive, while allowing the controller to divest of a sufficient proportion of equity to diversify wealth and permit a level of controller benefit extraction (which may, importantly, be non-pecuniary, as well as pecuniary, in nature) through ownership of enhanced-voting shares that encourages the controller to remain in control and perhaps day-to-day management.[164]

Even though the controller-bonding hypothesis has been described in terms of being a crucial benefit for inferior-voting shareholders, in certain circumstances it could be viewed as a detriment. For instance, if the relevant founder is not talented, given the wide scope granted to him or her through dual-class stock to run the business, the bonding effect could lead to the enduring presence of an underperforming CEO.[165] However, it is less likely that a dual-class firm IPO will be

[161] Böhmer et al. (2004) (n 160 above 119).
[162] Choi (2018) (n 157 above 59).
[163] C. Elson and C. Ferrere, 'Unequal Voting and the Business Judgment Rule' *Harvard Law School Forum on Corporate Governance and Financial Regulation* (7 April 2018).
[164] See Section 6.4.2 later in this chapter.
[165] See the discussion on 'Management Entrenchment' in Section 6.2.4 earlier in this chapter.

successful if potential investors do not have faith in the talent and ability of the enhanced-voting shareholders. It is acknowledged that in certain cases investors may face a 'Hobson's Choice',[166] where, in a competitive market between fund managers, investors will be loath to forego an investment in a company with potentially excellent growth prospects,[167] especially in a generally weak or small market for IPOs,[168] but it is difficult to foresee that an IPO of a tech firm will proceed with dual-class structure if the investors do not have at least a measure of faith in the abilities of the founder. For example, although the decision by WeWork to abandon its IPO on short notice in 2019 will have been based partly upon market scepticism as to the ongoing business plan and finances of the company, an underlying distrust of the founder's abilities was exposed when, soon after, it was announced that the founder would resign as CEO and potentially relinquish his enhanced-voting shares.[169] Similarly, it is unlikely that Uber would have countenanced a listing prior to the removal of Travis Kalanick, whose behaviour had been very publicly denounced, as CEO, and unification of the dual-class structure to one share, one vote.[170] An implication of the market not accepting dual-class structure where they do not have faith in the enhanced-voting shareholders is that where successful dual-class firm IPOs do take place, there is a high likelihood that the public shareholders value the skills of the controller, and, therefore, will see significant benefits in that controller continuing to be bonded to the firm.[171]

The bonding hypothesis can also apply to management and employees. As has been iterated, with dual-class structure, the management team is insulated from outside influences; the inferior-voting shareholders cannot remove directors from the board, and the market for corporate control is theoretically less robust and, in any event, dictated by the controller.[172] Therefore, as with controlling shareholder one share, one vote structures, managers may be more secure in their positions in the knowledge that, to the extent the controller takes a long-term approach, they will not be removed as a result of short-term fluctuations in share price. As such, managers may be more likely to invest in firm-specific human capital, an essential element in the success of some types of firms.[173] Additionally, although a controller involved in

166 ISS M&A Deal Note (North America), 'The Tragedy of the Dual Class Commons' (13 February 2012) at 1 http://online.wsj.com/public/resources/documents/facebook0214.pdf.

167 Wen (2014) (n 77 above 1505); A. Winden, 'Sunrise, Sunset: An Empirical and Theoretical Assessment of Dual-Class Stock Structures' (2018) 3 *C.B.L.R.* 852, 899.

168 A. Anand, 'Governance Complexities in Firms with Dual Class Shares' (2018) 3 *Annal. Corp. Gov.* 184.

169 A. Edgecliffe-Johnson and E. Platt, 'WeWork Founder Trades Voting Power to Back SoftBank Rescue' *Financial Times* (21 October 2019) www.ft.com/content/b9312eee-f440-11e9-b018-3ef8794b17c6.

170 M. Isaac, 'Uber Sells Stake to SoftBank Valuing Ride-Hailing Giant at $48 Billion' *The New York Times* (December 28, 2017). www.nytimes.com/2017/12/28/technology/uber-softbank-stake.html.

171 Reddy (2020) (n 87 above 333–335).

172 See nn 59 and 99–103 above and accompanying text.

173 D. Denis and D. Denis, 'Majority Owner-Managers and Organizational Efficiency' (1994) 1 *J. Corp. Financ.* 91, 106; DeAngelo and DeAngelo (1985) (n 122 above 62); Fischel (1987) (n 104 above 137);

management may view higher executive compensation as a justified controller benefit (as described as a detriment earlier), if the controller is not associated with management, and management has confidence that the controller has faith in their skills and long-term strategy, executive compensation may be lower on the basis that, unlike with dispersed ownership one share, one vote firms, the firm does not need to compensate management for the risks that they will be dismissed pursuant to the caprice of short-term orientated dispersed shareholders or as a result of a predatory takeover offer.[174] Accordingly, where management is not associated with the controller, executive compensation tends to be lower in dual-class firms.[175] Other employees may also be influenced by the fact that the controller is 'bonded' to the firm, and this benefit is closely linked to 'Long-Termism', which is discussed in more detail later in this chapter. The long-term commitment of the controller can encourage the firm-specific human capital investment by employees so essential in companies with high asset specificity such as high-technology industries; the adoption of long-term projects by companies in such industries gives employees comfort that the company is committed to long-term relationships with those employees.[176] The success of the ownership structures of technology companies such as Google and Facebook may lie in the investment of human capital by employees into such organisations being supported by the ability of such companies to take a long-term approach – the controller is incentivised to take a long-term approach due to the competitive advantages generated by attracting and retaining the most talented staff, and dual-class structure enables the taking of such an approach. For example, in justifying the company's dual-class structure, in Google's 2011 Founders' Letter to Investors, it was stated, 'Our colleagues will be able to trust that they themselves and their labors of hard work, love and creativity will be well cared for by a company focused on stability and the long term.'[177]

Additionally, controlling shareholder companies are often associated with the development of strong and ingrained relationships with suppliers, customers and other stakeholders,[178] resulting from the long-term bonding of the controller to the firm. Indeed, the very presence of a family controlling shareholder may send

Smart and Zutter (2003) (n 31 above 103); Böhmer et al. (1996) (n 160 above 111); Reddy (2020) (n 87 above 330).

174 Gilson (2006) (n 68 above 20); C. Knoeber, 'Golden Parachutes, Shark Repellents and Hostile Tender Offers' (1986) 76 *Am. Econ. Rev.* 155, 160.

175 H. Mehran, 'Executive Compensation Structure, Ownership and Firm Performance' (1995) 38 *J. Financ. Econ.* 163, 179; M. Bertrand and S. Mullainathan, 'Are CEOs Rewarded for Luck? The Ones without Principals Are' (2001) *Q.J. Econ.* (August 2001) 901, 921; Holderness and Sheehan (1988) (n 66 above 335).

176 C. Mayer, 'Corporate Governance, Competition, and Performance' (1997) 24 *J. Law & Soc.* 152, 168; Maher and Andersson (1999) (n 101 above 28); Reddy (2020) (n 87 above 330–331 and 333).

177 Alphabet's 2011 Founders' Letter (31 December 2011) https://abc.xyz/investor/founders-letters/2011/.

178 This is particularly true of family-controlled companies – see Cheffins (2002) (n 149 above 363). Also see Mayer (1997) (n 176 above 168); Gilson (2006) (n 68 above 9). Generally, in relation to the benefits that dual-class stock can confer on tech-companies, see Reddy (2020) (n 87 above).

a message to potential contracting parties that the company's management can be trusted since they can be assumed to have a desire to manufacture long-lasting contractual relationships;[179] this is particularly beneficial where the relevant firm has important stakeholder relationships, such as with vital customers, suppliers or partners.[180] Also, if the customer and product markets associate the company's success and product quality with the involvement of the controller, the bonding of the controller to the firm can also improve the sales of a firm where ongoing support or service of the products sold is an important factor for customers.[181]

Notably, although the premium tier proposals of the UK Listing Review curtail the market for corporate control,[182] many of the bonding benefits described earlier will not be realised if those proposals are implemented. Under those proposals, founders will only be able to block takeovers and will not be able to ensure control over all shareholder resolutions of the company (including in relation to the composition of the board as a whole), and therefore public shareholders, through the proxy of share price, will continue to have an influence over management decisions. Controller benefits will, accordingly, be attenuated, diminishing the bond that a founder has to the company. Similarly, if shareholders can indirectly remove managers (by virtue of their powers over the composition of the board),[183] the management and employee bonding benefits described earlier will also be lessened, since the strategy of the company will only be insulated from the market for corporate control and not the caprice of the public shareholders. Even in relation to the market for corporate control, the five-year duration attached to the ability to block takeovers, under the proposals of the UK Listing Review,[184] will prejudice the capacity of the company to form long-term and ingrained relationships with other stakeholders, which is, otherwise, a key benefit of dual-class stock adoption. Summarising the UK Listing Reivew though, the ability to block takeovers is only half the story, and the complete benefits of disproportionate voting ownership to public shareholders can only be achieved with 'genuine' dual-class stock.

The bonding benefits of dual-class stock to public shareholders are especially pertinent in the tech industry, where the success of innovative, high-growth tech firms is often associated with the visionary leadership of a founder or founders, whether that be Mark Zuckerberg at Facebook, Evan Spiegel, Bobby Murphy and

179 R. Gilson, 'Controlling Family Shareholders in Developing Countries: Anchoring Relational Exchange' (2007) 60 *Stan. L. Rev.* 633, 643; Cheffins (2002) (n 149 above 363).

180 In the context of takeover defences generally, see K. Cremers et al., 'Staggered Boards and Long-term, Firm Value, Revisited' (2017) 126 *J. Financ. Econ.* 422, 442; L. Cen et al., 'Discipline or Disruption? Stakeholder Relationships and the Effect of Takeover Threat' (2016) 62 *Manag. Science* 2820, 2831; W. Johnson et al., 'The Lifecycle Effects of Firm Takeover Defenses' (2018) 1, 29 http://dx.doi.org/10.2139/ssrn.2808208; Mayer (1997) (n 176 above 168).

181 Santoro (2015) (n 146 above).

182 Under the UK Listing Review, an individual can be granted rights to block takeovers for up to five years post-IPO (see Section 1.5.7 of Chapter 1).

183 See nn 57–58 above and accompanying text.

184 See Section 1.5.7 of Chapter 1.

Reggie Brown at Snap, Jack Ma at Alibaba or Larry Page and Sergey Brin at Google. With the glue of controller benefits and insulation from removal provided by dual-class stock, investors can be confident that the founder will continue to be associated with the firm for an extensive period of time. The way in which such companies differentiate themselves from the rest of the market and the founder's self-perceived ability to outperform the market in the long term has been described as a factor of the founder's 'idiosyncratic vision'.[185] Even where an original founder does not remain as a day-to-day leader of the company, he or she can still serve in a leadership role as a board member, continuing to drive the strategic direction of the company aligned with his or her idiosyncratic vision. The founders of Google, for instance, remain as board members, executive committee members and employees of Google, and very much involved in the company's strategy even though they have stepped down from their CEO and president roles.[186] The bonding benefits of dual-class structure are evidenced by the juxtaposition that can be drawn between the decade and a half of financial problems that beset Apple, a one share, one vote firm, after one of the founders, Steve Jobs, left in 1985 following a dispute with the board,[187] and the continued incumbency of Mark Zuckerberg at Facebook, a dual-class firm, in the face of opposition from the board and shareholders to the acquisition of Instagram for $1 billion in 2012. By 2018, Instagram was valued at $35 billion,[188] and long-term orientated public shareholders will have financially benefitted from the founder being bonded to the firm.

6.3.4 *Higher Takeover Prices*

A corollary to beneficial takeovers being blocked is that when takeovers do occur, in the presence of a controlling shareholder, the offer price for those takeovers should be higher than would otherwise be the case in a dispersed ownership structure. Whether higher takeover prices where, essentially, a wealth transfer occurs from the buyer to the existing shareholders, are, holistically, efficient or beneficial is beyond the scope of this chapter; however, since the provenance of the prohibition of premium tier dual-class firms appears to relate to protecting public shareholders, the factor deserves consideration. In a mandatory bid regime, higher takeover prices could be considered a benefit to public shareholders, since they will be able to share in such higher takeover prices with the controller. One reason for takeover prices being higher in the presence of a controlling shareholder is the ability of the

185 Z. Goshen and A. Hamdani, 'Corporate Control and Idiosyncratic Vision' (2016) 125 *Yale L.J.* 560, 577.

186 Alphabet 2019 (n 65 above).

187 M. Weinberger, 'This is Why Steve Jobs Got Fired from Apple – and How He Came Back to Save the Company' *Business Insider* (31 July 2017) www.businessinsider.com/steve-jobs-apple-fired-returned-2017-7?r=US&IR=T.

188 CFA Institute, 'Dual-Class Shares: The Good, The Bad and The Ugly' (August 2018), at 8.

controller to negotiate the offer price with the bidder.[189] In a dispersed ownership situation, since the shareholders are dispersed, and therefore subject to collective action and free-rider issues,[190] they are not able to effectively negotiate with the bidder, and, instead, the negotiations take place between the board and the bidder (leading to a board-recommended or hostile bid), even though ultimately, in the United Kingdom, the decision to sell is that of, and the success of the takeover is dependent upon, the shareholders. The board of a UK-dispersed ownership company may well be motivated to negotiate strongly on behalf of the shareholders (since the executive directors will not want to be replaced by a new management team, and those directors will have a duty to negotiate the best price), but a number of extraneous factors will affect the decisions of those directors (such as severance pay), and, in a hostile bid scenario, the bidder will have effectively determined to go above the heads of the directors. The second reason is that dispersed ownership shareholders, which will generally possess less pertinent knowledge as to the business and prospects of the firm compared to insider controllers, may decide to sell to a bidder when the more financially beneficial outcome would be to retain the shares unless a much higher price is offered.[191] The third reason is that the bidder must compensate the controller for the loss of controller benefits, and so the price at which a successful offer may be triggered will need to be higher than would be the case in a dispersed ownership system where there is no controller extracting controller benefits.[192] Stulz (1988) mathematically modelled that bid premium increases with increasing insider ownership.[193] With controlling shareholder dual-class firms, as further modelled by Harris and Raviv (1998),[194] takeover prices should be even higher than with controlling shareholder one share, one vote firms – as the controller's voting/cash-flow divergence increases, the value of controller benefits to the incumbent controller also rises, meaning that the compensation that the controller will expect for selling its stake will further increase. In a mandatory bid regime like the United Kingdom, this would also lead to greater returns for all selling inferior-voting shareholders. The empirical evidence, generally, also suggests that takeover

189 Fischel (1987) (n 104 above 138); C. Bacon et al., 'The Board of Directors and Dual-Class Recapitalizations' (1997) 26 *Financ. Manag.* 5, 5. In relation to antitakeover devices generally: H. DeAngelo and E. Rice, 'Antitakeover Charter Amendments and Stockholder Wealth' (1983) 11 *J. Financ. Econ.* 329, 335; S. Linn and J. McConnell, 'An Empirical Investigation of the Impact of "Antitakeover" Amendments on Common Stock Prices' (1983) 11 *J. Financ. Econ.* 361, 395.

190 For further details on collective action and free-rider issues, see Section 5.4 of Chapter 5.

191 Lund (2019) (n 128 above 687); Z. Goshen and R. Squire, 'Principal Costs: A Theory for Corporate Law and Governance' (2017) 117 *Colum. L. Rev.* 767, 784; Gilson (2006) (n 68 above 11).

192 See n 89 above and accompanying text. Under the proposals of the UK Listing Review (see Section 1.5.7 of Chapter 1), controller benefits will be less than with genuine dual-class stock, since the management team will not be insulated from the influence of public shareholders, and, therefore, even during the five-year post-IPO period when an individual can block takeovers, takeover prices will be less than where genuine dual-class stock has been adopted.

193 Stulz (1988) (n 93 above 33).

194 Harris and Raviv (1988) (n 93 above).

premia are higher in takeovers of dual-class firms compared to comparable one share, one vote firms.[195]

6.3.5 *Project Choice*

The incentivisation of dual-class controllers to pursue inefficient projects, described earlier in this chapter,[196] should be balanced against the possibility for dual-class structure to facilitate efficient projects. Although the insulation of management from extraneous influences was described as a detriment of dual-class stock (in Section 6.2.4 earlier in this chapter), that very insulation can also positively influence the types of projects that managers will entertain. For example, management will be less pre-occupied with wasting resources in signalling performance to public shareholders, and less likely to invest in projects with observable pay-offs that will produce lower returns than projects that are more challenging to monitor. Managers will also not be compelled to employ costly signalling devices such as dividend payments, share buybacks or leverage to inform outsiders that performance is robust where it is otherwise difficult to monitor.[197] Compared to one share, one vote dispersed ownership firms, managers may also be less likely to pursue projects that increase the costs of removing management, or produce immediate compensatory benefits to management, since they will have less fear in losing-out on deferred compensation as a result of dismissal or a takeover.[198] Chemmanur (2012) also suggested that dual-class structure can be beneficial where firms have choices between projects with high near-term uncertainty, but potentially large long-term upsides, and projects with low near-term uncertainty which may present clearer short-term benefits but are not as profitable in the long term.[199] Outside shareholders take longer to determine the possible success of projects with high near-term

195 Bauguess et al. (2012) (n 105 above 1249); Smart and Zutter (2003) (n 31 above 102); Bauguess et al. (2007) (n 105 above).

196 See Section 6.2.3 earlier in this chapter.

197 K. Lehn et al., 'Consolidating Corporate Control: Dual-Class Recapitalizations Versus Leveraged Buyouts' (1990) 27 *J. Financ. Econ.* 557, 564; Fischel (1987) (n 104 above 138); A. Alchian and H. Demsetz, 'Production, Information Costs, and Economic Organization' (1972) 62 *The American Economic Review* 777, 789; DeAngelo and DeAngelo (1985) (n 122 above 35); M. Cornett and M. Vetsuypens, 'Voting Rights and Shareholder Wealth: The Issuance of Limited Voting Common Stock' (1989) 10 *MDE* 175, 176.

198 J. Stein, 'Efficient Capital Markets, Inefficient Firms: A Model of Myopic Corporate Behavior' (1989) 104 *Q.J. Econ.* 655; Gilson (2006) (n 68 above 19); N. Mizik, 'The Theory and Practice of Myopic Management' (2010) 47 *J. Mark. Res.* 594, 596. Although, in specific circumstances, there may be incentives on a controlling shareholder to engage in earnings management for reasons not related to employment security or increased pay-outs under remuneration packages (see, for example, S. Lee et al., 'Earnings Management by Controlling Shareholders Who Plan for Stock Gifts: Korean Evidence' (2018) 25 *Asia-Pac. J. Account. E.* 313; Q. Hou et al., 'Performance Commitments of Controlling Shareholders and Earnings Management' (2015) 32 *Contemp. Account. Res.* 1099).

199 J. Chemmanur, 'Dual Class IPOs: A theoretical analysis' (2012) 38 *J. Bank. Finance* 305, 306.

uncertainty, valuing such projects less highly all things being equal, and, as such, management requires insulation from removal (whether by the public shareholders or as a result of a takeover), while share price may be undervalued, in order to pursue the more valuable project. The author predicted that this quality lends itself to industries such as newspapers, movies and those that require high R&D investment, and, therefore, those industries can benefit from the utilisation of dual-class structure.[200] Clearly, tech companies that require substantial R&D investment in projects, the ultimate success of which may not be observable to public shareholders, can accordingly benefit from the scope that dual-class stock grants their management teams to make such investments even when they impact short-term profits. Goshen and Squire (2017)[201] also noted that when dispersed shareholders are given rights that allow them to impinge upon management decisions, they may make poor decisions either due to issues of shareholder competence (for example, through being misinformed or lacking the expertise to adequately opine upon a major decision) or conflict (an example would be where the shareholders are short-term orientated or have conflicting interests),[202] which, again, could influence management to forsake high near-term uncertainty projects even though they will eventually be highly profitable. The authors noted that dual-class structure can alleviate those issues.[203] For example, it is unlikely that the management team of Facebook would have continued to pursue the acquisition of Instagram in 2012 in the face of a hostile shareholder (and board) body. The acquisition became a hugely successful acquisition for Facebook in the longer term.[204] It should be noted that, in relation to project choice, many of the benefits can also be identified in one share, one vote controlling shareholder firms, but, with dual-class structure, managers may be even less preoccupied with the observability of projects and the impact on short-term profits where the controller holds less of the equity.

6.3.6 *Post-IPO Equity Funding*

A further benefit is secured by dual-class stock over one share, one vote controlling shareholder structure in that investments by, and in, the firm may be promoted through the use of multiple classes of stock. Certain projects may require further funds, which a controlling shareholder may be unwilling to finance through equity if the controller's voting interest will be diluted.[205] This may precipitate the incurrence of debt in circumstances where equity financing may be more efficient for the firm and therefore

200 *ibid* 315; R. Davies et al., 'Measuring the Costs of Short-Termism' (2014) 12 *J. Financ. Stab.* 16, 18 also modelled that managers who are overly concerned about short-term performance metrics may forego otherwise profitable projects.
201 Goshen and Squire (2017) (n 191 above 767).
202 *ibid* 784. The authors labelled these 'principal costs'.
203 *ibid* 826.
204 See n 188 above and accompanying text.
205 K. Rydqvist, 'Dual-Class Shares: A Review' (1992) 8 *Oxf. Rev. Econ. Policy* 45, 51.

of benefit to all the shareholders.[206] Alternatively, a capital-constrained company may forego an otherwise profitable project if debt is difficult to source, which is often the case for long-term, possibly uncertain, projects common in the tech industry.[207] Dual-class stock would allow the firm to issue inferior-voting shares to obtain finance, or as consideration for an acquisition, without the controller losing control,[208] which therefore should encourage the controller to cause the company to invest in projects that are potentially profitable.[209] As referenced in Chapter 2, in the 1950s, numerous UK listed companies utilised non-voting stock as consideration for acquisitions. Dual-class stock also provides other forms of flexibility in acquisition structure. When General Motors' acquired EDS in 1984, the company adopted dual-class stock as a means of structuring the consideration payable to the sellers – an act that precipitated the NYSE's review of its prohibition of dual-class stock.[210] The use of multiple classes of stock enabled the issuance of inferior-voting shares to the sellers with discrete dividend rights that tracked the performance of the acquired business, without giving those sellers disproportionately high voting power in the acquiring entity.[211]

The expediency of dual-class stock can also be observed in the context of the UK Government's proposed laws on national security and investment.[212] As of the time of writing, a draft bill which has commenced its passage through Parliament proposes that acquisitions of businesses above certain thresholds should be subject to a national security test which could, if applicable, give the UK Government powers to block the acquisition or condition its closing on the fulfilment of remedial action. Although one of the proposed notifiable events relates to the acquisition of more than 15 per cent of the votes *or* shares in an entity,[213] the white paper that preceded the bill suggested that the primary concern is that a party prejudicial to national security may obtain a degree of control over the relevant entity.[214] If the final legislative provisions, and the related Secretary of State for BEIS Statement to be made pursuant to the legislation which will clarify when it is expected that

206 Bebchuk et al. (2000) (n 45 above 309).

207 Maher and Andersson (1999) (n 101 above 36). For further details on the lack of debt financing for high-growth tech companies, see Chapter 1.

208 Smart and Zutter (2003) (n 31 above 103); M. Partch, 'The Creation of a Class of Limited Voting Common Stock and Shareholders' Wealth' (1987) 18 *J. Financ. Econ.* 313, 323; G. Jarrell and A. Poulsen, 'Dual-Class Recapitalizations as Antitakeover Mechanisms: The Recent Evidence' (1988) 20 *J. Financ. Econ.* 129, 133; V. Dimitrov and P. Jain, 'Recapitalization of One Class of Common Stock into Dual-Class: Growth and Long-Run Stock Returns' (2006) 12 *J. Corp. Financ.* 342, 361; Bauguess et al. (2012) (n 105 above 1246); Burkart and Lee (2008) (n 92 above 11); Fischel (1987) (n 104 above 140).

209 S. Banerjee, 'Dual-Class Share Issues and Mitigating the Costs of Corporate Democracy' (2005) *Tulane University Working Paper* 1, 19.

210 See Section 2.3 of Chapter 2.

211 Santoro (2015) (n 146 above 148); Gordon (1988) (n 59 above 71).

212 See National Security and Investment Bill (November 2020).

213 *ibid*, s. 6(2).

214 BEIS, 'National Security and Investment: A consultation on proposed legislative reforms' (July 2018) at 35.

a transaction may be blocked,[215] are clearer that the concern is the acquisition of 'control', a dual-class structure could open up an entity to foreign investment[216] without national security concerns being triggered, since control will remain in the hands of the existing controller.[217] The promotion of dual-class stock could assuage the tension between protecting vulnerable British businesses, and encouraging their growth through foreign investment, post-EU withdrawal and during the post-2020 COVID-19 pandemic financial crisis.[218] Access to these sources of further financing by companies associated with national security issues can benefit all the shareholders as a whole, and dual-class structure is seen as beneficial in this regard in jurisdictions with even stricter foreign investment restrictions.[219]

6.3.7 *Long-Termism*

On 1 February 2016, Laurence Fink, CEO of asset manager BlackRock, the world's largest investor, stated in a letter to S&P-500 CEOs: 'Today's culture of quarterly earnings hysteria is totally contrary to the long-term approach we need.'[220] The sentiment of the comment was that in a dispersed ownership listed company, institutional shareholders were overly focused on quarterly results, leading to company management, looking to maximise pay-outs under their often short-term orientated remuneration packages, prioritising short-term shareholder profits rather than investing in long-term projects that could be profitable in the long term, but perhaps detrimental from a financial perspective in the short term. An oft-cited quality attributed to dual-class stock (and controlling shareholder one share, one vote firms), where the controller does not need to be beholden to outside shareholders with short-term proclivities, is that it engenders a long-term approach to business.[221]

215 National Security and Investment Bill (2020) (n 212 above), s. 3. BEIS has already suggested that the level of 'control' procured by an acquiror will be determinative (BEIS, 'National Security and Investment Bill: Statement of policy intent' (11 November 2020)).

216 Although the bill is technically not limited to foreign investment, its underlying premise is to block hostile foreign direct investment (see BEIS Press Release, 'New Powers to Protect UK from Malicious Investment and Strengthen Economic Resilience' (11 November 2020)).

217 Although beyond the scope of this chapter, it is submitted that foreign investment restriction legislation should consider the application of dual-class structure in more detail. For example, thought should be given to the application of the rules where enhanced-voting shares convert into inferior-voting shares as a result of sunset clauses (see Chapter 9), resulting in an increase in the proportion of votes held by the, potentially foreign, inferior-voting shareholders.

218 Crucially, though, the foreign control of which the UK Government will be wary is that over the composition of a relevant company's board, and a company adopting the proposals of the UK Listing Review would not be protected from such influence if a foreign shareholder were to acquire sufficient equity (see Section 1.5.7 of Chapter 1).

219 Cipollone (2012) (n 18 above 70).

220 BlackRock, 'Larry Fink's 2016 Letter to CEOs' www.blackrock.com/corporate/investor-relations/2016-larry-fink-ceo-letter.

221 For example, Fischel (1987) (n 104 above 139); DeAngelo and DeAngelo (1985) (n 122 above 35); G. Dent, 'Dual Class Capitalization: A Reply to Professor Seligman' (1987) 54 *Geo. Wash. L. Rev.* 725, 764; Choi (2018) (n 157 above 59); Goshen and Hamdani (2016) (n 185 above); L. Anidjar, 'Toward

The NYSE and NASDAQ listings of inferior-voting shares in Google, Berkshire Hathaway, Blackstone, Facebook and Mastercard, amongst others, were each characterised by the capital structures promoting efficiencies associated with boards being able to apply long-term approaches to the businesses of their companies.[222] In particular, Google, at IPO, stated, '... we have set up a corporate structure that will make it harder for outside parties to take over or influence Google. This structure will also make it easier for our management team to follow the long term, innovative approach emphasized earlier.'[223] Similarly, the founders of Snap stated that the public dual-class structure was being implemented to 'permit us to continue to prioritize our long-term goals rather than short-term results',[224] and Alibaba argued that the priority rights granted to founders over board appointments would allow the company to maintain its corporate culture and pursue long-term opportunities free from unreasonable demands to boost short-term profitability.[225] Even in the 1980s, when US firms adopted dual-class structure mainly to protect against a rampant hostile takeover market,[226] a poll of executives of dual-class firms found that, although the capability to raise capital and diversifying wealth without losing control weighed heavily on the minds of the executives when choosing a dual-class stock listing, the ability to pursue long-term interests over short-term profits was also a frequently raised reason.[227] At least founders seem to believe that dual-class stock can be beneficial to the long-term health of their companies. Taking a long-term approach, that is purportedly supported by dual-class stock, can particularly benefit technology companies. They are often involved in product innovation and, especially in their early growth-phase years, seek success through the exploitation of product cycles, which can increase R&D investment at the expense of short-term profits.[228]

Relative Corporate Governance Regimes: Rethinking Concentrated Ownership Structure Around the World' (2019) 30 *SLPR* 197, 205; Cipollone (2012) (n 18 above 71); Bebchuk and Kastiel (2017) (n 64 above 611); Cremers et al. (2018) (n 105 above 32); SGX Consultation (2017) (n 156 above 9); A. Friedman, 'The Promise of Market Reform: Reigniting America's Economic Engine' *Harvard Law School Forum on Corporate Governance and Financial Regulation* (18 May 2017) at 2; HKEX Concept Paper (2014) (n 151 above 23).

222 Cipollone (2012) (n 18 above 71).

223 Form S-1/A Amendment No. 8 to Registration Statement of Google Inc. (filed on 16 August 2004) at 29.

224 Form S-1/A Amendment No. 2 to Registration Statement of Snap Inc. (filed on 16 February 2017) at 167.

225 T. Holland, 'Alibaba's Plan to Stuff Board Hardly in Investors' Interests' *South China Morning Post* (28 August, 2013).

226 See Section 2.3 of Chapter 2.

227 Böhmer et al. (1996) (n 160 above 96 and 116). More recently, a study which used pre-IPO media coverage of a founder as a proxy for a founder's idiosyncratic vision found that firms with higher pre-IPO media coverage were more likely to adopt dual-class structure (A. Grinapell, 'Dual-Class Stock Structure and Firm Innovation' (2020) 25 *SJLBF* 40, 67).

228 Reddy (2020) (n 87 above 329–330); S. Kupor, 'Sorry CalPERS, Dual Class Shares Are a Founder's Best Friend' *Forbes CIO Network* (14 May 2013) www.forbes.com/sites/ciocentral/2013/05/14/sorry-calpers-dual-class-shares-are-a-founders-best-friend/?sh=11d05af112d9.

Biomed companies also similarly have long product cycles.[229] If founders are under pressure from equity market investors to maintain strong short-term profits and distributions, the ability of the founder to pursue such product cycles will be diminished.[230] Away from the technology and biomed industries, founders may need to maintain control to pursue a long-term, innovative vision that is not related to the invention of new products – for instance, innovative employee incentivisation mechanics, marketing campaigns, distribution processes or simply a confidence in one's ability to outperform all other competitors.

Although it is not proposed that a debate on stock market short-termism be presented here,[231] it should be noted that it is not conclusive that public shareholders do, in fact, prioritise short-term profits, or, indeed, that taking a long-term approach to business is overall beneficial to companies, shareholders and society generally. Both contentions are controversial issues. For example, although some studies suggest that institutional investors are besotted by short-term considerations, such as quarterly financials,[232] and that the markets are subject to irrational short-term bias with 'systematic' informational disparities leading to disproportionate short-term market behaviour,[233] other studies have noted that fund managers (and the investment consultants that advise them) do take into account long-term considerations such as R&D investment,[234] and that the influence of market short-termism on managerial behaviour may be overstated.[235] Even in the hedge-fund space, the accusation that activist investors generate purely short-term benefits has been challenged.[236] In relation to the benefits of long-termism, even if it is recognised

229 HKEX, 'Research Report: Listing Regime Reforms for Dual-Class Share Structure and Biotech Industry' (November 2018) at 8.

230 Google's founders, in justifying its capital structure, stated:

> 'Technology products often require significant investment over many years to fulfill their potential. For example, it took over three years just to ship our first Android handset, and then another three years on top of that before the operating system truly reached critical mass. These kinds of investments are not for the faint-hearted. We have protected Google from outside pressures and the temptation to sacrifice future opportunities to meet short-term demands.' (Alphabet (2011) (n 177 above)).

231 For a summary of the benefits of stock market long-termism see K. Willey, *Stock Market Short-Termism: Law, Regulation and Reform* (Palgarve Macmillan, 2019) at 195–218.

232 D. Goodhart and C. Grant, 'Making the City Work' (1988) 528 *Fabien Society* 1, 19.

233 See, for example, A. Shleifer, *Inefficient Markets: An Introduction to Behavioral Finance* (Oxford University Press, 2000); R. Gilson and R. Kraakman, 'The Mechanisms of Market Efficiency Twenty Years Later: The Hindsight Bias' (2003) *Harvard Law School Discussion Paper No 446* 1, 14; Moore and Walker-Arnott (2014) (n 59 above 421); Willey (n 231 above 130–147); Davies et al. (2014) (n 200 above 20).

234 B. Cheffins, *Company Law: Theory, Structure and Operation* (Oxford University Press, 1997) at 52–53; B. Bushee, 'The Influence of Institutional Investors on Myopic R&D Investment Behavior' (1998) 73 *Account. Rev.* 305, 322.

235 J. Abarbanell and V. Bernard, 'Is the US Stock Market Myopic?' (2000) 38 *J. Account. Res.* 221.

236 For example: L. Bebchuk et al., 'The Long-Term Effects of Hedge Fund Activism' (2015) 115 *Colum. L. Rev.* 1085, 1141; L. Bebchuk, 'The Myth that Insulating Boards Serves Long-Term Value' (2013) *Harvard Discussion Paper No*, 755 1, 29 *et seq*.

that short-term behaviour by boards can result in the prioritisation of distributions and share buybacks, and reduced investment in, for example, innovation and R&D, which may be essential to the long-term health of the company,[237] conversely, holding management's feet to the fire with respect to short-term performance can play an important signalling mechanism allowing shareholders to assess the performance and ability of management.[238] Notwithstanding the lack of resolution to the debates, in the context of evaluating dual-class stock, three aspects bear consideration. Firstly, even a mere perception that the markets are short-termist, whether justified or not, can influence managers, and a number of theoretical and empirical studies have found that managers in dispersed ownership firms make short-term orientated decisions as a result of at least a perception that the markets are myopic.[239] Secondly, even if the majority of the market takes a long-term approach, short-term shareholders can have a disproportionate effect on managerial behaviour. The eminent Kay Review, in 2012, which reviewed the United Kingdom's equity markets and their support of long-term decision-making, noted that 72 per cent of UK market turnover was attributed to hedge funds, high frequency traders and proprietary traders – actors often labelled as short-termists.[240] High market turnover of that type can have an effect on share price, and therefore an influence on management behaviour.[241] Finally, and perhaps most importantly, encouraging a long-term approach to business is a regulatory priority in the United Kingdom.[242] Therefore, from a policy perspective, engineering structures that are conducive to taking such a long-term approach will be essential.

How might dual-class stock enable long-termism? Management entrenchment and the absence of a market for corporate control, which were also notionally described as detriments earlier in this chapter, insulate management from the whims of short-term orientated investors, and, therefore, assuming that the relevant controller itself bears

237 G. Manso, 'Motivating Innovation' (2011) 66 *J. Financ.* 1823; N. Slawinski and P. Bansal, 'Short on Time: Intertemporal Tensions in Business Sustainability' (2015) 26 *Organ. Sci.* 531, 533; S. Cheng, 'R&D Expenditures and CEO Compensation' (2004) 79 *Account. Rev.* 305, 313.

238 R. Thakor, 'A Theory of Efficient Short-termism' (2016) http://ssrn.com/abstract=2821162; M. Burkart et al., 'Large Shareholders, Monitoring, and the Value of the Firm' (1997) *Q.J. Econ.* (August 1997) 693, 717.

239 For an account of the manner in which management of a dispersed ownership company can react to short-term-orientated shareholders with short-term-orientated behaviour, see Moore and Walker-Arnott (2014) (n 59 above 430 and 438); M. Jensen, 'Agency Costs of Overvalued Equity' (2005) 34 *Financ. Manag.* 5, 6; Ang and Megginson (1989) (n 160 above 305); A. Brandenburger and B. Polak, 'When Managers Cover their Posteriors: Making the Decisions the Market Wants to See' (1996) 27 *RAND J. Econ.* 523; Mizik (2010) (n 198 above 594).

240 J. Kay, 'The Kay Review of UK Equity Markets and Long-Term Decision Making: Final Report' (July 2012) at 38.

241 A. Shleifer and R. Vishny, 'Short Horizons of Investors and Firms' (1990) 80 *Am. Econ. Rev.* 148, 151; Bushee (1998) (n 234 above 328); B. Bushee, 'Do Institutional Investors Prefer Near-Term Earnings over Long-Run Value?' (2001) 18 *Contemp. Account. Res.* 207.

242 For example: Kay Review (2012) (n 240 above 20); HM Government, 'Building Our Industrial Strategy: Green Paper' (January 2017) at 64.

a long-term outlook in relation to the prospects of the company, the management team will not be fearful of losing their employment if short-term metrics are not positive.[243] Also, in relation to takeover-initiated changes of management, Stein (1988) modelled how the market for corporate control can cause management to be overly preoccupied with short-term share price in priority to the long-term interests of the company.[244] Management will be at the behest of those shareholders who may make misjudgements in accepting predatory takeover offers that are not in the best interests of those shareholders or the firm.[245] The presence of a controller eliminates these issues, and also creates (reinforced by the 'Bonding Hypothesis' described above) an environment beneficial for firms, including, in particular, tech firms, that need to invest in intangible assets and human resources, which are long-term assets the value of which may be misjudged by public shareholders.[246] It has been further speculated that innovation is promoted in companies where there is greater tolerance of short-term moribund share performance.[247] Effectively, entrenchment creates a permissive environment in which a company can take a long-term view to its business. On the other hand, the premium tier proposals of the UK Listing Review constitute a wasted opportunity, especially given the UK Government's erstwhile allusions toward promoting long-termism in companies.[248] Although the market for corporate control would be abated to a degree by a company adopting those proposals, the proposals do not insulate management from the existing public shareholders who, if they hold a majority of the equity, possess control over the constitution of the board.[249] Share price will still serve as a proxy for management performance, and, particularly in industries such as innovative tech fields where the long-term impact of management decision-making and investment may not be easily observable to public shareholders, the propensity for management to take long-term decisions will be curtailed by fear of removal. Even in relation to the market for corporate control, the UK Listing Review's proposals would only protect management for a period of five years post-IPO,[250] and, well before the expiry of five years post-IPO, the management team will already be concerned to ensure that share price is robust before such a period expires – hardly representative of long-termism. 'Genuine' dual-class stock is required to promote the long-termism sought.

It should be noted that it is not unequivocal that dual-class structure results in more long-term orientated companies than equivalent companies with dispersed ownership models. This uncertainty is apparent in assessing the European Commission's

243 M. Narayanan, 'Managerial Incentives for Short-Term Results' (1985) 40 *J. Financ.* 1469, 1479.
244 J. Stein, 'Takeover Threats and Managerial Myopia' (1988) 96 *J. Political Econ.* 61.
245 See n 191 above and accompanying text.
246 Gilson (2006) (n 68 above 1669); Ang and Megginson (1989) (n 160 above 305). In relation to the importance of human capital to tech firms, see nn 176–177 above and accompanying text.
247 GUBERNA Position Paper, 'Re-Designing Corporate Governance to Promote Innovation' (January, 2016) at 7; Manso (2011) (n 237 above 1852).
248 See n 242 above.
249 See Section 1.5.7 of Chapter 1.
250 *ibid.*

somewhat mercurial views on how to encourage 'long-termism'. In 2007,[251] the European Commission acknowledged the argument that controlling shareholders or entrenched boards would be more focused on long-term development, but dismissed it on the basis that in response to a questionnaire[252] on 'control-enhancing mechanisms' (such a dual-class structure), the majority of investors expressing dissatisfaction with such mechanisms were long-term investors.[253] However, by 2014,[254] the European Commission was advocating the use of additional voting rights and loyalty shares to enhance the influence of long-term shareholders – mechanisms that could enable controlling shareholder entrenchment. Empirical evidence of the long-term benefit provided by dual-class structure is similarly inconclusive. Certain studies have shown that dual-class firms, in various jurisdictions, are associated with greater capital expenditure or investment.[255] Jordan et al. (2016) also found that US dual-class firms had greater sales growth and R&D intensity (defined as R&D expenditure over assets) than one share, one vote firms, and that the trend was positively correlated with the controller's voting/cash-flow divergence.[256] Correspondingly, dual-class firms unifying into one share, one vote showed falls in sales growth and R&D intensity,[257] leading the authors to conclude that a decline in growth opportunities drives dual-class firms to unify, since the dual-class structure was no longer necessary or conducive for firm performance.[258] Further, it was found that US dual-class firms had significantly fewer short-term and transitory shareholders,[259] and were subject to fewer takeovers, providing circumstantial evidence that dual-class firms had fewer short-term pressures. Taking a different measure, Baran et al. (2017) found that an increasing voting/cash-flow divergence correlated with a greater quantity and quality of innovation as evidenced by more patent filings and citations, but that the positive correlation diminished over longer time periods.[260] However, other studies have shown that dual-class firms do not invest more in R&D than one share, one vote firms.[261] It should be

[251] EC (SEC(2007) 1705), 'Impact Assessment on the Proportionality between Capital and Control in Listed Companies' *Staff Working Document* (12 December 2007).

[252] ISS in collaboration with Sherman & Sterling LLP and the European Corporate Governance Institute as commissioned by the EC, 'Report on the Proportionality Principle in the European Union' (18 May, 2007).

[253] EC (2007) (n 251 above 32).

[254] EU Draft Report dated 19 December 2014 on the proposal for a directive of the European Parliament and of the Council amending Directive 2007/36/EC and Directive 2013/34/EU (2014/0121(COD)).

[255] Bauguess et al. (2012) (n 105 above 1251); Lehn et al. (1990) (n 197 above 577); Dittmann and Ulbricht (2007) (n 121 above 187).

[256] Jordan et al. (2016) (n 105 above 308).

[257] *ibid* 321 and 322.

[258] *ibid* 322.

[259] *ibid* 310.

[260] Baran et al., 'Dual Class Firm Structure and Innovation' (2017) https://ssrn.com/abstract=3183517.

[261] Arugaslan et al. (2010) (n 105 above 174); Mikkelson and Partch (1994) (n 105 above 197). Cremers et al. (2018) (n 105 above 19) found that one share, one vote firms spend more on R&D, although there were no significant differences in capital expenditure generally. In relation to antitakeover devices generally, it was also found that such devices correlate with a decrease in R&D investment (L. Meulbroek et al., 'Shark Repellents and Managerial Myopia: An Empirical Test' (1990) 98

noted, though, that 'investment' may not be a complete proxy for long-termism, and there are many aspects of short-term behaviour that do not relate to the foregoing of R&D and long-term investment. The level of sums invested by a company with a controller could also relate to the nature of expropriation; for example, on the one hand, basic tunnelling of cash-flow by a controller could leave less cash available for investment, whereas, on the other hand, if the relevant expropriation is by way of 'sweet-heart' deals, or through diversification or empire-building resulting in investments in inappropriate projects, such expropriation would be discernible by increased levels of investment.

Although the empirical evidence does not fully comport with greater long-termism, any inferences must take into account the diversity of controllers[262] since some controllers will have adopted dual-class structure to take a long-term approach (with a desire to spend more on R&D, for example) and others will have done so for different reasons (possibly with expropriation of inferior-voting shareholders in mind). Alternatively, the intentions of the controller may simply shift over time as the talents of the founder wane or control passes to heirs.[263] Therefore, the nature and identity of the controller is critical in ascertaining the effect on long-term strategy. It has been found that founder-CEO-controlled firms spend more on R&D than non-founder-controlled firms,[264] and R&D spending is generally less where corporate control has been inherited.[265] Another study discovered that founder-controlled firms are more, and heir-controlled firms are less, R&D intensive than dispersed ownership firms[266] (although the effects may be attributable to the fact that founder-CEO-controlled firms are generally younger). Similarly, in a meta-analysis of seventy-four studies on family firms, it was found that founder-led family firms invested more in R&D than non-family firms, but the trend was reversed for successor-led family firms,[267] emphasising that the identity of the controller can have a significant effect on the propensity for long-termism. The type of company, including its maturity, industry and market, can also have a bearing upon whether the presence of a controlling shareholder encourages 'long-termism'. For example, as alluded to earlier,[268] a dual-class firm may operate in an industry where the reputational advantages of such an approach can give the company a competitive

J. Political Econ. 1108, 1115; M. Johnson and R. Rao, 'The Impact of Antitakeover Amendments on Corporate Financial Performance' (1997) 32 *Financ. Rev.* 659, 681; R. Daines and M. Klausner, 'Do IPO Charters Maximize Firm Value? Antitakeover Protection in IPOs' (2001) 17 *J. L. Econ. & Org.* 83, 104).

262 Also see Chapters 5 and 7.

263 Also see nn 67–68 above and accompanying text.

264 R. Fahlenbrach, 'Founder-CEOs, Investment Decisions, and Stock Market Performance' (2009) 44 *J. Financial Quant. Anal.* 439, 446.

265 Morck et al. (2000) (n 67 above 345).

266 R. Anderson et al., 'Founders, Heirs, and Corporate Opacity in the United States' (2009) 92 *J. Financ. Econ.* 205, 212.

267 Essen et al. (2015) (n 67 above 13).

268 See text accompanying nn 176–177 above.

advantage, whether that be in relation to attracting talented employees[269] or forming stable relationships with long-term suppliers and customers.[270] A founder-controlled high-growth tech company may be more likely to utilise the qualities of dual-class structure to implement a long-term approach to business, whereas a mature non-founder managed manufacturing or retail company may have adopted dual-class stock for other purposes.

The support of long-termism through management entrenchment is also a quality of one share, one vote controlling shareholder structures, but the propensity may be amplified with dual-class structure since the controller will be less concerned by any short-term personal changes in net-worth correlating with share price movements. With one share, one vote, share price is apposite if the controlling shareholder intends to sell-down equity, but with dual-class structure, it is likely that the controller will already have disposed of a substantial proportion of its equity. Of course, if the market is indeed overall short-term orientated, inferior-voting share price may decline if short-term performance is poor, particularly if long-term value is not easily observable, but a diversified dual-class firm controller will be able to stay the course toward long-term success, and those less short-term orientated inferior-voting shareholders who continue on the journey with the controller will also be able to enjoy positive long-term returns. Accordingly, a mathematical model by Burkart et al. (1997) predicted that high-growth companies, particularly start-ups with low current earnings compared to future potential, are likely to be benefitted by, and prefer, dual-class structure.[271]

The flipside is that if the controller's ownership of equity is miniscule, it may be completely apathetic to share price. Although ignoring short-term share price fluctuations can be conducive to taking a long-term view of the business, the short-term share price can also provide a useful signalling mechanism,[272] and even promote better long-term performance by reducing managerial slackness.[273] There are two opposing views. A traditional supporter of dual-class structure may argue that share price fluctuations represent short-lived profit deficits in circumstances where the public shareholders, with informational deficiencies or with short-term horizons, cannot, or will not, fully appreciate, or price, the long-term benefits of managerial actions.[274] A traditional opponent of dual-class stock may, though, counter-argue that share price fluctuations represent a badly managed firm with little in the way of long-term prospects and a controller who has lost appetite for the business, is overly focused on egregious controller benefit extraction, or simply has

[269] See n 176 above and accompanying text.
[270] See n 178 above and accompanying text.
[271] Burkart et al. (1997) (n 238 above 718).
[272] See n 238 above and accompanying text.
[273] Bebchuk (2013) (n 236 above 45).
[274] Shleifer and Vishney (1990) (n 241 153).

a misguided belief that its long-term plan will be successful. Often, the long-term plans of the controller, and the long-term benefits of investment, may be masked and not easily discernible by outside shareholders, and therefore it may be impossible for the market to ascertain whether the controller's allusions to long-termism are merely a front for indolent or insidious behaviour, or an overly risky strategy that has little prospect of success. Although Chemmanur's (2012) model, discussed earlier in this chapter, showed that dual-class stock allows founders to pursue projects with high near-term uncertainty without fear of losing control, such projects are only predicted to yield higher cash-flows than projects with low near-term uncertainties if the founder is talented.[275] It can be difficult, though, for outside investors to discern the type and talent of the founder, and it has even been noted that a founder that has adopted dual-class structure primarily to expropriate inferior-voting shareholders could try to mimic a 'good' founder by implementing voluntary minority protections at IPO.[276]

As ever, a balance is in play. Although a dual-class founder will not fear a hostile takeover or shareholder-initiated removal as a result of declining share price, even with only a small equity holding, a dual-class controller is not completely dissociated from the economic health of the company. The controller may still gain substantial non-pecuniary benefits from the company remaining successful, in the short as well as the long term. Also, a controller intending to issue further equity for investment, financing or acquisition purposes, which may be required by high-growth tech firms, will desire that the equity is priced at a level that reduces the cost of capital.[277] Finally, although the controller's equity holding, as a constraining influence, has less of an impact on dual-class controllers than one share, one vote controllers,[278] unless the controller has reduced its equity ownership to a miniscule level, declining share price will have at least some effect on the controller's wealth. Therefore, given the difficulties for investors in ascertaining the nature and qualities of founders, it may, as endorsed in Chapter 9, be conducive to ensure that founders own more than minute levels of equity. By ensuring that the founder has more than trivial 'skin-in-the-game', an untalented founder or a founder focused on inferior-voting shareholder expropriation will suffer at least a non-inconsequential diminishment in wealth that could have a constraining effect on excessive pernicious controller benefit extraction and, in the case of untalented founders, incentivise the appointment of more talented third-party managers. The key, though, will be to ensure that the required level of retained equity is not so large that it inhibits the very ability of the controller to take the long-term approach enabled by dual-class stock.

[275] Chemmanur (2012) (n 199 above 306).
[276] *ibid* 306.
[277] See nn 85–86 above and accompanying text. Also see Section 8.3.1 of Chapter 8.
[278] See Section 8.3.1 of Chapter 8.

6.3.8 *Risk-Taking*

Closely connected with long-termism is the concept of risk-taking. With one share, one vote dispersed ownership firms, a regulatory prioritisation of robust monitoring (resulting in various mechanisms, such as independent directors, being implemented to substitute for a lack of scrutiny by dispersed shareholders) has been accused of blunting innovation in favour of curtailing the excesses of unfettered management.[279] Within such a culture of compliance, management is less likely to take the risks that are required to truly innovate and substantially improve returns. Although the monitoring mechanisms have been put into place in order to protect dispersed shareholders, given that those shareholders are generally well-diversified, it is likely that they would have a degree of appetite for risk in order to improve upside.[280] For a growing tech company, calculated risk-taking can be critical to success. Success is often predicated on the development of transformational and disruptive technologies, requiring a significant level of risk-taking.[281] Not all risks will pay-off, but in the innovative tech industry, a single big success can more than compensate for numerous failures. Two aspects of dual-class structure can encourage greater risk-taking and innovation, which could benefit all the shareholders in the company.

Firstly, even though the corporate governance requirements that seemingly inhibit risk-taking would still apply to premium listed dual-class firms (if permitted), their impact on the controller's decision-making (and risk-taking) will be reduced where the management team is entrenched.[282] For example, although the UK CGC recommends that at least half the board be comprised of independent directors,[283] as discussed earlier in this chapter and in Chapter 8,[284] in the presence of a controller with ultimate discretion over their continued incumbency, the genuine independence of those independent directors can be questioned, with them owing at least a degree of loyalty to the controller that has appointed them. Additionally, other aspects of the UK CGC which prioritise supervision of the management team over risk-taking and innovation will not have such a chilling impact on the ability of the management team to take risks. The UK CGC is premised on the concept of corporate governance disclosure, giving outside shareholders the information they need to instigate change if desired. However, in the presence of a controller with effective control over the voting rights in the company, corporate governance measures will have been implemented at the behest, or at least with the tacit

279 For example, S. Bianchini et al., 'Corporate Governance, Innovation and Firm Age: Insights and New Evidence' (2015) *GREDEG Working Papers Series* 2015–05 1; GUBERNA (2016) (n 247 above).

280 Cheffins (2002) (n 149 above 356).

281 B. Nagji and G. Tuff, 'Managing Your Innovation Portfolio' *HBR*. (May 2012), at 9; Reddy (2020) (n 87 above 331).

282 Smart and Zutter (2003) (n 31 above 103).

283 UK CGC, Provision 11.

284 See Section 6.2.4 of this chapter, and Section 8.2.5 of Chapter 8.

approval, of the controller, with the public shareholders possessing less influence than in one share, one vote dispersed ownership companies to influence modifications to the corporate governance arrangements of the company. Although the lesser effectiveness in controlling shareholder firms generally of independent directors and the UK CGC can be viewed negatively in not constraining the acts of controllers, it can also be viewed positively by giving controllers greater freedom to take risks.

Secondly, dual-class structure can enhance risk-taking from the perspective of the economic incentives of the controller. An analogy can be made to a wager hypothetical based upon the theories developed by Kahneman (2011).[285] This explained the common psychological loss aversion apparent amongst most individuals, and its exacerbation on single bets, compared to its mitigation when aggregated across multiple independent bets. For example, in its simplest form, consider a wager on the toss of a coin where a gain of £2000 is offered for heads, but a loss of £1000 is suffered for tails. In a single bet, it is inferred that the average person will reject the wager due to the loss aversion in losing £1000 weighing more heavily than the potential to win £2000. However, if such a person were offered multiple independent bets of the same nature, it is more likely that such a person will accept the aggregated wager. Although this is an extreme example, even with more complex scenarios and less stark differences between loss and gain, Kahneman showed that the aggregation of favourable gambles progressively moderates loss aversion by reducing the possibility of losses being sustained. Extending this to the corporate world, it is easy to foresee a scenario where management in a dispersed ownership one share, one vote firm turns down a single gamble on analogous terms to the coin toss, due to aversion to the potential loss – their employment could be under threat as a result of a short-term focus by a dispersed and fluctuating shareholder base.[286] The situation would be improved in a one share, one vote controlling shareholder scenario, where a long-term controller is present; such a shareholder has much to gain if management were to take many such independent gambles on such terms over the course of numerous years, assuming that the individual losses when incurred are not so large as to seismically imperil the future of the company. However, a competing influence is the undiversified nature of the controller's wealth – if a large proportion of the controller's wealth is invested in the firm, the controller's impulse to take such risks may be attenuated by the large paper losses that the controller could sustain in the short term if an individual 'bet' is not successful. With the controller's high exposure to the value of the company, management (which may include the controller, and even if it does not, will be influenced by the controller's views) may forego the pursuit of risky, potentially

[285] Kahneman (2011) (n 91 above 336).

[286] Similar to the discussion on 'Long-Termism' earlier in this chapter (nn 248–250 and accompanying text), the proposals of the UK Listing Review will not support risk-taking to the same degree as 'genuine' dual-class stock – unless a controller has retained significant equity (in which case the propensity for the controller to take risks may be diluted), in a company that has adopted the proposals of the UK Listing Review, management will be as apprehensive of the influence of existing public shareholders as in a one share, one vote dispersed ownership firm.

valuable, investments.[287] Empirical evidence does indeed suggest that one share, one vote controllers are statistically risk averse.[288] In practice, as with long-termism, the nature of the particular controlling shareholder and its appetite for a long-term perspective will be relevant. The propensity for risk-taking, though, can be significantly enhanced by the implementation of dual-class stock, where the controller has sold substantial equity to diversify while retaining control. The gambling hypothetical would remain apt, since the controller can purvey the aggregation of such individual decisions over an extended period of time, but, now, the controller, being better diversified, would not be burdened by tectonic shocks to its net wealth by individual decisions.[289] Essentially, by hedging its ownership of the firm, the controller can benefit all shareholders by not having to engage in value-decreasing hedging within the firm.[290] For a tech firm, if a talented founder can procure more, or more valuable, 'winners' than 'losers' through risk-taking, the overall long-term returns for shareholders will be greater than if those risks had been avoided. Empirically, Bauguess et al. (2012)[291] found that risk-taking (measured by the standard deviation of daily returns) was fostered in closely held firms after the implementation of dual-class stock and the divestment of significant equity by the controller, which was wealth-enhancing and beneficial to shareholders as a whole.[292] Of course, as even the worst Las Vegas gambler knows, risk-taking for risk-taking's sake will not be conducive to overall wealth. While risk-taking in a calculated manner can enhance wealth, it cannot be ignored that a dual-class controller out of his or her depth may take risks that destroy firm value in the short and long term; after all, the financial risk has shifted from the controlling shareholder to the outside shareholders.[293] Therefore, only sensible risks taken on an ongoing basis will be beneficial, which will very much depend upon the competence and perspicaciousness of the controller.[294] This highlights two factors which will be revisited in Chapter 9. Given the difficulties for public

287 A. Edmans, 'Blockholders and Corporate Governance' (2014) 6 *Annu. Rev. Financ. Econ.* 23, 33; also see Cheffins (2002) (n 149 above 357); C. Holderness, 'A Survey of Blockholders and Corporate Control' (2003) *FRBNY Econ. Policy Rev.* 51, 56; Ashton (1994) (n 7 above 927); *The Law and Finance of Corporate Acquisitions*, R. Gilson and B. Black (Foundation Press, 1995) at 784.

288 M. Faccio et al., 'Large Shareholder Diversification and Corporate Risk-Taking' (2011) 24 *Rev. Financ. Stud.* 3601, 3621 (risk was measured by the volatility of profitability). However, it was noted in C. Himmelberg et al., 'Understanding the Determinants of Managerial Ownership and the Link between Ownership and Performance' (1999) 53 *J. Financ. Econ.* 353, 368 that management ownership was itself a factor of firm characteristics (i.e. endogenic), such that a firm that takes greater risks would result in management desiring to own less equity.

289 Bauguess et al. (2012) (n 105 above 1245); Ashton (1994) (n 7 above 927); Gilson and Black (1995) (n 287 above 784); HKEX Concept Paper (2014) (n 151 above IV-8); Fischel (1987) (n 104 above 140); Hu and Black (2006) (n 3 above 852); Cipollone (2012) (n 18 above 69).

290 Hu and Black (2006) (n 3 above 852).

291 Bauguess et al. (2012) (n 105 above 1252).

292 *ibid* 1251.

293 Cipollone (2012) (n 18 above 69).

294 An analogy can be drawn to empirical evidence that suggests that takeover defences only benefit firm performance when the management team is talented (for further details, see the evaluation of dual-class stock empirical evidence in Chapter 7).

shareholders in assessing the qualities of controllers, it may be unwise to allow a controller to completely detach itself from the company's equity – a *de minimis* level of equity will still enable risk-taking, but not to the extent that the risks become purely speculative. Also, to the extent that public shareholders have decided (if they have a choice[295]) to invest in a dual-class firm based upon their faith in the controller, it would be prudent to protect them from future transfers of voting control to unexpected persons.[296]

6.4 THE DUAL-CLASS STOCK TRADEOFF

In this chapter, the theoretical detriments and benefits of dual-class stock structure, from the perspective of the inferior-voting shareholders, have been discussed. The remainder of this chapter deliberates upon the tradeoff between those benefits and detriments, and develops a formulation that treats such benefits and detriments as the consequences that materialise from the extraction of differing controller benefits. An evaluation of the empirical evidence on dual-class stock, as presented in the next chapter, will assist in ascertaining whether the tradeoff is generally shifted into a net-beneficial or net-detrimental position, and, subsequently, the concept of the new formulation of the tradeoff will be used to ascertain whether constraints can be used to tilt the tradeoff in a beneficial direction.

6.4.1 *The Tradeoff – Literature Review*

In Chapter 5, Gilson and Gordon's one share, one vote controlling shareholder tradeoff was outlined, which described the balance between the possible costs to public shareholders from the extraction of controller benefits, and the possible upside for public shareholders from the controlling shareholder monitoring management and reducing agency costs.[297] With the introduction of dual-class stock, the decrease in managerial agency costs in the form of increased monitoring to ensure performance and conduct is in line with shareholder value, and/or an equity linkage between management itself and share value, may no longer be extant, and the dynamics of controller benefit extraction are distorted. As a result, different tradeoffs apply, which have been recognised in differing guises by existing studies.

Taking into account the implementation of dual-class stock, Choi (2018) highlighted the importance of (i) aligning the controller's interests with those of the inferior-voting shareholders by ensuring that the controller holds sufficient equity;

[295] As discussed in Chapter 1, index tracker passive funds will be required to invest in dual-class firms if they are included on a relevant index.

[296] Notwithstanding that UK mandatory offer requirements provide a degree of protection to inferior-voting shareholders in this regard, Chapter 9 discusses the further justification for transfer-driven sunset provisions.

[297] Gilson and Gordon (2003) (n 4 above).

and (ii) securing the controller's long-term commitment to the firm.[298] The author noted that a tradeoff exists in relation to controller benefits – to the extent that controller benefits are large (in essence a manifestation of a large controller voting/cash-flow divergence), they reduce the alignment in (i), but enhance the long-term commitment in (ii). The balancing act presupposes that the inferior-voting shareholders value the contribution of the controller to the business, and that controller benefits bind the controller to the firm, which they will if they are substantial enough such that the value that the controller places in ownership outweighs the price it could achieve by selling its shares to a third party and exiting the business. Taking this theory to its natural conclusion would suggest that the tradeoff to be considered in order to achieve optimality involves ascertaining a firm-specific ideal voting/cash-flow divergence. As has been recently put: '... legislators must recognize that controlling shareholders may gain private benefits of control ... instead of trying to eliminate this, they should encourage it so long as it occurs at an efficiently optimal rate and incentivizes controlling shareholders to promote the company's best interests.'[299]

Goshen and Squire (2017) remarked upon the balance between principal costs and agency costs.[300] The authors extended the theme to dual-class structure, noting that agency costs are high in dual-class firms, since the controller can manage the firm in a self-serving way if it is insulated from direct control from outside shareholders, but what were described as 'principal costs' are low, since the outside shareholders, who may be prone to making irrational, uninformed or short-term decisions, are not able to interfere in the way the business is operated.[301] Again, the controller's voting/cash-flow divergence appears to be determinative in the tradeoff, and the 'principal-agency costs theorem' is therefore closely related to Choi's 'alignment-commitment theorem'. A large voting/cash-flow divergence could increase agency costs, while a small divergence could increase principal costs, since the controller will be more sensitive to share price movements and, therefore, the opinions of the outside shareholders. In reviewing empirical evidence, the authors noted that if managers were simply concerned about maintaining control, the voting/cash-flow divergence generally found in dual-class firms would be much more extreme.[302] The intimation is that the market has, through operation of a tradeoff, restricted the extent of the divergence to reduce agency costs by ensuring that the controller would still suffer at least some pain if it considered extracting controller benefits that were detrimental to firm value.

298 Choi (2018) (n 157 above 67).
299 Anidjar (2019) (n 221 above 245).
300 Goshen and Squire (2017) (see n 202 above and accompanying text).
301 *ibid* 806; Lund (2019) (n 128 above 716). In relation to an application of the 'principal-agency costs theorem' in the context of Snap, see B. Sharfman, 'A Private Ordering Defense of a Company's Right to Use Dual Class Share Structures in IPOs' (2018) 63 *Villanova Law Rev*. 1, 27; Anand (2018) (n 168 above 202); Lund (2019) (*ibid* 740).
302 DeAngelo and DeAngelo (1985) (n 122 above 55).

Evidence of the tradeoff can also explain the 'takeover defence/agency cost' versus 'optimal insider control' debate. Ang and Megginson (1989) explain that under the 'takeover defence/agency cost' hypothesis, insiders issue inferior-voting shares to insulate themselves from takeover activity and outside shareholder scrutiny, enabling them to act in a self-serving manner that is costly to outside shareholders. Under the 'optimal insider control' hypothesis, insiders issue inferior-voting shares to retain the ability to take decisions with a long-term perspective and to develop firm-specific skills, without fear of being removed, benefitting all shareholders.[303] The authors' empirical evidence lends support for both hypotheses. They found that most post-IPO recapitalisations by companies of one share, one vote into dual-class stock involved non-cash issuances of inferior-voting shares, which the authors stated possibly supports a primary purpose of management entrenchment, since no further funds were being generated for growth through the recapitalisation. However, such recapitalisations were also associated with positive abnormal returns for shareholders and, generally, post-recapitalisation, the voting/cash-flow divergence remained relatively stable, lending support to an inference that the primary purpose of recapitalisations was to benefit the firm as a whole. Although the authors did not describe a tradeoff as such, the difficulty in interpreting the study's empirical results can be alleviated through the application of tradeoff methodology. Extrapolating to IPOs by founder-led companies, a founder will decide to adopt dual-class stock to diversify wealth while retaining control, and that decision to retain control with a smaller equity holding is, in practice, a mixture of the 'takeover-defence/agency-cost' and 'optimal-insider-control' hypotheses – the decision has been made partly to enable self-serving behaviour, and partly to ensure the long-term success of the firm.[304] It is therefore unhelpful to create a distinction between the two hypotheses, when, in fact, a balance or tradeoff exists.

The aforementioned three dual-class studies are all suggestive of the existence of some form of tradeoff evident in the adoption of dual-class stock. In the next section, an attempt will be made to deduce a unifying theme between the studies, and it will be argued that a brightline determination that controller benefits are 'bad' for public shareholders, and other non-self-serving actions of controllers are 'good' for public shareholders, may not be a useful delineation. All behaviours of controlling

303 Ang and Megginson (1989) (n 160 above 303 and 305).

304 Chemmanur (2012) similarly noted that founders will have in mind both value creation and extraction of controller benefits. In modelling the behaviours of founders adopting dual-class stock, the author calculated that the extent of the founder's voting/cash-flow divergence also represents a tradeoff – the greater the divergence, the less the disciplining effect of equity ownership, but the greater the ability of the controller to create shareholder value and extract controller benefits. The author modelled that loss of discipline usually outweighs value creation when controller benefits are large, and so the driver toward a high voting/cash-flow divergence in such circumstances is the extraction of controller benefits rather than value creation; as such a cap should be placed on the maximum voting/cash-flow divergence permissible (n 199 above 315).

shareholders in dual-class firms are expressions of the extraction of controller benefits, but not all such benefits are truly personal or private to the controlling shareholder.

6.4.2 *The Dual-Class Stock Tradeoff in Terms of Types of Controller Benefits*

Throughout this book, the term 'controller benefits' has been used to describe how controller's cause their firms to take actions that are beneficial to the controller rather than the more traditional term 'private benefits of control'. The notion of 'private benefits of control' invokes a sense that the controller causes the company to take actions that are only beneficial to the controller. Private benefits of control, whether that be in the context of one share, one vote or dual-class stock, hinge on the fact that the controller can use its voting control to cause the company to take actions that are not beneficial to shareholder value since the controller does not own 100 per cent of the stock and therefore does not feel the full brunt of the actions on shareholder value. The efficiency (from the perspective of the controller) of extraction of such private benefits of control increases with dual-class stock as the equity held by the controller decreases. The natural assumption, which is sometimes more expressly articulated, is that any actions of the controller which are taken with the intent of benefitting the controller rather than purposefully to increase shareholder value are presumptively private benefits for the controller. However, the controller may take actions that are not primarily aimed at increasing shareholder wealth, but may, in the long term, have that effect. The term 'controller benefits' is therefore used in this book – it is acknowledged that the controller may derive certain benefits from being able to cause the company to take actions that are not necessarily driven by ensuring that share price remains robust, but such controller benefits may, in certain circumstances, create consequential benefits for public shareholders in the long run.

A better articulation of the dual-class stock tradeoff therefore involves viewing the arrangement as a tradeoff between pernicious and benign controller benefits, with the nomenclature in the common literature describing 'private benefits of control' slightly misleading. Controller benefits will be benign if the positive consequences of their extraction on public shareholders (as a result of the controller's benefits either being shared with the public shareholders or generating separate consequential benefits for public shareholders) are equal to or outweigh the negative consequences of their extraction on public shareholders, or if those controller benefits simply have no effect on shareholder wealth. In contrast, controller benefits will be pernicious if the negative consequences outweigh the positive consequences on public shareholders. Benign controller benefits may not, semantically, be private if they are shared with, or create consequential benefits for, the public shareholders. In order to achieve a net socially optimal state, a balance needs to be struck so that the controller can extract benign controller benefits, and, in order to persuade the founder to list (and bond the founder to the firm), even minimally pernicious controller benefits, while at the same time deterring the extraction of excessive pernicious controller benefits that can either discourage investment by outsiders or, to the extent outsiders have invested, expropriate the inferior-voting shareholders to a greater extent than the benefits that they secure.

The tradeoffs described in the literature earlier can be described in terms of controller benefits. Accordingly, in relation to Choi's 'alignment-commitment theorem', certain controller benefits may, in fact, undermine the long-term commitment of the controller to the firm, and, therefore, increasing the controller's voting/cash-flow divergence could be detrimental to both alignment and long-term commitment. For example, a relevant non-pecuniary controller benefit is the ability of the controlling shareholder to decide to take a back seat and pass control on to a family member or heir. The inferior-voting shareholders may not have invested in the firm on the basis that another individual will be managing the company, and that controller benefit, in fact, reduces both commitment and alignment to shareholder value. Similarly, increasing the controller's equity stake in order to align the interests of the controller with those of the public shareholders may on the face of it enhance 'alignment', but as discussed in this chapter, it may also limit risk-taking that could otherwise be beneficial to the company's long-term health and, therefore, long-term shareholder value. Risk-taking is a controller benefit that could create shared benefits with public shareholders. Therefore, the 'alignment-commitment' tradeoff can be analysed in the context of the types of controller benefits that may be extracted. The optimal situation will not be attained by only ensuring that the controller's voting/cash-flow divergence is at the 'correct' firm-specific level, but by also ensuring that constraints are in place to prevent or limit certain types of controller benefits that are more adverse to the interests of inferior-voting shareholders, but permit other controller benefits that are benign.[305] Similarly, Goshen and Squire's 'principal-agency costs theorem', in the context of dual-class stock, also benefits from being framed through the prism of types of controller benefits. The basic notion of the theory is that the grant of greater governance rights to outside shareholders can reduce agency costs but increase principal costs in dual-class firms. However, if certain controller benefits are benign or have beneficial consequences to outside shareholders, curbing such controller benefits through giving outside shareholders greater rights will increase principal costs without reducing agency costs. Therefore, the optimal balance can only be achieved by targeting the restriction of pernicious controller benefits rather than taking a scattergun approach. Finally, both the 'takeover defence/agency cost' and 'optimal insider control' hypotheses, which were outlined by Ang and Megginson, also relate to the extraction

[305] See Chapter 9. Choi (2018) does, in conclusion, recognise that constraints should be in place to prevent the controller extracting 'too much' controller benefits, but supports ex post judicial examination rather than implementing constraints that prevent egregious extraction in the first place (n 157 above 79).

of controller benefits by the insider. In the former 'takeover defence/agency cost' hypothesis, the controller's intent to insulate itself from the public markets to take self-serving actions is an extraction of controller benefits that is detrimental to other shareholders. Whereas, in the latter 'optimal insider control' hypothesis, the controller's decision to retain control to give it scope to take long-term decisions and develop firm-specific skills without fear of removal could be described as benign controller benefit extraction. A desire to procure the company's long-term success and invest in firm-specific skills and assets are, in and of themselves, controller benefits – the controller is taking such actions not necessarily because they will create shareholder value (especially when the controller's holding of equity is small) but for the sense of satisfaction and pride in building a successful business, and for the reputational gains that flow therefrom. If the controller possesses the requisite talent though, such controller benefits also generate consequential benefits for the firm as a whole, and can, therefore, be described as benign. Verifying which of 'takeover defence/agency costs' or 'optimal insider control' governs will be dictated by which of pernicious or benign controller benefits dominate.

A number of the benefits of dual-class stock outlined in this chapter can be framed as controller benefits that result in benign consequences – for example, the ability to take a long-term approach, take risks, possess freedom of choice in relation to projects, be judicious in whether to accept takeover bids, pursue greater prestige and focus on the core business of the company without pressure to diversify, all result in pecuniary or non-pecuniary benefits for the controller, but, in specific circumstances, can also generate beneficial outcomes for the public shareholders. Goshen and Hamdani's (2016) championing of dual-class stock presents a further example. They argue that an entrepreneur may value control with no intention to extract controller benefits,[306] and, instead, dual-class structure has been adopted to allow the controller to pursue its idiosyncratic vision. In fact, wishing to retain control to pursue an idiosyncratic vision is, in and of itself, a non-pecuniary controller benefit, and so, this 'ideological controller' is, in reality, a demonstration of balancing pernicious and benign controller benefits.

The time-dimension of the dual-class stock tradeoff should also be considered. Ang and Megginson noted that firms may unify dual-class stock into one share, one vote once they are no longer of benefit to the controller.[307] The discussion only really views such unification decisions through the eyes of the controller, since the controller will have to initiate any decision to unify the capital structure. However, from the perspective of the inferior-voting shareholders, the tradeoff may also change over time. The benign controller benefits that may have dominated at

306 Goshen and Hamdani (n 185 above 576).

307 Ang and Megginson (1989) (n 160 above 304). Also see Gilson (2006) (n 68 above 1670), who envisaged that life-cycle or intergenerational changes could result in controller benefits being of less value to an incumbent controller, resulting in greater efficiencies being garnered through breaking up the controlling position.

IPO may, over time, begin to be overshadowed by more pernicious elements. For example, management of the company may convey to a less talented team, the skills of a founder may gradually wane or the company may mature to an extent that short-term profit targets provide a useful signalling mechanism where growth has plateaued. This highlights the importance of not only constraining pernicious controller benefits but also fostering a unification of capital structure into one share, one vote, when the likelihood arises that pernicious controller benefits will outweigh those that are benign. Such 'sunset clauses', as discussed further in Chapter 9, operate to convert dual-class structure into one share, one vote based upon an acknowledgement that the occurrence of certain events are indicative of a greater risk that pernicious controller benefits will start to outweigh benign controller benefits.

Both Choi (2018) and Goshen and Squire (2017) indicate that their tradeoff concepts are firm-specific. When the tradeoff is reduced to a simple balance between types and levels of controller benefit extraction as outlined in this section, firm-specificity is still applicable. For certain types of firms, no optimal tradeoff may be possible with dual-class structure, and, instead, one share, one vote structure will be preferable. For example, for a mature company with an established product and stable market, the management team may not hold any firm-specific talents, and the long-term prospects and business plan of the company may be easily observable by the public markets. It is unlikely, for instance, that the managers will be so insightful that they are able to identify projects that are beneficial to the company in the long term that are not also evident to the public markets. The requirement that management be protected from removal by public shareholders in such a case is less persuasive, and, therefore, benign controller benefits may be sparse or non-existent, and, if dual-class structure is implemented, the extraction of pernicious controller benefits will dominate. Market forces may influence the decision to proceed with a one share, one vote structure, since investors may be unwilling to invest in a dual-class firm where there are no perceptible benefits to the outside investors in conceding to dual-class stock, such as in the absence of a visionary founder operating in an innovative or novel product market. For other types of firms, a positive tradeoff may be more easily discernible. Goshen and Hamdani (2016) arrive at a similar conclusion using a narrower formulation, noting that a balance needs to be struck between an entrepreneur's freedom to pursue its idiosyncratic vision through retaining control, and an investor's protection against expropriation by securing a level of control themselves.[308] The authors postulate that entrepreneurs and investors allocate cash-flow and voting rights appropriately to achieve the correct balance.[309] Accordingly, the obvious consequence of prohibiting dual-class stock from the premium tier is that one option that could assist in achieving the

[308] Goshen and Hamdani (2016) (n 185 above 586).
[309] *ibid* 587.

relevant balance is eliminated, meaning that in certain circumstances, the most efficient balance will not be possible.

6.5 CONCLUSION

Dual-class stock distorts the simpler dynamic of a controlling shareholder holding a majority of the voting and cash-flow rights in a one share, one vote firm. The distortion, driven by the fact that the controller of the majority of the voting rights no longer holds a proportionate level of cash-flow rights, can instigate positive and negative effects from the standpoint of outside shareholders. From a detrimental perspective, since the controller does not suffer commensurate pain from its actions, the distortion can increase the incentive on the controller to tunnel, extract high executive remuneration, make inefficient decisions, amplify non-pecuniary pernicious controller benefit extraction, block efficient takeover activity, and either continue to manage the firm when talents have waned or pass control on to unsuitable heirs. From a beneficial perspective, since the controller will be better diversified and less concerned as to the consequences of depressed short-term share price, the distortion can promote long-termism, risk-taking, investment in profitable projects with high near-term uncertainty, and greater core-business focus. The structure can also promulgate a bonding effect that ties a talented founder to the firm, increase offer prices when takeovers do occur, and support operational and acquisition financing through equity rather than debt. Importantly, as also discussed in Chapter 1, permitting dual-class stock can persuade founders to float their companies when they would otherwise be deterred, especially if the business of the relevant company entails long product cycles, asymmetric information distribution or unobservable projects. Encouraging the listing of firms where the benefits of the structure outweigh the detriments allows public investors to share in their success and growth, as well as creating companies that are able to pursue successful long-term, innovative visions without being inhibited by the whims of short-term orientated investors or the constraints on growth that could be imposed by debt or private equity funding.

Obviously, if the positive qualities of dual-class firms outweigh the negative aspects, overall a dual-class firm can be net-beneficial to public shareholders. A dual-class stock tradeoff exists which can be framed in terms of pecuniary and non-pecuniary controller benefits. The extraction of benefits by a controller can have beneficial, neutral or detrimental consequences on the interests of public shareholders. If the controller benefits that are benign (overall beneficial or neutral) outweigh those that are pernicious (overall detrimental), the structure will represent a net-beneficial system from the perspective of the inferior-voting shareholders. The positive qualities of dual-class firms are derived from the extraction of controller benefits that are also overall beneficial to, or have beneficial consequences for, inferior-voting shareholders. On a normative basis, the extraction of benign over pernicious controller benefits is more likely in certain types of companies, such as high-growth, tech firms. Furthermore, in relation to such firms, if dual-class structure is prohibited on the premium tier, as has been postulated by other tradeoff models, the most efficient structure conducive to their success will not be available. Introducing an option for tech companies that could both encourage further flotations and promote the success of such firms for the benefit of all shareholders is a strong argument for welcoming dual-class firms to the premium tier. Even if a company may, theoretically, be more successful listing as a one share, one vote firm rather than a dual-class stock firm, so long as benign controller benefits outweigh pernicious controller benefits, dual-class stock may still be preferable if it encourages the founder to list his or her firm in circumstances where he or she would otherwise not list as a one share, one vote firm.

However, it is not solely high-growth, innovative firms that choose dual-class structure. Although, in the United States, around half of dual-class stock listings since Google's IPO have been tech firms,[310] dual-class structure is also prevalent amongst companies in the media, entertainment and sports industries,[311] and the risk remains that some companies are choosing dual-class structure where the pernicious controller benefits outweigh the benign. That risk, though, will be mitigated by the market's determination of the merits of dual-class structure on a firm-specific basis. For every dual-class stock IPO of a Google, Facebook or Snap, examples exist of IPOs that did not proceed with dual-class stock, such as those of WeWork and Uber.[312] Institutional investors would not entertain those firms adopting dual-class stock on the public markets, determining that the extraction of pernicious controller benefits would likely outweigh that of benign controller benefits. The bias in US tech companies adopting dual-class stock in more recent years[313] may point to the market organically selecting the types of firms in relation to which institutional investors will tolerate dual-class stock. However, it is also certainly possible that firms where the tradeoff is tilted in a negative direction for public shareholders still slip through the net, especially where the public shareholders are not able to easily

310 S. Solomon, 'Shareholders Vote with Their Dollars to Have Less of a Say' *The New York Times* (4 November 2015) www.nytimes.com/2015/11/05/business/dealbook/shareholders-vote-with-their-dollars-to-have-less-of-a-say.html; J. Fisch and S. Solomon, 'The Problems of Sunsets' (2019) 99 *B. U. Law Rev.* 1057, 1068; S. Feldman, 'Companies Opting to Go Public Offer Investors Class A One-Vote-Per-Share Stock, While Founders and Other Insiders Retain the Class B Super-Voting Shares for Themselves' (2016) 47 *SRLR* 1342, 1342.

311 Smart and Zutter (2003) (n 31 above 105); Ashton (1994) (n 7 above 939); L. Enriques et al., 'The Basic Governance Structure: Minority Shareholders and Non-Shareholder Constituencies' in *The Anatomy of Corporate Law*, eds. R. Kraakman et al. (Oxford University Press, 2017) at 83; IRRC Institute and ISS, 'Controlled Companies in the Standard & Poor 1500: A Ten-Year Performance and Risk Review' (October 2012); Gompers et al. (2010) (n 82 above 1065).

312 See nn 169–170 above and accompanying text.

313 In one study, the authors simulated an index of US dual-class firms that had undergone IPOs between 2009 and 2019, and found that over 70 per cent of those companies were in communication services (including Facebook) or information technology industries (B. Anh et al., 'Synthetic Governance' (2020) 101, 132 https://ssrn.com/abstract=3645312).

ascertain the talents or intentions of the founder or the substance of the firm's long-term business plan. Even in recent years, dual-class stock has not been completely limited to the tech industry, and retail firms, such as Levi Strauss and Chewy, and hospitality industry firms, such as Shake Shack, have adopted dual-class stock since 2015. In the next chapter, though, the empirical evidence on dual-class firms will be evaluated with a view to identifying trends as to whether dual-class structure is, on average, being used for 'good or evil'. If the structure is generally generating positive performance, the justification to restrict the use of dual-class structure in the United Kingdom becomes even less credible.

Without pre-empting the evaluation of the empirical evidence, the issue remains that in specific cases the detriments could outweigh the benefits, even if, on average, dual-class stock were to be found to be unharmful to public shareholders. However, citing this as a justifiable reason to restrict such structures is tenuous. Dispersed ownership one share, one vote firms also present potential detriments, such as managerial agency costs and the propensity for directors to prioritise short-term profits over longer-term interests; in some cases, the detriments outweigh the benefits, yet the regulatory response is to implement measures that attenuate the detriments – for example, the use of performance-related pay to link managerial and shareholder interests, and the drafting of directors' duties and corporate governance codes to guide directors toward taking into account the long-term health of the company. A similar approach could be taken with dual-class stock, permitting the structure conditional upon the implementation of bespoke constraints that blunt the specific detriments of the structure.[314] Using the dual-class stock tradeoff methodology set forth in this chapter, constraints should be viewed through the prism of differing controller benefits. A balance must be achieved, since eliminating the extraction of controller benefits in their entirety would also moderate the extraction of benign controller benefits, thereby undermining both the reasons for which a controller would choose the structure and the possible benefits of the structure once listed. If the balance is not achieved and the constraints take on a scattergun approach, issuers will be unlikely to make use of the structure in a listed company environment. In Chapter 1, it was discussed that the UK Listing Review had proposed a form of disproportionate voting control on the premium tier that falls short of 'pure' dual-class stock;[315] the reticence of HM Treasury to recommend 'pure' dual-class stock will have been driven by a desire to mitigate some of the pernicious

[314] A. Gurrea, 'Theory, Evidence, and Policy on Dual-Class Shares: A Country- Specific Response to a Global Debate' (2019) *Ibero-American Institute for Law and Finance Working Paper Series* 3/2019 section 7 suggested that the approach to dual-class stock should be driven by the investor environment of the relevant jurisdiction – a spectrum could exist with, at one end, jurisdictions with strong investor protection laws and high levels of sophisticated investors accommodating dual-class firms without further constraints, and, at the other end, jurisdictions with weak investor protections and unsophisticated investors prohibiting dual-class stock. In between the margins, jurisdictions could permit dual-class stock with varying degrees of constraints.

[315] See Section 1.5.7 of Chapter 1.

controller benefits discussed in this chapter. However, also as discussed in this chapter, the constraints proposed by the UK Listing Review will attenuate the ability of a founder to extract benign controller benefits, and, in such circumstances, not only will founders be hesitant to adopt such structures,[316] but to the extent that companies do adopt such structures on the premium tier, public shareholders and founders alike will not realise the significant benefits that can be generated through the utilisation of dual-class structure. Caution must be taken in formulating limitations or restrictions attached to any premium tier approach to dual-class stock. It may even be acceptable to permit controllers to extract even pernicious controller benefits to the extent that they are not excessive and do not overshadow the benefits of the structure. For example, allowing controllers who are involved in management to extract remuneration (particularly if long-term performance-related) that exceeds, although not significantly, market norms could be a price that investors are willing to pay to be given the opportunity to invest in an innovative firm with great growth potential, managed by a talented founder. Equally, if the empirical evidence shows that dual-class firms are disproportionately discounted by the market, the founder may also view a pecuniary controller benefit such as high executive remuneration as acceptable compensation for the founder not receiving adequate recompense for shares sold on the market at the time of IPO. Achieving the correct balance is made even more challenging by the fact that the constraints must take into account different types of controller benefits, different types of firms and controllers, and variations related to the life-cycle of firms. Taking on that challenge, after evaluating the empirical evidence on dual-class firms in the next chapter, Chapters 8 and 9 turn to the varieties of constraints and their potential to effectively strike the correct balance.

[316] *ibid.*

7

The Empirical Evidence on Dual-Class Stock

99 per cent of all statistics only tell 49 per cent of the story.[1]

7.1 INTRODUCTION

In the previous chapter, conceptually, it was shown that in certain circumstances the dual-class stock tradeoff can be net-beneficial as a result of benign controller benefits outweighing pernicious controller benefits extracted by the controller. In this chapter, that theory will be tested by analysing empirical studies, relating to the 'performance' of dual-class firms. As discussed in Chapter 4, the focus of the evaluation will be on the effect that dual-class stock has on public shareholder wealth. Although even the very mention of the word 'empirical' can conjure a sense of dread in the mind of many a legal scholar, in this chapter, rather than engaging in a deep dive into specific empirical methodologies and formulae, empirical studies will be evaluated holistically, comparing the results and inferences from various studies with a view to developing concluding remarks as to the direction in which the dual-class stock tradeoff is likely pointed.

The empirical evidence on dual-class stock has long vexed commentators. Those who view dual-class structure as the harbinger of doom often interpret the empirical evidence as corroborating concerns that it is detrimental to outside shareholders.[2] Others, of a more positive demeanour, dwell on the inconclusiveness of the empirical evidence as supporting a school of thought that there is no unequivocal proof that dual-class stock is injurious to shareholders generally, and, in fact, dual-class stock may create benefits for certain firms and burdens for others.[3] Some commentators have further noted more recent empirical evidence indicating that dual-class

[1] R. DeLegge II, *Gents with No Cents* (Half Full Publishing Group, 2011).

[2] For example, L. Bebchuk and K. Kastiel, 'The Perils of Small-Minority Controllers' (2019) 107 *Geo. L. J.* 1453, 1471.

[3] For example, R. Adams and D. Ferreira, 'One Share-One Vote: The Empirical Evidence' (2008) 12 *Rev. Financ.* 51, 65; A. Anand, 'Governance Complexities in Firms with Dual Class Shares' (2018) 3 *Annal. Corp. Gov.* 184, 203.

stock enhances firm value, and therefore the possibility that the benefits of the structure outweigh the drawbacks.[4] Occasionally, the empirical evidence has been interpreted to form the testimony for preconceived predilections. However, there are numerous measures of 'performance', and when reviewing the empirical results from various studies in toto, a more byzantine portrait is perhaps emerging. Accordingly, empirical studies that test a variety of different measures of dual-class firm performance are critically evaluated in this chapter.

In the first instance, event-based studies that examine share price reactions to post-IPO recapitalisations by firms of one share, one vote structure into dual-class structure, and unifications of dual-class stock into one share, one vote, are reviewed. The evidence is mixed. However, event-based studies only examine momentary share price reactions, and the relevant share price fluctuations could be responses to other events surrounding the recapitalisation or unification. Furthermore, such studies may only be of historic fascination since, as will be noted, contemporary mid-stream recapitalisations from one share, one vote to dual-class stock are rare.[5] Therefore, after summarising the findings, and potential flaws, from event-based studies, rather than focusing on snapshots in time, this chapter will turn toward those studies that examine dual-class firms over longer periods of time.

The plethora of studies that examine firm valuations of dual-class firms and one share, one vote firms over periods of time are reviewed in detail. Although the evidence is not incontrovertible, generally such studies show dual-class firms to be associated with lower firm valuations than one share, one vote firms. Although the results could be interpreted to suggest that the dual-class stock tradeoff is shifted into a net-detrimental position in most cases, two caveats apply. Firstly, a number of studies also show positive effects of dual-class stock on firm valuation, sometimes when specific circumstances or firm qualities apply. Secondly, low firm valuations may not evidence expropriation or a poorly performing management team, but rather the market's attitude toward dual-class stock, with the market systematically discounting such firms in anticipation of future expropriation or poor performance that does not come to pass. The second caveat can be tested by evaluating two further varieties of study.

A handful of studies compare buy-and-hold stock returns of notional portfolios of dual-class firms to notional portfolios of matched one share, one vote firms. In most cases, portfolios of dual-class firm inferior-voting shares outperform portfolios of one share, one vote firms. The results of buy-and-hold stock return studies are not indicative of expropriation dominating over more beneficial aspects of dual-class firms. Therefore, either the discounts exposed by firm value studies are unjustified or

[4] For example, Y. Allaire, 'The Case for Dual-Class of Shares' (2019) *IGOPP Policy Paper No. 11* 1, 41 and 55. The authors did note, however, that taking recent and older studies as a whole painted a more inconclusive picture (*ibid* 36). Also see B. Anh et al., 'Synthetic Governance' (2020) 101, 121, https://ssrn.com/abstract=3645312.

[5] See nn 37 and 84–85 below and accompanying text.

they are applied by investors to ensure that they are compensated (through increased returns) for the risk that they may be expropriated (or burdened with a poor, entrenched management team). Finally, does that risk bear out in practice?

The last set of studies assess various measures of operating performance, mainly reflecting profitability of dual-class firms compared to one share, one vote firms, and, in general, there is little evidence that dual-class firms display worse operating performance than one share, one vote firms over time. This would suggest that the discounts being applied to dual-class firms are not justified by those firms performing worse than one share, one vote firms, and, therefore, those discounts are not warranted by a need for compensation to incur increased risk – those risks do not seem to transpire in the real world.

It will be concluded that the empirical evidence does not warrant the prohibition of dual-class firms from the premium tier. The market protects itself from the perceived risks of dual-class structure by pricing-in those risks, and, therefore, if the provenance of the premium tier prohibition of dual-class firms, as alluded to in Chapter 5, is to protect public shareholders, that protection is unnecessary where investors are organically protected and earn positive returns from investing in dual-class firms. Given the evidence suggesting that dual-class firm portfolios earn greater returns than one share, one vote firm portfolios, and that dual-class firms are at least as profitable as one share, one vote firms, it would seem that the market is overly discounting dual-class firms, and, in fact, the discussion should move toward reducing the cost of capital for dual-class firms, to, amongst other reasons, further encourage flotations. Those discussions continue in the subsequent chapters. It should be noted, though, that the picture is not simple. Several studies use greater levels of sub-sampling than others and deduce that dual-class stock is beneficial for certain types of firms, or in certain circumstances, but detrimental for other types of firms or circumstances. Time elements may also be pertinent, with divergences between studies possibly resulting from differences in the time periods studied. Also, more recent studies have been directed toward ascertaining whether the dual-class stock tradeoff changes over time on a firm-by-firm basis.

The majority of research in this area has been conducted on US firms, and, unfortunately, historic studies on UK dual-class firms conducted at a time when they were more widespread on the public markets, are sparse. However, the United States provides the most favourable analogy to the United Kingdom. The US equity markets are the closest to the United Kingdom in terms of the nature of ownership of publicly listed companies, and the profile of investors.[6] Additionally, the United Kingdom and United States are often characterised as strong investor protection jurisdictions[7] – a factor, as will be discussed, important in assessing the empirical

[6] See Section 2.3 of Chapter 2.

[7] The strength of investor protection in the United Kingdom and United States was deduced by an influential series of studies by La Porta et al. (R. La Porta et al., 'Legal Determinants of External Finance' (1997) 52 *J. Financ.* 1131; R. La Porta et al., 'Law and Finance' (1998) 106 *J. Political Econ.* 1113;

evidence and in developing policy. Given the pre-eminence of US studies, the overviews of the various categories of empirical studies in the following sections will note whether US listed or non-US listed companies have been studied in each case.[8]

7.2 A NOTE ABOUT DIVERSITY OF FIRMS AND CONTROLLERS

An obvious point, although one that is often ignored when discussing dual-class firms, is the possibly heterogeneous effect of dual-class stock, with it being beneficial to founders and public shareholders for some types of firms, and in certain conditions, and detrimental to public shareholders for other types of firms.[9] As well as firm qualities impacting upon whether dual-class stock is beneficial or detrimental to all shareholders, the identity and nature of the controller may be as, or even more, crucial.[10] These aspects can have an impact on the empirical evidence.

7.2.1 *Diversity of Firms*

In Chapters 1 and 6, it was deliberated that dual-class stock could be particularly beneficial for certain types of firms and industries, particularly tech companies. For example, dual-class stock can 'bond' controllers to the firm; this can be beneficial for firms where customers or suppliers associate the controller's involvement with success and product quality, which require employees to invest in significant firm-specific skills, or where the development of ingrained stakeholder relationships of trust and commitment is crucial.[11] Where investment in long-term projects with high near-term uncertainty, that may not be easily financed with debt, is critical to the success of a firm, dual-class structure may also enable such a firm to thrive.[12] At a more granular level, technology and biomed companies focused on product

R. La Porta et al., 'Investor Protection and Corporate Valuation' (2002) 57 *J. Financ.* 1147). However, in relation to the United States, some doubt was subsequently raised as to the strength of investor protections (for example, S. Djankov et al., 'The Law and Economics of Self-Dealing' (2008) 88 *J. Fin. Econ.* 430; H. Spamann, 'The "Antidirector Rights Index" Revisited' (2010) 23 *Rev. Fin. Studies* 467). Further studies have, though, explained this by suggesting that the strength of US protections lies in the accessibility and prevalence of private enforcement rather than the strength of the legal protections themselves (D. Katelouzou and M. Siems, 'Disappearing Paradigms in Shareholder Protection: Leximetric Evidence for 30 Countries, 1990–2013' (2015) 15 *J. Corp. Law Stud.* 127).

8 For a US-centric review of the empirical evidence, see B. Reddy, 'More than Meets the Eye: Reassessing the Empirical Evidence on US Dual-Class Stock' (2021) 23 *U. Pa. J. Bus. L.*

9 Adams and Ferreira (2008) (n 3 above 84); S. Smart and C. Zutter, 'Control as a Motivation for Underpricing: A Comparison of Dual and Single-Class IPOs' (2003) 69 *J. Financ. Econ.* 85, 88; Anand (2018) (n 3 above 206); S. Nüesch, 'Dual-Class Shares, External Financing Needs, and Firm Performance' (2016) 20 *JMG* 525, 527; K. Rydqvist, 'Dual-Class Shares: A Review' (1992) 8 *Oxf. Rev. Econ. Policy* 45, 53; Anh et al. (2020) (n 4 above 113).

10 D. Denis and D. Denis, 'Majority Owner-Managers and Organizational Efficiency' (1994) 1 *J. Corp. Financ.* 91, 93.

11 See Sections 6.3.3 and 6.3.7 of Chapter 6.

12 See Section 6.3.5 of Chapter 6.

innovation and with long product cycles may generate substantial value from the adoption of dual-class stock, by insulating managers from short-term share price declines while implementing the necessary long-term investments.[13] Even outside of the product sphere, companies with innovative visions that are not easily appreciated by the equity markets,[14] and high-growth companies (particularly start-ups) with low current earnings compared to future potential,[15] may be able to garner better performance and overall value through the use of dual-class stock. However, for other types of firms, such as a mature company with an established product and stable market, where the management team does not hold any firm-specific talents and the long-term prospects and business plan of the company are easily observable by the public markets, dual-class stock may not be correlated with a net-beneficial dual-class stock tradeoff.[16]

7.2.2 *Diversity of Controllers*

The identity and nature of the controller can also impact upon whether dual-class stock is beneficial or detrimental to all shareholders. For example, where the enhanced-voting shares are dispersed, issues prevalent in a controller being able to unilaterally direct the actions of the company (while holding a disproportionately low level of cash-flow rights) will not be present. Although, as discussed in the Introduction to this book, only controlling shareholder dual-class firms are considered throughout this book, many empirical studies do not make this distinction. Differences may also subsist between blockholders who are involved in management, compared to blockholders who are distinct from management.[17] However, at higher voting-ownership levels, a true controlling shareholder has the ability to control management indirectly, and the relevant distinction becomes blurred and is not as significant.[18] Furthermore, even with a controlling shareholder, the identity of that controller can have a bearing on empirical results. In the United States, the distinction between corporation-controlled and individual-controlled dual-class firms is not a significant factor since most of such firms are individual-controlled,[19]

13 See Section 6.3.7 of Chapter 6.
14 *ibid.*
15 *ibid.*
16 See Section 6.4 of Chapter 6.
17 HKEX, 'Concept Paper: Weighted Voting Rights' (August 2014) at IV-2.
18 K. Wruck, 'Equity Ownership Concentration and Firm Value: Evidence from Private Equity Financings' (1989) 23 *J. Financ. Econ.* 3, 16.
19 For example, R. Anderson et al., 'The Dual Class Premium: A Family Affair' (2017) 1, 3, https://ssrn.com/abstract=3006669 found, in examining Russell 3000 dual-class firms listed as of 2001, that only 11 per cent were not family/founder-controlled; Amoako-Adu et al.'s (2013) sample of dual-class firms (2001–2007) consisted of 83.2 per cent family-controlled firms (B. Amoako-Adu et al., 'Dual Class Discount, and the Channels of Extraction of Private Benefits' in *Advances in Financial Economics*, vol. 16, eds. S. Ferris et al. (Emerald Publishing, 2013) at 185). A more recent study assessing dual-class firms between 1994 and 2019 found that the most common controllers of dual-class firms are founders

but in other jurisdictions, the quality could have an impact, with studies showing that corporate-controlled dual-class firms are valued more by the market than individual-controlled companies.[20] Within the subdivision of individual-controlled firms, differences in firm performance exist between firms that are founder-controlled and those where control has passed to heirs or other family members,[21] and evidence suggests that the propensity to invest in R&D and long-term expenditure varies between the two types of controllers.[22] Differences may also relate to the extent to which a firm's worth is tied to the identity, and continued involvement, of the controller.[23] The dual-class stock tradeoff is more likely to be shifted in a beneficial direction with a visionary and talented founder.[24]

All of these considerations point toward what Holderness labelled the 'richness of blockholders'.[25] Taking things further, though, within broad categories of blockholders, there may be even more distinctions relating to the personal intents, ambitions, incentives, skills and altruism of the individual controller.[26] An individual controller of one firm may have a personal preference to prioritise the long-term wealth and success of the company, whereas an individual controller of another, otherwise identical, firm may prioritise short-term profit through expropriation of the inferior-voting shareholders. For example, for a media company, dual-class stock could allow the controller to procure equity investment while preserving the editorial freedom of the publication,[27] which could either improve profitability by inspiring greater public trust or could result in the controller pursuing a political agenda

(D. Aggarwal et al., 'The Rise of Dual-Class Stock IPOs' (2020) 1, 3, https://ssrn.com/abstract=3690670) – although the study found that a slim majority of dual-class firms were not founder-controlled, a large proportion of the remainder were VC- or PE-controlled, and, as discussed further in Chapter 9, often these firms adopt transfer-driven sunset clauses, meaning that when the VC or PE firms exit (usually not long after IPO), the selling parties' shares are converted into inferior-voting shares, often leaving the founders solely with enhanced-voting shares, and therefore in control; the authors also note that recent years have seen an increasing proportion of dual-class firms either being founder-controlled or joint founder/VC-controlled (*ibid* 28).

20 C. Holderness and D. Sheehan, 'The Role of Majority Shareholders in Publicly Held Corporations: An Exploratory Analysis' (1988) 20 *J. Financ. Econ.* 317, 344.

21 See Section 6.2.4 of Chapter 6.

22 See Section 6.3.7 of Chapter 6.

23 See the opening remarks of the CEO of the Hong Kong's SFC at the SFC's media luncheon on 19 March 2015, www.sfc.hk/edistributionWeb/gateway/EN/news-and-announcements/news/corporate-news/doc?refNo=15PR25 – 'Many have said that weighted voting rights makes sense where the whole enterprise value is completely tied up with the identity of a founder'; also see n 11 above and accompanying text.

24 See Section 6.3.3 of Chapter 6.

25 C. Holderness, 'A Survey of Blockholders and Corporate Control' (2003) *FRBNY Econ. Policy Rev.* (April 2003) 51, 60; also see A. Edmans and C. Holderness, 'Blockholders: A Survey of Theory and Evidence' in *The Handbook of the Economics of Corporate Governance*, eds. B. Hermalin and M. Wesibach (Elsevier, 2017) at 553.

26 By analogy to one share, one vote controlling shareholder firms, upon control transfers, the identity of the controller can have an effect on firm value (M. Barclay and C. Holderness, 'Negotiated Block Trades and Corporate Control' (1991) 46 *J. Financ.* 861, 877).

27 D. Ashton, 'Revisiting Dual-Class Stock' (1994) 68 *St. John's L. Rev.* 863, 939.

with complete disregard for the profitability of the company. A sovereign-controller could use dual-class structure to sell equity while maintaining control and cause the firm to enter into synchronicities with other entities controlled by the same state (particularly since the United Kingdom's related-party transaction rules do not apply as stringently to sovereign-controlled companies[28]), which is either beneficial to all companies involved or a means of tunnelling profits. Even in the technology sector, dual-class stock may either support an idiosyncratic vision, which requires indulgence of the mutability of product cycles to generate strong long-term earnings, or it may shelter a failing long-term vision, sacrificing short-term profitability without any prospect of a future turnaround in performance.

7.2.3 *Impact of Diversity on Empirical Studies*

Empirical studies that simply group dual-class firms and one share, one vote firms into uniform groups may see their results coloured by dual-class structure being, as is one share, one vote structure, beneficial for some types of firms and detrimental for others – the empirical evidence may therefore be inconclusive or skewed depending upon the matching criteria and sampling used by the relevant research.[29] Even those studies that match dual-class firms with similar one share, one vote firms will not assist in this regard if the results from each matched sample are then simply aggregated. More recently, though, studies have started to target the impact of dual-class stock on the performance of firms with specific qualities in an effort to identify whether, for certain firm qualities and types, dual-class stock promotes better operating performance, firm value or stock returns – this line of study will likely be more instructive going forward in ascertaining whether evidence can prove the normative argument that dual-class stock will be advantageous to the performance of those firms where expropriation of inferior-voting shareholders is either unlikely or likely to be substantially surpassed by improved performance. As discussed later in this chapter, trends can be observed in relation to high-growth firms, firms with low free cash-flow, and young firms, amongst others. However, whereas studies can control for the diversity of firm types, it is far more challenging to control for the diversity of controllers, and it has been noted that the academic literature has 'generally treated dual-class firms as a single monolithic "type"'.[30] Some characteristics, such as founder-controlled versus corporate-controlled firms, are easy to identify, but others, such as whether the involvement of the controller is viewed as critical to the success of the company, or the nature, characteristics and intents of the controller, are difficult to identify, and may not be observable.[31] These difficulties make it challenging, especially with relatively small sample sizes, to interpret empirical evidence as indicative that for certain types of firms dual-class stock is

[28] Listing Rules, Chapter 21.
[29] See nn 166 and 168 below and accompanying text.
[30] Aggarwal et al. (2020) (n 19 above 2).
[31] L. Dallas and J. Barry, 'Long-Term Shareholders and Time-Phased Voting' (2016) 40 *DJCL* 541, 589.

justified or unjustified. The empirical evidence should therefore be analysed in light of the diversity of firms and controllers that have implemented dual-class stock,[32] and the possibility that such diversity may result in the empirical evidence showing no correlation with capital structure as a result of cancelling out between those firms for which the specific structure is beneficial and those for which it is detrimental. The lack of profiling the 'nature' of the controller has been labelled the 'biggest missing factor affecting the probability of tunneling'.[33]

Although future research may, in time, fine-tune the degree of knowledge of dual-class firms to a level that allows better decisions as to whether dual-class stock should be permitted on a firm-by-firm basis,[34] it is fair to retain healthy scepticism that incontrovertible lines can be drawn. As remarked by Smart and Zutter (2003): 'Discerning which managers are entrenched to capture private control benefits and which are entrenched in the interests of shareholders challenges the empiricist.'[35] In any case, with the evidence that currently exists, the scope of reckoning should be whether the evidence is persuasive enough to warrant a prohibition of dual-class stock on the premium tier, and, if not, whether any form of dual-class firm admission to the premium tier should be accompanied by distinct protections.

7.3 EVENT-BASED STUDIES

Event-based studies explore the impact on the price of listed shares of recapitalisation events, where one share, one vote companies that have already been listed create dual-class structure, or of unification events, where existing listed dual-class structure is collapsed into one share, one vote. In relation to recapitalisations, the studies assess the price impact on one share, one vote shares that are already listed, and, in the case of unifications, the studies generally assess the impact on the price of inferior-voting shares after all shares become one share, one vote. Although the foundations of this book, as set out in Chapter 1, are focused on the adoption of dual-class structure at the time of IPO, with a view to attracting more firms to the public markets in the United Kingdom, empirical studies related to recapitalisations and unifications may provide some evidence as to how the equity markets react to dual-class stock. Given that institutional shareholders ostensibly oppose dual-class stock,[36] one may presume that

32 Similar points have been made by Ashton (1994) (n 27 above 959).

33 C. Chen et al., 'Board Independence as a Panacea to Tunneling? An Empirical Study of Related-Party Transactions in Hong Kong and Singapore' (2018) 15 *J. Empir. Leg. Stud.* 987, 1017.

34 An appeal for such evidence was made as far back as 1996 in E. Böhmer et al., 'The Effect of Consolidated Control on Firm Performance: The Case of Dual-class IPOs' in *Empirical Issues in Raising Equity Capital*, ed. M. Levis (Elsevier, 1996) at 116.

35 Smart and Zutter (2003) (n 9 above 103). Solomon expressed that it is impossible to discern whether a founder will utilise its superior skills to benefit all shareholders, or, instead, to extract controller benefits (D. Solomon, 'The Importance of Inferior Voting Rights in Dual-Class Firms' (2019) 2 *BYU Law Rev.* 533, 543).

36 The public criticism of dual-class stock made by institutional investors is discussed in Sections 2.2 and 2.3 of Chapter 2.

the market will react adversely to dual-class stock, reflecting investors' predictions of the future behaviour of the controller. One could argue that event-based studies are a pure indication of market reaction since they assess that reaction immediately, or close to immediately, after the relevant change in capital structure; however, as will be discussed further, the very fact that event-based studies illustrate only a snapshot in time means that the results can be contaminated by extraneous events occurring in and around the event. Furthermore, it should be noted that contemporary mid-stream recapitalisations of dual-class stock into one share, one vote are rare,[37] and, even when they do occur, event-based studies only gauge market-reaction to the events rather than whether, in fact, the new capital structure creates benefits or burdens for the company over time. As such, although noteworthy studies and their implications are considered next, other performance measures discussed later in this chapter may be more valuable in discerning the impact of dual-class stock on shareholder wealth.

7.3.1 *Summary*

Nine US studies and five non-US studies were reviewed. In summary, as shown in Figure 7.1, event-based studies display an inconclusive picture, although there is certainly a partial bias against dual-class stock. Unsurprisingly, given the nature of event-based methodologies, the results of several studies were heavily dependent upon other actions or events surrounding the relevant recapitalisation of one share, one vote into dual-class stock, or unification of dual-class stock into one share, one vote. Although a detailed analysis of the event-based studies is provided in the following section, since, as will be discussed in Section 7.3.3, the influence of extraneous events can significantly hamper the interpretation of data from event-based studies, we will not dwell on the inconclusive findings. Other forms of studies, which are presented in the subsequent sections of this chapter, will be more instructive in assessing dual-class stock.

7.3.2 *Detailed Analysis*

The pivotal US event-based study by Partch (1987)[38] explored recapitalisations by US listed one share, one vote corporations between 1962 and 1984, creating limited voting stock (and therefore becoming dual-class companies), straddling the period during which many US corporations were beginning to look to dual-class stock as a form of defence against hostile takeovers.[39] It was found that shareholder wealth was not affected by the announcement or creation of restricted stock.[40] Similar

[37] V. Dimitrov and P. Jain, 'Recapitalization of One Class of Common Stock into Dual-Class: Growth and Long-Run Stock Returns' (2006) 12 *J. Corp. Financ.* 342, 345.

[38] M. Partch, 'The Creation of a Class of Limited Voting Common Stock and Shareholders' Wealth' (1987) 18 *J. Financ. Econ.* 313.

[39] See Section 2.3 of Chapter 2.

[40] Partch (1987) (n 38 above 333).

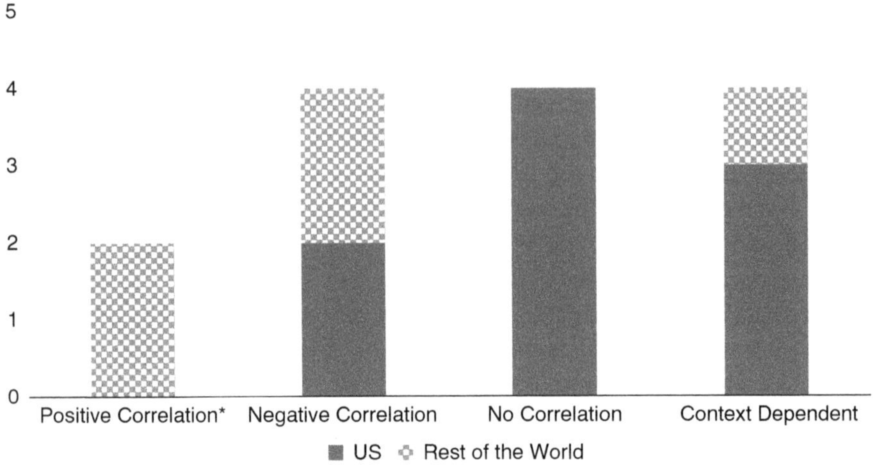

FIGURE 7.1 Dual-class stock event-based studies – *"correlation" relates to the market's reaction to the presence of dual-class stock, post- (pre-) recapitalisation of one share, one vote into dual-class stock (unification of dual-class stock into one share, one vote).*
** Includes a UK study even though it showed positive abnormal returns upon recapitalisation of one share, one vote into dual-class stock, and unifications of dual-class stock into one share, one vote (see 'Detailed Analysis' below).*

results were found by a number of subsequent studies which covered more extended periods of time.[41] As a note of caution, though, the results from historic studies from the 1980s will have been impacted by the shifting tides of the NYSE's attitude toward dual-class stock. During the NYSE's prohibition of dual-class stock, prior to the implementation of its moratorium on enforcement against companies recapitalising from one share, one vote into dual-class stock in 1984,[42] data may well have been distorted by the fact that any NYSE listed firm recapitalising into dual-class stock, in defiance of the prohibition, would have risked delisting by the exchange, which may have had an adverse effect on share price, masking any positive effect of the recapitalisation itself.[43] In contrast, Jarrell and Poulsen (1988)[44] in sampling recapitalisations between 1976 and 1987 found that recapitalisations from one share, one vote into dual-class stock had a negative effect on share price, driven by those firms that had recapitalised after the NYSE

[41] C. Bacon et al., 'The Board of Directors and Dual-Class Recapitalizations' (1997) 26 *Financ. Manag.* 5, 12; Dimitrov and Jain (2006) (n 37 above); M. Cornett and M. Vetsuypens, 'Voting Rights and Shareholder Wealth: The Issuance of Limited Voting Common Stock' (1989) 10 *MDE* 175 (although the authors found that recapitalisations had a positive effect on share price, the effect vanished when outlier companies were removed from the sample (*ibid* 181)).

[42] See Section 2.3 of Chapter 2.

[43] This distortion was acknowledged in G. Jarrell and A. Poulsen, 'Dual-Class Recapitalizations as Antitakeover Mechanisms: The Recent Evidence' (1988) 20 *J. Financ. Econ.* 129, 134.

[44] *ibid.*

introduced its moratorium. Those firms were dominated by NYSE listed firms, which were generally larger firms than those sample firms listed on other US exchanges, and had greater institutional investor, and less inside, ownership prior to the recapitalisation.[45] With lower inside ownership, the authors postulated that such firms were more likely to have adopted dual-class stock in response to hostile takeover activity (which was rampant at the time), since such insiders would not have been able to block takeovers prior to the recapitalisation, and the radically altered takeover probability created a negative market reaction.[46] Alternatively, another, simpler, explanation of Jarrell and Poulsen's results could be that investors were somewhat callow when pricing-in rare recapitalisations pre-moratorium and became more adroit over time in assessing the risks of dual-class stock post-moratorium.[47]

The extraneous events surrounding the relevant recapitalisation and the method by which it is implemented also have direct impacts on market reaction. For example, US studies have found that negative reactions were only observed for firms introducing dual-class stock post-IPO that subsequently issued further equity,[48] that did not offer dividend sweeteners,[49] or (in contrast to Jarrell and Poulsen's postulation above) where a stockholder had voting control prior to the recapitalisation (and was therefore able to compel the recapitalisation, and the potential to create a voting/cash-flow divergence, without the votes of the minority stockholders).[50]

Kim and Michaely (2018), in one of the very few modern US event-based studies (looking at recapitalisations into dual-class stock between 1971 and 2015), divided their sample into young (less than twelve years old) and mature (more than or equal to twelve years old) firms. They found that significant positive (negative) abnormal returns accrued to recapitalisations into dual-class stock of young (mature) firms.[51] The results suggest that firm age is a factor, with the market reacting positively to young firms adopting dual-class stock and negatively to older firms adopting dual-class stock. The authors postulated that market reaction is favourable when young firms switch to dual-class structure since it can insulate such firms from market pressures in a manner that is beneficial, but, for mature firms, the market recognises that the benefits of the structure are more limited and therefore overshadowed by the

45 *ibid* 143.

46 *ibid* 149.

47 P. Gompers et al., 'Extreme Governance: An Analysis of Dual-Class Firms in the United States' (2010) 23 *Rev. Financial Stud.* 1051, 1061; H. Kim and R. Michaely, 'Sticking Around Too Long? Dynamics of the Benefits of Dual-Class Structures' (2018) 1, 16, https://ssrn.com/abstract=3145209.

48 K. Lehn et al., 'Consolidating Corporate Control: Dual-Class Recapitalizations versus Leveraged Buyouts' (1990) 27 *J. Financ. Econ.* 557, 577.

49 J. Gordon, 'Ties that Bond: Dual Class Common Stock and the Problem of Shareholder Choice' (1988) 76 *Cal. L. Rev.* 1, 28–29. In fact, dividend sweeteners were generally implemented indirectly by imposing dividend discounts on those shares converting to enhanced-voting shares.

50 *ibid* 29.

51 Kim and Michaely (2018) (n 47 above 16).

substantial potential costs.[52] The authors did not empirically test whether there were variations in findings correlated with the period during which the relevant firms recapitalised into dual-class stock (such as prior to the NYSE's moratorium on dual-class stock or during a period of significant hostile takeover activity), but did control for potential temporal changes in market reactions by clustering standard errors at the year level.[53]

Looking at event-based studies from the opposite perspective, one may predict emergent patterns where firms with dual-class stock unify their structures into one share, one vote. Indeed, Smart et al. (2008) found that, for firms that completed US IPOs between 1990 and 1998, on average, firms that unified their dual-class structures into one share, one vote exhibited stock price rises.[54] The sample of unifying firms was small though, amounting to only thirty-seven firms.

Moving outside the United States, the only UK event-based study found that, between 1955 and 1982, during which dual-class firms were more common in the UK listed company world, on average, abnormal positive reactions transpired upon both announcements of recapitalisations of one share, one vote into dual-class stock, and unifications of dual-class stock into one share, one vote.[55] The results pose somewhat of a conundrum, with the market apparently viewing both one share, one vote and dual-class stock positively. The authors interpreted the results in terms of a firm's life-cycle. They further explained that, rather than in order to entrench management or enable subsequent nefarious behaviour, recapitalisations into dual-class stock were being created so that the insiders could act in the interests of the shareholders as a whole, and that dual-class structure could be representative of an intermediate form between closely held and dispersed ownership firms during which insiders were buying time in order to operate the company without interference from outside shareholders prior to resolving asymmetric information issues;[56] once such asymmetric information issues had been resolved later in the life of the company, reunification would occur, and the positive returns upon unification indicated that this was also beneficial to public shareholders as part of the natural life-cycle of the firm. Although the paper could provide useful evidence of the benefits of dual-class stock in the context of the United Kingdom, a number of uncertainties potentially reduce its saliency. For example, the study also assessed longer-term returns up to twelve months post-announcement, and it is not clear whether, post-recapitalisation into dual-class stock, the study assessed returns on the inferior-voting shares, the enhanced-voting shares or both. Seemingly, the study analysed the returns on the shares as a whole before and after the recapitalisations (although

52 *ibid* 16.

53 *ibid* 16.

54 S. Smart et al., 'What's in a Vote? The Short- and Long-Run Impact of Dual-Class Equity on IPO Firm Values' (2008) 45 *J. Account. Econ.* 94, 113.

55 J. Ang and W. Megginson, 'Restricted Voting Shares, Ownership Structure, and the Market Value of Dual-Class Firms' (1989) 12 *J. Financ. Res.* 301, 317.

56 *ibid* 317.

the currently prevailing trend is for firms to only list the inferior-voting shares, this study only analysed firms listing both classes of shares post-recapitalisation), in which case, the results could be skewed by excess returns being ascribed to the development of a premium on the enhanced-voting shares.[57] It is also not clear in relation to unifications of dual-class stock into one share, one vote whether returns were recorded on erstwhile inferior-voting shares or enhanced-voting shares, and the results may be influenced further by the fact that, in the vast majority of cases, compensation was paid to the holders of enhanced-voting shares.[58]

In Canada, upon recapitalisations of one share, one vote into dual-class structure, no decisive trend has been determined, with one study finding weak negative abnormal returns,[59] one also finding negative abnormal returns, generally, but with the effect reversed if accompanied by dividend increases,[60] and a further study finding significant positive returns.[61] In Germany, it was found that unifications from dual-class stock into one share, one vote resulted in significant positive abnormal returns that may have been underestimated since the unifications were partly anticipated.[62] The nuance to this study, though, is that, in Germany, during the time period covered by the study, only non-voting shares and one share, one vote shares were permitted, and non-voting shares were more akin to preference shares in the United Kingdom, since they were entitled to a minimum dividend prior to any distributions being made to the voting shares (after the voting shares have received the same dividend as the non-voting shares, the non-voting shares are then entitled to participate in any further distribution);[63] this renders the positive abnormal returns lower than they would have been had non-voting shares not been entitled to preferential dividends.

Therefore, the results of event-based studies are generally inconclusive. However, beyond the inconclusive results, it is, in any case, difficult to draw definitive conclusions from event-based studies generally, as discussed in the following section.

7.3.3 *Words of Warning*

Caution should be applied in using event-based studies to assess the merits and detriments of dual-class stock. Sample sizes in all such studies are small, and in some

57 In a sister paper, one of the same authors found that an average premium of 13.3 per cent was attached to the enhanced-voting shares of UK dual-class firms (W. Megginson, 'Restricted Voting Stock, Acquisition Premiums, and the Market Value of Corporate Control' (1988) *University of Georgia Working Paper* (cited *ibid* 303)).

58 Ang and Megginson (1989) (n 55 above 313).

59 V. Jog and A. Riding, 'Price Effects of Dual-Class Shares' (1986) 42 *Financ. Anal. J.* 58, 61.

60 E. Maynes, 'Reallocation of Voting Rights and Shareholders' Wealth' (1992) 25 *Can. J. Econ.* 538, 561.

61 L. Kryzanowski and H. Zhang, 'Introduction of Dual-Class Shares: Some Evidence on Canadian Pro-Rata Distributions' (1992) 1 *IRFA* 95, 102.

62 I. Dittmann and N. Ulbricht, 'Timing and Wealth Effects of German Dual Class Stock Unifications' (2007) 14 *Eur. Financ. Manag.* 163, 182.

63 *ibid* 171.

cases, extremely small.[64] It is also vital to note that event-based studies evidence the market's reaction to dual-class stock, rather than gauging the true performance of dual-class structure. Investors in the secondary market are simply pricing-in risk. Investors may underestimate risk or apply unjustified discounts based upon ideological concerns. The historically small number of such events could mean that investors are not experienced enough in judging them to be able to price effectively.[65] Investors may also apply discounts across the board without evaluating the individual circumstances of the company. Significantly, a large number of the studies straddle the period when dual-class stock was prohibited on the NYSE – therefore, for those companies that underwent IPOs prior to the NYSE relaxing its prohibition of dual-class stock (or at least prior to its moratorium on such structures), not only will the possibility of the company having to delist have impacted market reactions, but also the possibility of a subsequent restructuring of one share, one vote into dual-class stock would not have been factored into price at IPO, and the subsequent unexpected recapitalisation, to the extent that the market generally views such events unfavourably, will have caused a greater downward shock in share price as compared to where the probability of a recapitalisation occurring had already been incorporated into price.[66]

Further, although some studies use techniques to ascertain when pricing-in of the relevant event commenced, most studies only test share price movements over the course of a short window of the nature of only a few days prior to and after the announcement date. The size of the window used is sometimes arbitrary and there is a great deal of uncertainty as to when pricing-in commenced.[67] Additionally, event-based studies only provide a snapshot in time, rather than an indication of share price performance over extended periods – a perhaps more essential element in evaluating such structures, which is revisited later in this chapter. The market's perception of a company's dual-class structure may morph over time. For example, the qualities of a structure that are initially viewed as beneficial may gradually erode.[68]

Also, there are inherent biases in the event-based approach, which may positively or negatively affect share price. One of these is that the relevant event may be endogenous – the event may be being implemented as a result of the board anticipating a positive effect on operating performance going forward; therefore, in such a scenario, the market may view the event positively.[69] Alternatively, it has also been conjectured that managers may, in contemplation of impending poor

64 HKEX Concept (2014) (n 17 above IV-II); Dimitrov and Jain (2006) (n 37 above 345).
65 Dimitrov and Jain (2006) (n 37 above 345).
66 Gordon (1988) (n 49 above 26).
67 Dallas and Barry (2016) (n 31 above 585).
68 See Section 6.4.2 of Chapter 6.
69 Adams and Ferreira (2008) (n 3 above 64) – the authors presented this criticism as a reason for why positive abnormal returns were discovered in the United Kingdom for both recapitalisations and unifications by Ang and Megginson (1989) (n 55 above); Smart et al. (2008) (n 54 above 112).

performance, implement dual-class stock to protect themselves from removal or to divest of their own equity without losing control, and the market may be reacting to such signals of impending poor performance.[70] Market perception is clearly a material contagion in event-based studies, with there being many other external prompts for implementation of dual-class stock[71] – the market may simply be reacting to those other events rather than purely the recapitalisation. One study showed that a negative reaction to recapitalisation of one share, one vote into dual-class stock was only apparent when the relevant firm subsequently issued further equity.[72] It is possible, in such cases, that the market had correctly speculated that a recapitalisation into dual-class stock was indicative of greater potential for further equity issuances in the short term.[73] The market may have been reacting to this possibility rather than the recapitalisation itself, and often the market reaction is negative to further issuances.[74] Confusing the picture, in some cases, the market reaction may, in contrast, be positive to potential equity issuances, with changes in market sentimentality indicative of its perception of a firm that was previously cash-strapped recapitalising to raise further finance through the inferior-voting share issuance.[75] Unsurprisingly, dividend sweeteners mitigated negative market reactions to recapitalisations of one share, one vote into dual-class stock,[76] emphasising the importance of discerning the conditions surrounding the relevant event when only considering snapshots in time. Further highlighting the dangers inherent in drawing conclusions from event-based studies, negative reactions were exhibited where controllers unilaterally imposed dual-class structure on public shareholders[77] – rather than dual-class stock itself being called into question, it is possible that the negative reaction can be attributed to the public shareholders assuming that, where they have not been given the opportunity to opine on the recapitalisation, the relevant recapitalisation will have been adopted by the controller to extract pernicious controller benefits. Another bias is that the manner of implementation of the event can have a bearing on stock price. For example, where a recapitalisation is implemented by way of stock dividend, it is difficult to

70 K. Lins, 'Equity Ownership and Firm Value in Emerging Markets' (2003) 38 *J. Financ. Quant. Anal.* 159, 178; HKEX Concept (2014) (n 17 above IV-2); Nüesch (2016) (n 9 above 532).

71 HKEX Concept (2014) (n 17 above IV-8).

72 See n 48 above and accompanying text.

73 Lehn et al. (1990) (n 48 above 566 and 576).

74 As noted by Lehn et al. (1990) (*ibid* 576) in quoting a number of studies that showed negative market reactions to announcements of common stock offerings. Also see the citations in A. Pajuste, 'Determinants and Consequences of the Unification of Dual-Class Shares' (2005) *ECB Working Paper Series No. 465* 1, 34 – the author also viewed the phenomenon from the opposite perspective and determined that firms unifying dual-class stock into one share, one vote issue stock at the time of unification in order to mask the negative market reaction to equity issuances with the positive market perception of eliminating dual-class stock.

75 Dittmann and Ulbricht (2007) (n 62 above 167).

76 See nn 49 and 60 above and accompanying text.

77 See n 50 above and accompanying text.

isolate the recapitalisation from the positive effect of stock dividends generally.[78] Additionally, since insiders are not generally increasing their cash-flow rights in the relevant company upon a recapitalisation, investors may take this as a sign that insiders believe that the stock is overvalued, again resulting in a negative price reaction.[79] In circumstances where dual-class structure is being implemented as a form of takeover defence, results can be further skewed. On the one hand, downward share price pressure can result from the reduction in the probability of a takeover in the future that would otherwise generate a windfall for shareholders.[80] On the other hand, upward share price pressure can result from the proposed actions of the board indicating to outside shareholders that management foresees a bourgeoning takeover market for the company, particularly where management is attempting to increase its vote ownership.[81] In essence, it is difficult to separate the recapitalisation or unification event from other changes to the company that accompany it.[82]

The lack of more recent event-based studies also affects their contemporary relevance. Since Google's IPO, dual-class stock has become, at least in the United States, more prevalent, particularly in the technology sphere,[83] and as discussed in more detail in relation to firm valuation studies later in this chapter, investor perception of dual-class stock generally may have shifted over time. Modern-day studies would, therefore, be more helpful in assessing dual-class stock, but the narrow value and criticisms of event-based studies have limited, and will continue to limit, the number of modern-day studies. Additionally, in relation to recapitalisations, in the United States, apart from the three years immediately following the NYSE's moratorium on delisting recapitalising firms, such events have been few and far between (possibly due to companies now being able to implement dual-class stock at the time of IPO).[84] The small numbers of recapitalisations will limit the utility of modern studies, and, after a Delaware court decision on such recapitalisations,[85] it does not appear that there will be an upsurge in such events going forward.

78 Rydqvist (1992) (n 9 above 53) – the author specifically notes that the UK study by Ang and Megginson (1989) (n 55 above) mainly examined recapitalisations by way of stock dividends.

79 Lehn et al. (1990) (n 48 above 568).

80 L. Dann and H. DeAngelo, 'Corporate Financial Policy and Corporate Control: A Study of Defensive Adjustments in Asset and Ownership Structure' (1988) 20 *J. Financ. Econ.* 87, 95 found that the implementation of defensive takeover structures, generally, caused a 2–3 per cent share price decline.

81 *ibid* 114.

82 Adams and Ferreira (2008) (n 3 above 84).

83 See Figure 1.2 in Chapter 1; A. Gurrea, 'Theory, Evidence, and Policy on Dual-Class Shares: A Country-Specific Response to a Global Debate' (2019) *Ibero-American Institute for Law and Finance Working Paper Series* No. 3/2019 para. 5.1.3.

84 See, for example Dimitrov and Jain (2006) (n 37 above 348).

85 Recapitalisations into dual-class stock by one share, one vote controlling shareholder firms have been held to be 'conflicted transactions', which are subject to greater governance scrutiny (*IRA Trust FBO Bobbie Ahmed* v. *Crane*, C.A. No. 12742-CB (Del. Ch. Dec. 11, 2017)).

Given the substantial criticisms directed at event-based studies, apropos, this chapter will now turn toward the, possibly more decisive, empirical evidence that assesses dual-class firms over periods of time, and the conclusions developed in this chapter will draw mainly from firm valuation, buy-and-hold stock return, and operating performance studies.

7.4 FIRM VALUATION STUDIES

Firm valuation studies generally trace the value of a firm's stock (by market capitalisation), as compared to the firm's asset value, over extended periods of time. A number of studies measure firm value using Tobin's Q. Tobin's Q is the ratio of market value of stock to replacement cost of assets, and was originally developed as a determinant of investment in the macroeconomics sphere. However, the concept was appropriated by researchers looking for determinants of firm profitability,[86] who, given the difficulties in ascertaining replacement costs of assets, usually reduce Tobin's Q to the ratio of market value of stock to book value of assets. The concept was particularly attractive, since the use of market value in the numerator could reflect future expectations and assessments of risks.[87] Therefore, Tobin's Q can indicate whether the equity of a company is overvalued or undervalued compared to the value of its assets, and can be used as a proxy for firm value.[88] Unlike event-based studies which ascertain market reaction at a snapshot in time, theoretically firm valuation studies could reflect the manner in which a firm's assets are actually being managed. Market capitalisation can diverge from the value of a firm's assets, since, in an efficient market,[89] share price will be based upon investor predictions of future profitability,[90] which may bear

86 An early use of the concept in this manner can be seen in E. Lindenberg and S. Ross, 'Tobin's Q Ratio and Industrial Organization' (1981) 54 *J. Bus.* 1.

87 R. Bartlett and F. Partnoy, 'The Misuse of Tobin's Q' (2020) 73 *Vand. L. Rev.* 353, 369.

88 Technically, the numerator should also include the market value of the company's liabilities, and the denominator the book value of the company's liabilities, but it is common practice to assume that the two cancel each other out.

89 An efficient market is one where all public information is quickly incorporated into the price of securities (E. Fama, 'Efficient Capital Markets: A Review of Theory and Empirical Work' (1970) 25 *J. Financ.* 383, 383; for a review of the relevant literature, also see R. Gilson and R. Kraakman, 'The Mechanisms of Market Efficiency' (1984) 70 *Va. L. Rev.* 549, 549). More nuanced versions of the Efficient Capital Markets Hypothesis (ECMH) have subsequently been developed – the weak form (where all information from past share prices is incorporated), the semi-strong form (where all public information is incorporated) and the strong form (where public and non-public information is incorporated) (for a discussion on the forms of ECMH, see B. Cheffins, *Company Law: Theory, Structure and Operation* (Oxford University Press, 1997) at 56).

90 However, a body of study has doubted the genuine efficiency of the markets and suggests that share price may not reflect long-term performance, due to irrational short-term behaviours of investors and informational asymmetries which can be 'systematic' in nature, leading to disproportionate short-term market bias (for example, see A. Shleifer, *Inefficient Markets: An Introduction to Behavioural Finance* (Oxford University Press, 2000); R. Gilson and R. Kraakman, 'The Mechanisms of Market Efficiency Twenty Years Later: The Hindsight Bias' (2003) *Harvard Law School Discussion Paper No*

little resemblance to the value of the firm's assets. Accordingly, if Tobin's Q for a dual-class company is lower than '1', it could suggest that the market is discounting the value of its future cash-flow or earnings growth, as a result of anticipated expropriation by the controller or the presence of an entrenched underperforming management team.[91] Any negative market perception anticipating future expropriation of inferior-voting shareholders or poor management at the time of dual-class IPO or mid-stream recapitalisation into dual-class stock (as indicated by many event-based studies discussed above) should, if a sufficiently large sample is used over a robust period, be smoothed-out over time if expropriation does not actually occur or the management team performs above expectations, since one would, in an efficient market, expect investors to identify the potential for market-beating returns by investing in those firms, pushing up the price and eliminating the downward bias in share price. Alternatively, if expropriation of inferior-voting shareholders dominates, or if the management team underperforms (in circumstances where, as is the case with dual-class structure, management is insulated from removal), one would expect dual-class firms to continue to display low Tobin's Q values. Some authors have therefore described Tobin's Q as the 'capitalised value of agency costs'.[92]

Firm valuation studies commonly compare the firm value of dual-class firms to the firm value of matched one share, one vote firms with similar qualities and in similar industries. Although often not explicitly stated, for a majority of studies, the relevant quantification for market value of a dual-class company's stock is the value of the inferior-voting stock (grossed-up at the same per-share value in order to encompass the proportion of equity represented by enhanced-voting stock), since this better reflects the value accruing to outside shareholders[93] (and, in any case, often only the inferior-voting shares are listed[94]). Although such studies label this measure as 'firm value', in reality, total firm value equates to the sum of market value of the inferior-voting stock and enhanced-voting stock. However, for the purpose of this chapter, total firm value is not the vital determinant; rather the impact of dual-class stock on outside shareholders is the key consideration – the price of the inferior-voting shares will track predictions of future performance, whereas the price of enhanced-voting shares may also encompass the value of controller benefits.[95]

446 1, 14; M. Moore and E. Walker-Arnott, 'A Fresh Look at Stock Market Short-Termism' (2014) 41 *J. Law Soc.* 416, 421).

91 R. Morck et al., 'Management Ownership and Market Valuation' (1988) 20 *J. Financ. Econ.* 293, 294.

92 Y. Bozec and C. Laurin, 'Large Shareholder Entrenchment and Performance: Empirical Evidence from Canada' (2008) 35 *J. Bus. Finance Account.* 25, 33.

93 Adams and Ferreira (2008) (n 3 above 63).

94 Gompers et al. (2010) (n 47 above 1056).

95 ISS in collaboration with Sherman & Sterling LLP and the European Corporate Governance Institute as commissioned by the European Commission, 'Report on the Proportionality Principle in the European Union' (18 May 2007) at 12.

If dual-class stock is harmful to outside investors, one may predict that dual-class firms will consistently exhibit weaker Tobin's Q than one share, one vote firms, and, indeed, many studies discussed in the following sections find that dual-class firms are undervalued compared to one share, one vote firms. However, as will be discussed when interpreting the relevant studies, it is not clear that, in all cases, firm value is less for dual-class firms than one share, one vote firms, and, as discussed in Section 7.4.3 of this chapter, even where it is, it is not indisputable that this represents expropriation or poor management and, in fact, market perception is still a large contagion.

7.4.1 *Summary*

Twenty-nine separate dual-class stock firm value studies have been reviewed for the purposes of this section. Of those studies, one US study showed that dual-class stock structure is positively correlated with firm value.[96] Eleven studies (five US,[97] and six evaluating non-US jurisdictions)[98] found negative correlations between dual-class structure and firm value. Two further studies, one US,[99] and one non-US,[100] found that founder-control and family-control (including founder-control), respectively, was positively correlated with firm value, but the positive correlation was reduced by the adoption of dual-class structure. Another US study showed a negative relationship between firm value and dual-class structure,[101] until sub-sampling, after which the correlations/relationships varied in line with specific qualities. Five studies (one US study,[102] three rest-of-the-world studies[103] and one

96 Böhmer et al. (1996) (n 34 above).

97 Gompers et al. (2010) (n 47 above); Anderson et al. (2017) (n 19 above); Smart et al. (2008) (n 54 above); Amoako-Adu et al. (2013) (n 19 above); C. Hoi and A. Robin, 'Agency Conflicts, Controlling Owner Proximity, and Firm Value: An Analysis of Dual-Class Firms in the United States' (2010) 18 *Corp. Gov.* 124.

98 S. Claessens et al., 'Disentangling the Incentive and Entrenchment Effects of Large Shareholdings' (2002) 57 *J. Financ.* 2741; Lins (2003) (n 70 above); B. Maury and A. Pajuste, 'Multiple Large Shareholders and Firm Value' (2005) 29 *J. Bank. Financ.* 1813; M. King and E. Santor, 'Family Values: Ownership Structure, Performance and Capital Structure of Canadian Firms' (2008) 32 *J. Bank. Financ.* 2423; Pajuste (2005) (n 74 above); B. Lauterbach and A. Pajuste, 'The Long-Term Valuation Effects of Voluntary Dual Class Share Unifications' (2015) 31 *J. Corp. Financ.* 171.

99 B. Villalonga and R. Amit, 'How Do Family Ownership, Control and Management Affect Firm Value?' (2006) 80 *J. Fin. Econ.* 385.

100 R. Barontini and L. Caprio, 'The Effect of Family Control on Firm Value and Performance: Evidence from Continental Europe' (2006) 12 *Euro. Financ. Manag.* 689.

101 B. Jordan et al., 'Growth Opportunities, Short-Term Market Pressure, and Dual-Class Share Structure' (2016) 41 *J. Corp. Financ.* 304.

102 W. Mikkelson and M. Partch, 'The Consequences of Unbundling Managers' Voting Rights and Equity Claims' (1994) 1 *J. Corp. Financ.* 175.

103 V. Jog et al., 'Impact of Restricted Voting Share Structure on Firm Value and Performance' (2010) 18 *Corp. Gov.* 415; H. Cronqvist and M. Nilsson, 'Agency Costs of Controlling Minority Shareholders' (2003) 38 *J. Financ. Quant. Anal.* 695; B. Lauterbach and Y. Yafeh, 'Long Term Changes in Voting Power and Control Structure following the Unification of Dual Class Shares' (2009) 112 *Noto Di Lavoro* 1.

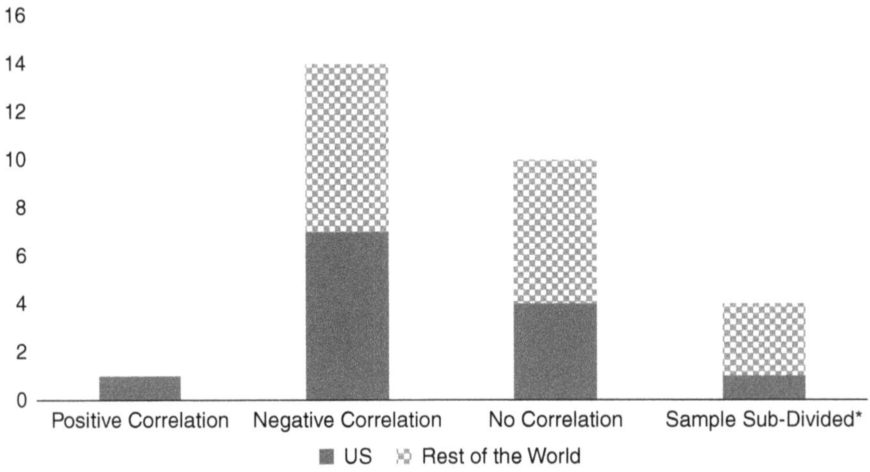

FIGURE 7.2 Dual-class stock firm value studies
** Indicates studies that did not assess a correlation between firm value and dual structure for the entire sample of dual-class firms, but, instead, assessed correlations between different sub-categories of dual-class firms and firm value.*

cross-country study which included the United States[104]) showed no statistically significant correlation between dual-class structure and firm value. Five studies (three US-specific,[105] and two non-US[106]) showed no correlation between firm value and dual-class structure, until sub-sampling, after which, the correlations/relationships varied in line with specific qualities. Four studies (one US-specific[107] and three non-US[108]) only assessed the dual-class stock/firm value relationship for separate sub-categories of firms, and found that correlation fluctuated with differing firm qualities or extraneous circumstances. Figure 7.2 graphically represents the results.

[104] La Porta et al. (2002) (n 7 above 1147).

[105] T. Chemmanur et al., 'Management Quality and Antitakeover Provisions' (2011) 54 *J. Law Econ.* 651; Kim and Michaely (2018) (n 47 above); M. Cremers et al., 'The Life-Cycle of Dual Class Firms: From IPO to Sunset' (2018) *ECGI Working Paper No. 550/2018* 1. It should be noted that Chemmanur et al. evaluated antitakeover devices (including dual-class stock) generally, and only assessed Tobin's Q at the time of IPO.

[106] Bozec and Laurin (2008) (n 92 above); Nüesch (2016) (n 9 above);

[107] R. Anderson et al., 'Founders, Heirs, and Corporate Opacity in the United States' (2009) 92 *J. Financ. Econ.* 205.

[108] M. Bennedsen and K. Nielsen, 'The Principle of Proportional Ownership, Investor Protection and Firm Value in Western Europe' (2006) *ECGI Working Paper No. 134/2006* 1; M. Holmén, 'Foreign Investors and Dual Class Shares' (2011) *Centre for Finance, University of Gothenburg Working Paper*; F. Braggion and M. Giannetti, 'Changing Corporate Governance Norms: Evidence from the Dismissal of Dual Class Shares in the U.K.' (2016) 1 https://ecgi.global/sites/default/files/working_papers/documents/SSRN-id2138949.pdf.

7.4.2 *Detailed Analysis*

A high-level review of the studies summarised in the previous section suggests that the empirical evidence swings toward a finding that dual-class firms exhibit lower firm values, with the majority of studies showing a negative correlation between dual-class structure and firm value, and only one study showing a positive correlation. A detailed evaluation illuminates more nuance. The period of the relevant study may influence the results obtained. Examining the US studies, Gompers et al. (2010) (GIM) is the classic, much cited, study offering evidence of a negative correlation between voting/cash-flow divergence and firm value, and examined a period between 1995 and 2002.[109] Smart et al. (2008), examining 1990–1998, a similar period to GIM, also deduced a negative correlation.[110] However, Kim and Michaely's (2018) study, examining an extended period (1971–2015) which straddled the GIM sampling period of 1995–2002, found no significant correlation between dual-class structure and firm value.[111] Similarly, Cremers et al. (2018),[112] examining a period from 1980 to 2015, also found no correlation overall. Kim and Michaely attributed the variance from GIM's results to the longer sample period (1971–2015) – when the GIM sampling period was replicated, the authors were able to corroborate the GIM results. Therefore, it would appear that the relevant sampling period is relevant, and, perhaps, investor sentiment shifts over time. How that pattern has shifted over time is difficult to discern, especially when studies examine time periods of differing, often overlapping, lengths. Böhmer et al. (1996)[113] found a positive correlation for a much shorter and earlier period (1984–1988), and Mikkelson and Partch (1994)[114] found no correlation for an earlier period from 1976 to 1987. In contrast, Jordan et al. (2016)[115] affirmed the GIM results for a longer period that commenced at a similar time to GIM, but also encompassed later years (1994–2011). A recent study, isolating later years (2001–2015), by Anderson et al. (2017),[116] found a negative correlation. The results do tend to suggest that, at least in the United States, the period from the mid-1990s onward has been mainly associated with negative correlations between firm value and dual-class structure. However, the lack of certainty is emphasised by Chemmanur et al. (2011),[117] which found no significant relationship between the two qualities for the period 1993–2000. Further research in this area would be welcome, since there are several reasons why there may be significant differences in the Tobin's Q reaction over different historical periods. Investor perception of dual-class firms may have changed, which could

[109] Gompers et al. (2010) (n 47 above).
[110] Smart et al. (2008) (n 54 above).
[111] Kim and Michaely (2018) (n 47 above).
[112] Cremers et al. (2018) (n 105 above).
[113] Böhmer et al. (1996) (n 34 above).
[114] Mikkelson and Partch (1994) (n 102 above).
[115] Jordan et al. (2016) (n 101 above).
[116] Anderson et al. (2017) (n 19 above).
[117] Chemmanur et al. (2011) (n 105 above).

be a product of the investor landscape changing, through, for instance, increased institutional investor pre-eminence.[118] Alternatively, as discussed later in relation to abnormal stock returns during the Asian financial crisis,[119] changing economic conditions, such as during global financial crises, may alter the incentives for expropriation by controllers. The types of firms embracing dual-class stock may also impact the results – with dual-class stock possibly being more beneficial to certain types of firms as compared to others, as trends change in the types of firms adopting the structure, firm value results will fluctuate accordingly. Since Google's IPO in 2004, as discussed in Chapter 1, the trend in the United States has seen a rapid rise in tech companies adopting dual-class stock, whereas pre-Google, dual-class firms were dominated by media companies.[120] Beyond the possible time-range effect, differences in the techniques used by individual studies, which may have improved over time, to match dual-class firms to similar one share, one vote firms may also explain the divergences in results between individual studies.[121]

It should be noted that Hoi and Robin (2010),[122] who found a negative correlation between firm value and dual-class stock, showed that the intensity of the negative correlation increased with the proximity of the controller to management, to the extent that where the controller was not involved in management at all, a positive correlation was found between firm value and dual-class structure. However, the sample size for dual-class firms where the controller was an outsider was very small.[123] Furthermore, Anderson et al. (2017),[124] who found a negative correlation overall between dual-class stock and firm value, found a positive correlation between firm value and dual-class structure where the corporation was not family- (including founder-) controlled; however, again, the sample size for non-family-controlled dual-class firms was very small.[125]

118 In the United States, institutional investors held 28.2 per cent of the equity of NYSE listed corporations in 1970, rising to 41.4 per cent in 1990 (NYSE Factbook data as published by NYXdata), and another study determined that institutional shareholders held, on average, 24 per cent of a NYSE firm's equity in 1980, rising to 44 per cent in 2000 (R. Sias et al., 'Changes in Institutional Ownership and Stock Returns: Assessment and Methodology' (2006) 79 *J. Bus.* 2869, 2877). As of 2018, institutions owned 62.4 per cent of US equities (The Securities Industry and Financial Markets Association, 'Capital Markets Fact Book 2019' (2019) at 60, www.sifma.org/wp-content/uploads/2019/09/2019-Capital-Markets-Fact-Book-SIFMA.pdf), although that figure may even be understated, since the figure indicated for 'households' may also include institutions, such as holdings by non-profit organisations, and presumably certain indirect retail ownership through institutional funds (R. Chan and J. Ho, 'Should Listed Companies Be Allowed to Adopt Dual-Class Share Structure in Hong Kong?' (2014) 43 *Comm. L. World Rev.* 155, 175; C. McGrath, '80% of Equity Market Cap Held by Institutions' *Pensions & Investments* (25 April 2017), www.pionline.com/article/20170425/INTERACTIVE/170429926/80-of-equity-market-cap-held-by- institutions).

119 See nn 203–204 below and accompanying text.

120 Gurrea (2019) (n 83 above para. 5.1.3).

121 Allaire (2019) (n 4 above 8).

122 Hoi and Robin (2010) (n 97 above).

123 *ibid* 128 – from a sample of 241 firms with dual-class structure between 1999 and 2000, in only 7 per cent of the cases was the controller outside of the management team.

124 Anderson et al. (2017) (n 19 above).

125 *ibid* 3 – in the authors' sample size, only 1.1 per cent were not family/founder-controlled.

Outside of the United States, definitive evidence is a little more elusive, and often the studies cover multiple, often overlapping, jurisdictions. The studies comprise a mix of those assessing the pure effect of dual-class stock, those assessing the effect of a divergence between voting and cash-flow rights (no matter the implementing mechanism) and those assessing the long-term effect of unifications into one share, one vote. Having expressed those caveats, generally it would appear that dual-class structure in East Asia, Western Europe and emerging markets is negatively correlated with firm value. The assertion is not indisputable, since both La Porta et al. (2002),[126] in examining twenty-seven wealthy economies, and Cronqvist and Nilsson (2003),[127] in isolating Sweden, found that a divergence between voting and cash-flow rights had no effect on firm value. As with the United States, the sampling period, and external shocks in specific years, may be decisive – in Sweden, Holmén (2011)[128] only found a negative correlation post-1992 after rules restricting foreign investment were relaxed. In Canada, the evidence is inconclusive – King and Santor (2008)[129] and Jog et al. (2010)[130] used similar initial samples and sampling periods, yet the former found a negative correlation and the latter found no correlation. A difference between the two studies is that the former study only included family (including founder) firms; however, the latter study controlled for family ownership, and, in any case, most controlled dual-class firms in Canada are family/founder-controlled.[131] The difference in results between the two studies is therefore somewhat puzzling, but could be owed to differences in methodologies and firm-matching criteria. In Israel, no statistical effect on firm value was found through unifications.[132]

A number of studies have, helpfully, sub-sampled firms and results, further emphasising that the specifics of the market, firms and controllers may heavily influence results, diminishing the possibility of formulating a universal dogma as to the effect of dual-class structure generally. An interesting aspect of the study by Bennedsen and Nielsen (2006) is that the negative correlation between dual-class structure and market-to-book value was only apparent in jurisdictions with high levels of investor protection.[133] This would, on first glance, seem counter-intuitive, since one may assume that investor protection regulations will protect inferior-voting shareholders and therefore reduce opportunities for expropriation. The explanation given by Bennedsen and Nielsen is that in high investor protection jurisdictions, managerial agency costs are less, and therefore the benefits of dual-class stock in palliating such costs are commensurately less, leading to the

126 La Porta et al. (2002) (n 7 above).
127 Cronqvist and Nilsson (2003) (n 103 above).
128 Holmén (2011) (n 108 above).
129 King and Santor (2008) (n 98 above).
130 Jog et al. (2010) (n 103 above).
131 *ibid* 434.
132 Lauterbach and Pajuste (2015) (n 98 above).
133 Bennedsen and Nielsen (2006) (n 108 above 18).

detriments dominating in terms of valuation.[134] However, the explanation should be taken with care, since investor protection should not be treated as a uniform block, with there being a variety of different investor protection types that protect against distinct abuses. Different types of investor protection will have different consequences. It is acknowledged that investor protections that reduce one share, one vote managerial agency costs will negate certain of the comparable benefits of dual-class stock (to the extent that the controller's equity stake is large enough[135]), but further investor protections related specifically to the protection of inferior-voting shareholders from expropriation by enhanced-voting shareholders will moderate the detriments of dual-class stock. In any case, this discussion highlights an important qualification to empirical studies – what is found in one jurisdiction does not necessarily parallel effects in other jurisdictions.[136] Very little empirical work has been conducted in the United Kingdom, leaving the US empirical efforts as the best guess scenario.

Two studies (one US-centred) found that although dual-class firms show better firm value than one share, one vote dispersed ownership firms, the positive effects were driven by family or founder ownership rather than the capital structure itself, with the relevant premia reduced when dual-class stock was adopted.[137] The US study by Villalonga and Amit (2006) found that founder control (but not descendant control) had a positive effect on firm value,[138] the level of which was reduced by the adoption of dual-class stock. However, founder-controlled dual-class firms still showed better Tobin's Q than non-founder-controlled one share, one vote firms. Similarly, the non-US study showed that family-controlled firms displayed better firm valuations than non-family-controlled companies, and the attenuation of the effect by the adoption of dual-class stock was not so great as to eliminate the positive bias of family-control compared to non-family-control firms generally.[139] Although the studies showed dual-class stock to have a negative effect on founder-controlled companies and family-controlled companies, respectively, given that there is a preponderance of dual-class firms owned by family members or founders,[140] and the contention that dual-class structure can persuade such founders to list their companies,[141] dual-class stock should not be viewed negatively in such circumstances. Even if dual-class structure seemingly reduces firm value for family/founder-owned controlling-shareholder one share, one vote firms, so long as the overall

[134] *ibid* 19.

[135] As discussed in Section 5.6 of Chapter 5, if the controller's equity ownership is small, the potential for a controlling shareholder to reduce agency costs also wanes.

[136] HKEX Concept (2014) (n 17 above IV-II); Bennedsen and Nielsen (2006) (n 108 above 28); Jog et al. (2010) (n 103 above 416); Adams and Ferreira (2008) (n 3 above 67); Gurrea (2019) (n 83 above section 7).

[137] Villalonga and Amit (2006) (n 99 above 406); Barontini and Caprio (2006) (n 100 above 703).

[138] Villalonga and Amit (2006) (n 99 above 406).

[139] Barontini and Caprio (2006) (n 100 above 703).

[140] See n 19 above.

[141] See Section 1.5.2 of Chapter 1.

effect compared to one share, one vote dispersed ownership firms is positive, dual-class stock can be beneficial in promoting the listing of more of such controlling shareholder firms.[142] Potentially decisive in the consideration, though, is that the study by Villalonga and Amit (2006) only showed positive correlation between founder-controlled companies and firm value, and not where control had been transferred to descendants. From a policy perspective, thought should therefore be directed as to whether restrictions should be placed upon the identity of individuals who can hold dual-class stock, and the ability of founders to subsequently transfer control.[143] Effective restrictions that could be employed on the premium tier are discussed in Chapter 9.

Other studies have also shown the importance of separating various traits. Chemmanur et al. (2011)[144] found that US firms with high-quality management[145] displayed greater firm valuations if they implemented antitakeover provisions (which included dual-class stock), resonating with the normative bonding hypothesis benefit of dual-class firms discussed in Chapter 6. On the other hand, since a determinative factor was the quality of management, lower-quality managers may be adopting antitakeover provisions primarily in order to protect themselves, ahead of forthcoming poor performance foreseen by those managers,[146] and, accordingly, correlate with lower firm valuations. Jordan et al. (2016)[147] found that the general finding of lower Tobin's Q for US dual-class firms was not upheld when splitting firms into high- and low-growth. Only low-growth dual-class firms continued to show lower Tobin's Q than matched one share, one vote firms, but for high-growth firms, dual-class structure had a positive effect on firm value. Again, the results resonate with the normative analysis in Chapter 6 – where a firm is in a high growth-phase with numerous investment opportunities, dual-class structure enables the controller to pursue long-term investment absent of the influences of short-term shareholders. Two studies (one US, one Canadian) indicated that low dual-class firm Tobin's Q may be driven by those dual-class firms with high free cash-flows, suggesting that high free cash-flows result in greater opportunities for expropriation.[148] Since free

142 Barontini and Caprio (2006) made the same point in their study (n 100 above 721).

143 For example, see A. Winden, 'Sunrise, Sunset: An Empirical and Theoretical Assessment of Dual-Class Stock Structures' (2018) 3 *CBLR* 852, 927; B. Reddy, 'Finding the British Google: Relaxing the Prohibition of Dual-Class Stock from the Premium-Tier of the London Stock Exchange' (2020) 79 *CLJ* 315, 342; Marc Moore, 'Designing Dual Class Sunsets: The Case for a Transfer-Centered Approach' (2020) 12 *W&M BLR* 93, 145.

144 Chemmanur et al. (2011) (n 105 above).

145 The authors used characteristics related to education, experience, CEO dominance, median tenure and tenure heterogeneity as determinants of management quality (*ibid* 661–662).

146 An analogy can be drawn to one of the similar endogenous factors noted for event-based studies earlier that could affect the rationale for converting one share, one vote into dual-class stock (n 70 above and accompanying text).

147 Jordan et al. (2016) (n 101 above). The authors used sales growth and R&D intensity as proxies for firm growth.

148 Bozec and Laurin (2008) (n 92 above); Amoako-Adu et al. (2013) (n 19 above 196).

cash-flow represents earnings after investment in assets, a company with a high free cash-flow could be one with high levels of profitability but which does not use those profits for further investment. As such, it may be possible to equate this study with Jordan et al. (2016) – if the company is not in a growth-phase, which requires long-term investment, profits are more likely to be diverted by the controller, making dual-class structure detrimental to other shareholders. Similarly, Nüesch (2016) found that dual-class firms, in Switzerland, showed positive correlation with Tobin's Q if cash-flow was not sufficient to meet investment opportunities.[149] The author provided a different explanation – a controller of a firm requiring further equity investment would be constrained by market forces from expropriating in order to reduce the firm's cost of capital,[150] and continued to suggest that, therefore, dual-class stock should be encouraged for fast-growing firms to promote firm-specific investment and stable management, but that low-growth firms should adopt one share, one vote to mitigate against the risks of expropriation.[151] Future research could assist by further investigating the reasons for high free cash-flow in those dual-class firms showing lower firm value. Additionally, Anderson et al. (2009)[152] noted the significance of high-quality disclosure. Using bid-ask spread as a proxy for asymmetric information among investors, and analyst errors as a proxy for information availability, transparent US dual-class firms showed a positive correlation with firm value, with a negative correlation for those with opaque disclosure protocols. Reverse causation may be a significant issue, though, since poor disclosure may be a result of managers attempting to obscure controller benefit extraction that is detrimental to the company. However, greater levels of disclosure can make it more difficult to conduct the more egregious types of expropriation, including those that are fraudulent or represent disguised related-party transactions. As discussed in Chapter 9, greater mandated disclosure could, therefore, reduce the cost of capital for dual-class firms.

Two further US studies, which showed no statistically significant differences in firm value between dual-class firms and matched one share, one vote firms when evaluating their entire samples, after sub-sampling, also indicated that the fundamentals of the dual-class firm may play a part in firm value. While Cremers et al. (2018) found that dual-class firms showed higher firm valuations than matched one share, one vote firms at IPO, the divergence narrowed over time to the extent that dual-class firms showed lower firm value than matched one share, one vote firms six years after IPO.[153] In a similar manner, after sub-sampling, Kim and Michaely (2018) found that only older (twelve or more years old) dual-class firms showed worse firm valuations than one share, one vote firms, and younger (less than twelve years old) dual-class firms

149 Nüesch (2016) (n 9 above 542).
150 *ibid* 546.
151 *ibid* 547.
152 Anderson et al. (2009) (n 107 above).
153 Cremers et al. (2018) (n 105 above).

actually had better Tobin's Q values than young one share, one vote firms.[154] The two studies measure slightly different qualities – degradation in valuation over time post-IPO as compared to degradation in valuation over the entire lifetime of the firm. Nonetheless, the studies indicate a time dimension suggesting that to the extent dual-class structure is beneficial for a firm, the net-beneficial position erodes over time (although the submission earlier that the market's perception of dual-class structure has a historical dimension could impact the results). This could also tally with the findings described earlier for high-growth firms, with the presumption that younger firms will, on average, have greater growth-rates than more mature firms. The policy implication, as discussed further in Chapter 9, is that inferior-voting shareholders may require greater protection as a firm ages, but for at least some part of a firm's life, dual-class stock may be beneficial (or at least the market perceives it to be beneficial) to all shareholders. The general proposition that variations of performance occur over time raises a criticism of the empirical studies on firm value, and, in fact, other measures of performance.[155] As noted by HKEX, studies attempt to deal with this issue by either assuming that such differences will even out over large samples, or by attempting to match firms with similar qualities, ages or time since IPO.[156] The former solution is often impaired by small sample sizes (partly a product of dual-class firms forming only a minority of all listed firms in many jurisdictions), and the latter suffers from differences between studies in methodology of selection of firms, identification of characteristics and description of qualities. Even if firms were adequately matched with respect to age, the issue subsists that any individual firm within a sub-sample assessed during a discrete period of time may be in the midst of poor or good performance for reasons unrelated to its structure.[157] Although some studies attempt to match firms on the basis of characteristics such as sales growth in order to compare firms in similar economic situations, the characteristics used are fairly crude and do not appreciate the level of complexity required to adequately compare 'apples to apples'. There may in fact be no way to attain the matching required without sample sizes becoming unfeasibly small.[158]

In overview, taking the United States, where the majority of research has been undertaken, and where the investor profile bears similarity to the United Kingdom, the prevailing inference is that dual-class structure is negatively correlated with firm value. The time periods over which studies were conducted may have had an, albeit as yet indeterminate, influence. For the rest of the world, again, it seems that the studies trend toward a negative correlation between firm value and dual-class stock. However, more discrete correlations may be occurring on a jurisdiction-by-jurisdiction basis,

154 Kim and Michaely (2018) (n 47 above).

155 L. Bebchuk and K. Kastiel, 'The Untenable Case for Perpetual Dual-Class Stock' (2017) 4 *Va. Law Rev.* 585, 630.

156 HKEX Concept (2014) (n 17 above IV-2).

157 *ibid* IV-1.

158 Cremers et al. (2018), for example, noted in their study that sample size was significantly diminished by their use of extensive matching (n 105 above 17).

with the level and type of investor protection existing in the relevant jurisdiction impacting upon the effect of dual-class stock. Caution should be exercised, though, in drawing broad conclusions, since studies in the United States and the rest of the world have presented a more nuanced picture when firms are sub-sampled, with specific firm- and controller-characteristics potentially determining whether dual-class structure creates positive or negative impacts on firm value. For example, it is possible that high-growth and young firms, in fact, have higher firm values than similar one share, one vote firms, with the positive correlations dissipating with a decline in growth opportunities and age. Future research may better define in what instances, and for which firms, dual-class stock is likely to be net-beneficial or net-detrimental to public shareholders, but, for the time being, based on the evidence at hand, it would appear that, overall, dual-class firms are generally valued lower than similar one share, one vote firms. If, as alluded to earlier, one of the drivers of low firm value is expropriation over time, it is possible that the data represents an environment where specific types of firms, such as high-growth and young firms, use dual-class stock for net-beneficial reasons, whereas other types of firms implement the structure for the purposes of detrimental expropriation, but, overall, it would appear that for dual-class firms as a whole, the dual-class stock tradeoff leans in a negative orientation. However, as discussed in Section 7.4.3 next, it is not unequivocal that lower Tobin's Q for dual-class firms represents expropriation or poor management, and, as with event-based studies, market perception may still be a significant factor.

7.4.3 *Words of Warning*

A broad interpretation that firm valuation studies trend toward a finding that dual-class stock is associated with public shareholder expropriation and/or underperforming management teams should be qualified. Although, unlike event-based studies, firm valuation studies do not orbit around the vicissitudes in and around the occurrence of specific events, they do still suffer from other endogeneity issues. Certain types of company or certain qualities may lend themselves to the choice of dual-class stock,[159] which in turn have their own effects on firm value independent of capital structure.[160] As an example, if high-growth companies are more likely to select dual-class stock,[161] a positive impact on firm valuations for dual-class firms could be generated by there

[159] Adams and Ferreira (2008) (n 3 above 62); H. Hu and B. Black, 'The New Vote Buying: Empty Voting and Hidden (Morphable) Ownership' (2006) 79 *S. Cal. L. Rev.* 811, 852; C. Li et al., 'Ownership Structure and the Cost of Corporate Borrowing' (2011) 100 *J. Financ. Econ.* 1, 10.

[160] J. Fisch and S. Solomon, 'The Problems of Sunsets' (2019) 99 *B. U. Law Rev.* 1057, 1073.

[161] Also noted by Cremers et al. (2018) (n 105 above 31). Both Jordan et al. (2016) (n 101 above 307) and Lehn et al. (1990) (n 48 above 571) interpret their empirical evidence as showing that firms with greater growth opportunities choose dual-class stock. The situation is, though, complicated, since a competing dynamic where a company has plentiful investment opportunities is a desire to ensure low costs of capital, which would be promoted by one share, one vote (Adams and Ferreira (2008) (n 3 above 67).

being a greater prevalence of quickly growing companies in the group. Most studies control for this type of endogeneity and match dual-class firms to groups of similar one share, one vote firms, but it can be very difficult to isolate relevant qualities on a firm-by-firm basis. Typical control variables are firm size and sales growth.[162] Certain studies, particularly those that are cross-country-orientated, control for jurisdiction and industry.[163] Others also control for family ownership and the ability to dominate voting,[164] as well as firm age.[165] Clearly, there are a large number of endogenous variables that influence the choice of dual-class structure, and, as noted by Adams and Ferreira (2008), many studies do not control for endogeneity properly.[166] Further research could focus on ascertaining whether there are any trends in the exact qualities of firms choosing dual-class stock – so far, studies have been inconclusive in identifying such trends.[167] Differences in controls and matching methodologies also create difficulties in comparing separate studies, as can differences in how the proportionality of cash-flow rights to voting rights is detected and measured.[168] It is even difficult to isolate the effects of the voting/cash-flow divergence from the individual and separate effects of voting rights concentration and cash-flow rights concentration.[169] Categorical proof of causation between capital structure and firm value is therefore elusive. Additionally, it has been contended that, if capital structure choice is perfectly efficient, the best capital structure for the relevant firm will be chosen in each case;[170] this would lead to inconclusive empirical evidence, since, in such an event, no overall positive or negative correlation to capital structure will be found.[171] For example, for a firm where short-term signalling is more important, a one share, one vote structure may be optimal, whereas dual-class stock could be optimal for firms where long-term strategy is more conducive.[172] That said, efficiency of capital structure choice is certainly not a given,

162 Adams and Ferreira (2008) (n 3 above 76).
163 For example: Bennedsen and Nielsen (2006) (n 108 above).
164 For example: Bozec and Laurin (2008) (n 92 above).
165 For example: Kim and Michaely (2018) (n 47 above).
166 Adams and Ferreira (2008) (n 3 above 85).
167 Chapter 6 (see, for example, Section 6.3.7) notes the inconclusiveness of studies seeking a correlation between dual-class stock and, for example, R&D investment and growth-rate.
168 Adams and Ferreira (2008) (n 3 above 85); ISS Report (2007) (n 95 above 12); Allaire (2019) (n 4 above 8).
169 Adams and Ferreira (2008) (n 3 above 85). The difficulty in separating the individual effects of changing voting rights and cash-flow rights on firm value when evaluating the effect of the divergence between voting and cash-flow rights is highlighted by the fact that La Porta et al. (2002) (n 7 above) found a positive correlation between cash-flow rights and firm value, and Cronqvist and Nilsson (2003) (n 103 above) found a negative correlation between voting power and firm value, but neither found any effect of voting/cash-flow divergence on firm value.
170 H. Demsetz and K. Lehn, 'The Structure of Corporate Ownership: Causes and Consequences' (1985) 93 *J. of Polit. Econ.* 1155, 1156; Lehn et al. (1990) (n 48 above 566).
171 Z. Goshen and R. Squire, 'Principal Costs: A Theory for Corporate Law and Governance' (2017) 117 *Colum. L. Rev.* 767, 814.
172 M. Burkart et al., 'Large Shareholders, Monitoring, and the Value of the Firm' (1997) *Q. J. Econ.* (August 1997) 693, 718.

and the credibility of the concept can be questioned – for instance, the inferior-voting shareholders may not anticipate the intentions of a controller to implement dual-class stock to enable the extraction of pernicious controller benefits. Additionally, subsequent to choosing a structure at IPO, whether that be dual-class stock or one share, one vote, the structure that is most efficient for the firm may change over time; however, it is not simple from a corporate law perspective to switch capital structure post-IPO, and the potential for such a switch to occur will also be subject to the ideological desires of those who are enfranchised to make the decision.[173]

Further, pointed criticism can be levied against firm valuation studies where they use estimates for Tobin's Q. As mentioned, as a result of difficulties in ascertaining the replacement value of assets, often 'book value' is used as a substitute in the denominator of Tobin's Q, meaning that such studies are not using a true Tobin's Q measure.[174] This can create discrepancies within studies, since firms use varied techniques to book the value of assets, including different depreciation schedules and inventory accounting rules.[175] Furthermore, although a Tobin's Q that deviates from '1' can, as discussed earlier, reflect discounted future cash-flow or earnings growth, it could also reflect the market's valuation of a variety of other intangible assets,[176] not necessarily related to the market's assessment of the capital structure of the firm. Intangible assets not only include future growth and good management but can also encompass elements such as goodwill, position in the market and patents held.[177] Certain other intangible assets are also 'unbooked assets' and not included in book value; for instance, complex products such as financial derivatives are not booked,[178] and, importantly, expenditure on R&D, knowledge and intellectual property are often not capitalised.[179] Extraneous divergences also exist between firms in relation to the booking of intangible assets – for example, differences can exist in the manner in which goodwill is booked between businesses that build, versus those that buy, intangible assets.[180] Although Tobin's Q was described earlier as the 'capitalised value of agency costs',[181] the measure can be very noisy,[182] reflecting the market's valuation of unbooked intangible assets, or the nature of assets (such as investment opportunities attached to such assets) rather than, as

173 Claessens et al. (2002) noted that it is extremely unlikely that firms would be able to nimbly change capital structure mid-stream, post-IPO, in response to changing circumstances (n 98 above 2764).
174 Bartlett and Partnoy (2020) (n 87 above 393).
175 *ibid* 394.
176 Morck et al. (1988) (n 91 above).
177 *ibid* 296.
178 Bartlett and Partnoy (2020) (n 87 above 394).
179 *ibid* 396. Some researchers therefore prefer to use 'Total Q', a measure which also includes, in the denominator, an estimate for the replacement value of intangible capital that is not reflected on the firm's balance sheet (*ibid* 398). Cremers et al. (2018) (n 105 above 30) utilised Total Q as a robustness check against results derived using Tobin's Q.
180 Bartlett and Partnoy (2020) (n 87 above 397).
181 See n 92 above and accompanying text.
182 Morck et al. (1988) (n 91 above 296); Bartlett and Partnoy (2020) (n 87 above 371).

supposed by Morck et al. (1988), necessarily based upon an assessment of the management team's qualities, level of entrenchment and whether the relevant assets are being managed well.[183]

Finally, and most importantly, an alternative explanation for low Tobin's Q could be the market's perception of dual-class structure, upon IPO or recapitalisation from one share, one vote to dual-class structure, enduring long after the IPO or recapitalisation – if investors, on a firm-by-firm basis, categorically presuppose that the structure will be abused by the controller eventually (as also suggested by those event-based studies that showed negative reactions), investors would view the discount to be a reasonable reaction to having to assume that risk. Such behaviour could explain the overall negative correlation found in certain studies rather than there being an overall tendency toward detrimental expropriation. In a UK study, for instance, it was found that the level of the premium attached to one share, one vote firms was positively correlated with the level of negative media coverage of dual-class firms, even where such negative coverage was not associated with increased expropriation behaviour in dual-class firms.[184] For those studies showing divergent results between different types of firms, the market may perceive that specific types of firms (or controllers) present either lower risks of expropriation, notwithstanding dual-class structure, or overcompensatory benefits as a result of dual-class structure. A key challenge, as with event-based studies, is determining the validity of dual-class firm valuations, and therefore ascertaining whether differences in firm valuations between dual-class firms and one share, one vote firms truly represent the balance between beneficial and detrimental qualities of dual-class structure or merely represent the market's perception of dual-class stock. An answer can be garnered by scrutinising the actual performance of firms, from the perspective of both actual firm operating performance and buy-and-hold stock returns, to which we turn next.

7.5 BUY-AND-HOLD STOCK RETURN STUDIES

In the 1980s, dual-class structure was mainly appraised on the basis of event-based studies, and, in more recent times, judging by the preponderance of Tobin's Q studies, firm valuation has been used as a proxy for the sagacity of dual-class firms, with the presumption that such studies determine whether dual-class structure is beneficial or costly to public shareholders. However, that premise can be tested further by establishing whether public shareholders who invest in dual-class firms are, in fact, better or worse served than those who invest in one share, one vote firms. Long-term buy-and-hold stock return studies can be conducive in this regard in that they ascertain whether a public shareholder investing in a notional portfolio of dual-class firm inferior-voting shares for a period of time will receive higher or

183 Mikkelson and Partch (1994) (n 102 above 188).
184 Braggion and Giannetti (2016) (n 108 above 26).

lower returns than the same shareholder investing in a notional portfolio of matched one share, one vote firms. Unlike event-based studies, buy-and-hold stock return studies track longer-term shareholder returns which are uncontaminated by extraneous transitory influences. Although only a handful of studies track this performance measure, they provide useful further testament by augmenting firm valuation studies, thereby enabling an assessment as to whether differences in firm values between dual-class firms and one share, one vote firms correlate with the returns actually earned by shareholders. For example, given that the trend of firm valuation studies is toward a negative correlation between dual-class structure and firm value, if dual-class firms are being discounted correctly (thus embodying lower future firm performance), the differences in firm value between dual-class firms and one share, one vote firms should reflect anticipated differences in performance over time, and, therefore, there should not be substantial differences between returns received by portfolios of dual-class firms compared to one share, one vote firms. Investors will acquire inferior-voting shares at a lower price, in order to receive a similar return to what they would have received had they invested in a similar one share, one vote firm instead.

7.5.1 *Summary*

Figure 7.3 summarises the findings from eleven buy-and-hold stock return studies. Six studies (all US) found that long-term[185] buy-and-hold returns were greater for dual-class firms than one share, one vote firms[186] although one of those studies provided a result, which was only economically and not statistically significant[187]). Two US studies,[188] and one Canadian study, did not find any abnormal returns,[189] and one US study, not included in Figure 7.3, was inconclusive, finding negative stock returns for dual-class firms (relative to matched firms) in the first calendar year after recapitalisation from one share, one vote into dual-class structure and positive

185 The subset of studies on buy-and-hold stock returns generally assess those returns over periods of three to eight years after IPO or recapitalisation from one share, one vote into dual-class stock. Three studies that were reviewed exercised longer time periods not necessarily commencing from IPO or recapitalisation – Anh et al. (2020) (n 4 above) examined the period from 2009 to 2019, Anderson et al. (2017) (n 19 above) examined 2001–2015 and Jog et al. (2010) (n 103 above) examined 1996–2005.

186 Dimitrov and Jain (2006) (n 37 above 347); Böhmer et al. (1996) (n 34 above 109); Anderson et al. (2017) (n 19 above 23); S. Bauguess et al., 'Shareholder Diversification, Corporate Risk Taking, and the Benefits of Changing to Differential Voting Rights' (2012) 36 *J. Bank Finance* 1244, 1251; Anh et al. (2020) (n 4 above 134); Chemmanur et al. (2011) (n 105 above 681). Chemmanur et al. assessed antitakeover devices (including dual-class stock) generally. A US study that found US dual-class firms to outperform the MSCI index between November 2007 and August 2017 has not been included in the examination of studies due to difficulties in ascertaining its academic rigour (D. Melas, 'Putting the Spotlight on Spotify: Why Have Stocks with Unequal Voting Rights Outperformed?' *MCSI* (2018), www.msci.com/www/blog-posts/putting-the-spotlight-on/0898078592).

187 Bauguess et al. (2012) (n 186 above 1251).

188 Smart et al. (2008) (n 54 above 106); Cremers et al. (2018) (n 105 above 24).

189 Jog et al. (2010) (n 103 above 425).

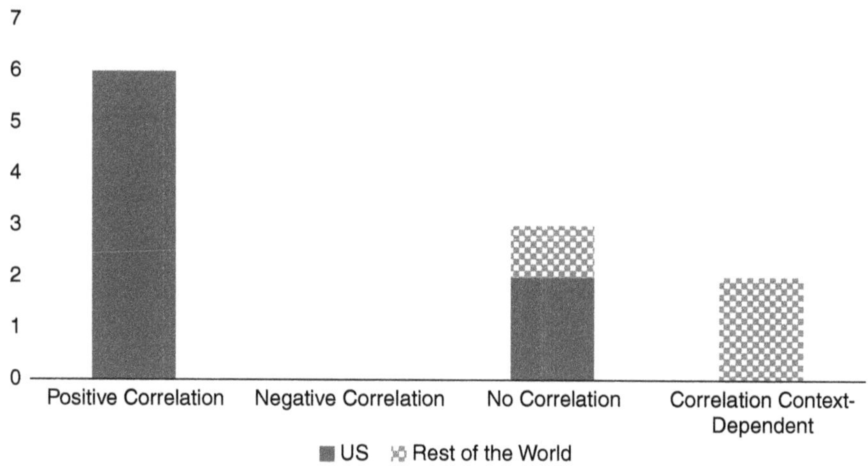

FIGURE 7.3 Dual-class stock buy-and-hold stock return studies

returns in calendar years two through four[190] (however, none of the results for each of the four calendar years post-recapitalisation were statistically significant enough for the authors to form a conclusion). Two studies (both non-US) found that the difference between portfolios of dual-class firm inferior-voting stock and one share, one vote firm stock only varied in specific circumstances.[191]

Certain Canadian studies have been excluded from the analysis in this section – Allaire (2019) cited six Canadian studies that examined the stock performance of dual-class firms compared to one share, one vote firms over five-, ten-, fifteen- or eighteen-year periods, all of which suggested outperformance by dual-class firms.[192] However, as the author notes, such studies are flawed in their univariate nature – merely comparing all dual-class firms to all one share, one vote firms does not take into account firm-level differences and other potential variables.[193] A further old study by a Canadian asset manager found that TSX dual-class stock portfolios slightly underperformed one share, one vote portfolios;[194] again, however, the study did not use matching (a critical oversight since the study recognises that dual-class stock is concentrated in specific industries[195]), and the authors acknowledge their bias

190 Mikkelson and Partch (1994) (n 102 above 191).

191 Braggion and Giannetti (2016) (n 108 above 31); M. Lemmon and K. Lins, 'Ownership Structure, Corporate Governance, and Firm Value: Evidence from the East Asian Financial Crisis' (2003) 58 *J. Financ.* 1445, 1455.

192 Allaire (2019) (n 4 above 38).

193 *ibid* 9.

194 Burgundy Asset Management Ltd., 'The View from Burgundy: Second Class Owners?' (September 1996) at 3, www.burgundyasset.com/wp-content/uploads/Second-Class-Owners-September-1996.pdf.

195 *ibid* 2.

against dual-class stock and the fact that they had not applied an academic level of precision to the study.[196]

7.5.2 *Detailed Analysis*

As with event-based and firm valuation studies, any studies that assess stock returns must be linked to risk pricing-in/share price discounting. If data presents abnormal positive long-term buy-and-hold stock returns from dual-class firms, it would tend to suggest that investors are overestimating the risk of dual-class stock and therefore overzealously discounting stock. Similarly, negative abnormal returns would suggest overoptimism on the part of investors. Most of the buy-and-hold stock return studies show that portfolios of dual-class firm inferior-voting stock earn public shareholders greater returns than similar portfolios of one share, one vote firm stock. Although a significant number of such studies also showed no correlation, intriguingly, none[197] show dual-firm portfolios to generate lower returns than one share, one vote firms.

Detailed analysis of the various studies reveals certain, possibly important, provisos. The study by Bauguess et al. (2012) only showed a positive correlation between dual-class stock and returns where controllers had sold-down equity at the time of adoption of dual-class stock (recapitalisations from one share, one vote into dual-class stock in this case).[198] Those who are antagonistic to dual-class firms would consider the reduced levels of 'skin-in-the-game', resulting from a controller selling-down equity, to indefensibly increase the incentives on the controller to extract controller benefits to the detriment of the company, but the higher levels of returns suggest that overcompensatory benefits to outside stockholders are generated when a controller diversifies wealth. As discussed in Chapter 6, that diversification can empower the controller to cause the company to take greater risks and pursue a successful long-term vision. Dimitrov and Jain (2006) found that their findings of a positive correlation between dual-class stock and returns were heavily influenced by those firms that issued further equity after recapitalisation.[199] The results conform to the hypothesis that dual-class structure is particularly beneficial to high-growth firms, since equity issuances could be indicative of a desire to fund further growth. Similarly, assuming that younger firms will more likely be growth-phase companies, Anh et al. (2020) found that the higher returns associated with dual-class firms could be driven by firms which have undergone IPO most recently.[200]

Two non-US studies suggested that returns vary depending upon external environmental conditions. In the United Kingdom, Braggion and Giannetti (2016) showed

196 *ibid* 1.

197 Ignoring a single Canadian study for the reasons discussed in the text accompanying nn 194–196 above.

198 Bauguess et al. (2012) (n 186 above 1251).

199 Dimitrov and Jain (2006) (n 37 above 360).

200 Anh et al. (2020) (n 4 above 136). Note, however, that the study by Anh et al. only matched dual-class and one share, one vote firm portfolios by industry. Furthermore, it would appear that greater returns for firms earlier in their listed lives were at the expense of greater volatility (*ibid* 136).

that during periods of negative media coverage of dual-class firms, discounts were applied to firm valuations of dual-class firms,[201] which were accompanied by greater average monthly stock returns for portfolios of dual-class firms compared to one share, one vote firms.[202] This is a good case study on the impact of market perception on firm value studies discussed in Section 7.4 earlier. When dual-class firms are faced with negative headlines, the market discounts dual-class firms, but such discounts overestimate the risks posed, resulting in higher returns from dual-class portfolios. A study by Lemmon and Lins (2003), though, did show that, in certain circumstances, discounts of dual-class stock may be justified – the study, spanning East Asia, showed abnormal negative returns for portfolios of dual-class firms during the East Asian financial crisis,[203] which were not apparent before the financial crisis.[204] The logic extolled was that when investment opportunities evaporated during the crisis, it either became more lucrative for dual-class controllers to expropriate inferior-voting shareholders rather than cause the relevant company to invest in the business, or the incentives on controllers to expropriate inferior-voting shareholders increased as the options to otherwise create equity upside became vanishingly small due to an absence of investment opportunities for the relevant company. A constructive area for further study would be to assess stock returns of dual-class firms in periods or circumstances where expropriation is potentially incentivised in order to ascertain scenarios where greater investor protection is required. With such information in hand, investors could be granted greater regulatory protections upon certain events developing. This line of thinking is further discussed in Chapter 9.[205]

Unfortunately, the studies on long-term buy-and-hold returns do not often distinguish between types of firms to the same extent as found in some firm valuation studies discussed earlier in this chapter. It would be interesting to deduce whether positive returns are also garnered for those types of firms which show a positive correlation between dual-class structure and firm valuation. If no abnormal positive returns are generated, it is possible that the market does not apply a discount that represents the risk of expropriation (or alternatively does not require a stock return premium to compensate for risk) where certain types of firms implement dual-class structure. If there are positive abnormal returns, though, it could mean that the market is still overly discounting dual-class stock, but since the market perceives those risks as being outweighed by the substantial benefits that dual-class structure can confer on those types of firms, the discount is not reflected by an overall negative correlation with firm value. Although there is a positive correlation with firm value, the price does not appreciate the full upside of dual-class stock, resulting in

201 See n 184 above and accompanying text.
202 Braggion and Giannetti (2016) (n 108 above 31).
203 Lemmon and Lins (2003) (n 191 above 1455).
204 *ibid* 1465.
205 See Section 9.6.5 of Chapter 9.

positive stock returns comparable to similar one share, one vote firms. The theme is revisited in Section 7.7 of this chapter.[206]

Overall, however, outside of specific economic conditions, based on the available research, there is certainly no robust evidence that outside investors are earning lower returns from dual-class firms than one share, one vote firms, and, at least in the United States, the fact that the trend, albeit from a small number of studies, is in the direction of positive abnormal returns intimates that investors are overly discounting dual-class stock. Therefore, at the very least, it would appear that investors are adequately protecting themselves from the potential risks inherent in dual-class structure, and may, in fact, be earning a premium from investing in dual-class firms. Firm valuation studies suggest that the market is mainly pricing dual-class firms at a lower price than one share, one vote firms, yet a majority of buy-and-hold stock return studies show that such firms are producing better returns than one share, one vote firms; this alludes to investors discounting dual-class firms out of fear of excessive expropriation, but those fears not materialising over time.[207] Alternatively, institutional investors possibly expect a stock return premium over time just for taking the risk of investing in dual-class firms.[208] Although the fear of the risks that institutional investors apparently hold is not so considerable that they shun dual-class firms,[209] they will require a reward for doing so. If concerns regarding shareholder wealth maximisation are dissuading regulators in the United Kingdom from welcoming dual-class firms, such concerns are not borne out by the empirical evidence.[210]

7.5.3 *Words of Warning*

The conclusion applied to buy-and-hold stock return studies above should be tempered by their possible limitations. Although sample sizes are not small, only

206 See nn 315–317 below and accompanying text.

207 Holmén (2011) (n 108 above 16) noted, in the context of an influx of foreign investors into the Swedish markets, that such investors applied a discount to dual-class firms independent of actual expropriation. Also see F. Braggion and M. Giannetti, 'At the Origins of the Non-Voting Shares' Discount: Investor Preferences vs. Fundamentals' (2012) at 1, 23, https://pdfs.semanticscholar.org/a48e/53a18141d21de29615ed9cdc4e472c6e2c5a.pdf which studied pricing differences between voting and non-voting stock and found that the discount applied to non-voting stock was unjustified by ex post returns, opining that the discount was applied simply as a result of investor preference for one share, one vote. Lauterbach and Pajuste (2015) noted that the market overestimated the agency cost benefits of controlling shareholders unifying their dual-class stock into one share, one vote (n 98 above 173).

208 Anderson et al. (2017) (n 19 above 19); Gordon (1988) (n 49 above 74).

209 Finding that institutional investor ownership in dual-class firms was the same or greater than such ownership in one share, one vote firms: Anderson et al. (2017) (n 19 above 28); Smart et al. (2008) (n 54 above 99); Smart and Zutter (2003) (n 9 above 98); Dittmann and Ulbricht (2007) (n 62 above 191). Finding slightly less institutional ownership of dual-class firms: K. Li et al., 'Do Voting Rights Affect Institutional Investment Decisions? Evidence from Dual-Class Firms' (2008) 37 *Financ. Manag.* 713, 720; J. Kim et al., 'Multi-Class Shares Around the World: The Role of Institutional Investors' (November 2018) *Unpublished* 1, 19, http://finance.darden.virginia.edu/wp-content/uploads/2018/08/KMX_Multi-Class-Shares-and-IO_2018_11_04.pdf.

210 Anderson et al. (2017) (n 19 above 8).

a handful of studies have been conducted in this sphere, and many of those that have been completed do not cover the most recent period of the US tech industry's embrace of dual-class structure. Buy-and-hold stock return studies may also suffer from endogeneity, in a similar manner to firm valuation studies. As with firm valuation studies, these aspects of endogeneity can be moderated by controlling for diverse variables using appropriate matching between dual-class firms and one share, one vote firms, but it is challenging to conclusively determine causation by perfectly matching against all potential variables without acutely reducing sample size.[211] For example, it is quite possible that, since dual-class structure is being prolifically adopted in the United States by high-growth tech firms, in more recent studies, a sample of dual-class firms could encompass a disproportionate number of high-growth firms as compared to a sample of one share, one vote firms. Better stock return results may, thus, be driven by high-growth firms, rather than dual-class structure. Although it is possible to control for such effects, indications of high-growth can be varied and obscure. Correspondingly, the potential inferences from two of the buy-and-hold stock return studies discussed earlier that dual-class stock is especially beneficial for high-growth firms[212] may be flawed. Relatedly, as discussed in relation to firm valuation studies, further research on the impact of time periods would be instructive, since the types of firms choosing dual-class structure will have evolved over time.

Finally, concurring with the discussion on diversity at the start of this chapter, portfolios of dual-class firms (even if grouped into firm-specific qualities) collate all such dual-class firms together notwithstanding the fact that some controllers will have implemented the structure, from the perspective of shareholders as a whole, for beneficial reasons, and some for detrimental reasons. Whether long-term buy-and-hold stock performance is positive or negative will depend not only on firm-specific qualities but also on the intentions of the controller, and the economic environment in which the company operates (as shown by Lemmon and Lins (2003)).

As already mentioned, event-based studies, firm valuation studies and long-run buy-and-hold stock return studies are all influenced by the market perception of dual-class stock. This chapter now turns toward assessing whether the results of these studies are aligned with the actual operating performance of dual-class firms over time.

7.6 OPERATING PERFORMANCE STUDIES

Operating performance studies scrutinise the business operations of dual-class firms by comparing accounting measures of performance between dual-class and one share, one vote firms. By combining data related to measures of firm value and buy-and-hold stock returns with those of business performance, a more elaborate picture

211 Indeed, it was noted in Cremers et al. (2018) that sample size was significantly diminished by their use of extensive matching (n 105 above 17).

212 See nn 199–200 above and accompanying text.

can be painted of the impact of dual-class structure and the reasons therefor. Several accounting measures of firm performance have been used by assorted studies, and, accordingly, such variations should be a consideration in comparing them (hence the greater detail in the study descriptions in Section 7.6.2). If dual-class structure is associated with a net-detrimental dual-class stock tradeoff, where, for example, the controller manages the company primarily to extract pernicious controller benefits, one may expect that operating performance will be similarly negatively correlated; however, as mentioned next, the evidence does not support that assertion.

7.6.1 *Summary*

Twenty-one operating performance studies were reviewed. Eight studies (seven US studies,[213] and one Canadian[214]) showed a positive correlation between dual-class stock and operating performance, although two of those US studies only showed positive results where, respectively, the controller had divested of equity or the company had subsequently issued further stock. Ten studies showed no correlation between dual-class structure and operating performance (four US studies,[215] and six studies from the rest of the world[216]), and three non-US studies showed a negative relationship between operating performance and dual-class structure (although in one of those studies, only family-controlled firms, which showed better operating performance than non-family-controlled firms, were evaluated).[217] Figure 7.4 illustrates the findings.

7.6.2 *Detailed Analysis*

A number of US studies have shown dual-class firms to display better operating performance than one share, one vote firms. Cremers et al. (2018), using six-yearly snapshots between 1985 and 2015, found that dual-class firms had greater return on assets (ROA)[218] and return on equity (ROE)[219] than matched one share, one

[213] O. Arugaslan et al., 'On the Decision to Go Public with Dual Class Stock' (2010) 16 *J. Corp. Financ.* 170; Cremers et al. (2018) (n 105); Böhmer et al. (1996) (n 34 above); Lehn et al. (1990) (n 48 above); Bauguess et al. (2012) (n 186 above); Dimitrov and Jain (2006) (n 37); Chemmanur et al. (2011) (n 105 above). Chemmanur et al. assessed antitakeover devices (including dual-class stock) generally.

[214] Jog et al. (2010) (n 103 above).

[215] G. Morey, 'Multi-Class Stock and Firm Value: Does Multi-Class Stock Enhance Firm Performance? A Regression Analysis' *CII Publication* (May 2017); Mikkelson and Partch (1994) (n 102 above); Smart et al. (2008) (n 54 above); Kim and Michaely (2018) (n 47 above).

[216] King and Santor (2008) (n 98 above); Bozec and Laurin (2008) (n 92 above); Nüesch (2016) (n 9 above); Bennedsen and Nielsen (2006) (n 108 above); Pajuste (2005) (n 74 above); Lauterbach and Yafeh (2009) (n 103 above 20).

[217] Cronqvist and Nilsson (2003) (n 103 above); Holmén (2011) (n 108 above); Barontini and Caprio (2006) (n 100 above).

[218] ROA is effectively EBITDA divided by assets.

[219] ROE is effectively net earnings over equity.

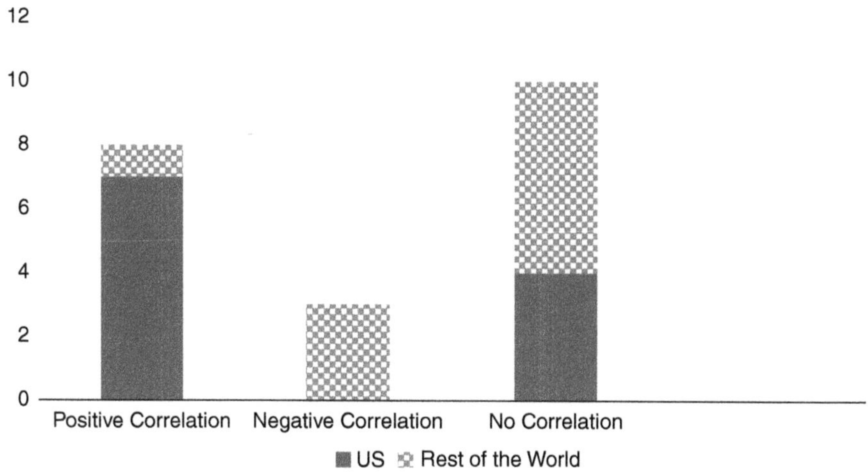

FIGURE 7.4 Dual-class stock operating performance studies

vote firms.[220] Sales growth was not statistically different for such firms.[221] Böhmer et al. (1996) found that dual-class firms, between 1984 and 1988, generated greater net operating income (effectively EBITDA) and ROA than one share, one vote firms in the year after IPO and through three years after IPO, while sales and assets were not statistically different.[222] Therefore, dual-class firms were able to produce better operating results with similar sales and assets growth. Beyond three years post-IPO, the rate of decline of ROA, ROE, and the ratio of net operating income to sales was significantly less for dual-class firms compared to one share, one vote firms.[223] Arugaslan et al. (2010) also found that, for US IPOs between 1980 and 2008, dual-class firms had higher profit margins[224] than industry-matched one share, one vote firms in the year after IPO.[225] Chemmanur et al. (2011) found that although all US firms displayed, through the fourth year post-IPO, declining OIBD[226] over assets, OIBD over sales, ROA and profit margin, those that had implemented antitakeover provisions (which included dual-class stock) saw lower rates of decline.[227] Similar to their results in relation to firm value described in Section 7.4.2 of this chapter, the authors also found that those firms with high-quality management outperformed all other types of companies across nearly all tested years post-IPO if they had also implemented strong

220 Cremers et al. (2018) (n 105 above 18).
221 *ibid* 19.
222 Böhmer et al. (1996) (n 34 above 112 and 114).
223 *ibid* 114.
224 Ratio of the difference between sales and earnings after interest and tax to sales.
225 Arugaslan et al. (2010) (n 213 above 177).
226 Operating income before depreciation *plus* interest income.
227 Chemmanur et al. (2011) (n 105 above 675).

antitakeover provisions.[228] It should be noted that the study by Bauguess et al. (2012) found no correlation when grouping all firms recapitalising into dual-class structure,[229] but, given that the premise of this book discussed in Chapter 1 is that dual-class stock enables founders to divest of investment while retaining control, it has been included in Figure 7.4 under the positive category, since statistically significant increases in industry-adjusted ROA were found for those firms where the recapitalisation also entailed the incumbent controller selling-down equity.[230] The authors suggested that increased operating performance was a product of controller diversification, through dual-class structure, leading to businesses being managed in a manner beneficial to both outsiders and insiders. As discussed in Chapter 6, such diversification supports risk-taking and greater core-industry focus by dual-class firms which may drive the increased operating performance.[231] Dimitrov and Jain (2006) found similar ROA and ROE and greater growth-rate for dual-class firms post-recapitalisation compared to matched one share, one vote firms, where those dual-class firms subsequently issued equity after the recapitalisation, suggesting that dual-class firms could grow in a way that their competitor firms could not, while maintaining steady profitability.[232] With higher-growth and similar profitability, the authors opined that total profits must be growing at the same rate as the growth-rate, meaning that dual-class stock likely allows those firms to take advantage of investment opportunities in a value-enhancing manner, which manifests itself in, as also found by the authors, higher abnormal returns over time for investors.[233] Lehn et al. (1990), examining recapitalisations between 1976 and 1987, found that EBITDA divided by sales significantly increased in the periods of one year before to one year, two years and three years after recapitalisation from one share, one vote into dual-class structure,[234] but that the positive results were concentrated within those firms that issued further equity (the results were statistically insignificant for those that did not).[235] It should be noted, though, that the studies by Lehn et al. and Dimitrov and Jain could have been affected by endogeneity with the further stock issuances driving better performance, rather than dual-class structure itself. Outside of the United States, one Canadian study also deduced a positive correlation between operating performance and dual-class stock, with Jog et al. (2010) finding that dual-class firms had marginally better ROA than one share, one vote firms[236] (although the statistical significance faded in the regression study[237]).

[228] *ibid* 676.
[229] Bauguess et al. (2012) (n 186 above 1249).
[230] *ibid* 1251.
[231] See Sections 6.3.8 and 6.3.2, respectively, of Chapter 6.
[232] Dimitrov and Jain (2006) (n 37 above 358–359 and 363).
[233] *ibid* 363 (also see 'Buy-and-Hold Stock Return Studies' earlier).
[234] Lehn et al. (1990) (n 48 above 577).
[235] *ibid* 578.
[236] Jog et al. (2010) (n 103 above 422).
[237] *ibid* 425.

A smaller set of US studies have found no significant difference in operating performance between dual-class and one share, one vote firms. Smart et al. (2008) in investigating ROA and EBITDA over book equity in the five years post-IPO,[238] and Mikkelson and Partch (1994) using an ROA proxy in the four years post-recapitalisation from one share, one vote to dual-class stock[239] were two such studies. Mikkelson and Partch had tried to replicate the positive dual-class firm operating performance results from Lehn et al.'s study (referenced earlier), and the authors attributed the discrepancy from the earlier study to differences in matching criteria. One further study,[240] showing no correlation between operating performance and dual-class stock, measured return on invested capital (ROIC),[241] which gauges how efficiently a company uses its capital to produce returns by linking earnings to investment projects.[242] The author equated high ROIC with long-term firm performance,[243] and suggested that the results show that dual-class stock is not required in order to deliver long-term performance.[244] However, ROIC can also equate to short-term comportment – a company that substantially invests in long-term R&D may suffer low ROIC as compared to companies that invest in projects that will bear immediate returns.[245] Therefore, it is difficult to construe the results in terms of short- and long-termism. If anything, the results add another strand to the inconclusiveness of studies attempting to correlate capital structure with R&D investment.[246] The results do, though, suggest that, on average, the controllers of dual-class firms do not abuse their positions to cause such firms to invest in projects that are detrimental to outside shareholders to any greater extent than is seen in one share, one vote firms. Kim and Michaely (2018) found no statistical difference overall in ROA and operating margin[247] between dual-class firms and matched one share, one vote firms through a long sampling period of 1971 to 2015,[248] but found that young (less than twelve years old) dual-class firms had statistically better operating margins than young one share, one vote firms, and mature (greater than or equal to twelve years old) dual-class firms had statistically worse operating margins than mature one share, one vote firms.[249] The authors stated that this evidences that dual-class stock can improve operating margins in young firms, but that such margins decline at a greater rate than one share, one vote

238 Smart et al. (2008) (n 54 above 107).
239 Mikkelson and Partch (1994) (n 102 above 190).
240 Morey (2017) (n 215 above 23).
241 ROIC is effectively operating income (adjusted for tax) divided by total debt and shareholder equity *less* cash.
242 D. Benoit, 'The Hottest Metric in Finance: ROIC' *Wall Street Journal* (3 May 2016), www.wsj.com/articles/the-hottest-metric-in-finance-roic-1462267809.
243 Morey (2017) (n 215 above 2).
244 *ibid* 31.
245 Benoit (2016) (n 242 above).
246 See Section 6.3.7 of Chapter 6.
247 Operating income before depreciation over sales.
248 Kim and Michaely (2018) (n 47 above 11).
249 *ibid* 17.

firms. Outside of the United States, a larger number of studies found no difference in operating performance between dual-class stock and one share, one vote firms. In Canada, King and Santor (2008) found no statistically significant effect on ROA,[250] and Bozec and Laurin (2008) also found that, generally, a divergence between voting and cash-flow rights did not cause statistically significant differences in ROA, ROIC or ROE.[251] The study by Bozec and Laurin deserves further attention though, since when the sample was split into companies with high and low free cash-flow, the voting/cash-flow divergence had a statistically significant negative effect on all three measures of performance for high free cash-flow companies.[252] The results were even more pronounced where the controller held less than or equal to 25 per cent of the cash-flow rights.[253] The authors concluded that weaker performance results where a controller has both the incentive (through a large voting/cash-flow divergence) and the opportunity (as a result of high free cash-flow) to expropriate inferior-voting shareholders.[254] On a similar note, in Switzerland, Nüesch (2016) found no correlation overall between dual-class stock and operating performance, but did find that ROA was positively correlated with dual-class structure for those firms that required external financing (the correlation was negative for those that did not).[255] Presumably, where external financing was required, the opportunities for expropriation of inferior-voting shareholders were less and the consequences of increased costs of capital were more. In Western Europe, Bennedsen and Nielsen (2006) did not find any correlation between disproportionate control and ROA,[256] and Pajuste (2005) found that ROA and ROE did not significantly change for firms unifying dual-class stock into one share, one vote.[257] Although Pajuste found that sales growth for such dual-class firms unifying into one share, one vote would significantly improve post-unification, when comparing those firms to non-unifying dual-class firms with matched investment opportunities no significant differences were found in sales growth.[258] Unifying firms also had lower leverage and tended to issue equity in the year after unification.[259] The authors ascertained that dual-class firms unify not because eliminating the dual-class stock structure will improve the operating performance of the firm, but in order to lower their costs of capital when equity financing is required to finance investment opportunities (which has become expensive due to discounting by investors).[260] Pajuste's theory shows conformity to the history of dual-class stock in

250 King and Santor (2008) (n 98 above 2429).
251 Bozec and Laurin (2008) (n 92 above 39).
252 *ibid* 39.
253 *ibid* 44.
254 *ibid* 44.
255 Nüesch (2016) (n 9 above 541).
256 Bennedsen and Nielsen (2006) (n 108 above 26).
257 Pajuste (2005) (n 74 above 33).
258 *ibid* 34.
259 *ibid* 34.
260 *ibid* 35. This also chimes with the findings of Lauterbach and Yafeh (2009) in Israel where dual-class firms that unified structure into one share, one vote were, prior to unification, underperforming other

the United Kingdom, where a number of companies, which had issued non-voting stock prior to any informal or formal prohibition by the regulators, enfranchised non-voting stock as a result of high costs of capital.[261] In Israel, Lauterbach and Yafeh (2009) found dual-class firms that unified into one share, one vote to have statistically lower ROAs, before and after unification, than those that did not unify.[262] It would therefore seem that unifying firms had worse operating performance prior to unification than other dual-class firms, and if it were expected that unification would improve performance, this was not apparent in practice. Such firms were performing poorly for reasons other than their capital structure.

In relation to negative correlations, although Barontini and Caprio found that dual-class stock reduced the operating performance, as measured by ROA, of family-controlled firms in Continental Europe, those family-controlled firms still outperformed non-family-controlled firms on the same measure.[263] As with the discussion earlier on firm value, this could be seen in a positive light on the basis that dual-class stock encourages family-controlled firms to list.[264] Only two other studies, both Swedish, indicated any negativity between dual-class stock and operating performance. Cronqvist and Nilsson (2003) found a negative effect,[265] and Holmén (2011) found a weakly negative effect.[266] The results may be attributable to the unique qualities of the Swedish public markets where dual-class firms form a majority by market capitalisation, and nearly a majority in number, of listed firms.[267] In such an environment, where dual-class stock has become normalised, there may be a lesser proportion of firms listing with dual-class stock for which the structure is more obviously beneficial than compared to a market such as the United States, where institutional investors will likely require more persuasion to invest in dual-class companies.

In overview, operating performance studies, at least in the United States, are largely in favour of a positive correlation with dual-class stock. The picture is more inconclusive for the rest of the world (where fewer studies have been conducted), but there is certainly no trend suggestive of a pattern that dual-class firms operate worse than one share, one vote firms. Even outside the United States, certain studies that showed no correlation overall did show positive relationships between operating performance and dual-class stock for firms with low free cash-flow[268] and those with

dual-class firms – it is possible that such firms required further equity financing due to poor performance and unification was required to reduce the costs of capital (n 103 above).

261 See Section 2.2 of Chapter 2.

262 Lauterbach and Yafeh (2009) (n 103 above 20).

263 Barontini and Caprio (2006) (n 100 above 703).

264 See n 142 above and accompanying text.

265 Cronqvist and Nilsson (2003) (n 103 above 712).

266 Holmén (2011) (n 108 above 11).

267 Committee on Capital Markets Regulation, 'The Rise of Dual Class Shares: Regulations and Implications' (April 2020), www.capmktsreg.org/wp-content/uploads/2020/04/The-Rise-of-Dual-Class-Shares-04.08.20-1.pdf.

268 See n 252 above and accompanying text.

external financing requirements,[269] qualities often attendant to high-growth tech firms. Ignoring a Continental Europe-wide study that only evaluated family-controlled firms, only in Sweden[270] did firms with voting/cash-flow divergences perform worse than those without. Taking the US and non-US studies together, certain studies suggest that better operating performance is found in dual-class firms that have higher-quality management,[271] have implemented the structure in conjunction with the controller selling-down equity to diversify wealth,[272] require external financing,[273] or which issue further equity at the same time or subsequent to the implementation of dual-class stock.[274] It is, therefore, likely, as with other types of studies, that certain firm characteristics allow some dual-class firms to significantly outperform one share, one vote firms. However, those studies also showed that when the relevant qualities were not sub-sampled, and all dual-class firms were taken as a whole, overall either there was no difference in performance between dual-class firms and one share, one vote firms or those dual-class firms with characteristics that enable them to outperform one share, one vote firms carry the whole sample to an overall positive correlation (albeit a weaker positive correlation than when solely considering those firms with the relevant qualities).

Reverting to the dual-class stock tradeoff, the empirical evidence does not resonate with a net-detrimental tradeoff position, where excessive expropriation or poor performance by an entrenched management team prevail, and seemingly adduces that dual-class firms perform operationally at least as well as one share, one vote firms. It therefore does not appear that the managers of dual-class firms (as compared to one share, one vote firms) overall either manage those firms less assiduously[275] or make investment decisions that are worse for outside shareholders,[276] both of which would be reflected by poorer operating performance. Just taking operating performance studies in isolation, dual-class controllers, notwithstanding the fact that they may retain voting control, do not use their privileged (and entrenched) positions to make business or investment decisions that prioritise their interests over those of inferior-voting shareholders to the extent that it (net) negatively affects the profits of the company as compared to similar one share, one vote companies. The lack of a negative correlation between operating performance and dual-class stock does not exclude the possibility that detrimental expropriation is still taking place, but any

269 See n 255 above and accompanying text.
270 See nn 265 and 266 above.
271 See n 228 above and accompanying text.
272 See n 230 above and accompanying text.
273 See n 255 above and accompanying text.
274 See nn 232 and 235 above and accompanying text.
275 Arugaslan et al. (2010) (n 213 above 177). The ability to shirk could also be considered to be a controller benefit. Although managers in one share, one vote firms could also shirk, the tendency is reduced in one share, one vote dispersed ownership firms by the use of performance-related remuneration packages, and in one share, one vote controlling shareholder firms by the large equity exposure of the controlling shareholder to poor management performance.
276 Böhmer et al. (1996) (n 34 above 115).

expropriation taking place that could affect the generation of operating profits is matched or overshadowed by the positive effects on profitability engendered by dual-class structure.

7.6.3 *Words of Warning*

A number of issues identified in relation to event-based, firm valuation and buy-and-hold stock return studies may also apply to operating performance studies. For example, even with extensive matching, endogeneity once again rears its ugly head. A company that implements dual-class stock may be a firm that is already high-performing. Indeed, in order to persuade investors to forsake their voting rights and still invest in the company at a reasonable price, the investors may need to know that the company is high-performing compared to other firms where there are less governance risks. As an example, in Israel, firms that unified their dual-class stock into one share, one vote were performing worse than other dual-class firms before the unification[277] – perhaps those firms unified since they were no longer able to raise equity capital at a reasonable price once performance had declined. On the other hand, in contrast to the postulation in Section 7.5.3 of this chapter that better buy-and-hold stock returns could be driven by a disproportionate number of high-growth firms adopting dual-class structure, often high-growth tech corporations will be pre-profit businesses,[278] and therefore could drive mean operating performance downward rather than upward. Again, ascertaining the effects of endogeneity is challenging without further research.

Another endogenous aspect to consider is whether better operating performance is being driven by the fact that dual-class firms are mainly family (including founder) owned.[279] There is some evidence that family-controlled firms show better 'financial firm performance' than non-family-controlled firms,[280] invest more in R&D where the controller is the founder[281] and show better operating performance than non-family-controlled firms.[282] Surprisingly, very few dual-class studies control for family ownership.[283] Further research on the effect of dual-class stock on family-controlled firms would be a valuable contribution to the discussion, although not essential for the purposes of considering the premium tier prohibition of dual-class stock – so long as dual-class firms, which are overwhelmingly family/founder-owned, show improved operating performance compared to one share, one vote firms generally,

277 Lauterbach and Yafeh (2009) (n 103 above).
278 HKEX, 'Concept Paper: New Board' (June 2017) at 15.
279 See n 19 above.
280 M. van Essen et al., 'How Does Family Control Influence Firm Strategy and Performance? A Meta-Analysis of US Publicly Listed Firms' (2015) 23 *Corp. Gov.* 3.
281 See Section 6.3.7 of Chapter 6.
282 King and Santor (2008) (n 98 above 2424); Barontini and Caprio (2006) (n 100 above 703).
283 Family-ownership is included as a controlled variable in the non-US studies of Pajuste (2005) (n 74 above), Bozec and Laurin (2008) (n 92 above) and Jog et al. (2010) (n 103 above).

dual-class structure should be welcomed in the context of enabling and encouraging founders to retain control as explained in Chapter 1. If dual-class structure can encourage founders to list their firms, the fact that dual-class samples include a disproportionate number of overperforming founder-controlled firms is not necessarily fatal to inferences that dual-class structure is effectual in creating value for outside stockholders. A repercussion, though, is that consideration should be given to situations where enhanced-voting shares are transferred to third parties, or even where ownership is passed from the original founder to other family members.[284] This is discussed further in Chapter 9. Finally, the diversity of firms may also affect results, since grouping all dual-class firms together, as most of these studies have done, does not distinguish between different types of firms, nor the intentions, agenda and inclinations of the controller.

Two salient issues should also be further considered. Firstly, a number of the studies only assess operating performance within a relatively short period of time from IPO or recapitalisation (usually within five years), potentially masking longer-term performance deficiencies. Kim and Michaely (2018) identified that older dual-class firms may, in fact, underperform compared to older one share, one vote firms.[285] Therefore, it is possible that the better performance of dual-class firms is finite and may recede over time, and further studies in this area would be welcome. Secondly, the possibility remains that expropriation could also be taking place after profits have been generated.[286] In effect, the company is operating at a level comparable to one share, one vote firms, but having generated similar or better operating profits, the controller simultaneously or subsequently extracts pernicious controller benefits, resulting in a lower firm valuation, since profits that would otherwise have accrued to the outside shareholders are expropriated by the controller. However, many types of pernicious controller benefit extraction through, for example, the controller abusing its entrenched management position to invest in pet or inefficient projects, paying itself high levels of remuneration, shirking or dedicating time as a manager to other unrelated enterprises, making decisions that benefit the reputation or self-image of the controller more than the interests of the company, or making poor acquisitions, would likely affect profitability.[287] The fact that operating performance seems to remain robust for a period of time after implementation of dual-class stock concords with either such extraction not taking place or taking place at such low levels that it is overshadowed by the operating performance benefits conveyed by the structure. Certain types of pernicious controller benefits could, though, be extracted

284 Also see n 143 above and accompanying text. In relation to evidence that firms perform worse when control has been passed by a founder to heirs, see Section 6.2.4 of Chapter 6.

285 See n 249 above and accompanying text. It should also be noted, though, that Böhmer et al. (1996) (n 34 above), using different measurements of performance over a shorter and earlier time period, found that dual-class firm performance declined less than one share, one vote firm performance in the period three years post-IPO (see text accompanying n 223 above).

286 Bennedsen and Nielsen (2006) (n 108 above 26).

287 Cronqvist and Nilsson (2003) (n 103 above 714).

after-operations. Potentially, in low investor protection jurisdictions, if related-party transaction regulations, legal enforcement and accounting standards are lax, profits could be tunnelled to the controller or its related-parties; particularly, if such tunnelling involves outright stealing, operating performance may continue to appear robust even though expropriation of the public shareholders is occurring. However, in developed jurisdictions, such as the United States, where most of the studies have been conducted, it is unlikely that such widespread stealing could occur.[288] The United States embraces resilient auditing standards and anti-fraud laws, and, with respect to related-party transactions, or conflicted transactions as they are labelled in the United States, the US courts uphold strong conflict of interest standards.[289] In any case, it is difficult to contemplate how such extraction could occur without eventually harming profits in future years, which would, in contradiction to the empirical evidence, be reflected by a negative overall correlation between operating performance and dual-class structure. As referenced in Chapter 6, instances of prohibited or fraudulent extraction by controllers of dual-class firms in developed jurisdictions are rare.[290] It is accepted that in low investor protection jurisdictions, it is possible that the results of operating performance studies may not (if they only comprise small samples over short time periods) reflect expropriation of public shareholders occurring after-profits. However, in a jurisdiction such as the United States, with strong accounting standards, a pervasive financial press and a robust enforcement environment, after-profits controller benefit extraction cannot explain why dual-class stock is generally negatively correlated with firm value, even though operating performance of dual-class firms is at least as good as, and in many cases better than, one share, one vote firms.

288 *ibid.*

289 For example, in Delaware, if conflicted transactions are challenged by stockholders with no interest in the transaction, alleging that directors or officers have breached their fiduciary duties, the courts can subject the transaction to an 'entire fairness review' (L. Bebchuk and A. Hamdani, 'Independent Directors and Controlling Shareholders' (2017) 165 *U. Pa. L. R.* 1271, 1282; *Weinberger* v. *UOP, Inc.*, 457 A.2d 701, 703 (Del. 1983)). Under an entire fairness review, unless specific processes have been followed by the company, the 'business judgment rule', pursuant to which the courts will otherwise defer to the judgment of management will not be applied (*Kahn* v. *Tremont Corp.*, 694 A.2d 422, 428 (Del. 1997); *Weinberger* v. *UOP, Inc.*, 426 A.2d 1333, 1346 (Del. Ch. 1981)). If the transaction has been approved by a committee of independent directors, the burden of proof in relation to the entire fairness standard shifts to the plaintiff (*Kahn* v. *Tremont Corp.*, 694 A.2d 422, 428 (Del. 1997)), although in the presence of a controlling shareholder, Delaware case law has been mixed in relation to whether a transaction can be 'cleansed' in this way (the Courts appear to take into account any ties that the independent directors may have to the controller that could impact genuine independence – Bebchuk and Hamdani (*ibid* 1289)). The burden can also be shifted if the company pre-approves the transaction through a majority of the minority vote (*Kahn* v. *Lynch Communication Systems, Inc.*, 638 A.2d 1110, 1115–1116 (Del. 1994)). In the context of controlling shareholder firm mergers, the Courts have recognised a dual-approval process such that if a committee of independent directors approves the transaction and it is further approved by a majority of the minority shareholders, an entire fairness review standard will no longer apply and the courts will revert to the business judgment rule (see *Kahn* v. *M&F Worldwide Corp.*, 88 A.3d 635, 644 (Del. 2014); J. Rosenberg and A. Lewis-Reisen, 'Controlling-Shareholder Related-Party Transactions Under Delaware Law' *Harvard Law School Forum on Corporate Governance and Financial Regulation* (2017) at 1, 8).

290 See the discussions on Adelphia and Hollinger International in Section 6.2.1 of Chapter 6.

The following concluding section continues with a discourse on what an amalgamation of the event-based, firm value, buy-and-hold stock return and operating performance empirical evidence tells us about dual-class firms.

7.7 CONCLUSION

The empirical evidence on dual-class stock presents a plethora of data to unpack. Therefore, this conclusion has been broken up into sections to obviate what would otherwise result in a rather impenetrable discussion. Although, at first glance, the empirical evidence may appear somewhat disparate, general trends can be observed, from which, notwithstanding the words of warning cautioned earlier, general conclusions can be formed. Finally, based upon those general conclusions, a roadmap forward will be introduced.

7.7.1 *General Trends*

The empirical evidence from event-based studies is inconclusive, but, as discussed, the significant impact of extraneous events surrounding changes of capital structure in such studies makes it problematic to interpret results and form conclusions, and such studies are, therefore, mainly excluded from the discussion that follows. The general trend in firm valuation studies is that dual-class structure leads to discounted share prices, although when splitting out particular qualities, it does appear that the market's distaste for such structures is ameliorated for certain types of firms. In contrast to the negativity surrounding firm valuation studies, it seems that the trend in buy-and-hold stock return and operating performance studies is certainly not negative. Arguably, although with a small sample of studies, US buy-and-hold stock return studies even trend toward a positive correlation with dual-class stock, and, with respect to operating performance, many studies, particularly in the United States, also show better operating performance for dual-class firms compared to one share, one vote firms. It is challenging to make robust conclusions when taking the different forms of empirical studies separately. However, when analyses of the trends are combined, a more coherent whole can be constructed. Given the highlighted issues with diversity, endogeneity and reverse causation, the most useful studies are those that research more than one aspect of firm performance, since they amalgamate performance aspects over the same samples of companies using the same methodologies and matching criteria. Smart et al. (2008),[291] Bennedsen and Nielsen (2006),[292] King and Santor (2008)[293] and Pajuste (2005)[294] are intriguing in this regard, and representative of the overall

[291] Smart et al. (2008) (n 54 above).
[292] Bennedsen and Nielsen (2006) (n 108 above).
[293] King and Santor (2008) (n 98 above).
[294] Pajuste (2005) (n 74 above).

trends.[295] They all seem to show that although dual-class firms display lower firm values compared to one share, one vote firms, this is not due to lower operating performance after the structure is implemented. Additionally, the study by Anderson et al. (2017)[296] was also redolent of the holistic trends, showing that dual-class structure correlates with greater stock returns but lower firm value.

7.7.2 *Explaining the General Trends*

The conundrum to be explained is why dual-class firms seem to show lower firm valuations than one share, one vote firms, but are not negatively correlated with buy-and-hold stock returns and operating performance? With respect to operating performance, as discussed earlier,[297] in weak investor protection jurisdictions, it is possible that expropriation of inferior-voting shareholders occurs after-profits, in which case operating performance may appear robust even while shareholder value is eroded, leading to lower firm values. However, in strong investor protection jurisdictions, such as the United States, where most of the studies have been conducted, it is unlikely that after-profits expropriation is taking place on a widespread basis, and, even if it were, it would not explain the corresponding greater buy-and-hold stock returns that most US studies show are earned by dual-class firm portfolios as compared to one share, one vote portfolios. Therefore, a more likely explanation is that outside investors perceive dual-class stock to represent an incentivisation structure where the extraction of controller benefits by the controller that are detrimental to the company outweighs the benefits that the structure presents in enabling the controller to manage the business in a manner that is beneficial to all shareholders. As such, investors apply a discount to dual-class firms to protect themselves from potential expropriation that may cause a future decrease in profitability in circumstances where they are powerless to remove inside management.[298] The logic is that by applying the relevant discount to stock price, once the relevant expropriation takes place, the investors are not prejudiced and should earn similar returns to firms with one share, one vote structure. However, with most US studies finding that those investors earn greater returns by investing in portfolios of dual-class firms than portfolios of similar one share, one vote firms, it is possible that the discounts in many cases are too high. The study by Anderson et al. (2017)[299] is pertinent, since it examined both buy-and-hold stock returns and firm valuations for the same sample of dual-class firms; dual-class firms had lower firm

[295] Also note that Barontini and Caprio (2006) (n 100 above) showed that dual-class structure reduced firm value and operating performance in family-controlled firms, but those firms still showed greater firm value and operating performance than non-family-controlled firms (nn 139–142 and 263–264 and accompanying text).

[296] Anderson et al. (2017) (n 19 above).

[297] See nn 286–290 above and accompanying text.

[298] Smart et al. (2008) (n 54 above 113).

[299] Anderson et al. (2017) (n 19 above).

values than matched one share, one vote firms, but produced higher average buy-and-hold annual returns over a period between 2001 and 2015. It would seem that investors protect themselves 'too much'. They are earning a premium by investing in dual-class firms. Investors may view such immoderate returns as compensation for taking the risk that excessive expropriation may occur at some point in the future,[300] but it is not justified – investors do not deserve a 'reward' or compensation for taking the risk that expropriation which exceeds the benefits of the structure will occur at some point in the future, since most operating performance studies do not show dual-class firms to be less profitable than one share, one vote firms, and, in the United States, mainly better operating performance is shown to accrue to dual-class firms. The expected excessive expropriation does not in fact come to pass.[301]

7.7.3 *Are There Other Justifications for the Discounts Applied to Dual-Class Firm Values?*

On first blush, taking the empirical evidence as a whole, it does not appear that the discounts applied to dual-class firms are warranted, since, overall, most studies show that the returns accruing to dual-class firm inferior-voting shares are greater than those accruing to one share, one vote firm shares, and operating performance studies show that dual-class firms perform at least as well as, if not stronger than, one share, one vote firms. In certain circumstances, though, arguments could perhaps be made that discounts on dual-class firm values are justified. The study by Kim and Michaely (2018), for example, suggests that after a certain period of time during a dual-class firm's life-cycle, operating performance starts to diminish to the extent that such firms underperform one share, one vote firms[302] (although it should be noted that a much earlier study with a shorter sampling period showed dual-class firm operating performance declining at a lower rate than one share, one vote firms[303]). Additionally, other studies suggest that in certain situations, whether that be as a result of general financial conditions (such as during an economic financial crisis)[304] or as a result of firm-specific conditions (such as where the firm has high free cash-flows),[305] the incentives and/or opportunities for pernicious controller benefit extraction increase, which may lead to decreased stock returns or operating performance. Either discrete shocks lead to an environment in which pernicious controller benefit extraction in dual-class firms becomes more likely, or at some

300 See n 208 above and accompanying text.

301 Also see Bauguess et al. (2012) (n 186 above), who showed increased operating performance for 'controller equity sale' firms recapitalising into dual-class structure to correspond with large economically significant (although not statistically significant due to the small sample size) buy-and-hold stock returns over the same period of time.

302 See n 249 above and accompanying text.

303 See n 223 above and accompanying text.

304 See nn 203–204 above and accompanying text.

305 See n 252 above and accompanying text.

point in a dual-class firm's life-cycle, the benefits of the structure that drive stock returns and/or operating performance are dominated by the detriments. Where expropriative behaviour is incentivised, discounts may be justified, and perhaps it is for those situations that investors will only invest at discounted prices in case a firm slips into a position where expropriation is incentivised.[306] However, this can be punitive for those dual-class firms that will never actually shift into a negative tradeoff position. Even in relation to firm age, it is difficult to maintain that the operating performance of all dual-class firms will disproportionately decline as they become older and eventually slip into negative tradeoff territory. Therefore, although those discounts could be justified for certain types of firms or in certain situations, since the empirical evidence from firm valuation studies shows dual-class firms (usually across a wide range of types and ages) to be, on average, discounted, even though, on average, they show at least as good operating performance and buy-and-hold stock returns compared to one share, one vote firms, those discounts are not being applied with sufficient preciseness.

If discounts are being applied indiscriminatorily, then how to explain those studies that show that, for certain types of firms, dual-class firms are valued greater than one share, one vote firms – that would suggest that the market is becoming more sophisticated and granular in recognising those firms that present lesser risks, rather than simply applying a staple discount across the board. For example, studies have indicated that dual-class firms may show either greater or similar firm valuations than one share, one vote firms, where those firms have better quality management,[307] constitute the rare cases where they are not controlled by family controllers,[308] are high-growth firms,[309] have low free cash-flow,[310] require external financing,[311] are more transparent in their disclosures,[312] are younger[313] or have only recently undergone IPO.[314] However, outside of those firms the market appears to significantly discount dual-class firms in a manner generally unjustified by performance and stock returns. Furthermore, even where the market recognises the benefits of dual-class structure, it may still be applying a discount; for example, Böhmer et al. (1996)[315] found that dual-class firms were both valued more than one share, one vote firms and produced larger buy-and-hold stock returns than one share, one vote firms, and Nüesch (2016)

306 In some jurisdictions, lower firm value may result from dual-class firms being forsaken by a large proportion of individuals, driving down share price. However, at least in the United States, it appears that institutional investors do not shun dual-class firms (see n 209 above), and, therefore, lower firm valuation reflects the lower price at which investors are willing to purchase stock.

307 Chemmanur et al. (2011) (n 105 above).

308 Anderson et al. (2017) (n 19 above); Claessens et al. (2002) (n 98 above).

309 Jordan et al. (2016) (n 101 above).

310 Bozec and Laurin (2008) (n 92 above).

311 Nüesch (2016) (n 9 above).

312 Anderson et al. (2009) (n 107 above).

313 Kim and Michaely (2018) (n 47 above).

314 Cremers et al. (2018) (n 105 above).

315 Böhmer et al. (1996) (n 34 above).

found that the positive correlation between dual-class structure for firms requiring external finance and firm performance was much greater for ROA than Tobin's Q.[316] Similarly, in relation to antitakeover mechanisms (including dual-class stock), Chemmanur et al. (2011) showed that positive abnormal buy-and-hold stock returns attach to high-quality management firms with antitakeover devices that also showed valuation premia.[317] Therefore, positive or neutral dual-class correlations with firm value may not fully respect the significant outperformance shown by many of those types of firms. In those cases, the overall positive effects of dual-class stock on firm value mask the discounts being applied. Further research combining firm valuation, buy-and-hold stock returns and operating performance appraisals across sub-samples of dual-class firms, distinguished on the basis of firm and controller qualities, will be valuable in discerning the market's treatment of specific types of dual-class firms. Pertinently, though, a survey of 445 worldwide institutional investors with over $4.9 trillion of assets under management found that 80 per cent of such investors routinely expect a discount on any company employing control-enhancing mechanisms such as dual-class stock,[318] and, in Sweden, it was found that valuation discounts were only applied to dual-class firms after foreign investment rules were relaxed, even though there were no commensurate changes in operating performance. Both sets of findings are indicative of large institutional investors seeking indiscriminatory dual-class firm discounts that impact dual-class firms on a wholesale basis.[319]

An alternative explanation for low firm valuations in the face of high operating performance is that investors may apply a discount to dual-class firms due to the ability of the controller to effectively veto takeovers that could otherwise earn investors a windfall to market price; however, again, such a discount is not empirically justified, since the empirical evidence is inconclusive as to whether takeovers of dual-class firms are in fact less prevalent than one share, one vote firms,[320] and, to the extent that takeovers do occur, the windfalls to investors are generally greater.[321] As such, it is unlikely that such concerns can fully explain the discrepancy in firm values of dual-class firms when compared to their operating performances.

[316] Nüesch (2016) (n 9 above 542).
[317] Chemmanur et al. (2011) (n 105 above).
[318] ISS Report (2007) (n 95 above 88).
[319] Holmén (2011) (n 108 above). A recent study, though, suggests a more nuanced dynamic when it comes to firm valuations than conventionally expected, and found that for founder-controlled firms, IPO valuations positively correlated with the founder's voting/cash-flow divergence, but negatively correlated with the square of the founder's voting/cash-flow divergence (Aggarwal et al. (2020) (n 19 above 34)). The insinuation is that the market recognises the benefit of a founder implementing a voting/cash-flow divergence in principle, but will penalise the firm if the divergence becomes too extreme. Although the study did not assess Tobin's Q over time or specifically compare dual-class to one share, one vote firms, it does bring into stark focus the potential need to protect existing public investors from a possible decline in share value if the founder's voting/cash-flow divergence reduces post-IPO (see Section 9.6.4 of Chapter 9).
[320] See Section 6.2.6 of Chapter 6.
[321] See Section 6.3.4 of Chapter 6.

7.7.4 So What Does the Empirical Evidence Tell Us?

So what does the empirical evidence mean for the potential for dual-class stock on the premium tier? Importantly, no broad pattern has emerged that suggests that dual-class stock harms outside investors from the perspective of both buy-and-hold stock returns and operating performance. On the contrary, there is some evidence that dual-class stock is beneficial to outside investors with a number of buy-and-hold stock return and operating performance studies showing dual-class firms to perform better on those measures than one share, one vote firms. Even though there are certainly flaws in much of the empirical evidence (as described in the 'Words of Warning' sections earlier in this chapter), and the numbers of empirical studies, particularly in the area of buy-and-hold stock returns, are small, it is instructive that there are very few studies that give any suggestion that dual-class firms perform worse than one share, one vote firms on buy-and-hold stock return and operating performance measures. If the policy priority is simply the protection of public investors, it does not seem that those investors require 'saving from themselves' so to speak – the empirical evidence does not suggest that dual-class firms are riskier investments than one share, one vote firms, and even to the extent that there are potential risks in dual-class stock, generally, investors apply a discount to dual-class firms, purportedly to protect themselves.[322] No institutional investor would describe itself as meek or naïve, and in jurisdictions with high levels of sophisticated investors, such as in the United Kingdom, those investors are well-placed to protect themselves through discounts, and, therefore, especially if additionally buttressed by robust investor protections, the justification to permit dual-class stock is stronger.[323] Less sophisticated investors also benefit from those discounts, since with institutional investors comprising the vast majority of investors in the UK public company market,[324] such discounting by institutional investors will filter into the market price of the shares. Similarly, passive index-tracker funds, which have no choice but to invest in dual-class firms if they are included on a relevant index,[325] would also invest on the basis of prices moderated by the discounts applied by active investors. Although in individual circumstances the discount applied may underestimate risks,[326] on average it seems that investors are pricing-in their risk, and, if anything, the average discount applied by outside investors is not justified. The dual-class stock tradeoff does not have a negative tilt, yet investors continue to discount dual-class firms.

322 The validity of a policy goal to prohibit dual-class stock as a result of lower firm value when operating performance is not weaker was questioned by Bennedsen and Nielsen (2006) (n 108 above 28).

323 A similar argument was made by Gurrea (2019) (n 83 above para. 7.2).

324 If individuals, charities and public sector bodies are excluded, UK and global institutions hold the remainder of UK equities, amounting to 77.77 per cent of UK listed shares as of 31 December 2018 (Calculated using data from: ONS, 'Ownership of UK Quoted Shares: 2018' (January 2020)).

325 See Section 1.5.4 of Chapter 1.

326 See, for example, nn 203–204 above and accompanying text.

As discussed in Chapter 5, protecting public investors from controlling shareholder abuses is the principal concern of the UK regulators when considering dual-class stock on the premium tier. If the evidence, in fact, shows that investors are able to financially protect themselves from the risks of abuse, one may suggest that the premium tier should open the doors to dual-class stock, and enjoy the commensurate benefits from attracting more listings. However, simply flinging open the doors may not be the answer to attract the plethora of listings, especially in the tech sphere, which the regulators desire. The empirical evidence indicates, especially when considering the United States as an equity market similar to the United Kingdom, that the share prices of dual-class firms would be subject to significant discounts. In a variation on the 'market for lemons' theme, if investors are not able to ascertain where on the dual-class stock tradeoff see-saw an individual firm will place, they will seek protective discounts no matter the quality of the firm and even if the controller only intends to extract benign controller benefits.[327] In a pure 'market for lemons', the 'good' sellers of equity will be deterred from entering the market, leaving a market dominated by 'bad' actors. In the context of dual-class stock, a vicious circle could develop, since high costs of capital could even motivate greater extraction of pernicious pecuniary controller benefits post-IPO in an attempt by the controller to compensate itself for having previously sold equity at IPO at a lower price than would have been the case under one share, one vote.[328] Clearly, though, given the empirical evidence on buy-and-hold stock returns and operating performance, unlike a pure 'market for lemons': (i) not all 'good' dual-class firm controllers are deterred from listing, meaning that, in many cases, the value to the controller of benign controller benefits outweighs the lower valuations of equity; and (ii) the market may be organically protected from the worst dual-class firms to a degree by rejecting some 'bad' dual-class firms – those firms will abandon dual-class structure if it appears that institutional investor interest in the flotation will be low.[329] However, although a pure 'market for lemons' may not emerge, the higher costs of capital for dual-class firms could still have substantive repercussions. As discussed, the market does, to a degree, identify some firms which investors perceive to present lower risks as dual-class firms, but, on the whole, the market does not seem to sufficiently identify 'good' controllers (considering the large discounts applied to dual-class firms, even though, overall, buy-and-hold stock returns, and, arguably, operating performance is better for such firms). Accordingly, the possibility remains that some 'good' potential dual-class firm controllers will eschew flotations if costs of capital are high. One empirical study found that the dual-class stock discount is greater the smaller the firm.[330] This is a critical consideration in the context of attracting tech firms to the premium tier. With, as outlined in Chapter 1,

327 G. Akerlof, 'The Market for "Lemons": Quality, Uncertainty and the Market Mechanism' (1970) 84 *Q. J. Econ.* 488; Cheffins (1997) (n 89 above 130).

328 Gordon (1988) (n 49 above 74).

329 For example, see the discussions on WeWorks and Uber in Section 6.3.3 of Chapter 6.

330 A. Grinapell, 'Dual-Class Stock Structure and Firm Innovation' (2020) 25 *SJLBF* 40, 65.

British tech firms regularly being acquired by foreign companies, if the cost of capital for a growing tech firm is too great, the danger will continue to subsist that such a firm will be bought out by a larger foreign firm before it has even had the opportunity to grow to a size at which the cost of capital on the premium tier becomes feasible. Even if that firm does list rather than succumbing to a buyout, it will do so at a later stage, precluding public investors from participating in significant early growth.[331] Additionally, for a dual-class firm that does list on the premium tier, continued high costs of capital could result in the controller unifying the share structure to one share, one vote at a time when it may be more beneficial to long-term success to continue with a dual-class structure (especially if the relevant company is seeking equity finance to grow).[332]

7.7.5 *Does the Empirical Evidence Prove that Dual-Class Stock Is Superior to One Share, One Vote?*

A combination of the buy-and-hold stock return and operating performance studies could be interpreted as exposing the myth of one share, one vote, and that, instead, firms and investors would be benefitted by founders always choosing dual-class stock over one share, one vote at IPO. However, the empirical evidence only compares existing dual-class firms to existing similar one share, one vote firms. It certainly cannot be categorically said that those firms that did list with dual-class stock have performed better than they would have done had they listed with one share, one vote. There may not be an accurate method in testing that contention. However, as discussed in Chapter 1, in the United Kingdom, at least in the technology sphere, those firms that would otherwise avail themselves of dual-class stock do not appear to be nevertheless listing as one share, one vote firms. If dual-class structure does not harm public investors, it is rational to liberalise the market to increase the chances that large private UK tech companies will list and give public shareholders the opportunity to garner positive returns. Investors are better off with those firms listing with dual-class stock, than not listing at all.[333]

The United States, as ever, provides a reasonable testing ground. In a study of long-term US stock market returns, Bessembinder (2018) found that the net gain for the US stock market between 1926 and 2016 can be attributed to only 4 per cent of its listed companies.[334] The study emphasises the importance of investing in the most successful companies for stock market investors. If the market misses out on investing in a vanguard company, it can significantly impact investor wealth. For example, total returns on Google stock, fifteen years after its IPO, were around 400 per cent, compared to approximately 250 per cent for the S&P 500 during the

331 See Section 1.5.5 of Chapter 1.

332 Also see n 260 above and accompanying text.

333 A similar argument was made by Anh et al. (2020) (n 4 above 137).

334 Henrik Bessembinder, 'Do Stocks Outperform Treasury Bills?' (2018) 129 *J. Fin. Econ.* 440, 456.

same period.[335] During that period, Google became the third largest company in the world by market capitalisation.[336] Similarly, total returns on Facebook stock soared by 400 per cent in the seven years after its IPO in 2012, compared to approximately 170 per cent for the S&P 500 during the same period.[337] Three of the twenty best-performing stocks of the last decade have been dual-class corporations.[338] Further, a study examining the S&P 500 noted that had the index included new dual-class stock issuers since 2017, when, as discussed in Chapter 2, such firms were excluded from the index,[339] returns would have been significantly higher for a notional investor tracking the index.[340] Extrapolating from such considerations, in the context of sunset clauses,[341] Sharfman (2019) noted the importance of ensuring that the best performing firms are able to adopt the governance structures that give them the optimum opportunities to succeed – '... inhibiting one company from becoming the next Alphabet or Facebook, it is one company too many'.[342] Even if it were the case that those dual-class firms that have listed in the United States could have generated greater shareholder returns if they had listed as one share, one vote firms, if the availability of dual-class stock instigates firms to list in the first place, given that, overall, it appears that investors in dual-class stock are not harmed, a prohibition of dual-class stock can become self-defeating for investors.

7.7.6 *The Way Forward*

Based upon the empirical evidence, dual-class firms do not, overall, financially harm public shareholders. In Chapter 6, a dual-class stock tradeoff was formulated

335 Anna Hecht, 'If You Invested $1,000 in Google 10 Years Ago, Here's How Much You'd Have Now' *CNBC* (8 October 2019), www.cnbc.com/2019/10/08/what-a-1000-dollar-investment-in-google-would-be-worth-after-10-years.html.

336 Tim Bradshaw and Adam Samson, 'Alphabet Overtakes Apple as World's Third-Biggest Company' *Financial Times* (3 January 2019), www.ft.com/content/56ad7d64-0f66-11e9-acdc-4d9976f1533b.

337 Anna Hecht, 'If You Invested $1,000 in Facebook at Its IPO, Here's How Much Money You'd Have Now' *CNBC* (25 October 2019), www.cnbc.com/2019/10/25/what-a-1000-dollar-investment-in-facebook-ipo-would-be-worth-now.html.

338 Philip van Doorn, 'These are the 20 Best-Performing Stocks of the Past Decade, and Some of Them Will Surprise You' *MarketWatch* (28 December 2019), www.marketwatch.com/story/these-are-the-20-best-performing-stocks-of-the-past-decade-and-some-of-them-will-surprise-you-2019-12-09. Regeneron Pharmaceuticals, Constellation Brands and Charter Communications are the three dual-class corporations in the list of the twenty best-performing stocks of the last decade.

339 S&P Dow Jones Indices, 'S&P Dow Jones Indices Announces Decision on Multi-Class Shares and Voting Rights' (31 July 2017), www.spice-indices.com/idpfiles/spice-assets/resources/public/documents/561162_spdjimulti-classsharesandvotingrulesannouncement7.31.17.pdf?force_download=true; see Section 2.3 of Chapter 2.

340 B. Sharfman and V. Deluard, 'How Discretionary Decision-Making Has Created Performance and Legal Disclosure Issues for the S&P 500 Index' (2021) 1, 33, https://papers.ssrn.com/sol3/papers.cfm?abstract_id=3794306.

341 For further detail on sunset clauses, see Chapter 9.

342 B. Sharfman, 'The Undesirability of Mandatory Time-Based Sunsets in Dual Class Share Structures: A Reply to Bebchuk and Kastiel' (2019) 93 *South. Calif. Law Rev. Postscript* 1, 10.

based upon the theoretical benefits and costs to public shareholders of dual-class stock. Moving into reality, the bulk of the empirical evidence suggests that the dual-class stock tradeoff is tilted in a positive (or at the very least, neutral) direction, where benign controller benefits generally outweigh (or at least equal) pernicious controller benefits. Of course, there will be instances where dual-class firms fail, or where dual-class stock for a particular firm is not the optimum structure and the dual-class stock tradeoff is tilted in a negative direction. However, the same is true of one share, one vote firms – one share, one vote, like dual-class stock, has, for public shareholders, possible benefits, such as greater public shareholder influence over management, and possible costs, such as agency costs and potential short-term outlooks. Investors often hold diversified portfolios,[343] which insulate those investors from those firms that do fail, whether that be in the one share, one vote or dual-class stock worlds. Even if those investors only held portfolios of dual-class stock, so long as they were diversified across all dual-class companies, they will, based upon the empirical evidence, likely earn positive returns. The empirical evidence does not support a prohibition of dual-class stock from the premium tier, and, with a view to attracting more listings, especially of high-growth tech companies, the FCA should support the adoption of dual-class stock on the premium tier.

However, harking back to the earlier discussion on the 'lemons trade',[344] even though the empirical evidence shows that dual-class firms make lemonade, the market assumes it is investing in lemons, and, therefore, it would be shrewd to take a cautious approach. The premium tier is a conservative market that is only just now seriously contemplating dual-class stock after decades of formal or informal prohibition, with a powerful institutional investor base, which, as remarked in Chapter 2, is openly sceptical to dual-class stock. Ushering in the new world of dual-class stock in an unrestricted manner may not be a prudent approach, since the relaxation of the premium tier prohibition of dual-class stock will inevitably provoke a backlash from the UK institutional investor community. The path toward dual-class stock could be smoothed by accompanying the introduction of dual-class stock with carefully formulated limitations as to their use, which will deter and prevent the most egregious types of pernicious controller benefit extraction. Cognisant of the scepticism directed at dual-class stock by the institutional investor community, those limitations or restrictions should sufficiently constrain the controllers of dual-class stock companies to give institutional investors the confidence that they will not be excessively expropriated. In a manner of speaking, this would be a similar approach to that taken with respect to one share, one vote controlling shareholder companies listed on the premium tier – those companies are permitted to list, provided that they conform to heightened corporate governance requirements that notionally protect public shareholders from

343 With respect to the benefits and optimality of diversification as an investment strategy, see H. Markowitz, 'Portfolio Selection' (1959) 7 *J. Financ.* 77.

344 See the discussion on the variation of the 'market for lemons' theme earlier (nn 327–329 above and accompanying text).

abuse.[345] Furthermore, in a world of premium listed dual-class firms, regulation, judiciously applied, could be used to assuage concerns of investors that they are participating in the 'lemons trade', and therefore reduce the costs of capital for dual-class issuers, since the level of discount required by inferior-voting shareholders will be necessarily less. The FCA has the opportunity to not only enhance the listing possibilities for founders through the use of dual-class stock but also further promote listings in the United Kingdom by providing an environment in which the costs of capital for dual-class firms are lower than would otherwise be the case (and potentially lower than other jurisdictions where regulatory protections for inferior-voting shareholders are lower). Lower costs of capital should attract better-quality dual-class firms to the market and, once listed, they will not be pressured into prematurely unifying into one share, one vote to generate further finance for growth at a fair price.

Ideally, any restrictions that accompany the welcoming of dual-class firms should be shaped around the indicators of greater expropriation incentivisation or likelihood. Formulating those restrictions is challenging given the available empirical evidence. Even with respect to the time-dimension, and giving investors greater protection as a firm ages, it is highly unlikely that a dual-class firm's performance declines merely because it is becoming older.[346] It is likely that changes, such as shifts from founders to heirs, diminishing investment opportunities and waning CEO powers, are occurring for which time is simply a proxy.[347] As studies become more sophisticated (particularly in relation to sub-sampling), a more complex picture may emerge, assisting in the determination of whether brightline rules can be developed to delineate between types of firms for which, or contexts in which, dual-class stock will generally be overall beneficial or costly to outside shareholders,[348] and how those qualities shift over time. However, the desire for

345 For examples of the existing restrictions and corporate governance requirements imposed on premium tier controlling shareholder companies, see Chapter 8.

346 However, in one study, the SEC compared post-IPO firm values of dual-class firms which had implemented mechanisms that convert them into one share, one vote after specific periods of time ('time-dependent sunset clauses'), with firm values of perpetual dual-class firms. In preliminary results, the former were found to outperform the latter from two years after IPO (see R. Jackson Jr. Speech, 'Perpetual Dual-Class Stock: The Case against Corporate Royalty' (15 February 2018, San Francisco, California). However, there are numerous reasons to explain the results that do not necessarily relate to the governance of those firms (B. Sharfman, 'On Governance: SEC Commissioner Robert Jackson and Perpetual Dual Class Shares' *The Conference Board* (2018), www.conference-board.org/blog/environmental-social-governance/Robert-Jackson-Perpetual-Dual-Class-Shares?blogid=3), and it would be useful for further research to assess the contrast in operating performance between sunset and non-sunset dual-class firms over extended periods of time. A sufficiently robust sample set may not, though, be available yet, since firms have only started adopting time-dependent sunset clauses in anything but negligible numbers recently (for further detail on sunset clauses, see Chapter 9).

347 W. Johnson et al., 'The Lifecycle Effects of Firm Takeover Defenses' (2018) 1, 5, http://dx.doi.org/10.2139/ssrn.2808208.

348 Adams and Ferreira (2008) also suggest further work in this field (n 3 above 84). Further research would be welcomed on the effect of external economic shocks, transparency, growth opportunities and levels of free cash-flow.

further research should not delay the emergence of dual-class firms on the premium tier. Restrictions could be fine-tuned over time, and, as has been the course followed in jurisdictions such as Hong Kong, Shanghai, Tokyo, Singapore and India, dual-class stock could be permitted with broad and flexible restrictions, since more granular empirical evidence that is specifically relevant to the jurisdiction in question will only be available once dual-class firms have become more widespread locally. Importantly, though, restrictions must tread a fine line between protecting inferior-voting shareholders and maintaining the attractiveness of such structures to controllers. If restrictions are so severe that they eliminate nearly all controller benefits, including those that are benign or only mildly malign, founders will remain reticent to list their firms, obviating the purpose of permitting dual-class stock in the first place. The proposals of the UK Listing Review[349] provide a case in point of an approach that prioritises protection of public shareholders to the substantive detriment of many of the benign controller benefits sought by founders.[350] As discussed in Chapter 1, the restrictions are so severe that the proposals cannot be considered to be 'genuine' dual-class stock, will unlikely satiate the needs of founders and will not attract the plethora of high-growth company listings envisaged.[351] With more balanced restrictions attached to 'genuine' dual-class stock, IPOs can be encouraged without seriously prejudicing public shareholders, and, accordingly, in Chapter 9 some of the potential varieties of inferior-voting shareholder protections are discussed with a view to scoping out a balanced protection package for inferior-voting shareholders in dual-class firms. Prior to that discussion, though, the next chapter will outline, and scrutinise the effectiveness of, the already existing UK regulations and constraints that could protect inferior-voting shareholders if dual-class firms became established on the premium tier.

349 See Section 1.5.7 of Chapter 1.
350 See Section 6.5 of Chapter 6.
351 Section 1.5.7 of Chapter 1; also see *ibid.*

PART III

Formulating a Policy on Dual-Class Stock

8

The Existing Constraints

... the passions of men will not conform to the dictates of reason and justice, without constraint[1]

8.1 INTRODUCTION

In the previous chapter, it was noted that the empirical evidence does not support the prohibition of dual-class firms from the premium tier. Dual-class firms, on average, appear to operationally perform at least as well as one share, one vote firms, and a number of studies suggest that investment in dual-class firms can result in greater returns than investment in similar one share, one vote firms. The receipt of greater returns is partly a manifestation of the market overly discounting dual-class firms when not warranted by the ensuing operating performance of such firms. Excessive discounting, and the corresponding increase in the cost of capital, can create indirect injurious effects, deterring the listing of dual-class firms, incentivising pernicious controller benefit extraction in listed dual-class firms and encouraging premature unifications of dual-class stock into one share, one vote at a time when the company is seeking growth through equity issuances. Furthermore, it is unfair for benign controllers to suffer for the sins of pernicious controllers by the application of uniform discounts across all dual-class firms. Some empirical evidence suggests that the discount applied by the market may be tempered for certain types of dual-class firms, but the research is in its nascent stages, and it is currently not conclusive that the market is adept at identifying which firms will be net-beneficial and which will be net-detrimental to public shareholders. Even in those cases where the market has seemingly applied a premium to particular dual-class firms compared to one share, one vote firms, research has shown that, based upon returns and operating performance, the premium is not sufficient and, therefore, the market may in fact still be discounting dual-class firms due to the risks perceived in investing therein.

[1] Alexander Hamilton (under the pseudonym, Publius), *The Federalist No. 15* (The Independent Journal, 1 December 1787).

It was further asserted in the previous chapter that the excessive discounts applied to dual-class firms could be reduced if the fears that investors have regarding being expropriated or lumbered with an underperforming entrenched management team could be assuaged. By constraining the abilities of a controller to expropriate inferior-voting shareholders or by granting governance rights to inferior-voting shareholders, those fears could be moderated. Not only would inferior-voting shareholders be protected from the worst potential excesses of controllers but also the costs of capital for dual-class firms would be reduced. In this Part III, therefore, a roadmap for the opening up of the premium tier to 'genuine' dual-class stock (rather than the 'dual-class-light' proposals of the UK Listing Review[2]) will be proposed, emphasising the need to accompany the relaxation of the premium tier rules with appropriate controller constraints and conditions. However, before suggesting possible regulations and constraints, it is apposite to consider the adequacy of existing aspects of the United Kingdom's legal, regulatory and market environment in potentially constraining the actions of dual-class controllers if dual-class stock were permitted on the premium tier. The relevant constraints are outlined in this chapter in the context of dual-class stock, divided into three main types: (i) legal/regulatory restrictions; (ii) market constraints; and (iii) 'psychological' constraints.

8.2 LEGAL/REGULATORY RESTRICTIONS

Laws and regulations already exist in the United Kingdom that could curtail the powers of dual-class controllers, if dual-class firms were welcomed on to the premium tier, and, echoing the sentiment of Holderness and Sheehan noted in Chapter 5, protect 'small' shareholders from harm.[3] Unsurprisingly, since those laws and regulations have not been specifically formulated with dual-class firms, and in some cases not even with controlling shareholders generally, in mind, a number of flaws are apparent in their efficacy in potentially constraining the acts of controllers of dual-class firms.

8.2.1 *Directors' Duties*

In the United Kingdom, directors owe duties, and their application can, in theory, constrain the extraction of controller benefits. Directors who owe their appointments to the controller may not, in practice, conduct themselves in a truly independent fashion,[4] but if he or she were to act in a manner that primarily serves the interests of the controller to the detriment of the company, that director would be breaching his or her duties. The relevant duties that could be breached include the

[2] See Section 1.5.7 of Chapter 1.
[3] C. Holderness and D. Sheehan, 'The Role of Majority Shareholders in Publicly Held Corporations: An Exploratory Analysis' (1988) 20 *J. Financ. Econ.* 317, 318. See Section 5.3 of Chapter 5.
[4] See Section 6.2.4 of Chapter 6.

duties to act in a way that the director considers, in good faith, would be most likely to promote the success of the company for the benefit of its members as a whole, to exercise independent judgment, to exercise reasonable care, skill and diligence and to avoid conflicts of interest.[5] In the normal course, those duties are owed to the company,[6] and only in very rare situations do directors owe duties to shareholders.[7]

Since the duties are owed to the company, the company is the proper plaintiff in such actions,[8] and, therefore, decisions to make a claim against a director for breach of duty is in the hands of the internal management organ of the company,[9] which, in most cases, is the board.[10] It is easy to suspect that directors serving on the same board may be reluctant to sue their own brethren, and, in many cases, the directors will have colluded together to cause the company to take the actions being challenged, making it even more unlikely that the directors will commence a claim against themselves. With those undercurrents in mind, shareholders have been imparted with a secondary avenue of enforcement through the statutory derivative claim procedure, pursuant to which shareholders can pursue a claim for negligence, default, breach of duty or breach of trust on behalf of the company.[11] With a dual-class firm, since any shareholder in the company can commence a derivative claim, it would appear that inferior-voting shareholders could possess a significant method by which to constrain and deter directors from managing the company primarily to extract controller benefits on behalf of the enhanced-voting shareholders. However, a number of hurdles must be succumbed to progress the derivative claim procedure.[12] Firstly, a two-step process must be respected prior to the substantive case being heard, commencing with the Court considering an application for leave, followed by a leave hearing. The application for leave will only be successful if the case identifies a prima facie claim based upon negligence, default, breach of duty or breach of trust,[13] and, at the leave hearing, the Court can dismiss the case on the basis of mandatory[14]

5 CA 2006, ss. 172, 173, 174 and 175, respectively.

6 CA 2006, s. 170(1); also see *Percival* v. *Wright* [1902] 2 Ch. 401.

7 Such as where the director (i) is dealing directly with, and acting as the agent of, the shareholders (*Allen* v. *Hyatt* (1914) 30 TLR 444); (ii) has been placed in a position of trust and confidence (by analogy to the New Zealand case of *Coleman* v. *Myers* [1977] 2 NZLR 255); or, potentially, (iii) in a takeover context, has a special relationship with the relevant shareholder (by analogy to the Australian case of *Brunninghausen* v. *Glavanics* (1999) 32 ACSR 294). See also *Vald Nielsen Holding A/S* v. *Baldorino* [2019] EWHC 1926.

8 *Foss* v. *Harbottle* (1843) 67 ER 189; *Prudential Assurance Co. Ltd.* v. *Newman Industries Ltd. (No. 2)* [1982] Ch. 204, 210.

9 *ibid*; *John Shaw & Sons (Salford) Ltd.* v. *Shaw* [1935] 2 KB 113; *MacDougall* v. *Gardiner* (1875) 1 Ch. D. 13.

10 Model PLC Articles, article 3.

11 CA 2006, ss. 260–264.

12 With the uncertainties inherent in clearing the hurdles prior to commencing the substantive derivative claim case, shareholders may be deterred from making use of the procedure (J. Armour, 'Derivative Actions: A Framework for Decisions' (2019) 135 *LQR* 421).

13 CA 2006, s. 261(2); *Iesini* v. *Westrip Holdings* [2011] 1 BCLC 498.

14 CA 2006, s. 263(2).

and discretionary[15] factors. Secondly, although derivative claims have become more accessible from a procedural and standing perspective since they took on a statutory footing,[16] from a practical perspective, for a shareholder with only a small interest in the relevant company, the potential benefits of making a claim will likely be far outweighed by the efforts and costs involved (since any successful remedy will accrue to the company itself[17]). If the inferior-voting shares are dispersed (which would likely be the case in the United Kingdom [18]), most shareholders will, individually, only hold small equity interests. Furthermore, it would be just as beneficial for that shareholder to 'free-ride' on the efforts of another shareholder (since the benefits of a successful claim that accrues to a shareholder will be the same regardless of the identity of the shareholder instigating the derivative claim).[19] Additionally, an aggrieved shareholder of a listed company may determine that it is more pragmatic to simply sell its shares on the market and exit, rather than commence a derivative procedure.[20] Thirdly, the Courts have historically shown significant judicial deference to the operational decisions of directors,[21] making successful claims challenging. Finally, although the Courts have the power to cause a company to indemnify a shareholder for the costs of pursuing a derivative claim on its behalf,[22] an indemnity will only be granted if it is required to ensure that a strong case that would otherwise not be commenced is pursued.[23] Therefore, if the claim is weak or if the shareholder in question has sufficient resources, the Court may not grant such an indemnity. The lack of certainty as to indemnification, and the 'loser-pays' civil procedure rules apparent in the United Kingdom,[24] pursuant to which the loser in a civil action is, as a general rule, required to pay the costs of the successful party, can increase the potential costs for small, inferior-voting shareholders. For all these reasons, shareholders may be deterred from commencing derivative claims against directors.

15 CA 2006, s. 263(3).

16 Prior to codification under CA 2006, derivative claims could only be pursued by shareholders under restrictive case law exceptions (see *Foss* v. *Harbottle* (1843) 67 ER 189).

17 *Spokes* v. *Grosvenor Hotel Co.* [1897] 2 QB 124, 128.

18 In relation to the dispersed ownership nature of the UK capital markets, see Section 2.3 of Chapter 2.

19 For a succinct description of the free-rider issue, see J. Gordon, 'Ties that Bond: Dual Class Common Stock and the Problem of Shareholder Choice' (1988) 76 *Cal. L. Rev.* 1, 44.

20 These practical deterrents may explain why, since derivative claims took on a statutory footing under the CA 2006, from a search on 26 March 2020 of the English case law database of Lexis Library using the terms 'derivative claim', 'plc' and 'Companies Act 2006', there have only been four instances where a minority shareholder of a UK public company has applied for leave to commence a derivative claim, and in all of those cases leave was refused (*Mission Capital plc* v. *Sinclair* [2008] EWHC 1339; *Bridge* v. *Daley* [2015] EWHC 2121 (Ch); *Robert Glew & Denton and Co Trustees Ltd and another* v. *Matossian-Rogers and others* [2019] EWHC 3183 (ch); *Kallakis* v. *AIB Group plc and Others* [2020] EWHC 460 (Comm)).

21 *Smith* v. *Fawcett* [1942] Ch. 304, 306; *Burland* v. *Earle* [1902] AC 83, 93.

22 *Wallersteiner* v. *Moir (No. 2)* [1975] QB 373.

23 *Smith* v. *Croft* [1986] 1 WLR 580.

24 CPR, Rule 44.2(2)(a). The Court does, though, have the discretion to make costs orders that deviate from strict loser-pays requirements (CPR, Rule 44.2(2)(b)).

The strict legal rules surrounding director liability should also not be taken in isolation. It has been identified that the greater the costs of taking legal action, the greater the level of self-dealing in which a controlling shareholder can engage before being subject to legal action.[25] Therefore, not only the strict legal rules applicable need to be considered, but also the practicalities of enforcing such rules. Owing to a weak litigious culture in the United Kingdom,[26] the legal constraints on the actions of controllers are not buttressed by effective enforcement, as compared to, for example, the United States.[27] Additionally, even if derivative claims are commenced, directors may not overly fear them, since they are often protected from out-of-pocket expenses by directors and officers (D&O) insurance policies and company indemnities.[28] Combined with the hurdles to commence derivative claims, it is therefore improbable that directors' duties will sufficiently deter the extraction of controller benefits by dual-class controllers.

8.2.2 *Unfair Prejudice*

Another theoretical English law protection that would be available to inferior-voting shareholders is the action of 'unfair prejudice'.[29] If a controller is extracting excessive controller benefits, an inferior-voting shareholder could claim that the affairs of the company are being conducted in a manner that is unfairly prejudicial to that shareholder.[30] Although unfair prejudice could result from non-compliance with a company's articles of association or other breaches of legal rights (to the extent that a shareholder is unfairly prejudiced by those breaches), the common law has also developed the remedy to encompass situations where informal rights have been breached even though there has not been any breach of legal rights.[31] Historically, such non-legal rights were claimed on the basis of a non-observance of the legitimate

25 Commentary by M. Huson in C. Holderness and D. Sheehan, 'Constraints on Large-Block Shareholders' in *Concentrated Corporate Ownership*, ed. R. Morck (University of Chicago Press, 2000) at 174.

26 The litigious culture and effectiveness of enforcement of corporate law by shareholders in the United Kingdom is discussed further in Section 9.3 of Chapter 9.

27 R. Gilson and B. Black, *The Law and Finance of Corporate Acquisitions* (Foundation Press, 1995) describes how, in the United States, minority shareholders are not, as a matter of strict legal law, well-protected, but in the context of corporate acquisitions, lawyers are risk averse owing to the litigious culture in the market, and generally advise clients to treat minorities fairly rather than to risk 'busted deals'.

28 D&O insurance and indemnities from companies in favour of directors against legal costs and damages (subject to certain limitations) are expressly permitted under CA 2006, ss. 232–234. See B. Cheffins and B. Black, 'Outside Director Liability across Countries' (2006) 84 *Texas L. Rev.* 1385; B. Black, 'The Legal and Institutional Preconditions for Strong Securities Markets' (2001) 48 *UCLA Law Rev.* 781.

29 CA 2006, s. 994.

30 *ibid.*

31 *O'Neill and Another* v. *Phillips and Others* [1999] 1 W.L.R. 1092 at 1099.

expectations of a shareholder,[32] but a more recent and restrictive interpretation requires the existence of an informal understanding between parties that results in an exercise of certain rights being subject to equitable considerations which would make the exercise of such rights unjust.[33] An inferior-voting shareholder could claim that the understanding when investing in the company was that the controller would not extract personal benefits, and excessive extraction is an unconscionable breach of that expectation. However, the Courts have generally been reluctant to entertain unfair prejudice claims against listed companies due to a desire to protect the 'credibility' of the public markets by ensuring that investors can rely upon all investor rights being exhaustively delineated in publicly available documentation.[34] Therefore, short of discriminatory fraud against an individual shareholder or the development of opt-out class action suits,[35] it is unlikely that unfair prejudice will form the basis of an effective inferior-voting shareholder protection in premium listed companies.[36]

8.2.3 *Takeovers*

On takeovers, public shareholders in UK listed companies are well-protected. In relation to public companies with registered offices in the United Kingdom, the Isle of Man or the Channel Islands[37] with securities traded on, inter alia, the Main Market, mandatory offer rules apply where any persons acting together in concert acquire shares carrying 30 per cent or more of the voting rights in that company; such persons must make an offer for all the remaining shares of each class in the company, at not less than the highest price offered for a particular class of shares in the twelve-month period prior to the offer.[38] Where an incumbent major shareholder already holds more than 30 per cent, but no more than 50 per cent, of the voting rights, it must make a similar offer if it (together with persons acting in

32 *Re Saul D Harrison & Sons plc* [1994] B.C.C. 475 at 490.

33 *O'Neill and Another* v. *Phillips and Others* [1999] 1 W.L.R. 1092 at 1102.

34 *Re Blue Arrow plc* [1987] Ch.D. 585; *Re Tottenham Hotspur plc* [1994] 1 BCLC 655; *Re Astec (BSR) plc* [1998] 2 BCLC 556 (note, though, that *dicta* suggests there may be scope to pursue an unfair prejudice claim, even in publicly listed companies, in instances of serious abuse of powers (*Re Saul D Harrison & Sons plc* [1994] B.C.C. 475 at 18 and 31) or serious mismanagement (*Re Macro (Ipswich) Ltd.* [1994] 2 BCLC 354 at 406)). Also see B. Cheffins, 'The Undermining of UK Corporate Governance (?)' (2013) 33 *OJLS* 503, 528.

35 Opt-out class action suits are discussed in more detail in Section 9.3 of Chapter 9. If the relevant act of the controller has unfairly prejudiced all public shareholders, the argument that the claim undermines the credibility of the public markets has less weight.

36 Also see the discussion on relationship agreements later in this chapter (n 85 below and accompanying text).

37 Takeover Code, Introduction Section 3. The Takeover Code also applies to public and, in certain circumstances, private companies, even if not currently listed, with registered offices and central management and control in the United Kingdom, the Channel Islands (in certain circumstances in relation to Guernsey) and, in certain circumstances, the Isle of Man (*ibid*).

38 Takeover Code, Rule 9.

concert) acquires an interest in any other shares which increases the percentage of shares carrying voting rights in which it is interested. Upon mandatory and voluntary bids, with multiple classes of shares, offers made for each class of shares must be 'comparable'.[39] 'Comparable' does not necessarily mean 'identical', and the Takeover Panel must be consulted,[40] but, prima facie, the Takeover Panel will insist that the ratio of the offer values be equal to 'the average of the ratios of the middle-market quotations taken from the Daily Official List over the course of the six months preceding the commencement of the offer period'.[41] Where the enhanced-voting shares are unlisted, the Takeover Panel would not be able to apply the voting premium formula in assessing 'comparable' price, if, for instance, a bidder triggers the Takeover Code's mandatory offer requirements by acquiring unlisted enhanced-voting shares. In such circumstances, it is difficult to envisage that the Takeover Panel will not insist that the same price be paid for equal equity interests, requiring that the price paid per listed inferior-voting share be the same as the highest price paid per unlisted enhanced-voting share. Indeed, the Takeover Panel confirmed in the case of Deliveroo's dual-class stock IPO on the standard tier[42] that upon any takeover offer, in order to be 'comparable', offers for enhanced-voting and inferior-voting shares would have to be made at the same price and on the same terms.[43] In practice, if dual-class firms were permitted on the premium tier, it is likely that the Takeover Panel would always require an applicant to specify in its issuer prospectus at the time of IPO exactly how the comparable pricing regime will apply to the inferior-voting shares. For example, the Takeover Panel may require simply confirmation that 'comparable' price means 'equal' price (as was the case with Deliveroo's IPO on the standard tier), or require the applicant to specify that the enhanced-voting shares will convert into inferior-voting shares on a 1:1 basis upon any transfer of such shares that triggers a change of control (essentially requiring a bidder to pay the same price for all classes of shares).[44]

39 *ibid* Rule 14.1.

40 *ibid* Rule 9.5.

41 *ibid* Notes to Rule 14.1.

42 See Section 1.5.6 of Chapter 1.

43 Deliveroo Holdings plc, 'Prospectus for the Offer of up to 384,615,384 Class A Shares at an Offer Price Expected to be between 390 and 460 pence per Class A Share and Admission to the Standard Listing Segment of the Official List and to Trading on the Main Market of the London Stock Exchange' (March 2021) at 175.

44 By way of analogy, the company British Energy granted a right to a UK Government entity in 2003 to convert certain payments due into convertible shares, the aggregate voting rights in relation to which would be restricted to 29.9 per cent to avoid the triggering of mandatory offer requirements. The terms of the convertible shares required them to be converted into ordinary shares upon a transfer, which led to the price payable per share being equal between convertible shares and ordinary shares when the company was acquired by EDF in 2009 (see Lake Acquisitions Limited (a wholly owned subsidiary of EDF S.A.), 'Recommended Offers for British Energy Group plc' (24 September 2008)). As a more recent example, The Hut Group, a standard listed company with classes of shares with differing voting rights in specified situations (see Section 1.5.5 of Chapter 1), outlined in its IPO issuing prospectus details as to how the Takeover Code will apply to its different classes of shares upon a takeover offer

Therefore, for companies to which the Takeover Code applies, it would not be possible for a bidder to acquire a stake giving effective control of the company without making an offer on similar terms to all the shareholders in the company. The relevance of this critical regulation is discussed throughout this book. For example, it prevents inferior-voting shareholders being subjugated to a new controller without first having the option to exit at a presumably fair price, and, therefore, to a degree, prevents a new third-party controller which was not contemplated by shareholders at the time of investment, from acquiring control of the enhanced-voting stock without the inferior-voting shareholders having the opportunity to sell on similar terms to the original controller. Furthermore, as discussed in Chapter 6, the regulation at the very least limits the level of any control premium that could be extracted by a dual-class controller upon a takeover of that company.[45]

In the context of dual-class stock, though, certain holes appear in the existing Takeover Code mandatory offer rules. For example, the Takeover Code does not protect inferior-voting shareholders where, albeit rarely, the controller merely sells a proportion of the enhanced-voting shares such that no new controller, or group of connected controllers, acquires a greater than 30 per cent interest. In such a situation, the erstwhile controller could lose overall control of the company, with control being in the hands of a small, but unassociated, group of shareholders. The inferior-voting shareholders would still be in a position where they have no influence over the management team of the company, but that management team would now be selected by a group of shareholders, rather than the original controller in which the inferior-voting shareholders had placed their faith at the time of IPO. Family transfers could also be problematic, since gifts of shares that would result in a person acquiring more than 30 per cent of the voting rights in the company will not automatically trigger a mandatory offer – the Takeover Code specifies that the Takeover Panel should be consulted in such cases,[46] and even if the Takeover Panel were to demand a mandatory offer, it is not obvious what offer price would be stipulated. Additionally, as discussed earlier, although, in the case of a triggering acquisition of unlisted enhanced-voting shares, it is likely that 'comparable' would be interpreted to require that an offer for listed inferior-voting shares is made at the same price offered for enhanced-voting shares, the position is not free from doubt. Finally, after the expiry of the UK/EU Withdrawal Agreement, the Takeover Code ceased to apply to those EEA companies listed on the Main Market which were previously subject to the requirements of the Takeover Code, and, therefore,

(THG Holdings plc, 'Prospectus for the Offer of up to 376,273,998 Ordinary Shares at an Offer Price of 500p per Ordinary Share and Admission to the Standard Listing Segment of the Official List and to Trading on the Main Market for Listed Securities of the London Stock Exchange' (10 September 2020) at 248), taking into account the loss of enhanced rights attached to the founder's 'special share' upon a transfer of that share (except upon a transmission of the special share to the founder's beneficiary upon his death) (THG Prospectus (*ibid* 21)).

45 See Section 6.2.7 of Chapter 6.

46 Takeover Code, Note 12 to Rule 9.1.

a company from outside of the United Kingdom, Isle of Man or Channel Islands may not be subject to equivalent mandatory offer requirements even though listed on the Main Market.[47] That final potential hole in the mandatory offer rules may be overstated though, since EU Member States are required to implement mandatory offer requirements (albeit, the thresholds at which they are triggered are Member State specific).[48] Therefore, if dual-class stock were to become permitted on the premium tier, although the mandatory bid rules of the Takeover Code would not apply to all dual-class firms, for a large number of companies, inferior-voting shareholders are likely to enjoy similar protections.[49]

8.2.4 *Relationship with the Controller*

Chapter 11 of the Listing Rules applies to transactions between a company and a 'related-party',[50] the definition of which includes a substantial shareholder (which, importantly in the context of dual-class stock, is based upon voting, rather than equity, ownership)[51] and its associates. Such transactions, above certain materiality thresholds,[52] must at least be confirmed by the company's sponsor to be fair and reasonable to its shareholders and disclosed upon the entering into of the transaction, or, if large enough, be pre-approved by shareholders independent from the related-party.[53] Premium listed companies are required to appoint a sponsor to advise the issuer on its listing obligations, and to give assurances to the FCA that

47 The Takeover Panel, Code Committee Response Statement RS2018/2, 'The United Kingdom's Withdrawal from the European Union' (6 March 2019) at 10. In relation to the transition period, see UK/EU Withdrawal Agreement, articles 126–132.

48 Takeover Directive, article 5. For example, 30 per cent thresholds apply in Germany, France, the Netherlands and Spain, with a 25 per cent threshold applying in Italy (Bonellierede, Bredin Prat, De Brauw, Hengeler Mueller, Slaughter and May and Uría Menéndez, 'Guide to Public Takeovers in Europe' (June 2016)).

49 As of 31 July 2020, from 1116 companies listed on the Main Market, 907 companies were registered in the United Kingdom, the Channel Islands or the Isle of Man, and 60 were registered in an EU Member State (derived from data disclosed in LSE, 'Issuer List' (31 July 2020), www.londonstockexchange.com/statistics/companies-and-issuers/companies-and-issuers.htm).

50 For the definition of 'related party', see LR 11.1.4R.

51 Subject to certain disregarded interests, a 'substantial shareholder' is any person who is entitled to exercise, or to control the exercise of, 10 per cent or more of the votes able to be cast on all or substantially all matters at general meetings of the company (or of any company which is its subsidiary undertaking or parent undertaking or of a fellow subsidiary undertaking of its parent undertaking) (LR 11.1.4R).

52 Transactions in the ordinary course of business are excluded under LR 11.1.5R, as are transactions where the class test percentage ratios are less than 0.25 per cent (n 53 below). A detailed analysis of the class tests is beyond the scope of this article, but they broadly follow a classification of the size of a transaction against the size of the company in accordance with a gross assets test, a profits test, a consideration test and a gross capital test pursuant to LR 10 Annex 1.

53 Listing Rules, Chapter 11. If the transaction in question is of a size large enough such that, upon the application of 'class tests' (*ibid*), the 'percentage ratio' for any class test is 5 per cent or more, independent shareholder approval of the transaction is required prior to the company entering into that transaction (LR 11.1.7). If all such class test percentage ratios are less than 5 per cent, but one or

the issuer's responsibilities thereunder are being met.[54] The sponsor must be a person approved by the FCA to provide sponsor services, and who must be an authorised person (under FSMA 2000, s.31) or member of a designated professional body,[55] and, therefore, owes duties to act appropriately. In certain circumstances,[56] the materiality thresholds are disapplied in the presence of a controlling shareholder,[57] further strengthening the effectiveness of the constraint. The regulations would protect inferior-voting shareholders from the most extreme varieties of tunnelling,[58] since a dual-class controller holding the enhanced-voting shares will not be able to simply extract significant controller benefits by entering into personally beneficial transactions with the company, unless the sponsor has confirmed the fairness and reasonableness of the transaction, or, in the case of very large transactions, the inferior-voting shareholders have consented. The application of the related-party transaction rules forms a more effective deterrent to tunnelling than directors' duties, since the FCA can directly sanction directors and companies for breaches of the rules.[59]

Additionally, under International Accounting Standards (IAS),[60] related-party transactions, regardless of size, must be disclosed by Main Market listed companies in their annual reports.[61] Furthermore, under the DTRs,[62] as amended pursuant to the EU's SRD II, listed companies incorporated in England and Wales[63]

more are above 0.25 per cent, independent shareholder approval is not required, but prior to entering into the transaction, the company must obtain confirmation from its sponsor that the transaction is fair and reasonable to its shareholders and the transaction must be publicly disclosed as soon as possible upon entering into the transaction (LR 11.1.10R). If all class test percentage ratios are less than or equal to 0.25 per cent, the Listing Rules requirements do not apply (LR 11.1.6R and LR 11 Annex 1). It should be noted, though, that for 'sovereign controlled commercial companies' (where a State exercises or controls 30 per cent or more of the voting rights), neither sponsor confirmation nor shareholder pre-approval are required, even for large transactions (LR 21.5.2R).

54 LR 8.2.

55 LR 8.6.

56 See n 79 below and accompanying text.

57 For these purposes, subject to certain disregarded interests, a 'controlling shareholder' is any person who exercises or controls on their own, or together with any person with whom they are acting in concert, 30 per cent or more of the votes able to be cast on all or substantially all matters at general meetings of the company (LR App 1.1).

58 For further discussion on 'tunnelling', see Section 6.2.1 of Chapter 6.

59 Breaches of the Listing Rules can attract censure and fines enforced by the FCA, or in serious circumstances, a suspension or cancellation of the issuer's listing (FSMA 2000, ss. 91 and 77).

60 Companies with their securities listed on an EU-regulated market must prepare their consolidated accounts in conformity with the IASs (Application of International Accounting Standards Regulation, article 4). Although the United Kingdom has left the EU, as of the time of writing, the requirement is also reflected in CA 2006, s. 403.

61 IAS 24. For these purposes, 'related party transaction' is defined to be any 'transfer of resources, services, or obligations between related parties, regardless of whether a price is charged' (IAS 24.9). The definition does not exclude transactions that are 'in the ordinary course of business' or 'concluded on normal market terms'.

62 The rules of the FCA's Disclosure Rules and Transparency Rules sourcebook.

63 DTR 1B.1.10R.

must disclose details of all proposed material related-party transactions[64] no later than the date on which the terms of the transaction are agreed, obtain board pre-approval for the transaction and ensure that no director who is an associate of the related-party is involved in the board pre-approval.[65] The definition of 'related-party' for these purposes follows the International Financial Reporting Standards and includes any person who has control or significant influence over the company,[66] and a transaction will be 'material' if it is 5 per cent or more on the basis of certain class tests,[67] which are broadly similar to those set out in the Listing Rules.[68] The Listing Rules separately extend the DTR requirements, except for the requirements in relation to board pre-approval, to foreign-incorporated premium listed companies.[69]

Although the related-party transaction regulations should on paper provide inferior-voting shareholders with a degree of comfort that they will not be excessively expropriated in dual-class firms, the current effectiveness of those regulations should be considered when formulating dual-class stock policy. In the context of one share, one vote controlling shareholder firms, the regulations have not prevented controversies at premium listed companies such as ENRC, Asia Resource Minerals, Exillon Energy, Fraser Group and Ferrexpo.[70] Those controversies arose from either the related-party regulations not covering the relevant transactions or the nature of the transactions creating obfuscation as to whether the relevant thresholds had been satisfied, resulting in such transactions being unintentionally or, perhaps even intentionally, not treated as related-party transactions by the company in question.[71] Additionally, loopholes emerged with respect to the limited breadth of the definition of 'associate' under the Listing Rules, which, in relation to a transaction between a company and a family member of the controlling shareholder, only encompasses the controller's spouse, civil partner or child. Therefore, broad scope still exists for a controller to cause a company to enter into transactions with certain family members without being subject to requirements for sponsor endorsement or independent shareholder approval of related-party transactions.[72] In contrast, under IAS, related-party transactions must be disclosed if the transaction is between the company and a close member of the controller's family, potentially

[64] The definition of 'transaction' is included in DTR 7.3.3R, and, for practical purposes, is similar to the definition under IAS 24 (n 61 above), except that it excludes transactions 'in the ordinary course of business' and concluded on 'normal market terms'.

[65] DTR 7.3.8R.

[66] IAS 24.9.

[67] DTR 7.3.7R; DTR 7 Annex 1.

[68] See n 52 above.

[69] LRs 9.2.6CR and 9.2.6DR (the provisions also apply to standard tier companies – LRs 14.3.25R and 14.3.26R).

[70] B. Reddy, 'The Fat Controller: Slimming Down the Excesses of Controlling Shareholders in UK Listed Companies' (2018) 38 *OJLS* 733, 757 *et seq*; also see Section 5.3 of Chapter 5.

[71] Reddy (2018) (n 70 above).

[72] *ibid* 751 and 760, in relation to Fraser Group (formerly Sports Direct) and ENRC, respectively.

embracing a wider group of family members as compared to the Listing Rules.[73] As such, as discussed further in Chapter 9, it may be prudent to bolster the related-party transaction regulations under the Listing Rules in the context of dual-class firms.

With the related-party transaction regulations portending a dysfunctional marriage, the 'relationship agreement' represents the 'pre-nup'. In 2014, following controlling shareholder controversies such as at ENRC,[74] the Listing Rules were amended to require that, in the presence of a controlling shareholder (which would include a controller of voting rights in a dual-class firm[75]), a premium listed company must enter into a 'relationship agreement' with the relevant controller,[76] pursuant to which the controller must agree that: (i) any transactions with the controller or any of its associates will be conducted at arm's length and on normal commercial terms; (ii) neither the controller nor any of its associates will take any action that will have the effect of preventing the company from complying with its obligations under the Listing Rules; and (iii) neither the controller nor any of its associates will propose or procure the proposal of a shareholders' resolution that circumvents the proper application of the Listing Rules.[77] The requirement to implement a relationship agreement impacts the application of the related-party transaction regulations, since a breach of the obligation to put in place a 'relationship agreement' with a controller, or in the case where a relationship agreement has been implemented, a breach of the independence provisions therein, results in the disapplication of the usual thresholds[78] that trigger the related-party transaction regulations.[79] Therefore, for example, if a proposed related-party transaction with a dual-class controller were not on 'arm's length terms', constituting a breach of the relationship agreement, it would require pre-approval by the other shareholders no matter its size and even if the transaction were in the company's ordinary course of business. It should be noted, though, that 'arm's length terms' is likely to only require that a transaction has been negotiated by the relevant parties on an independent basis without duress, on terms that could be obtained in a commercial transaction between two unrelated parties, but not necessarily better than the deal that the company could have achieved by transacting with another third party.[80] Therefore, the requirement that transactions be conducted

73 'Close members of the family' is defined as 'those family members who may be expected to influence, or be influenced by, that person in their dealings with the entity' (IAS 24, para 9).

74 For example, in 2011, two independent directors were ousted from the board by controlling blockholders acting in concert, after their criticism of the company's corporate governance and questioning of the independence of the chair. One ousted director described the company as 'more Soviet than City'.

75 For the definition of 'controlling shareholder' see n 57 above.

76 LR 6.5.4R and LR 9.2.2ADR(1).

77 LR 6.5.4R.

78 See nn 52 and 53 above.

79 LR 11.1.1AR and LR 11.1.1CR.

80 Reddy (2018) (n 70 above 752).

on arm's length terms will not provide complete protection from tunnelling through related-party transactions that do not otherwise exceed the thresholds triggering operation of the related-party transaction regulations under the Listing Rules. Other than the impact on the related-party transaction requirements, the influence of relationship agreements may be superficial. Under the Listing Rules, the FCA does not possess any clear direct enforcement powers with respect to breaches of relationship agreements. It is purely a contractual arrangement between the company and the controller, and, therefore, prima facie, the company has the right and responsibility to enforce any breach. In a controlling shareholder scenario, though, the appetite of a board under the control of the controller to enforce a breach against the controller may be slight. Even the independent element on the board may be reluctant to impel enforcement.[81] It could be argued that a failure to enforce such a breach would be a dereliction of the directors' duties,[82] but, as discussed earlier, there is little incentive for an inferior-voting shareholder with a small shareholding in the company to commence a derivative claim in relation thereto. With respect to unfair prejudice,[83] although such claims have been notoriously difficult in the publicly listed company sphere,[84] there is cogency in the argument that an inferior-voting shareholder could have a personal claim for unfair prejudice against a company that does not enforce a breach of a relationship agreement,[85] but this would be a new, and as yet untested, aspect of unfair prejudice case law.

Notwithstanding the imperfections, the related-party transaction regime does provide existing safe harbour for inferior-voting shareholders from the most egregious forms of tunnelling. However, such regulations do not prevent the controller from abusing its entrenched position to extract other controller benefits, as summarised in Chapter 6, which fall short of related-party transactions.

8.2.5 *Independent Directors*

Independent directors are non-executive members of the board, theoretically free from bias or conflicts, such as pre-existing associations with a controller, that could impact on their ability to make decisions on behalf of the company on a truly independent basis.[86] Not only can independent directors positively monitor executives in dispersed

81 See Section 6.2.4 of Chapter 6.

82 Potentially breaches of CA 2006, ss. 172, 173 and 174 (n 5 above and accompanying text).

83 CA 2006, s. 994 (see nn 29–33 above and accompanying text).

84 See n 34 above and accompanying text.

85 Cheffins (2013) (n 34 above 529) – since the terms of a relationship agreement are publicly available to existing and prospective shareholders, in theory, the credibility of the public markets (*ibid*) could still be preserved notwithstanding an unfair prejudice claim by a minority shareholder harmed by the breach of a relationship agreement or by the non-enforcement of the terms of a relationship agreement by the company against its controlling shareholder.

86 For examples of the types of conflicts that could prejudice the independence of directors, see UK CGC, Provision 10.

ownership systems,[87] but, if they are genuinely independent, they could also act as a monitoring mechanism curtailing the worst excesses of controllers in dual-class firms.[88] The UK CGC, which applies to premium listed companies, urges that at least half the directors on the board, not including the chair, be non-executive directors that the board considers to be independent.[89] The chair must also be independent upon appointment.[90] In determining the independence of a director, a relevant consideration under the UK CGC is whether such director is a representative of a significant shareholder.[91] Therefore, if dual-class stock were permitted on the premium tier, a dual-class company in full compliance with the UK CGC would, in theory, have implemented checks and balances to constrain the acts of its controller through majority board voting being carried by directors independent from the controller.

However, the UK CGC is applied on a 'comply-or-explain' basis, meaning that a company subject to the code is not mandatorily required to comply with the provisions. Under the Listing Rules, a premium listed company is required, in its annual report, to disclose how it has applied the UK CGC's principles, and whether it has complied with the UK CGC's provisions, and if it has not complied with the provisions, explain the reasons for non-compliance.[92] The success of 'comply-or-explain' rests upon the concept of disclosure – the UK CGC elicits disclosure to shareholders of corporate governance arrangements who can then take action to instigate change to the extent that they are dissatisfied. In the presence of a controller, though, disclosure is less consequential, since the corporate governance arrangements will have been implemented at the behest, or with the tacit approval, of the controller. Although, absent such disclosure, the public shareholders would be in the dark, there is very little power in the hands of those non-controlling shareholders to instigate change once enlightened. The only factor that could compel the controller to cause the company to comply are equity market forces which create downward pressure on share price, but, as discussed later in this chapter, equity market forces may not be especially potent in the context of dual-class stock.[93] A second issue can, though, also prejudice the sanctity of compliance by a dual-class firm; that is the propensity for companies to merely 'box-tick' against the provisions, and therefore comply with the form, but not the substance, of the provisions and principles.[94] Although the company may be disclosing that it has appointed sufficient independent directors, the independence of which are determined in the sole discretion of the board, in practice the provenance of their acts and decisions may

87 See Section 6.2.4 of Chapter 6.
88 See Section 9.7.3 of Chapter 9.
89 UK CGC, Provision 11.
90 *ibid* Provision 9.
91 *ibid* Provision 10.
92 LRs 9.8.6(5)R and 9.8.6(6)R.
93 See Section 8.3.1 later in this chapter.
94 For a summary of the concept of, and issues related to, 'box-ticking', see B. Reddy, 'Thinking Outside the Box – Eliminating the Perniciousness of Box-Ticking in the New Corporate Governance Code' (2019) 82 *MLR* 692.

not be genuinely independent.[95] More controversially, a controller could appoint directors who are known to, and supportive of, the controller, even though not directly tainted by the factors set out in the UK CGC stated to potentially prejudice independence. Such issues also materialise in one share, one vote controlling shareholder companies, and in response to such perils, the Listing Rules, in 2014, granted a modicum of privilege to minority shareholders of premium listed companies in the appointment of independent directors. Where a premium listed company has a controlling shareholder,[96] the election or re-election of independent directors must be separately approved by both the 'independent' (non-controlling) shareholders and the full body of shareholders.[97] If any such election or re-election is not approved pursuant to this dual-voting mechanism, and the company desires to persevere with the relevant election or re-election, a further vote must be held at a meeting at least 90 days but not more than 120 days after the original vote,[98] and the relevant director, if already an existing appointee, may remain on the board during the interim period.[99] The resolution will be passed at the subsequent meeting by a simple majority of votes exercised (including the votes of the controlling shareholder). If dual-class firms emerged on the premium tier, the same appointment requirements would apply to them, and the inferior-voting shareholders would have the right to opine on the suitability of directors designated by the board to be independent. However, the fact that the controller can, ultimately, impose its will with respect to the appointment of the relevant director dilutes the efficacy of the rules, and, as discussed in Chapter 6, the legitimacy of independence of such directors can be tainted.[100] In fact, when premium listed one share, one vote controlling shareholder companies have lost, or have come close to losing, the vote of the independent shareholders on individual independent director appointments, in most cases, the controller has exercised its voting power (at the subsequent shareholders' meeting where the initial vote has been lost) to ensure that such directors remain in place for a significant period of time.[101] In anticipation of a similar dynamic emerging if dual-class firms were permitted on the premium tier, in Chapter 9 possible modifications to the independent director requirements for dual-class firms are discussed.

8.2.6 *Amendments to the Articles of Association*

The articles of a company incorporated in England and Wales may be amended by a special resolution of its members.[102] Therefore, in the first instance, if a dual-class

95 *ibid* 713.
96 For the definition of 'controlling shareholder', see n 57 above.
97 LR 9.2.2ER.
98 LR 9.2.2FR.
99 LR 9.2.2DG.
100 See Section 6.2.4 of Chapter 6.
101 Reddy (2018) (n 70 above 744–747).
102 CA 2006, s. 21.

controller were to hold at least 75 per cent of the voting rights in the company, it would be able to amend the constitutional documents to, potentially, include provisions that are personally beneficial to it and smooth the path toward controller benefit extraction. There are two caveats, though, that could, in some instances, potentially protect inferior-voting shareholders. If the proposed change to the articles embodies a variation of 'class rights', a special resolution of the class affected is also required (unless a different procedure is compelled by the articles).[103] This could protect against discriminatory changes being imposed by the controller to the rights attached to inferior-voting shares in a dual-class firm. In the context of a one share, one vote firm, the nature of 'class rights' have often been narrowly defined by the Courts, being limited to special rights (rather than rights attached to all shares or members[104]) attached to shares or held in the capacity as a member.[105] A distinction has also being drawn by the Courts such that acts that only affect the enjoyment of rights will not be considered to be a variation of those rights.[106] However, if the proposed variation discriminately varies the distinct rights of the inferior-voting shareholders and not the enhanced-voting shareholders, it is likely that class rights would be deemed to be varied.[107] Also, although, unlike in the United States,[108] controllers do not formally owe duties as shareholders in the United Kingdom,[109] minority shareholders could possibly take comfort from a common law protection that requires decisions to amend the articles to be taken bona fide for the benefit of the company as a whole.[110] Therefore, a decision by a controller to exercise its votes to amend the articles in a manner purely personally beneficial to it could be challenged by the other shareholders. It should be noted, though, that there is a high bar to successful challenges to the bona fide standard, since the inferior-voting shareholders would have to show that no reasonable person would have come

103 CA 2006, s. 630.

104 *Cumbrian Newspapers Group Ltd.* v. *Cumberland & Westmorland Herald Newspaper & Printing Co Ltd* [1987] Ch. 1.

105 *ibid.* In relation to the distinction between rights held in the capacity as a member, as opposed to in some other capacity, see *Eley* v. *Positive Government Security Life Assurance Co. Ltd.* (1875) 1 Ex. D. 20.

106 For example, *White* v. *Bristol Aeroplane Co* [1953] Ch. 65; *Hodge* v. *James Howell & Co* [1958] The Times, 13 December; *Greenhalgh* v. *Arderne Cinemas Ltd and another* [1946] 1 All ER 512; *Dimbula Valley (Ceylon) Tea Co Ltd* v. *Laurie and another* [1961] Ch. 353.

107 *Cumbrian Newspapers* (n 104 above). However, in relation to the relevance of class rights upon recapitalisations of one share, one vote into dual-class stock, see nn 120–123 below and accompanying text.

108 *Ivanhoe Partners* v. *Newmont Mining Corp.*, 535 A.2d 1334, 1344 (Del. 1987). The Courts have equated the role of controlling shareholders to that of boards due to the level of influence they exert over the company and the board, hence the imposition of fiduciary duties (*Abraham* v. *Emerson Radio Corp.*, 901 A.2d 751, 759 (Del. Ch. 2006)). The extent of the fiduciary duty owed by controlling shareholders is not clear, and case law generally only recognises the duty in the context of conflicted transactions (K. Berchem et al., 'Duties of Controlling Stockholders – Murky Waters: Tread Carefully' *Akin Gump Strauss Hauer & Feld LLP Articles* (June 2012) at 2).

109 *Estmanco (Kilner House) Ltd.* v. *Greater London Council* [1982] 1 W.L.R. 2 at [10].

110 *Allen* v. *Gold Reefs of West Africa Ltd.* [1900] 1 Ch. 656.

to the same decision approving the relevant amendment to the articles.[111] Furthermore, there is broad scope for a controller to argue that amendments to the articles that are beneficial to the controller will, in fact, also benefit the company.[112]

8.2.7 *Post-IPO Recapitalisations of One Share, One Vote into Dual-Class Stock*

As discussed in Chapter 2, although the NYSE employs a broadly permissive attitude toward dual-class stock, it does limit the capacity of one share, one vote companies that are already listed on the exchange to convert or 'recapitalise' into dual-class stock if such a conversion will disparately reduce or restrict the voting rights attached to existing shares.[113] The concern is that public shareholders who have invested in a company on the basis of one share, one vote could see their voting rights reduced either directly, by the voting rights attached to their shares being restricted to a lesser standard than one share, one vote, or indirectly, by the issuance of new shares with enhanced-voting rights or the discriminatory conversion of insiders' shares into shares with enhanced-voting rights. Even where those public shareholders had knowingly invested in a controlling shareholder structure, their assessment of the risks and rewards inherent in the structure will have presumed that the controller holds an equivalent level of equity to its voting rights. As discussed in Chapter 5, the shift to dual-class stock could substantively change the balance of benefits and costs for public shareholders, with the basis on which shareholders have invested dramatically altered.[114] A shareholder may be content to allow a certain controller to maintain control so long as the controller is constrained by a sufficient equity ownership, but may not have any appetite to contemplate the same controller maintaining control with a disproportionately lower percentage of the equity. The situation is further exacerbated where the recapitalisation involves the issuance of enhanced-voting stock to parties that the public shareholders had not even contemplated would acquire control rights. Although public shareholders always possess the option to sell their investment, as discussed in Chapter 7, the mere announcement that a recapitalisation is going to occur can result in a fall in share price.[115] Additionally, post-IPO mid-stream recapitalisations from one share, one vote into dual-class stock can be particularly insidious, since, as also discussed in Chapter 7, the recapitalisation may be effected in response to specific events, and the rationale for the change into dual-class stock can relate to the controller selling equity and

111 *Shuttleworth* v. *Cox Bros. & Co.* [1927] 2 KB 9; as confirmed in: *Greenhalgh* v. *Arderne Cinemas Ltd.* [1951] Ch. 286, *Citco Banking Corp.* v. *Pusser's Ltd.* [2007] 2 BCLC 483 and *Re Charterhouse Capital Ltd* [2015] EWCA Civ 536.

112 For example, see the judgment in *Re Charterhouse Capital Ltd* [2015] EWCA Civ 536.

113 See Section 2.3 of Chapter 2.

114 See Section 5.6 of Chapter 5.

115 See Section 7.3 of Chapter 7.

entrenching control in contemplation of future poor performance, or in order to extract pernicious controller benefits.[116] The adoption of dual-class stock at IPO gives potential investors the opportunity to fully evaluate the merits of an investment in the relevant structure at that time, rather than a post-IPO recapitalisation into dual-class stock where the structure is imposed on existing investors, and, as such, the NYSE treats the latter more severely than the former. If the premium tier were to permit dual-class stock, consideration should turn to whether such structures should only be permissible if adopted at IPO or whether post-IPO recapitalisations should also be accepted, and, if so, whether recapitalisations that disparately reduce the voting rights attached to existing shares should be permitted. Of clear relevance is the extent to which currently applicable laws and regulations enable an existing controller to effect a recapitalisation of its company from one share, one vote into dual-class stock.

If existing premium tier companies were permitted to recapitalise into dual-class stock, currently applicable English law provides some protection against prejudicial recapitalisations by companies incorporated in England and Wales, but the level of protection varies depending upon the manner of the recapitalisation. The creation of a new class of shares would first need to be reflected by an amendment to the articles of association of the relevant company, which itself requires a super-majority special resolution vote of at least 75 per cent.[117] This would apply to either a conversion of existing shares or an issuance of new shares. With respect to a conversion of existing shares by a one share, one vote firm, a controller with sufficient voting rights to carry the amendment to the articles (in which case the company would have sailed close to the wind of a breach of the free-float rules, absent an exemption[118]) could unilaterally pursue such a recapitalisation. Having created a new class of shares, a controller could develop a voting/cash-flow divergence either by converting the ordinary shares held by public shareholders into inferior-voting shares, or by converting a portion of its own ordinary shares into enhanced-voting shares. The controller could then sell-down equity while retaining control. One may challenge such a discriminatory modification of rights to be a variation of class rights requiring approval by the public shareholders.[119] However, it is by no means clear that the common law supports such a proposition. In relation to converting publicly held shares into inferior-voting

116 See Section 7.3.3 of Chapter 7.
117 CA 2006, ss. 21 and 283.
118 In order to float on the Main Market of the LSE, at least 25 per cent of the shares to be listed must, by the time of their admission, be in public hands, and the relevant issuer must continue to comply with such requirement (see LRs 6.14R, 9.2.15R and 14.2.2R). Therefore, it is eminently possible for a one share, one vote firm to list with a controller holding up to and including 75 per cent of the shares. In any case, the FCA may lower the threshold for particular issuers upon request. In fact, the FCA has lowered the threshold for a number of controlling shareholder companies, such as ENRC, Ferrexpo and Fresnillo, in the past.
119 See nn 103–107 above and accompanying text.

shares, although the Courts have been inclined to deem class rights to include distinct rights held by specific shareholders, even if not attached to specific types of shares,[120] in this case, the right in question is not distinct, since all shareholders in the company, prior to the conversion, will have held equivalent voting rights.[121] It is not, therefore, free from doubt that such an act would be considered to be a variation of class rights. The determination that class rights have been varied is also uncertain where the controller converts a portion of its own ordinary shares into enhanced-voting shares, since the rights attached to shares held by the public shareholders have not been directly varied – only the enjoyment of those rights has been indirectly affected by the controller's, now, enhanced-voting rights.[122] Indeed, this was exactly the situation that occurred in the case *Citco Banking Corp NV* v. *Pusser's Ltd* (albeit involving a company incorporated in the British Virgin Islands).[123] It could perhaps be argued that the underlying amendment of the articles of the company to create the new class of shares is not bona fide for the benefit of the company, and is therefore, as discussed earlier, invalid[124] if undertaken in contemplation of a discriminatory conversion of shares, but, again, it is by no means certain that the common law supports such a determination.[125]

A scheme of arrangement could also potentially be used to discriminatorily convert shares into new classes, but it is more likely that the public shareholders would enjoy protection in such circumstances. Such a procedure would require a majority in number representing 75 per cent of the votes exercised in a meeting of

[120] *Cumbrian Newspapers* (n 104 above [23]).

[121] *ibid* [15]. However, it would seem perverse for a situation where the shares of public shareholders are discriminately converted into inferior-voting shares not to be considered to be a variation of class rights, and some commentators have argued that class rights should also include fundamental shareholder rights, such as voting, dividend and returns of capital upon a winding up, whether or not such rights are uniform amongst share classes (for example, see *Gower: Principles of Modern Company Law*, 11th edition, eds. P. Davies et al. (Sweet & Maxwell, 2021) at 510).

[122] In *Hodge* v. *James Howell & Co* [1958] C.L.Y. 446, CA, The Times, it was held that a new issuance of preference shares that ranked ahead of ordinary shares and behind existing preference shares did not vary the class rights of the existing classes of shares, even though the value of the existing classes would be affected. However, in *Greenhalgh* v. *Arderne Cinemas Ltd* [1946] 1 All ER 512, although it was held that a subdivision of one class of shares did not affect the class rights of another class of shares even though the subdivision diluted the voting power of that second class, the leading judge, in *obiter dictum*, suggested that class rights may have been varied if the application of one share, one vote had been changed (Lord Greene Mr. at 516).

[123] *Citco* (n 111 above). However, also see *obiter dictum* by Pennycuick J. in *Rights and Issues Investment Trust Ltd* v. *Stylo Shoes Ltd and Others* [1964] 3 All ER 628 at [631], where it was suggested that an amendment to the articles that doubled the votes attached to management shares could have required a class approval of the ordinary shareholders if the holders of the management shares had not (as they had in this instance) voluntarily declined to exercise their votes on the resolution.

[124] See nn 108–112 above and accompanying text.

[125] In *Citco* (n 111 above), the relevant amendment to the articles that created the new class of enhanced-voting shares, prior to the discriminatory conversion, was not considered to be contrary to the benefit of the company. However, the judgment expressly noted, and may have been influenced by the fact that, the relevant vote would have been carried on the facts even if the beneficiary of the enhanced-voting rights had not voted his shares.

each separate class of members to approve the transaction.[126] The determination of classes in the context of schemes of arrangements is more flexible than the determination of class rights under the common law. Since the minority and majority members would be treated differently in this case, it is likely that they would form separate classes for the purpose of schemes of arrangement.[127] Furthermore, the Court would then be required to approve the transaction,[128] which entails the Court ascertaining that members of each class could have reasonably come to the same decision,[129] and therefore were not motivated by ulterior personal interests.[130] Although it is unlikely that a Court would refuse to sanction a scheme that has been approved by the relevant classes except in the most extreme cases (and, even then, evidential issues would pertain), at least the Court procedure adds another layer of integrity to the process. In the United States, recapitalisations of one share, one vote into dual-class stock may also effectively require approval by the minority shareholders,[131] but the NYSE has maintained its prohibition of discriminatory recapitalisations on the assumption that dangers subsist that public shareholders could be coerced into approving the transaction[132] (through, for example, sweeteners, concerns that other shareholders will approve the transaction and benefit more extensively than those that do not, the ability of management to control the proxy agenda, and collective action issues hindering diffuse shareholders from acting together to ensure that they vote as a block in their interests), and that shareholders who voted against the transaction could still see their shares disenfranchised. As a result, the NYSE continues to maintain a prohibition against recapitalisations where shareholders are disenfranchised. The same argument made in the United States could also be made in the United Kingdom in relation to schemes of arrangement, in that the outside shareholders could be coerced into voting for the recapitalisation; however, the voting thresholds are so high in the United Kingdom, requiring one or more super-majority votes, that a large number of shareholders would need to be persuaded, and, on the modern-day LSE, most investors are sophisticated. It is therefore unlikely that a controller of a listed company could use a scheme of arrangement to effect a recapitalisation from one share, one vote to dual-class stock without the significant support of savvy institutional investors. In

126 CA 2006, s. 899(1).

127 *Re Hawk Insurance Company Ltd* [2001] EWCA Civ 241.

128 CA 2006, s. 899.

129 *Re Dorman Long & Co Ltd* (1934) 1 Ch. 635.

130 *Re T&N Ltd* [2004] EWHC 2361 (Ch); *Carruth* v. *Imperial Chemical Industry* [1937] AC 707.

131 Recapitalisations into dual-class stock by controlling shareholder one share, one vote firms have been held to be 'conflicted transactions', which are subject to greater governance scrutiny (*IRA Trust FBO Bobbie Ahmed* v. *Crane*, C.A. No. 12742-CB (Del. Ch. Dec. 11, 2017)).

132 See R. Gilson and J. Gordon, 'Controlling Controlling Shareholders' (2003) 152 *U. Pa. L. Rev*. 785; R. Ruback, 'Coercive Dual-Class Exchange Offers' (1988) 20 *J. Financ. Econ*. 153; Gordon (1988) (n 19 above 47); D. Ashton, 'Revisiting Dual-Class Stock' (1994) 68 *St. John's L. Rev*. 863, 912; S. Bainbridge, 'The Short Life and Resurrection of SEC Rule 19C-4' (1991) 69 *Wash. U. L. Q*. 565, 581.

fact, since the time when the US studies that framed the coercion issues were published, the investor profile in the United States has also become far more institutionalised, meaning that, even on the NYSE, it is unlikely that a large enough proportion of shareholders would be coerced in such a way to act against their own interests.[133]

Other mechanisms that could be utilised by a controller to implement a post-IPO, mid-stream voting/cash-flow divergence include splitting existing shares into two classes of shares,[134] distributing a new class of stock to existing shareholders as part of a stock dividend or bonus issue of shares,[135] or simply issuing new inferior-voting or enhanced-voting shares pursuant to a further cash issuance.[136] Again, if new classes of shares are being created, a special resolution to amend the articles would also be required, but a controller with 75 per cent of the votes (although, as aforementioned, absent an exemption, the controller will, in such a case, be close to breaching free-float requirements[137]) could pass the relevant resolution.[138] Having created a structure consisting of inferior-voting and enhanced-voting shares, the controller could subsequently create its voting/cash-flow divergence by disposing of inferior-voting shares. With enhanced-voting shares in existence, the environment becomes more conducive to retaining control while disposing of equity. The approach was taken by Google, in 2014, by creating a new class of non-voting stock post-IPO to reinforce its existing dual-class stock structure. Since all shareholders would be treated equally, separate class resolutions would not be required, allowing a controller with sufficient voting power to induce the recapitalisation. Even more controversially, a controller with sufficient voting power to pass special resolutions could disapply pre-emption rights[139] and issue itself with enhanced-voting shares for cash, thereby disenfranchising the other shareholders. In such a case, again it is by no means clear that the class rights of existing shares would be deemed to be varied, requiring a separate special resolution of the class affected,[140] and, even if it were

[133] When the NYSE re-evaluated its policy on one share, one vote in 1984, it noted that the original reasons for prohibiting dual-class stock had faded due to the growing proportion of sophisticated investors (as well as changes to the regulatory environment and increased minority shareholder protections through mechanisms such as audit committees and independent directors) (T. O'Neill, 'Rule 19c-4: The SEC Goes Too Far in Adopting a One Share, One Vote Rule' (1989) 83 *Nw. U. L. Rev.* 1057, 1064 f/n 55; Ashton (1994) (n 132 above 897)).

[134] An ordinary resolution is required to subdivide the stock (CA 2006, s. 618). This would require a majority vote (CA 2006, s. 282).

[135] Ordinary resolutions would be required to grant the directors authority to allot shares (CA 2006, s. 551), and, if the Model PLC articles apply, to approve the stock (or 'scrip') dividend or bonus issue (Model PLC Articles, article 78).

[136] An ordinary resolution would be required to grant authority to allot shares (*ibid*).

[137] See n 118 above and accompanying text.

[138] See n 117 above and accompanying text.

[139] A special resolution is required to disapply pre-emption rights (to the extent not already disapplied in the articles in relation to a specific authority to allot shares) (CA 2006, s. 571; LR 9.3.11R).

[140] See n 122 above and accompanying text.

required, the class affected would comprise all the existing shares in the company, possibly allowing the same controller to carry the vote.[141]

Therefore, although meaningful public shareholder protections (particularly in relation to schemes of arrangement) are in place in the United Kingdom relating to post-IPO, mid-stream recapitalisations, it is still possible that a controller, with sufficient voting control, could implement a recapitalisation into dual-class stock without substantial approval by minority shareholders, which could, eventually, enable the controller to create a large divergence between its voting and cash-flow rights. Also pertinent is that the recapitalisation mechanics described earlier are premised on statutory and common law, rather than regulatory, rules and, therefore, only apply to companies incorporated in England and Wales. If dual-class stock were permitted on the premium tier, a one share, one vote company incorporated in another jurisdiction, listed on the Main Market, may be subject to less strict rules pertaining to a recapitalisation into dual-class stock. Accordingly, a consideration of post-IPO mid-stream recapitalisations of one share, one vote companies into dual-class stock should accompany any discussion on the admission of dual-class firms to the premium tier – a matter revisited in Chapter 9.

8.3 MARKET CONSTRAINTS

Many of the market mechanisms that can discipline managers in one share, one vote firms can also play a role in constraining the actions of controllers of dual-class firms; among these are the equity markets, debt markets and product markets. In contrast, as discussed in Chapter 6, the disciplining effect of the market for corporate control is eroded in the presence of a controlling shareholder.[142]

8.3.1 *Equity Markets*

As alluded to in Chapter 6,[143] the equity markets can, in theory, act as a disciplining mechanism – if a controller of a dual-class firm regularly expropriates inferior-voting shareholders, the inclination for investors to invest as inferior-voting shareholders will significantly diminish, or to the extent investors are prepared to make equity investments, the price at which they will invest will be substantially lower.[144] Equally, with

141 However, case law suggests that at a class meeting to approve a variation of class rights, class members must exercise their votes bona fide in the interests of the class as a whole (*Re Holders Investment Trust* [1971] 1 WLR 583).

142 See Section 6.2.6 of Chapter 6.

143 See Sections 6.2.5 and 6.3.7 of Chapter 6.

144 As identified in a number of studies in relation to controlling shareholders generally, see A. Shleifer and R. Vishny, 'A Survey of Corporate Governance' (1997) 52 *J. Financ.* 737, 749; R. La Porta et al., 'Legal Determinants of External Finance' (1997) 52 *J. Financ.* 1131, 1149; M. Maher and T. Andersson, 'Corporate Governance: Effects on Firm Performance and Economic Growth' *Organisation for Economic Co-Operation and Development* (1999) at 1, 18; L. Bebchuk et al., 'Stock Pyramids, Cross-Ownership, and Dual Class Equity: The Mechanisms and Agency Costs of Separating Control from

inferior-voting shareholders lacking the ability to change the management team, upon inferior-voting shareholder expropriation, share price can be further depressed as a result of such investors pursuing an exit option and selling their shares. Similar share price declines may follow actions that unnerve public shareholders by feeding their fears that the structure may be more susceptible to greater extraction of controller benefits, such as where the firm does not comply with the UK CGC. Declining share price can represent a significant constraining mechanism on one share, one vote controlling shareholder firms where the controller owns a substantial equity tranche. Not only will a decline in share price substantially impair the shareholder's financial wealth, but it will also prejudice the ability of that shareholder to partially or fully exit at an acceptable price in the future. However, the effectiveness of the equity markets as a dual-class controller constraining mechanism in this regard can be seriously questioned. A dual-class controller will become less concerned as to how any decline in share price affects its personal assets (decreasing the constraining effect), as its voting/cash-flow divergence increases and the equity ownership of the controller decays. One of the principal reasons for a controller adopting dual-class stock is to diversify its wealth to allow it to operate the company free from concerns related to declining share price.

The equity markets will, though, continue to have a constraining effect on dual-class controllers in another sense, since there is an incentive to treat inferior-voting shareholders fairly in order to keep open the option to tap the equity markets for further finance in the future at low capital costs – a potentially critical consideration for high-growth tech firms requiring funding for R&D and further growth. The ability of the equity markets to constrain controllers can be blunted, however, due to difficulties inherent in the pricing-in of expropriation or risk. Underwriters[145] can impact upon share price, and the demand for shares by the controller itself (where the controller needs to subscribe to shares in order to maintain control upon a fresh issue of shares) can increase share price.[146] Additionally, the market may not be perfectly efficient, with asymmetric information issues preventing the market determining the correct price for stock in controlling shareholder companies.[147] This can

Cash-Flow Rights' in *Concentrated Corporate Ownership*, ed. R. Morck (University of Chicago Press, 2000) at 305.

145 T. Wen, 'You Can't Sell Your Firm and Own It Too: Disallowing Dual-Class Stock Companies from Listing on the Securities Exchanges' (2014) 162 *U. Pa. L. R.* 1495, 1506.

146 M. Giannetti and Y. Koskinen, 'Investor Protection, Equity Returns, and Financial Globalization' (2010) 45 *J. Financ. Quant. Anal.* 135, 136 and 146. Additionally, since the FTSE-indices only update constituents and weighting quarterly, if the expropriation occurs prior to an update, passive index trackers may still be required to invest in the relevant share issuance, bumping-up price (J. Fisch et al., 'Passive Investors' (2018) *U. Penn. Inst. Law & Econ. Research Paper* No. 18–12 1, 40).

147 L. Bebchuk, 'Foreword: The Debate on Contractual Freedom in Corporate Law' (1989) 89 *Colum L. Rev.* 1395, 1406; V. Brudney, 'Corporate Governance, Agency Costs, and the Rhetoric of Contract' (1985) 85 *Colum L. Rev.* 1403, 1423; also see Fisch et al. (2018) (n 146 above 43); R. Adams and D. Ferreira, 'One Share-One Vote: The Empirical Evidence' (2008) 12 *Rev. Financ.* 51, 83. In relation to inefficient markets generally, also see A. Shleifer, *Inefficient Markets: An Introduction to Behavioural Finance* (Oxford University Press, 2000); R. Gilson and R. Kraakman, 'The Mechanisms of Market Efficiency Twenty Years Later: The Hindsight Bias' (2003) *Harvard Law*

be further exacerbated by the controller obscuring the nature and extent of expropriation.

8.3.2 *Debt Markets*

Debt markets can also have a disciplining effect. Jensen and Meckling (1976) noted the disciplining and monitoring effect of debt on management, generally,[148] and there is no reason for the theory not to extend to dual-class firms. If, for example, due to nervousness on the part of investors to become inferior-voting shareholders, a firm is not able to raise further finance on the equity markets, it is possible that debt will be the only option to finance further growth. In such an event, debt covenants can prohibit firms from taking certain actions without debtholder consent, possibly constraining the ability of controllers to extract controller benefits. A debtholder may insist on working capital covenants, restrictive covenants limiting levels of distributions and indebtedness,[149] and even restrictions on transaction size. At least more extreme extractions of controller benefits could breach the debt covenants, and the need to service debt payments without the onset of insolvency can also limit the extent to which the controller can extract controller benefits from the company to the detriment of firm profitability. Additionally, the controller of a firm reliant on debt financing may be hesitant to excessively abuse minority shareholders, since a reputation for expropriation could affect the creditworthiness of the firm, increasing the interest rates (and fees) attached to debt and strength of covenants required by creditors upon future excursions to the debt markets. The constraining effect of debt on controller benefit extraction by controlling shareholders generally has been modelled, suggesting the converse supposition that a controlling shareholder will reduce the level of debt in order to extract greater controller benefits.[150] In contrast, a further study, examining dual-class firms between 1994 and 2010, suggested that debt may be used by dual-class firms to signal to the market that management is subject to debt constraints, and, thereby, reduce their costs of capital in the equity market.[151] However, debt covenants will still give controllers a large degree of flexibility since they will target protection against existential threats which prejudice the ability of the company to pay off the debt, rather than day-to-day expropriation. They will also not assuage inferior-voting shareholder concerns that an underperforming management team will become entrenched, and, in an extreme case, the controller of a dual-class

School Discussion Paper No 446 1, 14; M. Moore and E. Walker-Arnott, 'A Fresh Look at Stock Market Short-Termism' (2014) 41 *J. Law Soc.* 416, 421.

148 M. Jensen and W. Meckling, 'Agency Costs and Ownership Structure' (1976) 3 *J. Financ. Econ.* 305, 338.

149 *ibid* 338.

150 H. Bruslerie, 'Does Debt Curb Controlling Shareholders' Private Benefits? Modelling in a Contingent Claim Framework' (2016) 58 *Econ. Model.* 263.

151 A. Dey et al., 'Disproportional Control Rights and the Governance Role of Debt' (2016) 62 *Manage. Sci.* 2581.

firm may not fear a breach of debt covenants since the decrease in value of the firm caused by an acceleration of the debt will have less of an effect on the controller's wealth as its cash-flow interest in the company falls. Similarly, a potential increase in the cost of debt or imposition of unfavourable terms as a result of a decrease in creditworthiness caused by a reputation for excessive expropriation will have less of a constraining effect on a controller that only holds a small proportion of the equity.

8.3.3 *Product Markets*

Finally, in theory, the product markets can have a constraining effect on controlling shareholders, although, as discussed in this section, that effect may again be diminished when dual-class stock is introduced. Product market competition has been labelled as a managerial monitoring mechanism in one share, one vote dispersed ownership systems.[152] In a monopolistic market, it has been hypothesised that one share, one vote dispersed ownership firm managerial agency costs will be higher, since the value of the 'pot' into which managers can dip is larger, giving managers more 'slack'[153] – a competitive product market reduces those agency costs, since slackness or consumption of perquisites by managers readily reduces profits, exposing managers to the possibility of removal and the market for corporate control.[154] Although managerial entrenchment applies in the presence of a controller, other aspects of product market competition could also act as a monitoring mechanism that inhibits the extraction of controller benefits.[155] Firstly, if controllers extract substantial pecuniary controller benefits, it is possible that the quality of the firm's products will suffer, leading to a loss of market share and diminishing firm performance[156] (thereby reducing the value of the controller's equity stake). In extreme cases, the threat of insolvent liquidation can discipline not only managers of dispersed ownership firms, but also controlling shareholders. Secondly, if controlling shareholders regularly and egregiously expropriate minority shareholders, this could cause a reputational issue, making it more difficult for the firm to contract with third-party suppliers and customers.[157] Thirdly, increased product market competition increases the verifiability and transparency of prices, making it more

152 C. Holderness et al., 'Were the Good Old Days That Good? Changes in Managerial Stock Ownership since the Great Depression' (1999) 54 *J. Financ.* 435, 457.

153 M. Roe, 'Rents and Their Corporate Consequences' (2001) 53 *Stan. L. Rev.* 1463, 1468.

154 *ibid* 1473.

155 A. Dyck and L. Zingales, 'Private Benefits of Control: An International Comparison' (2004) 59 *J. Financ.* 537, 539.

156 *ibid* 577.

157 Holderness and Sheehan (2000) (n 25 above 152); R. Gilson, 'Controlling Family Shareholders in Developing Countries: Anchoring Relational Exchange' (2007) 60 *Stan. L. Rev.* 633, 648 – although the author noted that this mechanism is dependent upon a strong financial press to report behaviour, and acknowledged that there is nothing to suggest that behaviours vis-à-vis minority shareholders are more effectively disclosed and communicated than simply the quality of the firm's products and behaviours directly toward suppliers and customers.

difficult for controlling shareholders to extract resources by way of manipulated accounting without legal or reputational consequences.[158] However, the vigour of product market constraints may be stifled in dual-class firms as the controller's voting/cash-flow divergence increases, since the controller will be less concerned as to firm performance issues from a wealth perspective if that controller is diversified and has only a small percentage of its wealth invested in the equity of the firm. Nevertheless, although not related to pure monitoring or constraints, in competitive markets, the opportunities for expropriation may be less, since free cash-flow from which the controller can extract is potentially less plentiful than in monopolistic markets.[159] The extraction of controller benefits by dual-class controllers should, therefore, be less in jurisdictions or industries where product market competition is strong, and empirical evidence has suggested this to be the case.[160]

8.3.4 *Interplay between Market Forces and Voluntary Constraints*

Market forces can also influence the voluntary implementation by controllers of other constraints on their behaviours. By voluntarily implementing structural constraining mechanisms, the market may view the ownership structure more favourably, and, therefore, the cost of capital may be reduced. Those structural constraints may also smooth the firm's path toward debt financing, and instil greater trust in the product markets. In the United States, some dual-class firms have, as noted in Chapters 6 and 9, voluntarily implemented inferior-voting shareholder protections that result in the structure reverting to one share, one vote upon the occurrence of certain events, even though the provisions are not strictly required by law or regulation.[161] This is an example of market forces in action, since the voluntary adoption of the relevant provisions can signal to investors that the firm is likely to sit on the net-beneficial side of the dual-class stock tradeoff,[162] which will attract investors and reduce the firm's cost of capital.

8.4 PSYCHOLOGICAL CONSTRAINTS

In Chapter 6, the extraction of non-pecuniary controller benefits was identified as a potential hazard to inferior-voting shareholders.[163] However, those same controller

158 Dyck and Zingales (2004) (n 155 above 576).

159 Roe (2001) (n 153 above 1468); Maher and Andersson (1999) (n 144 above 26).

160 Dyck and Zingales (2004) (n 155 above 582) – equating strength of competition laws to strength of product market discipline. Conversely, though, it has also been noted that minority shareholders will be more concerned about controller benefit extraction in competitive product markets, since the total value of the 'pie' to share is smaller than in a monopolistic market (Roe (2001) (n 153 above 1489)).

161 See Sections 6.2.7 of Chapter 6 and 9.6 of Chapter 9.

162 The 'market for lemons' problem expressed in Chapter 7 (see, for example, Section 7.7.4) can be mitigated through such signalling mechanisms (B. Cheffins, ed., *Company Law: Theory, Structure and Operation* (Oxford University Press, 1997) at 164).

163 For example, see Section 6.2.5 and of Chapter 6.

benefits can also form constraints around more extreme pecuniary controller benefits. For example, even if the effectiveness of market constraints may be blunted in dual-class firms, a controller may otherwise be psychologically incentivised to maintain a good reputation if it values the fame and prestige garnered through controlling a high-profile company that could be lost if the controller becomes known for excessively expropriating the inferior-voting shareholders or leading the company into a precarious financial position. It has also been noted that reputation can bear heavily on the decisions of family firms, since the controller will be seeking to preserve the reputation and legacy of the family name as well as his or her own reputation.[164] The presumed reputational constraints on family firms can give those firms a business advantage in jurisdictions with weak investor protection and commercial laws.[165]

Additional 'psychological' mechanisms that could reduce controller benefit extraction are public opinion and social norms.[166] Increased disclosure of egregious behaviour can constrain such behaviour through public outrage;[167] and social or moral norms in a country can constrain controllers on the basis that expropriative behaviour is simply not acceptable in the moral climate of the relevant jurisdiction. When assessing the constraints on controller benefits in particular jurisdictions, such psychological constraints should not be overlooked.[168] The United Kingdom enjoys independent, extensive media coverage, and a well-developed financial press, which will reinforce psychological constraints of this nature.

8.5 CONCLUSION

A plethora of legal and regulatory requirements exist in the United Kingdom, some of which have been specifically formulated to constrain the acts of controlling

164 P. Flocos, 'Toward a Liability Rule Approach to the "One Share, One Vote" Controversy: An Epitaph for the SEC's Rule 19c-4?' (1989–1990) 138 *U. Pa. L. Rev.* 1761, 1777; Holderness and Sheehan (2000) (n 25 above 151); Gilson (2007) (n 157 above 643). However, R. Pollak, 'A Transaction Cost Approach to Families and Households' (1985) 23 *J. Econ. Lit.* 581, 587 cast doubt on whether reputation would be an effective constraining mechanism (other than in the case of gross expropriation or malfeasance) on individual family-member managers, since the family would not, in effect, ostracise a family member for mere shirking, slack performance or minor infractions.

165 Gilson (2007) (n 157 above 643).

166 Dyck and Zingales (2004) (n 155 above 539).

167 The term 'outrage costs and constraints' was coined in this context in L. Bebchuk and J. Fried, *Pay without Performance* (Harvard University Press, 2004) at 5.

168 For example, M. Holmén and J. Knopf, 'Minority Shareholder Protections and the Private Benefits of Control for Swedish Mergers' (2004) 39 *J. Financ. Quant. Anal.* 167, 168 found that although Sweden has poor corporate governance laws, the levels of expropriation by controlling shareholders is low – this was hypothesised to be as a result of the existence of extralegal institutions. Consistent with this, Sweden is fifth in the world for newspaper circulation (a proxy for public opinion – Dyck and Zingales (2004) (n 155 above 577)), and rates very low for crime rates (a suspected proxy for social norms – J. Coffee, Jr., 'Do Norms Matter?: A Cross-Country Examination of the Private Benefits of Control' (2001) *Columbia Law School, The Center for Law and Economic Studies, Working Paper No. 183* 2151, 2153).

shareholders generally, and could, therefore, potentially constrain the acts of dual-class controllers. Although certain of the rules are generally applicable, a subset is only applicable to premium listed companies, emphasising the greater levels of corporate governance expected of those firms. Even absent the legal and regulatory constraints, a dual-class controller would not have a free hand to act nefariously. A variety of market and psychological constraints also potentially constrain behaviour. However, the potency of market constraints in dual-class firms will be diluted to an extent by the diminution of the controller's equity restraint. The lack of the constraining effect of a significant equity holding (as would subsist in a one share, one vote controlling shareholder firm) can create a hole in the package of constraints that protects public shareholders, and therefore, in turn, the flaws and lacunae evident in the legal and regulatory protections identified in this chapter become more critical. In light of this, the next chapter will assess other possible types of constraints that could bolster the inferior-shareholder protection package. However, with a view to encouraging further UK listings, particularly of high-growth tech firms, any such constraints must be constructed with caution, since shifting the dual-class stock tradeoff into positive territory cannot come at the cost of eliminating all the controller benefits that would otherwise encourage a founder to list with dual-class structure. With that proviso in mind, a roadmap toward a cogent premium tier approach to dual-class stock is presented in the final chapter.

9

A Balanced Protection Package for Inferior-Voting Shareholders

She tasted the largest bowl, which belonged to the Big Bear, and found it too cold; then she tasted the middle-sized bowl, which belonged to the Middle-sized Bear, and found it too hot; then she tasted the smallest bowl, which belonged to the Little Bear, and it was just right, and she ate it all.[1]

9.1 INTRODUCTION

In the previous chapter the existing constraints on controllers that could protect inferior-voting shareholders, if dual-class firms were welcomed on to the premium tier, were expounded. It was noted that certain flaws in the legal and regulatory environment exist, and that market forces are progressively dented as the controller's voting/cash-flow divergence increases. In this chapter, a number of possible other forms of inferior-voting shareholder protections will be critically discussed, with a view to recommending an inferior-voting shareholder protection package for the United Kingdom if it were to relax its prohibition of dual-class firms from the premium tier. Although the UK Listing Review has already purportedly made concrete proposals for the introduction of dual-class stock to the premium tier, as discussed in Chapter 1,[2] the restrictions attached have led to the recommendation constituting a capital structure that falls far short of 'genuine' dual-class stock. In contrast, the minority protections prescribed in this chapter have been proposed with a view to protecting public shareholders without fatally eroding the orthodox characteristics of 'genuine' dual-class stock. A discussion of minority protections is critical in any consideration of dual-class stock, since it could be contended that one share, one vote is only a pivotal restriction in jurisdictions where minority shareholder protections are weak, but where such protections are strong, an outright prohibition of dual-class stock unnecessarily precludes the benefits that the structure

[1] R. Southey, 'The Story of the Three Bears' in *The Doctor* (Longman, Rees, Orme, Brown, Green and Longmans, 1837).

[2] See Section 1.5.7 of Chapter 1.

can offer.[3] In the face of sceptical institutional investors, judicious investor protections will smooth the path toward the premium tier introduction of dual-class stock, and also reduce the otherwise potentially high costs of capital for dual-class firms. Any protections that are introduced must be adequate to guard against the most nefarious elements of controller benefit extraction, but, at the same time, not be so restrictive to prevent the extraction of all controller benefits. As iterated in Chapter 6, the dual-class stock tradeoff can be framed in the context of the categories of controller benefits, and, therefore, those controller benefits that are benign, whether pecuniary or non-pecuniary, should be encouraged, whilst even those that are mildly malevolent can be tolerated so long as the structure is overall beneficial. If too many controller benefits were curtailed, the positive aspects of dual-class stock would be eliminated, and issuers would be discouraged from listing in the United Kingdom, making any such relaxation of the rules wholly worthless. As will be noted later in this chapter, certain protections that eliminate, or reduce the risk of, pernicious controller benefit extraction may be preferable from a theoretical or ideological basis, but they have not been proposed for adoption in the United Kingdom due to either intractable practical challenges in their real-world implementation,[4] or the danger that they will be so restrictive that issuers are unlikely to avail themselves of a relaxation of dual-class stock on the premium tier. As alluded to above, the proposals of the UK Listing Review, for example, potentially eradicate too many controller benefits, and, therefore, will deter many of the founders it is seeking to attract.[5] The discussion to follow mainly relates to the United Kingdom, and is pertinent to the United Kingdom's regulatory milieu. However, many of the themes are applicable in other jurisdictions, and the UK roadmap described later in this chapter outlines the merits (and negatives) of many of the commonly discussed inferior-voting shareholder protections that should be considered by policymakers of all jurisdictions where dual-class stock is permitted or being considered.

A balanced protection package offers inferior-voting shareholders a degree of protection from actual and potential expropriation (such that the discounts that would otherwise be applied to dual-class firms will be significantly reduced) while creating an environment in which founders will be willing to list their firms with dual-class stock by enabling them to retain sufficient flexibility to manage their companies in a manner that conforms to their long-term idiosyncratic visions.

[3] For example, B. Lauterbach and Y. Yafeh, 'Long-Term Changes in Voting Power and Control Structure following the Unification of Dual Class Shares' (2009) 112 *Noto Di Lavoro* 1, 23; M. Cremers et al., 'The Life-Cycle of Dual Class Firms: From IPO to Sunset' (2018) *ECGI Working Paper No. 550/2018* 1, 28; A. Winden, 'Sunrise, Sunset: An Empirical and Theoretical Assessment of Dual-Class Stock Structures' (2018) 3 *CBLR* 852, 909.

[4] In relation to the difficulties of the rule-making process, see B. Cheffins, *Company Law: Theory, Structure and Operation* (Oxford University Press, 1997) at 285–291.

[5] See Section 1.5.7 of Chapter 1.

9.2 THE RULE-MAKING CHALLENGE

9.2.1 *Mandatory, Presumptive or Permissive*

A key challenge when formulating a package of investor protections is to determine the most effective manner of implementation. Rules could be implemented on: (i) a mandatory basis; (ii) a presumptive basis, whereby default rules apply unless parties opt-out; or (iii) a permissive basis, whereby the rules only apply if parties opt-in.[6] In most cases, the presumptive approach will be advocated in this chapter, albeit with a nuance. It has been posited that the presumptive approach will generally be the most effective form of regulation, since parties save transaction costs by not having to formulate and negotiate a set of protections themselves in a scenario where they are widely accepted, but, invoking the no one-size-fits-all concept of corporations, parties can deviate when in their interests.[7] However, with dual-class stock, if the relevant rules could simply be waived by the issuer, given the control that the issuer has over the constitutional documents of the company as of IPO, and the voting power of the enhanced-voting shareholders post-IPO, the chances of opportunistic opt-outs are high; therefore, in many cases, the presumptive rules outlined in this chapter will be proposed on a basis whereunder the relevant protections can only be waived if both the enhanced-voting shareholders and a majority of the inferior-voting shareholders, post-IPO, agree. In a way, such presumptive rules could be described as 'sticky default', or even pseudo-mandatory, rules since there is only a minimal chance that a majority of inferior-voting shareholders would waive their rights.[8]

Purer mandatory rules, however, do have an important part to play in particular circumstances; for example where the protection of third parties is vital[9] or where self-serving or ill-advised opt-outs are likely.[10] It is unlikely that, given the sophistication of institutional investors in the United Kingdom, who dominate the equity markets,[11] a majority of public shareholders would waive a presumptive inferior-investor protection when not in their interests, but disclosure is an area where mandatory rules could be germane. Even sophisticated investors require adequate information disclosure regarding a particular company in order to make salient decisions.[12] In the context of the investor protection package, disclosure is vital to give potential investors the information that they require to ascertain whether, to the

6 Cheffins (1997) (n 4 above 217–263).

7 *ibid* 259.

8 A. Schwartz and R. Scott, 'The Common Law of Contract and the Default Rule Project' (2016) 102 *Va. Law Rev*. 1523, 1566.

9 Cheffins (1997) (n 4 above 244).

10 *ibid* 242.

11 If individuals, charities and public sector bodies are excluded, UK and global institutions hold the remainder of UK equities, amounting to 77.77 per cent of UK listed shares as of 31 December 2018 (calculated using data from: ONS, 'Ownership of UK Quoted Shares: 2018' (January 2020)).

12 Cheffins (1997) (n 4 above 246).

extent that they have a choice,[13] to invest in a dual-class firm, and to ensure that all pertinent information is readily available to all investors, including those without adequate resources to discover or extract the information by other means. Mandatory rules also ensure conformity across the market,[14] which reduces transactional costs for institutional investors when analysing dual-class firms on a case-by-case basis.

To the other extreme, in the United States, often the permissive approach is taken to dual-class stock investor protections. The permissive approach is particularly suited to fact patterns where a minority of market participants desire to adopt certain rules, but do not do so due to legal uncertainties.[15] Permissive rules benefit such participants by confirming the validity of those rules but save transaction costs for the majority of participants that would not desire to adopt them. In the United States, as further described later in this chapter, a number of dual-class firms do, voluntarily, implement sunset clauses which disassemble dual-class structure into one share, one vote when triggered; however, they are not particularly effective and can either allow controlling shareholders to maintain disproportionate control in perpetuity by avoiding the triggering of the clause or result in the dual-class structure persisting long past its sell-by date. They often present a veneer of altruism that, in reality, reflect the bare minimum limitations that should be implemented. In Canada, it was found that dual-class firms do not regularly establish substantial inferior-voting shareholder protections beyond those mandated by law.[16] Although in Chapter 8 it was noted how market forces could influence the voluntary adoption of constraints,[17] it has also been modelled that asymmetric information present at the IPO stage impedes the ability of the market to act as an effective constraint, meaning that in the absence of presumptive or mandatory rules, efficient corporate governance arrangements are not voluntarily adopted by issuers.[18]

Reverting to the theoretical foundation, the permissive approach applies well to the concept of permitting dual-class firms on the premium tier – by expressly confirming that such structures are permitted, the minority of issuers wishing to use such structures can do so – but in relation to investor protections, it is not clear that the balance of bargaining positions between all the players is sufficiently equal that they will be adopted voluntarily in cases where it is overall optimal to do so. One could challenge that *caveat emptor* applies, and, as with the approach taken in the

[13] Some potential investors may not have freedom of choice as to whether to invest in the relevant firm (see the text accompanying nn 19–22 below).

[14] Z. Condon, 'A Snapshot of Dual-Class Share Structures in the Twenty-First Century: A Solution to Reconcile Shareholder Protections with Founder Autonomy' (2018) 68 *ELJ* 335, 363.

[15] Cheffins (1997) (n 4 above 250).

[16] A. Anand, 'Governance Complexities in Firms with Dual Class Shares' (2018) 3 *Annal. Corp. Gov.* 184, 230.

[17] See Section 8.3.4 of Chapter 8.

[18] L. Bebchuk, 'Asymmetric Information and the Choice of Corporate Governance Arrangements' (2002) *Harvard Law School Discussion Paper No.* 398 1, 4.

United States, investors can choose whether to make investments in dual-class firms based upon an assessment of the inferior-voting shareholder protections that have (if any) been adopted voluntarily by the issuer. However, there are several factors that make it imprudent to take a purely *caveat emptor* approach to the United Kingdom's relaxation of the premium tier prohibition of dual-class stock. Firstly, not all investors have a choice regarding investing in dual-class companies. Post-IPO, index trackers will be required to invest in dual-class companies that are constituents of the relevant indices[19] (although for the principal indices, since they are formed of the largest companies by way of market capitalisation, if the dual-class firm has entered the relevant index, it can be indicative of a successful company, the stock of which the market values highly). Even at IPO, active investors may face what has been labelled a 'Hobson's choice',[20] where, in a competitive market between fund managers, investors will be reticent to miss out on an investment in a company with potentially excellent growth prospects,[21] especially in a generally weak or small market for IPOs.[22] Secondly, as presented in Chapter 7, numerous studies have shown that dual-class firms in the United States display significant pricing discounts as compared to one share, one vote firms,[23] which substantially increases the costs of capital for dual-class firms. With higher costs of capital, founders could be deterred from listing, dual-class firms could prematurely convert into one share, one vote, and founders of listed dual-class firms could succumb to seeking third parties to buyout the firm in the face of exorbitant equity financing costs which throttle future growth – the aspiration for a thriving listed tech company scene in the United Kingdom could be seriously hindered. The creation of broadly uniform inferior-voting shareholder protections across the market can result in a lowering of those costs of capital. Of course, as in the United States, dual-class firms could voluntarily adopt inferior-voting shareholder protections in an attempt to reduce costs of capital on a firm-by-firm basis. However, any such protections would likely be contractual or implemented through the constitutional documents of the issuer, and, therefore, not subject to regulatory oversight. The capacity for investors to granularly, and accurately, scrutinise the adequacy of contractual or constitutional protections on a firm-by-firm basis is low,[24] and could lead to universal discounts being applied to companies whether or not they have adopted the relevant provisions, or mispricing of protections that present a façade of robustness, but, in fact, are paper-thin in substance. Regulatory required protections, on the other hand, carry with them a degree of authoritative endorsement that the relevant protection conforms

[19] See Section 1.5.4 of Chapter 1.

[20] ISS M&A Deal Note (North America), 'The Tragedy of the Dual Class Commons' (13 February 2012) at 1, http://online.wsj.com/public/resources/documents/facebook0214.pdf.

[21] T. Wen, 'You Can't Sell Your Firm and Own It Too: Disallowing Dual-Class Stock Companies from Listing on the Securities Exchanges' (2014) 162 *U. Pa. L. R.* 1495, 1505; Winden (2018) (n 3 above 899).

[22] Anand (2018) (n 16 above).

[23] See Section 7.4 of Chapter 7.

[24] L. Bebchuk and K. Kastiel, 'The Untenable Case for Perpetual Dual-Class Stock' (2017) 4 *Va. Law Rev.* 585, 623.

to at least a minimum level of adequacy. Thirdly, as discussed further in this chapter, the litigation culture and environment in the United States is very different from that in the United Kingdom; it can act as a significant constraining mechanism on actions by controllers and thereby form a bedrock for the permissive approach in the United States. Introducing a broad, permissive approach to dual-class stock in the United Kingdom may result in differing consequences to those seen in the United States. Finally, and perhaps most importantly, institutional investors, especially UK institutional investors, are sceptical of dual-class stock, and relaxing the premium tier prohibition without complementary inferior-investor protections is likely to be met with resistance. Even though investors, as a self-protective measure, can apply discounts to dual-class stock, they will expect further protection, through the imposition of universally applicable mechanisms, from at least the risks of terminal expropriation. Without at least minimum levels of regulatory protection, the standing of the premium tier (and the FTSE UK-series indices) could be prejudiced. From a marketing perspective, the premium tier could also gain a competitive advantage by greater market confidence being instilled in dual-class firms listed in the United Kingdom, as compared to exchanges where only a disparate group of dual-class firms voluntarily adopt similar protections in a multiplicity of forms. All of these considerations erode the justification for a purely permissive approach in the United Kingdom, and a rational argument therefore exists, particularly in the early stages of permitting dual-class stock in a jurisdiction, to regulate rather than anticipating that inferior-voting shareholder protections will organically be adopted as a result of market forces.[25]

As such, a mixture of mandatory, presumptive and permissive rules may be appropriate. It is advocated that a presumptive approach be taken in most cases, since it gives institutional investors certainty that specific protections will be adopted, unless a majority of inferior-voting shareholders (and the controller) decline them (maintaining a degree of flexibility). Importantly, it should also have the effect of reducing discounts on inferior-voting shares across the board, since investors will be safe in the knowledge that all dual-class firms will incorporate the relevant protections unless public investors (or at least a majority of them) have determined that the risks inherent in disapplying them are outweighed by the benefits. In some cases, certain rules will be described in 'mandatory' terms, but with the ability of the FCA to waive the requirement in its discretion. No matter the approach, it is essential that any such protections are drafted so that they act as effectual restraints on controllers, but do not discourage beneficial listings nor unduly blunt the benefits that dual-class stock embraces.

25 Some have suggested that even the United States should follow the approach of Hong Kong and Singapore and implement safeguards on a legislative basis (Condon (2018) (n 14 above 362–364)).

9.2.2 *Legislative, Regulatory or Soft-Law*

Another challenge is determining what form rules should take – legislative, regulatory or soft-law. Legislative requirements, such as under the Companies Act 2006, benefit from statutory backing and legal enforcement, but, as a corollary to that substance, can take a long time to develop, must be approved by Parliament and will be subject to significant lobbying by interested parties.[26] Changes and amendments to legislation once on the books can similarly involve a protracted process, removing a level of flexibility in the rules to adapt nimbly to changing circumstances. The Companies Act 2006 also largely only applies to companies that have incorporated under the Act in England and Wales; it is difficult to effectively draft legislation with extraterritorial applicability. Furthermore, since legislation has the full force of the law, it is imperative that it encompasses certainty without vagaries, and, therefore, covers as broad a set of scenarios as possible – trying to cover all bases can result in substantially complex and labyrinthine statutes. Soft-law, such as the UK CGC comply-or-explain regime, is the most flexible, and it can provide broad rules with a great deal of leeway as to how companies implement them in practice. Although lobbying does occur, it is of a much lighter nature since issuers are able to deviate from the relevant rules so long as they explain why. A repercussion, though, is that issuers may not take the rules as seriously, and, as discussed in Chapter 8, the efficacy of the comply-or-explain approach, particularly in the context of controlling shareholders, can be doubted.[27] A happy medium is the use of regulatory rules that apply on a strict basis, but which are overseen by a regulator such as the FCA rather than comprising statutory law. Although new regulations, and material revisions to existing regulations, are usually preceded by consultation periods, the development time is far less protracted compared to statutory legislation, and the regulator has broad scope in the drafting and implementing of those rules. They do not enjoy the same strength of enforcement as statutory rules (although it should be noted that the FCA has statutory footing to enforce the Listing Rules) but can be regularly amended and refined over time. The Listing Rules are a good case-in-point,[28] and, since they relate to whether applicants will be admitted to the Main Market and the continuing requirements to remain admitted on the Main Market, they can encompass extraterritorial application.

Cognisant of the potential need for rules to evolve over time in response to evidence as dual-class firms become more prevalent on the premium tier, and that a not insignificant minority of premium listed companies are foreign-incorporated,[29] in most of cases, it will be proposed that provisions be implemented through

[26] Cheffins (1997) (n 4 above 178 *et seq*).

[27] See Section 8.2.5 of Chapter 8.

[28] Since 1966, there have been dozens of versions of the Listing Rules (previously known as 'Admission of Securities to Quotations' or 'Admission of Securities to Listing') and hundreds of inter-version amendments.

[29] As of 31 July 2020, from 1116 companies listed on the Main Market, 209 companies were registered in a jurisdiction other than the United Kingdom, the Channel Islands or the Isle of Man (derived from

the Listing Rules. As a condition of admission, the Listing Rules should specify that the FCA will expect that the constitutional documents of the relevant dual-class issuer will include relevant protective provisions, whether or not that issuer is locally- or foreign-registered.[30] The provisions would need to remain in those constitutional documents, and complied with, in order to maintain a premium listing.[31] Breach of the relevant protective provision would result in a breach of the constitutional documents of the company, which could, presumably, create rights of claim in the relevant jurisdiction for shareholders,[32] and a breach of the Listing Rules (which would allow the FCA to take administrative action).[33] The breach may also result in a contractual breach of the relationship agreement which must, under the Listing Rules, be mandatorily entered into between the controlling shareholder and the company.[34] Hong Kong, a jurisdiction with a significant number of listed foreign-incorporated companies,[35] has taken a similar approach to extraterritorial factors, requiring listed companies to replicate numerous Hong Kong-specific regulatory requirements in their constitutional documents as a condition of listing.[36] The relevant UK requirements should, generally, be included in a separate chapter of the Listing Rules that is only applicable to premium listed dual-class firms, so as not to be confused with requirements that would be applicable to all (including dual-class) firms. The concept of applying different listing rules to different types of companies is not novel. The Listing Rules already incorporate exclusions, exceptions and specific requirements for closed-ended investment funds,[37] open-ended investment companies[38] and sovereign-controlled commercial companies.[39]

9.2.3 *The Role of the FCA*

The role of the FCA in exercising 'primary market functions' will be critical. As earlier, it will be suggested that many of the protective measures should be

data disclosed in LSE, 'Issuer List' (31 July 2020), www.londonstockexchange.com/statistics/companies-and-issuers/companies-and-issuers.htm).

30 As an addition to LR Chapter 6 that cross-references the relevant protective measures. See, for example, LR 6.9.1

31 As an addition to LR Chapter 9 that cross-references the relevant protective measures.

32 Under English law, a breach of a company's articles will only create a right of claim in favour of a shareholder if the relevant breach affects the shareholder in its capacity as a member (*Hickman* v. *Kent or Romney Marsh Sheepbreeders Association* [1915] 1 Ch. 881; *Beattie* v. *E. F. Beattie Ltd.* [1938] Ch. 708) and is not held to be a mere internal procedural irregularity (*MacDougall* v. *Gardiner* [1875] 1 Ch. D 13).

33 Breaches of the Listing Rules can attract censure and fines enforced by the FCA, or in serious circumstances, a suspension or cancellation of the issuer's listing (FSMA 2000, ss. 91 and 77).

34 See Section 8.2.4 of Chapter 8.

35 D. Donald, *A Financial Centre for Two Empires* (Cambridge University Press, 2014) at 58 and 101 – as of 2014, only 13 per cent of HKEX listed companies were Hong Kong-incorporated.

36 *ibid* 103.

37 Listing Rules, Chapter 15.

38 Listing Rules, Chapter 16.

39 Listing Rules, Chapter 21.

implemented through Listing Rules that require the relevant provisions to be incorporated in the applicant's constitutional documents. The FCA is already able to request copies of an applicant's constitutional documents for review.[40] With the proposed protection package, the FCA may determine that it will need to review constitutional documents of dual-class applicants in more detail – alternatively, the FCA may take a looser approach, as it does in relation to many of the current requirements, and merely require that the applicant's sponsor confirm that the constitutional documents of the applicant include the necessary provisions. The latter approach may alleviate the burden on the FCA, and it is justifiable since the sponsor will be under a reputational and regulatory obligation to ensure compliance.[41] The issuer itself will also be eager to avoid the consequences of breaches.[42] Where it is proposed that the FCA retain discretion to waive what would otherwise be 'mandatory' requirements, this will impose a burden on the FCA, but it parallels the FCA's approach to the free-float rule, which can, and has, been waived for controlling shareholder firms.[43] The FCA should therefore be familiar with such a 'waiver process'.

More controversial would be to expand the role of the FCA in determining suitability of an applicant to list on the Main Market. Ideally, if dual-class stock were to be permitted on the premium tier, the FCA would play a discretionary role in whether to admit dual-class firms to the premium tier on a case-by-case basis, grounded upon broad firm and controller qualities. As discussed in Chapters 6 and 7 from both normative and empirical perspectives, dual-class stock will be more beneficial overall to shareholder wealth for certain types of firms, whereas other types of firms present riskier subjects for dual-class structure, where the potential costs to public shareholders are more likely to outweigh the benefits. As the gatekeeper to the Official List, the FCA could evaluate applicants and only permit an issuer to adopt dual-class stock to the extent that the company (and its controller) is of a type where the structure could present significant benefits to the success of the company and its public shareholders. The FCA already, to an extent, takes this approach to admissions, since it already confirms eligibility requirements (in coordination with the firm's sponsor) and reviews prospectus documents.[44] The UK Listing Authority, historically, always had the discretion as to whether to admit applicants, as evidenced by its previous informal resistance to the listing of dual-class firms.[45] Listing authorities in other jurisdictions, such as in Hong Kong, Singapore, China, India and Tokyo, have taken a discretionary approach to dual-class firms (as discussed later in this chapter), and in a competitive environment for

40 LR 3.3.7.
41 See Section 8.2.4 of Chapter 8.
42 See nn 33–34 above and accompanying text.
43 LRs 6.14R, 9.2.15R and 14.2.2R. The FCA has used its discretion to lower the threshold for a number of controlling shareholder companies, such as ENRC, Ferrexpo and Fresnillo, in the past.
44 LRs 3.3.1 and 3.3.3.
45 See Section 2.2 of Chapter 2.

listings, a mature and developed market like the LSE should be able to boast a regulator that is able to opine on admissions in a similar (albeit, as discussed later in this chapter, more flexible) way as in those other jurisdictions. It is acknowledged, though, that the current expertise and resources of the FCA will need to be enriched, which will take time, appetite and financial resources. The extra costs and resources required may well be a small price to pay to enable dual-class firm premium tier listings in a sensible manner, and, potentially, support the growth of tech companies in the United Kingdom. However, conscious of the possibility that a material expansion of the FCA as a regulatory body may be challenging in the short term, an alternative is proposed later in this chapter that would rely upon enhanced disclosure by dual-class stock applicants to the premium tier, enabling the market to better opine upon the suitability of the applicant as a dual-class firm. The FCA would, though, still have an important part to play in ensuring that disclosure is adequate and comprehensive.

9.3 WHAT'S NOT PROPOSED

Turning usual order on its head, this chapter will first define what is not proposed from a regulatory perspective, before outlining what is. Although the United States embraces a permissive environment for dual-class firms with little in the way of regulatory interference, it benefits from a litigious environment that is friendly to plaintiff shareholders wishing to instigate claims against directors and controlling shareholders. As compared to ex ante protections which are designed to limit the ability of, or incentives on, controllers to expropriate inferior-voting shareholders, at face value, the efficacy of ex post rights of actions and remedies can be doubted since, at that stage, damage has already been done and litigation can be costly.[46] However, crucially, the ease with which ex post claims can be made can also act as an ex ante deterrent to excessive controller benefit extraction. By way of example, when Facebook determined in 2016 that it would issue non-voting stock by way of a stock split, notionally to give the founder, Mark Zuckerberg, greater scope to divest of further equity while retaining control, two shareholders commenced litigation to attempt to block the change in capital structure.[47] With the threat of Court proceedings hanging heavily, the company abandoned the proposed stock split.[48] Similarly, although Google proceeded with its stock split in 2012 which created a new class of non-voting stock, in the shadow of litigation, the company agreed to pay a special dividend to shareholders upon any short-term decline in share price of non-voting stock to a value significantly

[46] A. Anand, *Shareholder-driven Corporate Governance* (Oxford University Press, 2020) at 69 *et seq.*

[47] T. Hals, 'Zuckerberg Nixes New Facebook Share Class after Shareholder Lawsuit' *Reuters* (22 September 2017), https://uk.reuters.com/article/uk-facebook-stock-zuckerberg/zuckerberg-nixes-new-facebook-share-class-after-shareholder-lawsuit-idUKKCN1BX306.

[48] Form 8-K Current Report of Facebook, Inc. dated 22 September 2017.

below that of one share, one vote stock.[49] In neither case were the suits finally litigated, but the plaintiff-friendly litigation environment will have had a constraining effect in a manner that would not be apparent in less litigious jurisdictions. The deterrent effect derived from the existence of an easily accessible litigation system in the United States has been noted in the context of the relaxation of dual-class stock prohibitions in Hong Kong, Singapore and Shanghai.[50]

In contrast, in the United Kingdom, 'loser-pay' rules can have a chilling effect on litigation in the corporate sphere. Under 'loser-pay' rules, the loser in a civil action is, as a general rule, required to pay the costs of the successful party.[51] Unless the plaintiff is sufficiently confident it will succeed in the relevant claim (which can be a challenge where the shareholder suffers from informational disadvantages relative to the company's board), it will be cautious about commencing litigation, further exacerbated by the fact that if the case is a derivative claim on behalf of the company, even if the plaintiff is successful, the remedies will flow to the company rather than the shareholder bringing and, possibly, funding the relevant claim.[52] In addition, while contingency-fee arrangements, which are effectively no-win, no-fee constructs where the lawyer receives a percentage of the award if successful, have been permitted in the United Kingdom since 2013, they have not, yet, become as all-pervasive as in the United States where law firms are more likely to offer clients such fee structures. Finally, the litigious culture in the United States is further fuelled by generous plaintiffs' lawyer awards,[53] and opt-out class action suits pursuant to which one or

49 Form 8-K Current Report of Google Inc. dated 30 October 2013.

50 For example, R. Chan and J. Ho, 'Should Listed Companies Be Allowed to Adopt Dual-Class Share Structure in Hong Kong?' (2014) 43 *Comm. L. World Rev.* 155, 177–179; H. Huang et al., 'The (Re) Introduction of Dual-Class Share Structures in Hong Kong: a Historical and Comparative Analysis' (2019) JCLS 1, 17 and 23; L. Lan and U. Varottil, 'Shareholder Empowerment in Controlled Companies: The Case of Singapore' in *The Research Handbook of Shareholder Power*, eds. Randall Thomas and Jennifer Hill (Edward Elgar, 2015) at 589; HKEX, 'Concept Paper: Weighted Voting Rights' (August 2014) at Appendix V, V-I; SGX, 'Consultation Paper on Possible Listing Framework for Dual Class Share Structures' (16 February 2017) at 8; J. Ho, 'Revisiting the Viability to Allow Dual-Class Share Structure Companies to List in the Financial Market of Hong Kong' (2018) 47 *Comm. L. World Rev.* 167, 181; K. Ho, 'Examining the Viability to Allow Dual-Class Share Structure Companies to List in the Financial Market of the People's Republic of China: Lessons and Experiences from Hong Kong' (2019) 1, 15, https://ssrn.com/abstract=3408873; M. Yan, 'Differentiated Voting Rights Arrangement under Dual-Class Structures in China: Expectation, Reality and Future' (2020) *Queen Mary Legal Studies Research Paper* No. 344/2020 1, 20.

51 CPR, Rule 44.2(2)(a). The Court has discretion to make costs orders that deviate from 'loser-pays' requirements (CPR, Rule 44.2(2)(b)).

52 CA 2006, s. 170(1). As discussed in Section 8.2.1 of Chapter 8, a shareholder may apply to the Court for an indemnity from the relevant company to commence a derivative claim on its behalf, but where the shareholder is a well-resourced institutional investor, the Court may not be receptive to such an approach.

53 In the United States, it has become customary for the plaintiff's lawyer to be awarded attorney fees upon either a judgment or a settlement if there is 'substantial or common benefit' to the corporation (M. Loewenstein, 'Shareholder Derivative Litigation and Corporate Governance' (1999) 24 *Del. J.*

more members of a class may sue or be sued as representative parties on behalf of all members.[54] In the United Kingdom, class actions (outside the competition law arena[55]) are severely limited and are, generally, commenced as 'group litigation orders' (GLOs),[56] which require claimants to initially commence individual claims[57] and 'opt-in' to the GLO.[58] As such, the UK system is not as conducive as the US system for entrepreneurial lawyers, in search of speculative, large plaintiff lawyer settlement awards, to commence actions on a contingency fee basis on behalf of large numbers of shareholders.

Focused changes to the civil procedural rules in the United Kingdom could lead to a more US-style litigation system that could provide inferior-voting shareholders with ex post remedies and deter controllers from pernicious expropriation. However, this represents a sledgehammer to crack a nut. A wholesale change in civil procedure will not just affect the corporate dynamic, but could result in unintended consequences throughout society. There does not appear to be an appetite in the United Kingdom to open the door to the opportunistic litigation that characterises the United States. Even with a discrete change affecting corporate litigation only, the UK corporate market would need to be prepared for a step change in corporate culture. The deterrent effect may also be overstated, since, with respect to directors' duties, the directors will not be overly concerned about personal liability if covered by company indemnities and/or third-party D&O insurance. It is therefore not proposed that civil procedure rules be modified.

Additionally, in Delaware, controlling shareholders owe a limited form of fiduciary duty to the company and the minority shareholders,[59] which, unless corporate governance protocols are followed, can manifest itself in the requirement of an

Corp. L. 1, 2); 'substantial benefit' has been loosely defined, and often the fees awarded are substantial compared to the actual benefit derived by the corporation. For example, in the 1996 case of *In re Caremark International, Inc. Derivative Litigation*, 698 A.2d 959 (Del. Ch. 1996), where a fairly weak derivative claim was settled pursuant to which the board merely agreed to make modest corporate governance changes and no monetary relief was awarded, the plaintiff's attorneys were awarded $816,000 (and $53,000 in expenses) (Loewenstein (1999) (*ibid* 5)).

54 US Federal Rules of Civil Procedure (2019 edition), Rule 23(a). Many States also have class action procedures similar to the federal rules (The Law Reform Commission of Hong Kong, 'Report: Class Actions' (May 2012) at 58).

55 Since 2015, opt-out class actions are permitted for breaches of competition law in front of the Competition Appeal Tribunal (Consumer Rights Act 2015, Schedule 8, Part 1).

56 CPR, Rule 19.10.

57 CPR, Practice Direction 19B, para. 6.1A.

58 *ibid* para. 6.2.

59 *Ivanhoe Partners* v. *Newmont Mining Corp.*, 535 A.2d 1334, 1344 (Del. 1987). The Courts have equated the role of controlling shareholders to that of the board due to the level of influence they exert over the company and the board, hence the imposition of fiduciary duties (*Abraham* v. *Emerson Radio Corp.*, 901 A.2d 751, 759 (Del. Ch. 2006)). The extent of the fiduciary duty owed by controlling shareholders is not clear, and case law generally only recognises the duty in the context of conflicted transactions (K. Berchem et al., 'Duties of Controlling Stockholders – Murky Waters: Tread Carefully' *Akin Gump Strauss Hauer & Feld LLP Articles* (June 2012) at 2).

entire fairness review of related-party (or 'conflicted') transactions.[60] Although the United Kingdom has implemented premium tier related-party transaction regulations,[61] their enforcement does not involve the Courts, and the scope of actions that may be contested by shareholders in the United States in a controlling shareholder scenario are more extensive than the United Kingdom's notion of related-party transactions and reinforced by the United States' litigious environment. For example, the actions by the shareholders of Facebook and Google discussed earlier in relation to proposals to issue non-voting stock[62] will have been based upon an argument that the capital restructurings (or 'reclassifications' in US parlance) were conflicted transactions that entrenched the existing controlling shareholders.[63] In the context of dual-class stock, an argument could be made that the United Kingdom should develop duties owed by controlling shareholders to the company and the other shareholders to enhance the protection of inferior-voting shareholders. However, extending fiduciary duties in the United Kingdom to the controlling shareholder may not be particularly effective. For example, if the duty is only owed to the company, shareholders may be impeded by some of the same challenges that face dispersed shareholders in enforcing directors' duties.[64] If the duty was owed directly to shareholders, the benefits of making a claim may still be outweighed by the potential costs for small, dispersed inferior-voting shareholders, unless there were also a correlating change in legal procedure to mirror the more litigation-friendly environment found in the United States, which is not contemplated by this

60 For example, in Delaware, if conflicted transactions are challenged by stockholders with no interest in the transaction, alleging that directors or officers have breached their fiduciary duties, the courts can subject the transaction to an 'entire fairness review' (L. Bebchuk and A. Hamdani, 'Independent Directors and Controlling Shareholders' (2017) 165 *U. PA. L. R.* 1271, 1282; *Weinberger* v. *UOP, Inc.*, 457 A.2d 701, 703 (Del. 1983)). Under an entire fairness review, unless specific processes have been followed by the company, the 'business judgment rule', pursuant to which the courts will otherwise defer to the judgment of management, will not be applied (*Kahn* v. *Tremont Corp.*, 694 A.2d 422, 428 (Del. 1997); *Weinberger* v. *UOP, Inc.*, 426 A.2d 1333, 1346 (Del. Ch. 1981)). If the transaction has been approved by a committee of independent directors, the burden of proof in relation to the entire fairness standard shifts to the plaintiff (*Kahn* v. *Tremont Corp.*, 694 A.2d 422, 428 (Del. 1997)), although in the presence of a controlling shareholder, Delaware case law has been mixed in relation to whether the transaction can be 'cleansed' in this way (the courts appear to take into account any ties that the independent directors may have to the controller that could impact genuine independence – Bebchuk and Hamdani (2017) (*ibid* 1289)). The burden can also be shifted if the company pre-approves the transaction through a majority of the minority vote (*Kahn* v. *Lynch Communication Systems, Inc.*, 638 A.2d 1110, 1115–1116 (Del. 1994)). In the context of controlling shareholder firm mergers, the courts have recognised a dual-approval process such that if a committee of independent directors approves the transaction and it is further approved by a majority of the minority shareholders, an entire fairness review standard will no longer apply and the courts will revert to the business judgment rule (see *Kahn* v. *M&F Worldwide Corp.*, 88 A.3d 635, 644 (Del. 2014); J. Rosenberg and A. Lewis-Reisen, 'Controlling-Shareholder Related-Party Transactions Under Delaware Law' Harvard Law School Forum on Corporate Governance and Financial Regulation (30 August 2017) 1, 8).

61 See Section 8.2.4 of Chapter 8.

62 See nn 47–49 above and accompanying text.

63 For example, see *IRA Trust FBO Bobbie Ahmed* v. *Crane*, C.A. No. 12742-CB (Del. Ch. Dec. 11, 2017).

64 See Section 8.2.1 of Chapter 8.

chapter. Further, adapting current statutory rules and judicial interpretation solely for dual-class firms, including the general deference given by the Courts to operational decisions of managers,[65] is a protracted and complicated process that may take disproportionate effort until such time that dual-class firms become more prevalent on the exchange, and is therefore not proposed in this chapter.

Another line of thinking by some commentators in the United States has raised the prospect that, for dual-class firms, the Courts should move beyond assessing fairness of procedure for self-dealing transactions to assessing genuine substantive fairness,[66] and even possibly applying a substantive fairness standard to all operational decisions.[67] Similar reasoning could be applied to the United Kingdom, and in the case of dual-class firms, the actions of directors, even outside of the related-party transaction sphere, could be scrutinised by the Courts more stringently upon being challenged.[68] However, requiring the Courts to discern whether a transaction is substantively fair in every case challenged by an inferior-voting shareholder, no matter the process taken in relation to the decision, can be onerous, requiring significant resource and expense to be incurred.[69] Even in the United States, it has been suggested that, although perhaps doctrinally persuasive, the Courts have little appetite to second-guess business decisions and are not well-placed to do so.[70] Moreover, a critical theoretical issue is that not every business decision will be a 'slam-dunk'. The ideal purpose of dual-class structure is to give the founder the space to think creatively, take risks and engage in a long-term approach. If the Courts could intervene in decisions at any stage, a founder could be sanctioned for one poor decision amongst many profitable decisions, undermining the benefits of dual-class structure.[71] Equally, if a decision is made with a long-term perspective, it is beyond credulity that the Courts would be able to evaluate whether poor interim performance is indicative of poor decision-making or whether the relevant decision will 'come-good' in the end; one of the reasons that the founder has implemented dual-class structure may be due to the long-term prospects of the business not being easily observable by the markets.[72] Such prospects will be equally (or more) unobservable to the Courts. A drastic change in jurisprudence to develop controlling shareholder fiduciary duties or enhanced scrutiny of business decisions by Courts is therefore not proposed.

65 *Smith* v. *Fawcett* [1942] Ch. 304, 306; *Burland* v. *Earle* [1902] AC 83, 93.

66 L. Bebchuk and K. Kastiel, 'The Perils of Small-Minority Controllers' (2019) 107 *Geo. L. J.* 1453, 1508.

67 C. Elson and C. Ferrere, 'Unequal Voting and the Business Judgment Rule' *Harvard Law School Forum on Corporate Governance and Financial Regulation* (7 April 2018) at 5; A. Choi, 'Concentrated Ownership and Long-Term Shareholder Value' (2018) 8 *HBLR* 53, 81.

68 In the normal course of events, English directors' duties case law has shown the Courts to apply judicial deference to managerial decisions of directors, and it is rare for the Courts to impugn the decisions of directors even if retrospectively they are found to be poor decisions (n 65 above).

69 Rosenberg and Lewis-Reisen (2017) (n 60 above 7).

70 *ibid* 6.

71 Also, see A. Grinapell, 'Dual-Class Stock Structure and Firm Innovation' (2020) 25 *SJLBF* 40, 84.

72 See Sections 6.3.5 and 6.3.7 of Chapter 6.

Rather than dwelling further on what is not proposed, next we move on to inferior-voting shareholder protections, which do not relate to substantive changes in law or civil procedure; such inferior-voting shareholder protections should be considered more seriously by the regulators. The protections can be broadly divided into restrictions on the eligibility to adopt dual-class stock, mechanisms that convert dual-class stock into one share, one vote in certain circumstances ('sunset' provisions) and constraints on the capacity or incentive of the controller to extract controller benefits ('sunrise' provisions). Although critically scrutinised in the context of a potential opening up of the premium tier to dual-class stock listings, the themes are relevant to any jurisdiction that permits or is considering permitting dual-class stock on its public markets.

9.4 RESTRICTING THE USE OF DUAL-CLASS STOCK TO SPECIFIC FIRMS OR CONTROLLERS (ELIGIBILITY)

Before discussing the inferior-voting shareholder protections that could be implemented once a dual-class firm has listed, thought should turn toward whether only certain types of firms or controllers should be permitted to adopt dual-class stock on the premium tier.

9.4.1 *Type of Firm Restrictions around the World*

A number of global exchanges have imposed restrictions of varying levels of specificity that limit dual-class stock to particular types of firms. In China, the SSE only permits dual-class firms on a segment dedicated to science and technology firms (the STI Board).[73] Initially, HKEX, in Hong Kong, similarly proposed a separate industry-specific board on which dual-class firms would be admitted with a view to attracting high-growth, early-stage, innovative companies.[74] The new board would only be open to 'new economy' companies – defined to be biotechnology, health care technology, internet and direct marketing retail, internet software and services, IT services, software, technology hardware, and storage and peripherals sector companies. Eventually, the proposal for a new board and the definition of 'new economy' were abandoned by HKEX.[75] The concern was that HKEX would just be pursuing listings in those industries in relation to which it was facing competitive pressure, rather than genuinely attempting to attract high-growth companies which are not restricted to specific

[73] Ho (2019) (n 50 above 26). The CSRC has published guidelines that will be used to evaluate the scientific and technology credentials of potential applicants to the STI (Yan (2020) (n 50 above 12)).

[74] HKEX, 'Concept Paper: New Board' (June 2017) at 26.

[75] In fact, HKEX had also previously dismissed an industry-defined limitation on dual-class structure (HKEX, 'Consultation Conclusions to Concept Paper on Weighted Voting Rights' (June 2015) at 29), and so it was not a surprise that the eventual relaxation of the dual-stock prohibition was not restricted to specific industries.

industries. Furthermore, the danger would exist that the relevant classification could be arbitrary and subjective, and create difficult issues for those companies that straddle a number of industries.[76] By way of example, Amazon is currently recognised as one of the largest and most successful technology companies in the world. However, at the time of its IPO, it's debatable as to whether it would have been classified as a retail, logistics or technology company. Similarly, in the United Kingdom, the companies Ocado and The Hut Group are variously described as tech and retail companies,[77] and Deliveroo, the only company, as of the time of writing, to list with genuine dual-class stock on the standard tier,[78] is as much a delivery service as a tech firm. Introducing an industry-limited route for dual-stock listings, such as solely for tech companies, would, therefore, create similar issues in the United Kingdom. It should be noted, though, that India has taken an industry-centric approach of sorts, but, importantly, has ingrained significant flexibility into the definition – dual-class stock will only be available for firms 'intensive in the use of technology, information technology, intellectual property, data analytics, bio-technology or nano-technology'.[79] Going forward, it will be interesting to examine the manner and flexibility in which India applies its industry restriction, and whether it can overcome the challenges identified by HKEX.

Although dual-class stock was not eventually restricted to particular industries in Hong Kong, in guidance, HKEX has stated that dual-class stock will only be suitable for listing by 'innovative' companies. The term 'innovative' requires a company to possess at least two of the following characteristics: (i) new and differentiated technologies or innovations; (ii) R&D should be a major activity of the business; (iii) the company's success should be attributable to unique features or intellectual property; and/or (iv) market capitalisation/intangible asset value should be disproportionately large compared to tangible asset value.[80] The intention is therefore to attract innovative firms to the exclusion of those companies which would find it more difficult to justify the need for dual-class stock.[81] The applicant must also be able to demonstrate a track record for high business growth.[82] However, even a restriction of dual-class stock to specific characteristics, such as 'innovative', rather than industries, is not without its perils – HKEX noted the difficulties in defining 'innovative'.[83] Also, the premise underlying HKEX's decision to admit dual-class firms is a desire to attract high-growth

76 *ibid* 29.

77 See Section 1.5.5 of Chapter 1.

78 See Section 1.5.6 of Chapter 1.

79 SEBI (Issue of Capital and Disclosure Requirements) (Third Amendment) Regulations, 2019, Rule 3(II).

80 HKEX Guidance Letter HKEX-GL93-18, 'Suitability for Listing with a WVR Structure' (April 2018) at para. 4.2.

81 HKEX Concept (2017) (n 74 above 23).

82 Growth will be objectively measured by 'operational metrics such as business operations, users, customers, unit sales, revenue, profits and/or market value (as appropriate) and [whether] its high growth trajectory is expected to continue' (HKEX Guidance (2018) (n 80 above para. 4.3)).

83 HKEX Concept (2017) (n 74 above 23).

firms,[84] but it is by no means clear that all high-growth firms are 'innovative'. For example, high-growth, early-stage companies in the media, sport and fashion industries could also benefit from dual-class stock, but these are not necessarily 'innovative' companies for the purposes of the eligibility requirements. Additionally, as acknowledged by HKEX, the categorisation of a firm being 'innovative' will change from industry to industry, market to market and even over time.[85] On balance, though, HKEX has determined that some form of definition is required to prevent riskier dual-class firms from the 'old economy' listing in Hong Kong. However, the definition of 'innovative' still derives from the types of industries in which the Hong Kong exchange is struggling to compete, rather than a substantive consideration of the micro-financial and historical details of the companies applying for quotation that could signify them to be high-growth companies, for which, as discussed in Chapters 6 and 7, the dual-class stock tradeoff would more likely be shifted in a net-beneficial direction. The SGX has introduced more flexibility than HKEX to its admission criteria by, instead, focusing on the business model of the company (including evaluating whether the company has a long-term plan that predicts high-growth), its operating track record, the level of participation of sophisticated investors and any other features of its business that may be benefitted by dual-class stock.[86] The TSE, in Japan, has also taken a potentially accommodating stance, stating that firms with dual-class stock will be admitted to the extent that, after examination, JPXR, the regulator, determines that dual-class stock is appropriate and necessary in the 'common interest of shareholders',[87] and will not approve dual-class firm admissions purely on the rationale that the structure provides stability to family-ownership[88] or otherwise provides protection from takeovers.[89] A non-exhaustive list of factors are considered, including the need for dual-class stock in the context of the controller's record and business performance of the firm, the period over which there is a need for dual-class stock, and the opinions of the firm's board and auditors on the need for dual-class stock.[90] Given the possible shortcomings of Hong Kong's approach as expressed earlier, it will be proposed (in Section 9.4.3 of this chapter) that the United Kingdom follows the more flexible approach of SGX and TSE but with a greater focus on the identity of the controller rather than the type of firm.

HKEX and Shanghai also impose higher minimum market capitalisation requirements for dual-class firms than one share, one vote firms.[91] It is not proposed that the

84 *ibid* 13, 18 and 23.
85 HKEX Guidance (2018) (n 80 above para. 4.2).
86 SGX, 'Consultation Paper: Proposed Listing Framework for Dual Class Share Structures' (28 March 2018) at 2.
87 Tokyo Stock Exchange, 'New Listing Guidebook: 1st and 2nd sections' (2018) at 142.
88 *ibid* 143.
89 *ibid* 146.
90 *ibid* 143.
91 HKEX requires dual-class firms to have a minimum capitalisation of HK$40 billion (or HK$10 billion with revenue of at least HK$1 billion in the last audited financial year); and the STI expects dual-class

LSE increase its market capitalisation threshold for dual-class firms,[92] since the size of the company is no guarantee that the benefits of the dual-class stock will outweigh the detriments (and empirical evidence in relation thereto is lacking), and a threshold of that nature would exclude young companies that would benefit from equity financing and prevent public shareholders from sharing in the future wealth of such companies from an early stage. The NYSE and NASDAQ, for instance, incorporate alternative minimum criteria options for the listing of both one share, one vote and dual-class firms, of which market capitalisation is just one. The size of a company would not offer assurances that inferior-voting shareholders would be treated fairly,[93] and, conversely, it can be argued that abuse by controllers of larger market capitalisation companies will have a greater impact on the market, as a result of such firms attracting a larger number of investors, and being more likely to be members of indices in which passive investors are required to invest.[94]

Continuing with the theme of eligibility requirements, if the policy priority is to attract the listings of high-growth companies which could benefit from dual-class stock (and in relation to which the dual-class stock tradeoff is more likely to be tilted in a positive direction for public shareholders[95]), one possible protection for public investors would be to restrict dual-class stock to high-growth firms, requiring that any applicant conforms to a pre-IPO quantitative growth profile threshold. However, such an approach would exclude any company which has a projected high growth-rate, which has not yet crystallised, and, in any case, further empirical evidence would be required to accurately determine the optimum growth-rate conducive to dual-class firm performance. Additionally, defining 'growth' satisfactorily for listing purposes would be challenging, and issuers could be incentivised to manipulate figures in order to satisfy the relevant threshold. Such a requirement is therefore also not proposed for the United Kingdom.

9.4.2 *Type of Controller Restrictions around the World*

Another type of restriction could limit the types of persons who may own enhanced-voting shares at the time of IPO. For example, a restriction could be implemented such that dual-class stock will only be permitted if the owner of the enhanced-voting shares is a founder, given that, as discussed in Chapter 6, the benefits of dual-class stock to companies and inferior-voting shareholders are most

firms to have a market capitalisation of at least RMB 10 billion (or RMB 5 billion with an operating revenue of at least RMB 500 million during the previous financial year).

92 As of the date of writing, the minimum market capitalisation for shares being listed by an applicant to the Main Market is £700,000 (LR 2.2.7R).

93 SFC: 'SFC Statement on the SEHK's Draft Proposal on Weighted Voting Rights' (25 June 2015), www.sfc.hk/edistributionWeb/gateway/EN/news-and-announcements/news/doc?refNo=15PR69.

94 *ibid.*

95 See Chapters 6 and 7.

likely to be evinced where the structure permits a founder to follow its long-term strategy. However, the possibility exists that the founder will have long gone, yet a new, equally visionary, management team is taking the company to new heights. Therefore, a better restriction would be to ensure that only persons substantially involved in the day-to-day management, and integral to the success, of the company may own enhanced-voting shares at the time of the listing. This would exclude the possibility of corporate owners and early-stage VC investors retaining enhanced-voting shares upon listing, unless, unusually, they were involved in the day-to-day management of the company.[96] HKEX, in its June 2017 concept paper, mooted restrictions on the types of persons who can hold enhanced-voting shares as a potential inferior-voting shareholder protection mechanism, but, at the time, it was still considering whether to take a disclosure-based or a mandatory-restrictions approach to public shareholder protections.[97] In its final decision on dual-class stock, Hong Kong provided, as part of its suitability requirements, that holders of enhanced-voting shares must have an active executive role and directorship at the time of IPO,[98] and such holders must have also materially contributed to the growth of the business. Post-IPO, the holders of enhanced-voting shares must merely remain as board members.[99] Similarly, in Singapore, the SGX, in considering whether dual-class firms should be admitted, assesses the role, contribution to the success of the business and level of active involvement in the business, of the proposed enhanced-voting shareholders,[100] and, post-IPO, requires that the holders of enhanced-voting shares remain as, not necessarily executive, directors.[101] Shanghai's STI Board requires that any holder of enhanced-voting shares must have made a 'material contribution to the development or business growth' of the company, but need only have been a director prior to IPO and continue to be a director post-IPO.[102] Tokyo will consider whether the knowledge and skills of the controller are essential to achieving the business plan of the company in the common interest of the shareholders, including an assessment of the involvement of holders of enhanced-voting shares in business development, R&D and recruitment,[103] and, post-IPO, will, in certain circumstances, also expect enhanced-voting shareholders to remain as directors and possibly even managers.[104] India is perhaps the strictest of all the jurisdictions, requiring that pre- and post-IPO

96 The UK Listing Review's proposals expressly restrict the holding of disproportionate voting rights, that enable the guarantee of a board seat and the blocking of takeovers, to individuals, but do not further limit who those individuals may be.

97 HKEX Concept (2017) (n 74 above 35).

98 HKEX Guidance (2018) (n 80 above para. 4.5(a)).

99 HK Listing Rules, Rules 8A.11 and 8A.17.

100 SGX Consultation (2018) (n 86 above).

101 SGX Mainboard Rules, Rule 210(10).

102 CSRC, 'Rules Governing the Listing of Stocks on the Science and Technology Innovation Board of Shanghai Stock Exchange (Revised in 2019)' (April 2019) at article 4.5.3.

103 Tokyo Guidebook (2018) (n 87 above 142–143).

104 *ibid* 144.

enhanced-voting shares may only be held by executives[105] (and subject to net-wealth thresholds at IPO[106]). As discussed next, concentrating on the identity of the enhanced-voting shareholders could be an effective inferior-voting shareholder protection in the United Kingdom.

9.4.3 *UK-Proposed Premium Tier Listing Criteria*

Turning to proposals for the United Kingdom. The discussion earlier asserts that it would be overly restrictive to limit dual-class stock to specific industries. However, it is clear from the normative analysis in Chapters 1 and 6, and, to a degree, from the empirical evidence in Chapter 7, that dual-class stock will at least likely be beneficial to certain types of firms more than others, and that certain firms will present greater risks that the detriments will shift the dual-class stock tradeoff into negative territory. Restrictions linked to the type of the firm, rather than its industry, could form an effective protection measure, but in developing a framework within which to assess such companies, it must not be so rigid that it excludes otherwise worthy companies, and, at the same time, not be so nebulous to cause market uncertainty. In discussing the Far East exchanges earlier, several criticisms were raised to introducing too much specificity. Therefore, a broader, balanced approach is proposed in this section whereunder any applicant should be required to justify to the FCA why dual-class stock is conducive to the success of the company.

It is also recommended in this section that the FCA should assess dual-class firms based upon the identities of the proposed enhanced-voting shareholders. A key benefit of dual-class stock, and closely aligned with the discussion in Chapter 1 on encouraging founders of tech firms to list in the United Kingdom, is that it enables a controller to diversify its wealth and raise equity finance while retaining the control that allows the continued pursuit of its idiosyncratic vision and the taking of a long-term approach. Assuming that such idiosyncratic, long-term approach has contributed to the success of the company pre-IPO, the listing gives public shareholders the opportunity to share in future success. Similarly, a further benefit of dual-class stock discussed in Chapter 6 is that it can bond the controller to the firm, and so, to the extent that the controller is integral to the success of the company, public shareholders can garner benefits from them knowing, and other stakeholders knowing, that the controller is bonded to the firm. If the holder of enhanced-voting shares is not a person integral to the success of the company, many of the benefits to the public shareholders espoused in Chapter 6 of giving that person a privileged, insulated and entrenched position in the company fall away. Similarly, from the perspective of the controller, it becomes less likely that only benign controller benefits will be extracted, since such a controller is unlikely to derive satisfaction

[105] SEBI (Third Amendment) Regulations, 2019 (n 79 above Rule 3(II)); SEBI (Listing Obligations and Disclosure Requirements) (Fourth Amendment) Regulations, 2019, Rule 3(VII).

[106] See n 231 below and accompanying text.

from steering and leading a company in accordance with a vision if that vision is largely created and progressed by other individuals. With a lower likelihood that the controller is extracting benign or acceptable non-benign controller benefits, the motives of the controller to maintain control can be questioned. The risks increase that the controller benefits that will be extracted will be excessively pernicious, and the incentive on the controller to ensure that the firm is managed in a way that intensifies the potential benefits of the structure are limited. Thus, the FCA should appraise the contribution of the proposed enhanced-voting shareholders to the success of the company. Relatedly, the FCA should also consider carefully whether the proposed enhanced-voting shareholders have been subject to compliance or conduct issues in the past (for example, previous convictions or disqualifications as directors), since such aspects could portend future poor behaviour.

In summary, the FCA should specify listing criteria based upon characteristics that limit dual-class structure to those firms with lesser risks that the detriments of the structure will outweigh the benefits. This will be based upon the type of the firm and the identities of the enhanced-voting shareholders. As stressed by the dual-class stock tradeoff discussion in Chapter 6, whether dual-class stock will be net-beneficial is a firm-specific factor, and it should therefore be incumbent on the FCA to assess whether an applicant is suitable to premium list with dual-class stock. It is noted that normative considerations discussed in Chapters 1 and 6, and empirical evidence discussed in Chapter 7, suggest that dual-class stock may be especially beneficial to high-growth and innovative companies. However, if other types of companies were able to persuasively justify the benefits of, and need for, dual-class stock, it would be capricious to refuse admission on the basis that the company does not conform to pre-existing strict definitions. Therefore, it is proposed that a flexible approach be promoted. Although this can create uncertainty for potential applicants, over time, the FCA can develop more comprehensive guidance with greater experience of the types of companies applying to list with dual-class stock. Greater certainty could be achieved if the FCA were to publish decisions to admit or not to admit applicants, together with reasons, but such a practice could deter applicants from seeking admission, since a particularly scathing report could either prejudice the likelihood of the applicant being approved on another exchange, or, to the extent admitted on another exchange, diminish the success of the flotation. The FCA should, though, at least express the aspects that it will consider when assessing suitability for admission with dual-class stock. On that basis, the following broad factors should be considered by the FCA, and guidance should be provided to potential applicants in this regard:

- Tracing the directors' duty under s. 172 of CA 2006,[107] the applicant must justify why the success of the company for the benefit of its members as a whole will be promoted by insulating, through the use of dual-class stock, the management team from the ability of the public shareholders to determine their composition – the

[107] See Section 8.2.1 of Chapter 8.

business model, product cycles, growth profile, observability of assets and long-term profitability, and projected business strategy should all be considered.

- The applicant must show a clean track record to-date, both in terms of compliance (to the extent that the company was subject to any regulatory requirements pre-IPO) and with respect to the conduct of the proposed enhanced-voting shareholders.
- The applicant must show that the skills, knowledge and talent of the proposed enhanced-voting shareholders are integral to the future success of the business, and evidence the significant contributions of the enhanced-voting shareholders to the success of the business to-date.

Although requiring that the skills, knowledge and talents of the proposed enhanced-voting shareholders be integral to the future success of the business could exclude a subset of dual-class firms from premium listings, at least in the initial stages of a relaxation of the rules, dual-class stock should be restricted to those firms to which the least risks of excessive pernicious controller benefit extraction attach. Such a proviso will also exclude many dual-class firms where the enhanced-voting shares are held by corporates (other than entities or trusts established by natural persons for tax-planning purposes).

The approach described does, though, impose significant responsibilities on the FCA. If enthusiasm to develop the FCA's resources and expertise to embrace the role envisaged is lacking, a secondary approach would be for the FCA to, instead, adopt a disclosure oversight role. The FCA could, in satisfaction of its existing responsibilities to review and approve issuer prospectuses, ensure that applicants for listing make relevant disclosures in relation to the three bullet points above. In effect, the applicant will be required to justify the need and legitimacy of dual-class structure for the type of firm, and the need for specific individuals to hold enhanced-voting shares. Potential investors can then use the information to discern whether the company in question has sufficiently justified the adoption of dual-class stock and, based upon the disclosures, in what direction the dual-class stock tradeoff is likely to be tilted. Although, retail investors and other unsophisticated investors may not possess sufficient expertise to make such determinations, and the danger exists that such investors may regard the FCA's approval of the relevant prospectus as an implicit regulatory seal of approval of the investment,[108] given the dominance of institutional investors in the market,[109] if sophisticated institutional investors are not persuaded by the company's disclosures, it is unlikely that sufficient support will be generated in the market for the IPO to proceed. In the United States, the abandonment of WeWork's IPO is a case in point.[110] Index trackers that are required to invest

108 B Reddy, 'Finding the British Google: Relaxing the Prohibition of Dual-Class Stock from the Premium-Tier of the London Stock Exchange' (2020) 79 *CLJ* 335.

109 See n 11 above.

110 See Section 6.3.3 of Chapter 6.

in the constituents of specific indices will also not be prejudiced, since they will only be compelled to invest in a firm after it has become a member of the relevant index, which can only occur after the IPO has completed, which, in turn, is contingent upon substantive non-index-tracker institutional investor support.[111] If the disclosure route were pursued, it would be imperative that the FCA takes an active role in ensuring that sufficiently detailed, and meaningful, disclosures are made, with the FCA requesting clarifications and further details to the extent necessary. Such a back-and-forth approach between the applicant and the FCA would lessen the risks that the procedure simply becomes a boilerplate exercise providing little in the way of useful information to potential investors.[112] The disclosure-based approach is not as rigorous as compared to the FCA acting as a gatekeeper in the way that HKEX, SGX and JPXR act in East Asia and will not prevent 'unworthy' dual-class companies entering the premium tier where institutional investors face the 'Hobson's Choice' dilemma described earlier in this chapter.[113] However, if the disclosure-based process were to be pursued in the first instance, it is an approach that could be reviewed over time, and if evidence emerges that material numbers of 'unworthy' dual-class firms are not being impeded from listing by the institutional investor filter, the FCA could then shift to a more prescriptive role.

Of course, applying the listing criteria at the time of admission is no guarantee that the state of affairs will not change post-IPO. For example, an enhanced-voting shareholder may transfer the enhanced-voting shares to another person, or an enhanced-voting shareholder may decide to play no further part in the business of the company going forward. The listing criteria will also not guarantee that a controller will not extract excessive pernicious controller benefits. Therefore, the listing criteria must be combined with other inferior-voting shareholder protections which are effective after listing as outlined in the following sections.

9.5 AS THE SUN SETS IN THE WEST, IT IS RISING IN THE EAST – LISTED COMPANY INFERIOR-VOTING SHAREHOLDER PROTECTIONS

In contrast to the United States, where, as discussed in Chapter 2, the attitude toward dual-class firms, particularly amongst institutional investors, has seemingly hardened in recent times, Hong Kong, Singapore, India, China and Tokyo have all recently relaxed their rules to permit dual-class firms to list. However, looking deeper, in fact, the West and the East are coming to somewhat of a shared understanding as to the risks and opportunities presented by dual-class stock. The universal

[111] Reddy (2020) (n 108 above 335–336).

[112] For example, the UK CGC has been accused of degenerating into a box-ticking, boilerplate disclosure exercise (B. Reddy, 'Thinking Outside the Box – Eliminating the Perniciousness of Box-Ticking in the New Corporate Governance Code' (2019) 82(4) *MLR* 692).

[113] See n 20 above and accompanying text.

thinking seems to be shifting to an environment where dual-class stock is permitted subject to the employment of mechanisms that protect public investors. The United States has, albeit by way of voluntary adoption, focused mainly on investor protections that are triggered some time after IPO and which result in enhanced-voting shares converting into inferior-voting shares (so-called sunset provisions). The major Asian exchanges have, on the other hand, taken a hybrid approach, partly adopting sunset provisions on a mandatory basis, but also prioritising the mandatory application of provisions that protect inferior-voting shareholders ab initio, effective and in force at the time of IPO (so-called sunrise provisions[114]). Solely relying on sunset provisions does not provide limits on a controlling shareholder from expropriating inferior-voting shareholders during the dual-class structure period. Equally, only depending upon sunrise provisions does not appreciate the shifting nature of the dual-class stock tradeoff, and the possibility that the purposes for which the structure was implemented and the benefits of the structure may eventually dissipate, leading to the dual-class stock tradeoff falling into a negative position over time or after the occurrence of specific circumstances. It is therefore proposed, as follows, that the United Kingdom, in relaxing its rules on dual-class stock, implements sunset and sunrise elements.

9.6 THE BALANCED SUNSET CLAUSE

The sunset clause is a term for a provision that removes, or dilutes, a right or power upon the occurrence of a pre-ordained event. In the context of dual-class firms, it relates to the dismantling of a dual-class structure into one share, one vote upon the occurrence of a specified event. Although often used generically, sunset clauses come in a variety of shapes and sizes. In the following sections, presumptive-rules governing transfer-driven, director-linked and ownership-linked sunsets will be recommended, and the challenges making the imposition of other event-driven sunsets and time-dependent sunsets impractical will be outlined.

9.6.1 *Time-Dependent Sunsets*

Perhaps the most basic type of sunset clause is one that is triggered upon the expiry of a period of time.[115] The constitutional documents of a dual-class firm may be drafted to provide that enhanced-voting shares (or all shares if non-voting shares have been issued) revert to one share, one vote a certain number of years after the IPO.

[114] While the term 'sunset' has been widely used in the literature, the term 'sunrise' is beginning to be used to describe initial provisions found and effective in the constitutional documents of dual-class companies at the time of IPO (for example, Winden (2018) (n 3 above)).

[115] R. Daniels and P. Halpern, 'Too Close for Comfort: The Role of the Closely Held Public Corporation in the Canadian Economy and the Implications for Public Policy' (1996) 26 *Can. Bus. L. J.* 11, 58.

Although time-dependent sunset clauses are rare,[116] they are frequently the topic of corporate governance discussions in the United States, and the CII has lobbied the NYSE to mandate seven-year sunset clauses for companies listing with dual-class stock.[117] In the United Kingdom, the standard listed company, The Hut Group, voluntarily implemented a time-dependent sunset of sorts, with the enhanced rights attached to the founder's 'special share' expiring three years after IPO,[118] and, similarly, the enhanced-voting rights attached to standard tier listed Deliveroo's enhanced-voting stock expire three years post-IPO.[119] In some cases, a time-dependent sunset clause may be subject to a vote of the inferior-voting shareholders, such that, usually at a time when the trigger of the clause is impending, a majority of the inferior-voting shareholders may waive the operation of the sunset clause for a successive period of time.[120] India is the first major jurisdiction that mandates time-dependent sunset clauses – dual-class companies must include provision for the conversion of the enhanced-voting stock into one share, one vote stock five years after IPO, with the inferior-voting shareholders being able to extend the period for one further five-year period.[121] Following the prescriptions of the Indian rules, and the examples of The Hut Group and Deliveroo, the UK Listing Review also proposes a mandatory time-dependent sunset clause for disproportionate voting rights on the premium tier (of five years post-IPO).[122] Although, as discussed in Chapter 1, those

116 In a study by Winden (2018) (n 3 above 870), it was found that, in the United States, time-dependent sunset clauses are rare – out of 139 dual-class firms from a sample of pre-2000 IPO S&P 500, S&P 400 and Russell-1000 stocks, and 2000–2017 IPO S&P 600 and Russell-2000 stock, only 25 had time-dependent sunsets (although there has been a significant increase since 2009). A more recent study of US IPOs between 1994 and 2019 found that only 8 per cent of US dual-class firms had adopted time-dependent sunset provisions (D. Aggarwal et al., 'The Rise of Dual-Class Stock IPOs' (2020) 1, 20, https://ssrn.com/abstract=3690670). In a study by Anand (2018) (n 16 above 228), out of eighty-five dual-class firms listed on Canada's TSX, as of 2015, forty-one had sunset clauses, but only two included time-dependent sunsets.

117 CII Letter to E. King, Chief Regulatory Officer, International Exchange Inc. (24 October 2018), www.cii.org/files/issues_and_advocacy/correspondence/2018/20181024%20NYSE%20Petition%20on%20Multiclass%20Sunsets%20FINAL.pdf; CII, 'Dual-Class Stock', www.cii.org/dualclass_stock. The lobbying may have had a market-driven effect, since, in 2017, six out of twenty-three, in 2018, five out of fifteen, in 2019, seven out of twenty-two, and, in 2020, eight out of seventeen dual-class firm IPOs included time-dependent sunsets (Council of Institutional Investors (CII), 'Dual-Class IPO Snapshot: 2017–2020 Statistics' (2021), www.cii.org/files/2020%20IPO%20Update%20Graphs%20.pdf). However, the duration of the relevant sunset period varies considerably on a firm-by-firm basis (CII (2019) (n 147 below)).

118 See Section 1.5.5 of Chapter 1.

119 See Section 1.5.6 of Chapter 1.

120 Helene Curtis is an example of a US dual-class firm with a time-dependent sunset that is renewable every five years (Winden (2018) (n 3 above 872)).

121 SEBI (Fourth Amendment) Regulations, 2019 (n 105 above Rule 3(VII)). Also note that the TSE expects that dual-class structures will dissolve once the need for the structure no longer exists (Tokyo Guidebook (2018) (n 87 above 143)) – a time-dependent sunset clause may satisfy such an expectation, but given the requirement's vagueness, many other forms of sunset clause could, instead, be potentially acceptable.

122 See Section 1.5.7 of Chapter 1.

proposals do not embrace 'genuine' dual-class stock per se,[123] they do show the UK regulator's current direction of travel if the premium tier prohibition of 'genuine' dual-class stock were to be relaxed.

The rationale for time-dependent sunsets is that the company mainly requires dual-class stock in the early years following an IPO to allow the controller to implement its vision for the company without fear of removal or other pressures from public shareholders if short-term profits are unexceptional.[124] As previously described, dual-class stock may be particularly beneficial for growth-phase companies. However, as the company matures, with product cycles completing, and business plans and core activities becoming ingrained, the need for dual-class stock becomes less persuasive, and the opportunities for pernicious controller benefit extraction become more dominant,[125] particularly if the controller reduces its equity stake over time.[126] A sunset clause of this type gives the controller the ability to pursue its idiosyncratic vision in the early stages of the company's growth, but balances this against the rights of minority investors, giving them the comfort that at a specific time in the future, once the company has matured, they will possess equivalent voting rights that allow them to potentially, depending upon the equity stake of the erstwhile controller, determine the composition of the board, and therefore the management team.

The study by Cremers et al. (2018) summarised in Chapter 7 is often put forth as justification for the use of time-dependent sunset clauses. To recap, the authors found that, on average, dual-class firms displayed a valuation premium over single-class firms at IPO, but the premium eroded over time to the extent that it became insignificantly negative six to nine years after the IPO.[127] Kim and Michaely (2018)[128] also found that although young dual-class firms (less than twelve years old) trade at a premium to, and are at least as efficient as, young one share, one vote firms, mature dual-class firms demonstrate lower valuations, operating margins, labour productivity and pace of innovation compared to mature one share, one vote firms. Additionally, in a speech by Robert J. Jackson Jr., then a commissioner of the SEC, findings were presented (albeit preliminary and non-peer-reviewed) that at IPO, and for two years thereafter, companies with and without sunset provisions showed similar valuation, but that by seven after IPO, those companies without sunset provisions traded at a significant discount to those with sunset provisions (which were presumably triggered in some cases).[129] However, caution should be

123 *ibid.*
124 See Section 6.3.7 of Chapter 6.
125 Bebchuk and Kastiel (2017) (n 24 above 605).
126 *ibid* 608.
127 Cremers et al. (2018) (n 3 above 30).
128 H. Kim and R. Michaely, 'Sticking Around Too Long? Dynamics of the Benefits of Dual-Class Structures' (2018) 1, 5, https://ssrn.com/abstract=3145209.
129 Commissioner Robert J. Jackson Jr. Speech, 'Perpetual Dual-Class Stock: The Case against Corporate Royalty' (15 February 2018, San Francisco, California).

applied to the empirical evidence. Firstly, the empirical evidence supporting time-dependent sunset clauses has been challenged on the basis that sufficient time has not passed to fulfil a thorough examination of modern dual-class structure, particularly in the tech sphere,[130] where dual-class firms are becoming increasingly prevalent.[131] Secondly, many aspects of those empirical studies examine firm value – as discussed in Chapter 7, firm value could simply reflect market sentiment rather than truly representing the actual performance of the relevant companies. Further research could more robustly investigate whether such changes in firm value over time are justified by operating performance. Finally, as discussed in Chapter 7, ascertaining causality is not simple, and the findings may not be a result of the waning powers of the controller or increased controller benefit extraction, but simply due to the types of companies that choose dual-class stocks – high-growth companies may be susceptible to more rapid deterioration over time.[132] Although some studies attempt to match dual-class firms to similar one share, one vote firms, matching will never be perfect when sample sizes are small and there are fundamental differences between the firms that choose dual-class stock and those that do not.

A key shortcoming of time-dependent sunsets is that the sunset period, which is determined at IPO, may be completely arbitrary in nature, not reflecting the optimum period of time.[133] The period may prove to be too long, with the detriments of dual-class structure outweighing the benefits long before the triggering of the clause, or it may prove to be too short, with the structure automatically falling away at a time when the company's long-term interests would be better served by the controller continuing to be able to direct its future with the freedom that dual-class stock presents.[134] The duration of the sunset is rarely born from a forensic examination of the characteristics of the company, such as maturity at IPO, age of the founder or time required to bring products to the market.[135] In any case, it may be impossible at the time of an IPO to predict the exact point in time when the motivations of the founder will diverge from the interests of the inferior-voting

130 J. Fisch and S. Solomon, 'The Problems of Sunsets' (2019) 99 *B. U. Law Rev.* 1057, 1074.
131 See Figure 1.2 in Chapter 1.
132 C. Loderer et al., 'Firm Rigidities and the Decline in Growth Opportunities' (2017) 63 *Manag. Sci.* 3000, 3005 – the authors find that Tobin's Q decreases with firm age, and speculate that this may be due to firms becoming more rigid over time, affecting their abilities to create, and take advantage of, growth opportunities – if the high valuation of high-growth companies is based upon imminent growth opportunities, the fall in Tobin's Q over time may be more acute as the firm becomes more rigid and less nimble, as compared to a firm that lists at a more mature stage with a robust and stable business.
133 Winden (2018) (n 3 above 917); D. Lund, 'Nonvoting Shares and Efficient Corporate Governance' (2019) 71 *Stanf. Law Rev.* 687, 739; Fisch and Solomon (2019) (n 130 above 1080); M. Moore, 'Designing Dual Class Sunsets: The Case for a Transfer-Centered Approach' (2020) 12 *W&M BLR* 93, 148.
134 Winden (2018) (n 3 above 917).
135 Fisch and Solomon (2019) (n 130 above 1081–1082).

shareholders.[136] Another potential drawback is that a forthcoming sunset expiry may amplify the incentives on the controller to extract controller benefits. The controller, fearing that the ability to extract significant controller benefits is soon to end, may determine that the rational course is to 'make hay while the Sun shines'.[137] Time-dependent sunset clauses could also give large customers or strategic partners cause for concern that the protection of their close relationships is only finite in time, attenuating one of the benefits for which dual-class stock was initially adopted.[138] Throughout the relationship, especially if the sunset duration is short, the counterparties may seek substitutes to the firm in the relevant business relationship, reducing the benefit that dual-class stock brings to the firm.

The weaknesses of time-dependent sunset clauses could, though, be mitigated. In relation to the sunset period being too long, there is an argument that in certain, more objective, circumstances, the sunset should be brought forward. This is further considered in the following sections in the context of other sunset clauses. In relation to the dual-class structure being unwound prematurely, as recommended by the Canadian Coalition for Good Governance (CCGG),[139] and as provided for under the Indian regulations,[140] inferior-voting shareholders could be granted the right to vote in favour of extending the structure for a period after the initial sunset, if the structure is still beneficial.[141] The effectiveness of this mechanism can be questioned, though, since shareholders may not vote for an extension even though it represents the best course of action for the company[142] due to the almost principled apathy of institutional investors to dual-class stock (and the fact that individual institutional investors may value control[143]). Similarly, even though, at the time of the sunset-vote, the inferior-voting shareholders may be better informed as to the abilities of the founder and the direction of the company than they would have been at the time of IPO, commentators have suggested that public shareholders could be just as likely to take a short-term view at the time of the sunset vote as they would in a one share, one vote firm, and, therefore, not support the founder's long-term vision.[144] Additionally, as the sunset trigger approaches, short-term shareholders, such as activist hedge funds, banking upon the elimination of the dual-class structure which removes the

136 *ibid* 1082.

137 Cremers et al. (2018) (n 3 above 40); Kim and Michaely (2018) (n 128 above 28); *ibid* 1083.

138 In the context of takeover defences, generally, see W. Johnson et al., 'The Lifecycle Effects of Firm Takeover Defenses' (2018) 1, 43, http://dx.doi.org/10.2139/ssrn.2808208. In relation to the capacity for the dual-class stock bonding hypothesis to create benefits for stakeholder relationships, see Section 6.3.3 of Chapter 6.

139 CCGG, 'Dual Class Share Policy' (September 2013) at 10.

140 See n 121 above and accompanying text.

141 Kim and Michaely (2018) (n 128 above 28); Anand (2018) (n 16 above 235).

142 Cremers et al. (2018) (n 3 above 41).

143 Fisch and Solomon (2019) (n 130 above 1085).

144 *ibid* 1085; B. Sharfman, 'The Undesirability of Mandatory Time-Based Sunsets in Dual Class Share Structures: A Reply to Bebchuk and Kastiel' (2019) 93 S. *Cal. Law Rev. Postscript* 1, 9; Moore (2020) (n 133 above 155).

controlling shareholder's insulation from hostile takeovers, may target the company and a potential windfall from a subsequent third-party takeover.[145] If the shareholders of the company at the time of the sunset extension vote are mainly short-termist in nature, it is unlikely that the capital structure would be preserved, and this is a clear risk that may hinder the efficient operation of a voting mechanic to extend a sunset period. The potential for a controlling shareholder to accelerate controller benefit extraction as the sunset closes in, and, indeed, throughout the life of the dual-class structure, would be mitigated by the inclusion of an inferior-voting shareholder vote (since the controller will recognise that excessive extraction of pernicious controller benefits will discourage inferior-voting shareholders from voting to extend the sunset period); however, the danger then exists that the controller's primary focus will shift from its idiosyncratic vision to ensuring maintenance of the dual-class structure and, thus, control.[146]

As of the date of writing, Texas Roadhouse, MaxLinear and Groupon are the only US listed dual-class firms with time-dependent sunset clauses that have triggered upon expiry.[147] All of these firms were subject to automatic unification, unconditional upon any shareholder vote. The share prices of Texas Roadhouse and MaxLinear did not show any significant trend in the lead up to unification, but, interestingly, the share price of Groupon plummeted in the lead up to its unification in 2016. Of course, other business issues may have contributed to share price decline, but it is worth noting that share price has not recovered to pre-unification levels as of the date of writing.[148]

Overall, unlike the UK Listing Review, it is not proposed herein that time-dependent sunset clauses form part of the United Kingdom's balanced protection package, and they should remain the preserve of voluntary adoption. In particular, the five-year specification under the UK Listing Review is prohibitively short. As referenced earlier, even CII, a conglomeration of US institutional investors traditionally antagonistic to dual-class stock,[149] has only lobbied for seven-year mandated sunsets.[150] A time-dependent sunset clause of such a short length could deter many founders from listing their firms with dual-class stock on the premium tier, knowing that they will only retain control for a period of five years, and, even to the extent that a founder were inclined to accede to such a sunset, an unintended consequence would be that such a founder may well wait until their firm is more mature before listing,[151] negating the aspiration of the UK regulators to attract firms to the LSE at an

145 Y. Allaire, 'The Case for Dual-Class of Shares' (2018) *IGOPP Policy Paper No. 11* 1, 47.
146 Sharfman (2019) (n 144 above 9).
147 CII, 'Companies with Time-Based Sunset Approaches to Dual-Class Stock' (February 2019), http://www.cii.org/files/2-13-19%20Time-based%20Sunsets.pdf.
148 Historic share price data obtained from MarketWatch, www.marketwatch.com/.
149 For example, see CII, 'Dual-Class Stock', www.cii.org/dualclass_stock.
150 See n 117 above.
151 B. Reddy, 'Up the Hill and Down Again: Dual-Class Stock and the UK Listing Review' (2021) 1, 27–28, https://ssrn.com/abstract=3812744.

earlier stage of their life-cycles.[152] Five years is also not redolent of the long-termism that dual-class stock could otherwise bring to firms.[153] Firms such as Google and Alphabet in the United States, which listed in 2004 and 2012, respectively, continue to innovate and create substantial shareholder value many years after listing. Even a longer mandated time-dependent sunset clause is mired in peril, since, as discussed earlier, determining the exact point in time, on a one-size-fits-all basis, that a firm is likely to slip into negative dual-class stock tradeoff territory is an impossible task, and successful, growing dual-class firms could easily be cut off at their knees before their primes. Time-dependent sunset clauses are crude mechanisms, and, notwithstanding the empirical evidence, the dual-class stock tradeoff may shift into negative territory before or well after any arbitrarily defined sunset time period. The turning-point will be firm-specific and will depend upon a variety of factors, including the maturity of the company at IPO, the potential length of product cycles and the time horizons of the controller.[154] The proponents of time-dependent sunset clauses are attempting to create a proxy for other indicators that dual-class stock has become net-detrimental. Time itself is not the relevant factor that blunts the benefits or amplifies the detriments, but rather specific qualities of the firm or controller are likely to change over time.[155] Harking back to the benefits of dual-class stock expounded in Chapter 6, over time, management teams may change, control may shift to different persons, the need for long-term relationships with specific customers or suppliers may recede, investment opportunities may decline, and the interest and skills of the founder may wane. All of these aspects are more likely to occur the longer the time that passes post-IPO, but it is not time per se that is causing firm performance to drop, and the time that it takes for those aspects to occur is very much firm-specific. A better formulated sunset protection would trigger upon events occurring that increase the risks that the structure will become net-detrimental or that materially change the terms on which the investors invested at the time of IPO. Such 'event-driven', including transfer-driven, director-linked and ownership-linked, sunsets are described in the following sections.

9.6.2 *Transfer-Driven Sunsets*

An alternative, or sometimes additional, type of sunset clause is one that is triggered upon the transfer of the enhanced-voting shares. As emphasised in Chapters 6 and 7, possibly the greatest influence on the dual-class stock tradeoff is the identity, nature and intentions of the controller. Those investors with freedom of choice will have bought into the founder's vision (or the vision of a successor to the founder) and would, perhaps reluctantly, be acquiescing to the dual-class structure on

152 The UK Listing Review at 19.
153 See Section 6.3.7 of Chapter 6.
154 Fisch and Solomon (2019) (n 130 above 1082).
155 Johnson et al. (2018) (n 138 above 31).

the basis that the controller as of the IPO date, and not another person, has unadulterated control of the company. They may well be investing on the basis of their assessment of the risks of expropriation by the individuals holding the enhanced-voting shares as of the date of IPO.[156] If the primary contention in favour of dual-class stock is that it gives a controller (especially a founder) the freedom to implement its long-term vision, the case falls away if the enhanced-voting shares are transferred to other persons, indicating a lack of commitment by the controller to his or her vision.[157] Therefore, it is proposed that the FCA should require the constitutional documents of dual-class stock applicants to include transfer-driven sunset clauses, such that any enhanced-voting shares transferred post-IPO should convert into inferior-voting shares, unless waived by a majority vote of those holders of inferior-voting shares who do not also hold enhanced-voting shares ('Independent Shareholders').[158] In the United States and Canada, it is not uncommon for dual-class firms to voluntarily adopt provisions in their constitutional documents that convert enhanced-voting shares into one share, one vote shares if they are transferred by the initial enhanced-voting shareholders.[159] By way of example, Facebook, Google, Snap and Lyft have all implemented provisions in their charters pursuant to which enhanced-voting shares will convert into inferior-voting shares upon transfers that are not 'permitted transfers'.[160] Hong Kong,[161] Singapore,[162] Tokyo,[163] India[164] and Shanghai's STI[165] all require that enhanced-voting shares automatically

156 Moore (2020) (n 133 above 142).

157 Winden (2018) (n 3 above 923).

158 In relation to a takeover of a dual-class firm, where the consideration for shares in the target is the issuance of new shares in the acquiror, an enhanced-voting shareholder selling enhanced-voting shares may itself, for UK tax purposes, also desire that its shares convert into inferior-voting shares at the time of the transfer to the acquiror. For example, such a conversion may be required in order to obtain stamp duty relief (Finance Act 1986, s. 77(3)(f)), or if it is important to the enhanced-voting shareholder to preserve Enterprise Investment Scheme relief (Income Tax Act 2007, ss. 247(5) and 257(5)) or tax relief on Enterprise Management Incentive scheme share options (Income Tax (Earnings and Pensions) Act 2003, Schedule 5, Part 6, para. 40(3)).

159 In the United States, transfer-driven sunset clauses have become more prevalent since Google's IPO (which implemented a transfer-driven sunset clause), with only twenty out of fifty dual-class firms listing before Google's IPO including restrictions on transfers of enhanced-voting shares, and seventy out of eighty-four dual-class firms listing after Google's IPO including such restrictions (Winden (2018) (n 3 above 881)). In Canada, transfer-driven sunset clauses are the most prevalent type of sunset clause – 44.44 per cent of the firms with sunset clauses in Anand's sample included transfer-driven sunset clauses (Anand (2018) (n 16 above 227)).

160 Amended and Restated Certificate of Incorporation of Facebook, Inc. (adopted 20 June 2016) (Facebook Charter), Article IV, section 3; Amended and Restated Certificate of Incorporation of Alphabet Inc. (filed 2 October 2015) (Google Charter), Article IV, section 2; Amended and Restated Certificate of Incorporation of Snap Inc. (filed 2 February 2017) (Snap Charter), Article V, section 6; Form S-1 Registration Statement of Lyft, Inc. (filed 1 March 2019) at 196.

161 HK Listing Rules, Rule 8A.18.

162 SGX Mainboard Rules, Rule 210(10).

163 Tokyo Guidebook (2018) (n 87 above 145).

164 SEBI (Fourth Amendment) Regulations, 2019 (n 105 above Rule 3(VII)).

165 CSRC Rules (2019) (n 102 above article 4.5.10).

convert into one share, one vote shares upon a transfer of those shares by the IPO-date holder. The UK Listing Review has also recommended that an individual with takeover-blocking and board seat rights, as permitted under its proposed premium tier reforms, should not be permitted to transfer those rights (with the relevant shares converting into regular ordinary shares upon a transfer).[166]

The requirement for transfer-driven sunset clauses in the United Kingdom could be challenged on the basis that mandatory offer requirements apply under Rule 9 of the Takeover Code.[167] Since transfer of control triggers a mandatory offer, notionally at a fair price, inferior-voting shareholders who do not approve of the new controller can simply exit by accepting the mandatory offer by the new controller. However, an inferior-voting shareholder may not desire to exit the investment, and may prefer to remain invested in a company with no effective controller, as would be the case if a transfer-driven sunset clause resulted in the enhanced-voting shares of the original controller converting into inferior-voting shares upon their transfer. Additionally, transfer-driven sunset clauses would still serve a purpose where the Takeover Code does not apply. For example, if the controller merely sells a proportion of the enhanced-voting shares such that no new controller, or group of connected controllers, acquires a greater than 30 per cent interest, the Takeover Code's mandatory offer provisions would not be triggered, even though the erstwhile controller may lose overall control of the company, with control now being in the hands of a small, but unassociated, group of shareholders. The management team would now be selected by a group of shareholders, rather than the original controller in which the inferior-voting shareholders had placed their faith at the time of IPO. Gifts of enhanced-voting shares by a founder to his or her heirs also may not trigger a mandatory offer under the Takeover Code, even if the result is a family member acquiring more than 30 per cent of the voting rights in the company – the Takeover Code specifies that the Takeover Panel should be consulted in such cases.[168] It is possible that the Takeover Panel could demand a mandatory offer, but it is not obvious what offer price would be stipulated. Therefore, transfer-driven sunset clauses are not redundant in the United Kingdom.

Various exceptions to transfer-driven sunsets are often included. For example, Google, Snap and Lyft, firms with multiple founders, include exceptions to their transfer-driven sunsets, permitting transfers between founders holding enhanced-voting shares as of the date of IPO, without the loss of privileged voting rights.[169] In Singapore, enhanced-voting shares may be transferred with impunity between members of a permitted-holder group approved by the listing authority pre-IPO, and Tokyo

166 UK Listing Review at 21. The UK Listing Review has, though, proposed exceptions for transfers for estate planning and charitable purposes (*ibid*).

167 For further details, see Section 8.2.3 of Chapter 8.

168 Takeover Code, Note 12 to Rule 9.1.

169 Google Charter (2015) (n 160 above section 2(f)(5)(iii)(1)); Snap Charter (2017) (n 160 above Article V, section 1.14); Lyft Registration Statement (2019) (n 160 above 196).

has indicated in guidance that it would be amenable to exemptions relating to transfers between existing enhanced-voting shareholders.[170] Although the centre of power between those enhanced-voting shareholders could therefore shift over time, at least at the time of IPO, the investors can assess the finite possibilities of controllers in the dual-class firm over the lifetime of the structure (and, to the extent that the Takeover Code applies, the inferior-voting shareholders could still enjoy a certain level of protection if the mandatory offer rules discussed later are triggered[171]). With multiple enhanced-voting shareholders, the ability to transfer enhanced-voting shares between themselves without loss of voting-rights may be important to fairly balance voting rights between the enhanced-voting shareholders when one enhanced-voting shareholder desires to sell shares to another, and it is proposed that such an exception should be incorporated in the United Kingdom. Exceptions for transfers to entities or trusts associated with the founder which may assist the founder from a tax-planning perspective are also acceptable,[172] although the enhanced-voting rights should not be protected unless the relevant entity or trust is fully controlled by the original founder. For example, Google and Snap permit unencumbered transfers to associated trusts and retirement plans, as well as entities controlled by transferors, and Lyft similarly permits transfers relating to estate planning and to charitable trusts to the extent that voting control remains in the hands of a founder or his spouse.[173] Hong Kong permits the original holder to transfer shares to entities that will hold the shares on its behalf,[174] and the UK Listing Review has also recommended exceptions in relation to transfers for estate planning and charitable purposes.[175] In the rare cases where the premium tier listing criteria proposed in this chapter[176] would permit a corporate enhanced-voting shareholder, that shareholder could also be permitted to transfer enhanced-voting shares to a parent, subsidiary or entity under common control (although any change of control of the enhanced-voting shareholder should trigger the sunset clause). Other more generous exceptions, that are sometimes adopted in the United States and Canada, could, however, run a cart-and-horses through the relevant protection, and they are not recommended hereunder – for instance, unencumbered transfers, exempt from transfer-driven sunset provisions, to family members of enhanced-voting shareholders.[177] Although a founder may believe that a family

170 Tokyo Guidebook (2018) (n 87 above 159).
171 See Section 9.8.2 of this chapter.
172 Winden (2018) (n 3 above 882–884 and 927).
173 Snap Charter (2017) (n 160 above, Article F, section 1); Google Charter (2015) (n 160 above, Article IV, section 2); Lyft Registration Statement (2019) (n 160 above 196).
174 HK Listing Rules, Rule 8A.18(2).
175 See n 166 above.
176 See Section 9.4.3 of this chapter.
177 The standard tier listed dual-class firm, Deliveroo, includes a transfer-driven sunset clause but with very wide exceptions for permitted transfers, including transfers to any family member of the founder (see Section 1.5.6 of Chapter 1). Although not entailing classic dual-class stock, at the UK standard listed company, The Hut Group, the enhanced rights attached to the founder's 'special share' will generally expire upon a transfer of that share, but with an exemption for a transmission of the special

member will be able to continue his or her legacy and vision, studies have shown that firm performance deteriorates when family members assume management from initial founders.[178] The possibility of unfettered transfers of enhanced-voting shares to family members created consternation, for example, at the US companies Viacom and CBS (which eventually merged).[179] There is no guarantee that an entrenched family member will possess the skills and abilities of the original founder behind whom the public shareholders had placed their faith by investing in a dual-class firm.

The use of transfer-driven sunset clauses can enable a controller wishing to further diversify its wealth to sell enhanced-voting shares in the market while more easily maintaining control, since any such enhanced-voting shares sold will be converted into inferior-voting shares in the hands of other shareholders. On the flipside, an unintended consequence is that a controller selling enhanced-voting shares which automatically convert into one share, one vote, will see the proportion of its voting rights reduce at a slower rate than the proportion of its equity rights, resulting in the controller's voting/cash-flow divergence increasing.[180] If the founder lists the company holding enhanced-voting shares only, while retaining substantially greater than 50 per cent of the voting rights, potentially the founder could, with a transfer-driven sunset clause in operation, sell a significant portion of equity while remaining above the 50 per cent level to retain absolute control, and therefore increase its voting/cash-flow divergence. A similar issue can transpire where a dual-class firm lists with a disparate group of investors holding all the enhanced-voting shares, but where the founders, at the time of IPO, do not hold effective voting control. The scenario emerged with the NYSE IPO of Pinterest, which implemented a capital structure comprised of enhanced-voting shares with twenty votes per share and one share, one vote inferior-voting shares, and adopted a transfer-driven sunset clause.[181] At the time of IPO, the founders held 13.4 per cent of the voting rights and 11.5 per cent of the cash-flow rights[182] – therefore, they did not hold effective control, and their voting/cash-flow divergence was not particularly severe. However, the other enhanced-voting shares were held by existing VC investors in the firm. As noted by Bebchuk and Kastiel (2019), VC investors operate within an investment horizon that requires them to liquidate their position within a relatively short period of time.[183] As the VC

share to the founder's beneficiary upon his death (THG Holdings plc, 'Prospectus for the Offer of up to 376,273,998 Ordinary Shares at an Offer Price of 500p per Ordinary Share and Admission to the Standard Listing Segment of the Official List and to Trading on the Main Market for Listed Securities of the London Stock Exchange' (10 September 2020) at 21).

178 See Section 6.2.4 of Chapter 6.

179 CFA Institute, 'Dual-Class Shares: The Good, the Bad and the Ugly' (August 2018) at 88.

180 By way of analogy: Bebchuk and Kastiel (2019) (n 66 above 1485).

181 Form S-1/A Amendment No. 2 to Registration Statement of Pinterest, Inc. (filed on 8 April 2019) at 182.

182 *ibid* 173.

183 L. Bebchuk and K. Kastiel, 'The Perils of Pinterest's Dual-Class Structure' *Harvard Law School Forum on Corporate Governance and Financial Regulation* (10 April 2019), https://corpgov.law.harvard.edu/2019/04/10/the-perils-of-pinterests-dual-class-structure.

investors exit their investments post-IPO, their enhanced-voting shares will convert into inferior-voting shares in the hands of the purchasers of those shares, thereby commensurately increasing the proportion of votes held by the founders who retain their enhanced-voting shares. It has been remarked that, as the VC investors of Pinterest exit, the founders will be able to hold over 50 per cent of the voting rights while holding less than 5 per cent of the equity.[184] A similar situation, albeit to a lesser extent, exists with Zoom – at IPO, the founder and other management together held around 37 per cent of the votes in the company, but upon a subsequent full exit by VC investors (and transfer-driven sunset clause conversion of their enhanced-voting stock into inferior-voting stock), the management team's voting control will increase to around 59 per cent without them having to increase their equity holdings.[185] Square, Veeva, Okta and RingCentral are also examples of corporations where the VC investors have all fully exited post-IPO – in each case, the founders' voting interests increased from below a majority of the votes to a majority of the votes (or, in the cases of Okta and RingCentral, to almost a majority of the votes), while their equity interests shrank considerably.[186] The consequences of a controller's voting/cash-flow divergence increasing could be mitigated by combining transfer-driven sunset clauses with ownership-linked sunset clauses (as described later),[187] which convert all shares into one share, one vote upon the equity ownership of the enhanced-voting shareholders falling below a specified threshold. Even though, with a combination of transfer-driven and ownership-linked sunset clauses, voting control could still shift, at least the inferior-voting shareholders will know, at IPO, the entire universe of possible enhanced-voting shareholders who may hold control in the future, and that they will not be able to create an extreme diminution in their equity ownership. In any case, with the premium tier listing criteria proposed,[188] it would be unlikely that VC investors would hold enhanced-voting shares on the premium tier.

A further unintended consequence of transfer-driven sunset clauses is that the enhanced-voting shares become more liquid, since the controller can sell those shares to a third party without that person procuring control over 30 per cent of the votes and triggering a mandatory offer; therefore, the 'bonding benefits' of dual-class stock diminish.[189] However, the substantive benefits of transfer-driven sunset clauses

[184] *ibid.*

[185] Data derived from Form S-1/A Amendment No. 2 to Form S-1 Registration Statement of Zoom Video Communications, Inc. (filed 16 April 2019) at 121.

[186] See Table 1.1 in Chapter 1.

[187] Another mitigating mechanism is a transfer-driven sunset clause that converts all enhanced-voting shares into inferior-voting shares only when control is transferred to another person. However, such a clause could prejudice non-transferring enhanced-voting shareholders, and it would still permit unencumbered transfers of enhanced-voting shares that do not trigger a change of control (whereas, as earlier, the rationale underlying the proposal for transfer-driven sunset clauses is that enhanced-voting shares should only be held by the initial enhanced-voting shareholders at IPO).

[188] See Section 9.4.3 of this chapter.

[189] See Section 6.3.3 of Chapter 6.

outweigh their marginal effects on the bonding hypothesis – the economic incentives on the founder to exit are, in any case, low if it only holds a small proportion of the equity (and has already substantially crystallised its investment in the company), and if the founder exited the company, with a transfer-driven sunset clause in operation, at least the ability to determine the composition of the board would revert to all the shareholders acting as a collective.

9.6.3 *Director-Linked Sunsets*

As well as the transfer-driven sunset providing, subject to exceptions, that enhanced-voting shares will only retain their enhanced-voting rights in the hands of the original holders, enhanced-voting rights could additionally be linked to continued involvement in the company as either a manager or a director.[190] After all, even though the premium tier listing criteria proposed earlier requires that holders of enhanced-voting shares must, at the time of IPO, be integral to the success of the company, if, post-IPO, the relevant founder is no longer involved in the company, after, for instance, resignation or retirement as a manager or director, there is little justification for that person continuing to hold enhanced-voting rights in order to ensure the pursuit of his or her idiosyncratic vision. It would not be unreasonable for the inferior-voting shareholders to argue that their acceptance of dual-class stock is based upon their trust in the founder to be intrinsically involved in the strategy of the company. Also, as discussed in relation to the premium tier listing criteria earlier,[191] if the controller is not actively involved in the company, the likelihood that the dual-class structure is being maintained to extract pernicious controller benefits increases. Similar considerations also applied to the UK Listing Review's approach to its premium tier proposed takeover-blocking and board seat rights – such rights would only be available to persons who remain as directors.[192] It is therefore proposed that, in relation to the inferior-voting shareholder protection package laid out in this chapter, any holder of enhanced-voting shares of a premium listed dual-class firm must continue to serve as a director of the company (or in the rare cases where the listing criteria permits a corporate enhanced-voting shareholder, that shareholder must ensure that it maintains a representative on the board). The Listing Rules should provide that the dual-class firm's constitutional documents must require that upon termination of the relevant directorship (whether by resignation, retirement, removal, death or incapacity), the enhanced-voting shares of such a person will convert into inferior-voting shares unless otherwise waived by majority vote of the Independent Shareholders.

190 Winden (2018) (n 3 above 878).
191 See Section 9.4.3 of this chapter .
192 UK Listing Review at 21. Unlike the proposals in this chapter, the UK Listing Review also requires that any holder of such rights be an individual.

A nuance to this theme is whether a holder of enhanced-voting shares should also be required to be involved in the day-to-day management of the company and not merely remain as a non-executive director of the company post-IPO. The counter-argument is that the founder may still play a significant role in the prospects of the business, such as in a chair role, after retiring from management, and, in the United States and Canada, management-linked sunset clauses of this type are rare[193] (although death and incapacity sunsets have become more common in the United States in recent years, including at the companies Google, Facebook, Snap and Lyft[194]). Hong Kong,[195] Singapore[196] and Shanghai's STI[197] all only require that enhanced-voting shareholders have been actively involved in the management of the company pre-IPO, and, post-IPO, merely require such holders to remain as, potentially non-executive, directors of the company. Tokyo has taken a stricter approach, although drafted in flexible terms – if the dual-class structure has been implemented to ensure the continued involvement of a person in the management of the company, then the structure in its entirety will convert into one share, one vote upon that person ceasing to be a director and manager within the company.[198] India, taking the theme further, expressly requires the holders of enhanced-voting shares to be executives, both pre- and post-IPO.[199] The rationale behind the more stringent approach is that although it is appreciated that a non-executive director, particularly the chair, could make a significant contribution to the strategy and vision of the company going forward, there is no assurance that such a non-executive would not in fact take a passive or laissez-faire role and delegate the pursuit of the company's vision to the management team and remainder of the board. In such a case, the presence of the enhanced-voting shareholder on the board only serves as window dressing and ingraining disproportionate control in that individual could allow the dual-class stock tradeoff to tilt into negative territory. However, there are theoretical

193 Only three of the firms surveyed by Winden included sunset clauses where enhanced-voting rights were tied to continued employment (Winden (2018) (n 3 above 878)). In Canada, slightly more firms – four of Anand's sample (7.41 per cent) – included such clauses (Anand (2018) (n 16 above 227)). Facebook requires that all enhanced-voting shares be converted into inferior-voting shares if the founder resigns or is terminated for cause as an 'approved executive officer' (Facebook Charter (2016) (n 160 above Article IV, section 3).

194 Winden (2018) (n 3 above 875) – although only 5 per cent of Winden's sample of dual-class firms listed before 2000 had death/incapacity sunset clauses, the number rose to 22 per cent for firms listed in the first decade of the twenty-first century, and 57 per cent in the second decade. For example, Google (Google Charter (2015) (n 160 above Article IV, section 2)), Snap (Snap Charter (2017) (n 160 above Article V, sections 5 and 6)), Facebook (Facebook Charter (2016) (n 160 above Article IV, section 3)) and Lyft (Lyft Registration Statement (2019) (n 160 above 196)) include death and/or disability sunsets.

195 HK Listing Rules, Rule 8A.11.

196 SGX Mainboard Rules, Rule 210(10).

197 CSRC Rules (2019) (n 102 above article 4.5.3).

198 Tokyo Guidebook (2018) (n 87 above 144).

199 SEBI (Third Amendment) Regulations, 2019 (n 79 above Rule 3(II)); SEBI (Fourth Amendment) Regulations, 2019 (n 105 above Rule 3(VII)).

and practical challenges to this approach. Such a requirement could lead to a founder, unwilling to relinquish control rights, being more likely to remain in a CEO position well after his or her entrepreneurial talents have waned. It is debateable whether the founders of Google would have stepped down from their respective CEO and president roles if they would have had to simultaneously relinquish control.[200] Instead, the founders could usher in a fresh, talented successor into the position of CEO, while maintaining the control that enables them to remain as active board members and ensure that the company continues to pursue their vision.[201] Further, from a practical perspective, it will be close to impossible to formulate effective rules. Presumably, the basic requirement would be for the enhanced-voting shareholder to be party to an executive employment contract with the company. Definitional issues will pertain, though, as to whether a particular individual is in a position of sufficient seniority, and giving an individual a title does not guarantee substantive active involvement by that individual. The controller can have sufficient control over the board such that the board does not dismiss the controller from its 'management' role, even if that 'manager' takes a completely passive role within the company. Given the significant consequences attached to the determination (in effect the controller would lose control of the company), precision is required so that it can be made on an objective basis. The level of precision required to be adopted by whoever is charged with making that determination, whether it be the regulator or independent directors, would be extremely difficult to legally frame without the risk of any such determination being challenged by controllers prejudiced by its application. Requiring that the enhanced-voting shareholder was intrinsically involved in the management of the company pre-IPO is simpler to implement, since the FCA, in ascertaining whether an applicant should be admitted, would be acting upon historic evidence supplied by the issuer covering a substantial period of time. Therefore, for the United Kingdom, given the practical hurdles, post-IPO, only director-linked mandatory sunset clauses are proposed hereunder, which trigger upon the enhanced-voting shareholder ceasing to be a director rather than ceasing to be a manager.

From a separate perspective, ensuring that any enhanced-voting shareholder is also a director does co-opt other protective measures. Such a shareholder would, in a company incorporated in England and Wales, be subject to the duties of directors as codified by statute,[202] and with respect to a foreign company listed on the Main Market, at least in most jurisdictions, directors owe some sense of duty to their companies.[203] Although, as

200 Alphabet, 'A Letter from Larry and Sergey' (3 December 2019), https://blog.google/inside-google/alphabet/letter-from-larry-and-sergey.

201 *ibid.*

202 See Section 8.2.1 of Chapter 8.

203 For example, see Practical Law Company, 'Corporate Governance and Directors' Duties: Global Guide', https://uk.practicallaw.thomsonreuters.com/Browse/Home/International/CorporateGovernanceandDirectorsDutiesGlobalGuide?transitionType=Default&contextData=(sc.Default)&firstPage=true&comp=pluk. In relation to Hong Kong and Singapore, see HKEX, 'Research

discussed in Chapter 8, relying on the enforcement of directors' duties as a deterrent is not without its pitfalls, with director-linked sunset clauses in situ, at least investors will know that any holders of enhanced-voting shares will be subject to duties requiring them to act in the interests of the company in their capacity as directors.

9.6.4 *Ownership-Linked Sunsets*

Another possible variety of sunset clause would be a provision that links the maintenance of enhanced-voting rights to the equity ownership of the founder, limiting the extent of the controller's voting/cash-flow divergence.[204] The importance of such a sunset clause is emphasised when the controller owns both enhanced-voting and inferior-voting shares, giving the controller an augmented opportunity to sell-down further equity post-IPO whilst retaining control.[205] The provision could operate either by a total reversion of the founder's shares into one share, one vote upon the founder selling down too much equity or by converting only such proportion of the founder's enhanced-voting shares into inferior-voting shares to ensure that the minimum equity-to-voting ratio is maintained (although, in the latter case, the risk persists that the controller will be able to retain effective control, even though less than majority control, while only holding a nominal equity level). The reasoning behind minimum equity ownership mechanisms is explained by the normative consideration that with less 'skin-in-the-game', the less aligned the interests of the controller with those of the public shareholders and the greater the incentives to extract pernicious controller benefits.[206] A similar position (although only triggered upon a takeover) can be attained through the use of breakthrough provisions which allow a bidder to acquire control of the board if it acquires a threshold percentage of the equity.[207] Dual-class firms are required to implement breakthrough provisions in Tokyo with a presumptive threshold of 75 per cent,[208] effectively resulting in the controller having to own more than 25 per cent of the equity to be able to insulate the firm from takeovers. Subject to Member State opt-out, the EU has also specified the

Report: Listing Regime Reforms for Dual-Class Share Structure and Biotech Industry – Summary' (April 2018); and SGX Consultation 2018 (n 86 above 5).

204 For example, AMC includes provision such that all the enhanced-voting shares will convert into inferior-voting shares upon the controller (together with its affiliates) holding less than 30 per cent of all the share capital in the company.

205 Even if the controller only owns enhanced-voting shares at IPO, a scenario could emerge where the controller owns both enhanced-voting and inferior-voting shares after a scrip dividend of inferior-voting shares to all shareholders post-IPO (Bebchuk and Kastiel (2019) (n 66 above 1483)). A UK public company can authorise the directors to allot further shares in the company by way of ordinary resolution (CA 2006, s. 551), meaning that a controller with over 50 per cent of the voting rights can authorise a pro rata distribution of inferior-voting shares, assuming that such shares have already been 'created' in the articles.

206 See Section 5.6 of Chapter 5.

207 For further details on breakthrough provisions, see Section 2.4.3 of Chapter 2.

208 Tokyo Guidebook (2018) (n 87 above 159).

implementation of breakthrough provisions at the 75 per cent level,[209] although, as of the date of writing, only three Member States – Estonia, Lithuania and Latvia – have applied the rules.[210] Google has implemented an ownership-linked sunset provision contractually – each founder has contractually agreed that he will not dispose of Class C non-voting stock to the extent that such disposal will result in him holding a greater number of Class B shares (voting stock with ten votes per share) than Class C shares.[211] A breach of the agreement automatically results in the conversion of such portion of the founder's Class B stock to one share, one vote Class A stock that will ensure that he does not hold more Class B stock than Class C non-voting stock. The provision endures until the founders together hold less than 34 per cent of the voting rights in the company. The intention of the provision is to ensure that while the founders have effective control of the company, they are not able to excessively increase their voting/cash-flow divergence.

Another technique to ensure that enhanced-voting shareholders possess sufficient skin-in-the-game is to require 'minimum voting ratios' to limit the ratio of 'votes-per-enhanced-voting share' to 'votes-per-inferior-voting share'. This measure is closely related to ownership-linked sunset clauses, but is a sunrise clause that is instigated ab initio at the time of IPO. By limiting the ratio in this way, a cap is set as to the size of the potential voting/cash-flow divergence. For example, AMEX once provided,[212] and Hong Kong,[213] Singapore,[214] India,[215] Shanghai's STI[216] and a number of European jurisdictions[217] currently provide, that they will not permit dual-class firms to list unless such a ratio is no greater than 10:1, preventing a controller from being able to own more than 50 per cent of the votes without at least 9.1 per cent of the equity. In Canada, the CCGG has recommended that dual-class firms should require enhanced-voting shareholders to have a 'meaningful equity ownership stake', which will depend upon the context, but is generally considered by the CCGG to constitute a ratio of no more than 4:1 (which would require a controller with 50 per cent of the voting rights to hold at least 20 per cent of the equity).[218] The Chartered Financial Analysts Institute (CFA), a global association of investment

209 See Takeover Directive, article 12(1) and article 11(4).

210 Report from the Commission to the European Parliament, the Council, the European Economic and Social Committee and the Committee of the Regions, 'Application of Directive 2004/25/EC on Takeover Bids' at 3.

211 Transfer Restriction Agreements dated 2 October 2015 (see Form 8-K of Alphabet Inc. dated 2 October 2015).

212 J. Seligman, 'Equal Protection in Shareholder Voting Rights: The One Common Share, One Vote Controversy' (1985–1986) 54 *Geo. Wash. L. R.* 687, 705, fn 90.

213 HK Listing Rules, Rule 8A.10.

214 SGX Mainboard Rules, Rule 210(10)(d).

215 SEBI (Third Amendment) Regulations, 2019 (n 79 above Rule 3(II)).

216 CSRC Rules (2019) (n 102 above article 4.5.4).

217 For example, Sweden, Denmark, Hungary and Switzerland (Bebchuk and Kastiel (2019) (n 66 above 1505)).

218 CCGG (2013) (n 139 above 8).

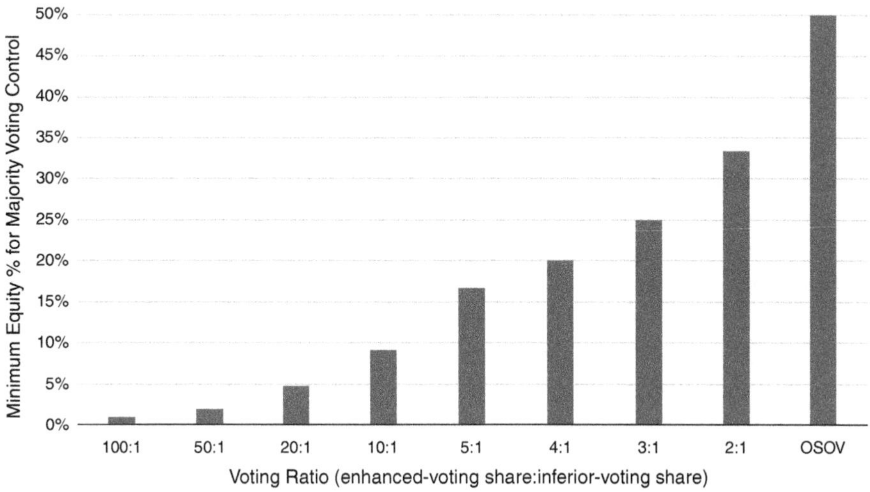

FIGURE 9.1 Equity ownership required for majority control varying by voting ratio *(Author created)*

professionals, has recommended a preferred ratio of 3:1, or, at most, 5:1.[219] The UK Listing Review, perhaps influenced by the fact that its proposals do not constitute 'genuine' dual-class stock and instead would only permit the holding of takeover-blocking and board seat rights on the premium tier, has proposed a much more relaxed ratio of 20:1,[220] meaning that an individual could decisively retain the relevant rights while holding only approximately 4.8 per cent of equity.[221] Figure 9.1 shows how minimum voting ratios correspond to minimum levels of equity that a controller would have to retain to ensure majority control.

However, it does not necessarily follow that a 20:1 ratio, for example, will result in the controller only holding 4.8 per cent of the equity. Indeed, the controller may voluntarily retain a greater level of equity, or may even be contractually required to continue to hold a certain level of equity, as is the case with Google. Equally, the controller may be content to hold effective control (below majority-control), which would be possible with potentially far less than 4.8 per cent of the equity. Therefore, rather than basing the protection on the potential voting/cash-flow divergence, a

219 CFA Institute (2018) (n 179 above 64).

220 UK Listing Review at 21.

221 With 'genuine' dual-class stock, a 20:1 ratio would enable an enhanced-voting shareholder to maintain majority voting control with only a nominal level of equity. It is hereby maintained that such a voting ratio would be largely ineffective in tempering the extraction of pernicious controller benefits by enhanced-voting shareholders. The UK Listing Review has, therefore, likely settled on a high voting ratio on the basis that the scope for controller benefit extraction is already substantially reduced by its proposed structure essentially only constituting takeover blocking and board seat rights rather than 'genuine' dual-class stock (see Section 1.5.7 of Chapter 1). For a critical evaluation of the UK Listing Review's voting ratio requirements, see Reddy (2021) (n 151 above 30–36).

more effective approach would be to tailor the provision to the equity actually held by the controller, which is the approach taken by ownership-linked sunset clauses – if the percentage of cash-flow rights held by the holders of enhanced-voting shares falls below a threshold, the dual-class structure converts into one share, one vote. Hong Kong[222] and Shanghai,[223] for example, also require that the holders of enhanced-voting shares hold at least (or more than, in the case of Shanghai) 10 per cent of the cash-flow rights in the company. If an equity ownership restriction were to be imposed for dual-class stock on the premium tier, it would be better, and sufficient, to solely tie this to the level of cash-flow rights actually held by the controller from time-to-time. Determining whether the relevant threshold represents sufficient 'skin-in-the-game' to constrain the controller from disregarding the interests of the inferior-voting shareholders, though, is a rather ethereal consideration. Albeit with a small sample size, Bebchuk and Kastiel (2019) found that the vast majority of the companies they studied that had implemented such sunset provisions permitted the original enhanced-voting shareholders to sell-down their equity to 10 per cent or less before the clause would be triggered.[224] The authors intimate that the incentives to extract controller benefits are significant at levels higher than 10 per cent,[225] and, therefore, controllers can sell-down equity to a dangerous level, from the perspective of extraction incentives, without the enhanced-voting shares converting into inferior-voting shares. The authors' presumptions though were based upon a computation of the level of diminution to the value of the controller's equity holding caused by controller benefit extraction that the controller would be willing to accept for a given value of controller benefit extraction. Calculations are rarely quite so black and white in practice though, with it seldom simple to predict the monetary value of controller benefits or the effect of their extraction on equity value. Additionally, with robust related-party transaction regulations, anti-fraud laws and audit requirements, such as in the United States and the United Kingdom, it is unlikely that a controller will simply extract value through tunnelling, and, in fact, the main sources of controller benefit extraction will relate to, as discussed in Chapter 6, the pecuniary and non-pecuniary benefits inherent in leading the company in a manner where shareholder wealth maximisation is not a primary concern of the controller. In many cases, therefore, 10 per cent of the equity could represent a material level of skin-in-the-game to constrain controller actions. Nevertheless, the authors did find that some founders could, notwithstanding the existence of ownership-linked sunset clauses, reduce their equity to extreme levels; for example, the founders of the US firms Snap[226] and Zynga, Inc.[227] are able to

222 HK Listing Rules, Rule 8A.12.
223 CSRC Rules (2019) (n 102 above article 4.5.3).
224 Bebchuk and Kastiel (2019) (n 66 above 1490).
225 *ibid* 1490.
226 *ibid* 1456.
227 *ibid* 1479.

reduce their equity stakes to 2.8 and 0.15 per cent, respectively, before the relevant sunset clauses are triggered. In Table 1.1 in Chapter 1, it was shown that for the twenty largest US dual-class firms for which information was publicly and readily available,[228] equity ownership by the enhanced-voting shareholders had declined since IPO to an average of 14.7 per cent. Therefore, even if the controller's equity tranche is substantial at IPO, unless an adequate ownership-linked sunset clause is included, the controller can dispose of equity significantly over time while maintaining control. An ownership-linked sunset clause should be set at the appropriate level so as to not permit the controller's equity ownership becoming so trivial that the controller can extract controller benefits without suffering material equity-value pain, while at the same time not being so restrictive to prevent a controller from selling shares on the market in the future while retaining control (since such a restriction may discourage the founder from listing in the first place).

The market capitalisation of the company will be relevant – 10 per cent of a company with market capitalisation of £10 billion is obviously much more skin-in-the-game than 10 per cent of a company with market capitalisation of £1 million. Hong Kong has acknowledged this distinction by stating that its 10 per cent enhanced-voting shareholder equity ownership threshold may be lowered for companies with market capitalisation of HK$80 billion or more.[229] Further complications are introduced, though, by the fact that market capitalisation could vary over time. In particular, if the company were to undergo further, successive equity issuances in order to raise finance, the market capitalisation of the company would grow – if the controller is required to maintain a threshold percentage of the total equity in the company (a so-called dilution ownership-linked sunset), the controller's absolute level of skin-in-the-game may have to be increased over time to retain control. Unlike Google's 'divestment' ownership-linked contractual sunset clause, such 'dilution' sunset clauses could lead to a perverse incentive on the controller to pursue non-equity financing, such as debt, to avert a dilution of the controller's equity which could result in a loss of control upon the triggering of the sunset clause.[230] The extent to which an individual controller will be influenced by the threshold equity can also take on a more granular consideration – for example, if the controller has made substantial profits from the relevant company by significantly disposing of equity pre-IPO, and therefore possesses significant wealth, the equity threshold may not have a material impact on the behaviour of that controller post-IPO. Other business interests and investments of the controller may also be germane, and it becomes impossible to cover all bases when developing a brightline

228 Information collated from the most recently available (as of 17 September 2020) publicly filed documents – current ownership information was available for nineteen of those firms.

229 HK Listing Rules, Rule 8A.12.

230 Yelp and Pure Storage are two US-listed companies which unified dual-class structure into one share, one vote as a result of dilution provisions (CII (2019) (n 147 above); J. Aycock, 'Yelp Caught in M&A Chatter, Up 2.6%; Ends Dual-Class Shares' *Seeking Alpha* (23 September 2016), https://seekingalpha.com/news/3210618-yelp-caught-m-chatter-2_6-percent-ends-dual-class-shares).

rule. India has attempted to recognise the dwindling efficacy of an equity constraint with increasing controller wealth by providing that enhanced-voting shareholders, pre-IPO, must not have a collective total net wealth (not including the shares held in the relevant company) of more than 500 crore rupees (circa £50 million as of the time of writing)[231] – a corollary, however, is that highly successful founders who have divested of substantial equity will not be able to utilise dual-class stock at IPO notwithstanding huge valuations being ascribed to their companies. Such a hard provision, with no flexibility, could hinder the listings of unicorns.

These considerations make formulating a mandatory uniform de minimis equity holding challenging. Therefore, it is recommended hereunder that the FCA replicate its approach to the free-float rules.[232] The FCA should specify the relevant level required generally with a proviso that it can be lowered (or possibly increased) by the regulator on a case-by-case basis. Since the relevant threshold could be waived, it should be set relatively high, but not so high that issuers dismiss a premium listing out of hand. Judging by the lack of dual-class listings in Tokyo,[233] 25 per cent (which is effectively mandated in Tokyo through the requirement for breakthrough mechanisms) may be too high. It is hereby proposed that the default minimum threshold be set at 15 per cent. The requirement would be imposed in the form of an ownership-linked sunset clause, such that the company will be required to implement provisions in its constitutional documents that automatically convert enhanced-voting shares into inferior-voting shares upon equity holdings falling below the relevant level, unless otherwise waived by a majority vote of the Independent Shareholders. The restriction enforced on a particular dual-class firm should require the enhanced-voting shareholders to hold a specific proportion of the total equity as of IPO, with the sunset clause triggering upon the relevant holder selling such number of shares that would result in it holding less than the number of shares corresponding to the relevant threshold proportion of the *IPO-date* issued equity (as adjusted for future non-cash stock splits, bonus shares and reorganisations). This would therefore operate as a divestment sunset clause, and the enhanced-voting shareholders would not be subsequently disadvantaged by future cash issuances of stock. In determining whether the equity threshold should be lowered or increased for a specific issuer, the FCA should make that assessment by predicting the absolute value of the equity that would be held by the enhanced-voting shareholders (if a 15 per cent threshold were applied) based upon an estimated IPO-date monetary value. The FCA would need to appreciate the balance between the mandated equity holding acting as an adequate constraint over the actions of the controller, and not undermining the desire of a controller to crystallise value and diversify

231 SEBI (Third Amendment) Regulations, 2019 (n 79 above Rule 3(II)).

232 The free-float rules require at least 25 per cent of any listed class of shares to be in public hands, unless an exemption is granted (n 43 above).

233 See Section 2.4.3 of Chapter 2.

wealth, or attenuating the long-termism benefits and the propensity for a controller to take risks and innovate. The FCA could assess evidence provided by the issuer relating to the expected market capitalisation of the company post-IPO and the existing wealth of the enhanced-voting shareholders. Although, in theory, the FCA should consider applicants on a case-by-case basis, it is acknowledged that, as a result of competitive pressures, one could speculate that the FCA would be more likely to, in most cases, lean toward lowering the minimum threshold, rather than increasing it, to compete with the 9.1-10 per cent cash-flow retention thresholds in the Hong Kong, India, China and Singapore markets. However, the FCA can still remain competitive with a 15 per cent threshold, since, unlike the 'dilution' sunsets of those jurisdictions, the 'divestment' sunset proposed herein would not require an enhanced-voting shareholder to continue to participate in fresh issuances to maintain equity ownership above a specific on-going threshold. Although the founders of behemoths like Facebook and Google, several years post-IPO,[234] have reduced their equity ownerships to below 15 per cent over time,[235] their percentages of equity will also reflect dilutions by multiple issuances post-IPO, which would not be taken into account when determining whether a divestment sunset has been triggered.[236] Notably, in the post-2000 period when dual-class IPOs, especially amongst the tech sector, have become more common in the United States,[237] Table 1.1 in Chapter 1 shows that in only two of the ten largest (by market capitalisation) post-2000 IPO firms have the founder(s) engaged in extreme diminution of equity ownership to below 10 per cent.[238] The premium tier will be able to maintain a competitive position with a 15 per cent divestment threshold, particularly with the option for the FCA to lower the threshold in creditable cases. With multiple enhanced-voting shareholders, the FCA could also impose individual minimum thresholds for each enhanced-voting shareholder (which in aggregate would equal the total minimum threshold specified) so that triggering of the ownership-linked sunset clause should, in most cases, only result in conversion into inferior-voting shares of those enhanced-voting shares held by the relevant enhanced-voting shareholder.

234 Facebook listed in 2012, and Google listed in 2004.

235 From the latest publicly disclosed information as of 17 September 2020, the founder of Facebook held 12.9 per cent of the equity, and the founders of Google held 11.4 per cent of the equity (see Table 1.1 in Chapter 1).

236 Google has, in fact, implemented a divestment sunset of sorts (n 211 above and accompanying text). Using data collated from the most recent (as of 17 September 2020) Form-4 and Form-5 insider trading filings, the equity ownership of Facebook's founder and Google's founders (adjusting for Google stock-splits post-IPO), represented approximately 17 per cent, and 25 per cent of the *IPO-date* equity, respectively.

237 See Figure 1.2 in Chapter 1.

238 As outlined in Table 1.1 of Chapter 1, from the latest publicly disclosed information (as of 17 September 2020), the founder of Twilio has reduced his equity to 5.2 per cent, and the founders of Okta own 8.9 per cent of the equity.

9.6.5 *Other Event-Driven Sunsets*

Transfer-driven, director-linked and ownership-linked sunset clauses are, in fact, subsets of event-driven sunset clauses, but sunset clauses could also be formulated such that they are triggered upon certain other events occurring. Some commentators have suggested that performance measures could be taken into account, such that enhanced-voting rights may be lost if, for example, profits, turnover or stock price remain depressed for an extended period of time,[239] or if the firm is consistently underperforming its industry peers over a period of five to ten years.[240] Such a sunset would flush out those founders who do not add value through their idiosyncratic vision and have adopted dual-class stock primarily to expropriate inferior-voting shareholders.[241] However, formulating the relevant measures is easier said than done, and even if that could be accomplished, reducing the formula to robust regulatory language is challenging, and, in any case, measures of accounting performance or turnover may not reflect the expropriation of inferior-voting shareholders after operating profits.[242] Stock performance or shareholder returns could be more appropriate measures, although the period over which any relevant decline should be assessed would be firm-specific. It may be impossible to categorically state that consistent industry-matched stock price declines over a period of, say, three years is indicative of the dual-class stock tradeoff becoming negative in all cases. In some cases, it could merely be indicative of a company significantly investing in projects with horizons much greater than three years, the potential success of which is unobservable to the public shareholders. Another triggering event could be linked to a firm growth-rate threshold, since some empirical evidence, as discussed in Chapter 7, suggests that dual-class stock is more likely to be conducive to firm performance for high-growth firms, and it appears that pernicious controller benefits increase, as the growth of those firms slows down.[243] Measures such as low free cash-flow, sales growth and high R&D intensity (all of which have been used as proxies for growth-rate, and correlated with better dual-class firm performance, in studies discussed in Chapter 7[244]) could be used as indicators of growth-rate. However, the outstanding empirical evidence on such factors is not sufficiently mature to develop specific thresholds. The onset of insolvency or the publication of qualified accounts have

239 Winden (2018) (n 3 above 928).

240 J. Chemmanur, 'Dual Class IPOs: A Theoretical Analysis' (2012) 38 *J. Bank. Finance* 305, 316.

241 *ibid* 316.

242 However, as discussed in Chapter 7, the prospect of post-operating profit extraction by controllers is limited in a UK legal and regulatory context.

243 Kim and Micahely (2018) (n 128 above 24).

244 See B. Amoako-Adu et al., 'Dual Class Discount, and the Channels of Extraction of Private Benefits' in *Advances in Financial Economics*, vol. 16, ed. S. Ferris et al. (Emerald Publishing, 2013); Y. Bozec and C. Laurin, 'Large Shareholder Entrenchment and Performance: Empirical Evidence from Canada' (2008) 35 *J. Bus. Finance Account.* 25; B. Jordan et al., 'Growth Opportunities, Short-Term Market Pressure, and Dual-Class Share Structure' (2016) 41 *J. Corp. Finance* 304.

also been suggested as triggering events,[245] although, by that stage, it may be too late for the inferior-voting shareholders to take effective action. Chapter 7 also noted the tendency, in certain jurisdictions, for expropriation to be incentivised during periods of economic shock. It would be unfair, though, for event-based sunset clauses to be triggered on the basis of events occurring outside the control of the relevant controllers, but during such periods, further research could define whether there are clear financial indicators that dual-class controllers are extracting excessive pernicious controller benefits. Ascertaining whether there are, generally, clear financial indicators prior to dual-class firms slipping into negative dual-class stock tradeoff territory is the 'holy-grail' of sunset clauses, and further research would be welcome, but with the currently available evidence, it is difficult to recommend a form of mandated 'one-size-fits-all' event-driven sunset clause based upon financial measures. Additionally, such clauses would have to be drafted carefully to avoid insidious incentives on the controller to engineer the company's finances in a manner that ensures that the performance-based provisions are not triggered,[246] and without greater certainty as to the relevant objective, measurable events, the ability of the controller to pursue a long-term vision could be undercut. Overall, therefore, it is not advocated that financial measure event-driven sunset clauses be regulatorily introduced in the United Kingdom.

It has also been suggested that inferior-voting shareholders could be protected if the enhanced-voting rights were lost upon the breach of fiduciary duty by the holder to the company or the shareholders.[247] In an English-law context, since shareholders do not, generally, owe any form of fiduciary duty to each other,[248] the clause would be triggered upon the breach of directors' duties – the clause would therefore have teeth only if the enhanced-voting shareholder in question was also a director, which would be the case with the imposition of director-linked sunset clauses as proposed earlier. There are obstacles, though, to an approach based upon breach of a director's duties. Firstly, shareholders would have to commence a derivative claim against the relevant director or directors on behalf of the company and obtain a Court decision confirming the breach. Secondly, as set out in Chapter 8, not only would the Court process be time-consuming and potentially expensive, but shareholder incentives and motivation to pursue derivative claims are often lacking, and Courts generally show a degree of deference to managerial decision-making.[249] On the other hand, it could be argued that, in the presence of an event-driven sunset clause, shareholders may be more incentivised to act collectively, since they would not only be pursuing

245 M. Teen, 'Say "No" to Dual Class Shares' The Business Times (November 2015, Singapore).
246 Winden (2018) (n 3 above 929).
247 *ibid* 929; Fisch and Solomon (2019) (n 130 above 1091).
248 *Estmanco (Kilner House) Ltd.* v. *Greater London Council* [1982] 1 W.L.R. 2 at [10].
249 See Section 8.2.1 of Chapter 8.

an award to the company (since financial awards in derivative claims flow to the company[250]) but also for the enhanced-voting rights to be unwound giving them the opportunity to remove an underperforming, significantly shareholder wealth-reducing, management team. Another possibility would be to require the adoption of event-driven sunset clauses that are triggered upon breaches of the Listing Rules or other regulatory provisions. Such event-driven sunsets should be simpler to implement than those linked to breach of fiduciary duty, since regulators will generally make administrative decisions quicker than the Courts, and implementing event-driven sunset clauses of this type could bolster the effectiveness of the Listing Rules as they pertain to dual-class firms, particularly in relation to the provisions currently relating to controlling shareholders. Overall, though, it is not advocated that the UK mandate event-driven sunset clauses triggered upon breaches of directors' duties or the Listing Rules. Above and beyond the hindrances created by the need to institute Court or administrative procedures to instigate their trigger, it would be concerning that even minor breaches could result in considerable consequences for the controller. Opportunistic shareholders may pursue claims for minor breaches to compel the triggering of the event-driven sunset clause. The rules could be formulated such that the sunset clause is only triggered upon 'material' breaches, but that precipitates issues regarding who should constitute a breach as 'material' and the objective basis upon which the determination would be made. No doubt, an appeals process would also need to be constituted, which would entail further administrative mechanisms. Therefore, although normatively attractive, event-based sunset clauses based upon breaches of directors' duties or the Listing Rules invoke numerous practical hurdles which would limit their application.

Another avenue for event-driven sunset clauses could be those that trigger upon the enhanced-voting shareholder being convicted of certain crimes that could portend poor behaviour in the context of the dual-class firm. Fraud and securities breaches could be relevant criminal offences, and precedent can be found in the United States, where the company Moelis & Co. voluntarily adopted such a clause.[251] However, in such cases, it is likely that the relevant person would be disqualified from acting as a director pursuant to directors' disqualification proceedings if the acts relate to companies[252] (subsequently triggering the director-linked sunset propositioned earlier), and it is therefore not proposed to introduce such clauses to the United Kingdom's balanced protection package.

[250] CA 2006, s. 170(1).

[251] Under the clause, the founder's enhanced-voting shares will convert into inferior-voting shares in the event that he is 'convicted of a criminal violation of a material U.S. federal or state securities law that constitutes a felony or a felony involving moral turpitude' (Amended and Restated Certificate of Incorporation of Moelis & Co. as filed on 21 April 2014, Article 4, section 2).

[252] Company Directors Disqualification Act 1986, s. 2.

9.6.6 Consequences of Sunset Clauses

In this chapter, transfer-linked, director-linked and ownership-linked sunset clauses have been proposed for dual-class stock on the premium tier if dual-class firms were to be welcomed on to the market. One consequence of such sunset clauses is that, to ensure that there are always voting shares in existence, the mechanics must specify that if triggering of a sunset clause will result in only non-voting shares being in issue, immediately prior to and after the triggering of that clause, all non-voting shares will be enfranchised into one share, one vote shares, so as to result in a simple one share, one vote firm after all the enhanced-voting shares have been converted.

The application of sunset provisions could also have a bearing on whether enhanced-voting shares can be listed. Hong Kong, Tokyo, Shanghai's STI and Singapore, for example, require the enhanced-voting shares to be unlisted. In the United Kingdom, the enhanced-voting shares would also need to remain unlisted, since under the free-float rules, at least 25 per cent of shares for which application for admission has been made must be in public hands;[253] taking the enhanced-voting shares as a separate class of shares, with a director-linked sunset clause, enhanced-voting shares will never be in public hands, since they would convert into inferior-voting shares in the hands of non-directors. Therefore, transfer-driven sunset mechanics should be structured so that enhanced-voting shares convert into inferior-voting shares immediately prior to the relevant transfer becoming effective, so that an enhanced-voting shareholder can offer listed inferior-voting shares to a third-party market participant, rather than a chicken-and-egg situation occurring such that the enhanced-voting shares cannot be sold on the market. An alternative mechanism, as adopted in India, is to provide that the enhanced-voting shares can be technically listed but locked-up until the conversion of such shares into inferior-voting shares.[254] Either way, as a further consequence, existing premium listed companies, such as Schroders and Hansa, which have already issued enhanced-voting shares to the public (with inferior-voting shares residing on the standard tier)[255] will not be entitled to 'upgrade' their inferior-voting shares to the premium tier upon a relaxation of the premium tier prohibition of dual-class stock. Both companies would no doubt desire to be able to premium list their inferior-voting stock, which would, additionally, be beneficial for the inferior-voting shareholders who would benefit from a bump in share price as a result of the stock being eligible for index inclusion,[256] but, since, under the proposals in this chapter, enhanced-voting shares can only be held by directors, upon any such upgrade to the premium tier, enhanced-voting stock held by non-directors would automatically convert into inferior-voting

253 LR 6.14.2R.

254 SEBI (Third Amendment) Regulations, 2019 (n 79 above Rule 3(IV)). Such a mechanism would also require an adjustment to the United Kingdom's free-float rules.

255 For an outline of the capital structures of Shroders and Hansa, see Sections 1.5.4 of Chapter 1 and 2.2 of Chapter 2.

256 In relation to the benefits of index inclusion, see Section 1.5.4 of Chapter 1.

stock – a consequence unpalatable to the enhanced-voting shareholders. In contrast, the Daily Mail and Deliveroo, which have only issued inferior-voting shares to the public (on the standard tier), with enhanced-voting shares remaining unlisted,[257] could potentially shift those inferior-voting shares to the premium tier, upon a relaxation of the premium tier rules, conditional upon the respective companies adopting the necessary protective measures proposed in this chapter (including ensuring that all enhanced-voting shareholders are directors).

Another consequence of the sunset proposals proposed in this chapter is that loyalty shares structures, which result in inferior-voting shares converting into enhanced-voting shares upon being held by a shareholder beyond a threshold period of time,[258] would not be compatible with director-linked sunset clauses, since loyalty shares do not discriminate between directors and non-directors when converting into enhanced-voting shares. However, as discussed in Chapter 3, the use of loyalty shares raises a subset of issues and challenges beyond those applicable to general dual-class stock, and, in particular, at IPO, public investors will not be able to incontrovertibly ascertain who will hold disproportionate control down the line when a loyalty share mechanism is in operation. Therefore, it is not proposed here that access to loyalty share mechanisms should accompany a premium tier relaxation of dual-class stock issuance, but the regulators could keep such an approach under review.

A final consequence of the proposed sunset package is that it will preclude a multi-class Google-esque structure that consists of enhanced-voting shares held by founders, and listed one share, one vote shares and listed non-voting shares held by founders and other shareholders. Under the proposed formulation, any shares with enhanced-voting rights compared to the lowest-voting shares must be held by directors. There are two main reasons for this approach. Firstly, without extending the director-linked sunset clause to apply to all shares with voting rights superior to the most inferior-voting shares, founders could, hypothetically speaking, issue themselves with enhanced-voting shares with, say, ten votes per share, which have to be held by directors, and mid-tier shares with, say, nine votes per share, which do not have to be held by directors. All other shareholders would hold one share, one vote shares. The founders could then transfer the highest-voting shares to third parties, whereupon they would convert into one share, one vote shares, leaving them with the mid-tier shares as now the highest-voting shares, but unencumbered by the director-linked sunset provision. Secondly, if non-directors were able to own mid-tier shares, the risk exists that disproportional control could reside, or could eventually reside, in the hands of non-director shareholders (especially after the top-tier voting shares convert into one share, one vote shares pursuant to the transfer-driven sunset clause propositioned earlier). The restrictions proposed would not prevent a

[257] For an outline of the capital structure of the Daily Mail, see Sections 1.5.4 of Chapter 1 and 2.2 of Chapter 2. For an outline of the capital structure of Deliveroo, see Section 1.5.6 of Chapter 1.

[258] See Section 3.8 of Chapter 3.

firm, at the time of IPO, constituting more than two classes of shares, so long as any enhanced-voting shares (as compared to the lowest voting shares in the company) are subject to the required sunset clauses, and therefore unlisted. This would allow, for example, the founders of a firm to hold enhanced-voting shares with different levels of voting rights between themselves, but all of those shares would convert into inferior-voting shares upon the triggering of sunset clauses, and no shares with enhanced-voting rights would be available to the public.[259] Although the capital structure adopted by Google (and once proposed by Facebook) would not be permitted, the restriction increases the likelihood that the dual-class stock tradeoff will be shifted in a positive direction. Moving forward, the FCA could consider relaxing this restriction based upon better evidence of outcomes from the United States (where Google-esque structures are permitted), and Hong Kong and Singapore (where Google-esque structures are prohibited), but, in the first instance, the door to dual-class stock should be opened cautiously in the interests of clarity and protecting public investors.

9.7 THE BALANCED SUNRISE PACKAGE

Sitting alongside sunsets, as per the approach in the major Asian jurisdictions, further protection could be imparted to inferior-voting shareholders by the inclusion of sunrise provisions, which are fully operational from IPO and safeguard against the more flagrant controller abuses without defenestrating the dual-class structure.

9.7.1 *Majority of the Minority Provisions*

One method of protection for inferior-voting shareholders would be to require that certain corporate actions be additionally approved by a majority of the votes (or possibly a supermajority if required by the underlying legislation) of the inferior-voting shares.[260] If the relevant corporate actions are selected carefully, this mechanism can prevent the controller from taking actions that could be substantially detrimental to the inferior-voting shareholders without their approval, curtailing certain types of controller benefit extraction. Hong Kong,[261] Singapore,[262] Shanghai[263] and India[264] have implemented protections such that all shares will be temporarily treated as one share, one vote upon votes on certain corporate

[259] Snap, for example, has issued three classes of shares, but only non-voting shares are available to the public, with the other two classes unlisted and owned by founders or initial investors (Form S-1/A Amended Registration Statement of Snap Inc. (8 February 2017) at 8).

[260] Bebchuk and Kastiel (2019) (n 66 above 1509); Anand (2018) (n 16 above 215) (eight of eighty-five TSX listed dual-class firms included 'majority of the minority' provisions (*ibid* 226)).

[261] HK Listing Rules, Rule 8A.24.

[262] SGX Mainboard Rules, Rule 730B.

[263] CSRC Rules (2019) (n 102 above article 4.5.10).

[264] SEBI (Fourth Amendment) Regulations, 2019 (n 105 above Rule 3(VII)).

actions. Although such a provision does not constitute a true 'majority of the minority' provision, it has similar effect, and respects the one share, one vote principle of decisions being passed by the majority of the equity. In many ways it is fairer than true 'majority of the minority' provisions, since it would otherwise be iniquitous to put a dual-class controller that has retained substantial equity in a worse position than a controlling shareholder in a one share, one vote firm. Denmark and Finland also implement general meeting voting requirements that blunt the voting advantages of enhanced-voting shares in relation to certain corporate actions.[265]

However, the Hong Kong, Singapore, China and India provisions create a potential problem from a UK perspective, since, if inferior-voting shareholders are able to propose resolutions (as discussed in Section 9.7.6 of this chapter), unless the enhanced-voting shareholders hold sufficient equity to block the resolution, it could be unilaterally passed by the inferior-voting shareholders, critically cutting across the control rights for which the controller has adopted dual-class structure.[266] It may be imperative for the controller to ensure that the inferior-voting shareholders cannot unilaterally effect corporate actions. The purpose of majority of the minority provisions is to prevent corporate actions being imposed by a controller on minority shareholders without their consent, rather than to enable minority shareholders to effect corporate actions without the consent of the controller. Therefore, it is proposed that the Listing Rules be amended to require that for certain resolutions, an *additional* voting approval be required where all the shares, even if they constitute non-voting shares (unless they are preference shares), are treated as one share, one vote shares. Accordingly, two votes would be required – a vote under corporate legislation, such as under CA 2006 and IA 1986, which would respect the superior voting rights of the enhanced-voting shareholders, and a second vote under the Listing Rules, which requires all shares to be treated equally from a voting perspective. In that way, the holders of a majority of the equity must approve certain corporate actions, without giving them unilateral powers of implementation.

In considering which corporate actions should be subject to the additional one share, one vote approval, it is crucial not to curtail the ability of the controller to manage the company in accordance with its long-term vision.[267] For example, the ability of the controller to cause the company to engage in large transactions or

265 Shearman & Sterling LLP, 'Proportionality between Ownership and Control in EU-Listed Companies: Comparative Legal Study' (18 May 2007) at 12.

266 In Chapter 1, the possibility for public shareholders to unilaterally prompt corporate actions was noted as a criticism of the premium tier proposals of the UK Listing Review and a potential deterrent to founders listing on the premium tier (see Section 1.5.7 of Chapter 1; also see Reddy (2021) (n 151 above 20–21)).

267 In Chapter 1, the potential ability of public shareholders to veto all corporate actions that require shareholders' approval was noted as a downside of the premium tier proposals of the UK Listing Review in the context of attracting founders to the premium tier (see Section 1.5.7 of Chapter 1; also see Reddy (2021) (n 151 above 18–20)).

acquisitions may be fundamental to the continuation of the controller's vision – an aspect, as discussed in Chapter 1, that would be encumbered under the proposals of the UK Listing Review.[268] The assessment to be made is whether the relevant action is of a nature such that the risk that the holders of a majority of the equity could be unfairly expropriated outweighs the importance that the controller attaches to the ability to effect the action in an unhindered manner. Amending the company's constitutional documents is an obvious example. Although inferior-voting shareholders in English-incorporated companies are notionally protected from harmful amendments to a company's articles or variations of class rights,[269] in practice, those protections are not particularly resilient,[270] and foreign-incorporated companies may not be subject to equivalent protections. Even though requiring an additional one share, one vote approval could limit the controller's ability to make minor constitutional changes that do not prejudice inferior-voting shareholder interests (such as procedures applicable to general meetings, distributions or director authorities), the danger of a controller with a disproportionately low level of financial exposure amending the articles in a manner detrimental to the financial interests of the company justifies this treatment. Attempting to make a distinction between minor and major amendments would introduce a great deal of uncertainty, so it is proposed that the additional one share, one vote approval mechanism be implemented in relation to any decision to amend the constitutional documents of dual-class firms.

Other corporate actions that primarily affect equity holders include winding-ups and waivers of pre-emption rights. A voluntary winding-up of the company can cut short the projected investment horizons of investors, and should, therefore, entail an additional one share, one vote approval in relation to the special resolution that is required to be passed.[271] The waiver of pre-emption rights should attract similar treatment, since any such waiver could result in the dilution of existing equity holders. The provision should be introduced as a super-equivalence requirement applicable to premium listed dual-class companies through amendments to LRs 9.3.11–9.3.12 of the Listing Rules.[272] In relation to auditors, currently, the audit committee is required to recommend auditors to the board,[273] and mandatory[274]

268 See Section 1.5.7 of Chapter 1. Since, under the UK Listing Review, a holder of disproportionate voting rights would only be able to exercise those rights on takeover decisions and personal board incumbency resolutions, decisions to enter into large 'Class 1' transactions (see *ibid*) would continue to require public shareholder approval unless such holder has retained a majority of the equity.

269 See Section 8.2.6 of Chapter 8.

270 *ibid*. Also, in relation to class rights, see Section 8.2.7 of Chapter 8.

271 IA 1986, s. 84. It should be noted that the Listing Rules already require a decision to delist a controlling shareholder premium listed firm to be approved by independent shareholders (LR 5.2.5R(2)).

272 LRs 9.3.11–9.3.12 are existing provisions under the Listing Rules governing the application and disapplication of pre-emption rights upon issuances of shares in premium listed companies.

273 CA 2006, s. 489A(3).

274 DTR 7.1.

and comply-or-explain-based[275] regulations dictate the composition of the audit committee. However, there is no proviso that the board selects the recommended auditor,[276] and the right for shareholders to approve the re-election of the external auditor at the AGM is an important protection.[277] If substantial pecuniary controller benefit extraction is taking place, the auditors will be best placed to identify tunnelling and quantify its extent, and should also be able to identify breaches of any related-party transaction rules, and potentially fraudulent transactions. The ability to approve the auditor protects those who have made financial investments in the company, and, therefore, the additional one share, one vote approval should apply to the appointment and removal of auditors of premium listed dual-class companies. Consideration could also be given as to whether reductions of capital should require additional one share, one vote approval. Reductions of capital are usually effected in order to create distributable reserves, reduce accumulated realised losses or to return surplus capital to shareholders. Under current legislation, a reduction of capital by a public company incorporated in England and Wales requires a special resolution, protecting the interests of the shareholders, and Court approval, protecting the interests of creditors (and also, to a lesser extent, shareholders).[278] However, discriminate reductions of capital where inferior-voting and enhanced-voting shares are treated differently could be effected by an enhanced-voting shareholder with sufficient voting power, and could prejudice public shareholders. A discriminatory reduction of capital of the enhanced-voting shares (which could give the holders the opportunity to expropriate profits of the company) may not trigger class right consent requirements of the inferior-voting shareholders,[279] and it is even uncertain that a discriminate reduction of capital of the inferior-voting shareholders would trigger class rights, given that inferior-voting and enhanced-voting shares would have uniform rights to capital upon a winding-up of the company.[280] Although a Court will also evaluate whether each class of shareholders is being treated 'equitably', it will likely only intervene if there is a significant risk to the relevant shareholders

275 UK CGC, Provision 24.

276 CA 2006, s. 489A(6).

277 CA 2006, s. 491.

278 CA 2006, s. 641. To an extent, the Court will also assess whether shareholders are being treated equitably (n 281 below and accompanying text).

279 Courts have tended not to regard indirect effects on classes of shares to be variations of class rights (see Sections 8.2.6 and 8.2.7 of Chapter 8).

280 It is unclear whether, even between different classes of shares, the variation of a right that is uniform between those classes would be considered to be a variation of a 'class right' under CA 2006, s. 630 absent specific provision in the articles – see Sections 8.2.6 and 8.2.7 of Chapter 8; also see *Gower: Principles of Modern Company Law*, 11th edition, eds. P. Davies et al. (Sweet & Maxwell, 2021) at 510. Even if a broader interpretation of class rights were taken, a reduction of capital of the inferior-voting shares would only be considered to be a variation of class rights if the reduction did not respect the rights of the shares upon a winding-up (for example, if the shares were reduced at par value) – *Scottish Insurance Corp* v. *Wilson & Clyde Coal Co* [1949] AC 462; *House of Fraser* v. ACGE *Investments Ltd* [1987] AC 38.

apparent at that time.[281] Furthermore, for a foreign-incorporated company, different rules may apply entirely. Therefore, it is proposed hereunder that the additional one share, one vote approval also be applied to reductions of capital of dual-class companies, unless the relevant reduction is being applied pro rata to equity holdings of all shareholders, to protect inferior-voting shareholders where all shareholders are not being treated equally.

Related to inferior-voting shareholder voting rights, Hong Kong,[282] Singapore[283] and Shanghai's STI[284] have, additionally, mandated that at least 10 per cent of voting rights must remain in the hands of Independent Shareholders. India takes an even stricter approach, requiring that the holders of enhanced-voting shares do not own greater than 74 per cent of the voting rights in the company,[285] thereby preventing the controller from unilaterally passing super-majority resolutions. It is not proposed to follow the Indian route, since preventing a controller from passing special resolutions in all instances will curtail the ability of the controller to pursue its vision and could deter the listing of dual-class firms; instead, concerns as to excessive power of controllers are better assuaged by introducing specificity to the types of resolutions that require an additional one share, one vote approval, as described in this section. The lower threshold requirements of Hong Kong, Singapore and Shanghai's STI, though, ensure that at least a sliver of control remains in the hands of public shareholders, while not introducing the stringent general curbs on voting power as in India. The lower threshold allows public shareholders to call general meetings and register their discontent with corporate actions by voting against the board on resolutions and rules out a 'Snap-style' structure where the public shareholders only hold non-voting shares.[286] However, in practice, the difference in governance powers between a dispersed group of public shareholders holding 10 per cent of the votes and public shareholders holding only non-voting shares is marginal. Even though 10 per cent gives public shareholders in Hong Kong, Singapore and Shanghai the ability to call general meetings, 10 per cent does not, in and of itself, give those shareholders further blocking powers. As discussed later in this chapter, the same protections could be more efficiently and effectively implemented by requiring that the company discloses inferior-voting shareholder votes, and ensuring that inferior-voting shareholders can propose resolutions at AGMs,[287] making an effective prohibition of non-voting shares unnecessary.

281 *Re Ransomes plc* [1999] 1 BCLC 775; *Re Ratners Group plc* [1988] BCLC 685; *Re Thorn EMI plc* (1988) 4 BCC 698; see Davies et al. (2021) (n 280 above 650).
282 HK Listing Rules, Rules 8A.9 and 8A.13.
283 SGX Mainboard Rules, Rules 210(10)(h) and 803A.
284 CSRC Rules (2019) (n 102 above article 4.5.7).
285 SEBI (Fourth Amendment) Regulations, 2019 (n 105 above Rule 3(VII)).
286 The 10:1 minimum enhanced-voting to inferior-voting ratio requirement in Hong Kong, Singapore, Shanghai and India would also rule out non-voting stock.
287 See Sections 9.7.5 and 9.7.6 later in this chapter.

9.7.2 *Restrictions on Further Share Issuances*

The issue of further shares by an existing dual-class firm should also be considered. The issue of further inferior-voting shares could allow the holders of enhanced-voting shares to divest of further equity over time. However, ownership-linked sunset clauses, as proposed earlier in this chapter, should assuage concerns that such issuances can be used to ingrain greater abuse of inferior-voting shareholders. The issue of further enhanced-voting shares, though, could result in the proportion of votes held by the inferior-voting shareholders as a group forming a smaller proportion of the total voting rights in the company. Although, earlier, the proposition that inferior-voting shareholders should hold a minimum proportion of the voting rights was rejected as part of the balanced inferior-voting shareholder protection package proposed in this chapter, if, at IPO, those inferior-voting shareholders do hold substantive voting rights as a group, they may expect that privilege to continue post-IPO. For example, at IPO, the public shareholders may hold at least some of the votes, which they may value in that it gives them the ability to block a special resolution (if they possess over 25 per cent of the votes[288]), or to require the calling of a general meeting of the shareholders (if they hold at least 5 per cent of the votes[289]). Hong Kong requires that the proportion that the enhanced-voting shares bear to the total share capital cannot change post-IPO,[290] and Singapore[291] requires that the ratio of the total voting rights attached to enhanced-voting shares to the total voting rights attached to inferior-voting shares may not change post-IPO. On Shanghai's STI, the ratio of the total voting rights attached to enhanced-voting shares to the total voting rights attached to inferior-voting shares may not be increased post-IPO, unless in connection with a proportional rights issue.[292] Tokyo goes further and specifies that it is unlikely that approval will be given for the issuance of further enhanced-voting shares post-IPO (although JPRX will assess proposals on a case-by-case basis).[293] As far as the United Kingdom is concerned, an outright prohibition of further issuances of enhanced-voting shares post-IPO for cash could have the unintended consequence of either encouraging capital structures consisting of non-voting shares (or shares with heavily depressed votes) or deterring the issuance, post-IPO, of inferior-voting shares, which could generate further equity financing for the company, since they would dilute the control of the enhanced-voting shareholders – even if they were to take up their pro rata share of any inferior-voting share issuance, since 'pro rata' would be tied to the proportion of inferior-voting shares

[288] CA 2006, s. 283.
[289] Members holding at least 5 per cent of the paid-up capital of the company (that carries the right to vote), or 5 per cent of the total voting rights in the company may require the directors to call a general meeting of the shareholders (CA 2006, s. 303).
[290] HK Listing Rules, Rule 8A.13.
[291] SGX Mainboard Rules, Rule 803A(3).
[292] CSRC Rules (2019) (n 102 above article 4.5.6).
[293] Tokyo Guidebook (2018) (n 87 above 161).

owned by the enhanced-voting shareholder, their voting control would likely be substantially diluted by the issuance (and even if the articles provided mechanisms to ensure that the enhanced-voting shareholders could participate to an extent necessary to maintain their voting percentage, they would have to expend greater resources to so participate than if enhanced-voting shares were also issued to them at the same time). Therefore, it is not proposed that further issuances of enhanced-voting shares for cash be prohibited, but the Listing Rules should require that the proportion that the enhanced-voting shares bear to the total issued shares in the company as of IPO cannot increase post-IPO (and, of course, that new enhanced-voting shares can only be issued to existing enhanced-voting shareholders so as not to circumvent the premise for the transfer-driven sunset), unless with the consent of the Independent Shareholders. Such a provision would permit further issuances of inferior-voting shares without complimentary issuances of enhanced-voting shares, but not permit, unless with Independent Shareholder consent, the issuance of enhanced-voting shares without an issuance of inferior-voting shares to ensure that the IPO proportion of enhanced-voting shares does not increase. To avoid pricing challenges where the enhanced-voting shares are unlisted, the price per enhanced-voting share in any such issuance should also not be any less than the price per inferior-voting share, to avoid enhanced-voting shareholders attempting to increase their equity holding at a discount. A requirement that the percentage of enhanced-voting shares as a proportion of the total issued share capital cannot increase post-IPO will also rule out the use of loyalty share structures, but, as already discussed, it is not proposed that loyalty shares be permitted on the premium tier at this time.[294]

9.7.3 *Independent Directors*

In a way related to majority of the minority provisions, another inferior-voting shareholder protection is the right to appoint a proportion of the board of directors. Commentators have noted the theoretical benefits of independent directors acting as a check-and-balance on the actions of controlling shareholders.[295] The conflict that needs to be monitored by independent directors shifts between one share, one vote dispersed ownership firms and controlling shareholder firms – from between management and shareholders to between the controller and public shareholders. In a dual-class firm, independent directors could constitute an important monitoring mechanism on the acts of the controller, as well as bringing the concerns of the public shareholders to the board. The empirical evidence on the effect of independent

[294] See Section 9.6.6 of this chapter. Also see Section 3.8 of Chapter 3.

[295] Daniels and Halpern (1996) (n 115 above 59) advocated that the board should take on more of a role monitoring any controlling shareholder, and that, therefore, regulations should provide for minimum numbers of outside directors who are sufficiently independent from both management and the controlling shareholder; also see J. Dahya et al., 'Does Board Independence Matter in Companies with a Controlling Shareholder?' (2009) 21 *J. App. Corp. Finance* 67, 76.

directors in controlling shareholder firms on firm performance is inconclusive,[296] and a plausible reason for such inconclusiveness is the level of scepticism directed at the independence genuinely exercised by such directors.[297] This emphasises the need to augment independent director appointment regulations by ensuring that those directors are truly independent within a dual-class structure.

On the premium tier, on a 'comply-or-explain' basis, at least half the board (excluding the chair) should comprise independent directors.[298] However, as mentioned in Chapter 8, notwithstanding the premium tier application of the dual-vote process to independent director appointments, the controller, ultimately, has the right to push through appointments against the objections of public shareholders.[299] Accordingly, even if a director has been designated to be independent by the board,[300] the independence of any such director can be doubted in the face of a controlling shareholder.[301] Based upon the commonality of premium tier one share, one vote controlling shareholders ignoring the negative votes by public shareholders against independent director re-elections,[302] this author has previously proposed that, in the presence of a controlling shareholder, independent shareholders should have a veto over the election and re-election of independent directors, such that their continuing tenures would depend upon both the controlling shareholder and the independent shareholders being satisfied with credentials and performance.[303] This should temper, to an extent, the tendency for such independent directors to display bias toward the controlling shareholder. Bebchuk and Hamdani (2017),[304] Pacces (2018)[305] and Gurrea (2019)[306] go much further and advocate that at least a certain

[296] For example – suggesting no effect of independent directors on firm performance: C. Bacon et al., 'The Board of Directors and Dual-Class Recapitalizations' (1997) 26 *Financ. Manag.* 5, 21; S. Arcot and V. Bruno, 'Corporate Governance and Ownership: Evidence from a Non-Mandatory Regulation' (2018) 3 *JLFA* 59, 77. Suggesting independent directors improve firm performance: Y. Yeh and T. Woidtke, 'Commitment or Entrenchment?: Controlling Shareholders and Board Composition' (2005) 29 *J. Bank. Financ.* 1857; B. Black et al., 'How Corporate Governance Affects Firm Value? Evidence on a Self-Dealing Channel from Natural Experiment in Korea' (2015) 51 *J. Bank. Financ.* 131; J. Dahya et al., 'Dominant Shareholders, Corporate Boards, and Corporate Value: A Cross-Country Analysis' (2008) 87 *J. Financ. Econ.* 73; L. Setia-Atmaja, 'Governance Mechanisms and Firm Value: The Impact of Ownership Concentration and Dividends' (2009) 17 *Corp. Gov.* 694, 705.

[297] See Section 6.2.4 of Chapter 6.

[298] UK CGC, Provision 11. In relation to 'comply-or-explain', see Section 8.2.5 of Chapter 8.

[299] See Section 8.2.5 of Chapter 8; LR 9.2.2ER and LR 9.2.2FR.

[300] UK CGC, Provision 10 provides guidance as to the situations where a director's independence may be prejudiced, including where such a director is a representative of a significant shareholder.

[301] See Section 6.2.4 of Chapter 6.

[302] See Section 8.2.5 of Chapter 8; B. Reddy, 'The Fat Controller: Slimming Down the Excesses of Controlling Shareholders in UK-Listed Companies' (2018) 38 *OJLS* 733, 744–747.

[303] Reddy (2018) (n 302 above 753).

[304] Bebchuk and Hamdani (2017) (n 60 above).

[305] A. Pacces, 'Procedural and Substantive Review of Related Party Transactions: The Case for NCS (Non-Controlling Shareholder)-Dependent Directors' (2018) *ECGI Law Working Paper No. 399/2018* 1.

[306] A. Gurrea, 'Towards a Credible System of Independent Directors in Controlled Firms' (2019) *Ibero-American Institute for Law and Finance Working Paper No. 1/2019* 1, 22.

proportion of independent directors should be appointed exclusively by independent shareholders. With one share, one vote, disenfranchising the controlling shareholder by giving minority shareholders exclusive appointment rights (as opposed to veto rights) could be heavy-handed, given that the equity ownership of the controlling shareholder should act as a buttress against the most extreme forms of abuse.[307] With dual-class stock, though, the argument for inferior-voting shareholder exclusive rights is stronger, since with a substantial proportion of the investment in the company being held by inferior-voting shareholders, it is arguably unpalatable that independent directors can be appointed by a minority (in terms of equity) shareholder.[308] As such, although the NYSE provides an exemption for controlling shareholder companies from complying with minimum independent director number requirements,[309] some commentators have recommended a disapplication of the controlling shareholder exemption where the controller does not own significant equity,[310] and that inferior-voting shareholders be given enhanced appointment rights for some independent directors as described earlier.

The concept of granting inferior-voting shareholders enhanced director appointment rights (or, equally, limiting the director appointment rights of enhanced-voting shareholders) is not a new one. The CCGG proposed a limit on the number of directors appointable by enhanced-voting shareholders of Toronto TSX listed dual-class companies.[311] AMEX, until 1993, required dual-class firms to grant the inferior-voting shareholders the right to appoint at least 25 per cent of the board of directors.[312] Italy requires listed companies to entitle public investors to appoint at least one director to the board and to propose a slate of nominees for that position,[313] and, in Israel, public companies must appoint at least two independent directors to the board in relation to which independent shareholders have veto rights.[314] In Singapore,[315] Hong Kong,[316] Shanghai[317] and India,[318] the regulators have mandated that dual-class firms should temporarily revert to one share, one vote when voting upon the appointment and removal of all independent directors.[319]

307 Reddy (2018) (n 302 above 755).
308 Winden (2018) (n 3 above 915).
309 Bebchuk and Kastiel (2019) (n 66 above 1510).
310 *ibid* 1510; Wen (2014) (n 21 above 1500).
311 CCGG (2013) (n 139 above 7).
312 Seligman (1985–1986) (n 212 above 704 fn 90).
313 Bebchuk and Hamdani (2017) (n 60 above 1291).
314 *ibid* 1292.
315 SGX Mainboard Rules, Rule 730(B).
316 HK Listing Rules, Rule 8A.24.
317 CSRC Rules (2019) (n 102 above article 4.5.10).
318 SEBI (Fourth Amendment) Regulations, 2019 (n 105 Rule 3(VII)).
319 In Singapore, under the SGX Mainboard Rules, Rule 210(5)(c), at least two members of the board must be independent directors (to be increased to at least a third of the board, with a minimum of two members, by 1 January 2022 (Code of Corporate Governance (6 August 2018) at footnote 7)). Under the HK Listing Rules, Rules 5.05 and 5.05A, at least a third of the board, with a minimum of three

Even if inferior-voting shareholders had the right to appoint a specific number of independent directors, the UK convention involves the board proposing the slate of directors on which shareholders vote; the inferior-voting shareholders would always be choosing from a group selected by the controller. An obvious drawback is that the nominees, if effectively proposed by the controller (even if that controller does not have appointment or removal voting rights), may feel beholden to the controller in some respect.[320] If inferior-voting shareholders are to be given the right to exclusively appoint independent directors to the board, the provision would be more effective if it also entitles such shareholders to nominate the directors for election to those positions.[321]

It is, therefore, proposed hereunder that the holders of a majority of the equity in premium listed dual-class firms should have the right to select up to two independent directors, who would be designated 'Inferior-Appointed Directors' and must submit for re-election on an annual basis. A simple majority of votes exercised, with all shares (including the enhanced-voting shares) treated on a one share, one vote basis, would be required to appoint, re-elect or remove any Inferior-Appointed Director. In the first instance, Inferior-Appointed Directors will be nominated by the controller for appointment or re-election at the AGM, and, in most cases, it is likely that the controller will enter into dialogue with major inferior-voting shareholders to ensure that any proposed candidates are acceptable.[322] However, to the extent that the appointment or re-election of nominees proposed by the controller is not approved (pursuant to the first stage of the current two-stage vote process applicable to independent directors in controlling shareholder firms), any shareholders holding between themselves at least 10 per cent of the equity should be entitled to nominate appointees to be voted upon by all the shareholders on a one share, one vote basis at an extraordinary general meeting (EGM) to be held between 90 and 120 days after the AGM (replicating the time frames for the current two-stage voting process).[323] Accordingly, the second vote on the Inferior-Appointed Directors will follow the same timeline for the second stage of the two-stage vote process currently applicable to controlling shareholder firms if independent directors have

members, must be independent directors. HKEX must approve any designation of independence (HK Listing Rules, Rule 5.07). Shanghai requires at least a third of the board to be independent directors, with a minimum of two (CSRC Zhengjianfa [2001] No. 102, 'Notice on Issuing the Guidelines for Introducing Independent Directors to the Board of Directors of Listed Companies' (16 August 2001) at article I(3)). India imposes super-equivalent provisions for dual-class companies, requiring them to ensure that at least half the board comprises independent directors (SEBI (Listing Obligations and Disclosure Requirements) Regulations, 2015, regulation 17(1)(b); SEBI (Fourth Amendment) Regulations 2019 (n 105 Rule 3(I)).

320 D. Lin, 'Beyond Beholden' (2019) 1, https://papers.ssrn.com/sol3/papers.cfm?abstract_id=3335195; Winden (2018) (n 3 above 915).

321 Bebchuk and Hamdani (2017) (n 60 above 1291); G. Loureiro, 'Monitoring the Board: Should Shareholders have Direct Proxy Access?' (2012) 12 *Quant. Anal.* 943.

322 Reddy (2018) (n 302 above 756).

323 In the case that, in the second vote, more than two nominees receive approval to be appointed as Inferior-Appointed Directors, those two nominees receiving the most affirmative votes would be appointed.

not been approved by the public shareholders. A difference from the current rules, though, is that the Inferior-Appointed Directors voted upon at the second stage may have been nominated by the public shareholders rather than the controller, and the resolution to appoint (or re-elect) those two Inferior-Appointed Directors can be passed unilaterally by the public shareholders (if they own a majority of the equity). It should be noted that this would be an option for Independent Shareholders, and the appointment of Inferior-Appointed Directors would not be mandated if the Independent Shareholders determine not to nominate appointees, or no appointee receives a majority of the votes (on a one share, one vote basis) exercised at the second-stage general meeting. It is important that the controller has the right to nominate appointees in the first instance (and the opportunity to convince major equity shareholders that they should be elected), to reduce the risk that the process could be hijacked by activist investors, particularly since studies have shown that dual-class firms that permit the inferior-voting shareholders to nominate and appoint a minimum number of directors to the board are frequently targeted by hedge funds and other activist shareholders.[324] One of the reasons for a controller to implement dual-class stock may be to avoid the potential for short-term activist shareholders to influence the company's business approach.[325] The rules would be implemented in the new Listing Rules chapter applicable to dual-class firms in a similar manner to the provisions relating to the appointment of independent directors in one share, one vote controlling shareholder firms under LR 9.2.2.

Although, with only two Inferior-Appointed Directors, those directors could easily be out voted by the remainder of the board, the purpose of dual-class structure would be undermined if inferior-voting shareholders were able to appoint a majority of the board and therefore seize control. Additionally, evidence suggests that the benefit of such a system lies in the qualities of the relevant independent directors and the information to which they are privy,[326] rather than their absolute numbers.[327] Accordingly, the Listing Rules should provide that any Inferior-Appointed Directors nominated should have financial and/or audit experience, and, if elected, must be appointed to the audit committee of the board (this will assist in ensuring that those directors receive information of a higher quality).

9.7.4 *Related-Party Transactions*

As discussed in the previous chapter, existing premium tier regulations require that related-party transactions exceeding certain thresholds be confirmed by the firm's

324 K. Kastiel, 'Against All Odds: Hedge Fund Activism in Controlled Companies' (2016) 1 *Colum. Bus. Law Rev.* 60, 90; Winden (2018) (n 3 above 916).

325 Winden (2018) (n 3 above 892).

326 J. Erickson et al., 'Board Composition and Firm Value under Concentrated Ownership: The Canadian Evidence' (2005) 13 *Pac-Basin. Financ. J.* 387.

327 C. Chen et al., 'Board Independence as a Panacea to Tunneling? An Empirical Study of Related-Party Transactions in Hong Kong and Singapore' (2018) 15 *J. Empir. Leg. Stud.* 987, 1007.

sponsor as being fair and reasonable to the shareholders as a whole, and even larger related-party transactions be approved by shareholders independent from the related-party.[328] However, it was also noted that potential flaws are present in the regulations that have created controversies in controlling shareholder firms, such as a narrow definition given to associates of the controlling shareholder in the context of family members (giving the controller broader scope to cause the company to enter into transactions with certain family members without being caught by the related-party transaction regulations under the Listing Rules), and confusion as to what transactions are covered by the related-party transaction regulations under the Listing Rules. This has led to a number of controversial transactions by premium tier one share, one vote controlling shareholder firms.[329] This author has, previously, proposed that in the presence of a controlling shareholder, (i) the definition of associate of a controlling shareholder should include not only a spouse, civil partner or child of the controller, but should be expanded to also include any relative of the controller, and any spouse or civil partner of any such relative;[330] and (ii) any related-party transaction, no matter its size or whether such a transaction is in the ordinary course of business, should be subject to confirmation by the company's sponsor that it is fair and reasonable to the shareholders as a whole.[331] The application of such requirements to dual-class firms are even more justifiable than to one share, one vote controlling shareholder firms, as the risk that the relevant related-party transaction is detrimental to the firm increases as the controller's equity constraint decreases, and, therefore, it is proposed that such requirements be adopted in the Listing Rules for premium listed dual-class firms. It is not, though, submitted that Independent Shareholder pre-approval should be implemented for all related-party transactions. Having to call a shareholders' general meeting and obtain pre-approval, with respect to every related-party transaction, would be a relatively onerous requirement on controllers and encumber the ability of the company to act nimbly,[332] potentially leading to management teams foregoing efficient projects that are overall beneficial to the firm,[333] or even discouraging controllers from listing their firms in the first place. The controller would also be subject to the caprice of inferior-voting shareholders who may, themselves, have individual agendas not necessarily in-line with the long-term vision of the founder. The lighter proposal that sponsor confirmation of fairness and reasonableness be obtained in all cases (with, as is already the case,

328 See Section 8.2.4 of Chapter 8.

329 *ibid*. Reddy (2018) (n 302 above 757 *et seq*); also see Section 5.3 of Chapter 5.

330 Reddy (2018) (n 302 above 756). For an example of an appropriate definition, see the definition under the FCA's Consumer Credit Sourcebook, which tracks the Financial Services and Markets Act 2000 (Regulated Activities) Order 2001 (as amended by the Financial Services and Markets Act 2000 (Regulated Activities) (Amendment) (No. 2) Order 2013, article 6), article 60(L).

331 Reddy (2018) (n 302 above 760).

332 *ibid* 761.

333 R. Gilson and A. Schwartz, 'Constraints on Private Benefits of Control: Ex Ante Control Mechanisms Versus Ex Post Transaction Review' (2013) 169 *J. Institutional & Theoretical Econ.* 160, 175.

Independent Shareholder approval only required for larger transactions outside the ordinary course of business) would be less draconian but still provide inferior-voting shareholders with an exacting degree of protection. As discussed in Chapter 8, the sponsor must either be authorised by the FCA or be a member of a designated professional body,[334] and therefore has reputational and regulatory incentives to undertake its duties thoroughly. The process with the sponsor could also be streamlined by permitting regular interrelated transactions to be covered by an overall umbrella confirmation, rather than individual confirmations being required for each specific transaction, or by permitting a general confirmation to be given for transactions with specific counterparties within predefined financial limits. If any Inferior-Appointed Directors have been appointed to the board, they can play an important role on related-party transactions by conveying any related-party transaction concerns to the sponsor. The Listing Rules should require the board to relate those Inferior-Appointed Director concerns to the sponsor. Such concerns should also be disclosed to the Independent Shareholders to the extent that the relevant related-party transaction requires, as a result of exceeding the existing thresholds, Independent Shareholder pre-approval. Also, as referenced in Chapter 8, since, at least for companies incorporated in England and Wales, material related-party transactions must, on a mandatory basis, be approved by the board of the company (excluding associates of the relevant related-party),[335] Inferior-Appointed Directors, if appointed, would be privy to such discussions. With the United Kingdom lacking the litigation culture of the United States, which will have resulted in the proportionately (based upon the size of the US economy) fewer US dual-class controversies as compared to UK controlling shareholder controversies, strengthening the United Kingdom's regulator-enforced related-party transaction regulations is a pragmatic approach to ushering in a new era of UK dual-class firms.

Consideration should also be given to the fact that, currently, the related-party transaction rules are largely disapplied for sovereign-controlled companies.[336] For sovereign-controlled dual-class companies, it would be prudent for the rules to be reasserted, since the mischief that could be derived from the existence of the controller's voting/cash-flow divergence becomes simple to achieve when there are no constraints around the transactions which the company can conduct with its controller.

9.7.5 *Disclosure of Inferior-Voting Shareholder Votes*

As earlier, Hong Kong, Singapore and Shanghai require at least a de minimis proportion of a company's voting rights be made available to the public[337] – the

334 See Section 8.2.4 of Chapter 8.

335 DTR 7.3.8R.

336 See Section 8.2.4 of Chapter 8.

337 See nn 282–284 above and accompanying text; India requires a much larger proportion of the votes to be held by outsiders (n 285 above and accompanying text).

contention is that if a non-negligible proportion of voting stock is made available to outsiders, even if they are in the minority, it will grant them a voice and the ability to put pressure on the controllers.[338] Furthermore, the FTSE Russell index, in fact, requires that 5 per cent of voting rights be held by outside investors for a company to be eligible for index inclusion.[339] Although there may be other good reasons to ensure the issuance of voting stock to outside investors,[340] it is a heavy-handed method of ensuring that outside shareholder voice is heard. Instead, it is proposed that the same purpose could be served more judiciously pursuant to a Listing Rules amendment requiring that, upon any resolution, a dual-class firm should disclose not only the result of the vote based upon the voting rights of the shareholders, but also the result of the vote had all shares been treated on a one share, one vote basis.[341] Although the resolutions will inevitably be passed, since the controller will be able to carry the resolution through exercising superior voting rights, by disclosing the votes of the inferior-voting shareholders, at least any obvious areas of discontent of the inferior-voting shareholders will be publicly highlighted. This would also give the inferior-voting shareholders a method of expressing general levels of dissatisfaction with the performance of the company or its management team, and awareness of controlling shareholder conduct can be raised. This could act as an incentive for inferior-voting shareholders to propose resolutions,[342] whereas, otherwise, they would be reluctant to do so since, without the benefit of voting-disclosure, no shareholder would likely expend effort in proposing resolutions that they will inevitably lose handily.[343] Although the resolution would still be lost, the disclosure of voting by inferior-voting shareholders could generate useful publicity.[344]

Whether such publicity will ensure that a dual-class firm changes its practices is uncertain. In the one share, one vote sphere, in some cases the loss of 'say-on-pay' advisory votes on directors' remuneration,[345] or public outcry generally, has resulted in changes being made voluntarily,[346] and a custom has developed whereby boards

338 Lund (2019) (n 133 above 744).

339 FTSE Russell, 'Voting Rights Consultation – Next Steps' (July 2017), www.ftse.com/products/downloads/FTSE_Russell_Voting_Rights_Consultation_Next_Steps.pdf.

340 For example, see Lund (2019) (n 133 above 716 *et seq*).

341 In relation to recommendations for Canada: Anand (2018) (n 16 above 237); Allaire (2018) (n 145 above 50). In relation to the United States: 'The absence of investor voice is ultimately an issue of accountability' (Winden (2018) (n 3 above 913)).

342 Later in this chapter (Section 9.7.6), it is proposed that inferior-voting shareholders be able to propose resolutions at AGMs.

343 Lan and Varottil (2015) (n 50 above 576).

344 With such an amendment to the Listing Rules requiring disclosure of public shareholder votes, FTSE Russell could also reconsider its 5 per cent public shareholder vote requirement for index inclusion (although the relevant requirement also pertains to ensuring adequate liquidity of securities, in relation to liquidity, the rule could be adapted to reference the free-float of equity rather than voting rights).

345 CA 2006, s. 439.

346 For example, the chair of the remuneration committee in 2009, and the CEO in 2012, resigned from Royal Dutch Shell and Aviva, respectively, after the loss of directors' remuneration report advisory

tend to discuss payment practices closely with shareholders prior to any such resolutions being proposed for vote.[347] The impact of dissenting votes will of course be more keenly felt by directors of one share, one vote dispersed ownership firms where their continued incumbency is subject to the support of the public shareholders, and in contrast, with a one share, one vote controlling shareholder, in relation to the two-stage vote system applicable to independent director appointments,[348] the disclosure of high levels of opposition by independent shareholders often in practice does not result in material changes being made to board composition by those companies.[349] Either way, at least the inferior-voting shareholders will possess a simple avenue with which to register discontent, and, even in relation to the appointment of independent directors in one share, one vote controlling shareholder firms, high levels of opposition can generate adverse headlines for the controller.[350]

'Say-on-pay' is another area where inferior-voting shareholder voting rights should be considered, since, as discussed in Chapter 6, excessive executive pay could be an avenue of controller benefit extraction. With the disclosure of votes regime recommended, the inferior-voting shareholders would be able to at least voice their discontent on executive pay when pay policy[351] and pay implementation[352] are voted upon by the shareholders as a whole. It is not proposed hereunder, though, that the additional one share, one vote approval process outlined earlier in 'Majority of the Minority Provisions' in Section 9.7.1 of this chapter be extended to 'say-on-pay'. Such a mechanism could be hijacked by activist investors looking to pressure a management team into taking actions favourable to the agenda of the activists.[353]

votes, and, in 2012, the CEO of Trinity Mirror resigned ahead of a planned shareholder revolt on pay. In 2016, the remuneration committee of BP used its discretion to reduce performance-related pay to which the CEO was otherwise entitled to avoid 'formulaic outcomes', after the company had lost the advisory vote on the implementation of the remuneration policy in the previous financial year. In 2017, the chair of Persimmon resigned after shareholder and public outrage toward the CEO's £110 million pay package, followed by the resignation of the CEO in 2018.

347 F. Ferri and D. Maber, 'Say on Pay Votes and CEO Compensation: Evidence from the UK' (2013) 17 *Rev. Financ.* 527, 546; R. Thomas and C. Van der Elst, 'Say on Pay Around the World' (2015) 92 *Wash. U. L. Rev.* 653, 730; CIPD Research Report, 'Executive Pay: Review of FTSE 100 Executive Pay Packages' (August 2017) at 2; KPMG Board Leadership Centre, 'Guide to Directors' Remuneration 2017' (December 2017) at 11.

348 See Section 8.2.5 of Chapter 8.

349 See n 302 above and accompanying text.

350 Reddy (2018) (n 302 above 746).

351 CA 2006, s. 439A.

352 CA 2006, s. 439.

353 Recently, there have been indications that activist investors, in pursuit of their agendas, are using governance-related issues as a means of attracting support from traditional investors and exerting personal pressure on directors (A. Mooney, 'Activists Become Wolves in Sheep's Clothing' *Financial Times* (21 July 2019), www.ft.com/content/bf1e6037-bbdd-3465-a0oc-d111e301624e). In relation to executive remuneration specifically, see J. Goldstein, 'Shareholder Activism and Executive Compensation' *Harvard Law School Forum on Corporate Governance and Financial Regulation* (18 June 2015); A. Ralph, 'Investors Revolt Over Executive Pay at De La Rue' *The Times* (26 July 2019), www.thetimes.co.uk/article/investors-revolt-over-pay-at-banknote-printer-de-la-rue-6x3r87tws.

Although the same tactic can be used in one share, one vote firms, one of the purposes of dual-class structure is to insulate the management team from such tactics.[354] Additionally, as contended in Chapter 6, allowing controllers to extract a non-egregious level of pecuniary controller benefits may be a tolerable price to pay to persuade founders to list and to realise the benefits of listed dual-class firms. It would be hoped that extortionate levels of directors' pay would be deterred by the potentially negative publicity generated by substantial symbolic votes against the relevant resolutions, and, in any case, evidence presented in Chapter 6 suggests that excessive executive remuneration is not generally a material channel of public shareholder expropriation in US dual-class firms. It is, therefore, not proposed that inferior-voting shareholders be given separate 'say-on-pay rights', but the point could be revisited after dual-class firms become more prevalent on the premium listed tier.

9.7.6 *Inferior-Voting Shareholder Proposed Resolutions*

Complimentary to the notion of disclosing inferior-voting shareholder voting is a discussion on the ability of inferior-voting shareholders to propose resolutions at AGMs and to call general meetings of shareholders. Hong Kong,[355] Singapore[356] and Shanghai[357] require that, in a dual-class firm, shareholders holding 10 per cent of the votes, where all shares are treated on a one share, one vote basis, be able to call a shareholders' general meeting. A similar right in the United Kingdom would allow inferior-voting shareholders to raise issues of concern and express discontent through a symbolic vote on the relevant resolutions (the votes would be 'symbolic' where the controller possesses sufficient votes to defeat the proposal). However, the ability to call general meetings at any time could be used by activists to disrupt the business of the firm, an outcome that a controller issuing, for example, non-voting stock would be keen to avoid. Such agitations to a controller attempting to pursue a long-term vision could deter issuers from choosing the United Kingdom as a destination for dual-class structure. Therefore, an unconditional inferior-voting shareholder right to call general meetings is not proposed. Other than where only non-voting stock has been issued to the public, it is likely that public shareholders will have sufficient voting power under CA 2006 (5 per cent of the votes)[358] to call a shareholders' general meeting in any case. If public shareholders will not possess sufficient votes to call a general meeting, it will be one of the considerations that

[354] Consequently, as discussed in Chapter 1, the premium tier proposals of the UK Listing Review, which do not enable founders to control the outcome of say-on-pay votes (and, apart from takeover and board incumbency resolutions, any other votes), are unlikely to satisfy the desires of founders to insulate management from public shareholders that would otherwise be possible through the use of 'genuine' dual-class stock (see Section 1.5.7 of Chapter 1).

[355] HK Listing Rules, Rule 8A.23.

[356] SGX Mainboard Rules, Rule 210(10).

[357] CSRC Rules (2019) (n 102 above article 4.5.7).

[358] See n 289 above.

potential investors will need to factor into their decision-making as to whether to invest in the company. It is, though, recommended that the Listing Rules be amended to require that the constitutional documents of premium listed dual-class firms include provisions that treat all equity shares (including non-voting shares, but excluding preference shares) on a one share, one vote basis in relation to any shareholder powers to propose resolutions to be heard at AGMs under the laws applicable to those companies.[359] This would enable inferior-voting shareholders, if they do own sufficient equity, to raise concerns on an annual basis, without being able to continually interfere throughout the year outside of the AGM forum.

9.7.7 *Greater Disclosure*

The importance of disclosure by dual-class firms is underlined by the enhanced disclosure requirements for dual-class firms imposed by Hong Kong, Singapore and Shanghai.[360] A study by Anderson et al. (2009) also found better firm valuation performance by dual-class firms compared to one share, one vote firms where such dual-class firms were transparent (as scored by an opacity index devised by the authors), with the opposite found for opaque dual-class firms.[361] In relation to financial information, at least under current legislation in the United Kingdom, the company's annual report must be circulated to all members of the company,[362] voting or non-voting, and, in relation to general meetings of the company, all members are entitled to notice of the relevant meeting and equality of information.[363] Inferior-voting shareholders could, though, benefit from more robust disclosure rules regarding the cash-flow interests of enhanced-voting shareholders and the extent to which enhanced-voting shareholders are able to reduce those cash-flow interests while retaining control,[364] given that the degree of the controller's voting/cash-flow divergence can influence the extent of controller benefit extraction.

Current regulations should already elicit a degree of pertinent information regarding share ownership. Since, under the proposals in this chapter, enhanced-voting

359 For a company incorporated under CA 2006, members holding at least 5 per cent of the voting rights, or at least 100 members with a right to vote and average sum paid-up per member of at least £100, can propose resolutions for a vote at the AGM (CA 2006, s. 338).

360 See Section 2.4 of Chapter 2.

361 R. Anderson et al., 'Founders, Heirs, and Corporate Opacity in the United States' (2009) 92 *J. Financ. Econ.* 205, 215. For further details, see Section 7.4 of Chapter 7.

362 CA 2006, s. 423.

363 CA 2006, ss. 310.

364 A quality that is not easy to discern from US disclosures (Bebchuk and Kastiel (2019) (n 66 above 1503)). This author can also testify that the collation of data for the purposes of discerning voting and cash-flow rights of US dual-class firm controllers (see Table 1.1 in Chapter 1) was not a simple process, requiring detailed review of extensive documentation and further processing of data; even then, for certain companies, disclosed information lacked clarity in relation to underlying trusts and family interests.

shareholders will be directors, they will be subject to LR 9.8.6(1)R, which requires the disclosure of directors' interests in the annual report; but the Listing Rules should be clarified to ensure that the information disclosed for dual-class firms is sufficiently clear and transparent to allow investors to ascertain not only the number of each class of shares owned but also the percentage that they represent of the total voting and cash-flow rights in the company.[365] Enhanced-voting shareholders will also be subject to disclosure requirements under Article 19 of MAR, under which directors must disclose any changes in interests in shares (subject to an annual de minimis threshold) – this would include enhanced-voting and inferior-voting shares, so the investors will receive the relevant information on changes in enhanced-voting shareholder ownership.[366]

However, greater clarity should be included in the offering prospectus of any dual-class firm proposing to list on the premium tier – the FCA's Prospectus Regulation Rules should be amended to require full disclosure of the capital structure (including details of the operation of sunset and sunrise provisions), the number and percentage of voting and cash-flow interests that will be held by substantial shareholders post-IPO and details outlining the maximum magnitude of voting/cash-flow divergence theoretically possible in the future under the proposed capital structure. Such information will give potential investors vital information as to where voting power lies, the personal financial equity investment of those with voting control and the extent to which controllers may reduce their equity involvement while retaining control. The Listing Rules should be amended to ensure that the same information is provided in the annual reports so that the information is updated for future investors.

9.8 FURTHER LISTING RULES AND TAKEOVER CODE CONSIDERATIONS

9.8.1 *LR 9.2.21 R*

Technically, the Premium Listing Principles do not prohibit a dual-class firm from listing inferior-voting shares on the premium tier while enhanced-voting shares remain unlisted, and, in this chapter, it has been proposed that the relaxation of the premium tier rules on dual-class stock should entail enhanced-voting shares remaining unlisted.[367] Therefore, upon such a relaxation, rather than amend the

365 Bebchuk and Kastiel (2019) (n 66 above 1502).

366 Any changes over the course of the financial year are also required to be disclosed in the annual report (LR 9.8.6(1)R). However, consideration should also be given to clarifying DTR 5 to ensure that changes in the cash-flow rights of major shareholders (whether or not directors) are disclosed, rather than merely voting-rights as currently required. Although enhanced-voting shareholders, as directors, would be required to disclose the relevant information under MAR and the Listing Rules, substantial inferior-voting shareholders would only be covered by the DTRs – this would give investors a fuller picture as to where the economic ownership of the company lies, which will be especially pertinent when enhanced-voting shareholders lose their privileged positions upon the trigger of sunset clauses.

367 See Section 9.6.6 of this chapter.

principles, the FCA would merely need to publicise its relaxation of the informal discouragement of dual-class firms noted in Chapter 2 (and that an issue of inferior-voting shares on the premium tier, with a retention by the controller of enhanced-voting shares, will not breach the spirit of the Listing Principles[368]), and that it welcomes the admission of dual-class firms to the premium tier so long as they adopt the measures described in this chapter. However, LR 9.2.21 R, which provides that certain matters relevant to premium listings must be approved only by the holders of premium listed shares, will need to be revised. Existing controlling shareholder provisions and the dual-class firm proposals under this chapter set out when separate votes of inferior-voting shareholders (or votes on a universal one share, one vote basis) should be required, and LR 9.2.21 R should therefore be modified to prevent a dual-class firm with unlisted enhanced-voting shares being prejudiced by certain further actions requiring approval by the holders of the premium listed inferior-voting shares.

9.8.2 *Takeover Code*

As discussed in Chapters 6 and 8, the mandatory offer and equal treatment requirements of Rule 9 of the Takeover Code are potentially important inferior-voting shareholder protections in dual-class firms, precluding the extraction of control premia and impeding inefficient takeovers. In relation to listed companies, though, the Takeover Code only applies to companies registered and traded in the United Kingdom, the Isle of Man or the Channel Islands.[369] Therefore, for foreign-registered companies, listing on the premium tier with dual-class stock, public shareholders will not enjoy those protections unless the foreign jurisdiction in question also imposes equivalent requirements.[370] However, in most cases, the application of transfer-driven sunset clauses will still prevent the extraction of control premia and obstruct (at least to the same extent as in a one share, one vote firm) inefficient takeovers, since, with enhanced-voting shares automatically converting into inferior-voting shares upon transfer, the holders of enhanced-voting stock will not be able to transfer disproportionate control to third parties.

In a particular set of circumstances, though, the transfer-driven sunset clause could be circumvented – if multiple persons, in a premium listed dual-class firm, hold enhanced-voting shares, a transfer of shares from one of those enhanced-voting shareholders to another would not, as a permitted transfer, trigger the transfer-driven sunset clause proposed in this chapter. This could prejudice inferior-voting shareholders since control could shift into the hands of an enhanced-

368 In relation to the spirit of the Listing Principles, see Section 2.2 of Chapter 2.

369 Takeover Code, Introduction Section 3. For further details on the applicability of the Takeover Code, see Section 8.2.3 of Chapter 8.

370 EU Members States, though, are required to implement mandatory offer provisions (Takeover Directive, article 5); also, see Section 8.2.3 of Chapter 8.

voting shareholder who did not have, prior to the relevant transfer, individual control over the company; the inferior-voting shareholders could rightly consider this to be a material change in circumstances that justifies the making of a mandatory offer for the remaining shares. The Takeover Code already acknowledges a similar scenario in the context of one share, one vote firms, where members of a concert party sell shares between themselves, resulting in a change in composition of the concert party. Where such sales result in a single member of the concert party crossing a relevant threshold, a mandatory offer requirement is triggered, unless waived by the Takeover Panel.[371] In deliberating a waiver, the Takeover Panel will consider, amongst other things, 'whether the leader of the group or the member with the largest individual interest in shares has changed and whether the balance between the interests in the group has changed significantly', and 'the relationship between the persons acting in concert and how long they have been acting in concert'.[372] For a dual-class firm to which the Takeover Code applies, the same considerations would be made upon a transfer of shares between enhanced-voting shareholders, who, as owners seeking to retain control amongst themselves as a collaborative group, may well be considered to be a concert party by the Takeover Panel.[373] However, for a foreign firm to which the Takeover Code does not apply, a hole exists since, in such a case, neither a mandatory offer nor transfer-driven sunset may be triggered. It could be proposed that, for the purposes of dual-class companies, Rule 9 of the Takeover Code be extended to all companies listed on the premium tier. However, it is unlikely that appetite exists to extend the Takeover Code in this way. Upon the expiry of the UK/EU Withdrawal Agreement, the Takeover Code ceased to apply to certain EEA companies.[374] The Takeover Panel ruled-out extending the Takeover Code generally to EEA companies post-EU withdrawal on the basis of difficulties in extraterritorial enforcement of the rules and decisions of the Takeover Panel, including the ability to seek compliance orders from the Courts,[375] and the potential for conflicts with local securities laws.[376] Although mechanisms could be developed to assuage the Takeover Panel's concerns regarding extraterritorial jurisdiction, the fact that the regulators are content for mandatory-offer provisions to only apply to locally registered listed companies suggests that the regulators are comfortable that a substantive public shareholder protective measure is not available to many listed

[371] Takeover Code, Note 4 to Rule 9.1.

[372] *ibid.*

[373] 'Persons acting in concert' comprise 'persons who, pursuant to an agreement or understanding (whether formal or informal), co-operate to obtain or consolidate control of a company or to frustrate the successful outcome of an offer for a company' (Takeover Code, Definitions).

[374] The Takeover Panel, Code Committee Response Statement RS2018/2, 'The United Kingdom's Withdrawal from the European Union' (6 March 2019) at 10. In relation to the transition period, see UK/EU Withdrawal Agreement, articles 126–132.

[375] CA 2006, s. 955.

[376] Takeover Panel (2019) (n 374 above 10).

companies. On that basis, it would be challenging to lobby for a different approach for dual-class firms specifically, which would require the formulation of complex mechanics and procedural rules. Another solution would be to limit the use of dual-class stock on the premium tier to United Kingdom, Isle of Man and Channel Islands companies. However, given that the 'hole' in the protection package relates to a very specific event, public shareholders will be fully informed as to the identities of potential controllers at IPO and it is likely that the large majority of dual-class companies will either be subject to the Takeover Code or be subject, if EU companies, to local mandatory offer requirements,[377] prohibiting foreign dual-class firms would be a disproportionate response and harm the prospects of the LSE competing for foreign listings. Therefore, the flaw in the protection package is noted, but it is not recommended that it be resolved; although it is an area that the FCA could maintain under review as dual-class firms become more prevalent.

For companies that are subject to the Takeover Code, certain amendments should be considered for the purposes of dual-class firms. For a dual-class firm, when a mandatory offer is triggered, or upon any takeover, the price to be offered for enhanced-voting and inferior-voting shares must be comparable, and, if both classes of shares are listed, will be calculated based upon middle-market quotation differentials between the two classes of shares.[378] Such a calculation is not possible if the enhanced-voting shares are unlisted. Currently, unlike coat-tail provisions in Canada, the Takeover Code does not expressly specify that, in such circumstances, inferior-voting shares must be priced identically to unlisted enhanced-voting shares in order to ensure that such a price is 'comparable'.[379] As referenced in Chapter 6, many US dual-class firms voluntarily adopt coat-tail provisions, limiting the levels of control premia in the United States; however, if dual-class firms were to become prevalent on the LSE, in order to forestall uncertainty as to whether the Takeover Code already provides sufficient protection against control premia, greater clarity should be articulated (therefore negating the need for voluntary adoption of coat-tail provisions). In relation to the standard tier dual-class stock listing of Deliveroo specifically,[380] the Takeover Panel confirmed that, upon a takeover, offers for inferior- and enhanced-voting shares would need to be at the same price and on the same terms to satisfy the 'comparable' requirements of the Takeover Code;[381]

377 See n 370 above. As of 31 July 2020, approximately 86 per cent of companies listed on the Main Market were registered in the United Kingdom, the Channel Islands, the Isle of Man or an EU Member State (derived from data disclosed in LSE, 'Issuer List' (31 July 2020), www.londonstockexchange.com/statistics/companies-and-issuers/companies-and-issuers.htm).

378 Takeover Code, Notes to Rule 14.1.

379 *ibid* Rule 14.1. As discussed in Chapter 8, it is likely, in any case, that the Takeover Panel would insist that the offering prospectus for a dual-class applicant outlines how different classes of stock will be priced on a takeover, but, if dual-class firms were to become more prevalent upon the opening-up of the premium tier, it would provide greater certainty if the 'comparable pricing regime' were clarified.

380 See Section 1.5.6 of Chapter 1.

381 Deliveroo Holdings plc, 'Prospectus for the Offer of up to 384,615,384 Class A Shares at an Offer Price Expected to be between 390 and 460 pence per Class A Share and Admission to the Standard Listing

however, greater clarity on a general basis would be welcome with the publication of general guidance to the effect that, for all premium tier dual-class firms, the enhanced-voting and inferior-voting shares would always be priced equally in such circumstances – much in the same way that coat-tail provisions apply in Canada.[382]

Another interesting interplay with Rule 9 of the Takeover Code is caused by the application of sunsets and the potential for a mandatory offer requirement being triggered by the conversion of enhanced-voting shares into inferior-voting shares. The Takeover Code does not expressly foresee such a scenario and should be clarified. Currently, outside of the specific context of dual-class stock, the Takeover Code broadly follows an approach such that a mandatory offer is not triggered where a person exceeds a triggering threshold through no action of their own. For example, if a person crosses a threshold as a result of the company redeeming or purchasing its own securities, or as a result of the enfranchisement of non-voting shares, that person is not normally required to make a mandatory offer, unless that person, at the time of acquiring the shares, had reason to believe that such a redemption or buyback, or enfranchisement, would take place, or, in the case of redemptions and buybacks, that person is a director.[383] Curiously, though, apparently in contrast to its approach to one share, one vote companies, in relation to the standard tier dual-class stock IPO of Deliveroo,[384] the Takeover Panel confirmed that if any person were to cross the Rule 9 threshold for a mandatory offer as a result of enhanced-voting shares converting into inferior-voting shares, that person would be required to make a mandatory cash offer for all the shares of the company (or, with the consent of the Takeover Panel, to dispose of sufficient shares to reduce its aggregate interest to below the Rule 9 threshold).[385] Presumably, the Takeover Panel erred on the side of simplicity and caution when faced with a rare 'genuine' dual-class Main Market standard tier IPO where the issuer had adopted a three year time-dependent sunset clause. Clearly any purchaser of, or subscriber to, stock in Deliveroo would be able to anticipate the forthcoming conversion of enhanced-voting shares into inferior-voting shares upon expiry of the time-dependent sunset clause. However, if dual-class firms were to become more prevalent, after a relaxation of the premium tier prohibition of such firms, the Takeover Panel should consider more detailed rules applicable on a broader basis. For firms that do adopt time-dependent sunset clauses, the mandatory offer provisions of Rule 9 of the Takeover Code should apply where a shareholder's voting ownership crosses the relevant threshold as a result of enhanced-voting shares converting into inferior-voting shares pursuant to the operation of that time-dependent sunset clause. In

Segment of the Official List and to Trading on the Main Market of the London Stock Exchange'(March 2021) at 175.

382 In relation to coat-tail provisions, see Section 6.2.7 of Chapter 6.

383 Takeover Code, Rule 37.1, Note 1 to Rule 37.1, and Notes on Dispensations from Rule 9, Note 6.

384 See Section 1.5.6 of Chapter 1.

385 Deliveroo Holdings plc (2021) (n 381 above 175).

relation to a crossing of the mandatory offer threshold as a result of the unanticipated operation of another type of sunset clause though (particularly one of the mandatory sunsets suggested in this chapter), different considerations apply. The cogitation is nuanced, and should be considered in light of whether the mandatory offer is imposed on enhanced-voting shareholders or inferior-voting shareholders.

There is cogency in the argument that the interests of inferior-voting shareholders should be protected, and mandatory bid requirements triggered, if one or more *enhanced-voting shareholders* cross a mandatory offer threshold as a result of another enhanced-voting shareholder's enhanced-voting shares converting into inferior-voting shares upon the trigger of a sunset through the actions of that enhanced-voting shareholder. Similar to transfers between enhanced-voting shareholders as discussed earlier, such a conversion could create a material change in the control dynamics of the enhanced-voting shareholder group. The enhanced-voting shareholders, if they are a close group of founders, would likely be aware of each other's intentions, or could ensure that they would be so aware by entering into contractual arrangements between themselves requiring the giving of adequate notice to each other of any actions that may trigger sunsets.[386] However, it is not hereby proposed that the Takeover Code abandons its 'no-fault' approach. Where one enhanced-voting shareholder's shares are converted into inferior-voting shares, all the remaining enhanced-voting shareholders will benefit from an increase in their proportion of the voting rights, rather than in the transfer scenario, where voting control could be manipulated into the hands of a specific enhanced-voting shareholder. Furthermore, if the mandatory offer rules were to apply in these circumstances, depending upon how votes are distributed, it could hinder the exit of an enhanced-voting shareholder without the other enhanced-voting shareholders having to make an offer for all the shares in the company, seek a waiver from the Takeover Panel (which would first require an approval by the Independent Shareholders[387]), or relinquish control by selling or voluntarily converting their enhanced-voting shares into inferior-voting shares (if power to do so has been retained under the constitutional documents). This could deter issuers from choosing the premium tier to list with dual-class stock, and a change to the Takeover Code in this respect is not proposed.

An *inferior-voting shareholder* could also cross a mandatory offer threshold as a result of enhanced-voting shares converting into inferior-voting shares, upon the triggering of sunsets, most probably as a result of a total conversion of all enhanced-voting stock into inferior-voting shares. Again, it is proposed that the Takeover Code retains its 'no-fault' approach, since, in effect, this mirrors the 'enfranchisement of non-voting stock' scenario already contemplated by the Takeover Code. Therefore, echoing the current treatment of non-voting stock enfranchisement, a minor

386 Such contractual arrangements would likely also include standstill and rights of first refusal provisions.

387 Takeover Code, Note 1 to Rule 37.1.

amendment to the Takeover Code should be made, in contemplation of dual-class firms with sunset clauses, to provide that a mandatory offer would only, generally, be required if the inferior-voting shareholder, at the time of acquiring inferior-voting shares, had reason to believe that such enhanced-voting share conversion would take place. An acquiring inferior-voting shareholder would, for instance, be deemed to have had such a belief at the time of acquisition where the relevant enfranchisement of inferior-voting shares occurs as a result of the operation of a time-dependent sunset clause. Another example would be where the founders have announced their retirement dates as directors (and therefore a subsequent conversion of their enhanced-voting shares into inferior-voting shares pursuant to the director-linked sunset will be pending) and an activist investor, such as a hedge fund, acting upon such information, acquires inferior-voting shares prior to the retirement dates, in an attempt to gain effective control. The provision should only be triggered where all enhanced-voting shares are to become inferior-voting shares (which is likely to be the case if an inferior-voting shareholder crosses the threshold in these circumstances), otherwise the perverse situation could occur where an inferior-voting shareholder is required to make an offer for the remaining inferior-voting shares, and takes the company private, without the acquiescence of a remaining, potentially large, enhanced-voting shareholder. Issuers should, though, be scrutinised at IPO on a case-by-case basis, since, especially where an issuer has voluntarily adopted a bespoke type of sunset clause, there may be good reason for the 'no fault' approach to be abandoned. In such cases, the relevant application of the Takeover Code should be expressly detailed in the IPO prospectus for the issuer, as is already customary for issuers with unusual capital structures.

9.8.3 *Limiting Dual-Class Stock to New Issuers*

Hong Kong,[388] Singapore,[389] Shanghai,[390] Tokyo[391] and India[392] all restrict dual-class stock to new issuers, and prohibit existing listed one share, one vote firms from recapitalising into dual-class stock. Although the NYSE does allow mid-stream recapitalisations of one share, one vote listed companies into dual-class stock, such recapitalisations will not be permitted if they have the effect of disparately reducing the voting rights of existing public shareholders.[393] As outlined in Chapter 8, for English-incorporated companies, minority shareholders do already enjoy some protections against majority shareholders unilaterally effecting discriminatory recapitalisations that result in premium listed one share, one vote firms converting into

388 HK Listing Rules, Rule 8A.05.
389 SGX Mainboard Rules, Rule 210(10)(c).
390 CSRC Rules (2019) (n 102 above article 4.5.2).
391 Tokyo Guidebook (2018) (n 87 above 140).
392 SEBI (Third Amendment) Regulations, 2019 (n 79 above Rule 3(II)).
393 NYSE Listed Company Manual, §313.00.

dual-class stock firms; however, circumstances do exist where a controlling shareholder with 75 per cent or more of the shares in a one share, one vote company[394] could unilaterally impose a dual-class stock structure on public shareholders (if dual-class stock were permitted on the premium tier), and, subsequently, create a controller voting/cash-flow divergence. Furthermore, the rules discussed in Chapter 8 that do protect public shareholders from discriminatory recapitalisations are specific to English-incorporated companies, and foreign companies may not be subject to equivalent procedures. Conceptually, mid-stream, post-IPO recapitalisations of one share, one vote firms into dual-class stock are problematic. A public shareholder will have invested in the relevant company based upon a one share, one vote system, and, even if a controlling shareholder is in situ, will have evaluated the investment having had regard to the significant equity constraint around the controller's actions. As discussed in Chapter 5, the development of dual-class stock substantively changes the dynamic within a controlled company.[395] In all likelihood, either a management team will become entrenched or an existing controller will divest of the equity that had, until then, acted as a constraining mechanism on its capacity to extract controller benefits. The discussion in Chapter 7 also raised the prospect that such mid-stream recapitalisations are often a prelude or a response to other events that allow management or a controller to protect itself in the face of such extraneous events to the detriment of the public shareholders.[396] Allowing substantive changes to the capital structure of premium tier companies in such a way will also make it challenging for investors to price the shares of one share, one vote controlling shareholder companies. The possibility of a future conversion into dual-class stock, particularly in a controlling shareholder firm where the controller has retained sufficient equity to decisively influence the recapitalisation process, will have to be factored into price, and, for those controlling shareholder firms already listed, share prices could be impacted. As referenced in Chapter 5, the UK regulators have always been distrustful of controlling shareholders, and, although certain restraints have been relaxed for sovereign-controlled companies, generally, since 2014, the trend has been to enhance minority shareholder protections in premium tier one share, one vote controlling shareholder firms. It is unlikely, therefore, that the regulators would be enthusiastic regarding midstream dual-class stock recapitalisations if dual-class firms were to be admitted to the premium tier, and, in any event, the premise of the proposed relaxation of the premium tier prohibition, as outlined in Chapter 1, is to encourage founders, particularly of tech companies, to

394 As discussed in Section 8.2.7 of Chapter 8, although a controller could own exactly 75 per cent of the shares (enabling the passing of a special resolution in a one share, one vote company), a controller will require an exemption from free-float requirements to hold *more than* 75 per cent of the shares in a Main Market listed company.

395 See Section 5.6 of Chapter 5.

396 See Section 7.3 of Chapter 7.

list on the LSE through the availability of dual-class stock on the premium tier at the time of IPO.

Therefore, it is proposed hereunder that the premium tier relaxation of the dual-class stock prohibition only be extended to firms with dual-class stock at the time of admission to the premium tier. To prevent a firm circumventing this condition by, for example, recapitalising from one share, one vote into dual-class stock on the standard tier or AIM and then graduating to the premium tier, the requirement should be drafted to ensure that dual-class firms will not be admitted to the premium tier unless dual-class stock had been adopted at the time of IPO (whether that be on the standard tier, premium tier, AIM or otherwise). Existing listed one share, one vote companies will not be entitled to recapitalise into dual-class structure and retain a premium listing, or become admitted to the premium tier subsequent to the recapitalisation. However, a company, such as Deliveroo, that adopted dual-class stock, at IPO, on the standard tier,[397] would be permitted to graduate to the premium tier (provided that it adopts the requirements of the balanced protection package proposed in this chapter).

9.9 CONCLUSION

If dual-class stock were permitted on the premium tier, this chapter has synopsised a clear package of protections that would provide safeguards for inferior-voting shareholders, combining regulatory restrictions with disclosure requirements, governance rights and an effective enforcement environment. The package comprises transfer-driven, director-linked and ownership-linked sunset clauses, additional approvals (where shares are treated uniformly as one share, one vote) for specific resolutions, conditions on the issuance of enhanced-voting shares post-IPO, independent director appointment rights for inferior-voting shareholders, a stronger related-party transactions regime, disclosure of inferior-voting shareholder voting, adapted AGM-resolution proposal mechanics, and an enhanced disclosure environment generally. Additionally, the FCA would have discretion as to whether to admit dual-class firms based upon broad admissions criteria, although it is acknowledged that in the absence of sufficient resources, the FCA could take a less prescriptive approach and, rather than act as a gatekeeper for dual-class firms, simply ensure that sufficient disclosure as to the rationale for dual-class stock is provided to investors. Minor changes have also been proposed to the Takeover Code, and dual-class stock would only be available to firms that adopt, or have adopted, dual-class stock as of IPO. The package gives inferior-voting shareholders greater comfort that they will not be egregiously expropriated, and that the dual-class stock tradeoff is more likely to swing in a positive direction. Accordingly, discounts applied to dual-class firms should be minimised, and costs of capital correspondingly reduced. The package

[397] See Section 1.5.6 of Chapter 1.

aims to make dual-class firm debacles rare and support the listing of dual-class firms (that may otherwise not list) without compromising the reputation of the premium tier. In the Appendix, a summary of the package is provided together with a comparison to other principal jurisdictions where dual-class stock is permitted.

The proposals outlined represent a balanced protection package for inferior-voting shareholders that treads the fine line between sufficient protection, on the one hand, and, excessive restrictiveness that could undermine the primary benefits for founders in issuing dual-class stock and deter founders from listing, on the other. Flexibility is preserved, since changes to statutory legislation are not proposed, with most of the proposals fulfilled by introducing provisions to the Listing Rules. The FCA can, periodically, keep under review the adequacy of the protections and the burdens that they impose on controllers. If the package slips across the fine line that is being negotiated, the FCA can make the necessary amendments to the Listing Rules in a more streamlined manner than would be the case with amendments to statutory legislation. Crucially, as summarised in the Appendix, the proposals are not more onerous than those imposed in jurisdictions that have recently opened-up to dual-class stock, such as Hong Kong, Singapore, China, Japan and India, and, in many respects, are more flexible. Even some NYSE dual-class firms have voluntarily adopted a number of the proposals. The fine line is evidenced by the experiences of those jurisdictions. Albeit based upon a short time span, dual-class firms have not been deterred from listing in Hong Kong by the restrictions implemented by HKEX, with blue-chip tech firms Xiaomi and Meituan-Dianping being attracted to the market, and Alibaba and Baidu 'coming home' by way of secondary listings. In contrast, as discussed in Chapter 2, Tokyo, which employs a restrictive breakthrough principle for dual-class firms, has not seen the flood of dual-class listings that it anticipated. India has imposed even more severe restrictions, with industry-specific requirements, and, for the first time for dual-class stock jurisdictions, the imposition of mandatory time-dependent sunset provisions. The course of India's experience will be keenly eyed by the FCA going forward, particularly in the context of the premium tier recommendations of the UK Listing Review, which also advocates a five year sunset for its proposed takeover-blocking and board seat-enabling rights.[398] As discussed in Chapter 1, the other features of the UK Listing Review's proposals which preclude the exercise of disproportionate voting rights on other forms of resolutions, including overall board composition decisions, may not attract the founders of high-growth companies to the premium tier as envisaged.[399] As such, the UK Listing Review, which falls short of constituting 'genuine' dual-class stock, is an example of regulation stumbling over the wrong side of the fine dividing line into excessive restrictiveness. The premium tier dual-class stock package that has been proposed in this chapter, however, should allow the LSE to be competitive in the

[398] See Section 1.5.7 of Chapter 1.
[399] *ibid.*

market for dual-class firms, while being sufficiently protective for inferior-voting shareholders so that the shift to dual-class stock permissibility will not be accompanied by widespread indignation.

Instead, it is contended that the package will enhance investor confidence in the premium tier for dual-class firms, and reduce the costs of capital for dual-class issuers that would otherwise be higher if the package were not implemented. Therefore, rather than making it less likely for a dual-class issuer to choose the premium tier, the package makes it more attractive. Overall, the opening of the premium tier to dual-class firms, together with the implementation of the balanced package, should achieve the goal of attracting more quality firms to the premium tier – firms that would otherwise not float. However, the FCA should monitor developments in other jurisdictions, and determine whether the restrictions that have been imposed on dual-class firms in those jurisdictions protect inferior-voting shareholders in practice, and/or the restrictions are so severe that applicants are rejecting those exchanges in favour of more permissive regimes, such as the NYSE and NASDAQ. It will be interesting, in the years ahead, to observe whether the restrictions imposed by, for example, Hong Kong result in lower costs of capital for dual-class firms compared to, say, NYSE, and whether that leads to NYSE issuers voluntarily adopting inferior-voting shareholder protections in an attempt to reduce their costs of capital. These factors will be pertinent to the FCA's ongoing review of the protective measures that are implemented in the United Kingdom upon a relaxation of the premium tier prohibition of dual-class stock.

Epilogue

If I can change and you can change, everybody can change.[1]

The search for the British Google has begun, with the UK Government and the FCA acknowledging a desire to support the growth of science and technology companies. However, Britain has a problem. When a UK technology company grows to a certain size, a founder wishing to float the company on the premium tier (the United Kingdom's most prestigious tier), to crystallise wealth and grow the company further, will be on the horns of a dilemma. The founder can list and lose control as ownership becomes dispersed, leaving management beholden to the whims of public shareholders and the market for corporate control, and potentially prejudicing the ability of the founder to pursue its long-term idiosyncratic vision; or alternatively, the founder can retain control post-IPO but limit his or her diversification of wealth and generation of equity financing for the company. Entering as a *deus ex machina*, dual-class stock would enable founders to achieve their diversification and equity financing goals, while continuing to maintain control. With, as of the time of writing, a fragile domestic economy, and competition from other exchanges which have long permitted, or have recently determined to permit, dual-class stock, the United Kingdom will be hamstrung if it does not remain nimble. Concerns appear to have played out in the technology domain, with numerous large British tech firms selling out to international peers rather than listing in the United Kingdom. UK public investors have not had the opportunity to share in the growth and success of such companies.

Although dual-class stock has been prohibited on the premium tier since its inception, the United Kingdom has taken the first tentative steps toward opening up the market. The UK Listing Review, published in March 2021, purportedly recommended that the FCA welcome dual-class stock to the premium tier. However, the use of the moniker 'dual-class stock' by the UK Listing Review is something of a misnomer. The proposals of the UK Listing Review restrict the

[1] Rocky Balboa, *Rocky IV* (Metro-Goldwyn-Mayer, 1985).

exercise of disproportionate voting rights to decisions pertaining to takeovers and the board seat of the holder of such rights. Traditional dual-class stock would permit the holder of enhanced-voting stock to exercise enhanced-voting rights on a wider gamut of shareholders' resolutions, including, most pertinently, board composition as a whole. Over and above a desire to block takeovers, other key factors in the choice of dual-class stock by founders of high-growth companies include the capacity to insulate the management team from the caprice of public shareholders (a capacity that is contingent upon the controller having unadulterated control over the composition of the majority of the board) and the capacity to ensure that corporate actions vital to the controller's vision can be undertaken without interference by public shareholders. Unlike exchanges that permit 'genuine' dual-class stock, the UK Listing Review proposals do not give controllers the control they seek when entertaining a dual-class stock listing. Accordingly, it is unlikely that the UK Listing Review will substantially move the needle in its mission to attract high-growth, early-stage firms to the United Kingdom's listed markets. However, the UK Listing Review proposals are a step in the direction of 'genuine' dual-class stock, and it would not be a leap for the premium tier to finally embrace more conventional dual-class firms.

Why would a founder be a 'control freak' in the first place? The answer can be framed around the notion of controller benefits. By retaining control, the founder can ensure that the company takes actions that create personal benefits for the controller. The theoretical benefits and detriments of dual-class firms can be painted in light of the types of controller benefits. Certain types of controller benefits are benign – they are overall either neutral to the public shareholders or create consequential benefits for public shareholders – which manifest themselves in the positive aspects of dual-class firms. Controller benefits are, otherwise, pernicious, overall negatively affecting public shareholders and therefore representing the detriments of dual-class firms. A tradeoff can be established such that where the benign controller benefits outweigh the pernicious controller benefits, dual-class stock will be beneficial for controllers and public shareholders. The tradeoff is firm-specific, and dual-class stock may be net-beneficial for some types of firms and net-detrimental for others. However, the same could also be said of one share, one vote. The regulator is shooting itself in the foot by ruling out an option for listed companies that represents the most beneficial capital structure for certain firms.

The key concern in admitting dual-class firms to the premium tier is that the structure could incentivise the nefarious extraction by controllers of pernicious controller benefits that overshadow benign controller benefits, leading to the expropriation of public shareholder interests, and the entrenchment of an underperforming management team that does not manage the company in a shareholder wealth maximising manner. Although similar issues are inherent in one share, one vote controlling shareholder firms, with the implementation of a wedge between the voting and cash-flow rights of the controller, the diminution of the equity constraint on the controller accentuates the negative aspects of the ownership structure.

However, the premium tier prohibition of dual-class firms does not stem from a forensic analysis as to whether controllers are likely to act in a negative manner, but rather an inclination of the regulators to kowtow to institutional investors. Sympathy can be offered to the FCA given the influential position of institutional investors in the UK public markets, but it is not credible that the admission of dual-class firms to the premium tier would result in the mass exodus of institutional investors from the LSE. Institutional investors, however grudgingly, do invest in US-listed dual-class firms in significant levels, and Hong Kong, Tokyo and Singapore have not seen a flight of investors since they introduced dual-class stock. If the premium tier prohibition is to continue, it would be better if it were based upon robust theoretical and evidentiary grounds.

If the empirical evidence were to suggest that the dual-class stock tradeoff is, in fact, shifted into a substantially net-detrimental position on average, the justification to disallow dual-class firms becomes more convincing. However, dual-class firms show at least as good, and in numerous studies, better, operating performance compared to one share, one vote firms. Many studies do, though, show dual-class firms to be valued less than one share, one vote firms. This suggests that investors are discounting dual-class firms to protect themselves from the perceived risks of the structure. Most pertinently, an argument that dual-class firms should be prohibited to protect investors quickly crumbles where the investors are organically protecting themselves by pricing-in their risk. Studies show that portfolios of dual-class firms earn investors returns at least on a par with, and in many cases greater than, portfolios of similar one share, one vote firms. Investors are not, on average, harmed by dual-class stock. If anything, the discounts that investors are applying are not warranted by operating performance or returns. From the perspective of issuers, excessive discounting disproportionately increases the costs of capital for dual-class firms, even where the structure has been adopted for purely benign reasons.

Therefore, empirical evidence does not support an outright premium tier prohibition of dual-class stock. However, especially in the early stages of any relaxation of the rules, simply opening the dam may not be the prudent approach. In such a case, dual-class firms would be significantly discounted, harming the equity financing of such firms, and even deterring their listings. By combining the acceptance of dual-class stock to the premium tier with the introduction of shrewdly formulated restrictions, investors can be given comfort that they will be protected from the most egregious aspects of expropriation and, accordingly, the costs of capital for dual-class firms will be reduced.

Any restrictions that are proposed need to tread a fine line between protecting public shareholders and, unlike the proposals of the UK Listing Review, giving controllers sufficient flexibility to enable them to extract benign controller benefits, such as the pecuniary and non-pecuniary controller benefits related to pursuing a long-term vision. If that line is not carefully observed, any relaxation of the rules may be rendered moot by those restrictions being too onerous to attract issuers. Prudence is crucial, but the overcautiousness of the UK Listing Review will be suffocating for founders. Taking these concerns into account, it has been proposed in this book that the premium tier be opened-up to 'genuine' dual-class stock alongside a balanced package of inferior-voting shareholder protections. The package acknowledges that certain events that occur over time could increase the risks that the dual-class stock tradeoff will shift into a net-detrimental position; when such events occur, enhanced-voting shares will automatically convert, in whole or in part, into inferior-voting shares. In that way, voting power can revert to the public shareholders when the risks of pernicious controller benefit extraction increase. The approach resonates with contemporary theoretical and empirical studies that suggest that dual-class stock is beneficial for young, growth-phase firms, with those benefits eroding with maturity, presumably after the occurrence of events that swing the dual-class stock tradeoff in a negative direction for public shareholders. The package also encompasses limited corporate governance measures that temper the extraction of pernicious controller benefits while the dual-class structure subsists. Finally, the package gives the FCA leeway in relation to whether to admit dual-class firms to the premium tier on a firm-by-firm basis, and/or requires substantive disclosure by potential premium tier applicants, recognising that controllers should justify the need for dual-class structure, and should show that those holding enhanced-voting shares have been, and are, integral to the success of the business. The presence of a visionary management team intrinsic to the prospects of the business with the ability, through the holding of enhanced-voting shares, to manage the business in accordance with a long-term vision is fundamental to many of the theoretical benefits of dual-class firms, and without that facet, greater perils subsist that the structure is being implemented to extract pernicious controller benefits. The protection package proposed would place the United Kingdom somewhere between the United States and the Asian markets in terms of permissiveness, and uses a regulatory methodology that retains scope for ongoing review and reform. Hong Kong, in particular, has attracted high-profile dual-class firms to its exchange notwithstanding taking a more restrictive approach, and, therefore, the protection package proposed for the United Kingdom should not have the contrary effect of debilitating the attraction of flotations that the introduction of dual-class stock to the premium tier is intended to achieve.

The evidence suggests that the United Kingdom's fear of 'founders without limits' is inflated, and by relaxing the premium tier prohibition of dual-class stock in conjunction with judicious restrictions, an environment can be created that supports the listing of UK businesses, while limiting the downsides. The package is by no means fool-proof, and controllers with insidious intentions may well still list their firms and expropriate public shareholders. However, the risks will be mitigated. Risks of public investors being harmed also apply to one share, one vote firms, and, therefore, the approach should mirror that taken toward dispersed ownership one share, one vote firms, where regulations and corporate governance mechanisms have been formulated to reduce, although not eliminate, agency costs. Even in the

United States, which adopts a more permissive dual-class stock environment, the empirical evidence suggests that, from an operating performance perspective, there are more dual-class firm 'winners' than 'losers'.

Although dual-class shares in the United Kingdom previously died a death in the last millennium partly as a result of institutional investor aversion to the structure, the UK boards adopting the structure at the time were doing so primarily to protect themselves from a burgeoning hostile takeover market and were mainly industrial and retail companies with easily observable long-term growth prospects, not redolent of contemporary, high-growth tech firms which can particularly benefit from the adoption of dual-class stock. However, dual-class stock is not a panacea to unearthing the elusive British Google. Founders may still see other benefits in selling their tech companies to foreign acquirors, such as high offer prices propelled by a weak pound, and the ability to create inter-company synergies through access to wider data. Additionally, relaxing the rules on dual-class firms will need to be integrated into a market that promotes innovation, entrepreneurship and long-termism. However, permitting dual-class stock on the premium tier does form one step in supporting the development of large, successful, growing British tech businesses, and enabling the public to participate in their success. The introduction of dual-class stock in a sensible manner could engineer a burgeoning market for such firms, thereby bolstering and enriching the British economy in uncertain times. Founders without limits will no longer be associated with limitless abuse, but, instead, with limitless possibilities.

Appendix

Comparison of Inferior-Voting Shareholder Protections on Major Dual-Class Stock Exchanges

Protection Measure	Chapter 9 Proposed UK Premium Tier Package	USA NYSE	Hong Kong	Singapore	Tokyo	China SSE	India	Canada TSX
Firm Type Restrictions	**Yes** Tracing the directors' duty under s. 172 of CA 2006, the applicant must justify why the success of the company for the benefit of its members as a whole will be promoted by insulating the management team from the ability of the public shareholders to determine their composition through the use of dual-class stock – the business model, product-cycles, growth profile,	**No**	**Yes** Applicants must be 'innovative' companies, possessing at least two of the following characteristics: (i) new and differentiated technologies or innovations; (ii) R&D being a major activity of the business; (iii) the company's success being attributable to unique features or intellectual property; and/or (iv) market capitalisation/intangible asset value being	**Yes** Applicant must be suitable for dual-class listing, and the following factors will be taken into account: (i) the business model of the company (e.g. that the company has a conceptualised long-term plan that contemplates ramping up growth at a fast pace); (ii) operating track record of the company or business; (iii) participation by sophisticated investors; and (iv) other features of	**Yes** Dual-class structure must be in the 'common interest of the shareholders' (such as to ensure that a specific person with appropriate knowledge and skill continues in management) and must not provide undue benefits to holders of enhanced-voting stock. Dual-class stock will not be permitted purely on the rationale that the structure provides stability to family ownership or otherwise provides	**Yes** Dual-class stock only permitted on the STI board, which is only accessible to 'science and technology' companies.	**Yes** Dual-class stock only available to companies 'intensive in the use of technology, information technology, intellectual property, data analytics, bio-technology or nano-technology'.	**No**

(continued)

Protection Measure	Chapter 9 Proposed UK Premium Tier Package	USA NYSE	Hong Kong	Singapore	Tokyo	China SSE	India	Canada TSX
	observability of assets and long-term profitability and projected business strategy should all be considered; and the applicant must show a clean track record to-date, in terms of compliance (to the extent that the company was subject to any regulatory requirements pre-IPO).		disproportionately large compared to tangible asset value. Applicant must also demonstrate a track record, and expected continued trajectory, for high business growth (objectively measured by operational metrics such as business operations, users, customers, unit sales, revenue, profits and/or market value).	the company or business that require dual-class stock.	protection from takeovers. It will also be considered whether the need for dual-class stock will remain relevant in the future, and whether the company, its board and its auditors recognise the need for dual-class stock.			
Controller Identity Restrictions	**Yes** The applicant must show a clean track record to-	**No**	**Yes** Each enhanced-voting shareholder must (i)	**Yes** The SGX will consider the role and contribution of	**Yes** The extent to which knowledge and skills of the	**Yes** Enhanced-voting shareholders must	**Yes** Pre-IPO, enhanced-voting	**No**

date, with respect to the conduct of the proposed enhanced-voting shareholders, show that the skills, knowledge and talent of the proposed enhanced-voting shareholders are integral to the future success of the business, and evidence the significant contributions of the enhanced-voting shareholders to the success of the business to-date.		have been materially responsible for the growth of the business, by way of his or her skills, knowledge and/or strategic direction in circumstances where the value of the company is largely attributable or attached to intangible human capital; (ii) be an individual who has an active executive role within the business, and has contributed to a material extent to the ongoing growth of the business; and (iii) be a director of the issuer at	intended enhanced-voting shareholders to the success of the company or business, and how actively involved they are in the company or the business.	controller are essential to achieving the business plan of the company in the common interest of the shareholders will be assessed, including consideration on the following basis: (i) is the controller the inventor of the company's technology and founder of the company? (ii) is the controller involved in, and does he or she influence business development, R&D and recruitment? and (iii) is the basis of the need for dual-class stock explainable in light of the record	be persons who have made material contributions to the development of the business.	shares must have been held by promoters or founders in executive positions, with total net worth (not including the shares) of no more than RS.500 crores.

(continued)

Protection Measure	Chapter 9 Proposed UK Premium Tier Package	USA NYSE	Hong Kong	Singapore	Tokyo	China SSE	India	Canada TSX
			the time of listing.		of the person and actual business performance of the applicant?			
Time-Dependent Sunset Clause	No	No	No	No	No (However, when the need for the dual-class structure no longer exists, the structure should be dissolved.)	No	Yes Five years, extendable for a further five years.	No
Transfer-Driven Sunset Clause	Yes	No	Yes	Yes	Yes	Yes	Yes	No
Director-Linked Sunset Clause	Yes	No	Yes	Yes	Yes (if the dual-class structure has been implemented to ensure the continued involvement of a person in the management of the company; although JPXR will consider exceptions on a case-by-case basis).	Yes	No	No

Management-Linked Sunset Clause	**No**	**No**	**No**	**No**	**Yes** (if the dual-class structure has been implemented to ensure the continued involvement of a person in the management of the company).	**No**	**Yes**	**No**
Ownership-Linked Sunset Clause	**Yes** At least 15 per cent of the issued equity as of IPO to be held on a continuous basis post-IPO (FCA to have discretion to increase or decrease threshold).	**No**	**Yes** Maximum 10:1 voting ratio, and enhanced-voting shareholders must hold at least 10 per cent of the equity (although HKEX may approve a lower percentage for high market capitalisation companies (e.g. over HK$80 billion)).	**Yes** Maximum 10:1 voting ratio.	**Yes** Either via sunset clause or application of break-through provisions – expectation that threshold set at more than 25 per cent of the equity.	**Yes** Maximum 10:1 voting ratio, and enhanced-voting shareholders must hold more than 10 per cent of the equity.	**Yes** Maximum 10:1 voting ratio.	**No**
Enhanced-Voting Shares to Remain Unlisted	**Yes**	**No**	**Yes**	**Yes**	**Yes**	**Yes**	**No** (However, enhanced-voting shares	**No**

(continued)

Protection Measure	Chapter 9 Proposed UK Premium Tier Package	USA NYSE	Hong Kong	Singapore	Tokyo	China SSE	India	Canada TSX
							locked-up until at least such time as they are converted into inferior-voting shares.)	
Majority of the Minority Provisions	**Yes** Two-Stage Vote for any proposal to: (i) amend the constitutional documents; (ii) voluntarily wind-up the company; (iii) waive pre-emption rights; (iv) re-elect the external auditor; and (v) reduce capital other than on a pro	**No**	**Yes** Voting rights will revert to one share, one vote on any decisions to (i) amend the constitutional documents; (ii) vary the rights attached to a class of shares; (iii) appoint and remove independent directors: (iv) appoint and remove	**Yes** Voting rights will revert to one share, one vote on any decisions to (i) amend the constitutional documents; (ii) vary the rights attached to a class of shares; (iii) appoint and remove independent directors; (iv) appoint and remove	**No** (However, dual-class issuers must implement mechanisms that protect the rights of inferior-voting shareholders from being disproportionately modified.)	**Yes** Enhanced-voting share voting rights to be identical to inferior-voting share voting rights on any decisions to (i) amend the constitutional documents; (ii) vary the voting rights	**Yes** Enhanced-voting share voting rights to be treated as one share, one vote on any decisions: (i) to amend the constitutional documents; (ii) to appoint and remove	**No** (Although TSX may, in its discretion, require that voting be carried out on a basis such that each shareholder will be permitted to exercise votes proportionate to its residual equity interest in the issuer.)

rata basis to equity holdings. First stage requires orthodox shareholder approval in accordance with CA 2006, respecting voting rights of shares; second stage requires approval by shareholders, with all shares treated on a one share, one vote basis.		auditors; and (v) voluntarily wind-up the company.	auditors; (v) effect reverse takeovers; and (vi) de list, or voluntarily wind-up the company.		attached to the enhanced-voting shares (requiring a super-majority vote); (iii) appoint and remove independent directors; (iv) appoint and remove auditors; and (v) combine, divide, dissolve, or change the legal form of the company.	independent directors; (iii) to appoint and remove auditors; (iv) on voluntary winding-ups or insolvency processes; (v) on related-party transaction approvals involving an enhanced-voting shareholder; (vi) to approve changes of control instigated by a voluntary transfer of enhanced-voting shares; (vii) to approve substantial value

(continued)

Protection Measure	Chapter 9 Proposed UK Premium Tier Package	USA NYSE	Hong Kong	Singapore	Tokyo	China SSE	India	Canada TSX
							transactions; (viii) on de-listings; (ix) on share buybacks; and (x) to utilise funds for purposes other than the company's business.	
Future Issuance Restrictions	**Yes** Proportion that the enhanced-voting shares bears to the total issued shares in the company as of IPO cannot increase post-IPO, unless with Independent Shareholder consent. Price per enhanced-voting share in any issuance	**No**	**Yes** Proportion that the enhanced-voting shares bears to the total share capital cannot increase post-IPO. Further enhanced-voting shares may only be issued, with prior HKEX approval, if offered to all shareholders pro rata to their	**Yes** Ratio of the total voting rights attached to enhanced-voting shares to the total voting rights attached to inferior-voting shares may not increase post-IPO. Further enhanced-voting shares may not be issued post-IPO, except	**Yes** Unlikely that approval will be given for the issuance of further enhanced-voting shares post-IPO (although JPRX will assess proposals on a case-by-case basis).	**Yes** Further enhanced-voting shares may not be issued, and the ratio of the total voting rights attached to enhanced-voting shares to the total voting rights attached to inferior-	**Yes** Further enhanced-voting shares may only be issued to existing holders pursuant to a bonus, split or rights issue.	**Yes** Further enhanced-voting shares may only be issued pursuant to a distribution to all holders of equity on a pro rata basis, although TSX will generally exempt the issuance of enhanced-voting shares that would maintain

	must not be any less than the price per inferior-voting share in the same issuance.		existing holdings, pursuant to a pro rata scrip dividend, or pursuant to a stock split or other capital reorganisation.	through rights issue, bonus issue, scrip dividend scheme or consolidation or subdivision of shares, in each case in conjunction with the issuance of inferior-voting shares and as approved by special resolution.		voting shares may not be increased post-IPO, except pursuant to a proportional rights issue.		(but not increase) the percentage voting position of an enhanced-voting shareholder, subject to any conditions TSX may consider desirable in any particular case (such as majority of the minority requirements, unless the right of enhanced-voting shareholders to maintain voting percentage has been publicly disclosed prior to the later of 6 November 1989 and IPO).
Voting Restriction	**No**	**No**	**Yes** Inferior-voting shareholders who do not also hold enhanced-voting shares must be entitled to exercise at least	**Yes** Inferior-voting shareholders who do not also hold enhanced-voting shares must be entitled to exercise at	**No**	**Yes** Inferior-voting shares must comprise at least 10 per cent of the voting	**Yes** Enhanced-voting shareholders may not hold more than 74 per cent	**No**

(continued)

Protection Measure	Chapter 9 Proposed UK Premium Tier Package	USA NYSE	Hong Kong	Singapore	Tokyo	China SSE	India	Canada TSX
			10 per cent of the voting rights.	least 10 per cent of the voting rights.		rights in the company.	of the voting rights in the company.	
Inferior-Voting Shareholder Independent Director Rights	**Yes** Two 'Inferior-Appointed Independent Directors' with financial and/or audit experience to be appointed by shareholders, on the basis of all shares being treated as one share, one vote. If board nominated nominees for Inferior-Appointed Independent Director roles are not approved in the first round, shareholders	**No**	**Yes** All shares to be treated on a one share, one vote basis on any decisions to appoint or remove independent directors. Independent directors to be subject to retirement-by-rotation every three years.	**Yes** All shares to be treated on a one share, one vote basis on any decisions to appoint or remove independent directors.	**No**	**Yes** All shares to be treated on a one share, one vote basis on any decisions to appoint or remove independent directors.	**Yes** All shares to be treated on a one share, one vote basis on any decisions to appoint or remove independent directors.	**No**

	holding at least 10 per cent of the equity can nominate nominees to be appointed as Inferior-Appointed Independent Directors in a second round of voting (again, with all shares treated as one share, one vote).							
Enhanced Board Requirements	**Yes** Inferior-Appointed Independent Directors to be members of the audit committee.	**No**	**Yes** Dual-class firms must implement a corporate governance committee, comprised of solely independent directors, to monitor compliance with the dual-class conditions, provide recommendations on potential conflicts with enhanced-voting shareholders and publish semi-	**Yes** Majority of the members of the audit, remuneration and nomination committees (as well as their respective chairs) to be independent directors.	**No**	**Yes** Board of supervisors to report annually on adherence to dual-class conditions and whether the enhanced-voting shareholders have abused their voting rights or damaged the	**Yes** At least half the board to be independent directors. Remuneration, nomination, risk management and stakeholder relationship committees to comprise at least two-thirds independent	**No**

(continued)

Protection Measure	Chapter 9 Proposed UK Premium Tier Package	USA NYSE	Hong Kong	Singapore	Tokyo	China SSE	India	Canada TSX
			annual reports on its activities. A dual-class firm must appoint a permanent compliance advisor and procure director, senior management and company secretary training on the risks of dual-class structures. Requirements on the roles of independent directors, and to implement a nomination committee composed of a majority of independent directors, that are otherwise imposed on a 'comply-or-			legitimate interests of investors.	directors, and audit committee to be comprised exclusively of independent directors.	

			explain' basis under a corporate governance code, are mandatory for dual-class firms. Chair of the nomination committee must be an independent director.					
Enhanced Related-Party Transaction Requirements	**Yes** Any Proposed related-party transaction, no matter its size or whether such transaction is in the ordinary course of business, must be subject to confirmation by the company's sponsor that it is fair and reasonable to the shareholders as a whole. Concerns of Inferior-Appointed Independent	**No**	**No**	**No**	**Yes** Controlling shareholder related-party transaction protections must be implemented by the issuer.	**No**	**Yes** All shares to be treated as one share, one vote on related-party transaction approvals involving an enhanced-voting shareholder.	**No**

(continued)

Protection Measure	Chapter 9 Proposed UK Premium Tier Package	USA NYSE	Hong Kong	Singapore	Tokyo	China SSE	India	Canada TSX
	Directors on related-party transactions to be related to firm's sponsor and (if independent shareholder approval is required under the Listing Rules) the Independent Shareholders. Related-party transaction exemptions for sovereign-controlled companies under the Listing Rules to be disapplied if the firm employs dual-class stock.							
Disclosure of Inferior-Voting Shareholder Voting	**Yes** Upon any resolution, a dual-class firm must (in addition	**No**	**No**	**No**	**No**	**No**	**No**	**No**

	to usual disclosure of the actual voting results) disclose the result of the vote had all shares been treated on a one share, one vote basis.							
Enhanced Inferior-Voting Shareholder Rights for Calling General Meetings of Shareholders	**No**	**No**	**Yes** Shareholders holding 10 per cent of the votes, where all shares are treated on a one share, one vote basis, can call a shareholders' general meeting.	**Yes** Shareholders holding 10 per cent of the votes, where all shares are treated on a one share, one vote basis, can call a shareholders' general meeting.	**No**	**Yes** Shareholders holding 10 per cent of the votes, where all shares are treated on a one share, one vote basis, can call a shareholders' general meeting. Shareholders holding 3 per cent of the voting rights may propose resolutions at the shareholders'	**No**	**No**

(continued)

Protection Measure	Chapter 9 Proposed UK Premium Tier Package	USA NYSE	Hong Kong	Singapore	Tokyo	China SSE	India	Canada TSX
						general meeting.		
Enhanced Inferior-Voting Shareholder Rights for Proposing Resolutions at the AGM	**Yes** All shares to be treated on a one share, one vote basis in relation to any shareholder powers to propose resolutions at the AGM under the laws of the relevant jurisdiction of incorporation of the company.	**No**	**No**	**No**	**No**	**Yes** Shareholders holding 3 per cent of the voting rights may propose resolutions at any shareholders' general meeting.	**No**	**No** (Although inferior-voting shareholders to be permitted to attend and speak at meetings of shareholders.)
Enhanced Disclosure	**Yes** 'Firm Type' and 'Controller Identity' (see above) justifications to be disclosed in offering prospectus and	**No**	**Yes** Disclosure of the dual-class structure on the front page of any documents issued by the firm, with	**Yes** Disclosure of the dual-class structure on the front page of any documents issued by the firm, with	**Yes** Purpose and need for dual-class stock to be appropriately disclosed in the initial listing application.	**Yes** Full disclosure at IPO and in periodic reports of the dual-class structure, its risks,	**No**	**Yes** Inferior-voting shares to be designated and marked as 'subordinate voting', 'restricted voting', or 'non-

future annual reports. Full disclosure in offering prospectus and annual reports of the capital structure (including details of the operation of sunset and sunrise provisions); the number and percentage of voting and cash-flow interests that will be or are held by substantial shareholders post-IPO; and details outlining the magnitude of the voting/cash-flow divergence theoretically possible under the proposed capital structure.		explanations within those documents for the rationale for the structure and the risks inherent therein. Interim and annual reports must disclose the holders of enhanced-voting shares and set out the circumstances when enhanced-voting shares may convert to one share, one vote shares, together with the impact of any such conversions. All dual-class firms to be designated with a dual-class stock marker.	explanations within those documents of the rationale for the structure and the risks inherent therein, and of decisions which will implement a one share, one vote process. Documents issued to shareholders or potential investors must disclose the holders of enhanced-voting shares, their holdings of, and voting rights attached to, enhanced-voting and inferior-voting shares and their total voting rights. All dual-class firms to be designated with		corporate governance implications and implemented investor protection measures.		voting' stock. Inferior-voting shareholders to receive the same information as is legally required to be disclosed to enhanced-voting shareholders.

(continued)

Protection Measure	Chapter 9 Proposed UK Premium Tier Package	USA NYSE	Hong Kong	Singapore	Tokyo	China SSE	India	Canada TSX
				a dual-class share stock marker.				
Coat-Tail Provisions	**Yes** (For companies to which the Takeover Code applies.) Clarification to be published that 'comparable' pricing on a takeover under the Takeover Code requires shares representing equal levels of equity to be priced equally. Also note transfer-driven sunset clauses above.	**No**	**No** (However, comparable offers must be made for different classes of shares, and any variation in pricing justified to the Takeovers Executive; also note transfer-driven sunset clauses above.)	**Yes** (Also note transfer-driven sunset clauses above.)	**No** (However, note transfer-driven sunset clauses above.)	**No** (However, note transfer-driven sunset clauses above.)	**No** (However, change of control approvals are conducted on the basis of all shares being treated as one share, one vote; also note transfer-driven sunset clauses above.)	**Yes** (Since 1987.)
Recapitalisations of existing listed one	**Yes** Firms must have adopted dual-	**No** However, voting rights of	**Yes**	**Yes**	**Yes**	**Yes**	**Yes** (Enhanced voting shares	**No** (However, TSX will not consent to

share, one vote firms into dual-class stock firms prohibited	class stock as of IPO.	existing share-holders cannot be disparately reduced or restricted through any corporate action or issuance.					must be in existence pre-IPO; only one class of enhanced-voting shares permitted; and only one share, one vote shares may be issued at IPO.)	a capital reorganisation or pro rata distribution of securities, which would have the effect of creating a class of restricted securities, or changing the ratio of outstanding restricted securities to common securities, unless the proposal receives minority approval.)

Index

Acquis Stock Exchange, 21, 47
  Main Market, graduation to, 47
Adaptimmune, 52
Adelphia
  controversies, 191
Age, Firm. *See also* Empirical Evidence, Dual-Class Firm performance: diversity of firms, importance of
  proxy for other characteristics, 306, 368
Agent Provocateur. *See* Fraser Group
AIM, 21, 46
  Main Market, graduation to, 47
Alibaba, 21
  board appointment rights, 120, 121
  founder, importance of, 221
  Hong Kong, secondary listing in, 95, 415
  long-termism, 227
  NYSE, IPO on, 91, 118, 121
Allianz
  cross-ownership, 131
Alphabet. *See* Google
Amazon
  controversies, 159
  tech credentials, 354
AMC
  sunset clause, ownership-linked, 377
AMEX, 88
  dual-class issuers, former conditions attached to, 86
  dual-class stock, permissibility of, 86
Amsterdam
  dual-class stock, admissibility of, 112
  loyalty shares. *See* Loyalty Shares
AMTD, 99
Android, 215
Antofagasta, 32
  controlling shareholder firm, as a, 167
Apple
  controversies, 159
  founder, resignation of, 221
Arbuthnot Banking Group, 47
ARM, 44
Articles of Association
  amendment, 325, 391
    class rights. *See* Class Rights
    recapitalisations, 328, 331
  Model Articles, application of, 24, 146
Asia Resource Minerals
  controversies, 170, 321
Australia
  dual-class stock, admissibility of, 15
Autolus Therapeutics, 52
Aveva, 33
Aviva
  executive remuneration, 195, 402

Baidu, 21
  Hong Kong, secondary listing in, 95, 415
Belgium. *See* Brussels
Berkshire Hathaway, 17, 227
Berle, Adolf, 84
  Berle and Means, 173
  Dodd/Berle debate. *See* Theory, Corporate
Big Tech, 16, *See also* Technology Companies
  bonding hypothesis, importance of. *See* Bonding Hypothesis
  controversies, 158–160
  diversification. *See* Diversification
  new economy, 33, 92
  pre-profit companies, 35, 60
  unicorns, 35, 39, 42, 45
BlackRock, 89, 226
Blackstone, 227
Bonding Hypothesis
  Big Tech, and, 220

controller benefits, impact of other, 217
dual-class stock, with, 149, 216
illiquidity, 216
takeover regulations, reinforcement with, 216
high executive remuneration, use of, 217
human capital investment by employees, leading to, 219, 232, 252
long-termism, and. *See* Long-Termism
management and employees, benefit to, 218
stakeholder relationships, benefit to, 219, 232, 252
sunset clauses, undermined by
transfer-driven, 373
technology companies, and. *See* Technology Companies
UK Listing Review, limitations under. *See* UK Listing Review
BP
executive remuneration, 195, 403
Breakthrough Provisions. *See* Sunset Clauses
British Energy, 317
British Insurance Association
dual-class stock, antagonism to, 75
Brussels
dual-class stock, limitations on the use of, 113
loyalty shares. *See* Loyalty Shares
Bumi plc. *See* Asia Resource Minerals
Burton Group, 15, 75
Business Roundtable, 88, 151, 157

Cash-Flow Rights
voting in US dual-class firms, divergence from, 27–28, 380–381
CBS. *See* Viacom
Charter Communications, 304
Chewy, 247
China. *See* Shanghai
Class Rights
articles of association, amendments to, 326, 391
recapitalisations, 328
Coase, Ronald, 152
Coat-Tail Provisions
Canada, 211, 409, 410
control premia, elimination of, 211
US, 210, 212, 409
Conglomerates
dual-class stock, lesser preponderance with, 215
dual-class stock, with, 196
inefficient decision-making, through, 195–196
non-pecuniary controller benefits, through, 202
Constellation Brands, 304
Constraints, Controller
articles of association, amendments to, 325–327
costs of capital, effect on, 306, 312, 336, 343, 414, 416
directors' duties, 312–315
director-linked sunset clauses, and. *See* Sunset Clauses: director-linked: directors' duties
formulation considerations, 306
independent directors, 323–325
market constraints. *See* Equity Markets, Debt Markets and Product Markets
voluntary constraints, causing adoption of, 212, 336, 342
psychological constraints. *See* Psychological Constraints
recapitalisations, regulations on dual-class stock, 327–332, 412
related-party transaction regulations, 192, 295, 319–323
unfair prejudice, 315–316
Control Premia, 208–212
coat-tail provisions, limiting through. *See* Coat-Tail Provisions
comparable pricing regime, limiting through. *See* Takeover Code
controller benefits, as valuation of, 212
empirical evidence, 211
mandatory offers, limiting through. *See* Takeover Code
UK Listing Review. *See* UK Listing Review
Control-Enhancing Mechanisms
board appointment rights, 120–122
Alibaba. *See* Alibaba
CA 2006 s. 168, comity with, 120
Premium Listing Principles, compatibility with, 121
cross-ownership, 128–132
Premium Listing Principles, compatibility with, 132
UK law, permissibility under, 128
derivative instruments, 132–136
collars, 133
equity swaps, 133
stock-lending, 132
loyalty shares. *See* Loyalty Shares
meaning, 119
preference shares. *See* Preference Shares
pyramid structures, 124–128
shareholders' agreements, 122–123
CA 2006 s.168, comity with, 122
listed companies, impracticability in relation to, 122
Premium Listing Principles, compatibility with, 123

Controller Benefits
benign, 212–238, 243, 245
beneficial related-party transactions. *See* Related-Party Transactions
bonding hypothesis. *See* Bonding Hypothesis
diversification. *See* Diversification
higher takeover prices. *See* Takeover Prices: dual-class stock, higher with
long-termism. *See* Long-Termism
post-IPO equity funding. *See* Equity Funding, Post-IPO
project choice. *See* Project Choice
risk-taking. *See* Risk-Taking
controlling shareholder firms, generally with. *See* Controlling Shareholders
incentive to extraction, dual-class stock as an, 184–185, 189
market forces, constrained through, 202
pernicious, 189–212, 245
control premia. *See* Control Premia
executive remuneration, high. *See* Executive Remuneration
inefficient decision-making. *See* Inefficient Decision-Making
management entrenchment. *See* Management Entrenchment
non-pecuniary. *See* Non-Pecuniary Controller Benefits
takeover probability. *See* Takeover Probability
tunnelling. *See* Tunnelling
private benefits of control, term used instead of, 188, 241
tradeoff, controlling shareholder. See Controlling Shareholders
tradeoff, dual-class stock, 188, 238–245, 249, 299, 304, 340, 385
alignment-commitment theorem, 238, 242
constraints, relevance of, 247, 306, 414
controller identity, 254
firm valuation studies, 250, 276
firm-specificity, 244, 245, 251, 253, 255–256, 276, 355, 356, 358, 359, 368
operating performance studies, 292
principal-agency costs theorem, 239, 242
takeover defence/agency costs and optimal insider control hypotheses, 240, 242
time dimension, 243, 362, 368
voting premia, relation to. *See* Voting Premia
Controlling Shareholders
agency costs, reduction of, 174
controller benefits, 168–172
controversies, 169–172
definition for purposes of this book, 10
definition, Listing Rules, 166, 192, 320
distrust of. *See* Controlling Shareholders: controller benefits
dual-class firms, average equity ownership in, 27, 28, 380, 381, 382
dual-class firms, corporate controlled, 253
dual-class firms, prevalence in, 8, 28
dual-class stock prohibition, as the provenance of the, 166–168
dual-class stock, fostered by, 213
dual-class stock, loss of equity constraint with, 32, 184–185, 238, 327, 333, 334, 336, 338
empirical evidence, 176–184
endogeneity, 182, 184
inconclusiveness of, 180–184
equity constraint, one share one vote, 32, 174, 184, 327
highest use value, 169
identity, importance of, 181, 232
independent directors. *See* Independent Directors
long-termism, and. *See* Long-Termism
management, involvement in, 270
permissibility on premium tier, 32, 167
private benefits of control. *See* Controlling Shareholders: controller benefits
restrictions under the Listing Rules, 167
risk-taking, and. See Risk-Taking
substantial shareholder, Listing Rules definition of, 319
takeover prices. *See* Takeover Prices
tradeoff, 175–176
types, 11, 253
Corporate Governance Code
box-ticking, 324, 361
comply-or-explain, 25, 324
directors, annual re-election of, 25
dual-class firms, reduced effectiveness in, 235, 324, 345
independent directors, 121, 235, 324, 396
independence, determination of, 323, 396
premium tier, application to, 49
Costs of Capital
controller constraints, effect of. *See* Constraints, Controller
debt, effect of, 334
expropriation, effect of, 332
inferior-voting shares, discounting of, 9, *See also* Empirical Evidence, Dual-Class Firm Performance: firm valuation studies
consequences, 302–303, 311, 343
reducing. *See* Constraints, Controller
technology companies. *See* Technology Companies
Countrywide

controlling shareholder firm, as a, 167
Cross-Ownerships. *See* Control-Enhancing Mechanisms
Cyberdyne, 101

Daily Mail, 52, 388
standard tier, demotion of non-voting stock to, 79
Daimler Benz
pyramid structure, 128
Debenhams, 215
Debt
consequences of, 36
costs of capital, effect on. *See* Costs of Capital
Indian dual-class firms, difficulties to source in, 110
private equity. *See* Private Equity
technology companies. *See* Technology Companies
Debt Markets
constraint, as a controller, 334–335
debt covenants, 334
DeepMind, 42, 215
Deliveroo, 24, 57–61, 63, 68, 388, 414
dual-class stock structure, 57, 65
index exclusion, 115
standard tier, listing on, 51, 54, 57
sunset clauses
director-linked, 57
interplay with mandatory offer rules, 410
management-linked, 57
time-dependent, 57, 59, 363
transfer-driven, 57, 371
takeover offer, pricing of share classes upon a, 317, 409
tech credentials, 354
Delphi Technologies, 52
Democracy, Shareholder, 143–150
fairness, equality and justice and, 143, 148
pass-along, puniness and crudeness arguments, 148
one person one vote, 144
political voting analogy, 143–148
residual claimants, shareholders as, 143
Derivative Claims, 313, 349, 385
impediments, 313, 385
Director-Linked Sunset Clauses. *See* Sunset Clauses
Directors
appointment and dismissal of directors in UK companies, 24–26, 120, 197, 200, 325, 396, 398
appointment and dismissal of directors in US companies, 24
board appointment rights as a control-enhancing mechanism. *See* Control-Enhancing Mechanisms
business judgment rule, US, 206, 295
disclosure of interests in shares, 405
dual-class stock
CA 2006 s. 168, comity with, 72
duties. *See* Constraints, Controller
derivative claims. *See* Derivative Claims
independent directors. *See* Independent Directors
judicial deference, UK, 207, 314
Disclosure Guidance and Transparency Sourcebook, The FCA Handbook's, 135, 406
Disclosure, Enhanced. *See* Sunrise Clauses
Disney
Twenty-First Century Fox, acquisition of, 125, 207
Dispersed Ownership
blockholders, influence of, 147, 166
collective action issues, 166, 173, 222, 330
dual-class stock, dispersed ownership of, 8–9, 253
free-riding, 173, 222, 314
ownership and control, separation of, 147, 152, 173, 184
rational apathy, 147, 173
risk-taking, and. *See* Risk-Taking
UK listed companies, prevalence among, 20, 81, 165
US listed companies, prevalence among, 20, 81
Diversification
Big Tech, 215
controlling shareholder one share one vote firms, 214
dual-class firms, 214
empirical evidence, 215
founders, by, 3, 16, 38, 119, 215
empirical evidence, 282, 288
Dodge Brothers, 83
DoorDash, 59
Dublin
dual-class stock, admissibility of, 113
loyalty shares. *See* Loyalty Shares

Easyjet
controlling shareholder firm, as a, 167
EDF, 317
EDS. *See* General Motors
Efficiency of Markets, 265
doubts, 184, 228, 265, 333
efficient capital markets hypothesis, 265
Eligibility Requirements, Dual-Class Stock, 353–361

Empirical Evidence, Dual-Class Firm Performance
buy-and-hold stock return studies, 279–285, 296
endogeneity, 285
controller, importance of types of, 252–256, 270, 273, 276, 285, 287, 294
family-ownership. *See* Family-Ownership
diversity of firms, importance of, 252, 273, 276, 292, 294, 298, 299
firm age, 259, 274, 289, 294, 298
growth-phase, 273, 276, 282, 285, 288, 290, 291, 293, 384
event-based studies, 256–265, 296, 327, 413
endogeneity, 262
firm valuation studies, 265–279, 296
discounts, consequences of. *See* Costs of Capital
discounts, possible reasons for, 280, 282, 283, 284, 294, 297–300
discounts, unjustified, 251, 297, 298, 299, 311
endogeneity, 276, 365
Tobin's Q. *See* Tobin's Q
tradeoff, dual-class stock. *See* Controller Benefits: tradeoff, dual-class stock
jurisdiction, importance of, 271
market perception, effect of, 285. *See also* Tobin's Q
matching, firm, 255
operating performance studies, 285–295, 296
endogeneity, 288, 293
time period, importance of study, 264, 269, 271, 282, 285
Endava, 21, 52
Endowment Effect
management entrenchment, leading to, 198
meaning, 204
non-pecuniary controller benefit, as a, 204
ENRC, 123, 172
controversies, 169–170, 321, 322
relationship agreement, founders', 123
Entire Fairness Standard, US
related-party transactions. *See* Related-Party Transactions: Delaware
two-step reorganisations, 212
Equity Funding, Post-IPO
dual-class stock, benefits of, 224–226
acquisitions, as consideration for, 74, 85, 225
national security issues, dual-class stock as a solution to, 225
R&D. *See* R&D
Equity Markets
constraint, as a controller, 332–334
expropriation, reaction to. *See* Costs of Capital
Euronext, 112
dual-class stock, rules on. *See* Amsterdam, Brussels, Dublin, Lisbon, Oslo and France
Evans Cycles. *See* Fraser Group
Event-Driven Sunset Clauses. *See* Sunset Clauses
Executive Remuneration
Aviva. *See* Aviva
bonding hypothesis. *See* Bonding Hypothesis
BP. *See* BP
controversies, 195
disclosure
UK, 194
US, 194
dual-class stock, high executive remuneration and, 193–195, 403
dual-class stock, moderation of management remuneration with, 218
empirical evidence, dual-class firms and, 194, 404
Fraser Group. *See* Fraser Group
Google. *See* Google
outrage constraints, 194, 402
Persimmon. *See* Persimmon
Royal Dutch Shell. *See* Royal Dutch Shell
say-on-pay
UK, 193, 402, 403
US, 193
Trinity Mirror. *See* Trinity Mirror
Exillon Energy
controversies, 171, 321

Facebook, 17
acquisitions, 215
controversies, 159
founder, importance of, 220
founder's equity, 383
human capital, investment in, 219
Instagram, acquisition of, 215, 221, 224
long-termism, 227
non-voting stock, proposed, 348, 351
returns, 304
sunset clauses
death and incapacity, 375
transfer-driven, 369
Family-Ownership
dual-class firm performance, effect on, 270, 272
dual-class firms, prevalence in, 253, 270
empirical evidence, 179, 272, 291, 293
founders, waning skills of, 198, 232
gravity of generations. *See* Family-Ownership: heirs
heirs, 199, 232, 254, 294, 371
empirical evidence, 199, 273, 294
reputation, importance of, 337
Farfetch, 21, 52

FCA
Main Market, as regulator of the, 22
mission, 28
Official List, 22, 72, 347
Ferrexpo, 32, 172
controversies, 171, 321
Fiat Group, 112
Fiduciary Duties
directors. *See* Constraints, Controller shareholders
Delaware, 326, 350
UK, discussion regarding, 351
UK, lack of in, 326, 351
Findel. *See* Fraser Group
First Data, 17
Fitbit, 215
Ford Motor Company, 17, 84, 100
Founder Skills
dual-class firms, importance in, 254
idiosyncratic vision, 221, 255
IPO, importance of founder talent at, 217, 368
waning. *See* Family-Ownership
Founder-Ownership. *See* Family-Ownership
Founders
dual-class firms, average equity ownership in. *See* Controlling Shareholders
France
dual-class stock, limitations on the use of, 110
loyalty shares. *See* Loyalty Shares
Fraser Group, 32, 175
acquisitions, 215
Agent Provocateur, 215
controlling shareholder firm, as a, 167
controversies, 171, 321
Debenhams, interest in, 215
diversification, 215
Evans Cycles, 215
executive remuneration, 195
Findel, 215
French Connection, 215
Game Digital, 215
House of Fraser, 15, 74, 75, 215
Kensington Health Clubs, 215
Sofa.com, 215
FRC
Corporate Governance Code. *See* Corporate Governance Code
Free-Float. *See* LSE
French Connection. *See* Fraser Group
Fresnillo, 32, 172
controlling shareholder firm, as a, 167
FTSE. *See* Indices
Future Enterprises, 107
Game Digital. *See* Fraser Group
GAN, 52
General Motors, 100, 114
EDS, acquisition with dual-class stock of, 85, 225
General Universal Stores, 74
Germany
dual-class stock, prohibition of, 110
Google
acquisitions, 215
Alphabet as new holding company, 16
capital structure, 16, 17, 388
non-voting stock, 16, 331, 348, 351
controversies, 159
executive remuneration, 195
founders, importance of, 59, 221
founders, resignations of, 199, 221, 376
founders' equity, 383
human capital, investment in, 219
IPO, 16
long-termism, 227
returns, 303
sunset clauses
death and incapacity, 375
ownership-linked, 378, 381
transfer-driven, 369, 370, 371
voting premia. *See* Voting Premia
Gravity of Generations. *See* Family-Ownership
Great Universal Stores, 78
Groupon, 17, 42
management entrenchment, 201
one share one vote, unification into, 17
sunset clause, time-dependent, 367
Gujarat NRE Coke, 107

Hansa, 52, 387
standard tier, demotion of non-voting stock to, 79
voting premia. *See* Voting Premia
Helene Curtis
sunset clause, time-dependent, 363
Hikma Pharmaceuticals, 175
Hill Review. *See* UK Listing Review
Hollinger International
controversies, 191
Hong Kong
competition from other exchanges, 91, 118
dual-class controllers, suitability of, 95, 357
dual-class issuers, 93
eligibility and suitability, 95, 354
market capitalisation requirements, 93, 355
dual-class stock
admissibility, 15, 53, 93
former prohibition, 91
history, 91

Hong Kong (cont.)
legislative permissibility, 91
listings, 95, 415
voting ratios. *See* Voting Ratios
enhanced-voting shares, restriction on listing of, 387
new issuers, restricting dual-class stock to, 93
SFC, 92
sunrise clauses. *See* Sunrise Clauses
sunset clauses. See Sunset Clauses
Hostile Takeovers
China, prevalence in, 104
Tokyo, prevalence in, 101
UK, prevalence in, 73
US, prevalence in, 85
House of Fraser. *See* Fraser Group
Hut Group, The, 54–67, 68, 149
index exclusion, 55, 115
premium tier, refusal of admission to, 54, 79
special share, 54, 363, 371
standard tier, listing on, 53, 54
sunset clauses
time-dependent, 55, 59, 363
transfer-driven, 371
tech credentials, 354

IHS Markit, 52
Independent Directors
appointments in UK companies. *See* Directors: appointment and dismissal of directors in UK companies, and Listing Rules: independent director appointments
controlling shareholder firms
empirical evidence, 395
ineffectiveness, 200, 395
NYSE requirements, 397
role, 395
Corporate Governance Code requirements. *See* Corporate Governance Code
flaws, 325
inferior-shareholder protection, as an. *See* Sunrise Clauses
Listing Rules requirements. *See* Listing Rules
roles, 200
India
dual-class controllers
net wealth thresholds, 108, 357, 382
suitability, 108, 357, 382
dual-class issuers
conditions attached, 108–109
eligibility and suitability, 108, 354
dual-class stock
admissibility, 15, 53, 108
history, 107–108
legislative permissibility, 107
voting ratios. *See* Voting Ratios
enhanced-voting shares, nature of listing of, 387
new issuers, restricting dual-class stock to, 108, 412
sunrise clauses. *See* Sunrise Clauses
sunset clauses. *See* Sunset Clauses
Indices
benefits of inclusion, 50–51
dual-class stock, consequences of exclusion of, 115–116
FTSE, 7, 50, 114
dual-class stock, limitations on, 89, 114
free-float, 402
standard tier issuers, exclusion of, 50, 55
index trackers, 7, 50, 343, 360
MSCI, approach to dual-class stock on, 89
S&P, prohibition of dual-class stock on, 89, 114
voting premia, effect on. *See* Voting Premia
Industrial Rayon Corporation, 83
Inefficient Decision-Making
conglomerates, formation of. *See* Conglomerates
dual-class firms, in, 195–197
empirical evidence, dual-class firms and, 196
non-pecuniary controller benefits, as a result of. *See* Non-Pecuniary Controller Benefits
one share one vote firms, in, 202
tunnelling, relationship with, 196
UK Listing Review, concerns under. *See* UK Listing Review
Inpex Corporation
golden share. *See* Tokyo
Instagram. *See* Facebook
Institutional Investors
dual-class stock, antagonism to, 75, 89, 160, 305
dual-class stock, prevalence of investment in, 160, 284
long-termism, and. *See* Long-Termism
prevalence. *See* LSE and NYSE
regulations, influence on, 76, 77
rise. *See* LSE
International Game Technology, 52
International Silver Company, 83
IPO
dual-class stock, consequences of, 27, 38
equity financing, as a source of, 35–36
foreign exchanges, listings by UK companies on, 52–54
one share one vote, consequences of, 26–27, 37–38
retail investors, 45
tech company listings, decline of UK, 33–35
UK decline, 33, 34
vanguard companies, importance of, 303
Ireland. *See* Dublin

Italy
  dual-class stock
    admissibility, 111
    limitations on use, 111
    voting ratios. *See* Voting Ratios
ITV, 15

Jain Irrigation Systems, 107
Japan. *See* Tokyo
Jenkins Committee, The, 76
Jensen, Michael
  Jensen and Meckling, 153, 173, 178, 334
Just Eat, 48

KAZ Minerals, 175
Kensington Health Clubs. *See* Fraser Group

Lemons, Market for, 302, 305
Lever Brothers, 136
Levi Strauss, 247
LinkedIn, 17
  takeover, 207
Lisbon
  dual-class stock, limitations on the use of, 113
  loyalty shares. *See* Loyalty Shares
Listing Rules
  enforcement, 320, 346
  independent director appointments, 200, 325, 396, 403
  Premium Listing Principles, 22, 79, 121, 406
  related-party transactions. *See* Related-Party Transactions
  relationship agreements. *See* Relationship Agreements
  sovereign-controlled companies, exemptions for, 172, 320, 346, 401, 413
  sponsor, firm, 319, 347, 401
  substantial transactions (Chapter 10), 63, 64, 140, 196, 391
Litigation Culture
  controller benefits, as a deterrent to the extraction of pernicious, 315, 348, 350, 401
  UK, 315
  US, 315, 344, 348, 349
Litigation Rules
  class actions, 316, 349
    group litigation orders, UK, 350
  contingency-fee arrangements, 349
  loser pays, UK, 314, 349
LivaNova, 52
Long-Termism, 172
  bonding hypothesis, and, 219
  controlling shareholders, facilitated by, 229
    empirical evidence, 232
  dual-class firms
    empirical evidence, 231
  dual-class stock IPO, as a reason for, 227
  dual-class stock, facilitated by, 226–234
  human capital investment by employees, leading to. *See* Bonding Hypothesis
  institutional investors, and, 228
  Kay Review, 229
  management and employees, benefits to. *See* Bonding Hypothesis
  management entrenchment, facilitated by, 229
  market for corporate control, facilitated by absence of, 229
  product-cycles, 227, 252, 255
  R&D. *See* R&D
  short-term signals, benefits of, 229, 233
  skin-in-the-game, importance of. *See* Sunset Clauses: ownership-linked
  stakeholder relationships, benefits to. *See* Bonding Hypothesis
  technology companies, benefits for. *See* Technology Companies
  UK Listing Review and limitations on. *See* UK Listing Review
Loyalty Shares
  Amsterdam, 112
  Brussels, 113, 137
  control-enhancing mechanism, as a, 137–140
  director-linked sunset clauses, and. *See* Sunset Clauses
  downsides, 139, 388
  Dublin, 113
  France, 111, 137
  Italy, 111, 137
  NYSE, 88, 137
  Oslo, 112
  political voting, analogy to, 146
  Portugal, 113
  premium tier, admissibility on, 137
  Spain, 112, 137
  Sweden, 112
LSE
  competition from local exchanges, 114
  dual-class stock
    decline, 75–78
    formal prohibition on premium tier. *See* Premium Tier
    former prevalence, 73
    informal prohibition, 77
  free-float, 48, 73, 84, 167, 172, 328, 331, 347, 413
    FTSE. *See* Indices: FTSE
  high-growth segment, 47–48
  hostile takeovers. *See* Hostile Takeovers
  institutional investors, prevalence of, 81, 301, 341

LSE (cont.)
institutional investors, rise of, 75
Main Market, 21
non-voting stock, prohibition on premium tier of. *See* Premium Tier
NYSE, comparison to, 81
premium tier. *See* Premium Tier
standard tier. *See* Standard Tier
Lyft, 18
sunset clauses
death and incapacity, 375
transfer-driven, 369, 370, 371

M&A
dual-class stock, acquisition consideration including. *See* Equity Funding, Post-IPO
dual-class stock, blocking of takeovers through, 45
public policy and national security, 42, 225
public-to-private, 44
strategic acquisitions, 41
UK, activity in, 42
Majority of the Minority Provisions. *See* Sunrise Clauses
Management Entrenchment
controlling shareholder firms, in one share one vote, 198
controversies, 198, 201
dual-class firms, in, 197–201
endowment effect. *See* Endowment Effect
impact over time, changing, 198
long-termism, and. *See* Long-Termism
non-pecuniary controller benefits, relationship to, 201
risk-taking, and. *See* Risk-Taking
tunnelling, relationship to, 201
UK Listing Review, limitations under, 198
Management-Linked Sunset Clauses. *See* Sunset Clauses
Manchester United, 52
NYSE, listing on, 96, 118
Mandatory Offers
EU, 205, 319, 407, 409
redemptions or buybacks or enfranchisement of shares, triggered by, 410
sunset clauses, triggered through operation of, 410–411
UK. *See* Takeover Code
Market Abuse Regulation, 135, 406
Market for Corporate Control
dual-class firms, lacking in, 207, 332
long-termism, and. *See* Long-Termism
meaning, 206
product markets and, 335
UK Listing Review and. *See* UK Listing Review
Market Forces, 148
Marks & Spencer, 15, 75
Mastercard, 227
Matomy, 48
MaxLinear
sunset clause, time-dependent, 367
Meckling, William
Jensen and Meckling. *See* Jensen, Michael
Meituan-Dianping, 95, 415
Mimecast, 52
Minimum Voting Requirements, Inferior-Voting Shareholder. *See* Sunrise Clauses
Moelis & Co.
sunset clause, event-driven, 386

NASD. *See* NASDAQ
NASDAQ, 88
dual-class stock, permissibility of, 86
National Security and Investment Bill, 225
Nest Labs, 215
Netherlands, The. *See* Amsterdam
New York Times, The, 17
News Corp., 199
management entrenchment, 201
Murdochs, 199, 201
Nike, 17
Non-Pecuniary Controller Benefits, 201–203
conglomerates, formation of. *See* Conglomerates
constraint, as a controller, 336
endowment effect. *See* Endowment Effect
inefficient decision-making, leading to, 196, 202
management entrenchment, leading to. *See* Management Entrenchment
market forces, constrained through, 202
takeover probability, effect on. *See* Takeover Probability
Norway. *See* Oslo
NYSE
competition from other exchanges, 85
dual-class stock
current treatment, 88
formal prohibition, 84
informal prohibition, 84
moratorium, 85
recapitalisation into, scope for. *See* Recapitalisations
relaxation of prohibition, 86–88
hostile takeovers. *See* Hostile Takeovers
independent directors. *See* Independent Directors

institutional investors, prevalence of, 81, 86, 269
LSE, comparison to, 81
NYSE America. *See* AMEX

Ocado, 33
tech credentials, 354
Oculus VR, 215
Okta
sunset clause, transfer-driven, 373
One Person One Vote, 82
One Share One Vote
Delaware default, 83
equality, based on, 71
UK default position, 72
unifications into, 75
empirical evidence. *See* Empirical Evidence, Dual-Class Firm Performance: event-based studies
Orchard Therapeutics, 52
Oslo
dual-class stock, limitations on the use of, 112, 113
loyalty shares. See Loyalty Shares
Ownership-Linked Sunset Clauses. *See* Sunset Clauses
Oxford Immunotec Global, 52

Passive Investors. *See* Indices: index trackers
Persimmon
executive remuneration, 195, 403
Pinterest, 18
sunset clause, transfer-driven, 372
Portugal. *See* Lisbon
Preference Shares
control-enhancing mechanism, as a, 136–137
dual-class stock, circumvention of a prohibition of, 102
voting/cash-flow divergence, as a means to, 136
Premium Tier
admission requirements, 48
continuing requirements, 49
controlling shareholders, permissibility of, 32
creation, 79
dual-class stock, prohibition of, 79–80
non-voting stock, prohibition of, 52, 79
Premium Listing Principles. *See* Listing Rules
significance, 46–54
Pricing-In. *See* Empirical Evidence, Dual-Class Firm Performance: firm valuation studies: discounts
Private Benefits of Control. *See* Controller Benefits
Private Companies
offers to the public, restrictions on, 45
relevance in the context of dual-class stock, 6
Private Equity
buyouts, 40
debt, incurrence of, 36, 40
exit, 41, 44
minority investments, 40
Product Markets
constraint, as a controller, 335
empirical evidence, 336
dispersed ownership firm management, as a constraint on, 335
market for corporate control, and the. *See* Market for Corporate Control
Project Choice
dual-class stock, enabling efficient project choice through, 223–224, 252
technology companies, enabling project choice in, 224
Prudent-Mean Voting, 145
UK, 71
US, 82
Psychological Constraints, 336–337
family firms, importance in. *See* Family-Ownership
outrage constraints, 337, 402
Public Companies
offers to the public, 6
public-to-private. *See* M&A
relevance in the context of dual-class stock, 2, 6–8
Pure Storage
sunset clause, ownership-linked, 381
Purpose of the Firm. *See* Theory, Corporate
Pyramid Structures. *See* Control-Enhancing Mechanisms

R&D
dual-class firms
empirical evidence, 231
dual-class stock, facilitated by, 224
economy, importance for, 35
empirical evidence, 232, 289, 293
equity funding, importance of, 36
long-termism, and, 227
technology companies, importance to, 203
Rank, 15, 75
Recapitalisations
articles of association, amendment to. *See* Articles of Association
class rights. *See* Class Rights
constraint, UK regulations as a controller. *See* Constraints, Controller
dual-class stock, into, 87, 327–332
criticism, 413

Recapitalisations (cont.)
empirical evidence. *See* Empirical Evidence, Dual-Class Firm Performance: event-based studies
flaws, regulatory, 332, 413
NYSE rules, scope under, 88, 327, 330
requirements, Delaware, 330
requirements, UK, 328–332
schemes of arrangement. *See* Schemes of Arrangement
Regeneron Pharmaceuticals, 304
Regus, 175
controlling shareholder firm, as a, 167
Related-Party Transactions
beneficial related-party transactions
dual-class stock, and, 213
sovereign-controlled companies, 213
controller constraint, regulations as a. *See* Constraints, Controller
controversies, 169–172, 191–192, 321, 400
Delaware, 49, 192, 295, 350, 352
DTRs, 320
enhanced provisions. *See* Sunrise Clauses
flaws, regulatory, 321, 400
IAS rules, 320, 321
premium tier, 49, 192, 319–323, 351, 399
class tests, 319
thresholds, 319
pyramidal stuctures, creation of, 125
relationship agreements, impact of. *See* Relationship Agreements
sovereign-controlled companies, exemptions for. *See* Listing Rules
Relationship Agreements, 49, 192, 322–323, 346
ENRC. *See* ENRC
flaws, 322
provisions, required, 322
related-party transactions, impact on, 192, 320, 322
Rolls-Royce. *See* Rolls-Royce
unfair prejudice, and. *See* Unfair Prejudice
Rightmove, 33
RingCentral
sunset clause, transfer-driven, 373
Risk-Taking, 235–238
controlling shareholders, and, 236
empirical evidence, 237
dispersed ownership, blunted with, 235, 236
dual-class stock, facilitated by, 237
empirical evidence, 237
management entrenchment, and, 235
skin-in-the-game, importance of. *See* Sunset Clauses: ownership-linked
technology companies, importance for, 235, 237
UK Listing Review, limitations under. *See* UK Listing Review
Rolls-Royce
ValueAct, relationship agreement with, 123
Royal Dutch Shell
executive remuneration, 195, 402
Rule-Making
legislative approach, 345
mandatory approach, 341
permissive approach, 342
problems with, 342
presumptive approach, 71, 341
regulatory approach, 345, 415
soft-law approach, 345

Saga
controlling shareholder firm, as a, 167
Schemes of Arrangement
recapitalisations into dual-class stock, 329
takeover context, 26, 205
Schroders, 52, 78, 387
standard tier, demotion of non-voting stock to, 79
voting premia. *See* Voting Premia
Sears Holdings, J., 73, 74
SEC
Rule 19c-4, 87
uniform voting standard, 87–88
Shake Shack, 247
Shanghai
competition from other exchanges, 104
dual-class controllers, suitability of, 357
dual-class issuers
conditions attached, 105
eligibility and suitability, 105, 353
market capitalisation requirements, 105, 355
dual-class stock
admissibility, 15, 53, 104
legislative permissibility, 104
listings, 106
voting ratios. See Voting Ratios
enhanced-voting shares, restriction on listing of, 387
hostile takeovers. *See* Hostile Takeovers
new issuers, restricting dual-class stock to, 105, 412
STI Board, creation of, 104, 353
sunrise clauses. *See* Sunrise Clauses
sunset clauses. See Sunset Clauses
Shareholder Primacy. *See* Theory, Corporate: purpose of the firm
Shell, 15

Singapore
competition from other exchanges, 96, 118
dual-class controllers, suitability of, 98, 357
dual-class issuers
conditions attached, 97–98
eligibility and suitability, 98, 355
dual-class stock
admissibility, 15, 53, 97
history, 96
legislative permissibility, 96
voting ratios. *See* Voting Ratios
enhanced-voting shares, restriction on listing of, 387
new issuers, restricting dual-class stock to, 97, 412
sunrise clauses. *See* Sunrise Clauses
sunset clauses. *See* Sunset Clauses
Skin-In-The-Game. *See* Sunset Clauses: ownership-linked
Sky, 125
Slack, 18
Snap, 17, 42, 103
capital structure
multiple share classes, 17, 389
founders, importance of, 220
long-termism, 227
sunset clauses
death and incapacity, 375
transfer-driven, 369, 370, 371
Sofa.com. *See* Fraser Group
Softbank, 40, 44
Spain
dual-class stock, limitations on the use of, 112
loyalty shares. *See* Loyalty Shares
Sports Direct. *See* Fraser Group
Square, 17
sunset clause, transfer-driven, 373
Stakeholder Pluralism. *See* Theory, Corporate: purpose of the firm
Stampede Capital, 107
Standard Tier
dual-class issuers, 51, 54–67
indices, exclusion from, 50, 55
issuers, consequences for, 48–51, 60
premium tier, differences from, 49
State Street, 90
Strength of Laws
UK, 190, 251
US, 190, 251, 295
Sunrise Clauses
coat-tail provisions. *See* Coat-Tail Provisions
definition, 362, 389
disclosure, enhanced, 274, 405–406
empirical evidence, 405
Hong Kong requirements, 94, 405
Shanghai requirements, 106, 405
Singapore requirements, 98, 405
Tokyo requirements, 102
UK Proposals, 348, 360, 406
enhanced-voting shares, restrictions on further issuances of, 394
Hong Kong requirements, 394
Tokyo requirements, 394
UK Proposals, 395
independent director appointment rights, 395–399
AMEX, erstwhile requirements of, 397
Hong Kong requirements, 94, 397
India requirements, 109, 397
Israel, 397
Italy, 397
related-party transaction regulations, and, 401
Shanghai requirements, 106, 397
Singapore requirements, 98, 397
UK Proposals, 398–399
inferior-voting shareholder voting disclosure, 401–404
UK Proposals, 402
majority of the minority provisions, 389–393
Canada, prevalence in, 389
Europe, 390
Hong Kong requirements, 94, 389
India requirements, 109, 389
Shanghai requirements, 106, 389
Singapore requirements, 98, 389
UK Proposals, 390–393
minimum voting requirements, inferior-voting shareholder
Hong Kong requirements, 94, 393, 401
India requirements, 108, 393
Shanghai requirements, 105, 393, 401
Singapore requirements, 97, 393, 401
proposed resolutions, inferior-voting shareholder, 404–405
Hong Kong requirements, 404
Shanghai requirements, 404
Singapore requirements, 404
UK Proposals, 404
related-party transaction provisions, enhanced, 399–401, *See also* Related-Party Transactions
independent director appointment rights, and, 401
India requirements, 109
sovereign-controlled companies, 401
Tokyo requirements, 102
UK Proposals, 400
say-on-pay, 403

Sunrise Clauses (cont.)
- shareholders' meetings, calling
  - Hong Kong requirements, 94
  - Shanghai requirements, 106
  - Singapore requirements, 98

Sunset Clauses
- breakthrough provisions
  - EU, 103
  - meaning, 103
  - ownership-linked sunset clauses, and. See Sunset Clauses: ownership-linked
  - Tokyo requirements, 103–104, 382, 415
- consequences, 387–389
- death and incapacity. *See* Sunset Clauses: director-linked
- definition, 362
- director-linked, 374–376
  - death and incapacity
  - Deliveroo. *See* Deliveroo
  - directors' duties, and, 376
  - Facebook. *See* Facebook
  - Google. *See* Google
  - Hong Kong requirements, 93, 357, 375
  - loyalty shares, and, 388
  - Lyft. *See* Lyft
  - management-linked. *See* Sunset Clauses: management-linked
  - multi-class share structures, limiting, 388
  - rationale, 374
  - Shanghai requirements, 105, 357, 375
  - Singapore requirements, 97, 357, 375
  - Snap. *See* Snap
  - Tokyo requirements, 102, 357, 375
  - UK Listing Review. *See* UK Listing Review
  - UK Proposals, 374, 376
  - US prevalence, 375
- event-driven, 283, 384–386
  - criminal offences, 386
    - Moelis & Co. *See* Moelis & Co.
  - extraneous events, 385
    - shortcomings, 385
  - fiduciary duty, breach of, 385
    - shortcomings, 385, 386
  - firm performance, 384
    - shortcomings, 384
  - growth-phase, 384
    - shortcomings, 384
  - insolvency, 384
    - shortcomings, 385
  - regulatory rules, breach of, 386
    - shortcomings, 386
  - Tokyo requirements, 102
- management-linked, 375–376
  - Canada, prevalence in, 375
  - Deliveroo. *See* Deliveroo
  - India requirements, 109, 357, 375
  - rationale, 375
  - shortcomings, 375
  - Tokyo requirements, 357, 375
  - US, prevalence in, 375
- mandatory offers, triggering. *See* Mandatory Offers
- ownership-linked, 300, 377–383, 394
  - breakthrough provisions, and, 377
  - Google. *See* Google
  - Hong Kong requirements, 94, 380, 381
  - ownership threshold, determining, 380–382
  - rationale, 377
  - Shanghai requirements, 105, 380
  - skin-in-the-game, importance of, 234, 237, 377, 380
  - Snap, 380
  - Tokyo requirements, 102, 103–104. *See also* Sunset Clauses: breakthrough provisions
  - transfer-driven sunsets, interplay with, 373
  - UK Proposals, 382
  - voting ratios. *See* Voting Ratios
  - Zynga. See Zynga
- time-dependent, 362–368
  - Canada, prevalence in, 363
  - Deliveroo. *See* Deliveroo
  - empirical evidence, 364
  - endogeneity, 365
  - extensions, 363, 366
  - Groupon. *See* Groupon
  - Helen Curtis. *See* Helen Curtis
  - Hut Group, The. *See* Hut Group, The
  - India requirements, 109, 363, 366, 415
  - MaxLinear. *See* MaxLinear
  - rationale, 364
  - shortcomings, 365
  - Texas Roadhouse. *See* Texas Roadhouse
  - time as a proxy for other characteristics. *See* Age, Firm
  - UK Listing Review. *See* UK Listing Review
  - US, prevalence in, 363
- transfer-driven, 238, 273, 294, 368–374
  - bonding hypothesis, undermining. *See* Bonding Hypothesis
  - Canada, prevalence in, 369
  - Deliveroo. *See* Deliveroo
  - exceptions, 370
  - Facebook. *See* Facebook
  - Google. *See* Google
  - Hong Kong requirements, 94, 369, 371
  - Hut Group, The. *See* Hut Group, The
  - India requirements, 109, 369

Lyft. *See* Lyft
mandatory offers, interplay with Takeover Code, 370, 371, 407
multi-class share structures, and, 388
Okta. *See* Okta
ownership-linked sunsets, interplay with, 373
Pinterest. *See* Pinterest
rationale, 368
RingCentral. *See* RingCentral
Shanghai requirements, 105, 369
shortcomings, 371, 372, 373
Singapore requirements, 97, 369, 370
Snap. *See* Snap
Square. *See* Square
Tokyo requirements, 102, 369, 370
UK Listing Review. *See* UK Listing Review
UK Proposals, 369, 371
US, prevalence in, 369
Veeva. *See* Veeva
Zoom. *See* Zoom
Sweden
dual-class firms, prevalence of, 113
dual-class stock
admissibility, 112
voting ratios. *See* Voting Ratios
loyalty shares. *See* Loyalty Shares

Takeover Code
applicability, 316, 318, 407, 408
comparable pricing regime
classes listed, with all, 78, 209, 317, 409
classes unlisted, with some, 78, 211, 409
control premia, limiting, 209, 318
requirements, 209
concert parties
definition, 408
dual-class stock, as a deterrent to the use of, 78
mandatory offers, 77, 125, 316–319
chain principle, 125
concert parties, transfers between, 408
control premia, limiting, 209, 318
flaws, 318, 370
inefficient takeovers, limiting, 204
takeover consideration, impact on. *See* Takeover Prices
transfer-driven sunset clauses, interplay with. *See* Sunset Clauses
Notes on the Amalgamation of British Business, 77
origins, 77
shareholders, equality of treatment of, 77
Takeover Panel, 77
Takeover Prices
controlling shareholders, higher with, 221
dual-class stock, higher with, 211, 221–223
empirical evidence, 222, 300
mandatory bid rule, consequences of, 221
UK Listing Review and. *See* UK Listing Review
Takeover Probability, 203–208, 300
controller benefits, compensation for loss of, 203
dual-class firm takeovers, examples of. *See* Takeovers
empirical evidence, dual-class firm, 207, 300
market for corporate control. *See* Market for Corporate Control
non-pecuniary controller benefits, effect of, 204, 208
takeovers, efficient, 203–204
takeovers, inefficient, 204–206
mandatory offers, limiting through. *See* Takeover Code
UK takeover mechanics, limiting through, 205
UK Listing Review and. *See* UK Listing Review
Takeovers
dual-class firms, examples of, 207
dual-class stock, probability with. *See* Takeover Probability
prices. *See* Takeover Prices
schemes of arrangement. *See* Schemes of Arrangement
takeover offer, 206
US two-step reorganisations, 212
Tata, 214
Tata Motors, 107
Technology Companies. *See also* Big Tech
bonding hypothesis, importance of, 220
Chinese companies, use of dual-class stock by, 21
costs of capital, relevance of, 333
debt, difficulties in sourcing, 35, 203, 224
dual-class stock, use of, 17–18, 19, 246, 365
listings, decline of UK. *See* IPO
long-termism, benefits of, 227, 230
pre-profit companies, 35, 60
project choice, enabling. *See* Project Choice
R&D. *See* R&D
risk-taking, and. *See* Risk-Taking
UK companies, use of dual-class stock by, 21
Tencent, 21
Tenured Voting. *See* Loyalty Shares
Tesla, 217
Musk, Elon, 217
Texas Roadhouse
sunset clause, time-dependent, 367
Theory, Corporate
Coase, Ronald. *See* Coase, Ronald
Dodd/Berle debate, 152, 158
Jensen and Meckling. *See* Jensen, Michael

Theory, Corporate (cont.)
purpose of the firm, 150–151
Business Roundtable. See Business Roundtable
dual-class stock, application to, 155, 157–160
managerialism, 87, 151
shareholder primacy, 151, 153, 155
stakeholder pluralism, 151, 152, 154
theory of the firm, 12
agency costs, 153, 173–174, 178, 184
contractarianism, 152–154
principal costs, 154, 224, 239
Theory of the Firm. See Theory, Corporate
Time-Dependent Sunset Clauses. See Sunset Clauses
Time-Phased Shares. See Loyalty Shares
Tobin's Q
criticism of use, 278
definition, 177, 265
firm value, proxy for, 265
market perception, effect of, 177, 276, 279, 283
significance, 177, 265, 267
Tokyo
dual-class controllers, suitability of, 357
dual-class issuers
conditions attached, 101–103
eligibility and suitability, 102, 355
dual-class stock
admissibility, 15, 53, 101
former prohibition, 100
history, 99–101
legislative permissibility, 99
listings, 103
enhanced-voting shares, restriction on listing of, 387
golden shares, 100
hostile takeovers. See Hostile Takeovers
keiretsu, 35, 99, 104
new issuers, restricting dual-class stock to, 102, 412
sunrise clauses. See Sunrise Clauses
sunset clauses. See Sunset Clauses
unit share system, 100
Toronto Stock Exchange
dual-class stock, admissibility of, 15, 53
Total Q, 278
Tradeoff
controlling shareholder, one share one vote. See Controlling Shareholders
dual-class stock. See Controller Benefits
Transfer-Driven Sunset Clauses. See Sunset Clauses
Trinity Mirror
executive remuneration, 195, 403
TSB
controlling shareholder firm, as a, 167
Tunnelling
controlling shareholders, one share one vote. See Controlling Shareholders: controversies
dual-class stock, 190–195
controversies, 190–192
executive remuneration, high. See Executive Remuneration
inefficient decision-making, leading to. See Inefficient Decision-Making
management entrenchment, leading to. See Management Entrenchment
related-party transaction regulations, constraining with, 192
Twenty-First Century Fox, 17
Disney, acquisition by. See Disney

Uber, 218, 246
UCloud, 106
UK CGC, 324, 333. See Corporate Governance Code
UK Listing Review, 2, 4, 6, 23, 57, 61–67, 80, 186, 340
bonding hypothesis, limitations on, 220
control premia, 211
disproportionate voting stock conditions, 61, 357
dual-class stock, deviation from 'genuine', 24, 39, 62–67, 69, 80, 114, 247, 307, 339, 415
early-stage companies, attraction of, 60, 66, 367
enhanced-voting rights, restrictions on the exercise of, 61, 62–66, 390, 391, 404, 415
inefficient decision-making, concerns over, 196, 197
long-termism, limitations on, 230, 368
management entrenchment, limitations on, 198
market for corporate control, and, 208, 220, 230
national security issues, ineffectiveness in relation to, 226
risk-taking, limitations on, 236
sunset clauses
director-linked, 61, 62, 374
time-dependent, 61, 66, 110, 220, 230, 363, 367, 415
transfer-driven, 61, 62, 370, 371
takeover prices, 222
takeover probability, 208
voting ratio, 61, 62, 379
UK Proposals
controller characteristics, 347, 358–361
dual-class issuers, eligibility and suitability of, 347, 358–361

enhanced-voting shares, restrictions on listing of, 387
Listing Rules, Premium Listing Principles and premium tier share approvals under, 406–407
loyalty shares, restriction on use of, 388, 395
multi-class shares structures, limitations on, 388
new issuers, restricting dual-class stock to, 412, 414
other jurisdictions, comparison to, 415
sunrise clauses. *See* Sunrise Clauses
sunset clauses. *See* Sunset Clauses
Takeover Code, 407–411
comparable pricing regime, 409
mandatory offers, sunset clauses triggering, 411
voting shares, ensuring existence of, 387
Unfair Prejudice
relationship agreements, and, 323
Unifications into One Share One Vote. *See* One Share One Vote
Unilever, 51
US IPOs
dual-class stock, acceleration of use of, 19

ValueAct
Rolls-Royce, director appointment right in, 123
Vanguard, 90
Veeva
sunset clause, transfer-driven, 373
Venture Capital, 37, 39
dual-class stock UK Proposals, and, 357, 373
dual-class stock, and, 372
exit, 41, 44, 372
Viacom, 17, 199
management entrenchment, 198
Redstones, 198, 199
sunset-clause, lack of transfer-driven, 372
Voting
cash-flow rights in US dual-class firms, divergence from, 27–28, 380–381
ordinary resolutions, 24
poll vote, 72
show-of-hands, 72
special resolutions, 25
Voting Premia
coat-tail provisions, effect of, 210, 211
controller benefits, relation to, 208, 210
Google, 210
Hansa, 210
index inclusion, effect of, 209
Schroders, 209
Voting Ratios, 378–379
AMEX requirements, erstwhile, 86, 378
Europe, 378
Hong Kong requirements, 94, 378
India requirements, 109, 378
Italy requirements, 111
Shanghai requirements, 105, 378
shortcomings, 379
Singapore requirements, 97, 378
Sweden requirements, 113
UK Listing Review. *See* UK Listing Review

WeWork
IPO, abandoned, 218, 246, 360
WhatsApp, 215
Whitbread, 15
unification into one share one vote, 78
Whitbread umbrella, the, 74

Xiaomi, 21, 95, 415

Yelp, 17
sunset clause, ownership-linked, 381
YouTube, 215

Zillow, 17
Zoom, 18
sunset clause, transfer-driven, 373
Zynga, 17
sunset clause, ownership-linked, 380

Ingram Content Group UK Ltd.
Milton Keynes UK
UKHW022022070723
424706UK00006B/7

9 781108 839358